D0214683

The New York
Botanical Garden
Illustrated Encyclopedia
of Horticulture

The New York Botanical Garden Illustrated Encyclopedia of Horticulture

Thomas H. Everett

Volume 5
G-Id

Garland Publishing, Inc.
New York & London

15 14 13 12 11 10 9 8 7 6 5 4 3 2 1

Library of Congress Cataloging in Publication Data

Everett, Thomas H
    The New York Botanical Garden illustrated encyclopedia of horticulture.

    1. Horticulture—Dictionaries. 2. Gardening—Dictionaries. 3. Plants, Ornamental—Dictionaries. 4. Plants, Cultivated—Dictionaries. I. New York (City). Botanical Garden. II. Title.
SB317.58.E94   635.9'03'21   80-65941
ISBN 0-8240-7235-9

PHOTO CREDITS

Black and White

Aluminum Greenhouses, Inc.: Lean-to with vertical sides, p. 1540. W. Atlee Burpee Company: *Geum* 'Lady Stratheden', p. 1475. Brooklyn Botanical Garden: Herb garden, with center knot, at Brooklyn Botanical Garden, p. 1656. Irving Kaufman Studios: Many houseplants benefit from being summered outdoors, p. 1720. Lord & Burnham, Inc.: Free-standing, even-span greenhouse with vertical sides, p. 1539; Free-standing, even-span greenhouse with sloping sides, p. 1540; Lean-to with sloping sides, p. 1540; A "window greenhouse" is ideal for many kinds of houseplants, p. 1715. Netherlands Flower Institute: *Galanthus nivalis flore-pleno*, p. 1425; Forcing hyacinths: (g) In full bloom, p. 1738. The New York Botanical Garden: *Gaultheria procumbens*, p. 1446; *Gentianopsis crinita*, p. 1460; Modern hybrid gladioluses, p. 1486; *Gleditsia triacanthos* (leaves), p. 1493; *Goodyera repens* in a native habitat, p. 1511; *Goodyera pubescens*, p. 1511; Young wedge grafts of three different cactuses, p. 1523; Veneer graft, holly (*Ilex aquifolium* variety on seedling understock), p. 1526; Rooted cuttings of a labrusca grape, p. 1532; Interiors of conservatories: (a) Succulent House, The New York Botanical Garden in 1942, p. 1537; *Gymnocalycium stuckertii*, p. 1568; *Gymnocladus dioica* (fruits), p. 1569; *Gynerium sagittatum*, p. 1571; *Hedyotis caerulea*, p. 1626; *Hedyotis purpurea*, p. 1626; *Hemerocallis* in a garden, p. 1649; Hybrid day lilies (both pictures), p. 1649; Herb garden at The New York Botanical Garden, p. 1656; *Hesperis matronalis* (flowers), p. 1665; *Howea forsterana*, p. 1723; *Hydrastis canadensis*, p. 1749. Alexander Timchula: Conservatories: (a) The Enid A. Haupt Conservatory, The New York Botanical Garden, p. 1536. United States Department of Agriculture: An electric-heated hotbed; cables in place ready for being covered with soil, p. 1707. Other photographs by Thomas H. Everett.

Color

Malak, Ottawa, Canada: An effective planting of hyacinths and pansies. The New York Botanical Garden: *Gaultheria ovatifolia, Habenaria blephariglottis, Habenaria ciliaris, Hepatica americana, Hesperis matronalis, Hesperocallis undulata, Hydrophyllum capitatum*. Other photographs by Thomas H. Everett.

Published by Garland Publishing, Inc.
136 Madison Avenue, New York, New York 10016

Printed in the United States of America

This work is dedicated to the honored memory of the distinguished horticulturists and botanists who most profoundly influenced my professional career: Allan Falconer of Cheadle Royal Gardens, Cheshire, England; William Jackson Bean, William Dallimore, and John Coutts of the Royal Botanic Gardens, Kew, England; and Dr. Elmer D. Merrill and Dr. Henry A. Gleason of The New York Botanical Garden.

Foreword

According to Webster, an encyclopedia is a book or set of books giving information on all or many branches of knowledge generally in articles alphabetically arranged. To the horticulturist or grower of plants, such a work is indispensable and one to be kept close at hand for frequent reference.

The appearance of *The New York Botanical Garden Illustrated Encyclopedia of Horticulture* by Thomas H. Everett is therefore welcomed as an important addition to the library of horticultural literature. Since horticulture is a living, growing subject, these volumes contain an immense amount of information not heretofore readily available. In addition to detailed descriptions of many thousands of plants given under their generic names and brief description of the characteristics of the more important plant families, together with lists of their genera known to be in cultivation, this Encyclopedia is replete with well-founded advice on how to use plants effectively in gardens and, where appropriate, indoors. Thoroughly practical directions and suggestions for growing plants are given in considerable detail and in easily understood language. Recommendations about what to do in the garden for all months of the year and in different geographical regions will be helpful to beginners and will serve as reminders to others.

The useful category of special subject entries (as distinct from the taxonomic presentations) consists of a wide variety of topics. It is safe to predict that one of the most popular will be Rock and Alpine Gardens. In this entry the author deals helpfully and adequately with a phase of horticulture that appeals to a growing group of devotees, and in doing so presents a distinctly fresh point of view. Many other examples could be cited.

The author's many years as a horticulturist and teacher well qualify him for the task of preparing this Encyclopedia. Because he has, over a period of more than a dozen years, written the entire text (submitting certain critical sections to specialists for review and suggestions) instead of farming out sections to a score or more specialists to write, the result is remarkably homogeneous and cohesive. The Encyclopedia is fully cross referenced so that one may locate a plant by either its scientific or common name.

If, as has been said, an encyclopedia should be all things to all people, then the present volumes richly deserve that accolade. Among the many who call it "friend" will be not only horticulturists ("gardeners," as our author likes to refer to them), but growers, breeders, writers, lecturers, arborists, ecologists, and professional botanists who are frequently called upon to answer questions to which only such a work can provide answers. It seems safe to predict that it will be many years before lovers and growers of plants will have at their command another reference work as authoritative and comprehensive as T. H. Everett's Encyclopedia.

John M. Fogg, Jr.
Director Emeritus, Arboretum of the Barnes Foundation
Emeritus Professor of Botany, University of Pennsylvania

Preface

The primary objective of *The New York Botanical Garden Illustrated Encyclopedia of Horticulture* is a comprehensive description and evaluation of horticulture as it is known and practiced in the United States and Canada by amateurs and by professionals, including those responsible for botanical gardens, public parks, and industrial landscapes. Although large-scale commercial methods of cultivating plants are not stressed, much of the content of the Encyclopedia is as basic to such operations as it is to other horticultural enterprises. Similarly, although landscape design is not treated on a professional level, landscape architects will find in the Encyclopedia a great deal of importance and interest to them. Emphasis throughout is placed on the appropriate employment of plants both outdoors and indoors, and particular attention is given to explaining in considerable detail the how- and when-to-do-it aspects of plant growing.

It may be useful to assess the meanings of two words I have used. Horticulture is simply gardening. It derives from the Latin *hortus,* garden, and *cultura,* culture, and alludes to the intensive cultivation in gardens and nurseries of flowers, fruits, vegetables, shrubs, trees, and other plants. The term is not applicable to the extensive field practices that characterize agriculture and forestry. Amateur, as employed by me, retains its classic meaning of a lover from the Latin *amator;* it refers to those who garden for pleasure rather than for financial gain or professional status. It carries no implication of lack of knowledge or skills and is not to be equated with novice, tyro, or dabbler. In truth, amateurs provide the solid basis upon which American horticulture rests; without them the importance of professionals would diminish. Numbered in millions, amateur gardeners are devotees of the most widespread avocation in the United States. This avocation is serviced by a great complex of nurseries, garden centers, and other suppliers; by landscape architects and landscape contractors; and by garden writers, garden lecturers, Cooperative Extension Agents, librarians, and others who dispense horticultural information. Numerous horticultural societies, garden clubs, and botanical gardens inspire and promote interest in America's greatest hobby and stand ready to help its enthusiasts.

Horticulture as a vocation presents a wide range of opportunities which appeal equally to women and men. It is a field in which excellent prospects still exist for capable entrepreneurs. Opportunities at professional levels occur too in nurseries and greenhouses, in the management of landscaped grounds of many types, and in teaching horticulture.

Some people confuse horticulture with botany. They are not the same. The distinction becomes more apparent if the word gardening is substituted for horticulture. Botany is the science that encompasses all systematized factual knowledge about plants, both wild and cultivated. It is only one of the several disciplines upon which horticulture is based. To become a capable gardener or a knowledgeable plantsman or plantswoman (I like these designations for gardeners who have a wide, intimate, and discerning knowledge of plants in addition to skill in growing them) it is not necessary to study botany formally, although such study is likely to add greatly to one's pleasure. In the practice of gardening many botanical truths are learned from experience. I have known highly competent gardeners without formal training in botany and able and indeed distinguished botanists possessed of minimal horticultural knowledge and skills.

Horticulture is primarily an art and a craft, based upon science, and at some levels perhaps justly regarded as a science in its own right. As an art it calls for an appreciation of beauty and form as expressed in three-dimensional spatial relationships and an ability to translate aesthetic concepts into reality. The chief materials used to create gardens are living plants, most of which change in size and form with the passing of time and often show differences in color and texture and in other ways from season to season. Thus it is important that designers of gardens have a wide familiarity with the sorts of plants that lend themselves to their purposes and with plants' adaptability to the regions and to the sites where it is proposed to plant them.

As a craft, horticulture involves special skills often derived from ancient practices passed from generation to generation by word of mouth and apprenticeship-like contacts. As a technology it relies on this backlog of empirical knowledge supplemented by that acquired by scientific experiment and investigation, the results of which often serve to explain rather than supplant old beliefs and practices but sometimes point the way to more expeditious methods of attaining similar results. And from time to time new techniques are developed that add dimensions to horticultural practice; among such of fairly recent years that come to mind are the manipulation of blooming season by artificial day-length, the propagation of orchids and some other plants by meristem tissue culture, and the development of soilless growing mixes as substitutes for soil.

One of the most significant developments in American horticulture in recent decades is the tremendous increase in the number of different kinds of plants that are cultivated by many more people than formerly. This is particularly true of indoor plants or house-plants, the sorts grown in homes, offices, and other interiors, but is by no means confined to that group. The relative affluence of our society and the freedom and frequency of travel both at home and abroad has contributed to this expansion, a phenomenon that will surely continue as avid collectors of the unusual bring into cultivation new plants from the wild and promote wider interest in sorts presently rare. Our garden flora is also constantly and beneficially expanded as a result of the work of both amateur and professional plant breeders.

It is impracticable in even the most comprehensive encyclopedia to describe or even list all plants that somewhere within a territory as large as the United States and Canada are grown in gardens. In this Encyclopedia the majority of genera known to be in cultivation are described, and descriptions and often other pertinent information about a complete or substantial number of their species and lesser categories are given. Sorts likely to be found only in collections of botanical gardens or in those of specialists may be omitted.

The vexing matter of plant nomenclature inevitably presents itself when an encyclopedia of horticulture is contemplated. Conflicts arise chiefly between the very understandable desire of gardeners and others who deal with cultivated plants to retain long-familiar names and the need to reflect up-to-date botanical interpretations. These points of view are basically irreconcilable and so accommodations must be reached.

As has been well demonstrated in the past, it is unrealistic to attempt to standardize the horticultural usage of plant names by decree or edict. To do so would negate scientific progress. But it is just as impracticable to expect gardeners, nurserymen, arborists, seedsmen, dealers in bulbs, and other amateur and professional horticulturists to keep current with the interpretations and recommendations of plant taxonomists; particularly as these sometimes fail to gain the acceptance even of other botanists and it is not unusual for scientists of equal stature and competence to prefer different names for the same plant.

In practice time is the great leveler. Newly proposed plant names accepted in botanical literature are likely to filter gradually into horticultural usage and eventually gain currency value, but this sometimes takes several years. The complete up-to-dateness and niceties of botanical naming are less likely to bedevil horticulturists than uncertainties concerned with correct plant identification. This is of prime importance. Whether a tree is labeled *Pseudotsuga douglasii, P. taxifolia,* or *P. menziesii* is of less concern than that the specimen so identified is indeed a Douglas-fir and not some other conifer.

After reflection I decided that the most sensible course to follow in *The New York Botanical Garden Illustrated Encyclopedia of Horticulture* was to accept almost in its entirety the nomenclature adopted in *Hortus Third* published in 1976. By doing so, much of the confusion that would result from two major comprehensive horticultural works of the late twentieth century using different names for the same plant is avoided, and it is hoped that for a period of years a degree of stability will be attained. Always those deeply concerned with critical groups of plants can adopt the recommendations of the latest monographers. Exceptions to the parallelism in nomenclature in this Encyclopedia and *Hortus Third* are to be found in the CACTACEAE for which, with certain reservations but for practical purposes, as explained in the Encyclopedia entry Cactuses, the nomenclature of Curt Backeburg's *Die Cactaceae,* published in 1958–62, is followed; and the ferns, where I mostly accepted the guidance of Dr. John T. Mickel of The New York Botanical Garden. The common or colloquial names employed are those deemed to have general acceptance. Cross references and synonymy are freely provided.

The convention of indicating typographically whether or not plants of status lesser than species represent entities that propagate and persist in the wild or are sorts that persist only in cultivation is not followed. Instead, as explained in the Encyclopedia entry Plant Names, the word variety is employed for all entities below specific rank and if in Latin form the name is written in italic, if in English or other modern language, in Roman type, with initial capital letter, and enclosed in single quotation marks.

Thomas H. Everett
Senior Horticulture Specialist
The New York Botanical Garden

Acknowledgments

I am indebted to many people for help and support generously given over the period of more than twelve years it has taken to bring this Encyclopedia to fruition. Chief credit belongs to four ladies. They are Lillian M. Weber and Nancy Callaghan, who besides accepting responsibility for the formidable task of filing and retrieving information, typing manuscript, proofreading, and the management of a vast collection of photographs, provided much wise council; Elizabeth C. Hall, librarian extraordinary, whose superb knowledge of horticultural and botanical literature was freely at my disposal; and Ellen, my wife, who displayed a deep understanding of the demands on time called for by an undertaking of this magnitude, and with rare patience accepted inevitable inconvenience. I am also obliged to my sister, Hette Everett, for the valuable help she freely gave on many occasions.

Of the botanists I repeatedly called upon for opinions and advice and from whom I sought elucidation of many details of their science abstruse to me, the most heavily burdened have been my friends and colleagues at The New York Botanical Garden, Dr. Rupert C. Barneby, Dr. Arthur Cronquist, and Dr. John T. Mickel. Other botanists and horticulturists with whom I held discussions or corresponded about matters pertinent to my text include Dr. Theodore M. Barkley, Dr. Lyman Benson, Dr. Ben Blackburn, Professor Harold Davidson, Dr. Otto Degener, Harold Epstein, Dr. John M. Fogg, Jr., Dr. Alwyn H. Gentry, Dr. Alfred B. Graf, Brian Halliwell, Dr. David R. Hunt, Dr. John P. Jessop, Dr. Tetsuo Koyama, Dr. Bassett Maguire, Dr. Roy A. Mecklenberg, Everitt L. Miller, Dr. Harold N. Moldenke, Dr. Dan H. Nicolson, Dr. Pascal P. Pirone, Dr. Ghillean Prance, Don Richardson, Stanley J. Smith, Ralph L. Snodsmith, Marco Polo Stufano, Dr. Bernard Verdcourt, Dr. Edgar T. Wherry, Dr. Trevor Whiffin, Dr. Richard P. Wunderlin, Dr. John J. Wurdack, Yuji Yoshimura, and Rudolf Ziesenhenne.

Without either exception or stint these conferees and correspondents shared with me their knowledge, thoughts, and judgments. Much of the bounty so gleaned is reflected in the text of the Encyclopedia but none other than I am responsible for interpretations and opinions that appear there. To all who have helped, my special thanks are due and are gratefully proferred.

I acknowledge with much pleasure the excellent cooperation I have received from the Garland Publishing Company and most particularly from its President, Gavin Borden. To Ruth Adams, Nancy Isaac, Carol Miller, and Melinda Wirkus, I say thank you for working so understandingly and effectively with me and for shepherding my raw typescript through the necessary stages.

How to Use This Encyclopedia

A vast amount of information about how to use, propagate, and care for plants both indoors and outdoors is contained in the thousands of entries that compose the *New York Botanical Garden Illustrated Encyclopedia of Horticulture*. Some understanding of the Encyclopedia's organization is necessary in order to find what you want to know.

Arrangement of the Entries

Genera

The entries are arranged in alphabetical order. Most numerous are those that deal with taxonomic groups of plants. Here belong approximately 3,500 items entered under the genus name, such as ABIES, DIEFFENBACHIA, and JUGLANS. If instead of referring to these names you consult their common name equivalents of FIR, DUMB CANE, and WALNUT, you will find cross references to the genus names.

Bigeneric Hybrids & Chimeras

Hybrids between genera that have names equivalent to genus names—most of these belonging in the orchid family—are accorded separate entries. The same is true for the few chimeras or graft hybrids with names of similar status. Because bigeneric hybrids frequently have characteristics similar to those of their parents and require similar care, the entries for them are often briefer than the regular genus entries.

Families

Plant families are described under their botanical names, with their common name equivalents also given. Each description is followed by a list of the genera accorded separate entries in this Encyclopedia.

Vegetables, Fruits, Herbs, & Ornamentals

Vegetables and fruits that are commonly cultivated, such as broccoli, cabbage, potato, tomato, apple, peach, and raspberry; most culinary herbs, including basil, chives, parsley, sage, and tarragon; and a few popular ornamentals, such as azaleas, carnations, pansies, and poinsettias, are treated under their familiar names, with cross references to their genera. Discussions of a few herbs and some lesser known vegetables and fruits are given under their Latin scientific names with cross references to the common names.

Other Entries

The remaining entries in the Encyclopedia are cross references, definitions, and more substantial discussions of many subjects of interest to gardeners and others concerned with plants. For example, a calendar of gardening activity, by geographical area, is given under the names of the months and a glossary of frequently applied species names (technically, specific epithets) is provided in the entry Plant Names. A list of these general topics, which may provide additional information about a particular plant, is provided at the beginning of each volume of the Encyclopedia (see pp. xvii–xx).

Cross References & Definitions

The cross references are of two chief types: those that give specific information, which may be all you wish to know at the moment:
Boojam Tree is *Idria columnaris*.
Cobra plant is *Darlingtonia californica*.
and those that refer to entries where fuller explanations are to be found:
Adhatoda. See Justicia.
Clubmoss. See Lycopodium and Selaginella.

Additional information about entries of the former type can, of course, be found by looking up the genus to which the plant belongs—*Idria* in the case of the boojam tree and *Darlingtonia* for the cobra plant.

ORGANIZATION OF THE GENUS ENTRIES

Pronunciation

Each genus name is followed by its pronunciation in parentheses. The stressed syllable is indicated by the diacritical mark ´ if the vowel sound is short as in man, pet, pink, hot, and up; or by ˋ if the vowel sound is long as in mane, pete, pine, home, and fluke.

Genus Common Names
Family Common Names
General Characteristics

Following the pronunciation, there may be one or more common names applicable to the genus as a whole or to certain of its kinds. Other names may be introduced later with the descriptions of the species or kinds. Early in the entry you will find the common and botanical names of the plant family to which the genus belongs, the number of species the genus contains, its natural geographical distribution, and the derivation of its name. A description that stresses the general characteristics of the genus follows, and this may be supplemented by historical data, uses of some or all of its members, and other pertinent information.

Identification of Plants

Descriptions of species, hybrids, and varieties appear next. The identification of unrecognized plants is a fairly common objective of gardeners; accordingly, in this Encyclopedia various species have been grouped within entries in ways that make their identification easier. The groupings may bring into proximity sorts that can be adapted for similar landscape uses or that require the same cultural care, or they may emphasize geographical origins of species or such categories as evergreen and deciduous or tall and low members of the same genus. Where the description of a species occurs, its name is designated in *bold italic.* Under this plan, the description of a particular species can be found by referring to the group to which it belongs, scanning the entry for the species name in bold italic, or referring to the opening sentences of paragraphs which have been designed to serve as lead-ins to descriptive groupings.

Gardening & Landscape Uses
Cultivation
Pests & Diseases

At the end of genus entries, subentries giving information on garden and landscape uses, cultivation, and pests or diseases or both are included, or else reference is made to other genera or groupings for which these are similar.

General Subject Listings

The lists below organize some of the encyclopedia entries into topics which may be of particular interest to the reader. They are also an aid in finding information other than Latin or common names of plants.

PLANT ANATOMY AND TERMS USED IN PLANT DESCRIPTIONS

All-America Selections
Alternate
Annual Rings
Anther
Apex
Ascending
Awl-shaped
Axil, Axillary
Berry
Bloom
Bracts
Bud
Bulb
Bulbils
Bulblet
Bur
Burl
Calyx
Cambium Layer
Capsule
Carpel
Catkin
Centrals
Ciliate
Climber
Corm
Cormel
Cotyledon
Crown
Deciduous
Disk or Disc
Double Flowers
Drupe
Florets
Flower
Follicle
Frond
Fruit
Glaucous
Gymnosperms
Head
Hips
Hose-in-Hose

Inflorescence
Lanceolate
Leader
Leaf
Leggy
Linear
Lobe
Midrib
Mycelium
Node
Nut and Nutlet
Oblanceolate
Oblong
Obovate
Offset
Ovate
Palmate
Panicle
Pedate
Peltate
Perianth
Petal
Pinnate
Pip
Pistil
Pit
Pod
Pollen
Pompon
Pseudobulb
Radials
Ray Floret
Rhizome
Runners
Samara
Scion or Cion
Seeds
Sepal
Set
Shoot
Spore
Sprigs
Spur
Stamen
Stigma
Stipule

Stolon
Stool
Style
Subshrub
Taproot
Tepal
Terminal
Whorl

GARDENING TERMS AND INFORMATION

Acid and Alkaline Soils
Adobe
Aeration of the Soil
Air and Air Pollution
Air Drainage
Air Layering
Alpine Greenhouse or Alpine House
Amateur Gardener
April, Gardening Reminders For
Aquarium
Arbor
Arboretum
Arch
Asexual or Vegetative Propagation
Atmosphere
August, Gardening Reminders For
Balled and Burlapped
Banks and Steep Slopes
Bare-Root
Bark Ringing
Baskets, Hanging
Bed
Bedding and Bedding Plants
Bell Jar
Bench, Greenhouse
Blanching
Bleeding
Bog
Bolting
Border
Bottom Heat
Break, Breaking
Broadcast
Budding
Bulbs or Bulb Plants

Gardening Terms and Information (Continued)

State Agricultural Experimental Stations
Stock or Understock
Straightedge
Strawberry Jars
Strike
Stunt
Succession Cropping
Sundials
Syringing
Thinning or Thinning Out
Tillage
Tilth
Tools
Top-Dressing
Topiary Work
Training Plants
Tree Surgery
Tree Wrapping
Trenching
Trowels
Tubs
Watering
Weeds and Their Control
Window Boxes

FERTILIZERS AND OTHER SUBSTANCES RELATED TO GARDENING

Algicide
Aluminum Sulfate
Ammonium Nitrate
Ammonium Sulfate
Antibiotics
Ashes
Auxins
Basic Slag
Blood Meal
Bonemeal
Bordeaux Mixture
Calcium Carbonate
Calcium Chloride
Calcium Metaphosphate
Calcium Nitrate
Calcium Sulfate
Carbon Disulfide
Chalk
Charcoal
Coal Cinders
Cork Bark
Complete Fertilizer
Compost and Composting
Cottonseed Meal
Creosote
DDT
Dormant Sprays
Dried Blood
Fermate or Ferbam
Fertilizers
Fishmeal
Formaldehyde
Fungicides
Gibberellic Acid
Green Manuring
Growth Retardants
Guano
Herbicides or Weed-Killers
Hoof and Horn Meal

Hormones
Humus
Insecticide
John Innes Composts
Lime and Liming
Liquid Fertilizer
Liquid Manure
Manures
Mulching and Mulches
Muriate of Potash
Nitrate of Ammonia
Nitrate of Lime
Nitrate of Potash
Nitrate of Soda
Nitrogen
Orchid Peat
Organic Matter
Osmunda Fiber or Osmundine
Oyster Shells
Peat
Peat Moss
Permagnate of Potash
Potassium
Potassium Chloride
Potassium-Magnesium Sulfate
Potassium Nitrate
Potassium Permagnate
Potassium Sulfate
Pyrethrum
Rock Phosphate
Rotenone
Salt Hay or Salt Marsh Hay
Sand
Sawdust
Sodium Chloride
Sprays and Spraying
Sulfate
Superphosphate
Trace Elements
Urea
Urea-Form Fertilizers
Vermiculite
Wood Ashes

TECHNICAL TERMS

Acre
Alternate Host
Annuals
Antidessicant or Antitranspirant
Biennals
Binomial
Botany
Chromosome
Climate
Clone
Composite
Conservation
Cross or Crossbred
Cross Fertilization
Cross Pollination
Cultivar
Decumbent
Dicotyledon
Division
Dormant
Endemic
Environment
Family

Fasciation
Fertility
Fertilization
Flocculate
Floriculture
Genus
Germinate
Habitat
Half-Hardy
Half-Ripe
Hardy Annual
Hardy Perennial
Heredity
Hybrid
Indigenous
Juvenile Forms
Juvenility
Legume
Monocotyledon
Monoecious
Mutant or Sport
Mycorrhiza or Mycorhiza
Nitrification
Perennials
pH
Plant Families
Photoperiodism
Photosynthesis
Pollination
Pubescent
Saprophyte
Self-Fertile
Self-Sterile
Species
Standard
Sterile
Strain
Terrestrial
Tetraploid
Transpiration
Variety

TYPES OF GARDENS AND GARDENING

Alpine Garden
Artificial Light Gardening
Backyard Gardens
Biodynamic Gardening
Bog Gardens
Botanic Gardens and Arboretums
Bottle Garden
City Gardening
Colonial Gardens
Conservatory
Container Gardening
Cutting Garden
Desert Gardens
Dish Gardens
Flower Garden
Fluorescent Light Gardening
Formal and Semiformal Gardens
Greenhouses and Conservatories
Heath or Heather Garden
Herb Gardens
Hydroponics or Nutriculture
Indoor Lighting Gardening
Japanese Gardens
Kitchen Garden
Knot Gardens

The New York
Botanical Garden
Illustrated Encyclopedia
of Horticulture

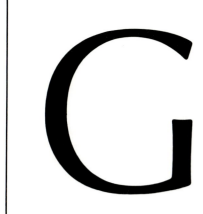

G

GAGEA (Gà-gea). Gageas are bulb plants related to *Lloydia*, natives of Europe, North Africa, and temperate Asia. They belong in the lily family LILIACEAE. The name commemorates Sir Thomas Gage, an English amateur botanist, who died in 1820. There are possibly seventy closely similar species, not really first class ornamentals.

Gageas are 2 to 10 inches tall, usually with one or two linear basal leaves and loose umbel-like clusters of small- to medium-sized blooms topping stalks with a few bracts. The flowers have six separate, spreading petals (more properly, tepals), in most kinds lustrous golden-yellow, with greenish-yellow undersides, that do not fall, but wither on the plant. There are six stamens and a solitary style. The fruits are capsules.

Hardy, spring-flowering *Gagea lutea* (syn. *G. silvatica*) has one, rarely two, basal leaves about ⅓ inch wide, three- to five-veined, and with hooded apexes. Its slender stalks, 4 to 10 inches tall, carry up to seven blooms ¾ to a little over 1 inch wide, and bright yellow, with a broad band of green down the outside of each petal. The stamens are about one-half as long as the petals. This inhabits open woodlands and meadows throughout most of Europe and parts of Asia. Somewhat more decorative, but not known to be cultivated, are *G. stellaris*, of southern Europe, and *G. alexeenkoana*, of the Balkans.

Garden Uses and Cultivation. Rock gardens and informal areas are most appropriate locations for gageas. Easily grown in well-drained soil of ordinary fertility and moisture content, they should be set about 3 inches deep and approximately the same distance apart, and should not be transplanted more often than necessary. So long as they are thriving it is better to leave them undisturbed. Propagation is by natural multiplication of the bulbs, and by seeds sown in sandy soil in a cold frame, as soon as they are ripe or in fall.

GAILLARDIA (Gaillàr-dia)—Blanket Flower. The entirely New World genus *Gaillardia* consists of twenty-eight species of annuals, biennials, and herbaceous perennials. It is most plentifully represented in the native floras of the southwestern United States and adjacent Mexico. There are two species in South America. Belonging to the daisy family COMPOSITAE, it has a name that commemorates Gaillard de Charentonneau, an eighteenth-century French patron of botany. The common name blanket flower alludes to the flower colors of some kinds resembling those of Indian blankets.

Gaillardias have short to long stems and more or less toothed leaves, alternate or chiefly basal. The showy, daisy-type, long-stalked flower heads have centers of fertile, purple disk florets. The ray florets are sterile and yellow or yellow and bronzy-red or brown, or purple. At their apexes they are three-toothed or three-lobed. The fruits are seedlike achenes.

Blanket flowers first came to the attention of Europeans when *G. pulchella* was introduced to France early in the 1780s and was cultivated in the Royal Botanical Gardens there. It is still one of the two most commonly grown gaillardias. The other is *G. aristata*. Other wild kinds introduced to cultivation from time to time have generated only ephemeral interest. Of prime horticultural importance is a group of hybrids between *G. pulchella* and *G. aristata* that originated spontaneously in a Belgian nursery about 1857 and to which the name *G. grandiflora* is applied. These intermediates between annual *G. pulchella* and perennial *G. aristata* behave as perennials. In vigor and ornamental value they are decidedly superior to their perennial parent.

An erect, branching, softly-pubescent annual 1 foot to 2 feet in height, *G. pulchella* has lanceolate, oblong, or spatula-shaped, thickish, nearly stalkless leaves, 1 inch to 2 inches long, and flower heads 2 inches across, with flat ray florets, rose-purple at their bases and yellow at their tips or sometimes wholly reddish-purple. The lower leaves are pinnately-lobed. This species, native from Virginia to Florida and New Mexico, is usually represented in

Gaillardia pulchella picta variety

gardens by its varieties *G. p. picta* and *G. p. lorenziana*. The former name covers horticultural selections notable for their large flower heads of various shades of color, the latter variety, which originated in Germany in 1881, is distinguished by having quilled or tubular ray florets, some of which are intermixed with the disk flowers. In the middle twentieth century, tetraploid variants of *G. p. lorenziana*, such as 'Tetra Fiesta' and 'Tetra Giant', were developed and these and other named horticultural varieties are described in seedsmen's catalogs as annual gaillardias.

The perennial *G. aristata,* native from Colorado to Oregon and British Columbia, was first described from a specimen collected by Lewis and Clark in 1806. It is 2 to 3 feet tall, branched, and more or less hairy. Its leaves are lanceolate to oblong or the lower ones spatula-shaped. They are 2 to 8 inches long and may be waved and lobed at the margins. The flower heads, 3 to 4 inches in diameter, have flat, yellow ray florets sometimes purple at their bases.

Gaillardia grandiflora variety

Perennial blanket flowers most commonly grown in gardens are varieties of the hybrid **G. grandiflora.** These are offered under many fancy varietal names such as 'Burgundy', 'Dazzler', 'General Patton', 'Portola', 'The Warrior', and 'Yellow Queen', and are listed and described in the catalogs of nurseries and seedsmen. It is of interest to note that hybrid populations have escaped from cultivation and in parts of the United States have established themselves along roadsides and railroads where neither parent species occurs naturally. Plants of *G. grandiflora* are intermediate between the parent species and usually combine the rich red coloring of *G. pulchella* with the perennial endurance of *G. aristata.* They seem, too, to have a hybrid vigor that causes them to be bigger and more robust than either parent.

Other gaillardias sometimes cultivated are these: **G. amblyodon,** of Texas, is a hairy, 2-foot-tall annual with scarcely lobed, stalkless leaves up to 3 inches long and 2-inch-wide flower heads with cinnabar-red ray florets. Annual *G. pulchella* 'Indian Chief', because of its flower color, is sometimes confused with this species. **G. comosa,** of Mexico, is a promising dwarf species with orange blooms. **G. lanceolata** is a variable native of the southeastern and southcentral United States of erect or diffuse habit and with flower heads with or without yellow to maroon ray florets. **G. multiceps** inhabits gypsum soils in the southwestern United States and is of compact growth. **G. parryi** has lemon-yellow blooms and is indigenous in Arizona. **G. suavis,** of Oklahoma, Texas, and adjacent Mexico, has globose, distinctly fragrant flower heads without ray florets.

Garden Uses. The cultivated blanket flowers are among the most attractive of summer flowers and are useful for cutting as well as for garden decoration. They are easy to grow, generally stand summer heat well, and are extremely resistant to drought. The annual kinds are also worth

growing in greenhouses for blooming in late winter and spring. All need full sun and are satisfied with fertile, well-drained garden soil. They are intolerant of wet, clayey ones. The perennial kinds are usually winter killed in such soils.

Cultivation. Choice varieties of perennial blanket flowers are best increased by careful division in early spring or early fall, by cuttings taken in summer, or by root cuttings in late winter or spring. They can be raised from seeds, but seedlings are variable and do not exactly reproduce the parent variety. Many seedlings, however, have beautiful blooms, and seed sowing is a popular means of raising perennial blanket flowers. Seeds are sown in May either in cold frames or in an outdoor seed bed, and the young plants are transplanted as soon as they are big enough to handle to a nursery bed in rows about 1 foot apart and with about 6 inches between the plants in the rows. By fall or the following spring the plants are large enough to transfer to their permanent locations. Routine care of perennial blanket flowers is not arduous. An annual application of a complete fertilizer in spring and regular surface cultivation or mulching around the plants to keep down weeds, promotes good growth. Faded flower heads should be removed promptly, and in very dry weather occasional applications of water are helpful. These plants need little or no staking. In regions of cold winters protection in the form of a light covering of salt hay or of branches of evergreens is advisable.

Annual blanket flowers are raised by sowing seeds in early spring, or in mild climates in fall, outdoors where the plants are to bloom. For cut flowers seeding may be done in rows 1 foot to 1½ feet apart. For decorative patches in flower gardens they may be broadcast. In either case the seeds are covered with soil to a depth of about ¼ inch, and the seedlings thinned to about 4 inches apart if in rows, to about 6 inches if in patches. An alternative method is to sow seeds indoors at a temperature of 55 to 60°F some six or seven weeks before the young plants are to be transplanted to their flowering locations, which may be as soon as all danger of frost is past, and to grow the young plants, spaced 2 inches apart in flats or individually in small pots, in a sunny greenhouse with a night temperature of 50°F, and day temperatures five to ten degrees higher, until planting-out time.

To have plants bloom in late winter and spring in greenhouses, seeds of the annuals are sown from September to January, and the seedlings are planted individually in small pots and are repotted into larger containers as growth demands. At their final potting they may be accommodated one in a 5-inch pot or three plants in a container 6 or 7 inches in diameter. Growing conditions should be those indi-

cated above as appropriate for raising young plants for outdoor gardens. When the final pots are well filled with healthy roots weekly applications of dilute liquid fertilizer are helpful. Early blooming is encouraged by lengthening the day by artificial illumination.

Diseases and Pests. Blanket flowers are subject to powdery and downy mildews, to a virus spotted-wilt disease, and to aster yellows. They may be infested with aphids, thrips, four-lined plant bug, and leafhoppers.

GALACTITES (Galactĭ-tes). One species of this group of three thistle-like annuals, biennials, and perennials, of the Mediterranean region and Canary Islands, is sometimes cultivated. The genus is related to *Cnicus* and belongs in the daisy family COMPOSITAE. The name is derived from the Greek *gala*, milk, in reference to the white juice and to the veins of the leaves.

The purple flower heads of *Galactites* are in clusters. They have ray florets larger than the fertile disk florets and like those of *Centaurea*, sterile. The fruits are seedlike achenes. The spine-pointed leaves have milky-white veins or blotchings, under surfaces with cottony hairs.

The species occasionally cultivated, *G. tomentosa* is an annual or biennial 2 to 3 feet tall with stems clothed with white cottony hairs. Its spiny, pinnately-lobed leaves are white-hairy on their undersides, more or less blotched with white above. The lilac-purple flower heads are 1½ inches in diameter. The bracts of the involucre (collar of leaflike bracts just behind the flowers) are spine-tipped.

Garden Uses and Cultivation. The most appropriate garden uses for this decorative species are for planting in groups in beds or borders of mixed flowers and for setting in irregular drifts in informal areas. The blooms are attractive as cut flowers and last well in water. Any ordinary garden soil satisfies. Full sun is needed. Sow seeds in early spring or in regions of mild winters in early fall. Thin the seedlings to 1½ feet apart. The plants need no special care and flower freely in high summer. They set seeds in abundance and if the ground where they grow is left undisturbed, self-sown seedlings are likely to appear in satisfying abundance the following year.

GALANTHUS (Gal-ánthus)—Snowdrop. Among the most pleasing small, hardy bulb plants, snowdrops rank highly in the estimations of discriminating gardeners. Most bloom in winter or very early spring, and provide welcome foretastes of garden delights to come. Of modest rather than blatant mien, they must be sought in the landscape to be enjoyed. Unlike crocuses, scillas, and glories-of-the-snow, they paint no patches of brilliant color in the garden. Comprising about twenty species, *Galan-*

thus belongs in the amaryllis family AMAR-YLLIDACEAE. Its members are inhabitants of Europe and western Asia. The name, alluding to the prevailing white or milky-white blooms, comes from the Greek *gala*, milk, and *anthos*, a flower. The bulbs of the common snowdrop, and probably other kinds, are somewhat poisonous.

Snowdrops have small bulbs from which sprout two or three narrow- to broad-strap-shaped, deciduous leaves and a stalk usually terminating in a solitary, nodding bloom. From snowflakes (*Leucojum*) the flowers of snowdrops differ in their stalks being solid rather than hollow and in their three inner perianth segments being markedly smaller than the three outer. All petal-like, the perianth segments are separate to their bases. There is no perianth tube. There are six stamens and one style. The fruits are angled capsules.

The common snowdrop (*G. nivalis*) is dainty and delightful. It has many variants, some recognized botanically, others bearing fancy (nonlatinized) names. The chief differences among this plethora of sometimes hard-to-distinguish varieties are the green or yellow patterns of the flowers. Undoubtedly some represent hybrids between the common snowdrop and other species. Typical *G. nivalis*, native to Europe and western Asia, is 4 inches to rarely 1 foot tall. It has usually two somewhat glaucous, slightly keeled, channeled, linear leaves about ¾ inch in width and in the bud stage flat or channeled, but not pleated. Its flowers, their inner petals deeply cleft at their apexes and with the cleft bordered with green, are about 1 inch long. This blooms in very early spring. Flowering in winter, *G. n. cilicicus* differs in the pedicels

(slender individual flower stalks) being shorter than the spathes (bracts) in the axils of which they arise, and in the leaves at flowering time being longer. Fall-flowering *G. n. reginae-olgae* blooms before its leaves, which are narrower than those of *G. nivalis* and are green with a central glaucous stripe, develop. Double blooms, less elegant than single ones, are borne by *G. n. flore-pleno*. Other more or less distinct varieties are *G. n. albus*, in which the green spot on the inner petals is nearly lacking; *G. n. atkinsii*, a very early flowering, tall variety; *G. n. lutescens*, with yellow-tipped inner petals; *G. n. pictus*, in which the outer petals have each a prominent green mark; *G. n. virescens*, similar, but with the outer petals also green-striped; *G. n. viridans*, the inner petals of which are green edged with white; and *G. n. viridapicis*, the outer petals of which are tipped with green. Other named varieties, including 'S. Arnott', tall and with scented blooms, and 'Straffan', which usually has two blooms on each stem, are listed and described in catalogs of specialist dealers in bulb plants.

The giant snowdrop (*G. elwesii*), a native of the mountains in Asia Minor, is another highly variable species. One variant, even larger than the typical kind, is *G. e. whittallii*, another, *G. e. maximus*, is distinguished by its twisted leaves. *G. e.* 'Cassaba' normally has two blooms on each stem. More robust than the common snowdrop and having larger bulbs, *G. elwesii* produces two upright, very glaucous leaves with hoodlike apexes. They are about ¾ inch wide. In the bud stage their edges are rolled inward. Its flowers are over 1 inch long, with broadly-ovate outer petals and oblong inner ones marked half-

way up from their bases and at their apexes with green.

Other kinds in cultivation include *G. plicatus*, of the Crimea. This rather late-flowering kind has large bulbs and a pair of glaucous leaves, flat in the bud stage and with recurved margins, and globular blooms over 1 inch long, the apexes of the inner petals of which are fringed with green. From *G. plicatus* variable *G. byzantinus* of Asia Minor differs in having the inner petals of its 1-inch-long blooms marked both at their apexes and bases with green. The margins of its leaves are recurved. Endemic to the island of Ikaria in the Aegean Sea, *G. ikariae* differs only slightly (the outer petals of its flowers are oblong-spatula-shaped instead of oblong-oval) from *G. i. latifolius*, which occurs in Asia Minor and the Caucasus. In the bud stage the two about 1-inch-wide leaves of these kinds have inrolled margins. The flowers, over 1 inch long, are dark green around the tips of the inner petals.

Garden and Landscape Uses. Snowdrops are splendid for naturalizing in lightly shaded places and in the open and for planting in rock gardens and other intimate areas where their blooms can be enjoyed to the fullest when nearly all around is unpromising and bleak. The flowers are admirable for use in small arrangements. In greenhouses and window gardens snowdrops can be gently forced into bloom a little ahead of their natural appearance outdoors, but they do not respond to hard forcing. Snowdrops appreciate cool, humid locations, and moist, but not wet soil that is mellow and fairly well supplied with organic matter. They seem to delight especially in sloping ground and

Galanthus nivalis

Galanthus nivalis flore-pleno

banks that assure good drainage as well as adequate moisture, and certainly such locations admit of their display to best advantage.

Cultivation. Selection of an agreeable site goes far to ensure success with snowdrops. Given the cool, moist environment they need, most kinds are likely to prosper and even proliferate. Under less happy conditions all that can be expected is sulky tolerance, and failure is more probable. Planting is done in early fall, the bulbs being set at a depth of 3 to 4 inches and about the same distance apart, but they should be spaced irregularly instead of in rows or other even patterns. As with all bulb plants, it is important not to remove the foliage until it dies naturally. This happens with snowdrops in early summer.

To have snowdrops early indoors, plant the bulbs closely together in pans (shallow pots) early in fall. Bury the containers to a depth of about 6 inches, in a bed of peat moss, sand, or similar material, in a cold frame or sheltered spot outdoors, and leave until January. Then bring them into a greenhouse or window where the night temperature is 40 to 50°F and that by day five to ten degrees higher. Keep them well watered. They will soon bloom. If, after flowering is through, they are grown under the same conditions until all danger of frost is past, they may be planted outdoors where they may be expected to bloom in future years. Snowdrops generally increase satisfyingly from offsets and are easily raised from seeds and bulb cuttings.

GALAX (Gà-lax). One of the most esteemed eastern North American wild flowers, the only species of this genus, *Galax aphylla*, is endemic to woods, chiefly in mountains, from Maryland to Kentucky, Georgia, and Alabama. Its leaves are familiar even to city folks who have little contact with growing plants and to others far from its natural range, for they are gathered commercially and are extensively employed by florists for wreaths, Christmas greenery, and other decorative purposes, and are a popular garnish for raw meats and fish in butcher shops and fish stores. This handsome plant belongs in the diapensia family DIAPENSIACEAE, a group now much less numerous than in former geologic times, related to the primrose family PRIMULACEAE, and including among cultivated plants *Diapensia* and *Shortia*. From these *Galax* differs in having its flowers in slender spike-like racemes. The name *Galax* is from the Greek *gala*, milk, and perhaps refers to the white flowers.

An evergreen, stemless, herbaceous perennial forming tufts of glossy, long-stalked, round or broadly-ovate leaves, 2 to 5 inches across with heart-shaped bases and rounded apexes, *G. aphylla* has erect, leafless flower stalks 1 foot to 1½ feet tall, crowded along their upper 2 to 4 inches

Galax aphylla

with numerous tiny white flowers. The corollas are cleft nearly to their bases into five segments, and the ten stamens, one-half of which are fertile and one-half sterile, have their filaments (stalks) united in their lower parts into a tube. The fruits are ovoid capsules. The intriguing feature of this plant is its beautiful leathery foliage that in fall matures to lovely shades of bronze and red, which it retains all winter.

Garden and Landscape Uses. Unlike a goodly number of eastern North American woodlanders, *Galax* is satisfyingly content to make its home in gardens; it domesticates with ready ease. For this we are grateful, for it is a delightful and charming plant, a most precious of groundcovers. It belongs in shaded places where the soil is acid and its content of decayed organic matter—forest debris such as leaf mold or peat moss or other reasonable substitute therefore—is high. This plant is a "natural" for gracing woodland gardens and rock gardens, for bordering shady paths, and for carpeting the ground in selected places beneath trees and shrubs.

Cultivation. Although *Galax* stands periods of relative dryness well, fair supplies of moisture at the roots encourage thrifty growth. And so does a mulch of organic matter, such as leaf mold or peat moss, maintained around the plants. Planting may be done in early fall or spring, spacing the plants about 9 inches to 1 foot apart. Propagation is easily achieved by seeds sown in a cold frame or nicely prepared bed outdoors that is unlikely to be disturbed. An acid, sandy peaty soil raked or sifted to a fine, level surface makes a good sowing bed. The seeds should be very lightly covered, and the bed kept uniformly moist and shaded from direct sun. Sowing is best done in fall or very early spring.

GALEANDRA (Gal-eándra). These pleasing orchids occur as wildlings from Florida to the West Indies, Mexico, and Brazil. There are twenty species, members of the orchid family ORCHIDACEAE. The name, from the Latin *galea*, a helmet, and the Greek *andros*, male, alludes to the stamen being crested.

The natural habitats of galeandras vary from branches and crotches of trees, where they perch as epiphytes (plants that

Galeandra devoniana

grow on other plants without taking sustenance from them), to loose forest soils. Sometimes they sit on mossy rocks. They fall rather neatly into two groups, those with fat and globular or slender and stemlike pseudobulbs that have long, narrow leaves, and leafless or apparently leafless kinds that have subterranean tubers. Members of the first group are more often cultivated. The flowers characteristically have large, showy, more or less flaring, trumpet-shaped lips. The sepals and petals are similar to each other.

The cylindrical or slightly spindle-shaped, stemlike pseudobulbs of deciduous *Galeandra devoniana* are in tufts and 2 to 4 feet tall or taller. Their lanceolate, keeled leaves are from 9 inches to over 1 foot long by up to 1½ inches wide. On stalks 6 to 8 inches long, the racemes of long-lived, 3- to 4-inch wide, fragrant flowers are borne in nodding or drooping, terminal racemes of several. They have widely-spreading to somewhat reflexed lanceolate sepals and petals that are dark purple or brownish-purple with contrasting yellow-green or green edges. These spread behind the showy, flaring lip like a stylized rising sun. The lip envelops the white column. It is 2 inches long, broadly-obovate, white, beautifully longitudinally striped with rosy-purple, and has a green spur. This is a native of Brazil and Venezuela.

Much less robust *G. baueri* (syn. *G. batemanii*), native of Mexico, Guatemala, and northeast South America, has slightly zig-zag pseudobulbs, their bottoms partly hidden by the persistent bases of the deciduous leaves. They are usually under 1 foot in length and have many pointed, linear to linear-lanceolate leaves up to 9 inches long by ¾ inch wide. The few-flowered racemes have bracted stalks up to about 1 foot long. From 2 to 3 inches in diameter, the long-lived, fragrant blooms have yellow-brown sepals and petals and a wavy-

edged, purple lip, with its basal portion white and purple. Sometimes, in a variant that perhaps should be distinguished as *G. b. floribus-luteus*, the lip is yellow, scarcely or not marked with purple.

An exceedingly rare native of southern Florida that occurs much more plentifully in tropical America and the West Indies, *G. beyrichii* is a terrestrial species that has erect stems up to 4 feet long, sheathed with bracts, and terminal racemes of greenish blooms 2 inches or more in diameter. The bell-shaped, crinkle-edged lip is white or greenish-white marked with crimson or reddish-brown lines. This species has tubers, but is without leaves.

Free-flowering *G. pubicentrum* of Amazonian Peru has clusters of slender, spindle-shaped, longitudinally-striped pseudobulbs 5 or 6 inches tall, with along their lengths more or less erect, narrow-linear leaves up to 6½ inches long and ½ inch wide. The long-lasting, fragrant flowers are 1½ to 2¼ inches long. They have light brown or brownish-green reflexed sepals and petals, and a large white, cream-white, or pink-tinged concave lip, lavender toward its apex and with a prominent, slender-funnel-shaped, greenish-yellow spur.

Galeandra pubicentrum

Garden Uses and Cultivation. These are very worthwhile components of orchid collections. They grow readily in intermediate- and warm-temperature greenhouses in well-drained pots in any of several loose, air-admitting rooting mediums. One consisting of approximately equal parts of turfy loam, osmunda fiber, coarse leaf mold, and one-half a part each of finely-broken crock (pieces of clay flower pots) and dried cow manure, with some crushed charcoal added, suits. Good light with only sufficient shade to prevent scorching of the foliage, high humidity, plenty of warmth, and ample supplies of water are needed during the season of active growth, at which time well-rooted specimens should be given dilute liquid fertilizer at regular intervals. Care must be taken not to allow water to lodge in the

leafy tops of the new growths. When the new pseudobulbs have matured, supplies of water are greatly reduced and the plants kept in a somewhat lower temperature and drier atmosphere until signs of growth beginning again are detectable. For more information see Orchids.

GALEGA (Galèg-a)—Goat's Rue. Half a dozen species of Europe, Asia, and Africa belong in *Galega* of the pea family LEGUMINOSAE. The name, from the Greek *gala*, milk, was applied in recognition of an old belief that the herbage is influential in stimulating milk production in goats, cows, and other animals.

Bushy, hairless, herbaceous perennials, galegas have alternate, pinnate leaves with a terminal and many lateral leaflets. The pea-shaped, purple-blue, blue, or white flowers are in terminal and axillary racemes. Each has a calyx with five nearly equal teeth, a broad standard or banner petal, and a pair of wing petals somewhat joined to the keel. The ten stamens are united. There is one persistent style. The fruits are slender pods.

Goat's-rue (*G. officinalis*), native from central Europe to Iran, is 2½ to 5 feet in height and has pretty leaves of eleven to seventeen oblong leaflets up to 2 inches long. The flowers are borne profusely in summer in erect, stalked racemes longer than the leaves. Purple-blue, about ½ inch long, many in each raceme, they are succeeded by reddish-brown seed pods 1 inch to 1½ inches in length. Variants are *G. o. alba*, which has white blooms, and *G. o. carnea*, with double pink flowers. The white-flowered variety is remindful of a decidedly superior white sweet-clover (*Melilotus alba*), the kind naturalized in

Galega officinalis

Galeandra baueri

many places along roadsides and waste places. Western Asian *G. bicolor* differs from *G. officinalis* in having flat rather than cylindrical seed pods up to 2½ inches long and in its flowers, in looser racemes, being bluish-white with a bluish-lilac standard petal. An intermediate hybrid between the last and *G. officinalis* named **G. hartlandii** (syn. *G. officinalis hartlandii*) has lilac-tinged flowers with a bluish-lilac standard petal, and foliage that when young tends to be variegated.

Garden and Landscape Uses. Although not one of the most outstanding herbaceous perennials, goat's-rue is hardy and is useful in perennial beds and informal areas. Its foliage is decorative and associates well with that of other plants. Its numerous spikes of bloom provide color and interest. The flowers are pretty for cutting and mixing with other kinds in arrangements.

Cultivation. Few plants are easier to grow than this. It thrives in any ordinary, well-drained garden soil in full sun and is easy to raise from seeds, which may be sown in a cold frame or outdoor bed in April or May. Transplant the seedlings as soon as they are big enough to handle comfortably into a nursery bed in rows 1½ feet apart, spacing the plants about 9 inches apart in the rows. The following spring they will be ready for transferring to their permanent flowering sites. Propagation can also be effected in spring or early fall by division, but the rootstocks spread slowly and unless increase is wanted there is no need to divide the plants except at intervals of several years.

GALEOBDOLON. See Lamiastrum.

GALINGALE. See Cyperus.

GALIUM (Gàli-um)—Sweet Woodruff or Waldmeister, Bedstraw. Scarcely among the most important of garden flowers, galiums belong in the madder family RUBI-ACEAE. There are about 300 species, natives of widely dispersed temperate regions and

Galium odoratum

mountains in the tropics. The name comes from the Greek *gala*, milk, and alludes to an ancient use of *Galium verum* as a curdling agent. It was also used for coloring cheese, and a red dye was extracted from its roots.

Galiums include annuals and herbaceous perennials, characteristically with slender, angled or cylindrical, often rough, weak stems. Their stalkless leaves are in whorls (circles of more than two). Usually bisexual, the tiny flowers are without or almost without calyxes. They have wheel-shaped, usually four-, but sometimes three-parted corollas, four or three stamens, and two styles. They are numerous and chiefly in axillary and terminal panicles. The fruits are dry or rarely somewhat fleshy.

Sweet woodruff or waldmeister (**G. odoratum** syn. *Asperula odorata*) is a charming, delightfully fragrant-flowered perennial useful as a groundcover in woodlands, rock gardens, and other places where the soil contains generous supplies of humus and is moderately moist, and there is light shade. It has many slender, erect, branchless stems, from 6 inches to 1 foot tall, and hairless, linear leaves 1 inch to 1½ inches long, ¼ to ½ inch wide, rough-toothed at their margins, in whorls of six to eight. In May it bears usually three-branched clusters of small pure white flowers. Sweet woodruff is used to flavor May wine and other beverages. Its leafy stems, pressed and dried between sheets of newspaper, turn black, become strongly fragrant of new mown hay, and can be used to scent linens. Sweet woodruff is native to Europe and Asia.

Two white-flowered bedstraws, similar in appearance and often confused in cultivation, are *G. mollugo* and *G. aristatum*. Natives of Europe, and the first naturalized in North America, both are sometimes known as false-baby's-breath. Perennials 1 foot to 3 feet tall, they form clumps of many erect stems, with bristle-tipped, single-veined, linear leaves in circles of six or eight. They have multitudes of small flowers in panicles suggestive of those of baby's breath (*Gypsophila paniculata*), although the blooms differ greatly in floral details. The leaves of **G. mollugo,** not over 1 inch in length, are not glaucous. Those of **G. aristatum** are up to 1½ inches long, and on their undersides usually glaucous. Also, the flowers of the last are in more open panicles than those of *G. mollugo*.

Northern bedstraw (**G. boreale**) is a variable native of much of the northern United States and parts of southern Canada. From the kinds dealt with above it differs in its leaves being in circles of four, in having three veins, and in not ending in bristles. It forms erect clumps 1 foot to 3 feet tall or somewhat taller. Its flowers are white.

Yellow bedstraw or Lady's bedstraw (**G. verum**), a native of Europe, North Africa, and Asia, is naturalized in North America.

Galium boreale

Galium verum

Galium olympicum

A sprawling or erect perennial, it has smooth stems 1 foot to 3 feet long, and lustrous leaves usually hairless above and minutely-hairy on their undersides, linear, and ½ to a little over 1 inch long in circles of six to twelve. The bright yellow flowers are profusely borne in crowded panicles.

Charming **G. olympicum** of Anatolia is a choice alpine that forms compact green cushions of hairless, four-angled stems 1 inch to 3 inches long and furnished with bristle-tipped, linear leaves in whorls (circles) of five or six. The tiny, nearly stalkless flowers, in clusters of two to six, produced in considerable abundance, are pink in bud, pure white when fully open.

Garden and Landscape Uses. The larger galiums are suitable for flower borders and naturalistic landscapes, and *G. verum*, which adapts to dry soils better than the others, for clothing banks and, if controlled to prevent its too rambunctious spread, for rock gardens. The sprays of flowers of several kinds are very nice for cutting to mingle with larger, heavier blooms, to lighten bouquets and arrangements. Low *G. olympicum* is suitable for alpine greenhouses and rock gardens.

Cultivation. Any ordinary garden soil suits most galiums; for *G. olympicum* a gritty, well-drained soil is needed. They do well in full sun or part-day shade. Increase is easily had by seed and by division. The kinds described are hardy.

GALLBERRY is *Ilex coriacea*.

GALLS. Galls are abnormal swellings of proliferated tissue on roots, trunks, twigs, leaves, and other plant parts. They are caused by a variety of irritants including insects, mites, nematodes, bacteria, and fungi. Galls occur on a wide variety of plants and assume a great many sizes, shapes, and colors. Many do no appreciable harm. If objectionable in appearance, hand picking or pruning may take care of these. Others are more serious, some extremely so. Control measures must be tailored to the causal agent and kind of plant. Ask a Cooperative Extension Agent or other local authority about these.

GALPHIMIA (Gal-phímia). Comprising about a dozen species of tropical American shrubs and small trees, *Galphimia* belongs in the malpighia family MALPIGIACEAE. The name *Galphimia* is an anagram of that of the related genus *Malpighia*.

These plants have opposite, undivided leaves and in racemes, branched clusters, or panicles, small yellow flowers with five each sepals and petals, the latter narrowed markedly to a claw at their bases, ten stamens, five of which are alternate with five shorter ones, and three styles. The fruits are capsules.

A shrub 4 to 6 feet tall, **G. glauca** (syn. *Thryallis glauca*) has reddish-hairy stems and short-stalked, ovate to elliptic, glaucous-green leaves 1½ to 2 inches long. The ¾-inch-wide, bright yellow flowers, many together in crowded terminal racemes, have two small bracts at or below the middle of the individual flower stalks. This is wild from Mexico to Guatemala. Up to 10 feet tall and native from Mexico to Peru, *G. gracilis* has elliptic-oblong to elliptic-lanceolate leaves 2 to 3 inches in length and with a pair of glands at the base. The ½-inch-wide, yellow flowers are loosely arranged, many together in terminal racemes. The stalks of the individual blooms have two small bracts near their tops.

Garden and Landscape Uses. This dainty shrub succeeds in a wide variety of soils and withstands drought and exposed locations. It does best in partial shade and is useful for the fronts of shrub borders, for facing down taller plantings, for foundation plantings, and for lawn beds. It is a pretty plant for growing in greenhouses either in ground beds or in pots, and has the merit of blooming while quite small.

Cultivation. The chief attention required is occasional pruning to keep the plant shapely, remove crowded branches and seed heads, and stimulate the production of new shoots. Pruning is best done at a time when the bush is out of bloom so that there is no interference with the flower display.

When grown in greenhouses galphimias do well in a minimum winter night tem-

Galls: (a) Spruce gall aphid

(b) Mossy rose gall

Galphimia glauca

perature of 50 to 55°F with a five to ten degree increase permitted during the day. The atmosphere should be moderately humid, but not excessively so. During the summer the plants may be placed outdoors in a lightly shaded location. Ordinary potting soil is suitable. Repotting and needed pruning is done in late winter or spring. Ordinarily, the first will be needed at intervals of two to three years only. In intervening years top dressing is all that is required. Water should be provided freely from spring to fall, less generously in winter, although the soil should never for long be dry. Specimens well rooted benefit from applications of dilute liquid fertilizer at about two-week intervals from spring to fall. Few plants are easier to propagate by seeds or cuttings than *Galphimia*. Both may be started in a temperature of about 60°F.

GALTONIA (Galtò-nia) — Summer-Hyacinth. The name of this South African genus commemorates the distinguished British anthropologist Sir Francis Galton, who died in 1911. It consists of four species, one well known in cultivation, and belongs in the lily family LILIACEAE. From *Hyacinthus* it differs chiefly in having more numerous seeds that are flattened and much crowded.

Galtonias are bulb plants with somewhat fleshy basal leaves and erect, leafless stalks with long, loose racemes of flowers. The blooms, white or white tinged with green, have short perianth tubes, six petals (more correctly, tepals), six stamens, and a solitary pistil. The fruits are somewhat triangular capsules.

The summer-hyacinth (**Galtonia candicans** syn. *Hyacinthus candicans*) has a common name and botanical synonym that suggests its affinity with *Hyacinthus*, which indeed exists, although the plant bears little overall resemblance to the hyacinths of spring. In gross appearance it seems more like a rather frail *Yucca*, although it belongs in a different family. Its bulbs are large and globose and its somewhat lax, four to six glaucous leaves strap-shaped, 2 to 3 feet long and 1 inch to 2 inches wide. The flower stalks rise to a height of 3 to 4 feet and carry as many as twenty to forty rather distantly spaced, fragrant blooms each 1 inch to 1½ inches long, narrowly-bell-shaped, and drooping. They are white.

Garden and Landscape Uses. This is an interesting and reliable plant where it is hardy, which means about as far north as Philadelphia, Pennsylvania. Under heavy mulch it may be wintered in the ground somewhat further north. It can also be successfully handled by lifting the bulbs each fall and storing them over winter as is done with gladioluses. The summer-hyacinth may be used effectively in borders and in groups among shrubs that do not root too aggressively. It associates well with architectural features. An interesting and effective use is to interplant it with *Yucca filamentosa*; in this way two distinct seasons of bloom are secured from the same patch of ground and the two species are perfectly congruous.

Cultivation. Summer-hyacinths are grateful for deeply spaded, fertile, well-drained soil and a sunny location. The bulbs are planted with their bases 6 inches beneath the surface, and it is important that there are a few inches of good soil below this into which the roots can ramify.

Early spring is the best time to plant and a spacing of 1¼ feet is about right. No special care is needed other than the removal of old flower stalks and, in fall, of dead foliage. A winter covering of salt hay, branches of evergreens, or other suitable insulation against deep-penetrating cold is desirable where frost is likely to reach the bulbs without this protection. If the bulbs are dug up and stored over winter they should be kept where the temperature is between 35 and 45°F. Propagation is by offsets, seeds, and bulb-cuttings.

GALVEZIA (Gal-vèzia). This genus of six or fewer species of the figwort family SCROPHULARIACEAE is related to snapdragons (*Antirrhinum*). Native from California to Peru, its name commemorates Jose Galvez, a Spanish administrator. Galvezias are shrubs or herbaceous perennials with leaves opposite or in whorls (circles of more than two) and flowers in terminal racemes. Their asymmetrical, tubular blooms have five-parted calyxes and strongly two-lipped corollas with their tubes pouched or spurred at their bases and their throats nearly closed with a prominence called a palate. There are four stamens in pairs, their stalks furnished with two rows of glands. The fruits are more or less spherical capsules.

The only kind cultivated is *G. speciosa* (syn. *Antirrhinum speciosum*), a native of California. A spreading, sometimes somewhat vining, evergreen shrub up to about 3 feet tall and twice as wide, this has short-stalked, thickish, elliptic to ovate, toothless leaves. They are in twos or threes and are ¾ inch to 1¾ inches long.

Galtonia candicans

Galtonia candicans (flowers)

The red, snapdragon-like flowers, ¾ to 1 inch long, form leafy, softly-pubescent racemes. In the wild G. speciosa favors dry, rocky soils. It blooms in spring.

Garden and Landscape Uses and Cultivation. The kind described is planted somewhat in California and is suitable for other mild dry climates. It is appropriate for the fronts of borders, for banks, and for native plant gardens. A sunny location and well-drained soil are requisite. Propagation is by seeds and by cuttings.

GAMBOGE. See Garcinia.

GAMOLEPIS (Gamó-lepis). To the daisy family COMPOSITAE belongs this South African genus of a dozen shrubs and herbaceous plants. They have alternate, usually deeply-pinnately-divided leaves. Solitary, stalked flower heads of disk and ray florets are typical of the group. The yellow or orange ray florets (often called petals) are in a single row, and are female. The disk florets are bisexual. The involucre (collar of leafy organs behind the flower head) consists of a single row of bracts joined for one-third or more from the bases to their tips. This characteristic is recognized in the generic name, which is from the Greek gameo, to unite, and lepis, a scale. The fruits are seedlike achenes.

Gamolepis tagetes

An annual up to 1 foot tall, **Gamolepis tagetes** is much-branched, wiry-stemmed, and free-flowering. Its leaves, 1 inch to 1½ inches long, are pinnately-divided into slender lobes, usually again toothed or lobed. About ¾ inch in diameter, the upturned, solitary flower heads are on stalks 2 to 4 inches long that arise from the tips of the branches. They have brilliant yellow or orange-yellow disks and rays. The bracts of the urn-shaped involucres are joined for over one-half their lengths.

A broad evergreen shrub 4 to 6 feet tall, **G. chrysanthemoides** produces over a long period, but most abundantly in spring, bright yellow daisies 1½ inches across.

The bright green, chrysanthemum-like leaves are obovate in outline, and deeply-pinnately-lobed or toothed. They are 2 to 3½ inches long.

Garden Uses and Cultivation. The very pretty and easily grown annual described above is attractive for edgings, the fronts of flower borders and for rock gardens, and similar uses. It may be raised from seeds sown early indoors to give plants for transplanting to the garden after danger of frost has passed, or by seeds sown outdoors in early spring and the seedlings thinned to leave those that remain to bloom where they were sown. About 6 inches between individuals is suitable spacing. Rather poor porous soil and a sunny location are suitable for G. tagetes. Like so many South African plants, it suffers in the very hot and humid summer weather characteristic of much of North America; nevertheless it withstands these hardships better than many of its sister South Africans and usually revives noticeably and satisfactorily with the coming of cooler nights in late summer and fall. In California and regions of similarly mild, dryish climates, G. chrysanthemoides succeeds so well that it frequently reproduces by self-sown seedlings. It is an interesting general-purpose flowering shrub that does well in sunny locations and is not fussy about soil. To ensure a neat, tidy appearance it needs pruning or shearing from time to time. It may be used as a formal hedge. This shrub is easily raised from seeds and from cuttings.

GANJA. See Cannabis.

GARAYARA. This is the name of hybrid orchids the parents of which include *Arachnis, Paraphalaenopsis,* and *Vandopsis.*

GARBANZO is *Cicer arietinum.*

GARBERIA (Gar-bèria). One endemic species of Florida comprises this genus of the daisy family COMPOSITAE. The genus is dedicated to Dr. Abram Paschal Garber of Pennsylvania, who died in 1881.

A freely-branched shrub about 6 feet in height, **Garberia fruticosa** has leathery, evergreen, spatula-shaped to broadly-obovate leaves up to about 1¼ inches long. The flower heads are without petal-like ray florets. They consist of pale purple to pink disk florets (the kind that form the centers of the flower heads of daisies). They are arranged in dense, flattish-topped clusters. The fruits are seedlike achenes.

Garden and Landscape Uses and Cultivation. Sometimes used as an ornamental, more particularly in naturalistic and semiwild surroundings, *Garberia* is little known beyond the region where it is native. It succeeds in sunny locations in well-drained sandy soil, and does well near the sea. Propagation is by seeds and by cuttings.

GARCINIA (Gar-cínia)—Mangosteen, Gamboge, Gelugor. One must travel to the tropics of southeastern Asia to enjoy at its best that most delicious and highly esteemed of tropical fruits, the mangosteen. The tree that bears it, *Garcinia mangostana,* is cultivated to a limited extent in the American tropics, but unfortunately, has not there provided generally very successful as a fruiting tree. Visitors to Bangkok, Singapore, Kuala Lumpur, and other sultry parts of Asia, if they are fortunate enough to be there when mangosteens are in season should not fail to sample them. It will be a memorable experience. Despite the similarity of names, the mangosteen is entirely different from the mango, a tropical fruit successfully cultivated throughout the American tropics and in Florida.

The genus to which the mangosteen belongs, *Garcinia,* consists of some 400 species, all natives of the Old World, and mostly Asian. They are trees and shrubs with leathery, evergreen leaves, and belong in the garcinia family GUTTIFERAE. Unisexual and bisexual flowers may develop on the same tree. The genus was named in honor of Laurent Garcin, a French physician, traveler, and botanist, who died in 1751. Its fruits, like those of oranges, are technically berries that, like oranges, after peeling divide readily into segments. The mangosteen is not, however, botanically related to the orange or other citrus fruits. In addition to those of the mangosteen the fruits of some other species of *Garcinia* are eaten in tropical Asia, but none approaches the mangosteen in quality. Another product of *Garcinia* is gamboge. This is a yellow pigment derived from a gum-resin and is obtained from more than one species including *G. cambogia* and *G. morella.*

The gelugor (**G. atroviridis**) is a tall tree with red blooms and fluted orange-yellow fruits. These are sliced, dried, and used in curries and with various foods, especially fish. They make excellent jelly.

The mangosteen (**G. mangostana**), native of the Malaya region, grows slowly, attains a height of about 30 feet, and is

Garcinia mangostana

Garcinia mangostana (fruit)

Garcinia xanthochymus (fruit)

well-branched and furnished with attractive glossy foliage to or nearly to the ground. Its pointed, elliptic-oblong, thick, leathery leaves are 6 to 10 inches in length and have many horizontal veins running from midrib to margin. The male flowers are three to nine together in terminal clusters, the bisexual ones are at the tips of the branches, singly or in pairs. They are about 2 inches in diameter and have four large, roundish sepals that are persistent and remain with the fruits and four fleshy, rose-pink, broadly-ovate petals. There are many stamens and a four-lobed, stalkless, eight-rayed stigma. Mangosteen fruits are rounded with slightly flattened ends. They average about 2½ inches in diameter and have a tough, thick rind that encloses five to seven juicy segments. If injured slightly the rind exudes a thick yellow juice, which soon hardens. The segments are pure white to ivory and slightly translucent. They contain few or no seeds. Another species cultivated to some extent in the American tropics, chiefly as an ornamental, is **G. xanthochymus** (syn. *G. tinctoria*), of India and Malaya. Up to about 40 feet tall, this species has leathery, pointed-oblong-elliptic leaves up to 1½ feet long. Its ¾-inch-wide, white flowers are succeeded by dark yellow, spherical fruits 2 to 3 inches in diameter.

Garden and Landscape Uses. The cultivated garcinias are good-looking, low, broad trees well furnished with attractive foliage. They make dense screens and are suitable for general landscape planting. In the American tropics they are grown experimentally, but otherwise are rarely cultivated. Some good fruiting trees of the mangosteen are at Summit Gardens in the Panama Canal Zone, and there also, are good examples of *G. cambogia* that fruit heavily. The mangosteen also fruits in Trinidad, Surinam, Jamaica, and Dominica. It is strictly tropical and cannot be expected to prosper outdoors in the continental United States. Despite many trials it has not been successful in Hawaii.

Cultivation. Not enough experience has been had with growing the mangosteen in the American tropics to make very strong pronouncements about its needs. There is evidence that the soil profoundly affects results. A stiffish clayey fertile earth is best. It should be decidedly moist, but well drained so that the roots have access to adequate fresh rather than stagnant water and so that superfluous moisture is drained away to a water table or reservoir a few feet beneath the surface. Mangosteens are commonly raised from seeds, but in view of the variability of the fruits, especially with regard to seediness, it would seem preferable to increase desirable seedless types by vegetative means. This can be done by inarching and by budding onto seedling understocks of the mangosteen or other species of *Garcinia*. For this purpose *G. cambogia* has proved successful, and mangosteens grown on it appear to thrive better in parts of the American tropics than own-root seedlings. Transplanting is a somewhat delicate operation and its successful accomplishment probably greatly influences the future well-being of the trees. It is recommended that the young plants be raised in pots and not be set in the open ground until they are 2 or 2½ feet tall. In their early stages young mangosteens should be shaded from strong sun. Established trees are either not pruned or may have their small interior branches removed annually to prevent overcrowding. A mulch is maintained over the ground around the trees and an annual application of fertilizer is given. Other species of *Garcinia* sometimes met with in special collections, such as *G. cambogia*, appear to be less demanding than the mangosteen.

GARDEN. There perhaps can be no unchallengeable definition of the word garden, but in general acceptance it connotes an area, usually enclosed or otherwise defined, devoted to growing plants more intensively and usually in much fewer numbers of each sort than implied by agriculture, forestry, or commercial orcharding. True, commercial vegetable production is frequently referred to as truck or market gardening and establishments where this is done as truck or market gardens, but such operations, especially since the introduction of machinery has made large areas necessary or at least desirable for success, are much more agricultural than horticultural.

Gardens then are generally private or public areas, usually landscaped and including lawns, trees, shrubs, and herbaceous flowering plants arranged for delight and pleasure and, in the case of vegetable and fruit gardens, for the supply of produce to the home. Some public gardens, notably botanical gardens, emphasize educational functions, others afford or stress opportunity for passive recreation. Home gardens enhance the livability of the environment, not only that of their owners and tenders, but of the neighborhood, and give opportunity for the pursuit of a delightful hobby and healthful recreation. The word garden derives from the same root as yard, the old English *geard* or medieval English *yerd*. It is of interest to note that in the United States a garden area adjacent to a building is frequently called a yard, but in Great Britain that word is now generally limited to describing a paved enclosure.

GARDEN CENTERS. In contemporary North America this term has two distinct meanings. The older and less frequent kind of garden center is in fact a horticultural society, a membership organization of people interested in gardening that maintains central facilities for meetings, lectures, flower shows, and similar events, usually has a library, sometimes a garden, and generally a professional staff to aid members and be of service to the general public. Such centers generally publish a bulletin. Outstanding examples of organizations of this kind are the Garden Center of Greater Cleveland, Cleveland, Ohio, and the Berkshire Garden Center, Inc., Stockbridge, Massachusetts.

Commercial garden centers, the numbers and popularity of which have increased tremendously since World War II, are in effect horticultural supermarkets. Mostly located

Commercial garden center: (a) Indoor sales area

(b) Outdoor sales area

in suburban areas and often associated with nursery and greenhouse businesses, they offer for sale, to a large extent on a pick up and carry away basis, as complete a line as possible or convenient of plants, bulbs, seeds, soil conditioners, fertilizers, pesticides, implements, tools, and other equipment and supplies needed by gardeners. Their popularity among shoppers is conditioned by the usual ready availability of parking space, the opportunity afforded to inspect in one place a very extensive stock of widely diverse items, and the fact that purchases can be carried away, thus eliminating waits and additional costs for delivery.

GARDEN CLUBS. The garden club idea and its development are peculiarly American, and although some mens' garden clubs exist, it is predominantly feminine. Its origin may be traced to the formation by a group of ladies in Athens, Georgia, in 1890 of the Athens Garden Club, its purpose to communicate knowledge and exchange experiences among its members about gardening. Following this, local groups elsewhere organized for similar purposes. In 1913 the Garden Club of America was founded at Philadelphia. An organization with social overtones of garden clubs that meet certain stringent accomplishment requirements, this has very substantially influenced the development of horticulture in the United States. Its member clubs and the parent body meet at regular intervals to hear lectures, exhibit flower arrangements, hold flower shows, and engage in other garden-related pursuits. Once a year the Garden Club of America holds a national convention. From time to time it sponsors garden tours for its members. It has accomplished a great deal in furthering the establishment and preservation of nature reserves, in promoting the conservation of natural beauty and of rare and threatened species, and in fostering and preserving the beauty of the American landscape. Its long, vigorously waged war against billboards has so far been only partially successful.

Coincident with the establishment of clubs that qualified for membership in the Garden Club of America other local groups of women interested in gardening formed similar clubs. The great majority of these are federated garden clubs, clubs that are members of statewide amalgamations of the type of the Federated Garden Clubs of New York State, which, founded in 1914, was the first of such organizations. The National Council of State Garden Clubs, Inc. serves as a link between many State Federations. Federated clubs engage in much the same activities as Garden Club of America clubs, stressing civic responsibilities with horticultural and conservation facets as well as engaging actively in the practice and promotion of gardening. The

Ohio Association of Garden Clubs, Inc. is another very active organization of this type. The Women's National Farm and Garden Association, Inc., with branches in most states, has done a great deal to stimulate interest in gardening.

Men's garden clubs gained prominence with the founding in 1932 of Men's Garden Clubs of America. Since then, interest in such clubs and accomplishments by them have steadily progressed, but the movement has not developed to the extent of womens' clubs. Most garden clubs have sponsored memberships.

GARDEN FRAMES. Cold frames and heated frames are simple devices in which plants are grown protected from full exposure to the weather. They are bottomless, boxlike structures fitted with light-admitting tops of glass or plastic that can be slid up and down, removed, or raised or lowered to ventilate the frame and allow working in it. The tops consist of one or more sections of convenient size called sash. Standard sash are 6 feet long by 3 feet wide, but amateurs are likely to find those of smaller dimensions, say 4 by 3 feet, easier to handle. The length of a more-than-one sash frame is the combined

Cold frame, with concrete walls and standard sash

Wooden cold frame, with standard sash

Home garden cold frames: (a) Sheltering young annuals and vegetables, sash removed

(d) A deep frame containing young hollies and camellias

The sash of this frame is of corrugated fiberglass

(b) Sheltering young tomato plants

Removable sash bars facilitate working inside the frame

Skeleton frames, with potted rhododendrons

(c) Hardening off young tomato plants, sash removed, lath shade over other plants in the frame

width of the number of sash plus that of narrow strips that project upward from the crossbars (sash bars) upon which the sash rest and act as separators and guide strips. It is often a great convenience if the sash bars are removable.

To shed rain the sash are installed with a downward tilt from back to front. A satisfactory slope for a 6-foot-wide frame is assured by having the rear wall 9 inches to 1 foot higher than the front. With a frame 4 feet wide, 6 to 9 inches is enough. For most uses a convenient height for the front wall is 9 inches to 1 foot. Special purposes, such as the accommodation of plants taller than these dimensions, may dictate the need for deeper frames, but higher front walls cause more of the interior to be in constant shade.

Construction materials for the walls may be wood or masonry. If the former, which is very satisfactory, use a moisture-resistant kind such as redwood or cypress. It may be painted or treated with a preservative nontoxic to plants. Never use creosote. For a long time, glass was the only acceptable material for sash and is still perhaps the most satisfactory for all purposes. Certainly, apart from breakage, it is the most long-lasting. But transparent and clear translucent plastics have gained much favor and serve well. They have the great advantage of being lighter than glass. Suitably sized panels of corrugated fiberglass can be used effectively. For temporary use, heavy-gage, clear polyethylene plastic can be employed. Glass panes must be overlapped slightly like those of a greenhouse roof so that they shed water without leaking it into the frame.

Condensation water on the underside of the sash builds up under some weather conditions. Unless prevented, it drips from the sash bars to the harm of the plants beneath. It may be circumvented by cutting on each side of each bar about ½ inch beneath the glass a ¼-inch-deep, longitudinal groove. Such drip grooves, as they are called, convey the condensed water to the sill on which the front of the sash rests and there discharge it.

Skeleton frames are frames without sash bars. When in position the sash are merely butted against each other. They are not as waterproof or weatherproof as conventional frames, but they serve very well as protection for many nearly hardy plants, such as pansies, forget-me-nots, and other spring bedding plants, and for seedlings and cuttings of shrubs. They are also very useful as way-stops to be used for hardening plants to be transferred from greenhouses to outdoors. Old railroad ties or even grass sod can be used as walls for skeleton frames, or they can be made of planks, cinder blocks, or other materials.

Pit frames, or pits as they are usually called, are frames with floors considerably below outside ground level, usually 2 to 4 feet lower. They are extremely useful for accommodating high plants in containers for overwintering and in some cases for summer growth. Their interiors are warmer in winter, cooler and more humid in summer, than outdoors. Also their occupants are easily protected from rain and too-strong sun.

There are various types of frames. They may be free-standing or backed against a wall or fence as lean-tos. They may have the usual top, sloping in one direction, or be span-roofed, with a center ridge from which lights slope downward in opposite directions. The lights may be removable or hinged at their tops so that they can be raised or lowered, but not taken off. The first type is the better for most purposes. Frames may be permanently located or practically so, or of such size, weight, and construction that they are portable and fairly easily movable from place to place.

Warm frame heated by hot water pipes, sash removed

Cold frames are heated only by the sun. Heated frames or warm frames are equipped to keep their interiors at least above freezing and often at higher minimums by electric heating cables, hot water pipes, or sometimes in large establishments steam pipes. Because of the difficulty of maintaining even temperatures with them, and the high temperatures near the pipes themselves, steam pipes are the least satisfactory. Heating cables are satisfactory in mild climates and where the temperatures to be maintained are not greatly higher than those outside. For all-purpose use hot water pipes are best. Hotbeds are frames in which the interior soil is warmed from below. For more about these see Hotbeds.

Locating frames needs some thought. They should be sheltered from wind, but not in low frost pockets or where water gathers. For many uses it is best that they face south, to benefit fully from the sun. But north-facing frames are advantageous in summer for such plants as primulas, cy-

clamens, gentians, and others that prefer relatively cool conditions and shade then. Rotting of wooden frames is prevented or greatly delayed by standing them on masonry foundations or on loose concrete blocks, cinder blocks, or bricks set partway into the ground, and also, by keeping them painted or treated with other wood preservatives. White interiors reflect the most light.

The floors, depending upon for what purpose the frames are to be used, may be of soil in which planting is done directly, of firmly packed gravel, finely crushed stone, cinders, or other material suitable for standing flats, pots, and tubs on, of a layer of sand, peat moss and sand, or cinders in which pot plants may be plunged (buried partway or to their rims), or of a similar layer of suitable material in which to plant cuttings. In any case, excellent subsurface drainage is necessary.

The chief uses of frames are these: to raise earlier annual and vegetable plants for setting outdoors than can be had by seeding outside; to raise somewhat earlier such vegetables as lettuce, radishes, scallions, asparagus, and cauliflowers and such flowers for cutting as asters, gladioluses, snapdragons, and tuberoses; to grow and overwinter biennials and plants grown as biennials, such as English daisies, forget-me-nots, pansies, polyanthus primroses, and wallflowers; to overwinter in pots young rock garden plants and choice and somewhat delicate alpine kinds; to store in winter larger container plants of kinds slightly tender and uncertain to survive outdoors; and to sow seeds of and propagate by cuttings a wide variety of herbaceous perennials, shrubs, and trees, and grow during their young stages the young plants so obtained.

Manipulate sash for ventilating with high regard for the frame's occupants. With tender, young plants be extremely careful in spring not to allow cold drafts to damage them. Observe the same precaution about drafts, cold or warm, with cut-

Ventilating: (a) Raising end of sash with a stepped wood block

(b) On a calm day, opposite ends of alternate sash may be raised

(c) On breezy days, sash may be raised on leeward sides only

tings during their rooting period. In their early stages do not ventilate at all unless absolutely necessary, and then only very little. Gradually increase the amount of ventilation as good root systems are developed.

Protection from cold, additional to that provided by the sash, can be given by covering them on cold winter nights with heavy mats of reeds, straw, or quilted material or with wooden shutters, or translucent polyethylene plastic film may be tacked on the undersides of the sash to gain a double-glazed or storm window effect. If the walls of the frames are thin, extra insulation can be assured by building around the frame about 1 foot away from it a temporary framework of wood or wire mesh and stuffing this with dry leaves or straw covered with plastic mulch or roofing paper to keep it dry. In the case of plants dormant through the winter, a layer of straw or salt hay may be strewn over them inside the frame. This also gives some shade from strong sun, which can be helpful to evergreen sorts.

Shade is often a requirement of plants grown in frames. This can be had by applying to the sash a mixture of one of the

Winter protection: (a) Sash may be covered with mats at night

(b) A light covering of salt hay over the plants in the frame provides shade and some protection from cold

(c) An outer wooden framework, the space between it and the permanent frame stuffed with hay or leaves, gives added protection against cold

paintlike shadings used on greenhouses, but easily removable shades made of wooden or aluminum laths or of Saran cloth are far better because they can be put on and off according to the dictates of the weather.

Management of frames naturally varies somewhat according to the purposes for which they are being employed, but certain principles are generally applicable. The chief dangers are excessive moisture, the buildup of too high interior temperatures, cold drafts on tender foliage, and exposure of the occupants to excessive cold.

Do not wet soil or plants unless moisture is surely needed, and so far as possible confine watering to bright weather and do it early enough in the day so that surface moisture dries before nightfall. When water is required saturate the soil, then give no more until there is need again. Newly transplanted seedlings, cuttings, and some other plants benefit from light overhead spraying with water during warm, sunny weather. If weather permits, keep the frame ventilated at least a little, more if possible, for some little time following watering. Excessive humidity inside frames is a tempting invitation to mildews, rots, and other diseases.

Prevent too high interior temperatures by well-timed ventilating. This is commonly done by pulling all or some of the sash part way down, or sometimes, to achieve more even circulation, by pulling down alternate sash and pushing the others up. Hinged sash are usually ventilated by propping their fronts on wooden blocks. In rainy weather this method is also used with sliding sash.

GARDEN-HELIOTROPE is *Valeriana officinalis*.

GARDEN-LEMON is *Cucumis melo chito*.

GARDEN LINE. An indispensable aid to gardeners is the garden line. Frequently one is improvised from a length of cord or string and a pair of short wooden stakes. Very much more professional is a line of strong, thin, braided cord with one end attached to a metal stake, the other to a reel that makes it possible to wind and unwind the line neatly and expeditiously.

Garden line and reel

Such reels can be bought, or made by anyone handy with tools. Garden lines are used in drawing seed drills, for marking out planting rows, and when laying out paths, flower beds, and other garden features.

GARDEN PLANNING. See Planning Gardens and Home Grounds.

GARDENER'S GARTERS is *Phalaris arundinacea picta*.

GARDENIA. The word gardenia is employed in the common names of these plants, which do not belong to the genus *Gardenia* (discussed in the next entry): paper-gardenia (*Tabernaemontana divaricata*) and wild-gardenia (*Rothmannia capensis*).

GARDENIA (Gardèn-ia) — Cape-Jasmine. Surely everyone is familiar with the delightfully fragrant gardenia flowers used so freely by florists and with the gardenia plants sold at Easter time. Those acquainted with southern gardens know the gardenia shrubs that grace and perfume them and with live oaks, camellias, and crape-myrtles conjure nostalgia for the Old South. All these gardenias are forms of a single species, the Cape-jasmine.

The genus *Gardenia* includes 250 species of shrubs and small trees of the madder family RUBIACEAE. They are natives of warm regions of the Old World. Their name commemorates Dr. Alexander Garden, a physician of Charleston, South Carolina and correspondent of the great Swedish botanist Linnaeus. He died in 1791.

Gardenias have leaves in pairs or occasionally in whorls of three or more. The flowers are solitary or in pairs from the leaf axils or ends of the shoots. Comparatively large, they have a persistent, lobed calyx and five to eleven waxy petals, usually white to yellow and in the bud stage twisted. There are five to nine stamens and one style. The stalkless fruits are fleshy or leathery berries.

Cape-jasmine (**G. jasminoides** syn. *G. florida*) and its varieties are by far the most popular. The colloquial name is a misnomer applied originally in the belief that it was native of the Cape of Good Hope, South Africa. Actually its home is southern China. In its typical form, *G. jasminoides* is an evergreen shrub 5 to 6 feet tall with glossy, leathery, usually lanceolate or obovate, short-stalked leaves up to 4 inches long. The flowers, about 3 inches across, are white, sweetly fragrant, often double (with more than the normal number of petals) and are borne in late spring and summer. The variety *G. j. fortuniana* (syn. *G. j. veitchii*) has larger blooms and these, in greenhouses, are produced in winter, from November onward. Horticultural developments of this are the varieties 'Belmont', 'Hadley', and 'McLellan's 23'. A low-grow-

Gardenia jasminoides

Gardenia jasminoides fortuniana

ing variety of G. jasminoides has been named G. j. prostrata, and G. j. variegata has its leaves margined with white.

The next best-known species is C. thunbergia, one of the most ornamental of South African native shrubs or small trees. It has whitish stems, short, stiff branches, and very long-tubed, white flowers 2½ to 4 inches across, with eight or nine spreading, overlapping petals. The elliptic or roundish, pointed, evergreen leaves, glossy green and variable in size, are sometimes up to 6 inches long. They are opposite or in whorls of up to five. The hard, woody, grayish fruits are distinctive. Egg-shaped, they are 2 to 5 inches long, contain many seeds, and remain on the trees for many years without opening to release their seeds. It is assumed that natural distribution of this species is by seed contained in fruits eaten by antelopes, which pass through the animals without detriment to the seed's vitality.

Less well-known kinds include these: G. carinata, of the Malay Peninsula, a shrub or tree up to 20 feet tall, has obovate to oblanceolate leaves up to 7 inches long, and singly or in pairs, fragrant flowers 3 inches in diameter that open creamy-white, change to buff-yellow. G. cornuta is a South African shrub with obovate to oblanceolate leaves up to 1½ inches long and solitary, six-petaled flowers with slender corolla tubes 2 to 2½ inches long. G. imperialis is a West African tree up to 60 feet tall. It has obovate leaves sometimes exceeding 8 inches in length and white,

Gardenia jovis-tonantis in Africa

Gardenia taitensis

3-inch-wide, solitary, five-petaled flowers with corolla tubes up to 8 inches long. G. jovis-tonantis, up to 15 feet in height and a small tree, is West African. It has obovate leaves up to 5 inches long and creamy-white, fragrant, eight- or nine-petaled flowers up to 3 inches wide. G. lucida, of India, is a small deciduous tree with elliptic-oblong leaves 8 to 10 inches long. The five-petaled flowers 3 inches in diameter that open white and then change to yellow have slender corolla tubes up to 2 inches long. G. pseudopsidium, a native of the Philippine Islands and up to 15 feet tall, has obovate leaves, and white, 2-inch-wide flowers with five or more petals. G. taitensis, a native of the Society Islands or other islands nearby, generally resembles

G. jasminoides, differing most noticeably in its single flowers having five to nine narrower petals that spread in pinwheel fashion. Its obovate leaves are 2½ to 4 inches long. G. tubifera, of the Malay Peninsula and Indonesia, is a small tree with obovate-lanceolate leaves up to 9 inches long and from the leaf axils solitary, 1-inch-wide flowers with six to nine petals. White when they first open, they change to yellow and finally orange. G. turgida, of India, is a deciduous, sometimes spiny tree up to 25 feet in height. It has elliptic-obovate to nearly round leaves up to 4 inches long and solitary, fragrant, white, short-tubed, five-petaled flowers 1 inch wide or a little wider. For plants sometimes named G. capensis and G. globosa, see Rothmannia.

Garden and Landscape Uses. Gardenias are among the choicest broad-leaved flowering shrubs. They have refinement and distinction and are justly rated highly as plants for shrub beds and borders and other garden purposes. They are attractive when espaliered.

North of coastal Virginia and parts of Maryland they are not hardy, being essentially plants for hot, humid summers and mild winters. In greenhouses gardenias are splendid for planting in beds or growing in containers, and are much cultivated for cut flowers. They are not good houseplants. Their environmental requirements are too exacting to make them at all reliable as such. Nevertheless, it does happen that they sometimes prosper for years in a home. This is when local conditions just happen to be right; much more frequently they gradually deteriorate and eventually die.

Cultivation. In regions favorable to their outdoor cultivation, gardenias are not difficult to manage. Popular *G. jasminoides* and its varieties and *G. thunbergia* respond especially well if given reasonable attention in the matters of site selection, soil preparation and maintenance, and suitable measures to control diseases and pests. For outdoor planting they are chiefly propogagated by cuttings 6 to 8 inches long, of previous season's shoots, made in winter and planted with two-thirds of their length below the surface in sandy peaty soil in a shaded location outdoors or in a cold frame. When 1 year old the young plants are ready for transplanting 2 to 3 feet apart in nursery beds to be grown on for use in landscape work. If they are to be cultivated for cut blooms, they may be left in the cutting rows for two years before they are transplanted to permanent beds and spaced 4 to 5 feet apart. In either case the soil should be deep and fertile and contain a fairly high content of organic matter. It must be on the acid side of neutral. A pH of 5.5 to 6.5 is satisfactory. It should be moderately moist at all times but not subject to waterlogging or flooding. Gardenias benefit greatly if a mulch of bagasse, peat moss, peanut shells, corncobs, or other suitable material is maintained around them. Pruning, attended to as soon as the flowering season is through, consists of thinning out weak shoots and shortening others. Specimens grown as landscape ornamentals need little regular pruning. Gardenias are rather heavy feeders and respond to applications of high-nitrogen fertilizers, but these should never be applied in such amounts that the roots are harmed. Only kinds with an acid reaction should be used. Organics such as cottonseed meal are excellent, but chemical fertilizers such as ureaform kinds can be used.

With age gardenias are apt to take on a somewhat "tired" appearance and to pro-

Gardenia jasminoides fortuniana variety as a pot plant

duce fewer and smaller leaves and flower buds. Then, fairly severe pruning combined with generous fertilizing is in order and will usually restore the plants to vigor. When transplanting a good rootball with soil attached should be retained.

In greenhouses gardenias are an exacting crop. The kinds chiefly grown for cut flowers are varieties 'Belmont', 'Hadley', and 'McLellan's 23' of *G. jasminoides fortuniana*. For ornamental pot plants, the smaller flowered *G. jasminoides fortuniana* is used. These plants are propagated by cuttings taken in midwinter from terminal shoots. The cuttings are made 3 to 5 inches long and are planted in a mixture of sand and peat moss in a propagating case in a greenhouse. Sufficient bottom heat is supplied by hot water pipes or electric heating cables to keep the rooting medium at 75°F; the air above is maintained at a temperature five to ten degrees lower, and very humid. Because canker disease gains entrance through wounds it is advisable not to increase the chances of this by removing the bottom leaves, as is usually done with cuttings of other kinds; the base of the cutting is cut cleanly across just beneath a node. When the cuttings have rooted, in four to six weeks, they are potted individually into 2½- or 3-inch pots. Immediately following potting the plants are returned to the conditions under which they rooted for two or three weeks and then are transferred to the sunnier and more airy conditions that favor the growth of established plants. Until mid-August all branches that attain a length of 6 inches have their tips pinched out to encourage branching.

Gardenias need a sunny, humid greenhouse where a night temperature of 62°F is maintained and the day temperature rises five to fifteen degrees, depending upon the intensity of the light. In bright weather lightly spraying the foliage with water, but never so late in the day that it does not dry before nightfall, encourages good growth. If gardenias are to be grown

in beds or benches for cut flowers, the young plants should be set in rows 1½ to 2 feet apart with 1¼ to 1½ feet between the plants in the rows. Soil consisting of three parts porous, fertile topsoil and one part peat, and having a pH of 5.5 to 6.5, is satisfactory. Unless it is free of nematodes, the soil should be steam-sterilized.

Routine care consists of maintaining high humidity at all times, except that a slightly drier atmosphere, but not to the extent that growth is checked, may be kept from late August to the end of September; this favors the initiation of flower buds. Early flowering can be further induced by shading the plants with black cloth from 5 P.M. to 8 A.M. for a three-week period beginning July 20th. During those parts of the year when night temperature can be controlled it should be maintained at 62°F. Under these conditions flowering begins in November or December and continues throughout the winter and early spring. Although the soil must never be permitted to become really dry, overwatering is to be guarded against as likely to reduce root efficiency and promote yellowing of the newer leaves. Similar yellowing can result from too high a pH value (an alkaline condition) of the soil or from lack of iron in the soil. The latter can be corrected by applying chelated iron dissolved in water at the rate of an ounce to twenty gallons and applied at a gallon to each five square feet of soil surface, or by applying iron sulfate at the rate of an ounce to every 6 square feet. Alkalinity can be reduced and acidity maintained by applications of sulfur to the soil. In florists' practice, gardenia flowers are cut without foliage, and leaves from lower on the plants are wired to them to form collars beneath the blooms. Great care must be used in handling the flowers, as even slight bruises develop into unsightly brown areas. The best results with florists' gardenias are from first-year plants. If they are grown on for a second season they should be pruned in May by cutting out all thin, weak shoots and shortening those left to 2 or 2½ feet. At this time, too, the plants in the benches or beds may be thinned by removing about twenty percent of them. If they are planted in staggered rows of alternately twos and threes across the beds or benches, as is usual, this is done by taking out the center plant in each row of three.

As houseplants *G. jasminoides fortuniana* and its varieties (the gardenias chiefly grown by florists in greenhouses) are not usually satisfactory. The only possibility of even partial success is to imitate as closely as possible the conditions described as needed for their satisfactory growth in greenhouses. The species *G. jasminoides* (the summer blooming kind often called *G. florida*) offers better chances of satisfaction. The best way is to winter it in a comparatively low temperature, 45 to 50°F being high enough, where light is good, but direct sunlight is not necessarily available; a cool, light cellar well away from the heating plant is a good place. During winter the soil is kept dryish and effort is made to hold the plants without encouraging them to grow. Under such conditions they may lose some foliage and the remainder may take on a yellowish hue. With the coming of spring the plants are pruned lightly, if this seems desirable, repotted or given new tubs, if such a change is needed, or are top dressed by having some of the surface soil taken away and replaced with a rich mixture. The plants are then moved to a warmer, light place and regular watering is resumed. As soon as steady warm weather arrives they may be put outdoors to remain until fall frost threatens. Throughout the summer they must be kept well watered and be fertilized regularly.

Diseases and Pests. Canker is the most serious disease of gardenias. It enters the plant through wounds and is controlled by avoiding breaking or bruising plant parts, by selecting cuttings from the top parts of the plants (these are less likely to be infected than lower shoots), and by steam-sterilization of the propagating medium and the soil. Leaf spots are usually the result of excessive wetting of the foliage at times when it does not dry fairly quickly. Nematodes causing root knot are the most serious pest. Steam-sterilization of all soils, pots, benches, etc., used, and the certainty that stock is free of infestation at planting time, are the only sure control measures in most areas. In the deep south, where it is hardy, G. thunbergia has proved quite strongly resistant to infestation by nematodes, and as an understock upon which to graft varieties of G. jasminoides has made possible their cultivation where otherwise they could not be grown. It is also more tolerant of limestone soils than G. jasminoides. Other pests include red spider mites and mealybugs.

GARLAND FLOWER. This is the common name of *Daphne cneorum* and *Hedychium coronarium*.

GARLIC. Widely used for flavoring and especially beloved by peoples of the Mediterranean region, garlic is *Allium sativum.* Rather obviously an onion relative, like onions it belongs in the lily family LILI-ACEAE. A distinctive feature of garlic is its bulbs, which when mature are encased in a thin, silvery-white or pinkish skin that contains readily separable, wedge-shaped parts called cloves. The cloves are used in the kitchen and, because the plant very rarely flowers or seeds, for propagation. The leaves are linear and flat. For giant-garlic see Rocambole. False-garlic is *Nothoscordum.*

Soil for this crop must be well drained, the location sunny. Fertile, sandy loam is best to its liking, but it is adaptable to most

Separating the cloves of a garlic bulb

Planting cloves of garlic

garden soils. Prepare it as for onions. Plant the cloves in early spring, or in mild climates in fall, setting them right side up, 1 inch to 2 inches deep, 3 to 4 inches apart in rows 1 foot apart. Summer treatment calls for nothing more than weed suppression, and until the bulbs are fully formed and begin to ripen, watering in dry weather.

Harvest the bulbs in summer or early fall when their foliage has died and become brown and dry. Pull them up and leave them on the ground until the tops are dry completely. Then, either braid the stalks, so that short ropes of bulbs result, or remove the tops and store the bulbs in a basket, bag, or box in a cool, dry place.

GARLIC VINE. This name is applied to *Cydista aequinoctialis* and *Pseudocalymma alliaceum.*

GARRYA (Gár-rya)—Silk Tassel Bush. This genus is unique as being the only one in the silk tassel bush family GARRYACEAE. Endemic from the western United States to Guatemala and the West Indies, it consists of eighteen species of nonhardy evergreen shrubs or small trees, often puzzling to identify with certainty as to species because in the wild they intergrade

freely where their territories overlap. The name *Garrya* commemorates Nicholas Garry, of the Hudson's Bay Company. A friend of the famous botanical explorer David Douglas, he died in 1830.

Garryas have opposite, undivided, lobeless, toothless, short-stalked leaves of rather leathery texture. Their small, unisexual flowers, the sexes on separate plants, are in pendulous, catkin-like, conspicuously bracted racemes or spikes. They are without petals. Male blooms are stalked, and are in threes from the bract axils, females are solitary and nearly stalkless. The males have four-parted calyxes, with the tips of the segments often joined, and four stamens. Female flowers have two-lobed calyxes, or none, and two styles. The fruits are one- or two-seeded, dark purple to black, dry berries with bitter flesh.

A shrub or small tree occasionally 25 feet high, but as known in cultivation usually considerably lower, *G. elliptica* is shapely. Its shoots are densely clothed with short hairs. The elliptic to broad-elliptic leaves, up to 3½ inches long or rarely longer, mostly have undulate margins. They are green and sparsely-hairy above, densely-felted with short, curly hairs on their undersides. Both male and

Garrya elliptica

Garrya elliptica (foliage and young catkins)

Garrya elliptica (mature catkins)

Garrya flavescens

female catkins usually are from 3½ to 6 inches long, but the males more often attain the greater length and are sometimes 1 foot long. Because of this the males are usually reckoned superior as flowering ornamentals. The spherical fruits, ¼ to nearly ½ inch in diameter, are white-hairy at first, but much of the hairiness is lost as the berries age. This is a native of dry soils from Oregon to California. The splendid horticultural variety 'James Roof' has catkins 1 foot long or a little longer. A hybrid between *G. elliptica* and West Indian *G. fadyenii,* named *G thuretii,* has narrow leaves up to 4 inches long, and slender spikes of female flowers.

Ranging from Washington to California and also favoring dry soils, **G. fremontii** differs from *G. elliptica* in the under surfaces of its short-stalked, oblong-elliptic to ovate, up to 2¼-inch-long leaves, which do not have undulate margins, being hairless or almost so. From 4½ to 9 feet tall, this is less ornamental than *G. elliptica.* Its young shoots are bristly-hairy. From 3 to 8 inches in length and yellowish, the male catkins are solitary or in clusters. The females are up to 2 inches long, or in fruit longer. The purple to nearly black, subspherical fruits are ¼ inch in diameter. The leaves of *G. fremontii,* which is sometimes called fever bush, skunk bush, and quinine bush, are sometimes used medicinally.

From 5 to 8 feet tall, *G. flavescens* has short-stalked, elliptic to elliptic-oblong leaves 1 inch to 2½ inches long, slightly hairy above, more so on their undersides. The flower spikes are pendulous, the males up to 2 inches long, the females not over one-half that. The fruits are grayish-hairy. This is native from Nevada to Utah, Arizona, and New Mexico. Variety *G. f. pallida* (syn. *G. pallida*), of California, differs in having distinctly glaucous rather than yellowish-green foliage. Native of Mexico and Guatemala, *G. laurifolia,* a shrub or tree up to 20 feet in height, has gray-hairy shoots

and lanceolate-oblong to oblanceolate-oblong leaves 2¼ to 6 inches long. Its dark blue fruits are ⅓ inch or somewhat less in diameter. In its home territory the bark of this is used medicinally.

The hardiest species, which may live outdoors about as far north as Philadelphia but is better adapted for drier regions in the southwest, is **G. wrightii.** Less ornamental than *G. elliptica,* or even *G. fremontii,* this is native from New Mexico to Texas, Arizona, and Mexico. From 3 to 10 feet tall, it has silky-hairy shoots and elliptic-oblong to broad-elliptic leaves up to 2 inches in length. Its racemes of blooms are 1½ to 3 inches long. The dark blue fruits are up to ⅓ inch in diameter.

Garden and Landscape Uses and Cultivation. Garryas are choice subjects for use where evergreens of good appearance can serve. They are especially effective in winter or very early spring when their catkins are making their best display. Garryas must have very well-drained soil. If it is too fertile the first blooming of the shrubs may be delayed for a few years. Garryas do best in sunny locations. Because they do not transplant readily it is advisable to keep young plants in pots or cans until they are set in their permanent locations. Not much routine attention is needed. A little trimming of long shoots to foster

shapeliness may be done in spring. Propagation is by seeds, layering, and by cuttings about 3 inches long made from firm but not hard shoots in summer and planted in a propagating bed in a cold frame or greenhouse or under mist.

GARRYACEAE—Silk Tassel Bush Family. The characteristics of this family of dicotyledons are those of its only genus, *Garrya.*

GAS INJURY. Small quantities of manufactured illuminating gas in the soil or atmosphere can seriously injure plants. It is the unburned gas seeping from broken or faulty pipes or burners or entering the air as a result of not igniting the burners immediately after they are turned on, not the results of combustion, that causes the trouble. The toxic substances in this gas, reportedly absent from natural gas, are carbon monoxide, hydrogen cyanide, and ethylene and related unsaturated hydrocarbons. Trees and shrubs in urban environments not infrequently suffer severely from underground gas leaks, especially when a layer of frozen soil prevents the gas from escaping into the atmosphere. Then it may travel long distances underground causing damage over a large area. Instances are recorded of gas from distant leaks traveling in this way and escaping through the unfrozen soil of greenhouses into the greenhouse itself and damaging or killing the plants there. It should be noted that although natural gas is not toxic to plants it may injure them by driving out and replacing needed air in the soil. Again, this is most likely to be serious when the surface soil is frozen. Signs of gas injury are gradual or sudden severe wilting of foliage, scorched foliage, and dying back of twigs and branches. Any of these signs can, of course, also result from other causes. If you suspect gas injury report your suspicions to the gas company immediately. For more information see Houseplants or Indoor Plants.

GAS PLANT is *Dictamnus albus.*

GASTERHAWORTHIA (Gaster-hawórthia). This is a genus of hybrids between *Gasteria* and *Haworthia*, of the lily family LILIACEAE. Its members are succulent, nonhardy perennials intermediate between the parent genera and with a name derived from theirs.

Attractive *Gasterhaworthia* 'Royal Highness' has much the appearance of *Haworthia margaritifera*. Its parent species are unknown, but probably one is *Gasteria verrucosa*. Forming compact, spiral rosettes of white-dotted, triangular leaves up to 4 inches long and 1 inch to 1½ inches wide at their bases, this robust plant increases freely by suckers. Its greenish-white flowers are ½ to ¾ inch long. Its parentage unknown, *G. bayfieldii* is a stemmed kind that suckers freely and has rosettes of spiraled leaves, triangular at their apexes, and 4 inches or so long by 1 inch wide or slightly wider at their bases. When young with leaves in two opposite rows, but at later stages spiraled, *G. holtzei*, the parents of which are *Gasteria verrucosa intermedia* and *Haworthia radula*, has abruptly tapering, lanceolate-triangular leaves with channeled upper sides. They are nearly 4 inches long by under 1½ inches wide and are green with white warts that, on the rounded to double-keeled undersurfaces, form crossbands.

Garden Uses and Cultivation. These are as for *Gasteria.*

GASTERIA (Gas-tèria). In their various forms not unlike haworthias and aloes, gasterias are small- to medium-sized South African succulents of considerable appeal. Often their leaves are beautifully marked and colored, and their blooms, although by no means showy, are not without interest and charm. The curious shapes of their curved, tubular, narrow-necked flowers, which have greatly expanded lower parts, are suggestive of tiny stomachs, and inspired the name, from the Greek *gaster*, a belly. These much swollen, curved flowers distinguish gasterias from aloes. From haworthias they differ in their blooms being red and yellow, not two-lipped, and having petals that do not spread widely. Gasterias belong in the lily family LILIACEAE; there are about seventy species. Hybrids between *Gasteria* and *Aloe* are named *Gastrolea*; between *Gasteria* and *Haworthia*, *Gasterhaworthia.*

Gasterias are stemless or short-stemmed, evergreen perennials with thick, fleshy, tongue-shaped, sword-shaped, or narrowly-triangular leaves, usually in two ranks or in spirals. Some kinds form rosettes, but even they, as young specimens, may have their leaves in two ranks. Dull or glossy dark green, commonly with white or pale greenish spots, the foliage on plants grown in full sun may become reddish. The nodding blooms are in slender racemes or panicles on more or less erect stalks. Most often they are muted reds or pinks, frequently with green tips. At their ends are six equal, suberect corolla lobes (petals). The six stamens do not protrude. The style is slender. The fruits are blunt-angled capsules.

Identification of gasterias is often difficult. This because of similarities between species, variations within species, and the different leaf shapes and appearances that individual plants assume at various ages and stages of growth. The difficulties of recognition are compounded in cultivated specimens by the fact that these plants hybridize with considerable enthusiasm and many specimens cherished by gardeners are likely to owe their origin to more than one parent species. As a aid to recognition, the species most commonly cultivated are divided below into three groups, according to their approximate habits of growth. Within the groups they are arranged alphabetically.

Kinds with leaves one above the other in two opposite rows include the following: *G. angulata* is stemless with spreading to incurved leaves up to 10 inches long by 2 inches wide, with double angles at each margin and with transverse bands of white dots. The young leaves are erect. *G. armstrongii*, stemless or brief-stemmed, has oblong, round-ended leaves up to 2 inches long by a little over 1 inch wide with white warts that run into each other. In old age this species becomes rosette-like. *G. brevifolia* is stemless with leaves more or less two-ranked and spreading, up to 6 inches long by 2 inches wide, very thick, rounded on their undersides, with white dots in horizontal bands and horny, toothed margins. The young leaves are erect. *G. caespitosa* is a clustered, short-stemmed kind, with spreading or up-pointing, tapering leaves up to 6 inches long by ¾ inch wide at the base with greenish spots. *G. disticha* (syn. *G. lingua*), stemless and freely suckering, has young leaves erect, the older spreading. The leaves, strap-shaped and 8 to 10 inches long by 2 inches wide, are thinnish, with flat upper sides and clear, roundish white dots in confused crossbars. *G. herreana* has very short stems and glossy leaves up to 6 inches long by 1 inch wide, curved upward at their three-angled, reddish or brown, toothed apexes, not keeled beneath, and with many spots randomly arranged on both sides. *G. maculata* is a

Gasteria armstrongii

Gasteria armstrongii (flowers)

Gasteria disticha

suckering kind with stems with thick, tongue-shaped leaves, nearly flat on their upper sides, and rounded below. They are 6 to 8 inches long, about 2 inches wide, and polished green with white spots that often merge and are in cross bands. In old specimens the leaves tend to be arranged spirally. **G. marmorata,** with stems 6 to 10 inches tall, has lanceolate, tapering leaves up to 6 inches long by approximately 1½ inches wide, and deep green with darker mottlings. **G. neliana** has a few tongue-shaped, rough leaves 6 to 8 inches long by under 1½ inches wide, slightly rounded above and below, with more or less distinct horizontal rows of whitish-green, merging dots. **G. obtusifolia** is stemless. Its fairly numerous stubby leaves, the younger erect, the older spreading, and toothed toward their tips, are up to 7 inches long by 2 inches

wide. Flattened above and with rounded undersides, they are green with horizontal bands of greenish-white spots. **G. planifolia** has glossy-green, randomly white-spotted, sword-shaped leaves 6 to 10 inches long and ¾ to 1 inch wide, on stems 6 to 10 inches long. **G. subverrucosa** has tongue-shaped leaves with both sides rounded, 8 to 10 inches long by 1¼ inches wide. The white dots, toward the leaf ends, are in horizontal bands, below they are scattered. **G. sulcata** has distinctly channeled, tongue-shaped leaves in two series. They are up to 4½ inches long by 1¼ inches wide and have few spots. **G. stayneri** is stemless and suckers freely. Its tongue-shaped to ovate-oblong, warty-surfaced leaves are dark green tinged coppery. Their upper sides are channeled, their undersides rounded. The warts are green and somewhat translucent. **G. verrucosa** suckers and forms clumps. Its leaves, up to more than 6 inches long by ¾ inch wide, and with triangular-pointed apexes, are channeled above and rounded on their undersides. They have many irregular, raised white warts that merge.

Leaves in spirals are characteristic of the following kinds: **G. colubrina** has stems 3 to 6 inches tall. Its dark green to purple, tongue-shaped leaves, about 10 inches long and 1¼ inches wide, are channeled above and have light spots that run together. **G. dicta** has short stems, and tongue-shaped leaves 4 to 5 inches long by 1¼ inches wide, with flat upper surfaces and two keels. They are green with warty dots. **G. excavata** has long-lanceolate leaves with hollowed upper sides, about 4½ inches long and 1 inch to 1½ inches wide. They are light green with whitish dots. **G.**

maculata suckers and has stems with shining-green, tongue-shaped leaves, spiraled to two-ranked, and 6 to 8 inches long. Nearly flat above, their undersides are hollowed and have two ridges. The plentiful pale dots merge and form distinct horizontal bands. **G. nigricans,** with very short stems, has usually spiraled, but sometimes two-ranked, smooth, tongue-shaped, glossy leaves 4 to 10 inches long and about 2 inches wide. Channeled above and below, dark green to reddish-brown, they have often indistinct white or greenish spots. **G. picta,** stemless or short-stemmed, has shining, black-green, pointed-tongue-shaped leaves 10 inches to 1¼ feet long and about 2 inches wide, toothed at their apexes, and with somewhat rounded upper sides and hollowed undersides. They have cross bands of white, merging spots. **G. pulchra** suckers from the base and has stems 6 inches to 1 foot tall. The narrowly-sword-shaped, tapering, three-angled leaves have hollowed upper surfaces and are usually almost in two ranks. They are 8 inches to 1 foot long, 1 inch wide, and glossy-green with irregular cross bands of whitish spots that run together. **G. retata** has stems 2 to 3 inches long and sword-shaped, flat-upper-surfaced leaves, with rounded undersides. They are almost or quite 1 foot long and up to 1½ inches wide. Toothed near their apexes, they have cross bands of merging white dots. **G. spiralis** has stems up to 6 inches long and glossy, tongue-shaped leaves 4 to 6 inches long and about 1 inch wide, with usually double margins. Green or reddish, they are marked with obscure white dots. **G. transvaalensis,** like **G. nigricans** which it somewhat resembles, is very short-stemmed and sometimes has

Gasteria verrucosa

Gasteria verrucosa (leaves)

leaves in two ranks. Dark green and lustrous, they are 4 to 5 inches long, 1 inch wide, and toothed at their tips. The markings are greenish-white spots in cross bands. *G. variolosa,* with a stem about 2 inches long, has tongue-shaped leaves 8 to 10 inches long and 1¾ inches wide with channeled upper sides and rounded lower ones marked with white spots that run together.

Kinds with leaves in rosettes include these: *G. batesiana,* stemless, has dark green, rough-surfaced, spiraled, pointed-tongue-shaped leaves, up to 6 inches long; they are three-angled and banded crosswise with whitish dots. *G. carinata* suckers abundantly. Its lanceolate, three-angled, rough-edged leaves, 5 to 6 inches long, are channeled on their top sides and keeled below. Dark green, they have horizontal lines of clear white warts, and form spiral rosettes. *G. croucheri* has tapering leaves 1 foot long or longer by 3 to 4 inches wide, with hollowed upper surfaces, and below, two off-center keels. They are green with white spots and toothed toward their apexes. *G. glabra,* stemless and suckering, has three-angled, lanceolate leaves 6 to 8 inches long and about 2 inches wide. They are green with white dots. *G. g. major* is similar, but has leaves 1 foot to 1½ feet long. *G. laetipunctata* is much like *G. carinata,* but smaller, and has narrower leaves.

Gasteria glabra major

Gasteria liliputana

G. liliputana suckers. It has dark green, greenish-white-spotted, glossy, lanceolate leaves 2 to 3 inches long. Their upper sides are hollowed, their under surfaces rounded and keeled. *G. prolifera* suckers abundantly. Its three-angled leaves, 8 to 10 inches long and about ½ inch wide, have small white dots. Their upper sides are channeled. *G. trigona,* stemless and suckering, has sword-shaped, bright green leaves with cross bands of white spots. They are 6 to 8 inches long by about 1½ inches wide and curved upward toward their ends. Their upper sides are channeled, their lower ones keeled.

Garden and Landscape Uses. Gasterias succeed outdoors only in desert and semi-desert regions where little or no frost occurs, in greenhouses, and as house and apartment plants. For the last uses they are attractive because their unusual, often angular, spreading forms fit well with modern furnishings and because they grow well in arid atmospheres. The smaller kinds are useful for dish gardens. Another point favors their use as houseplants; they do not need exposure to full sun. Indeed, too strong light can cause yellowing, reddening, and even scorching of the foliage, all of which indicate that life processes are disturbed and that the plant is suffering. For gasterias, good light yes, but with protection from the intense afternoon sun of summer. East and north windows are likely to afford good growing conditions, as are porches, lightly shaded greenhouses and, in summer a spot beneath a tree outdoors. They may even be grown indefinitely with only artificial light. In warm, dry climates they are suitable for lightly shaded spots in desert rock gardens.

Cultivation. Outdoors or indoors, the soil for gasterias must be one that drains freely. A nourishing, loamy earth is to their liking, one containing a moderate proportion of leaf mold or other organic material and plenty of coarse sand, grit, perlite, or finely chopped brick. Indoors, winter temperatures may range from 50 to 70°F, in summer normal outdoor temperatures suit. Watering must always be done with circumspection, especially when temperatures are low, but also from mid-June to mid-August when the plants are semi-dormant. Then, the soil should be kept nearly dry. At other seasons water regularly, but not excessively. Follow the practice of allowing the soil to become decidedly dryish, then give a thorough soaking. At all times a dry atmosphere is advantageous. Propagation is by offsets and leaf cuttings. Plants raised from seeds often prove to be hybrids. For additional information see Succulents.

GASTORKIS. See Phaius.

GASTROCHILUS (Gastro-chìlus). Formerly included in *Saccolabium* and still often

cultivated under that name, *Gastrochilus,* of the orchid family ORCHIDACEAE, consists of about twenty species of epiphytes (plants that perch on trees without abstracting nourishment from them). The genus is native from Japan to the Himalayas and Indonesia. The name comes from the Greek *gaster,* a belly, and *cheilos,* a lip. It alludes to the shape of the lip of the flower.

Usually compact, these orchids commonly have short stems from which develop aerial roots, a few leathery leaves, and umbel-like clusters of few blooms. The flowers, small to fairly large according to species, have subequal, spreading sepals and petals, the latter joined to the base of the column, and a three-lobed lip with a hemispherical pouched base. The side lobes are erect.

Beautiful, long-lasting, fragrant, waxy blooms are borne by *G. bellinus* (syn. *Saccolabium bellinum*), of Burma. This has stems usually not over 2 inches high, and up to eight narrowly-strap-shaped, stiff, leathery leaves, notched at their apexes, up to 1 foot long by 1¾ inches wide, but often smaller. Usually erect, the umbel-like flower clusters are of seven or fewer 1½- to 1¾-inch-wide blooms with greenish-yellow sepals and petals, prettily spotted or blotched with blackish-purple to reddish-brown, and a large white, fringed lip with an orange-yellow, reddish-purple-spotted center, and a tuft of hairs on each side. From the last, Burmese *G. bigibbus* (syn. *Saccolabium bigibbum*) differs in having 1-inch-wide, waxy, fragrant flowers in pendulous clusters of ten to twenty. Their sepals and petals are pale to golden-yellow with paler bases. The fringed, white lip has a yellow center and a few red markings at the edges of its blunt, broad, pouched base. The leaves, bright green, strap-shaped, and about 5 inches long by 1½ inches wide, are notched at their apexes. A natural hybrid between the species so far discussed, *G. bellino-bigibbus* (syn. *Saccolabium bellino-bigibbum*) is intermediate between its parents.

Its natural distribution extending from Malaya to Burma, the Himalayas, Sumatra, and Java, *G. calceolaris* (syn. *Saccolabium calceolare*) is short-stemmed. It has up to six leathery leaves, with two teeth at their apexes 4 to 7 inches long and ½ to ¾ inch wide. The waxy, slightly fragrant blooms, in short-stalked, umbel-like clusters, are ½ to ¾ inch across. They have greenish-yellow sepals and petals, spotted, blotched, or barred with reddish- or purplish-brown. The lip has a fringed, white blade with an orange center, and an orange-yellow basal pouch with a few red-brown spots. Akin to the last, but smaller, *G. platycalcaratus* (syn. *Saccolabium platycalcaratum*) is a short-stemmed native of Burma. Its few, oblong, 2-inch-long leaves, about ¾ inch wide, are notched at their apexes. Waxy and fragrant, the

Gastrochilus calceolaris

The parents of gastroleas are very few of the known species of *Aloe* and *Gastria*. One of the most prolific parents, *Aloe aristata*, crossed with *Gasteria nigricans* produced *Gastrolea bedinghausii* and *G. nowotnyi*; hybridized with *Gasteria verrucosa* it has given *Gastrolea beguinii*, *G. b. perfectior* (syn. *G. perfectior*), and *G. chludowii*; mated with *Gasteria maculata* it has produced *Gastrolea lapaixii*; and together with *Gasteria disticha* it is a parent of *Gastrolea simoniana*. Two gastroleas with *Aloe aristata* as one parent and the other unknown, are *G. prorumpens* and *G. quehlii*.

With *Aloe variegata* as one parent, *Gastrolea mortolensis* has *Gasteria acinacifolia* as its other. The result of crossing *Aloe variegata* with *Gasteria cheilophylla*, itself a hybrid, is *Gastrolea sculptilis*; of hybridizing *Aloe variegata* with *Gasteria candicans* is *Gastrolea smaragdina*. Hybrids of *Aloe variegata* and unidentified gasterias are *Gastrolea rebutii* and *G. pfrimmeri*. Either *Aloe variegata* or *A. serrulata* crossed with an unidentified gasteria produced *Gastrolea imbricata*.

Gastrolea rebutii

A hybrid between *Aloe striata* and *Gasteria acinacifolia* is named *Gastrolea derbetzii*. One between *Aloe striata* and *Gasteria verrucosa* is *Gastrolea lynchii*. Some doubt exists as to whether *Gastrolea pethamensis* is the offspring of *Aloe variegata* and *Gasteria carinata* or of the last named and *Gasteria verrucosa*; if the latter is true its proper name should be *Gasteria pethamensis*. A cross between *Aloe heteracantha* and *Gasteria acinacifolia ensifolia* is named *Gastrolea peacockii*.

Garden and Landscape Uses and Cultivation. These are the same as those suggested for *Gasteria*. Plantlets, which can be used for propagation, sometimes develop among the flowers. Their production can be encouraged by breaking off the ends of the bloom-bearing part of flower stalks.

crowded flowers are nine or fewer together in short-stalked clusters. About ½ inch wide, they have brown-spotted, yellow sepals and petals and a white lip with a greenish central patch.

Garden Uses and Cultivation. These are for orchid collectors. They require the same environments and care as *Aerides*. They resent root disturbance, abhor stagnant conditions of the rooting medium, and are best accommodated in baskets or pans suspended from the greenhouse roof. For more information consult Aerides, and Orchids.

GASTROCOCOS (Gastro-còcos). One species of the palm family PALMAE constitutes *Gastrococos*. Its generic name is derived from the Greek *gaster*, a belly, and the name of the palm genus *Cocos*. It alludes to the swollen middles of the trunks.

Native only of Cuba where it grows to a height of about 40 feet, **G. crispa** (syns. *Acrocomia crispa*, *A. armentalis*) has a slender, solitary, spindle-shaped trunk densely armed with rings of stout, nearly black prickles. Its many leaves are glossy-green above, grayish or bluish-green beneath. They have short, prickly stalks and many narrow leaflets, slightly notched at their ends. The central axis or rachis of the leaf may be prickly or smooth. The flowers are in stiff-branched clusters that become pendulous in fruit. They differ from those of *Acrocomia* in technical details. The largest of the two spathes is 3 to 5 feet long, narrow, woody, and covered with fine hairs. It has few or no prickles. The smooth, approximately globose fruits are about 1 inch in diameter. The seeds are edible.

Garden and Landscape Uses and Cultivation. This palm, in Cuba known as corojo or corozo, is distinct from the genus *Corozo*. Previously named *Acrocomia crispa* and *A. armentalis*, it has the same garden and landscape uses and needs the same cultivation as *Acrocomia*. For the best results locations in nearly full sun should be chosen and specimens set in their permanent locations while yet small. This palm prospers in southern Florida. For more information see Palms.

GASTROLEA (Gastro-lèa). Hybrids between *Gasteria* and *Aloe*, of the lily family LILIACEAE, are named *Gastrolea* (syn. *Gasteraloe*). They are succulent perennials. Most form clumps of stemless rosettes of more or less spiraled, fleshy, spotted or warted leaves and are intermediate in appearance between their parents. Their flowers, in racemes or loosely-branched panicles, also exhibit intermediate characteristics; they are tubular, but not, as in *Gasteria*, bellied, and are reddish with greenish tips.

GATES. Besides serving their primary purposes of allowing passage through barrier fences, walls, and hedges and entry into enclosures, gates can be charming aes-

Double wooden gate

Single wooden gates (above)

thetic features in gardens. Usually of wood or metal, they may be simple or of intricate design. Gates in fences should ordinarily be of the same material as the fence, but may differ from it in pattern.

The sizes, proportions, and designs of gates should harmonize with their surroundings. Those that serve as main entrances to imposing houses, estates, and parks may with good taste be much more elaborate than gates of lesser architectural importance and those associated with simpler landscapes. A mistake not infrequently made by suburban home owners is that of installing over-pretentious en-

Double wooden gates (above)

Single wooden gates (above)

Gaultheria procumbens

Single iron gates (above)

Double iron gates (above)

trance gateways. Particularly incongruous are those with masonry or stone pillars or arches, with perhaps short flanking sections of wall, installed to permit access through hedges or simple fences. Such barriers call for less elaborate gateways.

Gates may be single or double, high or low, of openwork to permit a clear view or solid to afford privacy. They may be plain or ornamented and self-closing by gravity, a spring, or chain and weight, or easily responsive to manual closing and latching.

Sturdiness and durability should be considered when selecting gates. It is important that they swing easily and close ac-

curately. Maintenance involving periodic painting or treating with some other preservative is needed by most types of gates. Gate posts, unless of masonry, are likely to need replacing at long intervals.

GAULTHERIA (Gaul-thèria) — Checkerberry or Wintergreen, Creeping-Snowberry, Salal. The name *Gaultheria* commemorates an eighteenth-century physician and botanist, Dr. Jean Francois Gaultier, of Quebec, Canada. It belongs to a genus of 200 species of hardy and nonhardy, low to large, evergreen shrubs of the heath family ERICACEAE and includes the creeping-snowberry, previously segregated as *Chiogenes*. The genus inhabits North and South America and Asia.

Gaultherias have alternate or rarely opposite, undivided leaves. Their bell- to urn-shaped small blooms have four or five sepals and the same number of corolla lobes (petals). There are ten stamens, one style, and one stigma. The true fruits are capsules, sometimes remaining dry and obvious, but usually enclosed in the enlarged, fleshy calyx in a berry-like structure commonly called, and henceforth here referred to as, the fruit. The blooms may be solitary but more often are in terminal or axillary panicles or racemes. Oil of wintergreen, obtained from *G. procum-*

bens, some other species, and strangely, also from the birch, *Betula lenta,* is used medicinally, to flavor candies and chewing gum, and to mask the unpleasant flavors of some medicines.

Checkerberry or wintergreen (**G. procumbens**), a matting creeper, has, from horizontal rhizomes, erect stems 4 to 8 inches tall with the foliage, often variegated, crowded near their tops. The short-stalked, hairless leaves, up to 2 inches in length by one-third to two-thirds as broad as long, are elliptic to oblong, their margins round-toothed or toothless. From a little under to a little over ⅓ inch long, the waxy-white, barrel-shaped, shallowly-lobed, nodding flowers are solitary from the leaf axils or rarely the shoot ends. Highly decorative, the bright scarlet fruits, ⅓ inch or slightly more in diameter, are edible. They have a spicy, aromatic flavor and are much sought as winter food by deer, grouse, and partridges. This species inhabits acid-soil, dry and moist woodlands from Newfoundland to Manitoba, Virginia, Minnesota, and Kentucky.

Creeping-snowberry, creeping pearlberry, or moxie (**G. hispidula** syn. *Chiogenes hispidula*) is a dainty species notoriously difficult to grow. Its leafy, prostrate stems without erect branches, are 8 inches to 1¼ feet long. Its short-stalked, broad-elliptic to almost round leaves, smooth above, on their undersides with sparse bristly hairs, are up to ⅓ inch or a little more in length. The few, bell-shaped, deeply-lobed flowers, with four sepals and petals, are ¹⁄₁₀ inch long. White and ⅓ inch more or less long, the fruits have a mild flavor of wintergreen. Creeping-snowberry inhabits wet woodlands and bogs from Newfoundland and Labrador to British Columbia, New Jersey, Pennsylvania, Michigan, and Minnesota and down the Appalachian Mountains to North Carolina.

Salal or shallon (**G. shallon**), a native from California to British Columbia and

Gaultheria shallon

Gaultheria semi-infera

Gaulthettya wisleyensis

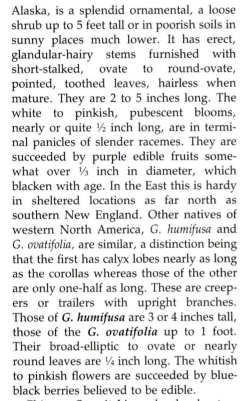

Gaulthettya wisleyensis (flowers)

Alaska, is a splendid ornamental, a loose shrub up to 5 feet tall or in poorish soils in sunny places much lower. It has erect, glandular-hairy stems furnished with short-stalked, ovate to round-ovate, pointed, toothed leaves, hairless when mature. They are 2 to 5 inches long. The white to pinkish, pubescent blooms, nearly or quite ½ inch long, are in terminal panicles of slender racemes. They are succeeded by purple edible fruits somewhat over ⅓ inch in diameter, which blacken with age. In the East this is hardy in sheltered locations as far north as southern New England. Other natives of western North America, *G. humifusa* and *G. ovatifolia*, are similar, a distinction being that the first has calyx lobes nearly as long as the corollas whereas those of the other are only one-half as long. These are creepers or trailers with upright branches. Those of *G. humifusa* are 3 or 4 inches tall, those of the *G. ovatifolia* up to 1 foot. Their broad-elliptic to ovate or nearly round leaves are ¼ inch long. The whitish to pinkish flowers are succeeded by blue-black berries believed to be edible.

Chinese *G. veitchiana,* hardy about as far north as Philadelphia, Pennsylvania, is best suited for moist soils. Up to about 3 feet tall, it has bristly-hairy shoots and lustrous, dark green, elliptic to oblong-obovate, bristly-toothed leaves 1½ to 3½ inches in length, ending in a short, glandular point, and bristly-hairy on the veins beneath. The white to pinkish, egg- to urn-shaped blooms, up to ¼ inch long, are in dense, hairy, axillary and terminal racemes 1 inch to 2 inches long. The fruits are indigo-blue. About as hardy as the last, *G. nummularioides* is a prostrate Himalayan species not over 1 foot tall. It has slender, bristly-hairy, interwoven stems furnished with two rows of ovate to nearly round leaves up to ½ inch long. The nodding flowers are solitary from the leaf axils. White, pink, or brownish-red and under ¼ inch long, they are hidden beneath the foliage. The ellipsoid, blue-black fruits are ¼ inch long or longer. Probably about

as hardy as the two preceding species, *G. semi-infera,* native from the Himalayas to southwest China, is up to about 6 feet tall. It has elliptic to obovate, finely-toothed leaves, flowers with five instead of the usual ten stamens common in the genus, and indigo-blue fruits.

Japanese *G. miqueliana* is a very good kind, hardy perhaps in sheltered locations in southern New England, but most commonly used in gardens in the Pacific Northwest. This has broad-elliptic to obovate, glandular-toothed leaves ½ inch to 1¼ inches long and tiny white, broad-urn-shaped blooms in nodding racemes 1 inch to 2½ inches long from the axils of the uppermost leaves. The fruits, white to pinkish, are about ¼ to nearly ½ inch in diameter. Very like the last, *G. cuneata,* of China, is distinguished by the ovaries of its flowers being not smooth but silky-downy.

Garden and Landscape Uses. Esteemed for their beautiful foliage and some kinds for their attractive fruits, gaultherias are excellent for inclusion with other acid-soil plants in lightly shaded shrub borders and beds, foundation plantings; the lower ones, in woodland and rock gardens and, where appropriate, native plant gardens. More rarely the nonhardy ones may be accommodated in cool greenhouses. They are best pleased with somewhat sandy soil containing abundant peat or similar organic residues and kept moderately moist.

Cultivation. Established plants need no particular care. They are aided if the ground is kept mulched with an organic material, such as leaf mold, peat moss, or rich compost. They appreciate deep watering at intervals during periods of dry weather. Increase is easy by division, by cuttings taken in late summer and planted in a propagating bed in a shaded, humid cold frame or greenhouse. Seeds sown in sandy peaty soil are also a satisfactory means of propagation.

GAULTHETTYA (Gaul-théttya). The name *Gaulthettya* was established to accommo-

date hybrids between *Gaultheria* and *Pernettya,* both of the heath family ERICACEAE. From their parents the hybrids differ, in intermediate fashion, in having fleshy calyxes about one-half as long as the fruits. The name is based on those of the parent genera.

Originated at the Royal Horticultural Society's gardens at Wisley, England where it first bloomed in 1929, *G. wisleyensis* (syn. *Gaulnettya* 'Wisley Pearl') is an evergreen shrub with alternate, elliptic-oblong to oblong-ovate leaves 1¾ to 3 inches long. Its pearly-white flowers, solitary or in short racemes of up to fifteen, have short glandular hairs. They are succeeded by maroon-red to wine-red fruits.

Garden and Landscape Uses and Cultivation. A rarity of interest to collectors of the unusual, *G. wisleyensis* is probably about as hardy as *Pernettya mucronata* and responds to similar conditions and care.

GAUNTLETTARA. This is the name of hybrid orchids the parents of which include *Broughtonia, Cattleyopsis,* and *Laeliopsis.*

GAURA (Gaù-ra). Only one of the eighteen species of *Gaura* of the evening-primrose family ONAGRACEAE is at all commonly cultivated. Native to North America and Ar-

Gaura lindheimeri

gentina the genus consists of herbaceous perennials, annuals, and biennials. From evening-primroses it differs in having small nutlike fruits that do not open to release the seeds instead of capsules that do. The name, from the Greek *gauros*, proud or superb, alludes to the attractive blooms of some kinds.

Gauras have alternate, undivided, stalked or stalkless leaves and small white or pink flowers in spikes or racemes. The blooms have four calyx lobes and the same number of clawed (narrowed to their bases), unequal-sized petals. The stamens are usually eight and the four-lobed stigma is surrounded by a ring or cup. The fruits have three or four ribs.

Native from Louisiana to Texas, **G. lindheimeri** is hardy at least as far north as New York City. It has erect, slender, more or less branched, hairy stems, and grayish-pubescent, lanceolate to spatula-shaped leaves with wavy, distantly toothed, rolled-back margins. The leaves are 1½ to 3½ inches long. The white flowers, about ¾ inch long, are in loose, branched or branchless spikes with only a few in each spike open at one time. Other species sometimes cultivated, all perennials, include **G. coccinea,** native from South Dakota to Mexico, with scarlet, pink, or white blooms ½ inch in diameter and oblong to lanceolate leaves up to 1½

inches long. This kind is 1 foot to 2 feet tall. Up to 5 feet in height, **G. parviflora,** which occurs as a native from South Dakota to Oregon and Mexico, is a pubescent plant with ovate-lanceolate leaves up to 4 inches long and pink blooms about ⅙ inch across. Ranging in the wild from Kansas to Mexico, **G. sinuata** is up to 3 feet tall and has toothed- or pinnately-lobed, linear or spoon-shaped leaves up to 3 inches in length. The pinkish flowers are about ⅓ inch long.

Garden and Landscape Uses. Gauras are appropriate for native plant gardens in their home territories and may be used to add interest to flower borders. They bloom over a long period in summer and fall and although certainly not blatant are showy enough to warrant mild attention from gardeners. The best kind is G. *lindheimeri*, an unobtrusive plant of airy grace that will appeal more to those who appreciate the unusual and somewhat rare than to seekers of brilliance.

Cultivation. Seeds sown in spring or early summer afford a ready means of acquiring plants. Gauras can also be increased by summer cuttings. They appreciate well-drained, moderately fertile soil and full sun. Planting is best done in spring or early fall, setting the plants 1 foot to 1½ feet apart.

GAUSSIA (Gaúss-ia). Two species of the Caribbean region are the only members of *Gaussia* of the palm family PALMAE. The name honors the German mathematician Karl Friedrich Gauss, who died in 1855.

These bisexual palms, related to *Pseudophoenix*, are little known in cultivation. Puerto Rican **G. attenuata,** up to 40 feet or more in height, has a slender, often slightly leaning trunk that from its base develops aerial prop roots with many short, spinelike projections. Its pinnate leaves, 4 to 6 feet long by 2 to 2½ feet wide, have many slender leaflets. The more or less egg- or cone-shaped flower clusters have lateral branches bearing orange-and-green flowers succeeded by round to pear-shaped fruits ½ inch long or slightly longer and red or orange-red. This inhabits rocky, limestone hills. Native to Cuba, **G. princeps** also favors limestone hills, often growing on inaccessible cliffs. It has a tall, slender trunk and the general aspect of a royal palm (*Roystonea*). Its fruits are red to purplish.

Garden and Landscape Uses and Cultivation. Little experience has been accumulated regarding the cultivation of these quite ornamental palms. Undoubtedly they need a humid, tropical climate and they may very well prosper if afforded the treatment successful with *Pseudophoenix* and *Chamaedorea*. They are primarily plants for the collector. For further information see Palms.

GAYA. See Hoheria.

GAYFEATHER. See Liatris.

GAYLUSSACIA (Gaylus-sàcia)—Huckleberry, Box Huckleberry, Dangleberry or Tangleberry or Blue Huckleberry, Buckberry. The "c" in *Gaylussacia* is pronounced as "sh." Gaylussacias belong to the heath family ERICACEAE. All of the approximately fifty species are natives of the New World, the majority inhabiting mountain regions in South America. Their name commemorates the French chemist Louis Joseph Gay-Lussac, who died in 1850. The common designation huckleberry, which properly belongs to this genus and preferably should be restricted to it, is often applied to low species of *Vaccinium*, notably to *V. hirsutum*, which is called hairy-huckleberry. The he-huckleberry is *Lyonia ligustrina*, the garden-huckleberry *Solanum nigrum*.

Huckleberries are deciduous and evergreen shrubs that often form colonies as a result of branches developing from spreading underground runners. Their short-stalked leaves are small, alternate, and usually toothless. Their white, pink, or red urn-to-tubular-bell-shaped blooms are in usually few-flowered axillary racemes. Each has a five-lobed calyx, a five-lobed corolla, and ten stamens. The blue or black fruits

Gaylussacia brachycera

are berry-like, about ⅓ inch in diameter, and edible though often insipid.

Cultivated kinds are all North American and, except one, lose their leaves in winter. The exception is the box huckleberry (*G. brachycera*), a choice creeping evergreen up to 1½ feet in height, native to wooded hillsides from Delaware and Pennsylvania to Kentucky and Tennessee. This is hardy at least as far north as Boston, Massachusetts. It differs from the majority of its race in that its leaves are not resinous-glandular and are finely-toothed. They are leathery, glossy-green, elliptic, up to 1 inch long, and hairless. The stems are conspicuously ridged below each leaf. The racemes are few-flowered and shorter than the leaves. Individual blooms are under ¼ inch long and white or pink. The fruits are dark blue. This desirable evergreen has much the aspect of the mountain cowberry (*Vaccinium vitis-idaea minus*).

Deciduous huckleberries are less useful garden shrubs than the box huckleberry. The most attractive is the dwarf huckleberry (*G. dumosa*), indigenous to wet sandy soils and bogs from Newfoundland to Florida and Louisiana. It has long, creeping stems from which spring erect branches up to 1½ feet tall. The nearly stalkless leaves, oblanceolate to obovate-oblong, and 1 inch to 1½ inches in length, have resin dots on their undersides only. They are lustrous green above, paler and hairy beneath. The open bell-shaped blooms, white to red, in loose, leafy-bracted, downy racemes, are about ¼ inch long. The fruits are black and downy. Other deciduous kinds, of lesser decorative merit, but sometimes cultivated, are the dangleberry, tangleberry or blue huckleberry (*G. frondosa*), the black huckleberry (*G. baccata* syn. *G. resinosa*), and the buckberry (*G. ursina*). Wild from New Hampshire to Ohio, Tennessee, Florida, and Alabama, *G. frondosa,* favors moist woods and thickets. Up to 6 feet in height, it has elliptic to oblong-obovate leaves about 1 inch long, with resinous glands on their undersides only. The racemes are ordinarily longer than the leaves and are of greenish-red-pur-

ple flowers that hang on threadlike stalks. They are succeeded by glaucous dark blue fruits that dangle on thin stalks and give reason to the common name. In the black huckleberry (*G. baccata*) the flower racemes are more compact and usually shorter than the leaves. The latter are glandular on both sides, elliptic to oblanceolate, and up to 2 inches long. The plants are about 3 feet in height. They have densely-sticky-resinous twigs and black fruits. This species inhabits sandy or rocky dry woods and thickets from Newfoundland to Quebec, Manitoba, Georgia, Alabama, Kentucky, and Illinois. Its variety *G. b. glaucocarpa* has larger fruits that are blue and covered with a waxy bloom (film). Variety *G. b. leucocarpa* has somewhat translucent white to pink fruits. Confined in the wild to North Carolina, the buckberry (*G. ursina*) is somewhat hairy and up to about 6 feet tall, with spreading branches and more or less obovate leaves 2 to 4 inches long. Its flowers are white or pinkish, its fruits glossy-black and sweet. They are much liked by deer, hence the name buckberry.

Garden and Landscape Uses. Except for the box huckleberry cultivated members of this genus are of minor decorative importance. The dwarf huckleberry is the best of the leaf-losing species. It is suitable for fronting shrub borders and for informal areas and native plant gardens. The other deciduous kinds may be used similarly. The box huckleberry is a gem that can be used effectively as a groundcover and as a choice item in rock gardens and other places. It is a neat, tidy, evergreen that well deserves its common name, bestowed because of the boxwood-like appearance of its foliage.

Cultivation. Sandy, peaty, not-too-dry, acid soils and part-shade suit most huckleberries, but the black huckleberry prospers under drier conditions and in full sun and the dwarf huckleberry takes kindly to soils too wet for most shrubs. None finds limestone to its liking. As with most members of the heath family, soil alkalinity spells poor health or death for huckleberries. Propagation is effected without difficulty by seeds sown in sandy peaty soil, and by using as divisions parts of the spreading clumps. Cuttings of half-ripened shoots inserted in summer in a greenhouse propagating bed or under mist are also successful. General care is minimal. Any pruning needed to shape or restrain may be done in late winter or spring. Like most plants of the heath family they benefit from having a permanent mulch of peat moss, compost, or other agreeable decayed organic material maintained over the soil.

GAZANIA (Ga-zània). The name *Gazania* honors Theodore of Gaza, who translated into Latin the works of Aristotle and Theo-

phrastus and who died in 1478. The genus it identifies belongs to the daisy famiy COMPOSITAE. It comprises about forty species, all African, the great majority, including all the sorts treated here, endemic to South Africa, mostly in coastal regions.

Gazanias are stemless or stemmed, nonhardy herbaceous perennials or less commonly annuals. Their leaves are all basal and in tufts or alternate on the stems. They are undivided, pinnately-lobed, toothed, or without lobes or teeth, often varying in these respects on the same plant. The medium-sized to large flower heads are solitary atop leafless stalks. Like those of daisies, they have a center of tiny disk florets, encircled by much larger, spreading, strap-shaped ray florets, and are backed by an involucre (collar) of linear or lanceolate leafy bracts. In *Gazania* the bracts, in two or more rows, overlap. Their bases are united into a cuplike or urnlike tube. The inner disk florets are dark colored and often sterile, the outer are bisexual and seed-producing. The ray florets are sterile and in a single row. The seedlike fruits are achenes. Like those of many African members of the daisy family, the flower heads of gazanias close at night and in dull weather.

Most commonly cultivated, *G. ringens* (syn. *G. splendens*), of neat growth, has linear-spatula-shaped leaves thickly clothed with silky-white hairs on their undersides. Often exceeding 3 inches in diameter, the flower heads have bright golden-orange to cream, pink, or ruby-red ray florets with at the base of each a black, brown, or mauve spot. Its precise geographical origin unknown, but surely South African, *G. ringens* has brief or up to 1-foot-long, more or less prostrate stems with upright branches, and lobeless or occasionally few-lobed, spatula-shaped to lanceolate leaves 3 to 5 inches in length, the blades of which taper into long, winged stalks. They have, except for the

Gazania ringens

Gazania nivea

midribs, densely-white-woolly-hairy undersides. Their upper sides are green and without hairs. The flower heads, on hairless stalks longer than the leaves, are 2½ to 3 inches wide. Their orange ray florets have at their bases a rich black spot decorated with a white eye. The tube of the involucre is much longer than the free apexes of its bracts.

Stemless or almost stemless *G. linearis* (syn. *G. longiscapa*) has lanceolate, lobeless, or pinnately-lobed leaves with white-woolly undersides, hairless or nearly hairless upper surfaces, and somewhat rolled-under, hair-fringed margins. The flower heads, 1½ to 3 inches in diameter, are on hairless stalks longer than the leaves. The ray florets are golden-yellow, often with a nearly black spot at their bases. The tube of the involucre, the outer bracts of which are fringed with hairs, does not exceed the free parts of the bracts in length.

Other kinds include these: *G. nivea* has a compact woody rhizome and very brief stems crowded with spreading, narrow-elliptic, perhaps sometimes pinnately-lobed leaves 1 inch to 1½ inches long, white-hairy on the undersides and sometimes hoary above. The flower heads, on stalks shorter than the leaves, have white-ray florets and yellow-disk florets. *G. pavonia* has short, branched stems and lanceolate to oblongish, usually pinnately-lobed, sometimes lobeless leaves up to 9 inches long, green and rough on their up-

per surfaces and white-hairy beneath. The large flower heads have bright orange ray florets with a black spot, sometimes with a lighter eye, at the base. The involucral bracts are blunt. *G. pinnata* has all basal, variously-shaped leaves. Mostly they are pinnately-lobed, less often lobeless. Up to 8 inches in length, they generally have rough upper surfaces and are white-hairy beneath. Some 3 inches or more in diameter, the flower heads, on stalks barely longer than the leaves, have orange ray florets, dark spotted at their bases. The bracts of the involucre are slender-pointed. Sometimes called the trailing gazanis, *G. uniflora* is about the size of *G. ringens* but differs in that it spreads rapidly by long, trailing stems that root freely into the ground. Its foliage is densely clothed with silvery-gray hairs. The plentiful 2- to 2½-inch-wide flower heads are yellow, orange, bronze, or white.

Garden and Landscape Uses. The gazanias discussed above are perennials, but may be grown as annuals. They are well adapted for flower gardens and rock gardens in warm, dry climates where little or no frost occurs as in California. They can also be used for summer display in regions where winters are too harsh for their survival outdoors by taking up the plants in fall and wintering them in a cool greenhouse, or under similar frostproof protection, or by raising new plants each year from seeds. Gazanias commend them-

selves for planting on banks, as edgings, in groups at the fronts of flower borders, and in beds by themselves. A warm, sunny location and well-drained soil, not too rich in nitrogen, make for the finest show of flowers. Constantly wet soil and high humidity in hot weather may cause the plants to collapse and rot.

Cultivation. Propagation is by division, usually done in spring, by cuttings taken in summer or early fall, and by seeds sown in early spring in sandy soil in a temperature of about 60°F. The seedlings are transplanted to flats or small pots and kept growing in a greenhouse or under equivalent conditions until the weather is warm and settled. Then they are planted where they are to bloom, spaced 9 inches to 1 foot apart. No special care is needed from then on. In regions of cold winters plants for stock are taken up before killing frost, potted in sandy soil, and wintered indoors where the night temperature is about 50°F and that by day not more than a few degrees higher.

GAZEBO. This is a summerhouse or similar structure located to afford a pleasing view of the surrounding landscape.

GEAN. This is a common name of *Prunus avium*.

GEIGER TREE is *Cordia sebestina*.

GEIJERA (Gèi-jera)—Australian-Willow. This genus of evergreen trees and shrubs inhabits Australia, New Guinea, New Caledonia, and the Loyalty Islands. It belongs to the rue family RUTACEAE and has a name commemorating a J. D. Geijer. It comprises seven species with alternate, undivided, often pendulous leaves and short, terminal panicles of small, yellowish-white flowers that have a persistent, five-parted calyx, five petals, five stamens, and united styles with a five-lobed, headlike stigma. The fruit are small five-seeded carpels.

The Australian-willow (*Geijera parviflora*) is a shapely, handsome tree 20 or 30 feet tall, with graceful, pendulous branches and drooping, hairless, short-stalked, gray-green leaves 3 to 6 inches long and usually not more than ¼ inch wide. Its loose, broadly-pyramidal panicles of nearly white blooms make a good display in spring. In Australia, because of the great fondness sheep have for its foliage, this species is often called sheep bush.

Garden and Landscape Uses and Cultivation. The Australian-willow is not hardy in the north, but is admirable for California and regions with similar mild climates. It withstands dry conditions well and is adaptable to various soils provided they are well drained. It is satisfied with conditions that suit *Citrus*. Propagation is by cuttings, which root slowly, and by seeds, which do not germinate readily.

GEISSORHIZA (Geisso-rhìza)—Sequins. The pleasant and fancifully descriptive name sequins is in South Africa applied to the flowers of *Geissorhiza*. Native only there and in Madagascar, the genus consists of more than sixty species of the iris family IRIDACEAE. Its name, from the Greek *geisson*, a tile, and *rhiza*, a root, was given because the bulblike organs of some species have tunics (coverings) that overlap like roof tiles.

Sequins have underground food storage parts (corms) that look like bulbs, but instead of being composed of concentric layers or of overlapping scales as are such true bulbs as those of onions and lilies, they are solid. The stems are slender, and branched or not. There are few leaves arranged in fans, their bases partly sheathing the stems. The flowers are in usually one-sided spikes. They have perianths with short, erect tubes and six nearly equal, spreading lobes (petals, or more properly, tepals). There are three symmetrically arranged stamens and a style with three short branches. The fruits are capsules.

Bright red-flowered *G. hirta* has a solitary, linear basal leaf up to 6 inches in length, and two leaves on its up to 1-foot-long stem. The raceme is of three to six blooms approximately 1 inch in diameter. They have yellow anthers. Pretty *G. rochensis* has flowers that, like those of *Babiana rubrocyanea*, have the lower halves of their petals crimson and the upper halves rich purple. This gives reason for the colloquial name wine cups applied both to the *Babiana* and the *Geissorhiza*. About 6 inches tall, this sort has narrow leaves and wiry stems with cup-shaped blooms about 1½ inches in diameter. Violet-blue to mauve-lilac flowers 1 inch to 1½ inches wide are borne by *G. secunda*. From 6 inches to over 1 foot tall, this has a usually branched, velvety-pubescent stem with two or three half-sheathing leaves that, like the two basal ones, which are 6 inches to 1 foot tall, are very slender. Its usually branchless stems 6 to 9 inches high, *G. splendidissima* has a pair of basal leaves about ¹⁄₁₀ inch wide and broader stem leaves. In loose, one-sided spikes of four or five, the bright purple flowers with yellowish-green throats are 1½ to 2 inches across.

Garden Uses and Cultivation. Geissorhizas are suitable for rock gardens in California-type climates and pots and pans (shallow pots) in greenhouses. They require the same conditions and attention as ixias, babianas and other South African bulb plants of that relationship. During their period of active growth ample supplies of water are needed. When dormant they are kept dry.

GEITONOPLESIUM (Geiton-oplèsium). Derived from the Greek *geiton*, neighbor, and *plesion*, near, the name of *Geitonople-*sium refers to the close botanical affinity of that genus to *Eustrephus*. Both are of the lily family LILIACEAE, or according to those who prefer to divide that assemblage, of the philesia family PHILESIACEAE. The inner petals of *Eustrephus* are fringed, those of *Geitonoplesium* not.

There is only one variable species, *G. cymosum* (syn. *Luzuriaga cymosa*) a twining, woody, evergreen vine, found in the wild from eastern Malaysia to the Philippine Islands, the Solomon Islands, Fiji, and Australia. The young stems of this kind grow for many feet before producing foliage. The leaves, on lateral branches, are linear to ovate and 2 to 4¼ inches long. The small, white, purplish-green, or reddish blooms, in loose, pendulous, terminal clusters or panicles, have six perianth segments (petals), six stamens, and a slender style. They are succeeded by handsome, shining, blue-black berries about ½ inch in diameter.

Garden and Landscape Uses. Only in warm, essentially frost-free climates does this vine succeed outdoors. It is best accommodated in fairly fertile, well-drained soil in partial shade. Supports around which it stems can twine are needed. It can be cultivated in pots, tubs, or ground beds in greenhouses and conservatories.

Cultivation. Once this plant becomes established no particular care is needed. Propagation is by seed. In greenhouses a winter night temperature of 50°F, with a rise of five to fifteen degrees by day, is sufficient. Whenever outdoor weather permits the greenhouse should be ventilated freely.

GELSEMIUM (Gelsèm-ium)—Carolina Yellow-Jessamine. Two of the three species of *Gelsemium*, of the logania family LOGANIACEAE, are natives of the United States, the other of eastern Asia and Indonesia. The best-known American is the Carolina yellow-jessamine. The name is an adaptation of *gelsomino*, the Italian name of the true jasmine (*Jasminum*).

Gelseminums are perennial, evergreen, hairless, twining woody vines with opposite or rarely whorled leaves and beautiful, sweetly fragrant flowers in axillary and terminal few-flowered clusters. The blooms have a five-lobed calyx, a tubular corolla with five spreading petals, five stamens, and a four-branched style. The fruits are capsules containing winged seeds.

Carolina yellow-jessamine (*G. sempervirens*) is sometimes 20 feet tall. It occurs natively from Virginia and westward to Texas, and ranges southward to Guatemala. Its lanceolate to ovate-lanceolate, short-stalked leaves are 1 inch to 4 inches long and glossy-green. The bright yellow blooms with orange-yellow throats are 1 inch to 1½ inches long and over 1 inch wide. The fruits are up to ½ inch long. Very similar *G. rankinii*, a native from North Carolina to Florida and Alabama, has leaves rounded rather than narrowed at their bases, flowers with narrower calyx lobes, and long-beaked fruits about ½ inch in length.

Garden and Landscape Uses. These are handsome vines, in mild climates excellent for screening porches and similar purposes where a neat and lovely twining climber of moderate growth can be used to good purpose. They can also be used as covers for steep banks and are interesting for greenhouse cultivation. Carolina yellow-jessamine and its relatives thrive in full sun or light shade in any soil of rather low to moderate fertility that is not excessively dry. Too abundant supplies of nitrogen encourage vigorous growth, but limit flower production.

Cultivation. No special demands are made of the gardener by gelsemiums. When grown as climbers they must be provided with suitable supports around which their stems can twine. Pruning to thin out crowded shoots, remove dead twigs, and restrain the vine to its allotted space should be done immediately after flowering or in very early spring before new growth begins. It is usually advantageous to prune quite severely. Propagation is readily achieved by cuttings and by seeds. Containers for gelsemiums should not be over-large in proportion to the size of the plants. Indoors, the yellow-jessamines seem to prosper best when their roots are somewhat confined. They bloom when young and as small specimens. A minimum winter night temperature of 45 to 50°F is appropriate.

Pests. Gelsemiums are subject to damage by mealybugs, scale insects, and whiteflies.

GELUGOR is *Garcinia atroviridis*.

GENIOSTOMA (Genió-stoma)—New-Zealand-Privet. The sixty species of this genus, distributed in the wild from Madagascar and Malaya to New Zealand, belong in the logania family LOGANIACEAE. Their name is from the Greek *geneias*, bearded, and *stoma*, a mouth and alludes to the hairs in the mouth of the corolla. One species, the New-Zealand-privet, is cultivated in California and similar mild-climate regions. It is the only kind native to New Zealand and is appropriately named, for it does, indeed, bear a close superficial resemblance to privet.

Geniostomas are opposite-leaved shrubs with small flowers in axillary clusters. Each bloom has a five-cleft calyx, a bell-shaped, five-lobed corolla, and five stamens. The fruits are dry capsules.

The New-Zealand-privet (*Geniostoma ligustrifolium*), up to 12 feet in height, has lustrous, hairless, pale green, pointed-ovate-oblong leaves 1½ to 3 inches long. The flowers, up to ⅛ inch in diameter and with recurved corolla lobes, are greenish-white and in small clusters. They have a comparatively large, two-lobed stigma. The rounded, pointed fruits are up to ¼ inch in diameter.

Garden and Landscape Uses and Cultivation. New-Zealand-privet affords a change from more common shrubs and may be used in most ways appropriate for shrubs. It prospers in ordinary soil and needs no special care. Propagation is by seeds and by cuttings.

GENIP. See Genipa and Melicoccus.

GENIPA (Gen-ìpa)—Genip, Marmalade-Box or Genipap or Jagua. To the madder family RUBIACEAE belongs this West Indian and tropical American genus of six species of trees. Its name is a Brazilian native one.

Genipas have large, opposite leaves and clusters of yellowish or white flowers with five or six spreading corolla lobes (petals). The fruits are technically berries. The name genip is applied also to the very different *Melicoccus bijugatus*.

The marmalade-box, genipap, or jagua (***Genipa americana***) is native to northeastern South America and the West Indies. In Puerto Rico it often occurs on moist limestone soils. A deciduous tree about 60 feet tall, with a dense spreading head, it is planted within its native range for shade and ornament and for its fruits, but is not widely known elsewhere. Its rather lustrous, short-stalked leaves are elliptic to obovate with pointed apexes. They are 4 inches to 1 foot long by 1½ to 4 inches wide. The light yellow, slightly fragrant flowers, in branched clusters, are about 1 inch long by one-half again as wide. They have five spreading petals that bend backward. There are five stamens and a pistil with a slender style and thicker stigma. The yellow-brown, lemon- to orange-shaped fruits, 3½ to 4½ inches long, are suspended singly on long stalks. Their flesh, soft when fully ripe, is sour, but edible. The fruits are eaten by livestock and are used to make marmalade and sometimes to prepare intoxicating as well as non-alcoholic drinks. The wood is used for many purposes including shipbuilding, furniture, cabinetwork, flooring, interior trim, veneer, and turnery. The flowers contain much nectar and are good bee pasture.

Garden and Landscape Uses and Cultivation. The marmalade-box is a stately tree worth planting for shade and ornament even where its fruits do not appeal as edibles (the taste for these is an acquired one). This tree needs humid tropical conditions and does best in a moist, loamy soil. Seeds are the usual means of increase. Budding onto seedling understocks can be done to multiply desirable varieties.

GENIPAP is *Genipa americana*.

GENISTA (Gen-ísta) — Broom, Dyer's Greenweed, Spanish-Gorse. As a common name broom is applied to *Cytisus* as well as *Genista*. Spanish-broom is *Spartium*. The genus *Genista* differs from *Cytisus* in its seeds being without a prominent strophiole (wartlike protrusion), also in its flowers having calyxes with a deeply-two-lobed, not merely toothed, upper lip. From *Genista* some modern botanists have transferred a number of more or less anomalous species to other genera, but for horticultural purposes it seems more useful to maintain the broader concept for *Genista* and include plants sometimes segregated as *Echinospartium*, and *Lygos*. Under this treatment *Genista* consists of perhaps ninety species. It belongs in the pea family LEGUMINOSAE and bears a Latin name used by Virgil. Geographically its chief center of distribution is the Mediterranean region, with representation in the native floras of most of western and central Europe, and adjacent Asia. From ancient times dyer's greenweed has been employed for dying cloth yellow and green. Its seeds are purgative. The name of the royal house of Plantagenet is derived from the custom of its founder, Geoffrey, Count of Anjou, wearing a sprig of genista (planta genista) in his cap.

Genistas are hardy and nonhardy, deciduous, spiny or spineless shrubs, with opposite or alternate, sparsely-foliaged, usually prominently ridged, often green branches. The leaves, usually opposite rarely alternate, and most commonly stalkless, are undivided or have three generally narrow leaflets. Undivided and trifoliate leaves not infrequently occur on the same plant and even the same branch. The flowers are in racemes, heads, or occasionally in opposite pairs. They are shaped like pea blooms. The upper lip of the calyx is deeply divided into two teeth, the lower into three usually shorter ones. The corolla has a broad-ovate or triangular standard or banner petal. Its wing petals are as long as the standard, the keel as long or longer. There are ten stamens joined by their stalks. The fruits are pods containing one to several seeds without wartlike appendages.

Dyer's greenweed (*G. tinctoria*) is highly variable and very hardy. Native throughout most of Europe and western Asia, it is naturalized from Maine to Virginia. Spineless, and in its typical form erect, it may be 6 feet tall or sometimes taller. It has alternate, undivided, slightly-hairy to densely-hairy, lanceolate, elliptic, or oblanceolate leaves usually over ⅖ inch long. The many yellow flowers, in branched or branchless racemes, are succeeded by usually hairless pods. Variety *G. t. depressa* is wide-spreading, not over

Genista tinctoria plena

8 inches high, with leaves rarely more than ⅖ inch long. Its flowers are few, its seed pods pubescent. Another shy bloomer, *G. t. prostrata,* is distinguished by having hairless or only slightly-hairy seed pods. From 2 to 4 feet tall, and erect, *G. t. ovata* (syn. *G. ovata*) has leaves generally more than ⅖ inch long, numerous flowers in racemes, and hairy pods. Double flowers are characteristic of *G. t. plena.*

Genista radiata

Genista sagittalis

Distinctive **G. sagittalis** (syns. *G. delphinensis, Chamaespartium saggitale*) is a ground-hugging kind hardy through most of New England. Never over 1 foot high and often lower, this native of Europe and western Asia has many branching green stems that flounder atop each other in all directions. Like those of the cactus genus *Epiphyllum,* they have slender, woody cores flanked by two broad, leaflike wings continuous or interrupted at the joints. Those of *G. sagittalis* are much narrower than the stems of *Epiphyllum.* About ¼ inch broad, like the cactus stems they function as leaves by photosynthesizing food and are responsible for the evergreen appearance of the plant. The true leaves are few, scattered, and deciduous. A dwarf variety *G. s. minor* is sometimes cultivated.

Kinds hardy, at least in sheltered places, in southern New England include several now to be described. The petty whin (**G. anglica**) is indigenous in Europe as far north as Sweden and Scotland. Erect to sprawling, and very spiny, with slender branches, and hairless shoots, this attains heights of up to about 2 feet. Its undivided, linear to oblong leaves are ¼ to ¾ inch long. In short, few-flowered racemes at the branch ends the ½-inch-long yellow flowers are produced in early summer. The seed pods are sickle-shaped, inflated, hairless, and ½ inch long. Variety *G. a. inermis* is without spines. About as hardy and as tall, nearly related **G. germanica** is erect and spiny. Native from Europe to central Russia, it is distinguished from the last by its shoots and undersides of the leaves being

hairy. The leaves are undivided, elliptic-oblong, and up to ¾ inch long. The yellow flowers, up to ½ inch long, with reflexed standard petals, occur in loose terminal racemes up to 2 inches long; they come in early summer. The one- to two-seeded, flattish, more or less hairy pods are between ¼ and ½ inch long. Variety *G. g. inermis* is without spines. Erect growth, opposite, spineless, very slender branches, and leaves of three leaflets ¼ to ¾ inch long by ¼ inch wide are characteristics of **G. radiata,** a native of central and southern Europe. A rounded bush 2 to 3 feet tall, in early summer this has heads of up to seven yellow flowers. The standard petals are hairless or with a line of hairs down their centers. In *G. r. sericopetala* the entire standards are silky-hairy.

Spanish-gorse (**G. hispanica**) is slightly less hardy than the kinds discussed immediately above. In sheltered locations it survives outdoors about as far north as New York City. Cushion-like and 1 foot to 2 feet tall, this has interlacing, prominently-spined branches, and hairy shoots. The leaves are confined to the flowering twigs. They are stalkless, ¼ to less than ½ inch long, and densely-silky-hairy on their undersides. One of the showiest of dwarf flowering shrubs, Spanish-gorse blooms profusely in early summer. About ⅓ inch

Genista hispanica

long and much less wide, its flowers are in crowded clusters of up to one dozen. The flattish, ovate seed pods have up to four seeds. This kind is native to southwestern Europe. Its variety *G. h. occidentalis* differs in the hairs of its stems and leaves lying flat and in its blooms being larger.

About as hardy as Spanish-gorse are *G. sylvestris* (syn. *G. dalmatica*) and *G. nissana.* Native of the Balkan Peninsula and Italy, **G. sylvestris** may be 1 foot in diameter, but does not exceed 6 inches in height.

Compact, it has angular, spiny branches. Its slender leaves ⅓ to ¾ inch long, with short-hairy under surfaces, are mostly on the lower parts of the shoots. The ⅓-inch-long bright yellow flowers are in terminal racemes 2 to 4 inches long. The one- or two-seeded pods are about ¼ inch in length. Very different **G. nissana** (syn. *G. nyssana*) is erect, spineless, and has branches that fork but little. It has densely-silky-hairy young shoots and leaves. The latter have three narrowly-linear to narrow-oblanceolate leaflets ½ to ¾ inch long. Its branches and leaves are alternate or nearly opposite. The flowers, in loose racemes 4 to 6 inches long, are in the axils of trifoliate leafy bracts. They are yellow, about ½ inch long, and have a hairy keel much longer than the standard or banner petal. The wing petals are hairless. Densely-hairy, the ¼-inch-long pods contain one or two seeds. This is an endemic of a restricted region of Yugoslavia.

Two other fine brooms, hardy about as far north as New York City or in sheltered locations somewhat farther north, are *G. pilosa* and *G. villarsii*. Both have yellow flowers with standard petals over ⅓ inch long. Not spiny, and usually 4 inches to 1½ feet tall, but sometimes higher, **G. pilosa** has procumbent and rooting, or suberect branches that when young, like the undersides of the leaves, are silky-hairy. The latter are stalkless or short-stalked, more or less folded, elliptic-oblong to ovate, and under ½ inch long. The long racemes of blooms terminate erect branches. The seed pods are up to 1 inch long. This is a native of Europe. Variety *G. p. prostrata* is 2 to 3 inches tall. A much-branched, spineless or weakly-spiny shrub, its stems and leaves densely clothed with silky hairs, **G. villarsii** (syn. *G. pulchella*) hails from the mountains of southern Europe. Its stalkless leaves are ⅓ inch long, or shorter, and narrowly-elliptic. The congested racemes have one bloom in the axil of each bract. This species, usually about 3 inches tall, and spreading, has stems that root into the ground. Its seed pods are hairy and about ½ inch long.

Genista pilosa prostrata

Almost treelike and up to 20 feet tall, **G. aethnensis** is without spines. It has opposite, rushlike branches that arch gracefully and become pendulous. The linear leaves are few, about ½ inch long, and somewhat silky-pubescent. Fragrant, the golden-yellow blooms, about ½ inch across, are in loose terminal racemes. They come in summer. Native of Sicily and Sardinia, sometimes called Mt. Etna broom, this is usually considered not hardy in the north, but in a sheltered location at The New York Botanical Garden a fine specimen lived for over twenty years.

Genista cinerea

Less hardy kinds adaptable only for regions of mild winters include several good garden plants, among them **G. cinerea**, of southern Europe and North Africa. One of the best, this is 3 to 10 feet tall, and has erect, pliable branches, finely hairy when young. Its stalkless, gray-green leaves, which are not very plentiful, are elliptic, oblanceolate, or obovate and about ½ inch long by ⅛ inch wide; they have silky-hairy undersides. The bright yellow flowers, solitary or in clusters of few, are on leafy branchlets from the leaf axils. They form racemes about 8 inches long. The standard petal is a little under ½ inch across, the wings and keel as long. The latter is silky-hairy. Distinguished by its branches being densely-white-hairy is *G. c. leptoclada*.

Extremely spiny **G. horrida** (syn. *Echinospartium horridum*), of the Pyrenees, withstands some frost, but not hard freezing. Ordinarily not over 1 foot tall, it forms a dense, compact, flat-topped cushion. Its stiff branches when young are silky-hairy as are the undersides of the leaves. The flowering branches are without terminal spines and usually have a pair, and sometimes two pairs, of yellow blooms up to ½ inch long. The pods are hairy.

The Genoa broom (**G. januensis**), of southern Europe, succeeds only in regions

Genista horrida

of fairly mild winters. Lovely and not over a few inches high, it forms broad mats or is sometimes erect. Its hairless, triangular stems usually have narrow, transparent wings. The flowering shoots are erect and have solitary clear yellow blooms in their upper leaf axils. Variable in shape and size, the leaves are undivided, linear-lanceolate to ovate and obovate, and ⅓ to 1 inch long or longer. They are without hairs. The 1-inch-long, hairless pods contain several seeds. Triangular stems and variable leaves distinguish this from closely related *G. lydia*. Generally under 1 foot tall and tufted, **G. sericea** is much-branched, and has narrowly-elliptic to obovate leaves, silky-hairy on their undersides, and from ¼ to 1 inch long. Their edges are inrolled. The flowers, in crowded terminal racemes on slender branches in late spring, are about ½ inch in length and have wing petals and keels, the latter silky-hairy, as long as the standard or banner petal. The densely-hairy pods, up to about ½ inch long, contain up to eight seeds. This species is a native of southern Europe.

Another beautiful, rather tender genista, native of the eastern Mediterranean region, is **G. lydia**. Typically prostrate, it has cylindrical or slightly-five-angled, hairless stems and undivided, sometimes

Genista lydia

clustered leaves, up to ⅓ inch long and narrowly-oblanceolate to oblong. Freely-borne in late spring at the branch ends, the flowers are few together in short racemes. The standard petal is about ⅓ inch long and wide, the wing petals and keel as long. The seed pods are hairless and from ¾ to 1 inch long. They contain up to eight seeds. Erect and loosely-branched, *G. l. rumelica* (syn. *G. rumelica*) is 1 foot to 3 feet in height.

A seacoast native of Spain and Portugal, **G. monosperm** (syns. *Lygos monosperma, Retama monosperma*) is a somewhat straggly species, 3 to 9 feet tall, with lax, rushlike, wide-spreading, pendent branches that when young are silky-hairy. The few leaves, ¼ to ¾ inch long and silky-hairy, are linear-lanceolate to narrowly spatula-shaped. The very fragrant flowers in short racemes scattered along the branches are from slightly under to a little over ½ inch wide. They come in spring and are milky-white and clothed with silky hairs. The ovate seed pods are about ½ inch long and end in very short points.

Garden and Landscape Uses. Genistas are showy, highly ornamental flowering shrubs, with few exceptions a little too tender to withstand northern winters, although a few prosper in warm, sheltered locations in well-drained soils. Such soil, poor in fertility rather than rich, and full sun, are desirable wherever genistas are planted, because such conditions simulate the environments under which they grow in the wild. As a group genistas do well in limestone soils. The taller kinds are suitable for beds, and particularly for slopes and banks, the smaller ones are delightful in rock gardens. They are basically dry-soil plants, intolerant of wetness and particularly of stagnant moisture about their roots. Climates such as are enjoyed in California and many part of the Southwest are ideal for these chiefly Mediterranean region shrubs.

Cultivation. Because of their long, deep, stringy roots genistas transplant very badly when old and long established. It is very advisable to set out only young specimens from containers. Spring is the best time to do this. In dry climates watering may be necessary during the first summer, but after that is not likely to be needed. Pruning calls for special understanding. The bushes should be looked over annually and any corrective cutting done promptly. It is fatal to allow the plants to go untended for years and then to attempt rehabilitation by severe pruning. Branches more than a year or two old rarely produce new shoots after they are cut back. They are more likely to remain as stubs and eventually die. Annual pruning (and not all will need this) may consist of thinning out older, crowded shoots and shortening the ends of any that tend to become straggly. Genistas that bloom before mid-June, on shoots of the previous

year, such as *G. hispanica*, are pruned as soon as they are through flowering, later-blooming ones that flower on shoots of the current year, are pruned in early spring. During their first and second years young specimens in containers benefit from pruning two or three times as a means of inducing desirable bushiness. The most satisfactory method of propagation is by seeds. Sometimes plants arise spontaneously near old ones from self-sown seeds. These can be dug up carefully, when quite small, and potted. Unless freshly gathered, it is well to soak the seeds in water for a day or two prior to sowing. Sowing may be done in a cold frame or cool greenhouse or in a protected bed outdoors. As soon as the seedlings have made their second pair of leaves they are carefully transplanted individually to small pots containing sandy soil. If seeds are not available increase can be had by layering and by summer cuttings made of firm side shoots taken with a thin sliver of older wood, a "heel," attached to their bases.

GENTIAN. See Gentiana. Other plants in which the word gentian is employed as part of their common names are these: catchfly-gentian (*Eustoma*), climbing-gentian (*Tripterospermum*), green-gentian (*Frasera*), horse-gentian (*Triosteum*), and prairie-gentian (*Eustoma grandiflorum*).

GENTIANA (Gent-iàna) — Gentian. Although many species occur in North America as natives, and a few of these and others are occasionally cultivated, gentians play a much less important role in gardens in North America than they do in those of northern Europe. There, along with saxifrages, primulas, and a few other groups, alpine species of gentians and some hybrids form the backbone of many rock garden plantings. In the northwestern United States and adjacent Canada many gentians find conditions agreeable and enjoy some popularity. In the northeastern and north-central states avid rock gardeners struggle with them to achieve a modicum of success. Constituting *Gentiana* of the gentian family GENTIANACEAE, this group consists of 350 species, natives of chiefly alpine and cool-climate regions throughout most of the world except Africa. It includes annuals, biennials, and hardy herbaceous perennials. It is named for Gentius, King of Illyria, who according to Pliny discovered the medicinal virtues of gentians. The plants sometimes called climbing gentians, referred by various authorities to *Gentiana* and *Crawfurdia*, belong in *Tripterospermum*. Other species, including the fringed-gentians, formerly included in *Gentiana*, and still often known as such, are now referred to *Gentianella* and *Gentianopsis*, under which they are treated in this Encyclopedia.

Gentians have lobeless, toothless, gen-

erally opposite, stalkless leaves. Usually blue, less commonly yellow or white, the solitary or clustered flowers are funnel- to bell-shaped. They have a usually five-cleft calyx. The corolla commonly has four or five flaring or erect lobes (petals), sometimes conspicuously fringed and generally with teeth, appendages, or membranous plaits in the bays between them. There are as many stamens as corolla lobes and two nearly stalkless stigmas. The fruits are capsules. The roots of *G. lutea* and *G. cruciata* are used medicinally. From those of the former a potent bitter liqueur is distilled. The gentians discussed below, unless otherwise stated, are hardy perennials.

The pine barren gentian (**G. autumnalis** syn. *G. porphyrio*), notoriously unamenable to cultivation, is a lovely native of moist sandy meadows and pine barrens from New Jersey to South Carolina. From 9 inches to 1½ feet tall, this has slender stems that rarely branch and linear to narrowly-oblanceolate leaves up to 2¾ inches long and generally not over ¼ inch wide. The flowers, usually solitary at the ends of the stems and branches, are bright blue spotted with bronzy-green. Their five petals spread widely in sunshine, close together in dull light. Rare *G. a. albescens* has white blooms.

Gentiana andrewsii

The closed gentian (**G. andrewsii**) has usually branchless stems 1 foot to 2½ feet tall. Its pointed, lanceolate to ovate-lanceolate, stalkless leaves are up to 6 inches long by nearly 1½ inches wide. In tight clusters of several nested among leaves and leafy bracts at the apexes of the stems and occasionally in the upper leaf axils, the flowers are blue, rarely white. Flask- or bottle-shaped and 1 inch to 1½ inches long, they never expand. Between the petals are broad, fringed plaits shorter than the petals. This inhabits wet woodlands, meadows, and shores from Quebec to Manitoba, New Jersey, and Missouri, and in the mountains of North Carolina.

Other eastern North American natives are *G. clausa* and *G. saponaria*. Much like

Gentiana saponaria

the closed gentian, **G. clausa** differs in the plaits between the petals being about as wide and long as the petals and two- or three-lobed. It occurs in damp soils from Maine to New York and New Jersey, and in the mountains to North Carolina. Also of this relationship, **G. saponaria** favors damp ground from New York to Florida and Louisiana, and in the north to Indiana, Wisconsin, and Minnesota. From 1 foot to 2 feet tall, it has lanceolate to oblong-lanceolate leaves up to 3 inches long. Its blue to white blooms, about 1¼ inches in length, have petals very slightly longer than the plaits between them.

Of western North American species, **G. calycosa** is perhaps the most beautiful. In the wild it frequents meadows, stream banks, and swamps usually at alpine and subalpine altitudes from the Rocky Mountains to the Sierra Nevada and other western mountains of California and Canada. From 4 inches to 1 foot tall, this forms clusters of stems with mostly seven to nine pairs of leaves usually more than one-half as wide as long. From pale to dark blue, more or less mottled or streaked with green, the upright, urn-shaped blooms are 1 inch to 1½ inches long. They have five erect petals with the plaits between them usually cleft into two to four teeth. The plant named *G. saxicola* is apparently no more than a variety of *G. calycosa* that prefers drier habitats. Its calyx lobes spread more widely. Wet soils in coastal regions from northern California to British Columbia are the natural habitations of **G. sceptrum.** Under good conditions this attains heights of up to 4 feet, or it may not be over 1 foot tall. It has thick, fleshy roots and stems with ten to fifteen pairs of oblong-lanceolate leaves 1¼ to 2½ inches long. The blue flowers, commonly streaked or dotted with green and 1 inch

to 2 inches long, have finely-toothed petals and alternating with them shorter, toothless plaits. From 6 inches to 1½ feet tall, very variable **G. affinis** has thickish roots and well-foliaged stems. The lower leaves are ovate, those above narrower. A native of foothills from northern California to Oregon and extending eastward to Alberta and Arizona, this has narrowly-lanceolate to oblong-lanceolate or elliptic-ovate leaves ¾ inch to 2 inches long by ¼ to nearly 1 inch wide. The flowers, deep blue frequently mottled or streaked with green, are about 1 inch long. Usually the plaits between the petals have two to five short teeth. Treated broadly, *G. affinis* includes

Gentiana lutea

Gentiana lutea (flowers)

variants sometimes segregated under such other names as *G. forwoodii, G. oregana,* and *G. parryi.*

The great yellow gentian (**G. lutea**), of Europe and western Asia, is a robust species that looks most un-gentian-like to those familiar only with lower, mostly blue-flowered kinds. Its rather glaucous foliage suggests that of *Veratrum viride.* Its spires of bloom call to mind those of certain lysimachias. The thick roots of old specimens of this gentian become turnip-like and weigh up to 25 pounds. Stout and stiffly erect, the hollow stems, 1½ to nearly 6 feet tall, are furnished with broadly-elliptic to ovate, conspicuously five- to seven-veined leaves 6 inches to 1 foot long, the lower ones stalked, those above progressively smaller, narrower, and stalkless. The 1-inch-long, stalked, golden-yellow blooms have extremely short corolla tubes. They have five to nine more or less spreading, pointed-lanceolate petals, separated almost to their bases and without plaits between them, about 1 inch long. Another yellow-flowered European of robust habit, the attractive spotted gentian (**G. punctata**) is a mountain species with deep taproots and rigid, erect, branchless stems 9 inches to 2 feet tall furnished with grayish-green, five- to seven-veined, elliptic leaves up to 4 inches long, the lower stalked, those above stalkless. The purple-spotted, pale yellow, stalkless, bell-shaped flowers, almost 1½ inches in length, have five to eight broadly-elliptic petals.

Gentiana punctata

Blue- or violet-blue-flowered Europeans, some extending into western Asia, include those now to be considered. The cross gentian (**G. cruciata**), its common and botanical names directing attention to its leaves being in four ranks and its blooms generally having four petals that spread to form a cross, is robust and rather coarse. It occasionally produces flowers with five petals. Its stems are up to 1½ feet long. The leaves are broad-elliptic to lanceolate, 2 to 4 inches long by up to ¾ inch wide.

Gentiana asclepiadea

Gentiana cruciata

Gentiana asclepiadea alba

They are three- or five-veined. The lower ones are stalked, those above stalkless. Barrel-shaped, the rather unexciting, dull blue flowers, ¾ to 1 inch long, are mostly partly concealed by the foliage. The cross gentian inhabits dryish pastures and open woodlands in limestone regions. The willow gentian (**G. asclepiadea**), lovely and accommodating, takes much more kindly to gardens in eastern North America than most exotic species. Native of damp soils in the moors, hills, and mountains in Europe, this forms clumps of gracefully arching, slender stems 9 inches to 1½ feet in length abundantly furnished with four or two ranks of lanceolate leaves 1½ to 3½ inches long and prominently five-veined. Its beautiful, stalkless, trumpet-shaped flowers, 1½ to 2¼ inches long, are usually solitary from the axils of the upper leaves. Rich dark blue and with five spreading petals, they are spotted inside with violet and lighter-striped on their outsides. Alternating with the petals are much shorter, cleftless plaits. Variety G. a. alba has white blooms. The marsh gentian (**G. pneumonanthe**) is a quite lovely wet-soil plant that develops erect, branchless, leafy stems 6 inches to over 1 foot tall. Its linear, one-veined leaves are ¾ inch to 1½ inches long, those low on the stems small and scalelike. Solitary or more commonly in clusters of up to seven, the bright blue flowers, striped green on their outsides, are terminal or from the axils of the uppermost leaves. Short-stalked and trum-

pet-shaped, they are 1 inch to 1½ inches long. Their petals are more or less erect rather than wide-spreading.

Dwarf alpine gentians of Europe include a few beautiful kinds tempting to rock garden enthusiasts. Here belong G. acaulis and G. verna, the first notorious for being capricious as to flowering. In some gardens

Gentiana acaulis

in climates suitable to its needs it blooms with cheerful exuberance, elsewhere in apparently identical environments it grows lushly, but obdurately refuses to flower. So closely related to *G. acaulis* are a few other species that some authorities treat them as subspecies or varieties. Here belong *G. alpina*, *G. angustifolia*, *G. clusii*, and *G. dinarica* among others. Collectively they are referred to as the *G. acaulis* complex. Typical **G. acaulis** (syns. *G. excisa*, *G. kochiana*) has basal rosettes of lanceolate, elliptic, glossy leaves 1 inch long or somewhat longer. The glorious deep blue blooms, on stalks 2 to 4 inches long, are upturned trumpets spotted with green in their throats and about 2 inches long. They have spreading, ovate, sharp-pointed petals. The anthers are united into a tube. Variable **G. verna** is native of much of Europe including Ireland, Scotland, and northern England and extends into arctic Russia. It forms tufts or mats of loose, non-flowering rosettes of foliage above which stretch to heights of about 4 inches the flowering stems each ending in a usually solitary bloom. The usually pointed, lanceolate to elliptic or broadly-ovate leaves have margins roughened toward their apexes. The two or three pairs of stem leaves are smaller and more spatula-shaped than the basal ones. The flowers typically are deep azure-blue, but variants occur in which the color ranges from pale to deep blue, sometimes with white throats. They have slender corolla tubes ¾ to 1 inch long and saucer-shaped faces about ¾ inch or somewhat more in diameter.

Among the most satisfactory low gentians are two species from western Asia and a hybrid between them that adapt well to gardens in northeastern North America. The species are *G. septemfida* and *G. lagodechiana*, which are so closely related that the last is sometimes treated as a variety of the first and named *G. s. lagodechiana*. The hybrid is named *G. hascombensis*. Native from Asia Minor to Iran, Turkestan, and the Caucasus, **G. septemfida** (syn. *S. cordifolia*) is more or less erect and up to 1 foot tall. Its pointed, five- or seven-veined leaves are up to 1¼ inches long by ½ inch wide. The flowers, several together at the stem apexes and narrowly-bell-shaped, are about 1½ inches long by one-half as wide across their faces. Mostly they are deep blue with spotted, paler throats, but they vary considerably in this respect. The deeply-incised plaits are nearly as long as the petals. In gardens variable *G. septemfida* is likely to be found growing under various names. From it and its variants **G. lagodechiana**, of the Caucasus, differs in its slender, leafy stems, prostrate except for their ascending tips and 6 inches to well over 1 foot long, having usually only one bloom at the apex. The leaves, up to 1 inch long and spaced about 1 inch apart, have short stalks and three chief veins. The lower ones are broadly-ovate with heart-shaped bases, those above are narrower and have rounded bases. Tubular-funnel-shaped, about 1½ inches long, and sharply narrowed at the base of the corolla tube, the flowers are deep blue with paler outsides, and on the petals and in their throats they have greenish spots.

Himalayan and western Chinese gentians include some of incredible beauty, but extremely exacting in their requirements for summers without suspicion of temperatures higher than 60 or 70°F and cooler at night, and with a definite appreciation of a humid atmosphere. Among such are **G. farreri**, in its finest expression with erect, trumpet blooms of purest turquoise-blue, but sometimes coming in degraded forms with flowers of washed-out blue. The lobes of the calyx are recurved and more than twice as long as the calyx tube. From a central rosette spread leafy stems 4 to 6 inches long. The leaves, about 1½ inches long, are narrow and recurved. At its best magnificent, related **G. sino-ornata** spreads gradually to form low mats of rooting stolons. It is studded in season with numerous solitary, stalkless or short-stalked, up-facing funnels of royal-blue darker than those of *G. farreri*, their insides blue with paler markings. The calyx has lobes less than one-half as long as the tube. The leaves, pointed-lanceolate and up to about 1½ inches long, increase successively in size from base to apex of the stolons, which are 6 to 8 inches long and have upturned tips. Unlike those of *G. farreri* the leaves of *G. sino-ornata* are not recurved. The flowers are 2½ inches long, one-half as much across their faces. Intermediate between its parents **G. macauleyi** is a very fine hybrid between *G. farreri* and *G. sino-ornata*. It is reported to prefer acid soil. Easy to grow but decidedly inferior as a decorative, **G. tibetica** of the Himalayas is a coarse, robust species 1 foot to 2 feet tall. It has lanceolate basal leaves up to 1 foot long by 3 inches wide, and smaller, narrower stem leaves the bases of which sheath the stems. The many tubular, greenish-white flowers, clustered near the

Gentiana septemfida

Gentiana lagodechiana

Gentiana farreri

Gentiana tibetica

tops of the stems, are 1 inch to 1½ inches long.

Northeastern Asia is home to late-summer-flowering *G. scabra* and closely allied *G. makinoi* and *G. sikokiana*. The typical species restricted to China, *G. scabra* is represented in Japan by *G. s. buergeri*, a superior vigorous variety 1½ to 3 feet tall with flowers 1½ to 2½ inches long. The more or less erect stems of **G. scabra**, 4 inches to 1 foot tall, are furnished with pairs of ovate leaves about 1½ inches long and with edges that are rough to the touch. Three longitudinal veins are clearly evident on their upper surfaces. The attractive bright blue flowers, from 1 inch to 1¼ inches long and facing upward, are in clusters of four or five at the tops of the stems and, usually in pairs, in the axils of the leaves. Endemic to the mountains of central Japan, **G. makinoi** is 1 foot to 2 feet tall. From *G. scabra* it is most readily distinguished by its paler blue flowers having calyxes with lobes of unequal lengths. Japanese **G. sikokiana** can be distinguished from *G. scabra* by the calyxes of its flowers, which are broadly-ovate rather than linear-oblong. Up to about 1 foot tall, this has four-angled stems furnished with pairs of elliptic leaves about 3 inches long. The blue or purplish-blue flowers, about 1½ inches long, are usually in threes at the apexes of the stems, with one or two blooms in the axils of the uppermost pair of leaves.

Several white-flowered gentians are natives of New Zealand Of these, **G. saxosa** may be grown by alpine plant enthusiasts. This has many stems up to 6 inches tall with at their ends rosettes of spatula-shaped, blunt, more or less fleshy leaves.

Gentiana scabra, cut stems in pot

The flowers are solitary or in clusters of up to five at the shoot ends. Broadly bell- to saucer-shaped, they are about ¾ inch in diameter. This species is less cold-hardy than the others that have been discussed.

Garden and Landscape Uses. Native America gentians other than western alpines include several that lend themselves to taming as garden plants. These are suitable for naturalizing in wild gardens, informal landscapes, and in rock gardens, under conditions approximating those under which they grow in the wild. Easiest to grow of the bottle gentian group is the eastern North American bottle gentian itself *G. andrewsii*. This adapts comfortably to moist, slightly acid and neutral soils in sun or slight shade and if undisturbed develops into considerable clumps that

Gentiana scabra (flowers)

bloom freely in late summer and fall. Some other eastern North Americans may be a little more difficult to establish, but are by no means impossible.

Alpine gentians, exotic kinds and native Americans, are treasures to be attempted by experienced rock gardeners only. As a group they are decidedly temperamental, difficult or impossible to satisfy in regions of hot summers. Among the most tractable, *G. scabra*, *G. septemfida*, *G. lagodechiana*, and *G. hascombensis* are suggested as suitable for ambitious beginners to employ to test their skills. These adapt well to a variety of soils, but are best satisfied with those that are gritty, well-drained, yet not lacking in moisture. They are benefited by a little shade from the full intensity of middle-of-the-day sun such as may be afforded by a nearby bush, shrub, or large rock. Similar environments may be tried for other alpine species. Unless you are dealing with a species that you know needs an alkaine soil or are making a test to determine if indeed a particular one does, provide a somewhat acid soil containing ample peat moss or leaf mold and coarse sand or grit. All in all, the best places to try out alpine gentians are rock gardens. Many kinds are most likely to succeed in moraines and in alpine greenhouses or cold frames. The willow gentian gives good results in woodland soil in semishaded places, a perfect companion for many primulas.

Cultivation. The chief consideration in growing gentians is to locate them happily. Once this is done and they are established their care makes few demands on the gardener. An annual top dressing with a soil agreeable to the species applied in early spring is helpful. In cold climates where there is little snow cover the winter protection of a loose strewing over them, after the ground has frozen, in fall of salt hay or branches of evergreens helps to minimize damage to the roots by alternate freezing and thawing. All species and some hybrids, although seedlings of the latter are likely to be somewhat variable, are easily raised from seeds. If fresh the seed may germinate promptly, but that of some kinds may take as long as a year. A few kinds, such as *G. verna* and *G. sino-ornata*, can be increased by division, and it is possible to root cuttings of some, including *G. septemfida* and its near relatives.

GENTIANACEAE—Gentian Family. The cultivated members of this dicotyledonous family of more than eighty genera and 900 species differ markedly in aspect and include, if the group is considered broadly, the aquatic bogbean (*Menyanthes*) and water snowflake (*Nymphoides*) as well as gentians and several other delightful ornamentals. Some authorities segregate kinds such as *Menyanthes* and *Nymphoides*, that have opposite leaves as the separate family MENYANTHACEAE.

Most members of the family are annuals or herbaceous perennials, less often subshrubs or shrubs. Their leaves are usually alternate, rarely opposite. They may be undivided or consist of more than one leaflet. The flowers are solitary or clustered and symmetrical. They come from the leaf axils or ends of the stems and usually have four or five, sometimes as many as twelve sepals, petals, and stamens and one style ending in a sometimes two-lobed stigma. The fruits are capsules or in rare cases berries. Cultivated members of the family include *Centaurium, Chironia, Eustoma, Exacum, Fauria, Frasera, Gentiana, Gentianella,* *Gentianopsis, Lisianthus, Menyanthes, Nymphoides, Sabatia, Swertia,* and *Tripterospermum.*

GENTIANELLA (Gentian-élla). Formerly included in *Gentiana,* but now treated as a separate genus, *Gentianella,* of the gentian family GENTIANACEAE, contains from 150 to 200 species of chiefly annuals and biennials together with a few herbaceous perennials. Its native range encompasses North America, South America, Europe, Asia, and New Zealand. The name is a diminutive of *Gentiana.* From closely related *Gentiana* and *Gentianopsis* this genus differs in its flowers lacking plaits or secondary lobes between the main ones of the corolla, and in the ovary being stalkless and the seeds smooth.

Gentianellas have branched, or less often branchless, frequently four-angled stems, and opposite, lobeless, toothless leaves. In short-stalked clusters of three to ten, the blue, lavender-blue, or white flowers have a tubular, four- or five-lobed calyx and a funnel-, bell-, or wheel-shaped corolla with five or less often four, toothless generally spreading lobes (petals). There are five or sometimes four stamens, one or no style, and two stigmas. The fruits are capsules.

Sorts cultivated, all annuals or biennials, include **G. amarella** (syn. *Gentiana amarella*), of northern North America, Europe, and Asia, which is variable. Usually branchless and from 6 inches to 1¼ feet tall, it has spatula-shaped basal leaves 1 inch to 1½ inches long and smaller, lanceolate stem leaves. About ½ inch long, the solitary and clustered flowers are light lilac-blue. **G. campestris** (syn. *Gentiana campestris*), of Europe and adjacent Asia, is variable; up to 1¼ feet tall, it has stalkless, ovate-lanceolate leaves ¾ inch to 1½ inches long. The ¾- to 1-inch-long flowers have a calyx with four lobes, two much smaller than the others, all broadest below their middles, and a four-lobed, bluish-lilac, purple, or white corolla. **G. propinqua** (syn. *Gentiana propinqua*), endemic from the northernmost United States, Quebec, and Newfoundland to the Yukon and Alaska and up to 1¼ feet tall, has elliptic to spatula-shaped basal leaves ¾ inch to 1¼ inches long and smaller stem leaves. Pale lilac to violet and solitary or in clusters of few, the ½- to ¾-inch-long flowers have calyxes with unequal lobes. **G. quinquefolia** (syn. *Gentiana quinquefolia*), of eastern North America, has stems 8 inches to 1½ feet tall, branched in their upper parts. Its stalkless, lanceolate to ovate-lanceolate leaves are ¾ inch to 1½ inches long. In dense clusters at the ends of the stem and side branches, the ¾- to 1-inch-long flowers are blue or sometimes white. **G. tenella** (syn. *Gentiana tenella*), of northern North America, Europe, and Asia, forms a basal rosette of elliptic, obovate, or spatula-shaped leaves 1 inch to 2 inches long and has a slender stem up to 6 inches tall, with solitary blue or white flowers less than ½ inch long at or near its apex, each with usually four calyx lobes and four corolla lobes each.

Garden Uses and Cultivation. Gentianellas are likely to appeal most to those who enjoy growing plants in wild gardens, rock gardens, along the fringes of woodlands, and in other naturalistic environments. Little is recorded about their cultural needs, but it would seem that success would be most likely by sowing seeds as soon after ripening as possible in patches of permanently dampish soil made ready by forking under generous amounts of peat moss or leaf mold and, if the soil is clayey, coarse sand or perlite as well. The young plants, except for any thinning out necessary to avoid undue crowding, should be left without transplanting to mature and flower.

GENTIANOPSIS (Gentian-ópsis)—Fringed-Gentian. formerly included in *Gentiana,* the about fifteen species of annuals and biennials that compose *Gentianopsis,* of the gentian family GENTIANACEAE, are natives of the northern hemisphere. From *Gentiana* they differ in not having small lobes or plaits alternating with the main lobes of the corollas of their flowers and in less obvious botanical details and from nearly related *Gentianella* in having flowers with four- instead of five-lobed corollas and in the lobes (petals) having fringed margins. The name, of obvious application, is derived from that of the genus *Gentiana* and the Greek *opsis,* like or resembling. The fruits are capsules.

The exquisite fringed-gentian of wet meadows, streamsides, and low, open woodlands from Maine to Ontario, Michigan, Pennsylvania, and Iowa, and in the mountains to Georgia, **G. crinita** (syn. *Gentiana crinita*) is 1 foot to 3 feet tall and

Gentianopsis crinita

has stems usually branched above and stalkless, ovate to lanceolate leaves. Its solitary or few to many bright blue flowers, terminal on the stems and branches and 1¼ to over 2 inches long, have deeply-fringed, wide-spreading petals. Resembling this species and favoring similar environments especially in limestone regions, *G. procera* (syn. *Gentiana procera*), sometimes called the lesser fringed-gentian, ranges as a native from Ontario to Wisconsin, New York, Indiana, and Iowa. From *G. crinita* it differs in having linear-lanceolate leaves and flowers with petals fringed only along their sides and toothed at their ends.

Native in moist meadows at high altitudes from Colorado to Arizona, *G. thermalis* is from 3 inches to 1 foot tall or somewhat taller and hairless, with erect stems. Its stalkless leaves, up to 1¼ inches long, are oblong to linear. Very showy, the blue-purple flowers 1 inch to 2 inches long have spreading, fringed petals.

Endemic to mountains in California, lovely *G. holopetala* (syn. *Gentiana holopetala*) is an annual or a biennial 3 inches to 1 foot high or higher and usually branched from its base. It has 1- to 1½-inch-long, obovate to linear leaves mostly toward the bases of its erect stems and a solitary, 1½- to 2-inch-long, bright blue flower with toothless or scarcely toothed corolla lobes terminating each stem.

Garden Uses and Cultivation. The plants of this genus are notoriously difficult to cultivate. Best prospects for success may lay in scattering freshly collected seeds on sites that as nearly as practicable provide the conditions the plants favor in the wild. Such sites are wet meadows, brook sides, and similar places.

GENUS. A botanical genus (plural genera) consists of a group of plants that resemble each other in critical details more closely than they do plants of other genera. Because of this they are presumably more closely related to each other than to other plants. A genus may be of one or more species and is identified by a distinctive generic name that forms part of the name or names of the species that compose it. Thus, the maidenhair tree belongs to the genus *Ginkgo*. It is the only species of that genus. Its name is *Ginkgo biloba*. By contrast the species of maple are numerous. All are included in the genus *Acer* and each is identified by a distinctive specific name the first word of which is that of the genus. The Norway maple is *Acer platanoides*, the sugar maple *Acer saccharum*, the sycamore maple *Acer pseudoplatanus*, and so on.

The formal establishment of a genus is based on botanical publication in accordance with internationally established procedures. But the acceptance of a genus and of the species it includes are subject to interpretation, and it is not unusual for equally competent botanists to hold different opinions. For example, some believe the giant suhuaro is sufficiently distinct from all other cactuses to warrant placing it in a genus of its own and name it *Carnegiea gigantea*. Others are of the opinion that it does not differ enough from *Cereus* to segregate it as a separate genus and so name it *Cereus giganteus*. So it is with many plants. In such cases it is not a matter of one name being right and the other wrong. The various names merely reflect different opinions as to the degree of fundamental variation needed to establish generic limits. It is important to emphasize that it is basic rather than gross or trivial characteristics that botanists employ in determining plant relationships. There are euphorbias for example, that in outward form closely resemble cactuses, to which they are not related, and bear little resemblance to poinsettias, which are of the same genus. As a practical matter gardeners and horticulturists in applying generic names follow standard authoratative literature available to them, but because of an unavoidable time lag this is not in every case in accordance with the latest scientific findings.

GEOGENANTHUS (Geogen-ánthus) — Seersucker Plant. Of the three or four species recognized as constituting this genus of the spiderwort family COMMELINACEAE, only one is known to be cultivated. The group, native to tropical South America, has a name presumably derived from the Greek *ge*, the earth, *genea*, birthplace, and *anthos*, a flower. It alludes to the location of the blooms.

Geogenanthuses are herbaceous perennials with rhizomes from which are produced more or less erect, branchless stems with, from their lower nodes, a few stem-clasping bracts, and, from the upper ones, two to four leaves with short stalks that enfold the stems. The leaves are crowded in terminal clusters. The flowers are in clusters that come from the bases of bracts low on the stem and actually burst through them. Each bloom has three sepals, three petals nearly equal in size that last for only a few hours, and five or six stamens, some of which usually have stalks hairy at their tops and some stalks that are hairless. The style is short. The fruits are capsules with angled seeds.

Seersucker plant (**Geogenanthus undatus**), native to the upper Amazon region, has been much confused with entirely different *Dichorisandra mosaica*. It has been mistakenly listed and grown as *D. m. undata*. From the dichorisandra this species is easily distinguished by the location and appearance of its flower clusters (those of the dichorisandra are in terminal showy clusters above the leaves) and in having two types of stamens and the foliage being very much undulated and seersucker-like in appearance and having pale, longitudi-

Geogenanthus undatus

nal stripes. The seersucker plant has stout, succulent stems, thickly clothed with brown hairs and 6 to 10 inches tall. Their bracts are reddish. Its evergreen, ovate leaves have blades that except for their margins appear to be smooth, but actually are densely covered with minute hairs. They are 3 to 4½ inches long and a little over 2 to 4 inches wide and have dark green upper sides banded along the longitudinal veins with silvery-green and under surfaces that are wine-red. The flowers have violet petals and are about ¾ inch across. There are three short, hairy stamens and two longer ones without hairs.

Garden Uses and Cultivation. The finding of this species, well over a century ago, growing in fissures of rocks at entrances to caves in Peru, suggests a practical use for it in tropical rock gardens, for which purpose it is ideally adapted. It is also a first-rate plant for cultivating in pots and pans (shallow pots) in tropical greenhouses and terariums. So long as a minimum temperature of about 60°F is maintained (it may with advantage be considerably above that), the atmosphere is highly humid, and there is shade from strong sun, no difficulty is likely to be encountered in growing the seersucker plant. The containers should be well drained and the soil one that contains an abundance of leaf mold, peat moss, or other decayed organic material and is kept evenly moist, but not saturated. Propagation is readily accomplished by cuttings. This species does not flower freely in cultivation and rarely sets seeds.

GEONOMA (Geonò-ma). Consisting of 150 or more species, *Geonoma*, of the palm family PALMAE, occurs natively only in tropical America including the West Indies. Although tropical, some of its species grow at considerable elevations and are subjected to comparatively low temperatures. In Colombia *G. aulacophylla* occurs at 10,600 feet. The name, from the Greek *geonomos*, skilled in agriculture, is of somewhat uncertain application.

In the wild geonomas chiefly occur as low plants and groundcovers in the shade of taller palms and other trees. They vary in height from a foot or so to as much as 20 feet and have solitary or clustered, reedlike, ringed stems; more rarely they are stemless. The leaves are pinnate or are undivided and have pinnate veins. When undivided their ends are deeply notched in fishtail fashion. When divided the segments are generally of unequal width, the ones toward the top of the leaf generally widest. The segments usually join the midrib without narrowing to a stalklike base. The branched or branchless flower clusters commonly come from the stem below the foliage and bear bisexual blooms with six stamens. There are two spathes, which often fall before the flowers open. The fruits are small, spherical, and black.

Native from Mexico to Panama, *G. interrupta* (syn. *G. binervia*) is up to 20 feet tall or taller. Its flower clusters are much-branched. Puerto Rican *G. gracilis* has a single stem up to 4 feet tall and a terminal crown of regularly-pinnate leaves up to 2½ feet long with numerous 1-foot-long leaflets about ½ inch wide, each with three veins. The flower clusters are long. Brazilian *G. pohliana* has a slender trunk up to 15 feet in height and narrow leaves 5 to 7 feet in length with leaflets of unequal width up to 1½ feet long. The flower clusters are short. Another Brazilian, *G. schottiana* also produces a slender stem up to 15 feet long, but its leaves are 1 foot to 3 feet in length and the long-pointed leaflets are about 10 inches long and under ½ inch wide.

Garden and Landscape Uses. In warm, humid regions geonomas are useful for planting outdoors where they receive shade and the soil is not excessively dry. They may be planted under trees and on the shady sides of walls and buildings. The lower ones are effective as underplantings, the taller growers as accents among lower-growing plants. In pots and tubs geonomas are effective house and greenhouse plants especially when they are young, and in greenhouses they grow well planted in ground beds. They tolerate low light intensities indoors better than many plants.

Cultivation. Geonomas are easy to grow if they are afforded a well-drained, but moist soil that contains generous amounts of decayed organic matter, such as compost, leaf mold, peat moss, or humus, and is kept always reasonably moist. In greenhouses they need a minimum winter night temperature of 55 to 60°F and night temperatures from spring through fall of at least 70°F. At all seasons day temperatures should be five to ten degrees above those maintained at night. The atmosphere must at all times be humid, and shade from strong sun must be provided. Biweekly applications of dilute liquid fertilizer, from spring through fall, are of great benefit to well-rooted specimens. Seeds sown in sandy, peaty soil in a temperature of 75 to 90°F afford a ready means of propagation. For additional information see Palms.

GERAEA (Gera-èa)—Desert-Sunflower. This genus of one annual and one short-lived herbaceous perennial is closely related to *Encelia* and is endemic to western North America. It belongs in the daisy family COMPOSITAE. The name *Geraea*, from the Greek *geraios*, old, refers to the white hairs of its achenes (seedlike fruits). Geraeas have alternate, usually toothed leaves and mostly panicled clusters of few yellow-flowered heads.

The desert-sunflower (*G. canescens*) is a native of California, Nevada, and Arizona, chiefly in desert regions. An annual, it usually branches from the base and is up to 2 feet tall. Its stems and foliage are white-hairy. The leaves are ovate to lanceolate or oblanceolate, up to 4 inches in length, and have toothless or few-toothed margins. The daisy-type flower heads, 1 inch to 1½ inches in diameter, are stalked and usually clustered, but sometimes are solitary. They have ten to twenty-one sterile ray florets.

Garden Uses and Cultivation. The desert-sunflower is an unusual and interesting annual for sunny flower beds and borders. It thrives in well-drained, dryish soil and blooms in summer. Sow seeds in early spring where the plants are to bloom and lightly rake them into the surface. Thin the seedlings to stand about 9 inches apart. Except for keeping down weeds, little or no care is needed. Water only in periods of drought.

GERALDTON WAX FLOWER is *Chamelaucium uncinatum*.

GERANIACEAE—Geranium Family. Certainly some geraniads, as members of the geranium family are called, are familiar to most gardeners; among them are pelargoniums and the plants popularly, but not botanically known as geraniums, both of the genus *Pelargonium*. Also belonging are the cranesbills (*Geranium*) and heronsbills (*Erodium*). A few geraniads provide forage and an oil used in perfumery is obtained from *Pelargonium odoratissimum*.

Five genera and 750 species are recognized as constituting this cosmopolitan family of dicotyledons. They include annuals, herbaceous perennials, subshrubs, and shrubs, most of which are hairy. They have opposite or alternate, divided, lobed or nearly lobeless, toothed, usually palmately-veined leaves. The flowers, rarely solitary, mostly in heads or branched clusters, are symmetrical or asymmetrical. The calyx is generally of five sepals, less frequently of four or eight. The corolla, typically five-petaled, but sometimes two-, four-, or eight-petaled, uncommonly is lacking. There are five, ten, or fifteen stamens or stamens and staminodes (nonfunctioning stamens) and three to five styles. The fruits are capsules. The genera of the family are *Erodium*, *Geranium*, *Pelargonium*, and *Sarcocaulon*.

GERANIUM. The genus *Geranium* and the pelargoniums commonly known as geraniums are dealt with, respectively, in the next two entries. In addition the word geranium forms part of the common names of some quite different plants including these: California- or velvet-geranium (*Senecio petasitis*), feather-geranium (*Chenopodium botrys*), mint-geranium (*Chrysanthemum balsamita*), and strawberry-geranium (*Saxifraga stolonifera*).

GERANIUM (Gerà-nium)—Cranesbill. The familiar subshrubby or in some instances shrubby, erect and trailing plants with more or less crowded heads of brilliant scarlet, pink, or white blooms commonly known as geraniums do not belong in the botanical genus *Geranium*. They are kinds of *Pelargonium*. Here we are concerned with the *Geranium* of botanists. Like *Pelargonium* it belongs in the geranium family GERANIACEAE. Of nearly cosmopolitan distribution in the wild, but chiefly concentrated in temperate regions, it comprises 400 species of annuals and herbaceous perennials, as well as a few soft-stemmed subshrubs, many weedy or for other reasons uninteresting to gardeners, a few attractive and good hardy flower garden and rock garden ornamentals. The name, alluding to the beaklike fruits, comes from the Greek *geranos*, a crane.

Geraniums have forked stems and opposite or alternate, generally roundish to kidney-shaped leaves most often fingered or lobed palmately (in hand-fashion), rarely pinnately. Those below are usually long-stalked. Upper leaves commonly have shorter stalks. The flowers, in pairs or loose arrangements, are symmetrical or nearly so (those of *Pelargonium* are often conspicuously asymmetrical). They have five separate sepals and five separate petals. The ten stamens all usually bear anthers (in *Erodium*, with which *Geranium* is often confused, there are only five anther-bearing stamens, the other five are represented by staminodes). In *Geranium* there are one, three, or five styles united at flowering time, but often separating later. They remain attached to the fruits. The latter, dry and capsule-like and at maturity with straight or arched rather than spiraled beaks, then shatter explosively into separate, one-seeded carpels, those of some kinds at the same time splitting to release the seeds. A distinction between *Geranium* and *Pelargonium* is that the flowers of the former are without spurs. In *Pelargonium* there is a spur fused to the flower stalk. It can be detected by the tiny lump on the stalk that usually denotes its

Geranium ibericum 'Johnson's Blue'

Geranium maculatum

end and by slicing across the stalk which makes visible the hollow center of the spur as well as that of the stalk.

Kinds suitable for beds and borders, hardy unless otherwise stated, include the relatively tall sorts now to be discussed. Its name alluding to the part of the Caucasus where it is native, not to the Iberian Peninsula, **G. ibericum** has thick rhizomes and stout, erect, hairy but not glandular stems, branched only in their upper parts. Its leaves, the basal ones long-stalked and few, the stem ones more plentiful, have angular-roundish blades 2 to 6 inches in diameter, cleft three-quarters to their bases into five or seven rhombic to obovate, coarsely-pinnately-lobed lobes. From 1½ to 2 inches in diameter and few together on hairy but not glandular stalks, the flowers are purple or blue-purple. They have broad petals slightly notched at their apexes, sometimes with a tooth on the bottom of the notch. Excellent varieties are *G. i. album*, with white flowers, *G. i. flore-pleno*, with double violet-blue blooms, and 'Johnson's Blue', with beautiful bright blue flowers. A very good hybrid, its parents *G. ibericum* and *G. platypetalum*, is **G. magnificum.** This has foliage much like that of *G. ibericum*, but differs in having glandular hairs on the flower stalks. Also, it is sterile and so does not produce seeds. This is often misnamed *G. ibericum*.

Magenta-pink to carmine-red blooms with wide-spreading petals are borne in dense clusters by **G. macrorrhizum,** of southern Europe. This 1- to 2-foot-tall species has stout rhizomes and leaves slashed to about three-quarters in from the margins into five- or seven-toothed, pinnately-cut lobes. The foliage when brushed

Geranium himalayense

against gives off an unpleasant scent. The flower stalks are densely-glandular-hairy. North American **G. maculatum** has thick rhizomes and usually branchless, erect stems. From 1 foot to 2 feet tall, this has deeply five- or seven-parted leaves 3 to 6 inches across, with coarsely-sharp-toothed lobes. The lower ones are long-stalked. Those above have shorter stalks. The 1- to 1½-inch-wide flowers, their rose-purple or magenta-pink petals not notched at their apexes, are two or more together on hairy, but not glandular stalks that come in twos or threes from the leaf axils. Native of Asia, **G. himalayense** (syns. *G. grandiflorum, G. meeboldii*) is 1 foot to 1½ feet tall. It has glandular-hairy stems with more or less reclining bases and long-stalked, deeply-five- to seven-lobed irregularly-toothed leaves 1½ to 1¾ inches in diameter. The flat flowers, displayed in bold, 1-

Geranium palmatum

foot-wide or wider clusters on glandular-hairy or hairless stalks are 1½ inches in diameter and lilac-blue with rosy-purple veining. Its foliage fernlike, shrubby-based **G. palmatum** (syn. *G. anemonifolium*), native to the Canary Islands and Madeira, is not hardy in the north, but is well suited for mild, dryish climates. It has essentially hairless large leaves palmately-cleft into five, or the upper ones into three, twice-pinnate segments. The big purple-red blooms are in twos on long, erect, hairless stalks that lift them well above the beautiful fernlike foliage.

Native of southwest Asia, **G. platypetalum** (syn. *G. ibericum platypetalum*) is exceptionally handsome. Approximately 2 feet tall, it has upright, glandular-hairy stems. Its leaves, which become bright orange-crimson in fall, are parted nearly to their bases into five or seven blunt, shallowly-toothed lobes. Deep purple and about 1½ inches in diameter, the flowers are in twos. Europe and temperate Asia are the homelands of **G. pratense.** From 1½ to 3 feet in height, this has pubescent stems glandular in their upper parts. Its long-staked basal leaves have nearly circular blades 3 to 6 inches wide divided into seven sharply-toothed lobes. The uppermost stem leaves are three-lobed and nearly stalkless. The glandular-hairy flower stalks, which become deflexed when seed pods develop, each have two clear lavender-blue to purple, cup-shaped flowers 1 inch to 1¾ inches wide, the petals sometimes slightly notched at their apexes. In variety *G. p. album* the blooms are white. The flowers of *G. p. album-plenum* are white and double. Those of *G. p. atropurpureum* are darker than those typical of the species. Armenian **G. psilostemon** (syn. *G. armenum*) well displays above its silvery foliage blooms of shocking bright magenta-pink with ebony-black blotches at the bases of the petals. They are carried on long stalks and have petals notched at their apexes. From 1½ to 3 feet in height, this has long-stalked, broadly-heart-shaped, five-lobed leaves, the lower ones 6 to 8 inches wide.

Geranium sanguineum

Common in old-time gardens, **G. sanguineum,** which is native throughout most of Europe, has horizontal rhizomes and more or less trailing, slender, white-hairy stems. It forms mounds up to about 1 foot tall and bears rather harsh magenta-pink flowers freely. Its leaves, mostly on the stems and 1½ to 2 inches wide or sometimes wider, are very deeply slit into five or seven pinnately-lobed lobes. The usually solitary flowers are 1 inch to 1½ inches in diameter. Very much lower than the typical species, *G. s. prostratum* (syn. *G. s. lancastriense*) has blooms similar in color. It is a useful rock garden plant.

Geraniums that like the last-mentioned varieties of *G. sanguineum* are adapted for rock gardens include beautiful silver-foliaged **G. argenteum,** a dwarf, tufted, deep-rooted native of limestone screes in moun-

Geranium sanguineum prostratum

tains of Italy and adjacent lands. Its densely-silky-hairy leaves are divided nearly to their bases into lobes, usually again deeply cleft into three narrow segments. The 1-inch-wide, cup-shaped blooms, silvery-pink with darker veinings, are on erect stems 4 to 5 inches tall. Very like the last except that its leaves are green is **G. cinereum.** This native of European mountains, including the Pyrenees and those of the Balkan Peninsula, has usually lilac-pink flowers with darker veinings.

Geranium cinereum subcaulescens

Geranium dalmaticum

Geranium renardii

Variety *G. c. subcaulescens* (syn. *G. subcaulescens*) differs in its flowers usually being deep reddish-purple. Resembling *G. macrorrhizum*, but considerably smaller and more delicate in appearance, **G. dalmaticum** (syn. *macrorrhizum dalmaticum*) is a charming native of Yugoslavia and Albania. A foot or so high **G. endressii** grows in wet places in southwestern France. It has creeping rhizomes. Perhaps a little too large and rampant for small rock gardens it may be given a place in outlying parts of bigger ones. This has hairy stems and leaves with blades 2 to 3 inches or more wide, cleft four-fifths way to their bases into five lobes. The bright pink flowers are without dark veinings. Caucasian **G. renardii** forms clumps up to 1 foot across and as tall or lower. Its conspicuously-veined, olive-green leaves have five rounded lobes. The violet-purple-centered flowers are in pairs. Native to New Zealand, **G. traversii** is a none-too-hardy kind that occasionally survives winters outdoors near New York City. It has deeply-lobed, roundish leaves and white flowers about ¾ inch wide. Himalayan **G. wallichianum** is a trailer up to 1 foot high or a little higher with stems up to 2 feet long. Its finely-hairy, kidney-shaped leaves are cleft into three or five deeply-lobed, toothed, segments. The lavender-pink, whitish-centered blooms, strongly veined with violet-purple, are 1½ to 2 inches in diameter. They are in pairs. 'Buxton's Variety' has exceptionally fine violet-blue flowers. Native of Siberia and Manchuria, **G. wlassovianum** is up to 1 foot tall. The upper parts of its stems are hairy. The roundish-kidney-shaped leaves are three- or five-lobed, the purple-violet blooms about 1¼ inches across.

Garden and Landscape Uses. The taller cultivated geraniums are useful as single specimens or in small groups at the fronts of flower beds and borders and for natu-

Geranium wlassovianum

ralizing in less formal areas. The low kinds are best in rock gardens and similar intimate plantings. The foliage of many kinds, even when they are out of flower, forms attractive foils for neighbor plants in bloom.

Cultivation. Geraniums adapt well to well-drained, not exceptionally dry, garden soils. For low rock garden kinds they are better if gritty and not over-rich in nutrients. Planting may be done in spring or early fall; the former is preferable in cold regions. Routine care is of the simplest, consisting of suppressing weeds, watering if the weather is dry, and promptly removing faded flowers to prolong the blooming season and to avoid the untidy appearance the seed heads produce. A yearly application of a complete garden fertilizer in spring is beneficial.

GERANIUMS. We are not concerned here with the botanical genus *Geranium*, which is considered in the preceding entry, but with the much better known and more popular geraniums of the window gardener, greenhouse gardener, and planter of window boxes and porch boxes, and in regions of cold winters and temporary summer flower beds, with the geraniums that in California and other warm, dry climates are perennial garden residents that riot in bright scarlets, crimsons, pinks, and whites without hint of the beautiful blues of the botanists' genus *Geranium*. These plants belong to the genus *Pelargonium*, and under that entry the species from which they have been derived are described. Here we deal only with the garden varieties and hybrids that constitute the populations commonly grown and universally recognized in English-speaking lands as geraniums. They fall into three main groups, bedding, zonal, or fish geraniums, ivy-leaved geraniums, and Lady Washington or Martha Washington geraniums. All have been derived from species native to South Africa. The scented-leaved geraniums of gardens have the same

geographical origin, but are generally of less complex ancestry. They are described and discussed under Pelargonium.

The story of geraniums begins toward the close of the seventeenth century. In 1652 the Dutch established near the Cape of Good Hope a calling station for ships trading with the East Indies. Its facilities included a large garden (now a public park in downtown Cape Town) to supply post personnel and provision ships with fresh vegetables. There can be little doubt that unfamiliar, colorful plants of the region attracted the attention of the gardeners and of some visiting seamen, especially ships' surgeons who in those days were generally botanically oriented, or that occasional ones were taken as novelties to Holland by the horticulturally minded Dutch. As early as 1690 one of the three prime parental stocks of our Lady Washington geraniums, *Pelargonium cucullatum*, was known in England, perhaps introduced via Holland or possibly brought in an English ship that called at the Cape. The other members of this group are *P. angulosum*, introduced to England in 1724 and *P. grandiflorum* in 1794. The ancestor of our ivy-leaved geraniums, *P. peltatum* is reported to have been brought to England in 1701. Benchmarks in geranium history were established in 1710 and 1714. In those years, respectively, *P. zonale* and *P. inquinans*, were introduced to England, the first by the Duchess of Beaufort, the other by Bishop Compton. These were to give rise, probably with later infusions from other species, to the vast variety of bedding or zonal geraniums we now enjoy and that must be numbered among the finest of South Africa's many glorious contributions to ornamental horticulture.

Early in the nineteenth century many species of *Pelargonium* were being grown in Europe and much hybridizing was being done, at first chiefly to produce varieties of Lady Washington geraniums. An interest in pelargoniums something akin to the earlier 'tulipmania' developed. This led to the publication between 1810 and 1820 of the five-volume *Geraniaceae* by Robert Sweet. This monumental classic contains 500 beautiful colored plates. It was during Sweet's time that interest in zonal geraniums began, an interest that expanded tremendously later and has continued unabated to the present day.

The first coming of geraniums to America is not recorded, but it is not improbable that it occurred fairly early. One likes to think that among the few possessions emigrants could take along with necessities for the tedious voyage some plant-loving wife might find place for a treasured geranium. Certainly other favorite plants have crossed the oceans under similar circumstances. Be that as it may, in 1786 John Bartram of Philadelphia had received plants of the Lady Washington type sent

from France by Thomas Jefferson. He had imported seeds of "geraniums" in 1760, but it is not clear whether they were of the kinds we are dealing with here or whether they represented other species of pelargoniums. Interest in geraniums in the United States was brisk during the first quarter of the nineteenth century and hundreds of kinds were grown, most if not all importations from Europe. Later American breeders entered the field and produced many outstanding varieties. This work is being continued.

Geraniums today are available in vast and increasing variety. As with many horticultural groups, old favorites may diminish in popularity, they may be completely superseded as newer varieties became available, or they may retain their places in the horticultural limelight. Popularity of some kinds, because of their adaptability to particular climates, is regional. Collectors of geraniums, and there are many in America, are likely to preserve and to prize older varieties as well as to welcome new ones. American breeders are active in developing these last and the International Geranium Society, founded in 1953, with its headquarters in California, as well as other specialist groups here and abroad stimulate interest in and disseminate information about geraniums, old and new. Because of this, it is not deemed helpful here to present a lengthy catalog of geranium varieties, some of which may soon be outdated, and others of which may be only of local importance. Some kinds will be listed. For more complete presentations of available varieties consult the catalogs of specialist dealers and the publications of geranium societies.

Bedding, zonal, or fish geraniums, those whose ancestry clearly stems back to *Pelargonium zonale* and *P. inquinans*, are for convenience grouped under the name *P. hortorum*, but gardeners more commonly call them zonal geraniums, bedding geraniums, or just geraniums. Their varieties are susceptible to grouping according to vigor, whether or not their foliage is variegated, and other characteristics. The most robust, sometimes referred to as the French type, have extraordinary large trusses of big flowers and thick-textured, large leaves.

Among the best plain-green-leaved bedding or zonal geraniums are these: 'Beaute Poitevine', semidouble pink flowers; 'Better Times', double red flowers; 'Fiat', rich salmon-pink, semidouble flowers; 'General Leonard Wood', single red blooms; 'Improved Ricard', bright light red, semidouble flowers; 'Irene', flowers crimson; 'Maxime Kovalevski', orange-scarlet flowers; 'Mme. Buchner', double white flowers; 'Olympic Red', bright red, semidouble flowers; 'Paul Crampel', single scarlet blooms; 'Radio Red', flowers double red; 'Salmon Supreme', flowers salmon-apri-

Green-leaved zonal geraniums: (a) 'Beaute Poitevine'   (b) 'Olympic Red'

Tricolor zonal geraniums: (a) 'Happy thought'

(b) 'Mrs. Henry Cox'

cot; and 'Snowball', flowers double-white.

Zonals with variegated leaves, sometimes listed as fancy leaf geraniums, include some of the most beautifully colored foliage plants of warm temperate and subtropical regions. Some flower quite handsomely and most satisfactorily, although rarely as splendidly as plain-leaved kinds. One old-time favorite, 'Mme. Salleron' does not bloom at all. The most brilliant of the variegated zonals are the tricolors, varieties in which the leaves display three colors.

Tricolor zonals include these: 'Happy Thought', leaves with creamy-yellow centers margined with brown and orange and edged with green, flowers red; 'Miss Burdett Coutts', ivory-white-edged, green leaves with a zone splashed with rose-pink, flowers scarlet; 'Mrs. Cox', narrowly-yellow-bordered leaves with a zone of brown splashed with red, flowers salmon-pink; 'Mrs. Pollock', yellow-margined, green leaves with a broad zone of bronze with red offsets, flowers scarlet; and 'Skies of Italy', pointed-lobed, creamy-yellow-margined, green leaves splashed with red and crimson, flowers red.

Zonals with white- or creamy-white-margined, green leaves include these: 'Flower of Spring', leaves with white borders of irregular widths, flowers scarlet; 'Hills of Snow', leaves with narrow, white

(c) 'Mrs. Pollock'

Zonal geraniums with white-variegated leaves: (a) 'Hills of Snow'

(d) 'Skies of Italy'

(b) 'Mme. Salleron'

Geraniums with bronzy-green to yellow-green leaves: (a) 'Bronze Beauty'

(b) 'Distinction'

margins, flowers small, double, rose-pink; 'Mme. Salleron', compact, with numerous long-stalked small leaves. This kind does not bloom. 'Mrs. Parker', compact, leaves with medium-wide white margins, flowers small, double, light rose-pink; and 'Wilhelm Langgluth', of spreading, low habit, flowers double, vermilion.

Yellow is the predominant color of the foliage of these zonals: 'Cloth of Gold', low, foliage golden to greenish-yellow, flowers scarlet; 'Crystal Palace Gem', leaves creamy-white to yellow with green centers, flowers scarlet; and 'Verona', foliage yellow to greenish-yellow, flowers rose-pink.

Bronzy-green to yellow-green foliage is typical of these: 'Alpha', leaves small, with rust-red borders, flowers red; 'Bronze Beauty', leaves with a narrow zone of reddish-brown, flowers light salmon-pink; 'Distinction', leaves with a very distinct narrow ring of brownish-black near their margins, flowers cherry-red; and 'Marechal MacMahon', leaves with a brown or rust-red zone well in from the margin.

Miniature or dwarf geraniums, compact, small-foliaged varieties of zonal types, are numerous and interest especially collec-

tors and window gardeners. A few notable ones of these are: 'Black Vesuvius', leaves blackish-green, flowers orange-scarlet; 'Brownie', leaves green with purple zone, flowers scarlet; 'Dopey', leaves green, tinged purple, flowers cerise-pink; 'Kleiner Liebling', leaves fresh green, flowers rose-pink; 'Mme. Fournier', leaves purplish-green to black-green, flowers scarlet; 'Pigmy', leaves light green, zoned, flowers double, red; and 'Sprite', leaves margined with white, flowers rosy-tangerine.

Novel-flowered geraniums include many varieties esteemed by collectors. Some, such as 'Fiat Queen', 'Fringed Poitevine', and 'Fringed Ricard' have petals with toothed edges and are sometimes called carnation-flowered geraniums. Kinds with more or less rosebud-like blooms are called rosebud geraniums. Here belong 'Apple Blossom Rosebud', 'Pink Rosebud', and 'Red Rosebud'. Cactus-flowered ge-

Miniature geranium 'Black Vesuvius'

Variegated ivy-leaved geranium

Lady Washington geranium

Zonal geraniums in a summer display outdoors

Pots of zonal geraniums brighten the corner of a terrace in summer

raniums have flowers with narrow, often twisted or curled petals. They include 'Poinsettia', 'Pink Poinsettia', and 'Rosette'. Bird's egg geraniums have flowers sprinkled with distinct pinhead-like dots of red or pink. They include 'Baudelaire', 'Curiosa', 'J. J. Knight', and 'Skylark'.

Ivy-leaved geraniums have slender, vinelike, more or less clambering, trailing, or pendulous stems, those of some varieties up to 6 feet long or longer. Their leaves are usually glossy, angular-lobed and have somewhat the aspect of those of English ivy, but are of lighter color. Ivy-leaved geraniums are less rigid and more graceful than the zonals. Their flowers, in slimmer-stalked, looser clusters, range from white through pinks and lavender-pinks to deep reds. There are single-, semi-double-, and double-flowered varieties. Here is a selection of ivy-leaved varieties. 'Apricot Queen', flowers double, salmon-pink fading to white at the center; 'Carlos Uhden', flowers bright red with white centers; 'Cesar Franck', flowers semidouble, rose-red suffused with orange; 'Galilee', flowers double, rose-pink; 'Joseph Warren', flowers double, rose-purple; 'Mexican Beauty', flowers semidouble, blood-red; 'Snowdrift', flowers double, white blushed pink at the bottom of the petals; 'Sybil Holmes', flowers double, deep silvery-pink. Specialist growers list many more as well as hybrids between ivy-leaved and zonal varieties.

Lady Washington or Martha Washington geraniums, also called Lady Washington or Martha Washington pelargoniums, keep alive as group names those of a mid-nineteenth-century variety originally known as 'Martha Washington', later as 'Lady Washington'. Abroad and to some extent in the United States they are known as re-gal and show pelargoniums. More technically they are identified as *Pelargonium domesticum*. These kinds differ from zonals and ivy-leaved geraniums. They have much woodier stems and their leaves are not zoned. Their flowers are often large, up to 3 inches in diameter, usually decidedly asymmetrical, and commonly are conspicuously ornamented with blotches of contrasting color. Many are reminiscent in form of the blooms of azaleas, petunias, or pansies. They also differ from zonals and ivy-leaved varieties in having a comparatively short spring and early summer season of bloom instead of one lasting practically throughout the year. In recent years many fine varieties have been raised by American breeders. Here is a selection: 'Azalea', flowers rose-carmine, lower petals lighter, upper with small dark blotch; 'Chorus Girl', flowers lavender with an orange-salmon-pink blotch, petals with ruffled edges; 'Cover Girl', flowers pale pink with deeper colored upper petals and a white throat; 'Dubonnet', flowers dark wine-red; 'Easter Greeting', early blooming, flowers bright red with a black blotch; 'Grand Slam', flowers brilliant red with a salmon-pink stalk, upper petals blotched with deep reddish-brown; 'Haile Selassie', flowers pinkish-lavender paling toward the petal margins, each petal with a brown blotch; 'La Paloma', flowers pure white; 'Marie Rober', flowers lavender-violet with large purple-black blotches; 'Mrs. Layal', flowers small, purple-violet, rose-pink, and white; 'Senorita', flowers salmon-red with paler, ruffled margins, upper petals reddish-brown.

Garden and Landscape Uses. The uses of the truly gorgeous plants we call geraniums are many and various. Their blooms are delightful for incorporating in nosegays and other floral arrangements, both old-worldly and more sophisticated. But it is as growing plants that they serve more commonly. Zonal or bedding geraniums of ordinary size and vigor are suitable for permanent outdoor planting in California and other warm, dry regions, and there and elsewhere as one-season occupants of summer flower beds, window boxes, porch boxes, urns, and other decorative containers. Where hardy outdoors, they make sizable subshrubs or shrubs and are well suited for espaliering against walls and other supports. Indoors, zonals are excellent pot plants for sunny windows in rooms not excessively hot and for

Head of a standard-trained geranium

Ivy-leaved geraniums outdoors in California

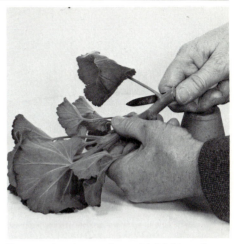

Propagating by cuttings: (a) Making the cuttings

greenhouses. In large greenhouses and conservatories, they may be trained in espalier fashion up posts and walls. These zonals also lend themselves for training as standards (tree-form specimens). Dwarf and miniature zonals are choice collectors' plants best adapted for greenhouse and window cultivation.

Ivy-leaved geraniums serve the same purpose as zonals, but are less widely used as furnishings for formal flower beds. Their more diffuse growth and trailing or pendulous stems fits them especially well as decorations for window and porch boxes, urns, and hanging baskets. In regions where they may be grown as outdoor perennials they are splendid for clothing slopes and banks and as espaliers. They are satisfactory greenhouse and window plants.

A hanging basket of an ivy-leaved geranium

Lady Washington geraniums are grown as permanent subshrubs or shrubs in warm, dry, essentially frost-free climates and are popular flowering pot and tub plants for ornamenting greenhouses, sunrooms, porches, and patios. They lend themselves well to training as standards.

Cultivation. Some statements about geraniums and their needs apply to all cultivated types. They are lovers of sunshine. They are intolerant of excessively high fall-to-spring temperatures. Night levels then of 50 or even 45°F, with daytime increases of five to ten or on very sunny days fifteen

degrees, suffice for carrying over well-established plants. Somewhat higher ones are needed for plants that are to be kept growing through the winter or that are to be brought into bloom then. For them 55 or even 60°F, at night with proportionate increases by day, are in order, but only if they are exposed to full sun or are given supplemental artificial light. A heavily humid, dank atmosphere is abhorrent to geraniums. On all favorable occasions ventilate the place where they are as freely as weather permits.

Soil for geraniums needs to be moderately heavy. Let it be decidedly loamy, slightly clayey, rather than too sandy. But be sure it is porous and well drained, neither pasty when wet nor likely to become waterlogged. See that it contains only moderate amounts of organic matter, not more than about one-quarter part by bulk of peat moss, leaf mold, or rich compost, and that it is fertile without being too rich in nitrogen. If unleached wood ashes are available mix them in at the rate of a quart or two to the bushel. This ensures a supply of needed potash. A pint of bonemeal to the bushel or superphosphate at about one-quarter that rate is also a good addition. Should the soil be excessively acid mix in a little ground limestone. This is especially appreciated by Lady Washington geraniums. When potting or planting, pack the soil firmly. This encourages short-jointed, stocky growth and discourages lankiness.

For summer display outdoors it is usually desirable to have well-grown plants of zonal and ivy-leaved geraniums in 4- or 5-inch pots at planting out time, which is after the last tulips have faded and it is safe to set out tomatoes and other warm season plants. To achieve such specimens take cuttings in September and after they have rooted plant them singly in 2½- or 3-inch pots. Keep them throughout fall and early winter in the lower temperatures suggested earlier, without pushing them, in a sunny greenhouse or window. In January or early

(b) Planting the cuttings

(c) A pot full of cuttings rooting

February pot them into 4-inch pots and increase the temperature slightly to encourage growth. When this has well started pinch out the tips of the stems to induce branching. After a few weeks some varieties may need a second pinching, and vigorous ones may benefit from transferring to pots 5 inches in diameter. Plants in 4-inch or smaller pots, suitable for bedding, can be had by taking cuttings in January or early February from old stock plants in the greenhouse, or by encouraging the plants

Zonal geraniums for summer display: (a) In 3-inch pots in greenhouse

Repotting a straggly zonal geranium: (a) Cut hard back in spring

(d) Under suitable conditions, new growth soon starts and a shapely plant results

(b) Transplanting to 5-inch pots

(b) Prick some soil away from around the roots

(c) Ready for transplanting outdoors

(c) Repot in a container just big enough to hold the roots

raised from fall-rooted cuttings to make sufficient growth so that, instead of merely pinching out the tips of their shoots to encourage branching, longer pieces can be cut off and used as cuttings. To avoid occupying greenhouse space unnecessarily commercial growers frequently rely upon cuttings shipped to them in January by specialist growers in California and from these produce good 4-inch pot plants by planting out time.

Larger specimens for planting in outdoor summer beds are had by wintering older plants indoors, trimming them to shape and repotting them in February, and growing them under the conditions advised for plants raised from cuttings. The plants so used may be specimens carefully dug from garden beds, cut back partway and potted and brought indoors

before the first fall frost or they may be plants raised from cuttings rooted in May or earlier of the previous year and grown throughout in pots.

As indoor plants and as container specimens for patios and similar places zonal and ivy-leaved geraniums are raised in the same manner as for summer beds, but instead of planting them in the ground for the summer they are potted into larger containers. Such specimens will need, in addition to the removal of faded blooms necessary with plants in beds, watering regularly and occasional fertilizing. They may also, ivy-leaved kinds especially, require staking. Take care not to keep the earth constantly saturated. Permit it to become dryish, but not to the extent that the foliage wilts, between waterings. When watering, drench the soil completely. Biweekly applications of dilute liquid fertilizer will ordinarily be sufficient. The objective in making these is to encourage steady growth, but not a too vigorous development at the expense of blooms. Be guided accordingly.

For winter bloom it is far better to raise zonal and ivy-leaved varieties especially for the purpose than to depend upon specimens that have bloomed through the summer. Take cuttings from March to May. When rooted, pot them individually in small pots and as root growth necessitates successively into bigger ones, giving them their final shift, into 5-, 6-, or 7-inch pots in late August. At an early stage pinch out the tips of the shoots to encourage branching. Repeat this once or twice, but not later than August. Throughout the summer keep the plants in a sunny spot outdoors with their pots buried nearly to their rims in a bed of sand or similar material. Treat them as recommended previously for indoor specimens for summer bloom except that until the end of September (the plants must of course be brought

To promote bushiness: (a) Discourage lanky shoots such as this

(b) By pinching out the terminal bud just beyond the first or second leaf in front of the developing flower bud

indoors before frost) pick off while quite small all flower buds. Indoors keep them in full sun where the temperature at night is 55°F and by day five to ten degrees higher depending upon the brightness of the weather.

Tree-form or standard zonal geraniums are easily developed. For preference choose vigorous-growing varieties. Root cuttings from March to May and grow the plants that result exactly as advised for winter-flowering specimens with the exception that you must not pinch out the tip of the main shoot. Instead, keep a single unpinched stem tied to a stake inserted firmly in the pot and as soon as they are discernible remove all side shoots and any flower buds that appear. Do not take off any leaves. When the stem has attained the height you want the trunk of your plant to be, 2½ to 3½ feet will usually be about right, pinch out its tip and allow three to five side branches to grow from its upper end. When these are 4 to 6 inches in length pinch out their tips and repeat this with subsequent branches until a good head is formed. Under good growing conditions fine standard specimens can be achieved in the second year.

Propagation of zonal and ivy-leaved geraniums is most usually by shoot cuttings or sometimes, when it is desired to secure as great an increase as practicable, by leaf-bud cuttings. Recently, however, excellent strains of seeds of zonals have become available and surprisingly good results are had by sowing these indoors about February and growing the young plants on in

the manner used for those raised from cuttings. Plants so obtained are not entirely uniform as to habit of growth or in form or color of bloom, but they flower profusely the first summer and produce a riotous display of color. By following this procedure the need for fall propagating and keeping plants through the winter is eliminated, and geraniums can be treated as annuals and raised as easily as petunias, wax begonias, and red salvias. Another advantage is that viral diseases are not transmitted by seeds, as they can be by cuttings.

Lady Washington geraniums are managed a little differently from zonals and ivy-leaved kinds. These have a season of partial rest after they are through flowering in late spring or early summer. In July or August prune them back quite severely, their branches to within three or four nodes or joints of their bases. Remove them from their pots, pick away as much old soil from among their roots as possible, and repot them into containers of the same or slightly smaller size, ones just big enough to accommodate the root mass. Make the soil firm. Water thoroughly and stand the plants in a lightly shaded greenhouse, cold frame, or sheltered spot outdoors. Avoid keeping the soil too wet, but spray the tops of the plants with water two or three times a day. Soon new shoots will appear. When these are about 3 inches long they may be taken as cuttings and planted in a greenhouse or cold frame propagating bed or under mist. When rooted, pot them individually in small pots. Grow the young

plants and the pruned-back older ones under conditions that suit zonal geraniums. Repot into larger receptacles as growth makes necessary, and pinch out the tips of the shoots when they are 5 or 6 inches long and those of the branches once again later. During fall and early winter considerable care must be exercised not to water too much, but increased water supplies will be needed as the days lengthen and the roots fill the final pots. From early March until the flowers begin to expand weekly applications of dilute liquid fertilizer are very beneficial.

After they are through blooming reduce the amount of water given by allowing longer intervals between applications. Let the soil become quite dry between soakings. Growth will cease and some of the foliage drop. That is all to the good provided the stems do not shrivel and dry. For this period of rest the pots can be put on their sides in a lightly shaded greenhouse or cold frame to be restarted into growth in late July or August. Lady Washington geraniums can be trained as tree-form specimens by the same procedures as zonals. Although usually multiplied by cuttings, they can also be had from seeds.

Pests and diseases of geraniums include aphids, caterpillars, mealybugs, mites, scale insects, black vine weevil, whitefly, and termites. These plants are subject to root rot, stem rot, and leaf spot diseases, as well as a number of virus infections. A dropsical-like condition called edema may develop in greenhouses, manifesting itself by spots at first appearing water-soaked,

Gerbera jamesonii

Gerbera jamesonii, garden varieties

later corky. It is the result of physiological disturbance in the internal water relations of the plant. Care to avoid excessive watering or the maintenance of too humid atmospheric conditions together with the exposure to as much sunlight as possible usually brings about improvement.

GERBERA (Gèr-bera)—Transvaal-Daisy or Barberton-Daisy. Only one species of this genus of seventy is well known to gardeners. The group, native from Africa and Madagascar to Asia and Bali, belongs in the daisy family COMPOSITAE. Its name commemorates the German naturalist Traugott Gerber, who died in 1743.

Gerberas are nonhardy, stemless, herbaceous perennials with, in rosettes, undivided, pinnately-lobed or lobeless leaves usually woolly-hairy on their undersides. Their solitary flower heads are on leafless, sometimes bracted stalks. They are of the daisy pattern, with a central eye of bisexual disk florets surrounded by one or two rows of often female, petal-like ray florets. If two rows, the inner is much shorter than the outer. The fruits are five-ribbed, seedlike achenes. Horticultural varieties with many more rows of ray florets are popular.

The Transvaal- or Barberton-daisy (*Gerbera jamesonii*) is hairy throughout. It has rosettes or tufts of spreading, fairly long-stalked, lobed or pinnately-divided leaves, with blades woolly-hairy on their undersides, 5 to 10 inches long. The flower stalks, 1 foot to 1½ feet tall, have heads up to 4 inches across, with orange or flame ray florets. Garden varieties have larger flowers with longer stems. Those of some varieties are semidouble or double. They come in white and in a wide range of

Gerbera jamesonii in a greenhouse bench

colors, including cream, yellow, orange, pink, red, and purple.

Garden and Landscape Uses and Cultivation. Besides other employments, these are among the most satisfactory flowers for cutting. Under reasonably good conditions they last three weeks in water. It is important not to cut the blooms until they are fully developed, and then to stand them upright in water. If they lie horizontally for only a few hours the heads bend upward, resulting in crooked stems. Because they open very few blooms at one time, although they produce over a long season, a sizable planting is needed to make possible any considerable gathering. For this reason gerberas are generally not well suited to the needs of operators of small greenhouses.

In dryish climates where little or no frost is experienced gerberas are satisfactory outdoors if conditions are reasonably to their liking. They are not choosy about soil so long as it is porous and fertile. Newly

set plants are rather slow to become established. The best results do not come the first year. Because it is important that water does not lodge and remain for long periods in the crowns, a sloping site is better than a flat one. In setting the plants take care to keep their crowns slightly above soil level. Excellent drainage is a must, and raised beds may be used to achieve this. Full sun is necessary. Gerberas do not thrive when crowded. They need space to spread their foliage without interference. Mulching to conserve soil moisture and to reduce the need for watering is very desirable.

In greenhouses, gerberas are grown chiefly in ground beds and deep benches. They do not produce enough blooms at one time to satisfy as ornamental pot plants. They do best in porous, moderately fertile, very slightly acid, sandy soil. Propagation is by division in spring. Do not set the plants so deep that soil will wash into the centers of the crowns. Plant them a foot or a little more apart each way. Water sparingly at first, generously after they are well rooted. Full sun, and airy conditions are needed at all times. A winter night temperature of 50 to 55°F, with a daytime increase of five to fifteen degrees, proportionate to the light intensity, is appropriate.

GERMAN. As part of common names this word is included in these: German-camomile (*Matricaria*), German catchfly (*Lychnis viscaria*), and German-ivy (*Senecio mikanoides*).

GERMANDER. See Teucrium. Germander speedwell is *Veronica chamaedrys*.

GERMINATE. To sprout or cause to sprout, to begin growth. Said of seeds and spores.

GERRARDANTHUS (Gerrard-ánthus). Five African species constitute *Gerrardanthus*, of the gourd family CUCURBITACEAE. The name, from that of a South African plant collector and the Greek *anthos*, a flower, commemorates W. T. Gerrard, who died in 1866.

These perennial, usually tuberous-stemmed vines have forked tendrils, and the leaves are thinnish, heart-shaped, or five-lobed. Their male and female flowers are on separate plants, and blooms have five-lobed calyxes, and deeply-five-parted, wheel-shaped corollas wth two of the lobes (petals) bigger than the others. Males have four stamens and a staminode (nonfunctional stamen). In female flowers there is a three-angled ovary, three short styles, and a two-lobed stigma. The fruits are elongated-cylindrical or three-angled.

Dry regions in East Africa are the home of *G. macrorhiza*, which has an above-ground, nearly globular to urn-shaped tuber up to about 8 inches across and slender climbing branches. The leaves are rather large and of two shades of green. The small flowers have no display value. The fruits are three-angled.

Garden Uses and Cultivation. Suitable for growing in collections of succulents, outdoors in frostless, desert, and semidesert regions, and in greenhouses, the species discussed above succeeds in sunny locations in very porous soil. Moderate supplies of water are needed while the plant is in active growth, none during the dormant season. Indoors, a winter night temperature of 55°F is suitable, with a daytime rise of five to ten degrees permitted. Propagation is by seeds and by cuttings.

GESNERIA (Ges-nèria). In using this name, which has also been spelled *Gesnera*, gardeners must be wary. Its application has been much abused. Most of the plants that in gardens have been known by it do not belong here. Often they are rechsteinerias, but kohlerias, rhytidophyllums, sinningias, and smithianthas have all been called gesnerias. Simple identifying characteristics are that gesnerias have alternate leaves, sometimes bunched tightly in basal rosettes, and are without tubers or scaly rhizomes. Their roots are fibrous. Belonging to the gesneria family GESNERIACEAE, and thus qualifying as gesneriads, the fifty species of *Gesneria* are mostly natives of the West Indies. A few are indigenous from Mexico to Colombia. The name honors the Swiss naturalist Conrad von Gessner, who died in 1565.

Gesnerias range from compact, short-stemmed perennials to tall shrubs. Their leaves are undivided. The flowers, commonly appearing in succession from the leaf axils, have five-lobed and angled or ribbed calyxes, tubular, cylindrical corollas with five lobes (petals), four fertile stamens, and one style. The fruits are capsules.

The first species discovered, *G. humilis* was rediscovered in Hispaniola in 1970 after having been lost to science and cultivation since shortly after its finding 277 years earlier. This low kind has oblanceolate leaves, and small, slightly nodding, greenish-yellow flowers shaped much like those of many sinningias.

Gesneria cuneifolia

Most frequently cultivated, *G. cuneifolia* is a native of Puerto Rico, Cuba, and Hispaniola. It inhabits shaded steep banks and limestone cliffs. When young, its habit of growth superficially resembles that of an African-violet, but its leaves are somewhat differently shaped and of thinner texture. Oblanceolate, with rounded or pointed apexes, and narrowing at their bases to short or scarcely evident stalks, they are up to 5 inches long by about 1¼ inches wide. They are green above. Their undersides are paler and have long, white hairs on the veins. The margins are coarsely-toothed. On thin, hairy stalks, the 1-inch-long flowers are usually bright red, tinged orange on the underside of the corolla tube, or they may be solid red or nearly pure yellow. Even smaller, *G. pumila* forms a tight rosette of glossy, green leaves and has pink-based white blooms large for the size of the plant and sometimes with six petals. The stamens have red stalks. This is a native of Jamaica. Another Jamaican, *G. acaulis* is a subshrub up to 1 foot tall with round-toothed to irregularly-lobed, hairy to hairless leaves up to 7 inches long by 1½ inches wide and with wrinkled surfaces. Usually many on stalks longer than the leaves, the green-stalked flowers are held horizontally. Red to orange with darker petals, they have the corolla tube bent at its middle.

A rare native of Puerto Rico, slightly woody-stemmed *G. pauciflora* is about 1 foot high. Its leaves, up to about 4 inches long by about one-quarter as wide, are dark green with paler undersides. About 1 inch in length, the flowers, in short-stalked clusters of up to six, are brilliant orange-yellow. Unfortunately the propagation of this fine species has proved perplexing. Also Puerto Rican, *G. citrina* has stems 8 inches to 1 foot long, and somewhat succulent, hairless, wedge-shaped leaves. Its clear yellow blooms, on slender, green stems, are about 1 inch long. Seeds of this species are reported not to germinate well.

A shrub up to 4½ feet tall, *G. saxatilis,* of the Dominican Republic, when first brought into cultivation was misidentified as *G. mornincola* and is still occasionally known by that name. Except for the leaf axils, this species is hairless. It has obovate to elliptic-obovate leaves up to nearly 1 inch long by ⅜ inch wide, toothed near their apexes. The solitary flowers have ½-inch-long, cylindrical corollas with non-protruding stamens. When first brought from its homeland, the Dominican Republic, *G. pedicellaris* was misidentified as *G. christii* and is still sometimes grown as such. This has erect to pendulous hairy stems up to 2½ feet long and wrinkled-surfaced, rough-hairy, irregularly-toothed leaves up to 5 inches long by 1¼ inches wide. Shorter than the leaves, the flowering stems carry up to six reddish-stalked, up-facing flowers with a red-lined, red to yellow tubular corolla.

Gesneria pedicellaris

Much taller kinds have been grown experimentally and by fanciers in the United States from about the middle of the twentieth century. Most are too large to appeal to other than gesneriad specialists who can accommodate them in a humid tropical garden or greenhouse. Here belongs *G. pedunculosa* (syn. *G. albiflora*), of Puerto Rico. A shrub 2 to 12 feet tall, usually favoring limestone soils in semishade, this has elliptic leaves 2 to 4 inches long and 1 inch to 2 inches wide. Its flowers, in clusters of up to four and cream to yellow, have long protruding stamens. Other tall kinds include *G. calycina*, *G. calycosa*, and *G. ventricosa*. To give some idea of the possibilities of gesnerias, the first of these was described by an American enthusiast who visited it in its native mountains in Jamaica as being "like a tree and has main stems as thick as my arm. The foliage and flowers occur only at the top like a feather duster. This requires looking skyward for a small green flower among the lush tropical growth all around." In fact, **G. calycina** is up to 20 feet tall, with a trunk circumference of more than 1 foot and short-stalked leaves up to 9 inches long by 2½ inches wide. The flowers, about 1 inch long, are greenish-white and have protruding stamens. Another native of Jamaica, **G. calycosa** is about as big as the last. Its leaves are up to 5 inches long by 2 inches wide. About 3 inches long, the pale green flowers are solitary in the leaf axils. A shrub up to 15 feet tall, **G. ventricosa** of the West Indies has short-stalked, pointed-elliptic to oblanceolate, irregularly-toothed leaves with blades 4 to 5½ inches long and up to 2 inches wide. Its orange-red blooms, in long-stalked clusters of few from the leaf axils, have curved corollas 1½ inches long, with the stamens long-protruding.

Gesneria ventricosa

Garden Uses and Cultivation. Gesnerias are adapted for outdoor cultivation only in the humid tropics. They are better known as greenhouse pot plants. Indoors they prosper where temperatures in winter are 55 to 60°F at night, and by day, depending upon the brightness of the weather, five to fifteen degrees higher, and where the atmosphere is highly humid. Their soil needs are met by a loose, nourishing mix that contains an abundance of organic matter, such as leaf mold or peat moss, and is made sufficiently porous by the addition of perlite or similar material to encourage the free passage of water. Stagnant, poorly aerated soil is anathema to gesnerias, many of which succeed under somewhat drier conditions at their roots than most gesneriads.

It is well to let the soil become dryish, but not to the extent that wilting results, between waterings. Neutral or at most slightly acid soil is more to the liking of these plants than soil with a lower pH. Some kinds, such as *G. pauciflora* and others that in the wild grow on limestone, are likely to prefer slightly alkaline earth. Good light, with shade from strong sun, is necessary for the best results. Dwarf kinds are satisfactory in artificial light gardens. Poor health or even death can result from soil that is too acid. Gesnerias come readily from seeds sown on soil and scarcely covered, or on the surface of milled sphagnum moss. A temperature of 70 to 75°F favors germination. Propagation by other means is a little more tricky than with most gesneriads. Cuttings root rather slowly in a greenhouse propagating bench, preferably with mild bottom heat. Air layering is successful, but slow. Kinds such as *G. cuneifolia* can be multiplied by carefully removing basal shoots, if possible with a few leaves attached, and using them as cuttings.

GESNERIACEAE—Gesneria Family. Certain members of this family of dicotyledons, notably achimenes, African-violets, columneas, episcias, and the plants commonly called gloxinias (*Sinningia*), are among the most popular greenhouse plants and houseplants. The group numbers 2,000 species accommodated in 120 genera, is almost exclusively tropical and subtropical. The genera *Ramondia* and *Haberlia* contain the only hardy kinds known in cultivation. None is useful other than for ornament.

Gesneriads, as members of the gesneria family are called, are mostly herbaceous or slightly woody perennials sometimes with tubers, but they include a few subshrubs and shrubs and some stem-rooting vines. The majority are forest denizens, growing in the organic debris that covers the ground or as epiphytes perched on trunks or branches. Usually opposite, much less commonly alternate or in whorls (circles of more than two), the toothed or toothless, undivided leaves are generally lobeless, in a few sorts pinnately-lobed. Sometimes solitary or in racemes, the mostly asymmetrical to nearly symmetrical blooms are more often in sprays or clusters. They are tubular, tubular with flaring petals, or bell-shaped. The calyx is five-cleft or five-lobed. The corolla, with five lobes or petals, is usually two-lipped. There are two, four, or rarely five stamens and sometimes staminodes (nonfunctional stamens). If four, the stamens are in pairs of unequal lengths. The single style is crowned with a sometimes two-lobed stigma. The fruits are capsules or berries.

Cultivated gesneriads include *Achimenantha*, *Achimenes*, *Aeschynanthus*, *Agalmyla*, *Alloplectus*, *Asteranthera*, *Bellonia*, *Besleria*, *Boea*, *Briggsia*, *Chirita*, *Chrysothemis*, *Codon-* *anthe*, *Columnea*, *Conandron*, *Corallodiscus*, *Diastema*, *Didymocarpus*, *Drymonia*, *Episcia*, *Gesneria*, *Gloxinia*, *Haberlea*, *Jankaea*, *Koellikeria*, *Koellikohleria*, *Kohleria*, *Loxostigma*, *Lysionotus*, *Mitraria*, *Nautilocalyx*, *Nematanthus*, *Niphaea*, *Opithandra*, *Paradrymonia*, *Ramondia*, *Rhabdothamnus*, *Rhynchoglossum*, *Rhytidophyllum*, *Saintpaulia*, *Sarmienta*, *Seemannia*, *Sinningia*, *Smithiantha*, and *Streptocarpus*.

GESNERIADS. This is an inclusive name for all plants of the gesneria family GESNERIACEAE. It may be pronounced with the hard "g" of girl or the soft one of generous. It is analogous to orchids for all plants of the orchid family. There are approximately 2,000 species of gesneriads accommodated in approximately 120 genera, some of the most familiar being *Achimenes*, *Columnea*, *Episcia*, *Saintpaulia*, *Sinningia*, *Smithiantha*, and *Streptocarpus*. Thus, both African-violets and florists' gloxinias are gesneriads.

Gesneriads range natively through most tropical and warm temperate, humid regions and a few, notably *Ramonda* and *Jankaea*, into cooler parts, even to alpine regions in the Pyrenees and Balkans, where they spend winters covered with snow. None is native to the United States. They vary amazingly in habit, flower color, and other easily observable characteristics. Recondite details of the ovaries and ovules are the chief characteristics used by botanists to separate *Gesneriaceae* from allied families. Consider the very different aspects of rosette-forming African-violets and ramondas, tuber-possessing florists' gloxinias, trailing, weak-stemmed aeschynanthuses, columneas, and episcias, and erect smithianthas and nautilocalyxes. Reflect on the great differences in flower sizes, shapes, and colors as presented by these and others. The obvious considerable differences extend to the fruits. Completely unlike are the long, slender, dingy pods of achimenes and the brightly-colored, berry-like fruits of *Codonanthe*.

Especially since the end of World War II gesneriads have gained popularity among amateur gardeners. Catering to the special interests of these are the African Violet Society of America, the American Gesneria Society, the American Gloxinia and Gesneriad Society, and less specialized, the Indoor Light Gardening Society of America.

GESNOUINIA (Gesnou-ínia). There is only one species of *Gesnouinia* of the nettle family URTICACEAE. It is endemic to the Canary Islands. The name is a commemorative one.

A tree up to about 20 feet tall, **G. arborea** has shoots and young leaves clothed with hoary hairs. The strongly-veined leaves are alternate, undivided, lobeless, and toothless. They are lanceolate, 2 to about 5 inches long by 1 inch to 2 inches

Geum quellyon variety

Geum 'Lady Stratheden'

wide. The minute, greenish flowers are unisexual, two males and a female with an involucre (collar of bracts) at the base of the group forming units that are assembled in large terminal panicles. Male flowers have four-parted perianths, four stamens, and a rudimentary ovary. Female blooms have a four-toothed perianth and a branchless style. The fruit is an achene enclosed by the perianth.

Garden and Landscape Uses and Cultivation. In southern California and other warm, dry regions the species described is sometimes planted as a decorative, and for its interest. It succeeds in ordinary locations and soils. Propagation is by seeds and by cuttings.

GEUM (Gè-um)—Avens. Containing forty species, a few of interest to gardeners, *Geum* belongs to the rose family ROSA-CEAE. A native of temperate and arctic regions of the northern and southern hemispheres, it has an ancient Latin name of no obvious meaning that was used for one or more of its kinds.

Geums are herbaceous perennials, the cultivated ones hardy. They have thickish rhizomes or rootstocks and more or less tufted basal foliage with smaller leaves scattered along the stems. The leaves are pinnate or pinnately-lobed with the terminal leaflet or lobe usually much bigger than the others. Solitary or several on branched stems, the white, yellow, orange, tawny, purplish, or red blooms often resemble those of potentillas. They

have saucer- to bell-shaped calyxes of five sepals with usually five bractlets alternating with them. There are generally five, sometimes six, petals, many stamens and pistils, the latter often crowded on a cylindrical or conical fleshy core. The styles are persistent and feathery, or they shed their upper portions, leaving behind persistent, hooked bases. The fruits are small achenes assembled in heads, those of kinds with persistent styles often resembling small feather dusters and much like seed heads of the pulsatilla group of anemones. These kinds were once segregated as the separate genus *Sieversia*. In closely related *Potentilla* the styles shed completely.

The most popular geums are varieties or possibly hybrids of *G. quellyon* (syn. *G. chilense*), a native of Chile, in gardens often misidentified as *G. coccineum*. The wild form is not reliably hardy near New York City, but the varieties attributed to it are. Glandular-hairy and 1 foot to 2 feet tall, *G. quellyon* has erect, irregularly-toothed basal leaves up to 1 foot long, with several pairs of unequal-sized lateral lobes and a terminal one approximately twice as long as the largest side leaflets. The stem leaves are considerably smaller, the uppermost represented by bracts. In erect, loose panicles, the up-facing, 1-inch-wide scarlet blooms have spreading petals and usually red-stalked stamens. The styles drop their upper sections. The flowers of *G. q. plenum* are double and scarlet. Two old improved varieties of this with semidouble blooms about 1½ inches wide

are scarlet-flowered 'Mrs. Bradshaw' and, with clear yellow blooms, 'Lady Stratheden'. Newer varieties or hybrids, are 'Fire Opal', with single reddish-orange flowers, 'Orangeman', with large orange blooms, 'Princess Juliana', which has semidouble, rich golden-orange flowers, and 'Red Wings', the semidouble blooms of which are bright scarlet.

True **G. coccineum,** of mountains of the Balkan Peninsula and Asia Minor, is scarcely known in gardens. It may have played a part as parent of some garden varieties of hybrid ancestry. From *G. quellyon* which commonly masquerades under its name, it differs in its lower leaves having only two or three pairs of small lateral leaflets and a sharply-lobed and toothed, kidney-shaped terminal one to three times as long or longer, as well as in the stalks of the stamens of its up-facing, long-stalked bright orange-scarlet blooms, two to four on each stem, being yellow. The petals spread. The upper parts of the styles are deciduous. Yellow-flowered *G. heldreichii* of gardens is very likely derived from *G. coccineum*. The scarlet-flowered kind called **G. sibiricum** is also probably a variant of that species. The plant grown in gardens as *G. bulgaricum*, but not the species to which that name rightly belongs, may also belong here.

Mountain avens (**G. montanum**) has stout, creeping rhizomes, but no stolons. Its basal, toothed leaves, up to 6 inches long, have a terminal leaflet considerably bigger than the three to six pairs of lateral

Geum montanum

ones, approximately 2 inches wide or a little wider. From 2 inches to 1 foot tall, or sometimes considerably taller, the flowering stalks carry small leaves and one to three golden-yellow, up-facing blooms 1 inch to 1½ inches wide. They have often six spreading petals. The persistent, long, feathery styles, which do not drop their upper parts, are about ¾ inch long. This species is a native of southern Europe.

Nodding flowers are characteristic of *G. bulgaricum*, of the mountains of the Balkan Peninsula, and water avens (*G. rivale*), of Europe, temperate Asia, and North America. A thick creeping rhizome, large basal leaves with small side leaflets, and a large kidney- to heart-shaped terminal leaflet characterize **G. bulgaricum.** The 1-inch-wide, bell-shaped blooms, three to seven on stems 1 foot to 1½ feet tall, have whitish to pale-yellow petals, notched at their apexes. Their styles, up to ½ inch long, are retained in their entirety. The bell-shaped, ½-inch-long or smaller blooms of **G. rivale,** two to five on a stem, have dark brownish-purple calyxes longer than the cream to purplish-pink petals. This has a short, thick rootstock and basal leaves with three to six pairs of small lateral leaflets and a larger, roundish terminal leaflet about 2 inches in diameter. The tops of the

Geum borisii of gardens

½-inch-long styles are deciduous. This inhabits wet meadows and swamps. Probably a variety, but perhaps a hybrid of it, **G. pulchrum** has yellow-petaled blooms.

Native of the Balkan Peninsula, **G. reptans** sends long reddish stolons from its rootstocks. Its pinnate leaves have deeply-pinnately-cleft leaflets, the terminal one not conspicuously bigger than the others. Up to about 6 inches in height, the flowering stalks carry usually one up-facing, bright yellow bloom 1 inch to 1½ inches in diameter, with spreading petals. The styles persist without shedding their tips. A hybrid between *G. reptans* and *G. bulgaricum*, named after King Boris of Bulgaria, **G. borisii** characteristically is intermediate between its parents and has bright yellow flowers, but the plant often grown under that name has orange-scarlet blooms that suggest *G. coccineum* as one of its parents. It is a good ornamental, 8 to 10 inches high.

Native at high altitudes in the mountains of New England and adjacent Canada, **G. peckii** is up to 1 foot tall or somewhat taller. Its long-stalked basal leaves have irregularly-toothed, shallowly-lobed, kidney-shaped to round terminal leaflets 2 to 4 inches in diameter. The six or fewer (sometimes there are none) deeply-cleft lateral leaflets are rarely ½ inch in length. The stem leaves resemble these. The flow-

ers, ¾ to 1 inch wide, have spreading, yellow petals. The styles, feathered at least in their lower parts, are not deciduous. An inhabitant of the mountains of North Carolina and Tennessee, **G. radiatum** is very similar.

Native from British Columbia to Alaska and northeastern Asia, and up to about 1 foot tall, **G. calthifolium** has basal leaves with a very large heart-shaped to kidney-shaped terminal lobe and either no lateral leaflets or only minute ones. The one to few flowers on each stalk are bright yellow

Geum rivale

Geum calthifolium

and 1 inch or somewhat more across.

Garden and Landscape Uses. The taller garden varieties of geums are excellent for the fronts of herbaceous perennial beds and borders, where they bloom chiefly in late spring and early summer, and for providing useful materials for flower arrangements. (Pick them before the blooms open fully.) Water avens and some others are suitable for native plant gardens. Low geums are excellent for rock gardens.

Cultivation. Water avens needs wet soil. Other kinds succeed in well-drained, preferably fertile ones that contain an abundance of organic matter. Most prefer sun, but succeed in part-day shade. For the best results divide and replant the species and older varieties about every third year. The newer garden varieties do better when left undisturbed longer. Routine care consists of fertilizing each spring, watering in dry weather, removing faded flowers, and in severe climates applying a light winter cover of branches of evergreens, salt hay, or similar loose protection. Propagation is by seeds sown indoors early or in a cold frame about May and by division, preferably done in late summer, possibly in spring. Some semidouble- and double-flowered kinds, such as 'Mrs. Bradshaw', come true from seed. Geums are not much subject to pests or diseases.

GEVUINA (Gev-uìna)—Chilean Nut or Chile-Hazel. Three species are recognized as constituting this genus, once believed to consist of only one native of Chile and Argentina. As now understood, the group is represented in the floras of South America, Australia, and New Guinea. It belongs in the protea family PROTEACEAE and has a name based on a native one of South America. It is sometimes spelled *Guevina*.

Gevuinas are trees with alternate, pinnate or twice-pinnate leaves with uneven numbers of leaflets. Their flowers are bisexual, and in pairs in fairly long axillary racemes. Without petals, they have cylindrical calyx tubes with four lobes (sepals). There are four stamens and an undivided style. The ovoid-spherical fruits are drupes (fruits structured like plums).

Chilean nut or Chile-hazel (*Gevuina avellana*) is a beautiful evergreen tree 30 to 40 feet in height. It has pinnate or twice-pinnate, glossy, leathery leaves 6 inches to 1¼ feet in length by about two-thirds as wide. The major leaf divisions number three to fifteen, each with as many as five leaflets. The final segments are ovate, from 1 inch to 7½ inches long, and the biggest up to 3 inches wide. They are sharply-toothed. The white, ivory-white, or sometimes reddish flowers are in racemes about 4 inches long. They come in summer and have protruding stamens. Cherry-sized, the fruits as they ripen change from coral-red to purple to black. They have edible kernals.

Garden and Landscape Uses. Where winters are nearly or quite frostless, as in California, the Chile-hazel is well worth planting for ornament and interest. It grows satisfactorily in ordinary soils and is propagated by seeds and by cuttings set in a greenhouse propagating bench or under mist. So far as is known this species has rarely if ever fruited in North America.

GHERKIN. The gherkins used in mixed pickles are small cucumbers (*Cucumis sativus*). The West Indian or bur gherkin is *Cucumis anguria*.

GHOST. This word appears as part of the common names of these plants: ghost flower (*Mohavea confertiflora*), ghost men (*Pachypodium namaquanum*), ghost weed (*Euphorbia marginata*), and Holy Ghost flower (*Peristeria elata*).

GIANT. This word appears in the common names of various plants including these: giant bamboo (*Dendrocalamus giganteus*), giant-bellflower (*Ostrowskia magnifica*), giant cactus (*Carnegiea gigantea*), giant helleborine (*Epipactis gigantea*), giant holly fern (*Polystichum munitum*), giant-hyssop (*Agastache*), giant-milkweed (*Calotropis gigantea*), giant orchid (*Grammatophyllum*), giant-reed (*Arundo donax*), giant-sequoia (*Sequoiadendron giganteum*), giant timber bamboo (*Phyllostachys bambusoides*), and giant water-lily (*Victoria*).

GIBASIS (Gib-àsis) A few of the ten species of the *Tradescantia* relative *Gibasis* are cultivated outdoors in warm countries, in greenhouses, and as window plants. The genus, endemic to the Americas, belongs in the spiderwort family COMMELINACEAE. Its name, from the Latin *gibber*, swollen, alludes to the calyxes of the flowers having swollen bases.

These plants are small to fairly large, sprawling to erect, more or less succulent herbaceous perennials, or sometimes perhaps annuals. They have stems thickened at the nodes (joints), and alternate, undivided, toothless leaves, grasslike or broader, their bases sheathing the stems. The flowers, in terminal or axillary, branched clusters, have three sepals, three petals of about equal size, six fertile stamens of almost equal lengths, and one style. The fruits are capsules.

A pretty trailer, with the lower parts of its slender zigzagged stems horizontal, their ends ascending or erect, *G. geniculata* (syns. *Aneilema geniculatum*, *Tradescantia geniculata*) is a native of lowland forests from Mexico to South America and of the West Indies. From 1 inch to 3½ inches long, its pointed, ovate to ovate-lanceolate stalkless or nearly stalkless leaves are usually hairy on both sides, densely so on the parts that sheathe the stem. The flowers, in open clusters with repeatedly forking,

Gibasis geniculata

very slender stalks, are white, and about ¼ inch across. Common in cultivation, a selected form of *G. geniculata* is known as, with fine disregard for the nativity of the species, Tahitian bridal veil. This has purple stems and pointed-lanceolate leaves not over 1 inch long, deep purple on their undersides, and hairless except at their very bases. Its flowers close at night.

Discovered in Mexico in 1971, *G. oaxacana* is nearly related to *G. geniculata*. From it it differs in having bigger (up to 4 inches long), more evidently stalked leaves, and in the stalked umbels of its flower clusters having three to eight rays instead of two. Two forms of this species are described, one with green and one with red undersides to the leaves. The white flowers, sometimes with a purplish center band, are ⅓ inch in diameter. Up to 1 foot high and with thickened, tuberous roots, *G. karwinskyana*, of Mexico, has somewhat glaucous, lanceolate leaves and pink flowers.

Garden and Landscape Uses and Cultivation. In frostless and nearly frostless, warm climates *G. geniculata* can be used as a groundcover in partial shade or sun. It succeeds in ordinary soil without special care. It is very easy to manage in pots and hanging baskets in ordinary well-drained soil kept moderately moist. A winter night temperature of 50 to 55°F is adequate, with a few degrees more by day. Propagation is simple by division, cuttings, and seeds. The other species described respond to the same culture.

GIBBAEUM (Gib-baèum). The fascinating stone plants or pebble plants of South Africa belong to several genera of the carpet-weed family AIZOACEAE, or according to another interpretation, to the mesembryanthemum family MESEMBRYACEAE. The genus *Gibbaeum* is one of this group. It consists of from twenty to thirty species, depending upon individual botanists' understandings of specific limits. The name, from the Latin *gibba*, humped, alludes to the forms of the plant bodies. The plant sometimes named *G. fissoides* is *Antegibbaeum fissoides*, and the one sometimes called *G. nebrownii* is *Imitaria muirii*.

Gibbaeum, undetermined species

Gibbaeums are low, tufted, succulent perennials often with subterranean woody rootstocks from the tops of which the many branches, ending in one or two pairs of generally markedly unequal-sized, fleshy leaves, sprout. Each pair of leaves constitutes a plant body, and these, depending upon species, are tightly or loosely clustered. In tightly-clustered kinds the leaves of each pair are joined, sometimes so completely that only a slight fissure at the apex indicates the separation. In others the main branches are longer and prostrate and produce erect secondary branches that may again branch, and the leaves of the plant bodies may be joined or almost completely separate. The flowers, daisy-like in aspect, but not in structure, are stalked and solitary. They have six sepals, numerous pink, red, or white petals, many stamens, and some nonfunctional stamens (staminodes). There are six or seven stigmas. The fruits are capsules.

Kinds with the pairs of leaves more or less equal in size and approximately as wide as long include hairless or apparently hairless *G. heathii* (syn. *Rimaria heathii*), *G. album*, and *G. petrense*. The first is variable and includes kinds that some botanists treat as separate entities under the names *G. blackburnii*, *G. comptonii*, and *G. luckhoffii*. Much resembling a close cluster of rounded, bluish or yellowish-green peb-

bles, each ½ inch to 2 inches in diameter, *G. heathii* has white to light red flowers, their color intensifying as the blooms age. They are ½ inch to 2 inches or slightly more in diameter. Very much resembling the last, **G. album** differs in its leaves being angular and keeled instead of rounded. They are always whitish-gray, usually glossy, and because of scarcely visible pubescence they are velvety to the touch. About 1 inch in diameter, the blooms are white to rose-pink. Clustered plant bodies, greenish to grayish rather than white, and more triangular-ovate, sharp-angled leaves distinguish *G. petrense* from *G. album*. The magenta-pink blooms of **G. petrense** are under ¾ inch in diameter. Closely similar to the last, **G. tischleri** has clusters of small, blue-green to gray, pebble-like plant bodies. Its violet-red blooms are about ¾ inch across.

Leaves about as wide as long, of nearly equal size, and usually obviously pubescent are characteristic of the three species next discussed. Closely allied *G. pilosulum* and *G. cryptopodium* have greenish-yellow, pebble-like, obovate plant bodies about 1 inch in diameter. Those of **G. pilosulum** have long, silky hairs at their tops, those of **G. cryptopodium** have fewer, short hairs or are sometimes hairless. The flowers of both are up to ¾ inch across and bright pink. Gray-velvety pubescence clothes the deepy-fissured pebble-like, sol-

itary or two or more closely crowded plant bodies of **G. dispar.** They are subglobose to ovoid and often have one of each pair of usually more or less keeled leaves considerably larger than the other. The flowers, about ¾ inch in diameter, have a single row of intensely violet-pink petals.

Leaves two to five times as long as wide, with those of each pair very unequal in size, are characteristic of the species now to be described. In *G. gibbosum*, *G. pubescens*, *G. shandii*, and *G. geminum* the leaves of each pair are joined except for a fissure. The first is without hairs, the others are pubescent. Plants once named *G. luteoviride*, *G. perviride*, *G. muirii*, and *G. marlothii*, are included in **G. gibbosum.** This forms clumps of plant bodies up to slightly over 2 inches tall, each of a pair of markedly unequal, blunt-angled, triangular leaves. The flowers, approximately 1 inch wide, have pale pink petals with purple mid-veins. The pubescent species belonging in this group can be separated into those in which the leaves are united except for a cleft or fissure between them at the apex and those joined at their bases only. A thick covering of down-pointing, white hairs distinguishes densely cushiony **G. pubescens.** This has repeatedly branching stems terminating in pairs of cylindrical-ovoid leaves up to 1 inch long. Its light to dark rose-purple blooms are 1 inch or more across. So closely similar is *G. shandii* to *G. pubescens* that only by examining them under a hand lens can they be surely separated. The hairs in **G. shandii** are branched and point outward from the leaf surface, those of *G. pubescens* are branchless, parallel with the leaf surface, and point downward. Wide mats of loosely arranged, quite prostrate, often rooting stems, each with several to many erect branches up to 2 inches long and with more or less club-shaped, velvety, greenish-gray plant bodies with the fissures well below their apexes, are characteristic of **G. geminum.** The blooms, with a single row of light rosy-purple petals, are approximately ½ inch wide.

Gibbaeum pubescens

Pubescent leaves two to five times as long as wide, those of each pair of unequal size, and united only at their bases, are typical of *G. pachypodium* and *G. angulipes*, which have three-angled leaves, and by *G. velutinum* and *G. schwantesii*, in which the leaves are broad, boat-shaped, and have curved apexes. The branches of **G. pachypodium**, which spread widely, support erect, minutely-pubescent, often reddish-tipped, greenish to greenish-gray, sausage-shaped leaves, flattened on their inner sides. The pale pink to reddish blooms are almost 1 inch wide. Also with prostrate, spreading stems, **G. angulipes** has keeled, somewhat three-angled, silvery or grayish, velvety leaves, the smaller of each pair about two-thirds the length of the longer. The flowers, ¾ to 1 inch wide, are reddish-purple.

Tufted and stemless, **G. velutinum** has crowded plant bodies with the larger leaf of each pair up to about 2 inches in length. The leaves are shaped like the prow of a boat and are gray-green or whitish. The blooms come from the angles formed between the old and new leaves. They are 1½ to 2 inches in diameter, and have two rows of white or reddish-tinged petals. The more or less boat-shaped leaves of the pairs of the loosely arranged green to yellowish-green plant bodies of **G. schwantesii** are very unequal in size. The larger are 2 to 2¾ inches long. The flowers come from ahead of the new pairs of leaves. They are 1¼ to 2 inches in diameter and have two rows of light red petals. The species identified as *G. haagei* is very like *G. velutinum*. It has broadly-triangular, sharply-three-angled leaves, the largest about 1½ inches long, and whitish flowers a little over 2 inches in diameter.

Garden Uses and Cultivation. Gibbaeums are for fanciers of choice succulents. Some do not take readily to cultivation, others do. In warm, dry, desert and semidesert regions where the climate approximates that of the South African Little Karoo, which is the home of the group, gibbaeums can be accommodated in rock gardens and similar places, but generally they are grown in well-drained pots or pans (shallow pots) in greenhouses or sometimes as window plants. They require the same care as *Lithops* and other stone plants and are easy to raise from seeds and cuttings. Their resting seasons vary somewhat according to species, but most usually are in summer. Then, the soil is kept dry. During the period of active growth periodic soakings are given, with the earth allowed to become almost completely dry before each. Very porous, gritty soil, to which has been added some crushed limestone, satisfies these interesting plants.

GIBBERELLIC ACID. One of a group of naturally occurring plant hormones called gibberellins that variously affect growth,

but most pronouncedly by stimulating it, gibberellic acid is the only one commercially available. In minute amounts it is employed to encourage certain low and dwarf sorts to grow bigger and to increase the size of the fruits and to promote seedlessness in grapes.

GIDDINGSARA. This is the name of hybrid orchids the parents of which includes *Ascocentrum, Euanthe, Renanthera, Vanda,* and *Vandopsis*.

GIFT PLANTS. Gift plants bought for holidays and other occasions need rather special care. Flowering kinds are usually in full bloom at the time of their arrival and often have come from congenial greenhouse surroundings to the harsher conditions of the home at seasons not especially suited to such moves. They therefore need special care.

Because their pots are likely to be full of roots, give particular attention to their moisture requirements. Do not let the soil dry, but avoid constant saturation. Watering by the immersion method is nearly always more satisfactory than top-watering. Do it at least once a week even if you water at the top in between.

Try to accommodate the new arrivals favorably. Avoid drafty places. Certain kinds, such as primroses, cinerarias, cyclamens, heaths, lily-of-the-valley, spireas, genistas, hyacinths, tulips, daffodils, lilies, narcissuses, hydrangeas, Christmas cherries, and Christmas peppers, need cool locations. A sun porch where the temperature does not go below 40°F at night nor above 65°F in the daytime suits them well. If you cannot provide this, select positions close to east or west windows and away from radiators, so temperatures will not be too high.

Gardenias, poinsettias, Christmas begonias, African-violets, and the zebra plant (*Aphelandra squarrosa*) prefer about 60°F at night, with a little more warmth in the daytime. They, too, need good light and abhor close proximity to heating units.

Naturally you want to keep flowering plants blooming as long as possible and,

in some cases, to retain them for future years. Some gift plants, including tulips, hyacinths, cinerarias, and poinsettias, have just one lot of blooms each season. Others, such as primroses and African-violets and cyclamens, produce a succession

(b) Zebra plant

(c) Tulips

Popular gift plants: (a) African-violet

(d) Hyacinths

(e) Easter lily

(h) Christmas begonia

(f) Christmas cherry

(i) Primrose

(g) Poinsettia

of flowers over a long period. The latter benefit from the application of very dilute fertilizer once a week. Those that have one lot of flowers only will not need this. In all cases remove all dead leaves and faded blooms promptly.

When your gift plant is through blooming, the treatment you accord it should depend upon its kind. Narcissuses of the Chinese sacred-lily, 'Paper White' and 'Grand Soleil d'Or' varieties and Roman hyacinths, tulips, lily-of-the-valley, Christ-

mas begonias, Christmas cherries, and Christmas peppers have no further usefulness. Discard them.

Only if you have a cool greenhouse or a sunporch so light that the conditions inside approximate those of a greenhouse with a night temperature of 40 to 50°F is it worthwhile attempting to keep over genistas, heaths, and cyclamens.

Forced hardy narcissuses and daffodils, hardy hyacinths, and Easter lilies may be retained for planting in agreeable positions in the garden. Easter lilies will usually bloom again in late summer. In mild climates, they will flower in succeeding years, too, but hard winters kill them. Hyacinths will produce small, loose spikes of flowers for two, three, or more succeeding springs. Daffodils and other hardy narcissuses will recover and bloom well in a couple of years and will continue to do so indefinitely with proper care.

Hardy bulbs that have been forced are not suitable for indoor cultivation again.

Success in preparing them for outdoor planting depends upon letting them retain their foliage as long as possible and keeping them watered and in a cool, light place from the time their flowers fade until their leaves die naturally.

Keep spireas (astilbes), roses, and hydrangeas well watered, and in a cool light place, until all danger from frost is passed. Then plant them in the garden. They are not suitable for retaining as pot specimens.

The principal flowering gift plants, sold by the florist that may be kept from year to year in the house are gardenias, poinsettias, azaleas, genistas, cyclamens, African-violets, and zebra plants. Success, of course, depends upon being able to provide agreeable environments and care for them.

Do not expect to succeed with all of these as easily or as well as does your florist, who has greenhouses at his command. Still, with careful attention, some houseplant growers do bring all these plants through successfully. Instructions for the care of these after they are through blooming are given under their appropriate entries in this Encyclopedia.

When foliage plants, such as dumb canes, English ivies, and philodendrons, are received, the main problem is to get them settled into their new environment without excessive loss of foliage. Selection of suitable locations, care in watering, and spraying their foliage with clear water two or three times a day are the best preventatives of leaf drop. Give them dilute fertilizer at regular intervals.

Dish gardens, often containing an assortment of plants that need different growing conditions, are popular. These are arranged by the florist to produce eye appeal, usually without much regard for the real needs of the plants. Often no adequate drainage is provided, and roots are crowded or cut.

The recipient of one of these can dismantle the "garden," pot the plants individually, and afford each the treatment it needs, or leave the plants in the dish to fight it out as best they may, merely removing those that become sick or die. It is usually possible to enjoy the garden as it is for a couple of weeks or sometimes considerably longer. Then before the first signs of poor health appear, you can dismantle the creation. Because they lack drainage, great care is needed in watering dish gardens to strike a happy balance between too much and too little.

GILIA (Gíl-ia). Many plants formerly included in *Gilia*, of the phlox family POLEMONIACEAE, now are placed in other genera including *Collomia*, *Eriastrum*, *Ipomopsis*, *Leptodactylon*, and *Linanthus*. Of the twenty to thirty species that remain fewer than ten, all annuals, are cultivated, three or four fairly commonly. The name of the ge-

Gaillardia pulchella

Gaultheria ovatifolia

Gazania pinnata

Galium verum

Gazania, undetermined species or variety

Gentiana scabra

Gloriosa rothschildiana

Basket of ornamental gourds

Grapes in vigorous early summer growth

Graptopetalum paraguayense, with *Sedum treleasii* behind

Gladiolus segetum

nus honors Felipe Luis Gil, a Spanish botanist of the late eighteenth century.

Gilias are mostly natives of western North America, some of southern South America. They are annual, biennial, or rarely perennial herbaceous plants with alternate often much-dissected leaves, those on the upper parts of the stems commonly conspicuously smaller than the lower ones. The flowers are solitary in the leaf axils or are in loose clusters, or compact heads. They have a five-parted calyx, a tubular, funnel- or bell-shaped corolla with five lobes (petals), five stamens, one style, and a three-lobed stigma. The fruits are capsules.

The most popular kinds include the bird's eyes (*G. tricolor*), a native of California, easily distinguished from other cultivated gilias by its three-colored flowers, which inspired its botanical name, and by its quite leafy stems. The upper parts of the plant are glandular. This kind is up to 2 feet tall and has leaves twice-divided into narrow segments. Its flowers, solitary or in clusters of two to five, are ½ to ¾ inch across. They are lilac or purple with a yellow to orange tube marked in its throat with a ring or five pairs of spots of purple. Native from California to British Columbia and Idaho, *Gilia capitata* is 2½

Gilia achillaefolia

Gilia capitata

feet tall, has slender stems, leaves cut twice or thrice into narrow segments, and light blue flowers in crowded globose heads about 1 inch across and with protruding stamens. In the typical species the heads consist of fifty to a hundred blooms, but in *G. c. abrotanifolia* the number in each varies from twenty-five to fifty. Similar to but easily distinguished from *G. capitata*, Californian *G. achillaefolia* grows to 2½ feet tall. It is often slightly sticky. Its fan-shaped clusters of blue flowers contain up to twenty-five blooms; their stamens do not protrude. In the typical species there are at least eight flowers in each head, in *G. a. multicaulis* two to seven smaller ones. Native of Peru, Chile, and Argentina, *G. laciniata* is somewhat like *G. a. multicaulis*,

but its corolla lobes are spreading rather than erect. Its flowers, in heads of few, are blue, lilac, or white. From 1 foot to 1½ feet tall, this sort has deeply-dissected leaves.

Other sorts sometimes cultivated include these: *G. caruifolia* is native to dry locations in California and Baja California. Its flowers, pale blue-violet, and often with a pair of purple spots at the base of each corolla lobe, have extremely short tubes and projecting stamens. Its leaves are twice- or thrice-times-divided. *G. latiflora* is a Mojave desert species up to 1 foot tall. Glaucous below, glandular above, it has strap-shaped, toothed to lobed basal leaves and much smaller stem leaves. The flowers, up to ⅞ inch long, are in loose clusters. Their corollas have purple tubes, yellow and white throats, and violet tips to the lobes. *G. latifolia*, a desert plant of California and Utah, may be distinguished from other cultivated gilias by its ovate to roundish, toothed or somewhat lobed leaves, its rank odor, and its cream (not white or blue) pollen. The insides of the flowers are bright pink, the outsides paler pink or buff. *G. leptomeria*, native from Oregon to California, Colorado, and New Mexico, has tubular flowers about ¼ inch long with stamens of equal length. Its basal leaves are up to 2 inches long, broadly-strap-shaped, toothed or lobed, and in rosettes. This sort, about

8 inches tall, is sticky-hairy throughout. Its flowers are white to pale rose-pink.

Garden Uses. Gilias are elegant annuals for growing outdoors in regions where they can be had in bloom during fairly cool weather. They soon lose their attractiveness and die under torrid, humid conditions. They are attractive as pot plants for decorating cool greenhouses in late winter and spring. Outdoors, they are interesting additions to flower beds and borders and in their native ranges are appropriate for including in gardens of native plants.

Cultivation. Gilias grow best in well-drained, porous soil of moderate fertility. They need full sun. Seeds are sown outdoors in spring or, in mild climates, in fall, where the plants are to bloom, and are raked into the soil surface. The resulting plants are thinned to stand 4 to 9 inches apart according to the vigor of the species. Little other care is needed. Weeds must be eliminated as they appear. The taller kinds may need a little support, which can be provided unobtrusively by pushing slender brushwood stakes into the ground between the plants when they are partly grown. Faded flower heads should be removed promptly. To have flowering plants in pots in late winter and spring, seeds are sown in September, those of the taller kinds in well-drained, 5-inch pots containing porous fertile soil; low-growing kinds can be accommodated in 6-inch pans (shallow pots). Eight or ten seeds are sown in each pot, more in each pan, and when the young plants are well up all except three or four from each 5-inch pot are pulled out, and low growing kinds in pans are thinned to 2 or 3 inches apart. The plants are grown throughout in full sun in a night temperature of 50°F. Daytime temperatures may be five to ten degrees higher, and on all favorable occasions the greenhouse should be ventilated to combat any tendency to a heavy, humid, oppressive atmosphere. Great care must be taken through the winter, especially in dull weather, not to water too much; it is better that the soil be dryish than excessively wet. But as spring approaches more generous waterings will be needed, and then those plants that have filled their pots with roots will benefit from an occasional application of dilute liquid fertilizer. Container-grown plants should be staked neatly, and well before their stems topple.

GILIBERTIA. See Dendropanax.

GILL-OVER-THE-GROUND is *Glechoma hederacea*.

GILLENIA (Gil-lènia)—Indian Physic, American-Ipecac, Bowman's Root. Natives of dry and moist upland woods in eastern North America, the only two species of *Gillenia* are members of the rose family Rosaceae. Their name commemorates Arnold Gillen, a German physician, who wrote about plants in the seventeenth century. Both are known by the colloquial name Indian physic; in addition, *Gillenia stipulata* is known as American-ipecac and *G. trifoliata* as Bowman's root. These plants were used by the American Indians as mild emetics.

Gillenias are deciduous, hardy, herbaceous perennials. They are summer-bloomers with rhizomes and erect, sometimes branched stems and nearly stalkless leaves, each of three leaflets. At the base of each leaf is a pair of stipules (small appendages), the character of which serves to distinguish between the two species. The flowers have a five-toothed calyx, five petals, and ten to twenty stamens. The fruits consist of five follicles.

The American-ipecac (*G. stipulata*), 1 foot to 3½ feet tall, is native from New York to Ohio, Illinois, Kansas, Georgia, and Texas. A sparsely-pubescent plant, its lanceolate leaflets, 2 to 3¼ inches long, narrow at both ends and are sharply-toothed. One to a few of the lowest leaves have deeply-divided leaflets and are fern-like. The white to delicate pink flowers, with five spreading linear to narrowly-oblanceolate petals up to ½ inch long, are in loose showers at and near the upper parts of the stems. They have ten or more stamens, most usually about twenty. In this species the stipules are broad-ovate, deeply-narrowly-toothed, leafy, and persistent. Bowman's root (*G. trifoliata*) differs in having small awl-shaped stipules that soon drop off, and the lowest leaves on its stems are similar to the upper ones. It is sparsely-pubescent or hairless, and its stems are usually branched above. The flowers are larger than those of the American ipecac; the petals are from slightly under ½ inch to nearly 1 inch long.

Garden Uses and Cultivation. The Bowman's root is the showier, but even it makes no great display. Nevertheless, these are interesting, attractive, and gracious additions to woodland gardens, native plant gardens, and like developments. They are satisfied with any reasonably good, somewhat acid soil and are very easily raised from seeds sown at any time. Light shade is appropriate. They need no special care.

GILLIFLOWER. This is an old-fashioned name for carnations (*Dianthus caryophyllus*), the English wallflower (*Cheiranthus cheiri*), and stocks (*Matthiola incana*).

GILMOURARA. This is the name of hybrid orchids the parents of which include *Aerides*, *Arachnis*, *Ascocentrum*, *Euanthe*, and *Vanda*.

GINGER. See Zingiber. Plants other than true gingers that have the word ginger as part of their common names are these: blue-ginger (*Dichorisandra thyrsiflora*), crape- or Malay-ginger (*Costus speciosus*), ginger-lily (*Hedychium*), orchid-ginger or small shell-ginger (*Alpinia mutica*), red-ginger (*Alpinia purpurata*), shell-ginger (*Alpinia speciosa*), torch-ginger (*Nicolaia elatior*), and wild-ginger (*Asarum*).

GINKGO (Gín-kgo)—Maidenhair Tree. The ginkgo or maidenhair tree is the only living representative of the ginkgo family Ginkgoaceae, a group that in ages past included many species. Abundant fossils prove that ginkgos were common when huge dinosaurs roamed the earth, 175 to 200 million years ago. Then and later they flourished on all continents. For long it was thought that *Ginkgo biloba*, a native of China, did not exist in a wild state, that it had been preserved in cultivation because it was a favorite in China for planting near temples, other religious sites, historic places, and tombs. This appears not to be the case for no mention of the tree is made in Chinese literature before the eleventh century, and recently reliable investigators have reported truly wild native ginkgos in China. The tree was taken from China to Japan probably nearly a thousand years ago. Early in the eighteenth century it was brought to Europe, the first specimen being planted in the botanic garden in Utrecht, Holland. It is believed that the earliest planting of this tree in America was in the garden of William Hamilton, near Philadelphia, Pennsylvania, in 1784. The name ginkgo is a corruption of a Japanese pronunciation of the Chinese ideograph for yin-hsing (silver apricot), the Chinese name of the tree.

The ginkgo under the most favorable conditions attains a height of 120 feet and huge girth. Usually it is smaller. When young, the tree generally is spirelike. As it matures it develops few or several, upright or spreading, massive branches, and a comparatively dense crown, but not one that casts heavy shade. Considerable diversity in branching habit and shape of the crown occurs even among ginkgos raised from seeds from the same parent tree. Individuals may be slender or wide-topped. Often they branch erratically, one or more limb reaching out at angles markedly different from the others. Sometimes one side of the tree is erect and the other has

Ginkgo biloba varies considerably in habit of growth: (a) With more or less pendulous branches

(b) With erect branches

Ginkgo biloba as a street tree, New York City

Ginkgo biloba (fruits)

Ginkgo biloba fastigiata

Ginkgo biloba (leaves)

spreading limbs. The branches, along most of their lengths, have short woody spurs (abbreviated branches) that increase in length only a fraction of an inch each year. Both these and the younger parts of the longer branches bear foliage. The leaves on the spurs are crowded, those on the longer shoots more distantly spaced. They are 1 inch to 2¾ inches long. The foliage is deciduous and unlike that of any other tree. Long-stalked, fan-shaped, more or less notched at the apex, and with numerous parallel veins, the leaves are remindful of the leaflets of maidenhair ferns, hence the name maidenhair tree. In fall they turn bright yellow. Ginkgos are unisexual with their flowers on the short spurlike branches that also bear leaves. The males, which consist of green stamens only, are in 1-inch-long catkins, the females, on stalks up to 2 inches long, consist of a pair of terminal ovules partly enclosed by basal collars. The primitive nature of the species is evidenced by the fact that the male reproductive cells or sperms are motile, as is true also of cycads, but not of other seed plants. In this respect cycads and ginkgo resemble ferns. The plumlike fruits, about ¾ inch long,

consist of a large seed encased in a thin fleshy layer, which is orange and malodorous when ripe. Variety *G. b. aurea* has golden foliage, *G. b. fastigiata* is a narrow and pyramidal tree, *G. b. laciniata* has larger, more deeply cut leaves than the typical kind, *G. b.* 'Mayfield' is a slender male sort, *G. b. pendula* has drooping branches, and *G. b. variegata* has leaves indistinctly variegated with yellow. In the Orient the seeds of ginkgo, freed from the pulp and washed and roasted, are a favorite article of diet. The wood of the ginkgo is used as a base of lacquer ware and for abacus beads and other small articles.

Garden and Landscape Uses and Cultivation. The ginkgo, hardy throughout most of New York and New England, is a distinctive tree for use as a single specimen and in avenues. It is extremely resistant to diseases and pests and is highly tolerant of city environments. In New York, Washington, Tokyo, and other cities it is used as a street tree. It prospers in any moderately fertile, well-drained soil and

can be transplanted safely even when quite big. Because the ill-smelling fruits are likely to prove nuisances it is usually advisable to plant male trees only, but as it is not practicable to determine the sexes of seedlings before they bloom, which is unlikely to be before they are twenty years old, young males can only be surely had by raising them from cuttings or grafts from known male stocks. Propagation is by seeds, cuttings, and grafting onto seedlings in the greenhouse in spring.

GINKGOACEAE—Ginkgo Family. The only representative of this family of gymnosperms is discussed and described under Ginkgo.

GINORIA (Gin-òria). This horticulturally little known genus of fourteen species of shrubs and small trees of the loosestrife family LYTHRACEAE is a native of Mexico and the West Indies. Its name honors Caroli Ginori, a former Governor of Leghorn, Italy and a patron of the botanical garden at Florence.

Ginorias are nonhardy shrubs with opposite leaves, and flowers with six-cleft calyxes, six petals, twelve stamens, and one style. The fruits are capsules.

A bushy shrub, *G. glabra,* of Cuba, is 4 to 10 feet tall or taller if trained as a vine. It has pointed-elliptic to pointed-ovate, hairless leaves up to 4 inches long and 1¼ inches wide, with a prominent mid-vein. The rose-pink to lilac flowers 1 inch to 1¼ inches wide are slender-stalked. Also Cuban, *G. americana* is a slightly hairy, sometimes spiny shrub 3 to 5 feet tall. It has short-stalked, opposite, ovate to lanceolate leaves ½ inch to 2½ inches long and slender-stalked, rosy-purple flowers ¾ to over 1 inch across. West Indian *G. rohrii,* up to 15 feet tall, has stems with short spines at the nodes and somewhat leathery, obovate to elliptic-ovate leaves up to a little more than 3 inches long. In umbels of two to eight from the leaf axils of wandlike branches, the flowers are white and ¾ to 1 inch across.

Garden Uses and Cultivation. In warm climates the sorts described may be used as general-purpose flowering shrubs. They prosper in ordinary soils, appreciate sunny locations, and are easily propagated by seeds and cuttings. In southern Florida *G. glabra* has survived 28°F.

GINSENG. Apparently without basis in fact, in many parts of the Orient ginseng is very highly esteemed for medicinal purposes and as an aphrodisiac. For its dried roots, marketed at extraordinarily high prices, there is an almost insatiable demand. The roots are those of Asian *Panax schinseng* and closely similar American *P. quinquefolius.* To meet the demand the American species has been collected from the wild and cultivated for export. Learning of the high prices ginseng commands in China and other Eastern countries, ambitious Americans sometimes suppose that its cultivation may provide a great profit and a quick way to fortune. Both are unlikely. Much skill, time, and care is needed to grow ginseng. It takes six or seven years from seed sowing to harvest, during which time more or less continual attention is needed. Also, the plants are subject to various diseases, including wilt and leaf spots. Certainly before embarking on ginseng cultivation as an enterprise the prospective grower should consult with and obtain the advice of his or her State Agricultural Experiment Station.

Ginseng prefers slightly acid, well-drained, deep, fertile soil, neither excessively sandy nor clayey. It should have a high organic content and be moderately moist. The best fertilizing procedure is to mix thoroughly with the soil liberal amounts of leaf mold or well-decayed compost. Bonemeal can also be used with advantage. Before sowing or planting, the beds should be steam-sterilized to eliminate disease organisms.

Fairly heavy shade is necessary and is supplied by lath shades or similar devices. Plants are raised from seeds, which, after harvesting, must never be allowed to dry. They are either sown immediately or mixed with slightly moist sand or peat moss and stored where the temperature is from 35 to 40°F until spring, and then sown in shaded cold frames. It is likely to be the summer of the following year before the seedlings appear. When the seedlings are one or two years old transplant them in spring or fall to their permanent placed in shaded cold frames or lath houses at a spacing of about 5 inches each way between individuals. Subsequent care includes repeated weeding and watering in dry weather. A 4-inch-thick mulch of leaves of deciduous trees placed over the beds after the ground is frozen to a depth of about an inch gives beneficial winter protection. The roots are dug in late summer or fall and cured for about a month at 60 to 90°F. They are then ready for marketing.

GIRASOLE is *Helianthus tuberosus*.

GIRDLING or RING BARKING. Sometimes also called bark ringing, this is a technique occasionally employed to check over-vigorous shoot production and to induce the cropping of fruit trees or more commonly grape vines. It may also be employed to encourage wisterias to bloom. Its effect is to interrupt the downward flow of sap that has been elaborated in the leaves and that contains sugars and nitrogenous materials, and the upward flow of nutrient-containing water.

Girdling for these purposes consists of removing a ring of bark ⅛ to ¼ inch wide from completely around a trunk (usually

Girdling or ring barking: (a) Remove a narrow ring of bark from round the entire trunk or branch, or

(b) Remove two strips on opposite sides of the trunk or branch, each going halfway around it, and one 3 to 4 inches above the other

(c) Cover the wounds with adhesive tape, or

below the lowest branch) or from a branch, or of removing two similar strips from opposite sides, each extending precisely one-half way around the trunk or limb and spaced 3 to 4 inches apart. The cuts are made down to, but not into, the underlying

(d) With tree wound paint

wood. The width of the strips removed must not be greater than will surely heal during the summer (girdling is done in spring, usually in May, when the sap is running freely so that the bark lifts easily without tearing). If the strips are too wide, and if no foliage is left below the operation, the roots will be starved and die.

Make the cuts with a sharp knife (a special double-bladed one is sometimes used for grape vines) or a sharp chisel. Remove the strips cleanly. To prevent entry of disease organisms, cover the wounds with adhesive tape and grafting wax or with tree wound paint.

A less severe procedure, called scoring, consists of making a cut through the bark completely around a shoot without removing any bark. This is mostly done to check the too-vigorous growth of young trees.

Tightening a wire around a trunk or branch has effects similar to girdling by bark removal and is sometimes done to persuade a too-vigorous wisteria to bloom. Loosen or remove the wire a year after its installation.

Except with grapes, girdling is less often done in America than Europe. There, its employment is chiefly on apples and pears. It is not recommended for plums, cherries, peaches, or other kinds of the genus *Prunus*.

GIRDLING ROOTS. Trees can be severely injured or even killed if their trunks, taproots, or large lateral roots are partially encircled by other roots so that movement of water and nutrients through them is severely impeded or cut off. The strangling effect, similar to that caused by a wire tied tightly around a branch and left for a few years, does not cause sudden death, but results in deterioration evidenced over a period of a few years by weak growth and dying back of branches that normally would be supplied by the girdled root.

Symptoms of severe girdling are not different from those that may result from other causes. If a taproot is choked the central leader of the tree is likely to grow poorly and eventually die back, if a large lateral root is strangled branches on its side of the tree behave similarly. In late fall before leaf drop the foliage of affected limbs is likely to be paler than normal and to drop early. Lack of an outward flare on one side of a trunk that at other sides spreads outward at about ground level may indicate the presence of a girdling root. Such roots may be near the surface or at greater depths.

Predisposing circumstances favorable to the development of girdlng roots include planting young trees that have been growing in containers so long that thick roots have spiraled around their interiors. It is important as far as practicable to straighten such roots at planting time. Pits or holes dug in hard, compacted, unkindly earth for the reception of trees and filled with good soil at planting time may cause roots to deflect or double back when they reach the hard earth and this increases the possibility of girdling. Cramping roots when planting instead of spreading them in normal directions may also encourage this defect.

A young tree with a horizontal root that unless cut away will eventually girdle the base of the trunk and severely harm the tree

Treatment of girdling roots is based on first locating the offender (when near the surface this can be done by a little careful digging) and then with a chisel cutting a section 2 to 3 inches long out of it where it joins a large lateral root or trunk. The removal of a piece instead of merely cutting through the root precludes the possibility of the severed ends growing together again. Apply tree wound paint to the cut surfaces.

GITHOPSIS (Githóp-sis). About six species of annuals indigenous to western North America constitute this genus of the bellflower family CAMPANULACEAE. The generic name is derived from that of the genus Githago, and the Greek opsis, meaning

similar to. The likeness to which attention is thus directed is in gross appearance only. The genera involved belong in quite different botanical families.

The genus Githopsis is characterized by its usually angled stems and inconspicuous, scattered, stalkless or nearly stalkless, narrow leaves. The flowers are terminal or arise from the axils of the upper leaves or originate in both ways. The persistent calyx is of five usually conspicuous sepals. The five-lobed corolla is tubular with spreading petals or is bell-shaped. There are five stamens and one style. The fruits are capsules.

One species, *G. specularioides,* native from California to Washington, is sometimes cultivated. Rarely exceeding 6 inches in height and softly-pubescent, this has stiff stems branched above their bases and small ovate to oblong, coarsely-toothed leaves. The bright blue flowers have slender tubes and spreading petals. They are both terminal and from the upper leaf axils. A variety with white flowers is *G. s. candida.*

Garden Uses and Cultivation. This charming little plant is interesting for growing in rock gardens and as edgings. It prospers in any ordinary garden soil in full sun, but does not tolerate very hot, humid summers. Seeds are sown in early spring where the plants are to bloom and the seedlings thinned to about 3 inches apart.

GLABARIA. See Litsea.

GLADDON or GLADWIN is *Iris foetidissima.*

GLADIOLUS (Gladì-olus). Few flowering plants are better known than gladioluses or, if you prefer the latinized plural, gladioli. Among summer-flowering bulb plants they stand supreme, magnificent for garden adornment and as cut flowers. Florists use them in vast numbers. Amateurs proudly exhibit them at flower shows. As with dahlias, irises, roses, and chrysanthemums their cultivation seems to have a particularly strong appeal for men. Many outstanding growers and breeders belong to what once, it seems rather amusingly, was referred to as the stronger sex. In addition to the magnificent and familiar summer-flowering gladioluses there are, as we shall see, a spring-blooming group adapted for outdoor cultivation in mild climates. Gladiolus fans and breeders also find it worthwhile to seek out and grow some of the horticulturally unimproved species. By some botanists the genus Acidanthera is included in Gladiolus, but that is not done here.

The name Gladiolus means a little sword. It alludes to the leaves and comes from the Latin gladius, a sword. Its classical pronunciation is Gladí-olus, but much more pop-

ular among English speaking peoples is *Gladi-òlus.* There are between 250 and 300 species. They belong in the iris family IRIDACEAE and are chiefly natives of tropical and South Africa with a smaller representation of kinds indigenous to the Mediterranean region. These last, common in grain fields and well known to the ancients, are occasionally grown. They had no part in the development of modern hybrid gladioluses.

We have called gladioluses bulb plants, but the swollen underground parts commonly known as bulbs are not such in the botanical sense. They are corms. True bulbs consist of concentric layers of scales that, like those of an onion, can be peeled, or consist of shorter scales that overlap like shingles on a roof as do those of lily

Here the corm that was planted has withered and the new corm is clearly evident above it

bulbs. The corms of gladioluses are solid and covered with thin, easily removable membranes. Unlike bulbs, the corms are not perennial. Each year the old ones shrivel and die, and new ones form above them. From them arise to heights of 1½ to about 4 feet deciduous, more or less leafy, mostly branchless, erect stems terminating in a spike of blooms. Generally sword-shaped and with many parallel, longitudinal veins, the leaves are commonly 1 inch to 2 inches wide, sometimes narrower, sometimes cylindrical. Each stalkless flower comes from the axil of a conspicuous bract. The blooms, ranging in size from 2 to 7 inches or more in diameter, come in white and a wide variety of pastel and bright colors with only good blues absent. Those of some species are fragrant. Each flower has a short- to long-tubed perianth of three outer petal-like sepals, and three inner petals, all six commonly referred to as petals although tepals is the better designation. The three upper petals are usually, but not always noticeably bigger than the three lower. There are three stamens and a slender style with three short arms or branches. The fruits are broad-cylindrical to obovoid capsules.

The history of modern gladioluses traces to the middle years of the eighteenth century when South African species were first brought to Europe in ships of the British and Dutch East India companies that called at Cape Town for water and supplies. The earliest introductions included *G. alatus, G. carneus* (syn. *G. blandus*), *G. recurvus,* and *G. tristis.* Other species followed, including in 1789 *G. cardinalis.* Experimental hybridization began in England about 1806, but without notable results. It was nearly two decades later before what became known as the *G. colvillei* hybrids were produced by hybridizing *G. tristis* and *G. cardinalis.* James Colville of England achieved this, and it is a remarkable tribute to the merit of the hybrids that after more than a century and one-half some of the original productions as well as a white-flowered mutant (sport) of one named 'The Bride' that appeared about 1871 are still grown. All of these early introductions and their hybrids bloom in spring and rest in summer. Their growing season is from fall to spring. Because of this they are without value as outdoor plants in regions of cold winters. In 1830 three summer-flowering species were introduced from South Africa to Europe. These were given the names *G. oppositiflorus* (soon wrongly named *G. floribundus*), *G. papilio,* and *G. natalensis* (syn. *G. psittacinus*). The first was used in Holland with *G. cardinalis* as a parent of a group of winter-growing, spring-blooming hybrids that attained no great popularity. Of far greater importance was the successful hybridizing in Belgium in 1837 of *G. natalensis* and *G. cardinalis.* This laid the foundation for modern hybrid summer-flowering gladioluses. The results of the Belgian cross were grouped as *G. gandavensis* hybrids. These, by crossing and recrossing among themselves and with other hybrid kinds gave rise to numerous named horticultural varieties. Later *G. gandavensis* varieties were crossed with various species to produce the very wide variety of summer-flowering gladioluses now cultivated. A group known as *G. nanus* hybrids, some of which, including charming 'Peach Blossom', are still offered commercially, were raised in the Channel Islands about the middle of the nineteenth century. These, like the *G. colvillei* hybrids, are winter-growing, spring-bloomers adapted for cultivation outdoors in mild regions only. Their parents are *G. cardinalis* and *G. scullyi* (syn. *G. venustus*) with later infusions of *G. tristis* and *G. carneus.* The *G. nanus* and *G. colvillei* hybrids are sometimes called baby gladioluses, a name likely to cause confusion between them and the quite different miniature summer-flowering varieties.

A great breakthrough came with the reintroduction from Africa to England in 1902 of *G. primulinus.* Although this had flowered at Kew Gardens in England as early as 1890, and the Kew authorities then referred to it as a "unique and brilliant discovery" that "ought to be the starting point for a new race of garden gladiolus," twelve years passed before its possibilities as a parent caught the imagination of gladiolus breeders. Then it was employed as a parent to produce varieties more graceful than any previously known and with flowers with their upper petals forming a distinct hood. At first known as *G. primulinus* hybrids, these have since been so mingled by hybridizers with varieties of earlier types that such separation is scarcely tenable. Never-

Gladiolus primulinus

theless some varieties that exhibit most strongly the influence of *G. primulinus* are still offered in catalogs as primulinus hybrids. The *G. primulinus* stock introduced in 1902 came from within reach of the spray of the Victoria Falls of the Zambesii River. The question has been raised as to whether in fact it is the same species as the one first described as *G. primulinus* that came from the grass lands of Tanganyika. The latest monograph considers both to be phases of *G. natalensis.* Whatever be its nomenclatural disposition, it was the Victoria Falls plant that was used so widely and effectively by hybridizers to create varieties of far greater grace and refinement than any previously developed.

Double-flowered gladioluses go back to 1947. The first of which notice was taken, believed to be a mutant or sport of a normal single-flowered variety, was named 'Multipetal No. 1'. By employing this as a parent, a number of double-flowered and semidouble-flowered varieties were developed in the United States.

Fragrance, a noticeable feature of the flowers of several South African spring-blooming species, has largely eluded the efforts of breeders of summer-flowering hybrids.

Once the relationships of hybrid gladioluses to ancestral species became greatly blurred as a result of crossing and recross-

ing between varieties of very mixed ancestry it became necessary to devise a new system of classification for horticultural varieties of gladiluses. As now accepted by the North American Gladiolus Council and the New England Gladiolus Society size of flower, for which they use the word floret, is the basis of such an artificial classification. Measured without spreading or flattening any of the petals, under 2½ inches in diameter characterizes a miniature gladiolus, 2½ to 3½ inches a small gladiolus, 3½ to 4½ inches a medium gladiolus, 4½ to 5½ inches a large gladiolus, over 5½ inches a giant gladiolus. The American Gladiolus Council, formed in 1945 as an affiliation of gladiolus societies (seventy-one in 1971), to a large extent assumed the responsibilities of the then fading American Gladiolus Society, founded in 1910. The active New England Gladiolus Society came into existence in 1920. These and other such societies have had tremendous influence in popularizing gladioluses in North America and in making the United States one of the leading countries in the breeding of new varieties.

Modern hybrid gladioluses

Cultivated gladioluses in the vast majority of cases are of hybrid origin. These are listed, adequately described, and often well illustrated in easily available catalogs of specialist dealers. Very few natural species are readily procurable, but gladiolus specialists, particularly those interested in breeding, may from time to time secure and grow a few in addition to those next to be described, most of which are available commercially.

Summer-blooming *G. byzantinus,* of the central and eastern Mediterranean regions, is 1½ to 3 feet tall. It has leaves approximately ½ inch wide and short-tubed,

Gladiolus byzantinus

in length by the white style. Variety *G. f. milleri* has flowers that are white at first and change to pale sulfur-yellow. They have purple streaks in their lower petals. Similar to *G. communis*, but more slender and with narrower leaves, **G. illyricus**, a native of Europe, is the only species indigenous to Great Britain. Its flower spikes differ from those of *G. communis* in being not one-sided and usually having fewer (not over ten), rosy-purple blooms 1 inch to 1½ inches long, with unequal upper petals. Native to southern Europe, North Africa, and the Middle East, **G. segetum** is 1½ to 3 feet tall. It has tapered, approximately ½-inch-wide leaves and one-sided

Gladiolus orchidiflorus

somewhat bell-shaped, bright purple-rose-pink flowers 1½ to nearly 2 inches long with nearly equal petals and the stalks of the stamens not longer than the anthers. The blooms are in one-sided spikes of up to ten. The seeds are flattened and winged. The flowers of *G. b. albus* are white. Also a summer-bloomer, **G. communis** is a southeastern European native common there in fields of grain. From 2 to 3 feet tall, it can be distinguished from the last by the stamens of its blooms having stalks longer than the anthers. Its pointed leaves are up to a little over ½ inch wide. More or less funnel-shaped, the short-tubed, bright rose-pink to rosy-purple or sometimes white flowers are about 2 inches long. Their petals are all similar. The seeds are broadly-winged. **G. floribundus** of South Africa blooms in late spring or early summer. From 1 foot to 1½ feet tall, it has rather broad, strongly-veined, sword-shaped leaves and loose spikes of four to twelve blooms displayed in two ranks. They are white suffused and veined with pink. The stamens, which have purple anthers, are slightly exceeded

Gladiolus segetum

Gladiolus tristis

spikes of up to about twelve rosy-purple flowers 1½ to 2 inches long. The stalks of the stamens are not longer than the anthers. The rounded seeds are without wings. South African **G. tristis** is a winter-growing, spring-blooming species with slender, nearly cylindrical, erect leaves often more or less spirally-twisted. Its flowers, sweetly fragrant, especially in the evening, are in slender, few-flowered spikes 1½ to 2 feet tall, overtopping the foliage. They have perianth tubes nearly 2 inches long and are yellowish-white veined or suffused with purple in their

Gladiolus undulatus

throats. Variety *G. t. concolor* has blooms of pure pale yellow without invasions of purple. Another winter-blooming native of South Africa, **G. orchidiflorus** has linear leaves up to 1 foot long and ¼ inch wide. Rather distantly spaced, its greenish-yellow to purple flowers, usually not more than six to a spike and about 1½ inches across have a strongly-down-arched upper petal about 1 inch long and ⅓ inch wide and much narrowed toward its base. The two side petals are shorter and ½ inch wide or wider. The lowest three petals are narrowly-obovate, point downward, and have an obovate blade and long claw. The stamens reach almost to the tips of the segments. **G. undulatus** is 1 foot to 1½ feet tall. A native of South Africa, it has three to five broadish sword-shaped leaves. In loose, zigzagged spikes of four to seven, its flowers have white to cream-yellow petals, carmine-striped inside on their lower parts. The upper petal is a little wider than the others and the lower petals are recurved.

Garden and Landscape Uses. Undoubtedly the most frequent use for gladioluses is as cut flowers. For this they are superb. They are also favorites for exhibiting at

Gladiolus floribundus milleri in South Africa

flower shows. They are also admirable for garden decoration especially as accent groups in mixed flower borders to supply color after early perennials, biennials, and short-season annuals have passed out of bloom. Although for the most part gladioluses are not hardy, the Mediterranean and European species will survive outdoors even in the vicinity of New York City, if in a sheltered location such as near the base of a south-facing wall and if given a heavy winter covering of leaves or some similar protection. In mild climates the winter-growing, late-spring-blooming nanus types or baby gladiolus varieties are highly useful for outdoor spring displays and for cutting. In greenhouses they serve similarly and may be flowered earlier.

Cultivation. If treated well, gladioluses are among the easiest flowers to grow. Choose sites in full sun, reasonably sheltered from wind. The soil must be well drained. If these conditions are met you can easily modify others to meet the needs of gladioluses. Consider first the preparation of the soil. For the best results spade, rototill, or plow to a minimum depth of 7 to 8 inches. Mix in generous amounts of compost, well-rotted manure, or other organic matter or turn under some few weeks before planting a green manure crop. The ideal to strive for is crumbly earth in good tilth, with adequate fertility, testing between pH 6 and pH 7. Soils that will grow good vegetables produce high quality gladioluses. Most growers prefer to apply fertilizers as top dressing or side dressing during the growing season instead of incorporating them with the soil before planting, but if the soil is low in nutrients it will pay to mix in a dressing of complete fertilizer during the initial preparation.

When to plant depends upon the variety and when the flowers are wanted. Make the first outdoor planting of summer-flowering gladioluses about the time deciduous trees are sprouting new foliage. To assure continuous bloom make successive plantings until the beginning of July. For the first and last plantings rely upon early varieties, those that bloom in sixty to seventy-five days. Betweentimes plantings may be of varieties needing longer growing periods. Space plantings at ten-day to two-week intervals, allowing a little more time between earlier plantings than later ones.

Use only healthy corms. Discard any obviously diseased or suspected of being infected with virus. If you buy planting stock be sure to get corms of blooming size. Pass up so-called bargain offers of substandard ones. They should be at least 1¼ inches in diameter, that is unless they are choice and probably expensive varieties you are intending to grow on to flower in their second year. Corms 1½ to 2 inches in diameter are generally more desirable than smaller ones.

Tall, deep corms with high centers are better than large, flat ones with hollowed upper surfaces. Do not worry if the outer skins part from the bulbs. Some growers remove these before planting to give them an opportunity to inspect the surfaces of the corms for signs of disease, but this is not generally necessary.

For exhibition quality blooms de-eye the corms before planting. This is not necessary for ordinary garden display or for those grown for cut flowers where two or more flower spikes from each corm are preferred to one bigger one. And it only pays for show purposes if you have first quality corms of choice varieties that are to be planted and grown under as nearly ideal conditions as possible. Given these, it can mean the difference between prize-winning blooms and also-rans. Each sizable gladiolus corm has about six eyes or potential growth buds. If all except the strongest are removed before planting the food stored in the corm and the growth energies of the plant are concentrated on supplying just one shoot with moisture and nutrients and, conditions being favorable, that responds with maximum growth

Planting patterns: (a) For cut flowers, in single rows spaced widely enough to permit surface soil cultivation by machine

(b) In double rows spaced for machine cultivation

(c) For cut flowers in a home garden, in rows spaced more closely for hand tool cultivation

(d) beginning to bloom in a cut flower garden, zinnias in foreground

(e) In a trial ground, in groups to admit evaluation of different varieties

and flower production. To de-eye, peel the corm and then with a sharp-pointed knife or potato peeler scoop out the unwanted eyes. In doing this cut deeply so that they are removed right to their bases.

Planting patterns and distances depend upon purpose. For cut flowers set the corms in rows 1½ to 2½ feet apart with 4 to 6 inches between corms. Or plant them the same distance apart in double rows 6 to 8 inches apart, with 2 to 3 feet separating the double rows. Relate planting depth to the size of the corms. Set the biggest 5 or 6 inches deep, at the greater depth in sandy soils, somewhat more shallowly in heavier ones. Depths of 3 to 4 inches are satisfactory for smaller corms. The measurements suggested are from the bases of the corms to finished ground level. When planting for display in mixed flower borders set the corms at the same depth, spaced 6 to 8 inches apart, in groups of six to twelve. A narrow-bladed trowel comes in handy for planting in the often rather restricted spaces between other plants.

Cultivating to destroy young weeds

Routine summer care is of the simplest. Keep weeds from growing by frequent shallow cultivation or, after the young shoots are well up, by mulching and by hand weeding along the rows and close to the plants. Water copiously at weekly intervals during dry spells. This is especially necessary if dry weather occurs during the first eight weeks, before the new corms are well developed and have good root systems of their own. About a month after planting apply a side dressing or top dressing of a complete fertilizer, for preference one rather rich in potash such as a 5-10-10, and repeat this just before the first flowers open. This will assist in the development of fine new corms that you will likely depend upon for planting the next year. Support may be given by staking or by hilling soil around the bases of plants in rows much as is done with corn. Do this when the growths are 9 or 10 inches tall by mounding soil to a height of 4 or 5 inches. Take care not to dig too deeply with the hoe to secure the soil for hilling.

Cutting gladiolus blooms is best done in early morning. If you intend to keep the corms for the following year do not take much foliage. Leave a minimum of four mature leaves to build up strong corms. Cutting may be done as soon as the lowest flowers show good color or after the first one or two have expanded.

Cutting blooms, leaving maximum foliage

Harvesting corms in readiness for storage must be done before the tops have turned completely brown and dead. Approximately six weeks after the blooms have faded is about the right time, but if frost comes it must be done sooner. To harvest the corms, loosen the soil along the rows or around groups of plants by inserting the prongs of a spading fork in the ground a few inches from them and prying them upward by bearing down on the handle. Then carefully pull on the stems to lift the corms from the earth. Remove the stalks from the bulbs promptly. Do this by twisting them off. Cutting tools may transmit virus diseases from infected to healthy corms. It is important to dry the bulbs immediately after they are harvested. This is done by spreading them in trays with screen wire bottoms, in shallow flats, or on burlap or similar material and leaving them for a few days in a sunny place outdoors or in a greenhouse. Winter storage should be in a dry place where the temperature holds as near 40°F as possible, and certainly not higher than 50°F. The corms may be spread in trays with wire mesh bottoms or filled into mesh bags or old nylon stockings and suspended.

Storing gladiolus corms: (a) Twist the tops off the newly dug plants

(b) Spread the corms thinly to dry in a sunny place for a few days

(c) Store in mesh bags, or in some other fashion, to assure free air circulation between the corms

Spring-blooming, winter-growing gladioluses are planted in fall, outdoors in frost-free and nearly frost-free climates, and in greenhouses. During their summer dormant period their corms are stored or, in dry climates, left in the ground. For outdoors, set the corms 3 to 4 inches deep and as far apart, or for cut flowers closer together in rows 1 foot to 1½ feet apart. If there is danger of frost penetrating to the corms or young shoots protect them with loose mulch, which must be removed gradually in spring. To established plantings apply each fall a complete fertilizer. Keep the beds free of weeds and do not cut the foliage down until it has died naturally after flowering. Lifting and replanting is necessary at intervals of a few years, as soon as overcrowding and reduction in the number of flower spikes produced begins to be evident. The best time to do this is as soon as the foliage dies. Sort the corms to size and revitalize the soil by spading or rototilling in compost, peat moss, or other organic conditioner as well as a dressing of slow-acting complete fertilizer.

Greenhouse cultivation in pots or pans (shallow pots) calls for planting in August or September. Space the corms so that the distance between individuals is about one-half the width of a corm. Five to eight corms will usually suffice for a container 5 or 6 inches in diameter. Make sure the pots or pans are well drained. Use fertile, porous soil packed moderately firmly. Set the corms with their tops an inch below the surface. After planting, water thoroughly and stand in a shaded cold frame or other cool place. It is a good plan to cover the soil surface with a layer of moss, peat moss, or similar material to prevent rapid drying. Water with some caution at first, but never permit the soil to become completely dry. Before there is any danger of the plants freezing move them to a sunny greenhouse where the night temperature is 45 to 50°F. There they will stay until they bloom, and afterward until their tops die and their season of dormancy begins. Day temperatures must not be more than five to ten degrees above those maintained at night. On all favorable days ventilate the greenhouse freely. As roots permeate the soil increase the frequency of watering. After the containers are filled with roots supply weekly applications of dilute liquid fertilizer. Discreet staking with wires or thin bamboo canes is likely to be needed. When blooming is over continue watering until the foliage begins to die naturally. Then gradually increase the intervals between applications until finally water is withheld entirely. Then store the corms dry either in the soil in which they grew, or removed from the soil in bags or shallow, mesh-bottomed trays in a shaded, cool place such as a cellar, until replanting time in early fall.

Propagation in home gardens is usually adequately secured by the natural multiplication of the corms. If faster increase is desired you may use cormels (tiny corms that develop around old ones) and, in the cases of species or if you are raising new varieties, seeds. Gladioluses can also be propagated by cutting the corms into pieces each with one eye, allowing these to dry in a warm place for about a week and then planting, but this is rarely practiced.

Cormels clustered at base of gladiolus corms

Raising plants from cormels is simple. Prepare the ground as for regular plantings and as early in spring as the soil can be readied set the cormlets ½ to 1 inch apart in furrows 1½ to 2 inches deep spaced 9 inches to 1 foot apart. Cormels do not always sprout readily unless treated before planting. One method of doing this is to soak them in cloth bags in tepid water overnight and the following morning spread them out in the sun; repeat this for about six or seven successive days prior to planting. Another recommended treatment is to keep the cormels for about two months prior to sowing in a refrigerator at a low temperature, but without allowing them to freeze. The cormels of some varieties of gladioluses will not sprout until the second spring after harvesting. Treatment of the growing cormels is as for regular corms. Seeds of gladioluses may be sown in an outdoor seed bed in spring or be started earlier indoors.

Pests and Diseases. The chief pests are aphids, mealybugs, nematodes, tarnished plant bug, thrips, and wireworms. Diseases include leaf and flower spot, various rots, and wilt. There are also a number of serious virus infections, among them aster yellows and tobacco ring spot.

GLAND, GLANDULAR. Glands are organs that secrete oils or nectar. Usually they are small, and often minute. Often they are at the tips of hairs, which are then identified as glandular hairs. The term glands is sometimes, but not quite correctly used for non-secreting glandlike bodies. A plant part that is glandular is furnished with glands.

GLANDULICACTUS (Glanduli-cáctus). By those who favor broader concepts of cactus genera than the inveterate "splitters," the plants that constitute this genus are included in *Echinocactus*. They are cataloged from time to time under *Ferocactus*. They belong to the cactus family CACTACEAE. The name *Glandulicactus* alludes to the presence of nectar glands on the plants, but that feature is not always absent from related genera. The genus is native to Texas and Mexico. There are two species.

Glandulicactuses are of medium size; spherical when young, they are cylindrical later. They have notched, rounded, high ribs with elongated areoles (regions from which spines develop) continued as gland-bearing grooves from the ends of which the flowers arise. The spines are numerous, and one or more of the centrals are hooked. Short and funnel-shaped, the blooms open by day. Their perianth tubes, like the ovary and fruits, are scaly.

The first species to be given the name of this genus *G. uncinatus* (syns. *Echinocactus uncinatus*, *Ferocactus uncinatus*) inhabits Mexico. It has slightly glaucous-blue, short-cylindric, usually solitary stems 4 to 8

inches high with nine to thirteen ribs. The spine clusters have three or four centrals, one, longer than the others, up to 3 inches long and hooked, and seven or eight radials. The brownish to maroon blooms are funnel-shaped and about 1 inch wide. A variety, native of Texas, with spine clusters with only one central up to 5 inches long is distinguished as *G. u. wrightii*. Mexican *G. crassihamatus* (syns. *Echinocactus crassihamatus*, *Ferocactus crassihamatus*) has stems with thirteen deeply-notched ribs and clusters of eight awl-shaped radial spines and five flattened centrals, one about 1½ inches long and hooked. The 1-inch-wide blooms are purple.

Garden Uses and Cultivation. These are attractive plants for collectors. They need desert conditions, full sun, and thoroughly well-drained, slightly acid soil. Excessive wetness or humidity is likely to cause rotting. For more information see Cactuses.

GLASS. Glass is sometimes used as an inclusive descriptive term for conservatories, greenhouses, hotbeds, and cold frames. Thus, reference may be made to plants under glass as distinct from those grown outdoors.

GLASSHOUSE. This is synonymous with greenhouse or conservatory.

GLASTONBURY THORN is *Crataegus monogyna biflora*.

GLAUCIDIUM (Glaucíd-ium). One spring-blooming species, a native of the mountains of Japan, is the sole one of this genus of the buttercup family RANUNCULACEAE. The derivation of its name is unclear.

Little known in American horticulture, *Glaucidium palmatum*, a relative of the goldenseal (*Hydrastis*) is a noble herbaceous plant 2 feet tall. Its erect, branchless stems from short, fat rhizomes have two or three leaves 4 inches to 1 foot across and palmately (like typical maple leaves), seven- to eleven-lobed, with the center lobe often thrice-cleft at its apex. The edges of the

Glaucidium palmatum

Glaucidium palmatum, in fruit

Glaucidium palmatum (fruit)

leaves are sharply-toothed. There is one, or rarely two, flowers to each stem. They are without petals. Their display is made by four broad, rounded pale mauve to violet or rarely white sepals that look like petals. The numerous stamens form a tight central cluster. The flowers are about 3 to 3½ inches in diameter and are succeeded by dry, usually paired, follicles (pods) containing many broadly-winged seeds.

Garden Uses and Cultivation. Not enough horticultural experience has been had to be precise about the uses and cultivation of this plant in America. It may be expected that *Glaucidium* would thrive best in partial shade in moist, but not wet woodland soils. In all probability it is best adapted for gardens in the Pacific Northwest, but it flourishes near New York City in cool, sheltered, north-facing locations.

GLAUCIUM (Glàuc-ium)—Horned-Poppy, Sea-Poppy. This genus of the poppy family PAPAVERACEAE consists of about twenty-five species of annuals, biennials, and short-lived perennials, which in gardens are almost invariably treated as annuals or biennials. Although not of first horticultural importance, some kinds have showy blooms and are attractive. The name *Glaucium*, derived from the Greek *glaukos*, gray-

ish-green, refers to the color of the foliage. Horned-poppies are natives of Europe and the Middle East extending to the Altai Mountains of Asia with Iran the chief center of their distribution. In parts of North America *G. flavum* is naturalized. The genus is closely related to *Dicranostigma*, but differs in having very long seed pods usually exceeding 4 inches with the seeds surrounded by a spongy material. Also, the petals mostly angle upward, rather than spread horizontally, to form a cup- or funnel-shaped flower. In color the flowers of *Glaucium* vary from yellow to scarlet; they are often blotched with brown or black at the bases of their petals. The flowers of *Dicranostigma* are invariably clear yellow.

Horned-poppies or sea-poppies are herbaceous plants containing yellow sap. They have basal rosettes of pinnately-lobed, usually glaucous and hairy leaves, and erect or somewhat lax, branched, leaf-bearing stems. Their long-stalked flowers are large and solitary; they have two early deciduous sepals, four petals, numerous stamens, and almost stalkless styles, this last characteristic distinguishing them from *Stylophorum*. From *Chelidonium* they are separated by the large size of their flowers and by technical differences.

The kind most likely to be met with in gardens is **G. flavum,** a native of maritime

regions in Europe, North Africa, the Canary Islands, and western Asia. The roots of this sort are poisonous. Its several stems attain a height of 2 to 3 feet and have upper leaves that clasp the stems. The golden-yellow flowers are about 2 inches in diameter, the seed pods 6 inches to 1 foot long. Closely related to *G. flavum*, but with somewhat smaller blooms, ranging in color from yellow to reddish, is **G. oxylobum.** This is not a seacoast species. Indigenous to Turkey, Iraq, Iran, and Afghanistan, it is perhaps not in cultivation. The plant usually cultivated as *G. corniculatum* (syn. *G. phoeniceum*) is the showier and more attractive **G. grandiflorum,** a red-flowered native of Turkey, Iraq, and Iran. The true *G. corniculatum* is very variable and is widely distributed through Europe and the Middle East. Its flowers range from yellow to scarlet and frequently have their petals marked with dark basal blotches that are sometimes margined with white. The blooms of this species usually are hidden among the foliage and this, together with their narrower petals, accounts for the plant being less decorative than *G. grandiflorum*.

Garden Uses. Although the blooms are large and individually showy, they last only about a day and usually not many open at once. This somewhat reduces the

Glaucium flavum

popular appeal of horned-poppies as garden ornamentals. Nevertheless, they can be quite effective grouped in informal parts of the garden as well as in borders of mixed flowers. The blooms have no value for cutting. These plants need full sun and thoroughly drained soil.

Cultivation. The most satisfactory method of handling these plants is as biennials. Seeds are sown in May or June outdoors and the seedlings transplanted to nursery beds in rows 1 foot apart, with 6 inches allowed between the plants in the rows. In September or October or early the following spring, they are transferred to the locations where they are to bloom at 1 foot to 1½ feet apart. Considerable care must be taken to retain as large balls of earth as possible about the roots during transplanting operations; like many members of the poppy family these resent root disturbance. An alternative plan is to sow seeds in September where the plants are to remain and thin the seedlings to a suitable distance apart. Success is also had from seeds sown in February or March in a temperature of 60 to 65°F in a greenhouse. The seedlings are potted individually in 2½-inch pots and are grown on in full sun in a night temperature of 50 to 55°F and daytime temperatures five or ten degrees higher until the weather is warm and settled; then, after being hardened by standing in a cold frame or sheltered place outdoors for a week or so, they may be planted in the garden.

GLAUCOUS. Covered with a thin layer of usually waxy, gray, gray-green, or blue-green particles that are easily rubbed off. Such a layer, conspicuous on the fruits of grapes and on many cactuses and other succulent plants, is sometimes called a bloom.

GLECHOMA (Glec-hòma)—Ground Ivy or Gill-Over-The-Ground. The name is sometimes spelled *Glecoma*. The green-leaved type of the not unattractive little *Glechoma hederacea* is best known to gardeners as a weed of lawns and other places. It is scarcely a cultivated plant; only its variegated variety is usually accorded that status. At one time included in *Nepeta*, from which it differs in its flowers being in the axils of regular foliage leaves instead of bracts, it is one of a genus of five species, all natives of Europe and temperate Asia. Their name is a modified version of the ancient Greek one for pennyroyal, *glechon*. This genus belongs in the mint family LABIATAE.

Glechomas are creeping or trailing perennial herbaceous plants with long-stalked round to kidney-shaped leaves and small blue flowers, usually in threes. Their short-stalked, asymmetrical blooms are tubular and have five-lobed calyxes and two-lipped corollas, the upper lip

shallowly-two-lobed. There are four stamens located just beneath the upper lip of the corolla; they are as long as the lip. The fruits consist of four small nutlets.

Ground-ivy or gill-over-the-ground (*G. hederacea*) is a lowly hardy plant that spreads extensively. Its stems and foliage are finely-hairy or smooth. The leaves are up to 1½ inches across with coarsely-scalloped edges and deeply-heart-shaped

Glechoma hederacea

Glechoma hederacea (leaves and flowers)

Glechoma hederacea variegata

bases. The blue flowers are in twos or threes. Variety *G. h. variegata* has green and white leaves.

Garden Uses. The variegated ground-ivy is splendid for hanging baskets, window boxes, and for growing in pots to trail over the edges of benches in cool greenhouses. It is less hardy than the green-leaved kind.

Cultivation. Most accommodating as to its needs, *G. h. variegata* roots readily from cuttings and grows vigorously in any ordinary soil. It responds to cool conditions, such as suit geraniums, in greenhouses, window gardens, and other frost-free places, and grows well outdoors in summer. Sun is not necessary, but good light is appreciated. In greenhouses and rooms the winter night temperature should not exceed 55°F; a few degrees lower is satisfactory. Day temperatures up to ten degrees above those maintained at night are appropriate. Good 4- or 5-inch pot specimens are obtained quickly by planting four or five rooted cuttings in each container. When the plants are about 4 inches tall their tips are pinched out to encourage branching. The soil should be always fairly moist. Well-rooted specimens benefit from regular applications of dilute liquid fertilizer. The chief pest is the red spider mite.

GLECOMA. See Glechoma.

GLEDITSIA (Gled-ítsia)—Honey-Locust or Sweet-Locust, Water-Locust or Swamp-Locust. Inhabiting North America, South America, Asia, and Africa, *Gleditsia*, of the pea family LEGUMINOSAE, comprises eleven species. An ancient genus in the Tertiary, it was much more common and widely distributed over the earth's surface than at present. Its name honors the German botanist Johann Gottlieb Gleditsch, who died in 1786.

Gleditsias are deciduous trees, often of large size, and commonly with trunks and branches furnished with large, branched or sometimes branchless spines that it is believed represent aborted branches. The leaves are alternate and pinnate or twice-pinnate without a terminal leaflet. In some kinds pinnate and twice-pinnate foliage occurs on the same tree. The small, greenish flowers, unisexual and bisexual ones usually on the same tree, are in racemes or less commonly panicles. They are not pea-shaped. Each has three to five sepals and petals, the latter of nearly equal size and not much longer than the sepals. There are ten separate stamens and a short style tipped with a large stigma. The fruits are pods containing one or more seeds.

The common honey-locust or sweet-locust (*G. triacanthos*) is sometimes called the three-thorned-acacia, this because of its formidable armament of strong, often branched thorns up to 4 inches or so long, and flattened at least toward their bases.

Gleditsia triacanthos

Gleditsia triacanthos (leaves)

Gleditsia triacanthos (fruits)

Native from Pennsylvania to Nebraska, Mississippi, and Texas, and hardy as far north as southern Canada, this is the largest tree of the pea family indigenous to the United States or Canada. Attaining a maximum height of 140 feet, it is graceful and broad-headed. Its ferny leaves have generally more than twenty remotely-toothed, oblong-lanceolate, usually pointed leaflets ¾ inch to 1½ inches long. The very short-stalked flowers are in slender racemes. The slightly curved seed pods, 9 inches to 1½ feet long and with sweetish pulp between the seeds, become twisted with age. Of particular interest to gardeners and landscapers are thornless variants of this species that come under the group named *G. t. inermis*. Here belong kinds named 'Moraine', 'Shademaster', 'Rubylace', and 'Sunburst', as well as others. The first two are especially good green-leaved selections. 'Rubylace' has deep purplish-red young foliage that changes to bronze-green as the season advances. The spring growth of 'Sunburst', a slower-growing, more compact tree, is bright golden-yellow. It dims and becomes green later.

The water-locust or swamp-locust (*G. aquatica*), native from South Carolina to Kentucky, Florida, and Texas, attains a height of about 60 feet. It has cylindrical, not flattened thorns. Its leaves are pinnate with twelve to eighteen slightly toothed, nearly hairless, ovate-oblong leaflets ¾ inch to 1¼ inches long, rounded or notched at their apexes, or are twice-pinnate. The short-stalked flowers are in racemes up to 4 inches long. The usually one-seeded pods are 1 inch to 2 inches in length. This kind is hardy to about as far north as New York City. An intermediate hybrid between it and *G. triacanthos* is named *G. texana.* This has straight seed pods up to 5 inches long.

Hardy about as far north as southern New England, *G. japonica,* of Japan and China, is up to 75 feet tall. It has thorns, often branched, flattened at least in their lower parts, and up to 4 inches long. Its leaves, approximately 1 foot long, usually have twenty or fewer leaflets ¾ inch to 1½ inches long or rarely longer, that have blunt or notched apexes. The flowers are short-stalked and in slender racemes. Twisted and rough-surfaced, the seed pods, about 1 foot long, have the seeds at their middles. Somewhat less hardy, *G. macracantha* hails from China. A tree up to about 50 feet in height, it has large spines flattened toward their bases and leaves of up to twelve ovate-oblong or rarely obovate, toothed leaflets, mostly 2 to 3 inches long, with hairs on the midribs above and on the undersides. The longish-stalked blooms, in racemes, are succeeded by seed pods 6 inches to 1 foot in length. Also Chinese and about as hardy as the last, is *G. sinensis.* Up to 50 feet tall, this has conical, often branched spines. Its leaves, up to 7 inches long, have eight to fourteen or occasionally more, blunt or somewhat pointed, toothed, ovate to oblong-ovate leaflets 1¼ to 3¼ inches in length, dull yellowish-green, and somewhat hairy. In slender, drooping racemes, the flowers are short-stalked. The nearly straight pods are 4½ to 10 inches long. The most spiny kind is *G. caspica.* A native of the Transcaucasus and Iran, this is up to about 40 feet tall. Its leaves are pinnate and have twelve to twenty toothed, elliptic leaflets up to 2 inches long; they sometimes are twice-pinnate. The curved seed pods are about 8 inches in length.

Garden and Landscape Uses. Honey-locusts are esteemed for their pleasing forms and graceful, delicate foliage, but are without other ornamental values. Neither flowers nor fruits are decorative, nor does the foliage assume bright fall color. By far the most popular kinds for garden and landscape planting are *G. triacanthos* and its thornless varieties. The latter are often preferred because they are without the vicious spines of the typical species. These thorns can cause problems in public and sometimes in private places. The 'Moraine' honey-locust and some other selections do not produce seed pods, and since such pods

Gleditsia triacanthos 'Moraine' as a young street tree

tend to be messy when they fall, this is another recommendation. Varieties 'Rubylace' and 'Sunburst' are planted chiefly for their colorful foliage. 'Sunburst' needs to be carefully placed otherwise its insistent, unusual color can be incongruous in the landscape. These honey-locusts stand city conditions well. The green-leaved kinds are especially much favored as street trees. One virtue is that their small leaves create no problems or hazards when they fall. They dry and tend to blow away. Because the leaves appear late in spring and drop in early fall, and the shade cast is light, grass grows better under honey-locusts than many trees. Because of this they are favorite lawn trees.

Cultivation. Honey-locusts respond to ordinary soils, the water-locust needing a moist one, and open locations. They transplant well. No regular pruning is needed, but any necessary to keep the trees shapely or restrain their growth may be done with impunity. Propagation of the species is by seeds, which germinate more surely and rapidly if before sowing they are filed or are steeped in a concentrated solution of sulfuric acid for two hours and then thoroughly washed in water. Selected varieties and rare species are increased by grafting or budding onto seedling understocks of *G. triacanthos*. Pests that are sometimes troublesome include the mimosa webworm and a pod gall, caused by a mite. Both affect the leaves.

GLEICHENIA (Gleich-ènia). Notoriously difficult to cultivate, species of *Gleichenia*, of the gleichenia family GLEICHENIACEAE, are native to Malaysia, Australia, New Zealand, Madagascar, and tropical America. There are more than 100 species. The name commemorates the German botanist W. F. Gleichen, who died in 1783.

Gleichenia, undetermined species

Gleichenias are ferns that much resemble *Dicranopteris*, but differ in the way in which the veinlets of their leaf segments fork and in the undersides of the fronds (leaves) being generally scaly instead of glaucous. They are vigorous creepers that spread by surface or slightly buried rhizomes to form great thickets. They have repeatedly forked, evergreen fronds with deeply-divided, pinnate leaflets. The fronds continue to grow and lengthen throughout their lives. The clusters of spore capsules, usually two or four on the undersides of the leaflets, are without indusia (covers).

Native from Mexico to the West Indies, South America, and New Zealand, *G. bifida* has wide-spreading rhizomes. Its fronds, which continue to elongate throughout their lives, fork repeatedly into pointed-narrow-linear, pinnate leaflets each with numerous narrow segments

Gleichenia bifida

arranged like the teeth of a comb along both sides of the midrib. The leaflets are up to 1 foot long or longer by 1½ to 2 inches wide. Malayan and Sumatran *G. linearis* (syn. *G. dichotoma*) has fronds with zigzag stems that repeatedly fork into two or three branches.

Garden and Landscape Uses and Cultivation. These are as for *Dicranopteris*.

GLEICHENIACEAE—Gleichenia Family. Five genera by some authorities included in the *Polypodiaceae* constitute the fern family GLEICHENIACEAE. They include about 160 species, mostly tropical and subtropical, but two extending as far north as Japan.

Unusual for ferns, the sorts of this family grow in sunny habitats. They form thickets of extensive, creeping rhizomes and usually leathery, often repeatedly forked fronds (leaves) with pinnately-lobed leaflets. The clusters of spore capsules are without covers (indusia). The only genera known to be cultivated are *Dicranopteris* and *Gleichenia*.

GLIRICIDIA (Gliric-ídia)—Madre de Cacao. Related to locusts (*Robinia*), from which they differ in having erect instead of drooping flower clusters and seed pods without wings and in other details, the ten species of *Gliricidia*, of the pea family LEGUMINOSAE, are warm-country trees and shrubs indigenous from Mexico to South America and Cuba. The name is from the

Latin *gliris*, a dormouse, and *caedo*, to kill, in allusion to some sorts at least being poisonous to rodents.

Gliricidias have pinnate leaves with an odd number of toothless leaflets, the upper ones of each leaf bigger than those below. The pink or white, pea-like flowers, in racemes or dense clusters, have large upper petals and incurved keels. The fruits are broadly-linear.

The only kind at all commonly cultivated is the madre de cacao (*G. sepium*), a native of Central America and Colombia. A tree up to 30 feet in height, this has leaves up to 10 inches long of seven to seventeen broad-oblong-ovate leaflets each 1 inch to 3 inches in length and often blotched on their undersides with purple or bronze. The ½- to ¾-inch-long flowers, which are attractive to bees and appear in spring before the leaves, are in racemes up to 6 inches long. They are pink or white usually marked with yellow or purple. The shiny brown seed pods are 4 to 6 inches long, have slightly thickened edges, and contain up to eleven seeds.

Called live fence post and quick stick, the madre de cacao is commonly used in Mexico and in Cuba, where it blooms in January and February, for fence posts. "Cuttings," consisting of stems 2 to 3 inches in diameter and several feet long, set with their bases in the ground, root readily and bloom the following season. Flowering fences of *Gliricidia* are a feature

Globba atrosanguinea

those of most cultivated members of the ginger family the plants and blooms are small. The latter are white, yellow, orange, or purplish. They have funnel-shaped, unequally-three-lobed calyxes, slender corolla tubes much longer than the calyxes, with three spreading or deflexed lobes, a large lip, two staminodes representing abortive stamens, one fertile, slightly petal-like stamen, and a long-projecting style. The fruits are capsules.

Kinds cultivated are *G. atrosanguinea*, of Borneo, and from Thailand, *G. winitii* and *G. schomburgkii*. From 1½ to 3 feet in height, **G. atrosanguinea** has lustrous green, slender-pointed, lanceolate or oblanceolate leaves 5 to 8 inches long and more or less downy on their undersides. Its panicles, about 2½ inches long, have blood-red bracts and elegant yellow flowers with corolla tubes about 1 inch long. From 1 foot to 3 feet tall, **G. winitii** has short, fleshy rhizomes and smooth green leaves, the lowermost represented by long sheathing bracts. The chief leaves have slender stalks up to 4 inches long and pointed-oblong blades up to 8 inches long. The golden-yellow flowers make a display over a long period. They are in loose, drooping panicles, up to 6 inches in length, with rosy-purple bracts, the largest 1 inch to 1½ inches long. The curved corolla tubes are about ½ inch long. This blooms in fall. About 1½ feet tall, *G. schomburgkii* has leaves about 5 inches in length, and panicles of red-spotted, yellow blooms with tubes ¾ inch long from the axils of light green bracts. The panicles are about 3 inches long.

Garden and Landscape Uses and Cultivation. Only in tropical and subtropical

of Cuban landscapes. In Hawaii, too, the madre de cacao blooms during the early months of the year. The tree, poisonous to rats and other rodents, but not to cattle, is also planted to shade coffee, clove, and cacao plantations; its name madre de cacao (mother of cacao) reflects this use. The beautifully grained, hard and durable wood of this tree is esteemed for cabinet-making and carpentry.

Garden and Landscape Uses and Cultivation. This is an attractive small ornamental flowering tree for tropical and nearly tropical climates. In general appearance in bloom it approximates the apple and peach trees of cooler climates and is seen to best effect against a background of dark evergreens such as araucarias or *Ficus*. The madre de cacao grows without difficulty in full sun in ordinary soil and is easily propagated by cuttings and seeds.

If its branches tend to become too long a more compact head can be induced by pruning them back quite severely.

GLOBBA (Glób-ba). Few of the fifty species of *Globba* are known to gardeners, and then usually only to those in the tropics or with tropical greenhouses. Predominantly forest plants, these inhabit a native range from Indomalaysia to southern China and belong in the ginger family ZINGIBERA-CEAE. The name comes from an Amboinan one *galoba*.

Globbas are ginger-like. They have slender rhizomes and clusters of leaves with sheathing bases. The leaf blades are slightly asymmetric. The flowers, of very unusual appearance, are in erect or arching and pendent racemes with, in the lowermost bracts of each, in place of flowers, usually small bulbils. Compared with

Globba winitii

Globba schomburgkii

climates where little or no frost is known can these interesting plants be grown permanently outdoors. In such regions they are useful for shaded places where the soil is fairly good and not exceedingly dry. Their flowers are useful for cutting. They last well in water. Globbas are also attractive for ground beds and pots in greenhouses and, where the atmosphere is not excessively dry, they may be grown as houseplants. They are rested in winter by keeping them dry in a temperature of about 55°F. Repotting is done in spring. At that time increase may be had by dividing the rhizomes. After repotting, the plants are started into growth in a temperature of 60 to 70°F, and watering is resumed, at first rather sparingly, but freely once new foliage is well initiated and growth is active. Summer applications of dilute liquid fertilizer encourage favorable development. Division and bulbils and seeds afford means of propagation.

GLOBE. The word globe is included as part of the common names of these plants: globe-amaranth (*Gomphrena globosa*), globe berry (*Ibervillea*), globe-daisy (*Globularia*), globe flower (*Trollius*), globe-mallow (*Sphaeralcea*), globe-thistle (*Echinops*), and globe-tulip (*Calochortus*).

GLOBULARIA (Globu-lària)—Globe-Daisy. Natives of the Mediterranean region, adjacent Asia, and the Canary Islands and Cape Verde islands, the twenty-eight species of *Globularia*, together with two species of *Poskea*, not cultivated, are the only members of the globularia family GLOBULARIACEAE. The name, from the Latin *globulus*, a small, spherical head, alludes to the clustered flowers.

Globularias include hardy and nonhardy herbaceous plants, subshrubs, and small shrubs. They have alternate, undivided, sometimes toothed, usually leathery leaves, and flowers in terminal, fluffy, moplike heads with or without an involucre (collar) of bracts at their bases. The individual blooms are small, and commonly blue or white. They have tubular, five-lobed, persistent calyxes and tubular two-lipped corollas with the upper lip short or nearly absent and the lower with three long lobes. There are four stamens in two pairs. The fruits are one-seeded nutlets.

Globularias hardy in the north include herbaceous perennial *G. vulgaris*, of southeastern Europe, a species once used as a source of a yellow dye. This, somewhat woody at its base, is from 2 inches to 1 foot in height. Its basal rosette leaves, about 1½ inches long, are long-stalked, broadly-elliptic, and notched or three-lobed at their pointed apexes. The few stem leaves are stalkless, lanceolate, long-pointed and about one-half as long as the basal ones. In heads rather under ½ inch in diameter are the bright blue, or more

Globularia repens

rarely lilac or white, flowers. The bracts of the involucre are long pointed. More commonly cultivated, and often misidentified as *G. vulgaris*, is **G. aphyllanthes** (syn. *G. willkommii*), native to southern Europe. This differs from *G. vulgaris* in not being as woody at the base, in having blunt basal leaves, and in the leaves on the flower stalks being short-pointed. Also from southern Europe, **G. nudicaulis** (syn. *G. alpina*) differs from those discussed above in its flower stalks being without leaves. This is up to about 6 inches tall, and has blunt-ended, oblong, round-toothed leaves. Its blue flowers are in comparatively large heads.

Mat-forming globularias that spread by creeping stems or stolons include several worth cultivating. Familiar is **G. trichosantha**, which has basal rosettes of short-stalked, spatula-shaped leaves with 1-inch-long blades usually three-toothed at their apexes, and stalks 6 to 8 inches long. The stalks are furnished with linear-lanceolate, long-pointed leaves or bracts, and terminate in heads ½ inch in diameter of light blue flowers. This species is native to Bulgaria, Turkey, and the Crimea.

Choicest of globularias are the dwarf, matting kinds that spread into miniature lawns of evergreen foliage above which rise on short or shortish stalks little balls of blue or steel-blue flowers. Here belong *G. cordifolia*, *G. meridionalis* (syn. *G. bellidifolia*), *G. repens* (syn. *G. nana*), and *G. incanescens*. A native of Europe and adjacent Asia, **G. cordifolia** is a cushiony subshrub 3 or 4 inches high, with rosettes of glossy, ovate to nearly round leaves, with rounded, notched or sometimes three-toothed apexes, and about 1 inch long. Atop leafless stalks about 2 inches long,

the flower heads are about ½ inch wide. White-flowered *G. c. alba* and pink-flowered *G. c. rosea* are charming. Lanceolate to obovate-lanceolate leaves usually short-pointed at their apexes distinguish **G. meridionalis,** of the Balkans, from *G. cordifolia*. Its leaves are 1 inch to 4 inches long, its flower heads are on long, leafless stalks. The plant commonly grown in gardens as *G. bellidifolia* and sometimes as *G. cordifolia nana,* is much smaller than this description allows and may represent a dwarf form of the species or perhaps is distinct. Not over 2 inches tall, it has leaves under ¾ inch in length, and powder-blue, nearly stalkless flower heads. Smallest of all, and also with nearly stalkless flower heads, **G. repens** of southern Europe is 1 inch to 1½ inches high. From ¾ inch long to very much smaller, its short-pointed leaves are lanceolate to obovate-lanceolate. The flower heads are about ½ inch wide. Glaucous-blue, ovate-spatula- to heart-shaped leaves

Globularia incanescens

are characteristic of cushion-like *G. inca-nescens*, native to southern Europe. Its 2-inch-long flower stalks have ovate to lanceolate leaves and are topped by light blue to violet-blue balls of flowers.

A much-branched undershrub, native of dry places in Europe and about 2 feet in height, *G. alypum* is not hardy in the north. It has rigid, leathery, lanceolate leaves with three-toothed tips and heads, ½ to ¾ inch wide, of fragrant flowers, each head sitting in a collar of bracts. This is a poisonous plant with violently purgative properties.

Garden Uses and Cultivation. Although they make no great splash of color, globe-daisies are worthwhile garden plants that have a quiet beauty. They are especially suitable for rock gardens and other intimate plantings. In general they are sun-lovers, but *G. nudicaulis* is not averse to a little shade. All require very well-drained soil and prefer dryish, gritty ones of a limestone character. In the north it is advantageous to protect these plants from strong winter sun and wind by placing over them cut branches of evergreens or some other covering that allows some light to reach them, and permits free air circulation. Increase is simple by seeds, division, and summer cuttings in a cold frame or greenhouse propagating bed.

GLOBULARIACEAE — Globularia Family. Two or three genera of which one is cultivated in rock gardens and similar places constitute the globularia family, a group of dicotyledons that are native to Europe, Asia Minor, North Africa, the Canary Islands, and the Cape Verde Islands. The species total about thirty. Members are herbaceous plants, subshrubs, or shrubs, with alternate, undivided leaves and tiny flowers crowded in heads or spikes with generally a collar (involucre) of bracts at the base. The blooms have five-lobed, persistent calyxes and two-lipped, five-lobed corollas with the lower lip often much smaller than the upper. There are four stamens in pairs of different lengths or much less frequently only two, and one slender style. The fruits are one-seeded nutlets. Only *Globularia* is cultivated.

GLOCHID. Minutely-barbed, hairlike or bristle-like spines, often easily detachable, are called glochids. They commonly occur in tufts on the areoles of cactuses of the *Opuntia* relationship.

GLOCHIDION (Glochíd-ion). This tropical genus, mostly of the Old World, but represented in the Americas and Australia, belongs in the spurge family EUPHORBIACEAE. It differs from related *Phyllanthus* in its female flowers having undivided styles and in technical details of its seeds. Its species, numbering 300, are trees and shrubs, none of much importance horticulturally.

The name, from the Greek *glochidos*, the point of an arrow, alludes to the leaves.

Glochidions have alternate, undivided, usually toothless leaves and from the leaf axils solitary or clustered, small, unisexual flowers, the males with up to eight sepals, the females with short, thick stigmas. The fruits are capsules.

Occasionally planted in southern California and other warm regions, *Glochidion album* (syn. *Phyllanthus albus*) is a shrub or small tree, native of the Philippine Islands. It has very short-stalked, oblong-elliptic leaves contracted to short points, which are hairy on their undersides and from 4 to 10 inches long by up to 4 inches wide. The small blooms are in clusters. The fruits are white. The ornamental uses and needs of this species are similar to those of *Phyllanthus*.

GLORIOSA (Glorió-sa) — Climbing-Lily, Glory-Lily. The very name of this group of lily relatives suggests the startling beauty of some of its kinds. Natives of warm parts of Africa and Asia, gloriosas are deciduous climbing plants well suited for growing permanently outdoors in warm climates, as summer vines where winters are colder, and for greenhouse cultivation. There are five species. They belong in the lily family LILIACEAE. The name derives from the Latin *gloriosus*, splendid. For gloriosa-daisy see Rudbeckia.

Gloriosas have distinctive tubers, slender, brittle, and usually with two long prongs that spread to form a V or an L; occasionally there are three prongs. From the ends of the arms of the tubers the new stems develop. These bear alternate, opposite, or whorled (in circles of more than

Tubers of *Gloriosa*

two), undivided, parallel-veined leaves that end in tendrils that attach themselves to suitable supports. The scentless, lily-like, long-stalked blooms arise singly from the upper leaf axils. They are red or yellow, or a combination of those colors, and have six spreading, reflexed, or sometimes erect perianth segments (commonly called petals, but more correctly tepals), with usually wavy or much crisped margins, six long stamens, and a slender style that at its base is bent at right angles. The fruits are capsules.

The two best known species are *G. superba*, of tropical Africa and Asia, and *G. rothschildiana*, of tropical East Africa. Both attain heights of 5 or 6 feet or sometimes more. The long-lanceolate to narrowly-ovate-lanceolate leaves of *G. superba* are 4

Gloriosa superba

Gloriosa superba lutea

Gloriosa rothschildiana

to 5 inches long and up to 1 inch wide. Its flowers, borne in late summer and fall, have very much crisped petals, yellow at first, but soon changing to orange-brown or red. They are 2 to 3 inches long and spread widely or are reflexed. Variety *G. s. lutea* is yellow-flowered. Even more showy, **G. rothschildiana** has down-facing flowers with strongly reflexed, scarcely crisped, but sometimes somewhat wavy margins to its petals, which are 2 to 3 inches long or longer, at first bright red and yellow, changing to red as the blooms age. The leaves are broadly-lanceolate to ovate-lanceolate, 5 to 7 inches long by 1½ to 2 inches wide. Variety *G. r. citrina* has clear citron-yellow blooms with small wine-red blotches at the bases of the petals. This species and its variety bloom earlier than *G. superba*.

Less commonly cultivated, **G. simplex** (syns. *G. virescens*, *G. plantii*), a kind widely distributed through tropical Africa,

is a summer-bloomer 3 to 4 feet tall. Its flowers have spatula-shaped petals, about 2 inches long, with slightly undulating, but not crisped margins. They are deep orange and yellow, or when grown in shade, clear yellow. Other species that may be cultivated are **G. carsonii**, of East Africa, which has blooms with recurving wine-purple petals edged with yellow especially toward their bases, 2½ inches long, and **G. verschuuri**, probably of East Africa. This last is up to 5 feet tall, compact, and has leaves wider than those of *G. rothschildiana*. Its shorter-stalked flowers have broad, reflexed, deep crimson petals with yellow bases and margins.

Garden and Landscape Uses. Gloriosas are gorgeous flowering vines for flower borders, fences, and grouping in spaces at the fronts of shrubberies in climates where they succeed outdoors. They are splendid for large tubs and other containers for decorating patios, terraces, and similar places,

and for greenhouses. They succeed in well-drained, nutritious soils, and are best contented when the ground and the lower parts of their stems are shaded and their upper parts reach into sunlight or part-day shade. Their flowers are excellent for cutting.

Cultivation. In warm climates where the tubers are not subject to freezing, gloriosas may be left undisturbed in the ground for years. Elsewhere, even in northern gardens where the growing season is not excessively short, they may be planted directly outdoors as soon as it is safe to set out tomatoes; they will bloom in summer or fall. The tubers are planted horizontally, or at a slight angle with the growing end up, at a depth of about 5 or 6 inches. When frost kills the tops the tubers are carefully dug and stored in dry peat moss or sand in a temperature of about 50°F through the winter. By digging time the tubers that were planted have withered and been replaced by new ones, the ones taken up in fall. It is of vital importance to handle them with great care; if their upper ends are broken off they will not grow again. As an alternative to planting directly outdoors the tubers may be started in pots indoors in a humid atmosphere in a temperature of 70°F and the plants set in the garden after the weather is warm and settled.

Containers, such as large pots, tubs, or boxes, for gloriosas must be well drained. They should be filled with fertile, porous earth. Several tubers are planted in each large container. In greenhouses this is done in February or March. The tubers are set horizontally at a depth of 3 or 4 inches. At first, watering is done cautiously, but as growth develops more liberal applications are in order, and when in full growth

Gloriosa rothschildiana citrina

Gloriosa simplex

Glottiphyllum, undetermined species

Glottiphyllum linguiforme

generous supplies are given. Applications of dilute liquid fertilizer are of benefit after the containers are filled with roots. Light shade from strong summer sun is advisable. From the time the tubers are started into growth the temperature should not be lower than 65°F, and at times may rise considerably higher. A humid, but not dank, atmosphere favors good growth. Supports around which the tendrils can twine are needed. Unless seeds are to be saved faded blooms should be removed promptly. In fall, when the plants show signs of going to rest, watering is gradually reduced, finally stopped, and the tubers are stored dry in the soil in which they grew or are taken from the soil and packed in peat moss or sand until it is time to start them into growth again. Propagation by seeds is easy, and the young plants bloom in their second year. An alternative method of increase is by offsets.

GLORY. The word glory occurs as part of the common names of these plants: Chilean glory flower (*Eccremocarpus*), glory bower (*Clerodendrum*), glory bush (*Tibouchina*), glory-lily (*Gloriosa*), glory-of-Texas (*Thelocactus bicolor schottii*), glory-of-the-snow (*Chinodoxa*), glory-of-the-sun (*Leucocoryne ixioides*), and glory-pea (*Clianthus formosus*).

GLOTTIPHYLLUM (Glotti-phýllum). An unusual genus of plants of a relationship that teems with such, *Glottiphyllum* belongs to the *Mesembryanthemum* association of the carpetweed family AIZOACEAE and comprises fifty species. Its name, alluding to the foliage and apt for most species, comes from the Greek *glotta*, a tongue, and *phyllon*, a leaf. Its members are all South Africans. Of one species, Dr. G. Schwantes, the great German student of South African stone

plants, windowed plants, and their like, wrote "when the sun shines through it looks like a translucent sea creature, overflowing its pot in all directions. In two ranks along its stems the leaves are set like greenish-yellow tongues, often tinged with a wonderful violet color or the purple of the dawn." That well describes many glottiphyllums. A few have leaves in four rather than two ranks and a few have opaque, chalky-white, usually pale green leaves.

Glottiphyllums, among the most intriguing of succulent plants, are low perennials with short, branching stems and opposite, very soft leaves containing much watery tissue. The leaves are tongue- or tentacle-like, one of each pair often longer than the other. Each shoot normally has two or three, less often four pairs of leaves. The stalked or stalkless, glossy-petaled, yellow or rarely white, solitary flowers are often fragrant and in aspect resemble daisies. In fact they are very different from daisies, for each is a single flower rather than a head of florets. The fruits are capsules.

The name *G. linguiforme* often seen on labels of plants in succulent collections belongs to a species rare in cultivation that has not been found in the wild since its discovery in the eighteenth century. Most plants grown as *G. linguiforme* are *G. longum*, closely related species, or hybrids of *G. linguiforme*. Apparently all plants of the true species are descendents by vegetative propagation of one individual. They do not set seeds to their own pollen and can only be propagated by cuttings. True *G. linguiforme* has four-ranked leaves 2 inches long or a little longer and at their widest about two-thirds as wide. Of a lively, lustrous green, they are shaped like thick, pointed tongues. The short-stalked, golden-yellow flowers are 2 to 2½ inches

Glottiphyllum linguiforme at Huntington Botanical Garden, San Marino, California

across. Because it so easily adapts to cultivation and grows with such abandon *G. longum* is one of the most commonly cultivated glottiphyllums. It has erect, tongue-shaped leaves 3 to 4 inches long by ¾ inch wide, with flat upper surfaces, and usually with pustular (warty) bases. The golden-yellow flowers, atop stalks 3 to 3½ inches long, are 2 to 3¼ inches wide.

One of the most unusual of the clan, *G. semicylindricum* has slender, curved, prostrate leaves that, except for being flattened somewhat at their sides and keeled at their apexes, are nearly cylindrical. They are up to 2 inches long by about ¼ inch in diameter, and have near their middles on their margins a pair of blunt tooth-like projections. The golden-yellow blooms are 1½ inches across. Another curious-looking kind is *G. depressum*. This has shoots with three or four pairs of two-ranked, prostrate leaves that sprawl in all directions. They are 3½ to 4 inches long by ¾ to 1 inch in diameter and have up-

Glottiphyllum depressum in South Africa

Glottiphyllum fragrans

Glottiphyllum latum

Glottiphyllum oligocarpum

turned tips. The yellow flowers are about 2¼ inches wide.

Other kinds included in choice collections are the following: *G. album* is distinguished by its white flowers. *G. armoedense* has glossy, fresh green, upcurving leaves in four distinct rows, those of each pair nearly equal in size, and almost 2 inches long by ¾ inch wide and ½ inch thick. The yellow blooms are almost or quite 2 inches across. *G. fragrans* has crowded, asymmetrically-tongue-shaped leaves 2 to 3 inches long or a little longer, 1 inch wide and ½ inch thick. Its flowers are stalkless, golden-yellow, and 3 to 4 inches in diameter. *G. herrei* has bluish-green or reddish leaves tending to be in four rows. Those of each pair are of unequal length. The longer one is incurved, about 2¼ inches long, by about 1 inch wide, somewhat under ½ inch thick, and compressed at the apex. The shorter leaf is spreading. The 3-inch-wide blooms are yellow. *G. latifolium* has light green leaves, slightly tinged with pink and speckled with dark, translucent dots. Those of each pair are unequal in length. The longer is about 3½ inches long by approximately 1½ inches wide, and up to ½ inch thick. The flowers are not known. *G. latum* has nearly stemless shoots with lustrous, straight or slightly curved, strap-shaped leaves in two ranks. The larger of each pair is 2 to 5 inches long and up to 1 inch wide. Their upper surfaces are flat or nearly so, their undersides are more or less rounded. The flowers, 1¾ to 2½ inches across, have bright yellow petals and deep yellow stamens. *G. oligocarpum* has prostrate stems with spreading, blunt, obscurely fine-hairy leaves, four to a shoot, in two rows, that look much like a cluster of pebbles. They are whitish-olive-green with, especially toward their tips, conspicuous dots, or are chalky-white. Of

Glottiphyllum regium

Glottiphyllum surrectum

unequal length, the biggest leaves are 1 inch to 1¾ inches long by one-half to two-thirds as wide as long, and somewhat less in depth. The smaller leaf of each pair is markedly rounded at the apex. The yellow blooms are about 2 inches across. *G. peersii* is remarkable for its erect, gray-green, often red-tinted leaves having white keels. One of each pair is nearly cylindrical and up to about 2 inches long, the other is triangular and under ½ inch long, its upper side hollowed or flat, its underside rounded. The bright yellow blooms are a little over 2 inches across. *G. regium* forms clumps of short shoots with pairs of erect to spreading leaves, the larger of each pair up to 6 inches long or longer. Their upper surfaces are flat to slightly concave, their undersides are rounded. From 2¼ to 2½ inches across, the flowers have golden-yellow petals and stamens with pale yellow stalks and orange-yellow anthers. *G. suave* is compact. It has bright green stems up to 4 inches long, and tongue- to strap-shaped leaves, not markedly spreading, up to 2 inches long, ¾ inch wide, and ⅓ inch thick. One leaf of each pair is decidedly keeled. The light yellow, stalkless blooms are about 2½ inches in diameter. *G. surrectum* has erect or spreading, awl-shaped to narrow-triangular leaves in four rows. Its flowers are yellow.

Garden and Landscape Uses and Cultivation. So long as they are not supplied with too much water glottiphyllums are among the easiest of the very fleshy members of the *Mesembryanthemum* relationship to grow. Excessive moisture soon results in rotting and complete disaster, or at best in the plants growing over-exuberantly and losing their characteristic forms. Only in warm, semidesert or desert climates can these plants be grown permanently outdoors. They are well adapted for inclusion in greenhouse collections of succulents and for sunny windows. As with all their relatives, excellent drainage and porous soil are essentials to success. Too generous treatment, not only in the application of water, but in the provision of rooting space and nutrients, is likely to produce specimens neither as beautiful nor as typical of their kinds as those raised under harsher conditions. Indoors, winter night temperatures of 45 to 50°F are adequate, with an increase of five to ten degrees by day permitted. Warmer environments at other seasons are in order, but always dry atmospheric conditions must be maintained. On all favorable occasions the greenhouse must be ventilated freely. The chief growing season is from about April to July. Then, watering is done moderately, less freely and with more caution at other seasons, and especially winter. Because glottiphyllums do not set seeds to their own pollen but produce them only after being fertilized with pollen from a plant of another seedling stock of the same or a different species, and because they hybridize readily, seeds from mixed collections, although they germinate well, are likely to result in progeny not truly representative of the seed parent. For the surest maintenance of true stocks rely for increase upon cuttings. These root with great ease in sand, perlite, or vermiculite.

GLOXINERA. See Sinningia.

GLOXINIA (Glox-ínia). The showy plants, commonly called gloxinias by gardeners and florists, belong to the genus *Sinningia* and are described under that name in this Encyclopedia. Their cultivation is discussed in the next entry, Gloxinias, Florists'. Quite distinct, although belonging to the same gesneria family GESNERIACEAE, is the botanists' genus *Gloxinia*, our concern here.

This consists of six species, natives of Central and tropical South America. Its name honors the eighteenth-century botanical author Benjamin Peter Gloxin.

Gloxinias are herbaceous perennials without tubers characteristic of sinningias. Instead, they have scaly rhizomes similar to those of *Achimenes*. Their long, leafy stems, erect or somewhat sprawling, have opposite, stalked leaves. Solitary or in groups of few from the leaf axils are borne quite large, nodding, bell-shaped blooms. These have a five-lobed calyx, a tubular corolla with five lobes (petals), four stamens, and one style. Encircling the ovary is a ringlike disk in place of five glands present in *Sinningia*. The fruits are capsules.

The only kind much known as a cultivated plant, and that less commonly than its merits deserve, is *G. perennis* (syn. *G. maculata*). This native of tropical South America, 1½ to 4 feet tall, has hairless, fleshy, often branched stems, usually

Gloxinia perennis

spotted with reddish-brown. Its long-stalked leaves, with blades 3 to 7 inches long by almost as wide as their lengths, and round-toothed or scalloped at their margins, are lustrous and slightly hairy above, paler and red or suffused with red on their undersides. Somewhat suggestive of those of Canterbury bells (*Campanula medium*), the mint-scented, bell-shaped blooms, solitary from the axils of the upper leaves and bracts, form in effect a terminal raceme. Densely-hairy on their outsides, they are 1 inch to 1½ inches long, and are soft lavender with a dark violet blotch at their bases inside. There is a patch of glandular hairs on the upper inside of the corolla. The lower petal differs from the others in being incurved, instead of spreading, and in having a toothed margin. The stamens do not protrude. The stigma is mouth-shaped. Native from Panama to Venezuela and Colombia, **G. pallidiflora** differs from *G. perennis* in having frailer stems without spots and smaller, paler blooms. Plants intermediate between it and *G. perennis* are not uncommon in cultivation.

Garden and Landscape Uses and Cultivation. In the humid tropics these are beautiful for lightly shaded places where the ground is rich in organic matter and during the growing season pleasantly moist. They are also handsome ornamentals for humid, warm greenhouses, blooming in late summer and fall. Coarse, rich soil that contains abundant humus is to their liking. Following a winter of complete dormancy in a dry condition the plants are removed from the old soil, repotted in a fresh mix, watered, and restarted into growth. They prosper under conditions that suit *Achimenes* and the florists' gloxinias (*Sinningia*). As growth necessitates, successive moves into larger containers are given during the season. Well-grown specimens from early starts may be finished in 8- or 9-inch pots. Attractive plants in 6-inch receptacles result from later starts. After the pots in which they are to flower are filled with healthy roots weekly applications of dilute liquid fertilizer are very helpful. When blooming is through the plants are gradually dried off and stored in the same way as achimenes and florists' gloxinias. Propagation is easy by division of the rhizomes, cuttings, leaf cuttings, and seeds.

GLOXINIAS, FLORISTS'. The plants discussed here do not belong in the botanical genus *Gloxinia*, dealt with in the previous entry, but rather in the related *Sinningia* of the gesneria family GESNERIACEAE. Among the most popular of summer-flowering tropical plants for growing in pots, they are admirable for embellishing greenhouses and conservatories and for employment as window plants. In favorable environments they produce a succession of handsome blooms over a period of many weeks.

Sinningia speciosa

Florists' gloxinias are horticultural derivatives of variable *Sinningia speciosa,* a native of Brazil introduced to England early in the nineteenth century. Characteristically they are deciduous perennials that have more or less globular tubers and usually short stems, although in some forms these may attain a length of 1 foot. The short-stalked, ovate to oblong-ovate, round-toothed, softly-hairy leaves are up to 8 inches long or longer and three-quarters as wide as their lengths. They have dark green upper surfaces and paler undersides.

Three chief types of these gloxinias are recognized, each including several to many varieties. Most popular is the Fyfiana group. Its sorts, the first raised in Scotland in 1845, have erect, up-facing,

Florists' gloxinias, three varieties of the Fyfiana group

Double-flowered florists' gloxinias of the Fyfiana group

Newly started plant of florists' gloxinia

symmetrical, bell- to bowl-shaped flowers that may be 3 inches long or longer and as wide and come in a broad range of colors, including lavender, blue, purple, pink, red, and mixtures of these, as well as in white. There are double- as well as single-flowered varieties. Varieties of the Maxima group, commonly called slipper gloxinias, the first of which originated in England in 1838, are less numerous than those of the Fyfiana group. From this group slipper gloxinias differ in having asymmetrical, decidedly nodding or pendulous, pink or white flowers. Also known as slipper gloxinias, the sorts of the Speciosa group are simply types of *Sinningia speciosa* as it occurs in the wild in its native Brazil. These are less showy than the sorts discussed above and appeal chiefly to collectors. In general they resemble varieties of the Maxima group but have smaller flowers, up to 1½ inches long, that are violet, red, or white with a red-spotted band of white or yellow within the corolla.

Cultivation. Gloxinias are not difficult to grow. They can easily be raised from seeds and propagated from leaf cuttings, or they may be started from tubers which are readily obtainable in late winter and spring from dealers in seeds, bulbs, and plants.

The chief concern is the provision of a favorable environment. This means suitable soil, a constant temperature of 65°F or higher, high humidity without the air being oppressively humid, and good light with a little shade from strong, direct sun. Be sure the soil contains about 50 percent leaf mold, peat moss, or other acceptable decayed organic material. The remainder of the mix should consist of equal parts of loamy topsoil and perlite or coarse sand, with a little dried cow or sheep manure and a sprinkling of bonemeal added. The finished mix should be slightly acidic.

If you begin with tubers either saved from the previous year or newly purchased, plant them in late winter or spring 2 to 3

inches apart in pots or flats of peat moss, leaf mold, or perlite so that they are barely covered. Keep them just moist in a temperature of 65 to 70°F. When new shoots are about 1 inch long and leaves begin to develop, pot the plants separately in well-drained 5- or 6-inch pots, setting them with the tops of their tubers level with the soil surface and about ¾ inch below the rim of the pot. Water rather cautiously at first without ever allowing the soil to dry out. Later, when roots have pervaded the soil, water more freely but avoid a constantly saturated condition. When flower buds begin to form begin applying dilute liquid fertilizer twice weekly but discontinue this after the blooms open. Maintain agreeable atmospheric humidity by frequently wetting down greenhouse paths and benches, but at all times avoid wetting the foliage. When the blooms open, their life span is increased if a somewhat cooler, airier atmosphere is maintained than during the main growing period.

After blooming ceases and the dormant season approaches, gradually increase the periods between waterings and eventually withhold water completely. Then, after the foliage has died, store the plants in the soil in which they grew by laying the pots on

After blooming, rest florists' gloxinias by storing them in a dry place

their sides beneath a greenhouse bench, in a cellar, or in some similar place where the temperature is 50 to 55°F.

To raise gloxinias from seeds, sow in February or March in well-drained pots or seed pans in a finely-sifted mix of equal parts of peat moss or leaf mold and sand or perlite. After pressing the mix into place and making its surface level, moisten the mix by immersing the containers nearly to their rims in water. Allow them to drain, and then scatter the seeds thinly over the surface and spread a little fine sand over them. Cover with a pane of glass or polyethylene film but do not shade with paper, as is often done with seeds of other plants. Gloxinia seeds germinate better in light than in darkness, but exposure to strong sun is harmful. As soon as the seedlings are visible remove the glass or polyethylene and, when the second pair of leaves has developed, transplant them individually to 2½-inch pots. Later, as growth suggests, repot them into 4-inch pots. Many will produce a few blooms in late summer but it will not be until the second year, following a winter of dormancy, before they give of their best.

Propagation by cuttings is easily achieved. Remove new shoots 1 inch to 2 inches long from started tubers by cutting them off with a sharp knife and planting in a greenhouse propagating case or pot containing perlite or coarse sand mixed with peat moss. Keep the cuttings in close, humid conditions until they have developed roots 1 inch to 2 inches long, then pot them separately in small pots. Leaf cuttings afford a ready means of propagation. Make these in summer from mature leaves. Cut across the junctions of the main veins on the undersides of the leaves and anchor the leaves to a bed of peat moss and sand by weighting them with small stones or pinning them with pieces of wire bent like hairpins. Alternatively, cut the leaves into wedge-shaped pieces, with the stem of the leaf forming the point of the wedge, and plant these at a slight angle, with their bases 1 inch beneath the surface, in a mixture of peat moss and perlite or sand.

Leaf cuttings: (a) Making the cuttings

(b) Planting the cuttings

Glyceria maxima variegata

Yet another method of propagation is to cut tubers that have been started into growth in spring into pieces, making sure that each piece has one or more shoots. After dusting the cut surfaces with powdered sulfer or ferbam, plant each piece separately in a small pot and, when that becomes filled with roots, in a larger one.

Diseases and Pests. The most serious diseases of these plants are rots resulting from excessive wetness of the soil and poor drainage. The most common pests are mites, thrips, and mealybugs.

GLYCERIA (Gly-cèria)—Manna Grass, Reed Meadow Grass. The twenty or more species of manna grasses (Glyceria) mostly inhabit cool parts of the northern hemisphere; some occur in South America, Australia, and New Zealand. Their name is derived from the Greek glykeros, sweet. It refers to the taste of the grains (seeds) of some kinds. Glycerias belong in the grass family GRAMINEAE. They occur in wet soils and shallow water.

Glycerias have rhizomes or creeping rooting bases to their stems. At first folded, the leaf blades flatten as they develop. The flower panicles, loose or dense, consist of many-flowered, stalked spikelets without awns (bristles).

The reed meadow grass (**G. grandis**), indigenous from Quebec and Nova Scotia to Virginia and westward across the continent, has clusters of erect stout stems up to 5 feet tall, and narrow leaves up to 1 foot long. Its loosely-branched flower panicles, with usually nodding apexes, are 8 inches to 1¼ feet long. The spikelets, five- to nine-flowered, are about ¼ inch long. European reed sweet grass (**G. maxima** syn. **G. aquatica**), a native of Europe and temperate Asia, has stout, erect stems 3 to 8 feet high, narrow leaves 1 foot to 2 feet long, and loose to rather compact, freely-branched, green or purplish flower panicles 6 inches to 1½ feet long. The spikelets are ¼ to ½ inch in length and four- to ten-flowered. In variety **G. m. variegata** (in gardens sometimes named **G. aquatica foliis-**

variegatis), the leaves are striped with white or cream.

Garden and Landscape Uses and Cultivation. The kinds described, the seeds of which are favorite foods of birds, are sometimes planted for decoration at watersides and in wet places. Provided the soil is always moderately moist, G. m. variegata will grow under ordinary flower border conditions. These grasses need no special care. They are propagated by seeds and division, the latter method being the only one applicable to the variegated-leaved variety.

GLYCINE (Glycì-ne)—Soybean. The soybean (Glycine max) is extensively cultivated as an agricultural crop for animal and human food, oil, and commercial uses. It has little horticultural importance except as a green manure, a cover crop to be turned under to enrich the soil. The soybean belongs to a genus of ten species of twining or erect plants of the pea family LEGUMINOSAE, natives of the tropics of the Old World. They have leaves with usually three, occasionally five or seven, leaflets. The white, pink, or purplish, pea-like flowers, in racemes from the leaf axils, are of no ornamental merit. The fruits are pods usually with constrictions between the few seeds.

Not known as a wild plant, the soybean (**G. max**) is perhaps derived from G. hispida, of eastern Asia. It is an erect, hairy annual, 2 to 6 feet tall, with usually some of its shoots vinelike, and having leaves with three leaflets. The white to purplish blooms, in racemes of five to eight, are succeeded by narrow, hairy seed pods generally with constrictions between the seeds. The name Glycine comes from one applied by the ancient Greeks to some other plant and is derived from glykys, sweet.

GLYCOSMIS (Gly-cósmis). The fragrance of the flowers, and of the leaves when crushed, give reason for the name Glycosmis, which is derived from the Greek glykys, sweet, and osme, a smell. A genus of

the rue family RUTACEAE, it consists of about sixty species, natives of Indomalaya.

These are evergreen shrubs or trees with alternate or nearly opposite, smooth-edged or vaguely round-toothed, leathery leaves, undivided or of an uneven number of pinnately-arranged leaflets. The small, fragrant, white flowers are in axillary or more rarely terminal panicles. Urn-shaped, they have five each sepals and petals and ten stamens. The fruits are small berries, those of some sorts edible.

An attractive kind naturalized on Key West, Florida, **G. parviflora** (syn. G. citrifolia), of southern China, Indochina, and Thailand, is a shrub or small tree up to 12 feet in height with green branches and alternate leaves of one leaflet and others with three or perhaps occasionally more on the same plant. The leaflets are elliptic with tapered ends, 3 to 8 inches long. The tiny flowers are in terminal and axillary clusters 1 inch to 2 inches long. Their calyx lobes are densely fringed with hairs, their petals are obovate. They have stamens with broad, white, club-shaped stalks and yellow anthers. The fruits, the juicy flesh of which is edible and has a sweet, carrot-like flavor, are semitransparent and orange-pink; they look like big, colored mistletoe berries. Each contains one or two large brown, orange-veined seeds. Ranging as a native from India to the Philippine Islands and Australia, **G. pentaphylla,**

Glycosmis pentaphylla

sometimes called the Jamaica mandarin-orange, is a shrub or small tree with leaves of five or fewer elliptic to ovate or obovate leaflets up to 4½ inches long, with pale undersides. From 1 inch to 1½ inches long, the clusters of white or pinkish flowers are rusty-hairy. The fruits are white to pinkish.

Garden and Landscape Uses and Cultivation. These are good-looking general purpose shrubs for the humid tropics and warm, moist subtropics. They are also worth growing as ornamentals in tropical greenhouses. Their fruits remain decorative for a long time. They are easy to grow in well-drained, reasonably fertile, moderately moist soil and are propagated by cuttings inserted in spring or early summer in a greenhouse propagating bench with mild bottom heat. Seeds provide an alternative means of increase. In greenhouses repotting is done in late winter or early spring, and any needed pruning to shape is done at that time too. In summer some shade from the strongest sun is appreciated.

GLYCYRRHIZA (Gly-cyrrhìza) — Licorice. Belonging to the pea family LEGUMINOSAE, this genus of temperate and subtropical America, Europe, Asia, North Africa, and Australia, comprises about fifteen species of herbaceous perennials and subshrubs. Its chief product, licorice, derived commercially from the underground rootlike stems and roots of *G. glabra*, and contained in other species, is used for flavoring candies, tobacco, and the beverages stout and porter, and in some kinds of fire extinguishers. It was well known to the Ancients, and was discussed by Theophrastus and named by Dioscorides. The name comes from the Greek *glykys*, sweet, and *rhiza*, a root, and alludes to the flavor of the rootlike subterranean stems.

Glycyrrhizas have pinnate leaves with uneven numbers of leaflets, and small pea-shaped white, yellow, violet, or blue flowers in dense, stalked or stalkless axillary racemes. Usually the stamens are joined in their lower halves in two groups. The fruits are few-seeded, glandular or spiny pods, slightly flattened or somewhat inflated.

Licorice (*G. glabra*), native from southern Europe to central Asia, is a coarse, hardy, very deep-rooting herbaceous perennial 2 to 3 feet tall that has leaves with nine to seventeen blunt, elliptical to oblongish leaflets. Its pale blue flowers, in stalked spikes shorter than the leaves, are borne in summer and fall. The pods are nearly or quite hairless and about 1 inch long. This species has become established as an escape from cultivation in some parts of California.

Wild licorice (*G. lepidota*) inhabits much of North America from Mexico to Canada. A coarse herbaceous perennial up to about 3½ feet tall, its stems are minutely-hairy to sticky. Its leaves have eleven to nineteen oblong or lanceolate leaflets. Those of the main leaves are 1 inch to 2 inches in length, those of side branches are smaller. In short racemes the pale yellow, ½-inch-long flowers are crowded. The pods, about as long as the flowers, are thickly clothed with hooked, bristly hairs.

Garden and Landscape Uses and Cultivation. Except for inclusion in collections of hardy plants used commercially licorice has little to recommend it to gardeners. Wild licorice may occasionally be included in plantings of native plants. For their best success these plants need deep, moist, fertile ground and sunny locations. Propagation is by seed.

GLYPTOPLEURA (Glypto-pleùra). One of two species of small annuals or biennials that compose this western North American genus of the daisy family COMPOSITAE may be cultivated. The name, from the Greek *glyptos*, carved, and *pleura*, side, alludes to the fruits.

These are low, compact, rosette plants with pinnately-lobed, white-edged leaves and many short-stalked, white or yellowish flower heads. The fruits are seedlike achenes.

Common in sandy soils in parts of California, Utah, and Arizona, *Glyptopleura setulosa* is very pretty. It has deeply-lobed, very short-stalked leaves up to 2 inches long, and creamy to lemon-yellow flower heads 1½ to 2 inches in diameter, with spreading petal-like florets.

Garden Uses and Cultivation. Little is recorded about the cultivation of this quite charming species. It may be expected to accommodate to sunny locations in sandy well-drained soil and would make a pretty plant for rock gardens. In regions of mild winters the seeds should be sown outdoors in late summer where the plants are to remain. Elsewhere sowing in very early spring would be worth trying.

GLYPTOSTROBUS (Glyptostrò-bus). One small tree of southern China is the only member of *Glyptostrobus*. It is similar to the swamp-cypress (*Taxodium*) and belongs in the taxodium family TAXODIACEAE. Like the swamp-cypress, it is one of few deciduous conifers, the others are dawn-redwood (*Metasequoia*), larch (*Larix*), and golden-larch (*Pseudolarix*). The name *Glyptostrobus* is derived from the Greek *glypto*, to carve, and *strobilos*, a cone. It alludes to the cones. This genus differs from *Taxodium* chiefly in its comparatively long-stalked cones and in their scales being elongated rather than rounded.

In the province of Canton, *G. lineatus* (syn. *G. pensilis*) grows along stream banks and in other damp places. It is believed, however, to have survived through the efforts of man. The Chinese plant it near their homes and rice fields in the belief that it brings good fortune. It is not known as truly wild anywhere. Apparently, it is a relic of vegetation now extinct as part of any spontaneous native flora. This tree attains a height of 50 feet or perhaps more and has somewhat pendulous lower branches. It has the delicate, feathery appearance of the swamp-cypresses and, as with them, its foliage in fall turns warm golden-brown before it drops. It has two kinds of shoots, persistent ones that are chiefly terminal and have axillary buds, and short, deciduous branchlets without buds in their leaf axils that drop with their leaves attached in fall. The leaves of the persistent shoots are small, scalelike, overlapping, and are arranged spirally around the shoots. Those of the deciduous branchlets are narrowly-linear, up to ½ inch long, and disposed in three rows. The cones are only on persistent shoots. They are ovoid or pear-shaped, ¾ to 1 inch long and about one-half as wide, on stalks ½ inch long or longer.

Garden and Landscape Uses and Cultivation. Not hardy in the north, *Glyptostrobus* can be cultivated successfully in the southern part of the United States and in other regions of mild winters. It is essentially a tree for special collections and for those interested in rare and unusual plants. It succeeds in any ordinary garden soil that is not dry, in full sun. The recommended means of propagation is by seeds sown in sandy peaty soil kept evenly moist. For additional information see Conifers.

GMELINA (Gmel-ìna)—Snapdragon-Tree. Asian, African, and Australian trees and shrubs constitute this genus of thirty-five species of the vervain family VERBENACEAE. The name *Gmelina* commemorates a German naturalist, J. Gottlieb Gmelin.

Gmelinas are spiny or not, have opposite leaves and racemes or panicles of yel-

Glycyrrhiza glabra   *Glycyrrhiza glabra* (foliage and fruits)

low or brownish, asymmetrical, two-lipped, tubular flowers each with a bell-shaped, five-toothed or toothless calyx, four or five petals, and four stamens in two pairs. The fruits are berry-like.

Sometimes called snapdragon-tree, *G. arborea,* of India and Malaya, deciduous and broad-headed, is up to 60 feet tall. Its young parts are covered with white pubescence. Its long-stalked, ovate-heart-shaped, pointed leaves up to 9 inches long are woolly on their undersides. Often the leaves of young specimens are toothed, but those of older trees are smooth-edged. The 1-foot-long panicles of snapdragon-like flowers, displayed when the trees are leafless or nearly so, come from the branch ends. The brownish to orange color of the fragrant blooms is that of four of the petals, a fifth bright yellow one is partly concealed. Orange-yellow and egg- or pear-shaped, the fruits are ¾ to 1 inch long. In India they are eaten. Their juice stains the fingers yellow. In its native lands deer browse the foliage of this tree and it is used as fodder for domestic animals.

From India and Ceylon comes *G. asiatica* (syn. *G. elliptica*). An often thorny shrub, this has lobeless or three-lobed, ovate to obovate leaves 2 to 4 inches long, and racemes up to 2 inches long of scentless yellow flowers about 1½ inches long. The ¾-inch-long fruits are yellow.

Garden and Landscape Uses and Cultivation. Only in climates as uniformly warm as those of southern Florida, southern California, and Hawaii can the trees and shrubs described above be expected to prosper. They stand little frost. Tall *G. arborea* is a fast grower, recommended as a street and shade tree. The bushy kind is useful as a shrub and hedge plant. Both thrive in ordinary soil in sun. Propagation is by seed.

GNAPHALIUM (Gnaph-àlium). Of nearly cosmopolitan distribution in the wild, *Gnaphalium,* of the daisy family COMPOSITAE, comprises about 200 species. The name, derived from the Greek *gnaphalon,* a lock of wool, alludes to foliage characteristics of some kinds. These plants are sometimes called cudweed.

Gnaphaliums are annuals, biennials, and herbaceous perennials. They have alternate, undivided leaves and flower heads of small, whitish or yellowish disk florets (the kind that form the eyes of daisies) without surrounding petal-like ray florets. The outer florets are female and slender, the inner ones coarser and bisexual. The fruits are seedlike achenes. For *G. lanatum* see *Helichrysum petiolatum.*

Annual or biennial *G. viscosum* (syn. *G. decurrens*) is up to 3 feet tall. Its more or less glandular stems are woolly-hairy for their entire lengths or at least in their flowering parts. The lanceolate leaves, up to 3 inches long and with white-woolly under-

sides, have blades continued as wings down the stems. The ¼-inch-wide flower heads are in panicles of clusters that terminate branches from the upper leaf axils. Similar *G. obtusifolium* differs chiefly in its leaves, which when crushed smell faintly of lemon, narrowing to their bases instead of reaching down the stems as wings. Both species are widely distributed in North America. Quite different, and native of damp soils in western North America, *G. palustre* is an annual, usually much branched from the base, and 2 to 8 inches or occasionally 1 foot tall. Loosely clothed with woolly hairs, it has, except for those associated with the flower heads, which are oblong or lanceolate, spatula-shaped leaves up to 2 inches long.

Perennial *G. sylvaticum* has branchless stems up to 2 feet tall. Their upper parts are slender, spikelike spires of yellowish flower heads with a brown spot on some or all of the bracts of the involucre (collar surrounding the florets). This inhabits woods and open places in high northern latitudes in America, Europe, and Asia.

Garden and Landscape Uses and Cultivation. Except for inclusion in gardens of native plants and for naturalizing in semi-wild areas gnaphaliums make little appeal. They are easy to grow, and are raised from seeds, or the perennials by division. The kinds described above are hardy.

GNIDIA (Gníd-ia). The 100 species of *Gnidia,* of the mezereum family THYMELAE-ACEAE, are inhabitants of Africa, chiefly

South Africa, Madagascar, Arabia, India, and Ceylon. The name, an ancient Greek one for the laurel (*Laurus*), is an adaptation of that of the town Gnidus in Crete.

These are evergreen shrubs, often of heathlike aspect, with opposite or alternate, usually small leaves and white, yellow, or less often red or violet flowers generally in terminal, stalked or stalkless heads or spikes, but sometimes solitary in the leaf axils. The blooms have a cylindrical, four- or five-lobed calyx, four, five, eight, or twelve smaller scalelike petals, eight or ten stamens, and a slender style. The dry fruits are enclosed in the persistent bases of the calyxes.

A graceful native of South Africa, *G. polystachya* (syn. *G. carinata*) is 4 to 7 feet tall. It has hairy shoots and alternate, hairless, linear leaves ¼ to ½ inch long by about 1/16 inch wide. Freely produced, the little yellow blooms are in densely-crowded, 1-inch-wide clusters.

Garden and Landscape Uses and Cultivation. The species described is a quite pretty all-purpose shrub for climates such as that of California. It prospers in sunny locations in ordinary well-drained soil. Propagation is by seeds and by cuttings.

GOA-BEAN is *Psophocarpus tetragonolobus.*

GOAT NUT is *Simmondsia chinensis.*

GOAT'S BEARD. This is a common name applied to *Aruncus* and to *Tragopogon pratensis.*

Gnidia polystachya

GOAT'S-RUE. This common name is used for *Galega officinalis* and *Tephrosia virginiana*.

GODETIA. See Clarkia.

GOETHEA (Goè-thea). A member of the mallow family MALVACEAE and closely related to *Pavonia*, Brazilian *Goethea* consists of five species. Its name compliments the German poet Johann Wolfgang von Goethe, who died in 1832.

Goetheas are evergreen shrubs with alternate, distantly-toothed or toothless leaves. They bear along the leafless portions of their stems and close to them numerous flowers that have usually six or sometimes fewer, pink or red, petal-like bracts enclosing the five-cleft calyx. There are five short petals and a column of united stamens. The style is ten-branched. The fruits are carpels.

Its stems erect and up to about 9 feet tall, *G. strictiflora* has short-stalked, distantly-toothed, ovate to broad-elliptic leaves approximately 6 inches long by nearly one-half as wide. When young they are minutely-hairy on their undersides. The abundant flowers have erect, 1-inch-long, pointed-heart-shaped strawberry-red and yellowish bracts.

Goethea strictiflora

Garden and Landscape Uses and Cultivation. The species described is attractive for outdoors in the tropics and subtropics, including southern Florida, and for growing in tropical greenhouses. It succeeds in ordinary soil in part-shade and makes an unusual and interesting ornamental. In greenhouses a winter night temperature of 55 to 60°F is appropriate with a daytime rise of five to fifteen degrees permitted. A humid atmosphere from spring to fall and shade from strong sun are requisite. In winter drier atmospheric conditions are in order and the soil should also be kept somewhat drier than at other seasons. Re-

potting is done in late winter. Well-established specimens benefit from fertilizing regularly through the summer. Propagation is easy by cuttings, air layering, and seeds.

GOLD and GOLDEN. As parts of the common names of plants these words are used in the following: basket-of-gold or golden-tuft (*Aurinia saxatilis*), gold crest (*Lophiola americana*), gold dust tree (*Aucuba japonica variegata*), gold fern (*Pityrogramma chrysophylla*), golden alexanders (*Zizia*), golden-aster (*Chrysopsis* and *Heterotheca subaxillaris*), golden barrel cactus (*Echinocactus grusonii*), golden bells (*Emmenanthe* and *Forsythia*), golden chain (*Laburnum*), golden currant (*Ribes aureum*), golden dewdrop (*Duranta repens*), golden drop (*Onosma echioides*), golden eardrops (*Dicentra chrysantha*), golden eggs (*Oenothera ovata*), golden-eyed-grass (*Sisyrinchium californicum*), golden feather (*Chrysanthemum parthenium aureum*), golden fleece (*Dyssodia tenuiloba*), golden glow (*Rudbeckia laciniata hortensia*), golden groundsel or golden ragwort (*Senecio aureus*), golden hedge-hyssop (*Gratiola aurea*), golden-larch (*Pseudolarix kaempferi*), golden-marguerite (*Anthemis tinctoria*), golden-rain tree (*Koelreuteria paniculata*), golden-saxifrage (*Chrysosplenium*), golden shower (*Cassia fistula*), golden star (*Chrysogonum*, *Hypoxis hygrometrica*, and *Triteleia ixioides*), golden stars (*Bloomeria*), golden top (*Lamarckia aurea*), golden wave (*Coreopsis basalis*), golden weather glass (*Hypoxis hygrometrica*), golden-yellow-hawkweed (*Tolpis barbata*), and Queensland gold blossom tree (*Barklya syringifolia*).

GOLDBACHIA (Gold-báchia). Botanists recognize half a dozen species of hairless annuals as composing this Asian genus of the mustard family CRUCIFERAE. One may occasionally be cultivated. The generic name commemorates the German botanist Karl Ludwig Goldbach, who died in 1824.

Goldbachias have undivided leaves, the upper ones stem-clasping. The white to purple flowers have four sepals, four petals spreading in the form of a cross, four long and two shorter stamens, and a short style ending in a two-lobed stigma. The seed pods are segmented (sometimes consisting of only one section) with one seed in each segment.

A semidesert species, *Goldbachia laevigata* is native of southeast Russia and central and southwest Asia. From 4 inches to 1 foot or a little more in height, perhaps more in cultivation, it has oblong to obovate leaves, those at the base stalked. The violet flowers, under ½ inch across, are in long racemes. The four-sided seed pods, markedly constricted between the seeds, are mostly of two or three segments.

Garden Uses and Cultivation. Of minor importance horticulturally, this species

may be planted in flower borders and informal areas. A sunny site and well-drained soil are needed. Propagation is by seeds sown in spring where the plants are to remain. The seedlings are thinned so that they do not unduly crowd each other.

GOLDEN FLEECE is *Dyssodia tenuiloba*.

GOLDENROD. See Solidago.

GOLDENSEAL is *Hydrastis canadensis*.

GOLDFIELDS is *Lasthenia chrysostoma*.

GOLDILOCKS is *Aster linosyris*.

GOLDTHREAD. See Coptis.

GOMESA (Go-mèsa). Brazil is home to all twelve species of *Gomesa*. So far as is known none in the wild crosses its boundaries. These are attractive tree-perchers (epiphytes) of the orchid family ORCHIDACEAE. They are related to *Oncidium*. Their name pays tribute to a Portuguese naval surgeon, Bernardino Gomez, who wrote about Brazilian plants. He died in 1803.

Gomesas have pseudobulbs with one to three leaves, and from their bases arching or pendulous stalks with racemes of many fragrant, interestingly-shaped, long-lasting, pale yellow, greenish-yellow or white blooms.

Most commonly cultivated, *G. crispa*, *G. planifolia*, and *G. recurva* are similar in habit, and have flowers about ¾ inch across, with spreading sepals and petals. They have close clusters of flattened, oblong pseudobulbs 2 to 4 inches tall each usually with a pair of strap-shaped, softish leaves that may be 8 or 9 inches long by 1 inch to 1½ inches wide or a little wider. The flowers of *G. crispa,* in gracefully arching racemes about 8 inches long, have wavy, widespreading sepals and petals, the lateral sepals united at their bases. The lip has two blunt keels at its base. The ra-

Gomesa crispa

Gomesa planifolia

Gomesa recurva

cemes of *G. planifolia,* up to about 10 inches long, arch pleasingly. The flowers are about as large as those of *G. crispa,* but have less wavy sepals and petals, and the side sepals are joined for two-thirds of their lengths. More crowded racemes of flowers about 1 inch wide are produced by *G. recurva,* which has nonwavy sepals and petals.

Garden Uses and Cultivation. Gomesias require conditions and care suitable for tropical oncidiums. They may be grown in pots or hanging baskets or on slabs of tree fern. For more information see Orchids.

GOMPHOLOBIUM (Gompho-lòbium) — The common name wedge-pea is applied in Australia to this genus of which there are about twenty-five species, all except one, in New Guinea, native to Australia. It belongs in the pea family LEGUMINOSAE. Its botanical name, from the Greek *gomphos,* club, and *lobos,* a pod, alludes to the club-shaped fruits.

Gompholobiums are small- to medium-sized, upright, evergreen shrubs with alternate leaves that are pinnate or consist of three or five leaflets that spread from a common base. Often large, the yellow to reddish-orange, pea-shaped blooms are solitary or in racemes. They are succeeded by inflated, bladder-like, nearly spherical or ovoid pods containing several seeds.

The golden glory wedge-pea (*G. latifolium*), perhaps the finest of its genus, has soft, very shortly stalked, hairless leaves each with three slender, flat leaflets 1 inch to 2 inches long. The brilliant light to deep yellow blooms, with fringed keels, are freely produced. They are 1½ inches in

diameter and solitary in the axils of the upper leaves. The upper or standard petal is 1½ inches wide, the lateral ones 1 inch long. The large wedge-pea (*G. grandiflorum*) is erect, up to about 3 feet tall, and has leaves with three narrow-linear leaflets. Its large yellow blooms, solitary or in twos or threes, are on short lateral shoots or are terminal on the branches. The bright yellow standard petal, ¾ inch long by twice as wide, is deeply notched at its apex. The lateral petals are smaller.

Garden Uses and Cultivation. For warm-temperate climates approximating that of southern California these shrubs are adaptable for sunny, well-drained locations. They are also sometimes cultivated in cool greenhouses. When well grown they are very beautiful in bloom. They require the same treatment as *Chorizema,* but are less easy to satisfy. Great care must be taken that the soil is never excessively wet for long periods or that it ever dries out. Propagation is by seeds, which should be prepared for sowing by pouring boiling water over them and allowing them to soak for twelve to twenty-four hours. Sow in a sandy peaty soil in a temperature of 60 to 65°F. Cuttings made in spring from moderately firm shoots may be rooted in a greenhouse propagating bench.

GOMPHRENA (Gom-phrèna) — Globe-Amaranth. Of the approximately 100 species of this genus of annuals and perennial herbaceous plants of the amaranth family AMARANTHACEAE, only one, the globe-amaranth (*Gomphrena globosa*), is commonly cultivated. Two or three others may be occasionally grown. The group is

chiefly a native of the American tropics and that is where the globe-amaranth probably originated, although its native habitat is not surely known. The name *Gomphrena* is derived from an ancient one for the amaranth (*Amaranthus*).

Gomphrenas are prostrate or erect hairy plants with opposite, undivided, lobeless leaves and bisexual flowers generally in stalked heads that are chaffy and of an "everlasting" character. Sometimes there is an involucre (collar) of bracts at the base of the flower head. The tiny flowers are five-parted. The fruits are small; technically they are utricles.

The globe-amaranth (*G. globosa*) is a bushy, erect, stiffish plant 1 foot to 2 feet tall, with oblong to ovate leaves 2 to 4 inches long, fringed at their margins with hairs. The heads of bloom have the gen-

Gomphrena globosa

eral appearance of those of clover and typically are brilliant amaranthine red-violet, but in garden varieties vary to slightly dingy-white, orange, pink, or red. Nearly globose and about 1 inch in diameter, the flower heads have two leafy bracts at their bases. They remain attractive for a very long period. Although not as crispy papery as most "everlastings," they may be dried and used as such. The name *G. g. nana* is applied to kinds that do not exceed 8 or 9 inches in height.

Other species that may be occasionally cultivated include *G. decumbens,* a sprawling annual from the warmer parts of North and South America that has oblong to oval leaves and globose flower heads with, at their bases, two white, winglike bracts. Attaining a height of about 2½ feet, *G. haageana* is truly a tender perennial, but may be and usually is treated as an annual. Native to Texas and Mexico, it is erect and has narrow, pointed-lanceolate leaves and bright yellow globular flower heads each about 1 inch in diameter. There are two light colored bracts to each head.

Garden Uses. The globe-amaranth is a very useful annual for outdoor beds and window and porch boxes; it can also be grown in pots as a summer-blooming ornamental. It blooms continuously for a long season and revels in hot weather. The flowers are useful for cutting. If they are to be used as everlastings they should be cut with long stems just before the heads reach their greatest maturity, be tied in small bundles, and be hung upside down in an airy, shady place to dry. The other species mentioned have similar uses, although neither is as compact or as neat in its habit of growth.

Cultivation. Globe-amaranths and other species of *Gomphrena* are raised from seeds. These may be sown directly outdoors as soon as the ground has warmed a little in spring, but a better and more usual procedure, especially in the north, is to sow seeds indoors some ten weeks before the young plants are to be transplanted to their flowering stations, which may be done when it is safe to set out geraniums, peppers, and other tender plants. In a temperature of 60 to 65°F the seeds germinate in ten or twelve days and the seedlings, as soon as they have developed their second pair of leaves, are spaced about 2 inches apart in well-drained flats of fertile porous soil. They are kept growing in a sunny greenhouse in a minimum night temperature of 60°F, this may rise five to fifteen degrees by day. For a week or two prior to planting them in the garden they should be hardened by standing them in a cold frame or sheltered spot outdoors. Spacing outdoors may be about 1 foot between individual plants of the globe-amaranth, slightly more between those of *G. haageana,* and up to 3 feet between plants of *G. decumbens.* These plants need full sun and a

fairly deep fertile soil that does not dry excessively. Summer care consists of weeding, and watering in dry weather. No staking is required.

GONGORA (Gon-gòra)—Punch and Judy Orchid. Gongoras are epiphytes (tree-perching plants that do not absorb nourishment from the trees they inhabit), natives from Mexico to Brazil and Peru. They belong in the orchid family ORCHIDACEAE. There are twenty species. The name commemorates a Bishop of Cordova, Spain, Don Antonio Cabellero y Gongora, who died in 1818.

These orchids have clusters of ovoid, conspicuously ridged pseudobulbs with, from the apex of each pseudobulb, two or sometimes one or three broad, longitudinally-pleated leaves much resembling those of the related genus *Stanhopea.* Often there are many aerial roots. The flowers are in loose, pendulous racemes, at times exceeding 3 feet in length, from the bases of the pseudobulbs. The racemes are of few to many often quite fantastically formed, interestingly colored, fragrant blooms, generally not over 2 inches wide. Unlike those of most orchids, the flowers commonly have their lips uppermost. Usually the sepals are slender, the lateral pair often strongly reflexed. The dorsal sepal, the one opposite the lip, is often smaller than the others. It is partly joined to the column. The petals, attached to the column, are frequently hornlike lobes, the central one pouched, or platelike and held vertically.

Gongora truncata

Mexican *G. truncata* has very short pseudobulbs. Its pendulous racemes of flowers, up to somewhat over 2 feet long, are of blooms nearly 2 inches wide, whitish and freely blotched with red. The lip is yellowish. The arching column is white spotted with red. Mexican *G. galeata* has light brown flowers with pointed, broad-ovate sepals, and a red lip. The blooms, usually under 2 inches wide, with gracefully arched

individual stalks, are in racemes 6 to 8 inches long. The pseudobulbs are about 1¾ inches long, the leaves up to about 1 foot in length by under 2 inches wide. The blooms of *G. armeniaca,* of Central America, are yellow to orange-yellow or light salmon, with some red spots and bars on the reflexed sepals. The large, fleshy lip is usually deeper colored than the other parts. The petals are minute. Similar in growth to the last, *G. cassidea,* of Central America, has loose racemes of greenish-brown to pinkish-brown flowers; the lips, usually of a brighter hue than the sepals and petals, are about 2 inches wide. The lip ends in two lobes. More robust than most gongoras, *G. quinquenervis,* of northern South America and Trinidad, has pseudobulbs 3 inches long and leaves up to 1½ feet long by 4 inches wide. The flowers, usually 2 inches or more in diameter, are in racemes that may be 2 feet long. The blooms are usually bright yellow more or less spotted with dark red. The lip is shorter than the lateral sepals. Some species previously included in *Gongora* are described under Coryanthes.

Garden Uses and Cultivation. Interesting plants for orchid fanciers, gongoras thrive outdoors in the tropics and in warm, humid greenhouses. They need essentially the same conditions and care as *Stanhopea,* and like members of that genus need a short period of dormancy in a somewhat lower temperature, during which time they are not watered, after the season's growth is mature. They are best accommodated in hanging baskets or in pans (shallow pots) suspended from the greenhouse roof. For more information see Stanhopea and Orchids.

GONIOLIMON (Gonio-límon). This genus of the plumbago family PLUMBAGINACEAE differs from closely related *Limonium,* with which by some authorities it is united, in the stigmas of its flowers being subspherical and headlike instead of slender-cylindrical. Like limoniums, its members are often known in gardens by the botanically discarded name *Statice.* There are twenty species of *Goniolimon,* natives from North Africa to Mongolia. The name comes from the Greek *gonia,* an angle, and *leimon,* a meadow. It alludes to the angled flower stems, and the habitats of some species.

Goniolimons are herbaceous perennials sometimes with short, woody stems. They have fairly broad, rather fleshy leaves in basal rosettes. The flower stems terminate in panicles of spikelets of two to six small blooms. Each flower has a persistent, funnel-shaped, papery, five-lobed, white calyx, five petals rarely as much as one-half as long again as the calyx, separate except at their very bases, but their lower parts overlapping to form a tube, their apexes shallowly notched, five stamens, their stalks dilated below, and five separate styles. The one-seeded, dry fruits are enclosed in the calyx.

Commonly occupying chalky or saline soils from eastern Europe to the Caucasus, *G. tataricum* (syns. *Limonium tataricum*, *Statice tatarica*) is 1 foot to 1½ feet tall. Its many, pale green, hairless, usually broad-lanceolate leaves have blades generally 4 to 6 inches long by 1 inch wide, sometimes smaller or bigger. They taper gradually to long stalks and end in a short, sharp point. The erect, strongly-angled flower stalks are more than twice-branched. The branches are rather broadly-winged and hairless or nearly so. The corollas of the blooms are violet.

From the last, *G. eximium* differs in its flower stalks being not more than twice-branched, the branches without wings and hairy. The leathery, hairless leaves have usually wavy margins and a brief point at the apex. Their blades are broad-lanceolate to obovate, up to 5 inches long by almost one-half as wide, gradually tapering into long stalks. The lilac-rose to violet flowers are in dense heads at the ends of the more or less recurved branches of the panicles. About 2 feet tall, this species is native of the steppes of central Asia.

Siberian *G. callicomum* (syns. *Limonium callicomum*, *Statice callicomum*), up to 2 feet tall, has oblong-elliptic to lanceolate leaves 1½ to 2 inches long and angled flowering stalks, branched above and bearing loose spikes of violet-rose-pink flowers. A native of central Asia and Siberia, *G. speciosum* (syns. *Limonium speciosum*, *Statice speciosum*), 1½ to 2 feet tall, has broadly-lanceolate to obovate leaves up to 3 or 4 inches long that narrow into the wide, flat stalks. The angled or winged flowering stalks support masses of short, crowded spikes of pink flowers.

Garden and Landscape Uses and Cultivation. These are as for *Limonium latifolium*.

GONIOPHLEBIUM. See Polypodium.

GONOLOBUS (Gonó-lobus)—Angle Pod. Several members of this New World group of about 200 species were previously included in *Vincetoxicum*, but that name is now restricted to European and Asian plants closely allied to *Gonolobus* and probably not cultivated in North America. Both genera belong in the milkweed family ASCLEPIADACEAE. The name comes from the Greek *gonia*, an angle, and *lobos*, a pod, and has reference to the seed pods of one species.

Perennial, twining, herbaceous and woody, milky-juiced vines constitute *Gonolobus*. They have opposite, mostly heart-shaped leaves and axillary clusters of often dark colored flowers with deeply-five-lobed calyxes and wheel- or bell-shaped corollas with five deep lobes (petals) and a flat disklike or cupped, dis-

tinctly or obscurely ten-lobed central corona (crown). There are five stamens joined to each other, and to the stigmas and two styles. The fruits are pods (follicles). For the kind sometimes named *G. carolinensis* see Matelea.

A tropical species called guayote is cultivated in Central America for its edible fruits. In Mexico the young fruits of several native species are eaten raw and cooked and are boiled in syrup to make sweetmeats. In California the guayote is hardy and blooms freely, but is reported not to fruit.

Inhabiting moist woodlands and thickets from Virginia to Indiana, Missouri, and southwards, *G. gonocarpos* (syn. *Vincetoxicum gonocarpos*) is a finely-hairy, high-climbing vine with heart-shaped to ovate-oblong leaves 4 to 8 inches long and often not one-half as wide. The brownish-purple to greenish-purple, starry blooms are in few-flowered, stalked clusters. They have petals ⅓ to ½ inch long. A distinguishing feature is that their calyx lobes have a few hairs at their tips only. The seed pods are smooth, sharply angled, and 3 to 5 inches long. The guayote (*G. edulis*), a native of Central America, is a creeping vine with hairy stems and oblong-lanceolate leaves up to 2½ inches long. It has three- to five-flowered clusters of blooms, on hairy stalks, with ½-inch-long, yellow petals and brown coronas. The pods are 4 to 5 inches long.

Garden Uses and Cultivation. As horticultural plants the hardy kinds of *Gonolobus* have small merit except for use in native plant gardens and semiwild areas. They succeed in dampish, fertile soil in light shade and are propagated by seeds. Not hardy in the north, *G. edulis* is for trial in frost-free climates only.

GONZALAGUNIA. See Dúggena.

Goodenia ovata

GOOBER. This is a common name, used mostly in the south, for the peanut (*Arachis hypogaea*).

GOOD KING HENRY. This is the name given in the British Isles to *Chenopodium bonus-henricus* once popular there as a leaf vegetable and its young shoots as a substitute for asparagus but now rarely grown. It is a hardy herbaceous perennial closely related to lamb's quarters (*C. album*), the latter in America sometimes gathered in the wild and cooked as a vegetable. Good King Henry, also called all-good and sometimes mercury, is not to be confused with *Mercurialis*. It grows well in fertile, dryish soil in sun and is easily raised from seed. As with asparagus, harvesting should not be done the first year and it should be restricted afterward so as never to denude the plants of foliage at any one picking.

GOODENIA (Good-énia). Annuals, herbaceous perennials, subshrubs, and a few shrubs constitute *Goodenia* of the goodenia family GOODENIACEAE. Except for one that extends into Indonesia and tropical Asia, the 110 species of this genus are exclusively Australian and Tasmanian. The name commemorates Dr. Samuel Goodenough, botanist and Bishop of Carlisle, England. He died in 1827.

Goodenias have all-basal or alternate leaves. In terminal racemes or in panicles from the leaf axils the asymmetrical flowers are yellow, purplish, or blue. They have five sepals, a five-lobed, more or less two-lipped tubular corolla slit on its upper side to its base, five stamens, and one style. The fruits are capsules.

A slender, erect subshrub or shrub 3 to 4 feet tall, its young shoots often clammy, *G. ovata* has broadly-lanceolate to ovate, or the lower roundish-heart-shaped, stalked, toothed, thin leaves 1¼ to 4 inches long by up to 1½ inches wide. The yellow flowers, with brown lines in their throats and many together in branched clusters, are ½ to ¾ inch long.

Garden and Landscape Uses and Cultivation. Goodenias are usable as ornamentals in mild Mediterranean-type climates, such as that of California, and can also be grown in cool greenhouses under conditions that suit acacias. They need a sunny exposure and well-drained, fertile, sandy peaty soil kept moderately moist, not saturated. Increase is by seeds and by cuttings, which root readily in spring in a greenhouse propagating bench or under mist.

GOODENIACEAE—Goodenia Family. The about 300 species of this family, mostly natives of Australia and Tasmania, but represented also in the native floras of New Zealand, islands of the Pacific, and tropical coastal regions elsewhere, are disposed in fourteen genera. Dicotyledons, they include shrubs and herbaceous plants with all basal foliage or with stems having alternate or rarely opposite leaves. Their asymmetrical flowers, in clusters, racemes, spikes, or solitary from the leaf axils, have five small sepals, a five-lobed corolla, five stamens, and one, sometimes two- or three-branched style. The fruits are generally capsules, less commonly nuts or drupes. Cultivated genera are *Goodenia*, *Leschenaultia*, and *Scaevola*.

GOODIA (Goòd-ia). This genus of two species is restricted in the wild to Australia and Tasmania. Its name commemorates Peter Good, an English botanical collector, who died in Sydney in 1803. Belonging in the pea family LEGUMINOSAE, goodias are evergreen shrubs. They have leaves of three leaflets and racemes of pea-like blooms. The calyxes have two upper lobes joined into a broad, blunt lip, with two erect teeth, and three smaller, narrower lower lobes. The ten stamens are united into a tube around the slender style. The fruits are flattish pods containing seeds with fleshy appendages.

Cultivated for ornament in California and other regions of mild winters, but not hardy in the north, **Goodia latifolia**, is much-branched, leafy, and 3 to 9 feet tall. Its shoots and undersides of its leaves are minutely-pubescent. The leaflets are obovate and ½ to a little over 1 inch long. The clear yellow flowers, with purple-red stains at the bases of their broad, rounded, notched standard or banner petals, are profusely borne in terminal and lateral racemes up to 4 inches long. The seed pods are long-stalked, and ½ to ¾ inch long. From the last, **G. pubescens** differs in being more conspicuously hairy and having smaller leaves and smaller flowers in shorter racemes.

Goodyera repens in a native habitat

Garden and Landscape Uses and Cultivation. These easily grown shrubs accommodate to a variety of well-drained soils and sunny locations. They need no regular pruning, but if any is deemed desirable to shape them or limit them to size it should be done as soon as blooming is through. Propagation is easy by seeds and by cuttings of firm shoots inserted in a greenhouse propagating bed or under mist.

GOODYERA (Good-yèra) — Rattlesnake-Plantain. This genus of forty or fewer species of ground orchids occurs wild in many temperate, warm-temperate, and tropical lands north and south of the equator. The only kinds likely to be cultivated in North America are those native to the continent. Its name commemorating John Goodyer, a British botanist, who died in 1664, *Goodyera* belongs to the orchid family ORCHIDACEAE.

Goodyeras are herbaceous perennials with short rhizomes and clusters or rosettes of basal leaves, those of many kinds netted with white veins in manners that give reason for the name rattlesnake-plantain. Their erect flower stalks, with several scalelike bracts, terminate in spikelike racemes of small, white or greenish blooms. Each flower has two petals joined to the upper of the three sepals to form a helmet that extends over the shorter, essentially lobeless lip. The corollas are more or less pouched at their bases. The two lateral sepals spread only at their tips.

The lesser rattlesnake-plantain (**G. repens** syn. *Epipactis repens*) occurs wild in Europe and temperate Asia as well as in woodlands through much of North America. It produces slender runners and has tiny, loosely arranged, white, greenish, or pinkish flowers in hairy-stalked, one-sided racemes up to 1 foot tall. Its broadly-ovate leaves are up to 1¾ inches long. In the form, sometimes distinguished as *G. r. ophioides*, commonest in America they are clearly white-veined. European populations have green foliage. Called Loddige's rattlesnake-plantain, **G. tesselata** (syn. *Epipactis tesselata*) is wild in woodlands in eastern and central North America. From *G. repens* it differs in its flowers, often spiraled along the racemes, being larger and much less deeply pouched at their bases and in having sharply beaked instead of blunt anthers. Also, it is bigger, and somewhat coarser.

Downy rattlesnake-plantain (**G. pubescens** syn. *Epipactis pubescens*) occurs in woodlands from southern Canada to Florida and Alabama. From other kinds described here it differs in being more densely-downy and in having crowded, cylindrical, downy-stalked racemes of bloom up to 1½ feet or slightly more in height. Its ovate-lanceolate leaves, up to 3 inches long, are netted with white veins. The anthers of the white flowers are blunt. About as tall as the last, **G. oblongifolia** (syns. *G. menziesii*, *G. decipiens*, *Epipactis decipiens*) is generally coarser than other kinds considered here. It has oblong-lan-

Goodyera pubescens

Gooseberries

Pruning gooseberries

ceolate to elliptic leaves up to 4 inches in length that have broad white midribs or are sometimes mottled in shades of green. The scarcely pouched, white or greenish flowers, over ¼ inch long, are in one-sided racemes. This inhabits woodlands throughout much of North America.

Garden Uses and Cultivation. Goodyeras are rarely cultivated. They are suitable for native plant gardens and such places where conditions similar to those they know in the wild can be given them. Careful division affords the best means of increase. For further information see Orchids.

GOOSE FLOWER. See Aristolochia.

GOOSEBERRY. In addition to being the name of some kinds of *Ribes* discussed in the next entry and under Ribes, the word gooseberry forms part of the common names of these plants: Barbados-gooseberry (*Pereskia aculeata*), Cape-gooseberry or husk-tomato (*Physalis*), Ceylon-gooseberry (*Dovyalis hebecarpa*), Chinese-gooseberry (*Actinidia chinensis*), gooseberry gourd (*Cucumis anguria*), gooseberry-tree or Otaheite-gooseberry (*Phyllanthus acidus*), and hill-gooseberry (*Rhodomyrtus tomentosa*).

GOOSEBERRY. Although among the most satisfactory fruits for pies, jams, and jellies, and some varieties for eating out of hand, gooseberries are little grown in North America. They are much more popular in the British Isles and other parts of northern Europe. One reason that limits their cultivation in the United States and Canada is that they are alternate hosts to the white pine blister rust disease. Because of this, their cultivation is prohibited in regions where white pines are important. Before planting gooseberries be sure to check that it is lawful to do so in your locality. Your Cooperative Extension Agent or your State Agricultural Experiment Station can advise you about this. Also, do not plant nearer than 1,000 feet to any pine tree that has needles (leaves) in clusters of five.

Gooseberries, like currants, belong to the genus *Ribes*, or by some authorities are segregated as the genus *Grossularia*. They are of two types, those called English gooseberries, derived from *R. uva-crispa*, and American gooseberries, varieties of *R. hirtellum*. There are also hybrids between the two types. English sorts bear larger fruits of very much better quality than the American kinds, but unfortunately are subject to a devastating, defoliating fungus disease called downy mildew to which American gooseberries are resistant.

Gooseberries are hardy, cool climate, bush fruits about 3 feet tall, with usually spiny stems, and palmately (in hand-fashion)-lobed leaves. Their fruits, much larger than currants and usually hairy, when ripe are green, yellow, or deep red, according to variety, and are tart or sweet. Gooseberries may be propagated from hardwood cuttings made after the leaves drop in fall or more surely by mound layering. They can also be raised from leafy cuttings made of firm shoots taken in summer. The first two methods are usually preferred. Grow the rooted cuttings in a nursery bed for one or two years then, in early fall or spring, set them in their permanent locations. Because gooseberries leaf out very early the spring planting season is a very short one.

They do well in any well-drained, fertile soil that suits vegetables; they prefer full sun, but tolerate light, part-day shade. Proximity to trees the roots of which compete with those of the gooseberries is highly detrimental. At planting time prune the young bushes quite severely, and set them 3 to 4 feet apart each way.

Because gooseberries are comparatively shallow-rooted they are likely to suffer in times of drought unless watering is done or moisture is conserved by mulching. The last is an excellent practice. Any acceptable organic material, such as compost, seaweed, or hay, suitable for mulching, or black polyethylene plastic may be used. To raise excellent crops you must give the bushes good care. Prune them in late winter or spring by cutting out all branches over three years old and all others except three or four of each that are three years old, two years old, and one year old respectively. Remove any branches that trail on the ground, that are broken or ill-placed, or that are infested with borers. So far as possible select for retention branches well placed to form a shapely bush that permits air and light to reach the interior.

Let the vigor of the bushes and appearance of the foliage be your guide as to the need for fertilizer. If good shoot growth is made and the leaves are of normal size or bigger, and dark green, fertilizer is not needed. If this is not so, apply a nitrogenous fertilizer or a complete garden fertilizer at rates appropriate for vegetables. On sandy and gravelly soils potash deficiency may result in the leaf edges browning. To counteract this keep an organic mulch around the bushes and apply sulfate of potash (not muriate of potash) at the rate

A span-roofed greenhouse, with one section shaded

Graptophyllum pictum

Conservatory (center) and greenhouses at Wave Hill gardens, Bronx, New York City

In a greenhouse, snapdragons for cut flowers

An attractive greenhouse display, in late winter, featuring azaleas, callistemons, camellias, cinerarias, geraniums, hippeastrums, hyacinths, primulas, streptosolens, and tulips

A greenhouse collection of bromeliads

A greenhouse collection of succulents

Lettuce and other salad crops thrive in this polyethylene plastic greenhouse

Guzmania lingulata

of 3 ounces to each 10 square feet. Pests and diseases that may attack gooseberries include borers, currant aphids, and gooseberry mildew. To control these, follow current recommendations of your State Agricultural Experiment Station or other competent authority, preferably one familiar with your region.

English varieties are 'Chautauqua', with large green berries, and red-fruited 'Fredonia'. American varieties are 'Downing', the fruits of which are light green, 'Poorman', with red fruits of large size and good quality, and 'Red Jacket' ('Josselyn'), which has medium-sized, reddish-green berries. Hybrids between English and American varieties include 'Clark', large-fruited and productive, and 'Oregon Champion', which has medium-sized green berries.

GOOSEFOOT. See Chenopodium.

GOPHER PLANT is *Euphorbia lathyrus*.

GOPHERS. In parts of the West these small mammals cause serious damage by burrowing and feeding on roots, bulbs, and other underground parts of plants. First evidence of their presence is likely to be a surface mound of finely pulverized earth, which may or may not have an opening in it, and which marks the top of a short burrow that branches from the one leading to a main burrow which runs horizontally at a depth of 6 inches to 1½ feet.

Trapping is generally the most effective means of dealing with gophers. Dig down to the main runway and set a trap in it at both sides of the excavation. Then fill the hole with fresh cut grass, carrot tops, or other succulent greens and block out light by covering this with a piece of board or soil. Check frequently and if necessary clear the traps of soil that a gopher, without being caught, may have pushed into them. Poison baits may also be used and beds of special importance may be protected by lining them with fine-mesh hardware cloth or chicken wire as recommended in the Encyclopedia entry Moles.

GORDONIA (Gord-ònia)—Loblolly-Bay. Of the about thirty species of *Gordonia*, of the tea family THEACEAE, all except one are Asian. The exception is the loblolly-bay of the southeastern United States. The tree previously named *G. alatamaha* is *Franklinia alatamaha*. The name commemorates an eighteenth-century London, England, nurseryman, James Gordon.

Gordonias are trees and shrubs with alternate, undivided, toothed or toothless leaves, and solitary, axillary blooms with five each sepals and petals, many stamens, and a slender style with a lobed stigma. The fruits are woody capsules.

The loblolly-bay (*G. lasianthus*) inhabits moist, fertile bottom-lands from Virginia to Florida and Louisiana. Developing a

Gordonia lasianthus

rather narrow, compact top, it is sometimes 75 feet tall, but is often lower and frequently does not exceed the dimensions of a large shrub. Its handsome, alternate, lustrous, dark green, short-stalked leaves are elliptic to oblanceolate, shallowly-toothed, and 3 to 6 inches long. The fragrant, white flowers, which open in succession over an extended summer season, are very beautiful. They are about 2½ inches in diameter and have petals and sepals pubescent on their outsides. The flower stalks are red, thickened toward their tops, and 2 to 3 inches long.

The southern Chinese **G. axillaris** is a large shrub with short-stalked, oblanceo-late leaves, with or without teeth at their margins, and 3 to 6 inches long. The creamy-white blooms are 2 to 3 inches in diameter.

Garden and Landscape Uses and Cultivation. Gordonias are not hardy in the north, but are useful and beautiful for planting in the south. They are esteemed for their fine foliage as well as for their blooms. The loblolly-bay is the hardiest and is generally suitable within its natural range and places with comparable climates. These trees and shrubs like best a fertile soil that contains a generous proportion of organic matter and does not lack for moisture. They may be propagated by seeds, layers, and cuttings of firm, but not hard shoots planted in a greenhouse propagating bench or under mist.

GORSE is *Ulex europaeus*. Spanish-gorse is *Genista hispanica*.

GOSSYPIUM (Gos-sýpium) — Cotton. Except in demonstration and educational collections of plants useful to man cotton is not grown horticulturally. It belongs to the genus *Gossypium* of the mallow family MALVACEAE. There are twenty species, stout annuals and herbaceous perennials or sometimes quite woody and nearly treelike perennials, natives of warm regions in both the Old World and the New World. The botany of domesticated cottons is not well understood. The name *Gossypium* is an ancient name of the Arabic species.

Gordonia lasianthus (flowers)

Most important of vegetable fibers, cotton consists of nearly pure cellulose. It was used as long as three thousand years ago in the Indus valley of Asia to make threads and fabrics, and before historic times the natives of South and Central America made similar use of native species. But it was not until the fifteenth century that Europeans became acquainted with cotton. Today it is an important crop in the southern United States, Peru, the Soviet Union, Egypt, and other warm-climate regions. In addition to the employment of the long fibers or lint for making thread and fabrics, the short fuzz or linters is used in the manufacture of photographic film, transparent wrapping materials, and explosives. Cottonseed oil, expressed from the seeds, is made into margarine and used in cooking. The residue from the pressing provides animal feed and fertilizer.

Gossypiums have large palmately-lobed or palmately-veined, undivided leaves with tiny translucent dots. There are conspicuous glands on their undersides, flower stalks, and involucres. The blooms are large and quite showy, white, yellow, or purplish, often changing from one color to another shortly after they open. Beneath the flower is a collar (involucre) of three to seven prominent, usually cleft or fringed, separate or joined, large leafy bracts. The calyx is lobeless or slightly five-lobed. There are five petals. The many stamens are united into a tube surrounding the single style. The fruits or bolls are capsules that open to disclose the smooth or fuzzy-hairy, nearly spherical seeds and, in cultivated kinds, abundant lint or floss fibers, called the staple, that are the cotton of commerce.

Upland cotton (**G. hirsutum**), most likely of tropical American origin, comprises the greater part of the cotton crop of the United States. There are both short staple and long staple varieties. Bushy, much-branched, and 2 to 5 feet tall, these are annuals or are cultivated as such. They have dusty-grayish-green, hairy, three-lobed leaves generally as broad or broader than long, 3 to 6 inches wide. The flowers, opening white or pale yellow and becoming pink or purplish, have involucres of deeply-lobed bracts at least twice as long as the 1½- to 2½-inch-long petals. Their columns of stamens are short, with the loosely arranged anthers on stalks of varying lengths. The seeds are densely covered with persistent, greenish fuzz. Jamaica cotton (**G. h. punctatum**) is a shrub, woodier than upland cotton and perennial, cultivated to some extent by Indians in Arizona and by native peoples in some other parts of the world, but otherwise of slight importance as a crop plant. This is native from Florida to Central America and the West Indies.

Sea Island cotton (**G. barbadense**), native to tropical America, is shrubby, 5 to 8 feet

Gossypium hirsutum, (flower)

tall, and hairy or hairless except on the leaf-stalks and on the veins on the undersides of the leaves. Its leaves, 3 to 6 inches long and as broad or broader, are cleft into three to five lobes at least one-half as long as the depth of the blade. The purplish-tinged, bright yellow flowers have involucres of five or more coarsely-shallowly-toothed bracts. The column of stamens is long, the anthers, on stalks of equal length, are in compact clusters. The seeds may or may not be covered with greenish fuzz. The lint or staple is long.

Other kinds, little cultivated in the United States, are Ceylon or Chinese cotton (**G. arboreum**), and Levant cotton (**G. herbaceum**). Also known as Indian tree cotton, **G. arboreum** is an annual or a subshrub or shrub up to 10 feet in height. Its leaves have usually five to seven primary lobes, which may again be lobed. Solitary from the leaf axils, the sometimes purplish-marked, pale yellow blooms have involucres up to one-half as long as the petals, with their bracts toothless or the upper ones only toothed. The long column of stamens has short-stalked anthers throughout its length. The seeds may or may not have short fuzz as well as lint. Native from Japan and China to Arabia and Africa, this kind is grown in many varieties in Asia and Africa. Levant cotton (**G. herbaceum**) is a bushy annual up to about 4½ feet tall. Probably a native of Asia Minor and Arabia, it has leathery leaves with conspicuously heart-shaped

Gossypium hirsutum, boll (fruit)

bases, five- or seven-lobed to less than half-way to the base of the blade. Mostly broader than long, the heart-shaped bracts of the involucre are toothed. The purple-centered, yellow flowers are of medium size. The seeds are angled. The fuzz and lint are gray.

Arizona wild cotton (**G. thurberi** syn. *Thurberia thespesioides*), a native of southern Arizona and Mexico, is an erect, 3- to 10-

foot-tall, very minutely-hairy perennial. Its leaves are three- to seven-lobed, the clefts between the major lobes extending nearly to the tops of the leafstalks. Shallowly cupped, with petals 1 inch long or a little longer, the flowers are white, becoming purplish as they age. The angular seeds are finely-hairy. The capsules are about ¾ inch in diameter. As is true of other wild cottons this produces no spinable lint.

Garden Uses and Cultivation. For educational display cottons are cultivated in botanical gardens and similar places, outdoors in warm climates and in greenhouses. Considerably north of where it is grown commercially cotton can be flowered outdoors, but to have it develop and mature its snowy bolls a long growing season is necessary. Grown as annuals, cottons succeed in ordinary soils, most satisfactorily in fertile ones. They need full sun. The seed is sown in spring outdoors after the ground is warmed where the plants are to remain, or it may be started indoors in a temperature of 70°F and the young plants carried along in pots in a warm, sunny greenhouse until a week or two after it is safe to plant tomatoes, and then planted in a warm, sheltered place in the garden.

GOURDS, ORNAMENTAL. Gourds is the name of the fruits, and plants that bear them, of certain members of the gourd family CUCURBITACEAE. Just which sorts qualify as gourds and which do not is a matter of interpretation. According to the broadest view cucumbers, melons, pumpkins, squash, and watermelons are gourds, but in North America these are not usually thought of as such and the term is pretty much restricted to hard-shelled kinds mostly not considered palatable and grown principally as decoratives and for use in craft work. The chief kinds belong in the genera *Cucurbita*, *Lagenaria*, and *Luffa*. Other genera of ornamental gourds are listed at the end of this entry.

Except as ornamentals gourds play no appreciable part in contemporary America, but in times past and to a lesser extent now, in the New World and the Old certain kinds were dried and put to many uses. They were employed as vessels for holding liquids and dry goods and were fashioned into such utensils as bowls, dippers, and spoons. Musical instruments and many other useful and decorative objects were made from them. Luffa gourds still enjoy some popularity as substitutes for sponges. So important were gourds to the ex-slave population that assumed control of Haiti after the overthrow of the French that their leader Henri Christophe pronounced them the standard currency of the country and as such they served for almost a year. An outcome was that the standard coin of Haiti is to this day called a gourde.

Garden and Landscape Uses and Cultivation. Gourds are vines suitable for adorning trellises, fences, arbors, arches, pergolas, and similar supports, or they may be allowed to sprawl on the ground. They are grown as annuals. Be sure to obtain the seeds from a reliable source. Inferior seeds that give plants with uninterestingly-shaped fruits are sold by some dealers. Gourds are subject to the same pests and diseases as cucumbers, melons, pumpkins, squash, and other cucurbits.

Because gourds do not transplant well, they are raised from seeds sown after the weather is warm and settled, where the plants are to remain, or are started three weeks to a month earlier indoors in a temperature of 70°F by sowing three seeds each in 4- or 5-inch pots of fertile soil. Before the seedlings begin to crowd all except the strongest in each pot is pulled out. Outdoors, sow in hills of six to eight seeds, spacing the hills about 8 feet apart. Thin the seedlings to four to each hill. If seeds of mixed varieties have been sown, when thinning leave some of the weaker as well as some of the stronger seedlings. If you do not you may remove all of some one variety. Take great care at planting time not to disturb the roots. Hot, humid weather, sunny locations, and fertile, well-drained soil, always sufficiently moist so that the foliage does not wilt, suits gourds.

Delay harvesting unless frost threatens, until the fruits are fully mature. Immature gourds do not keep well. Yellow-flowered gourds (*Cucurbita pepo olifera*) give evidence of ripeness by the stems at the point of attachment to the fruit beginning to shrivel and dry. White-flowered gourds of the calabash type (*Lagenaria siceraria*) are best harvested immediately before they begin to turn yellowish. Loofah or dishcloth gourds (*Luffa acutangula*) turn brown, become lighter in weight, and begin to harden their shells at maturity. Harvest by clipping the fruits with a piece of stalk attached to each. Bring them indoors at once and wash them with a mild, nonbleaching disinfectant to remove grime and organisms that may cause rotting, then put them in a warm, dry place to harden fur-

Gourds (male flower and fruit)

Gourds on an arbor

ther. For additional information about methods of preserving gourds and details of their cultivation consult Benincasa (white gourd or wax gourd), Coccinia (ivy gourd), Cucumis (gooseberry gourd and hedgehog or teasel gourd), Cucurbita (yellow-flowered gourds), Lagenaria (white-flowered gourds), Luffa (dishcloth or loofah gourd), and Trichosanthes (serpent, snake, or club gourd).

GOURLIEA (Gour-lièa). A solitary species of the pea family LEGUMINOSAE constitutes *Gourliea*, the name of which commemorates Robert Gourlie, who botanized in Argentina and died there in about 1882.

A hairless, rigid shrub or small tree up to 20 feet in height, with spines and spine-tipped branchlets, *G. decorticans* (syn. *G. spinosa*) is a native of Argentina and Chile, where it is known as chanar. It has pinnate leaves in clusters of three or four. They have three or four pairs of oblong-elliptic leaflets ¼ inch to 1½ inches long, and a terminal one. The red-streaked, yellow to orange-yellow, pea-shaped flowers, about ⅓ inch in length, are in short racemes from the leaf axils. They have a shortly-five-toothed or toothless calyx, five petals, ten stamens, and an incurved style. The brownish fleshy fruits with one or two seeds do not open.

Garden and Landscape Uses and Cultivation. Easy of cultivation, this may be planted for ornament in sunny locations outdoors in frostless or practically frostless climates. It grows satisfactorily in ordinary soils, including dryish ones, and is propagated by seed.

GOUT PLANT is *Jatropha podagrica*.

GOUTWEED or BISHOP'S WEED is *Aegopodium podagraria*.

GOVERNOR'S-PLUM is *Flacourtia indica*.

GRABOWSKIA (Grabòws-kia). Belonging to the nightshade family SOLANACEAE, this genus of up to one dozen species of spiny shrubs, is native to South America. Its name honors H. E. Grabowsky, botanical author and apothecary of Silesia, who died in 1842.

Grabowskias resemble lyciums, to which they are related. They have alternate, sometimes fleshy leaves and small blooms with five- or ten-lobed calyxes and short funnel-shaped corollas with five spreading lobes. There are five protruding stamens. The fruits are berry-like and contain two seeds.

Cultivated in California and elsewhere in mild, dryish climates, *Grabowskia boerhaaviaefolia* (syn. *G. glauca*) of Peru is 4 to 10 feet tall and of loose, spreading habit. Its arching or pendulous branches are armed with spines ¼ to ½ inch long. Short-stalked, and broad-elliptic, its obo-

vate or roundish, gray-green, fleshy, hairless leaves are up to 1½ inches in length. Solitary, or in short terminal or axillary clusters, the white or pale blue flowers, with spreading or reflexed petals, are about ¼ inch long and slightly more wide. They are borne in spring but make no effective display.

Garden and Landscape Uses and Cultivation. Of minor horticultural importance, the species described is grown for its botanical interest and for its gray foliage. It thrives in dryish soil in full sun and is easily propagated by cuttings and by seeds.

GRADING. Grading or contouring the ground is often necessary or desirable when making gardens and as a preliminary to landscaping homes. Properly done it can add immensely to the amenities of the area. Improperly or inadequately carried out it may bring troubles and distress or at best result in an unsatisfactory landscape and perhaps inordinately high costs.

The amount of grading needed in any particular situation can vary from none to elaborate land operations. If the latter are contemplated and the area is large, begin by having a topographical survey of existing conditions made and the results plotted on paper. With this as a basis and the proposed new contours also set down on

a plan, estimates of the amount of cutting (excavating) and filling can be made and amounts of new fill needed or excess material to be disposed of determined. Also, be sure to check on local laws controlling grading operations. In some communities it is required that plans be submitted and permission obtained if the work contemplated exceeds certain limits, which frequently include fills more than 3 feet in depth involving more than five cubic yards, slopes greater than 1 to 5 vertical to horizontal, and excavations more than 5 feet deep.

Home gardeners with small- to moderate-sized areas not in need of drastic contour changes need no elaborate preparation. They can usually achieve satisfactory results by the exercise of common sense and sound judgment and with the aid of some stakes, strings, and a reliable way of determining levels and grades. This last is important. The eye, and especially the unpracticed eye, can seldom be trusted to appraise grades correctly or even approximately. In addition to these appurtenances there will of course be needed equipment for moving earth. This may range from wheelbarrow and shovel to bulldozer.

Before you begin contouring on even a small scale determine the present grades

Determining grades: (a) With a surveyor's level

Landscaping around new houses often involves grading

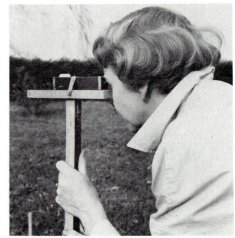

(b) With a hand sighting level

(c) With a carpenter's level

(c) Reading the level

Heavy equipment may compact clay soils to the extent that drainage is impaired

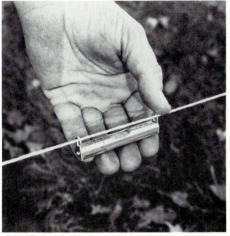

Establishing grades with a line level: (a) The level

(d) Raising or lowering the string at one end to determine the rise or fall between the two points

(b) The level positioned midway along a string stretched between two points

Driving temporary stakes so that their tops indicate the finished grade

other heavy equipment, even when covered with topsoil they will act as water-collecting basins inhospitable to most plants set over them. A first consideration then when contemplating changing grades is to make sure that adequate provision is made for drainage and run-off. Outlets may have to be developed.

The reprehensible practice of skimming all topsoil, selling or otherwise disposing of a considerable amount for use elsewhere, and then spreading a skimpy layer of 3 or 4 inches over tightly packed subsoil is followed by many development builders. This presents the landscaper and gardener with an extremely discouraging place to start. If you can possibly prevent such situations arising do so.

The only proper procedure when grading is to first skim all topsoil from the area and stockpile it, to be spread again after the under soil has been suitably contoured to a subgrade 6 to 8 inches or more below the finished grade. The minimum depth of topsoil for lawn areas should be 6 inches. For flower beds and borders and for shrubs and trees 8 inches to 1 foot or more is really needed.

Shaping ground for landscape effects calls for more than sympathetic regard for soil physics and application of engineering techniques. For pleasing results an appreciation of beauty is demanded. Just as surely as the plants employed and their placement, surface contours contribute to the rightness and soul-satisfying qualities of a landscaped area, be it natural, naturalistic, or more frankly formal. Avoid incongruous, drastic changes from one type of landscape to another, the peanut-brittle type of rock garden as a mound in a lawn, for instance.

From buildings, let the surface grade slope away and slightly downward for at least several feet so that water is directed away from instead of toward the structure. Grades between house and street of necessity are determined by the relative elevations of the two, but never permit an even

and especially which way surface water flows. You certainly will want this to be away from rather than toward the immediate vicinity of the house. For taking such measurements you may use such simple devices as a carpenters' level and a long straightedge spanned between stakes driven into the ground, a line level, a hand level, or on larger areas a surveyor's level.

Drainage, both surface and subsurface, is a prime consideration in all grading op-

erations. The finished grade must be such that rain and snow water does not collect where it will damage buildings, driveways, or paths or harm lawns, trees, shrubs, other plants, or the soil itself. This last is likely to result from erosion if the slope of cultivated ground, a vegetable garden, for example, is too severe. If low areas of clayey subsoil are compacted by bulldozers or

Before grading begins: (a) Remove topsoil

After establishing the subgrade, distribute topsoil in convenient piles and spread it evenly

(b) Stockpile it conveniently

(c) Then grade subsoil

slope downward from street to structure. Always it should rise toward the house. Where any very considerable difference of elevation must be accommodated between house and street, or on other short horizontal run, that is, if the rise or drop is steep, the need for one or more terraces supported by banks or retaining walls is generally indicated. Maximum slopes for banks supporting terraces should not be greater than 1 foot of rise for each 2 feet of horizontal distance, a 1 to 2 grade. If the

slopes are to be of lawn, a 1 to 3 grade makes for easier maintenance. Should the bank be high, the installation of a gutter along its top will divert run-off from slightly sloping ground above and so reduce the danger of the bank being exposed to erosion and washes.

After removing the topsoil, establish the new subgrade by cutting and filling, removing or adding material until the desired contours are achieved. Be sure to compact the fill enough to ensure a firm base for the topsoil. If land drains are to be installed take care of that next.

Before spreading the topsoil loosen the upper 6 inches to 1 foot of the subgrade with a fork or rototiller. This will not destroy the deeper compaction previously achieved and will enable the upper soil to mingle with the under at the point of junction instead of meeting it as a hard, impervious layer. If you can afford compost or other organic matter for admixture with the subsoil in areas where planting is to be done this is all to the good. After the topsoil is spread, graded, and made moderately firm leave its surface as coarse as possible. There is no need for fine raking until after trees and shrubs are planted or lawns are to be sodded or sown.

Important precautions to be taken when grading with heavy equipment relate to the avoidance of accidental disturbance or cutting of such utilities as sewers, leaching fields, gas pipes, and electric lines, and to

the protection of trees to be saved. Also, insofar as it can be scheduled, and this is a counsel of often unattainable perfection, if the soil is clayey operate on it only when it is reasonably dry and does not stick readily to tools and implements. Working such soil when it is wet alters its physical characteristics seriously for the worse and a long period of weathering and other treatment including the application of lime or gypsum may be needed to bring it back to a reasonably friable condition.

Trees to be saved should have their trunks well protected with heavy planks or stakes or by having large rocks set

During grading, protect trees from damage by contractor's equipment

around them some little distance from their bases. Do not permit earth to be scraped from over the root area. If the tree to be retained is in an area where the grade is to be lowered, slope the soil gently downward from the tree to well beyond the spread of its roots, which will be more than the spread of the branches, and leave it standing on a slight elevation.

A masonary well protects the trunk of this tree above the roots of which the grade has been raised

If fill must be placed over the roots and its depth is not more than a few inches all that is necessary is to circle the base of the trunk a foot or so away from it with loose rocks or concrete blocks to prevent the earth coming into contact with the bark, which can be fatal. If deeper fill is to be installed, the proper procedure is to build a masonry-walled well around the trunk 1½ to 2 feet from it. Also, use for the lower layer of the fill sand, gravel, crushed rock or similar material that will not compact to such an extent that the movement of water and air are seriously impeded. If the location is low it may be advisable before placing the fill to install several lines of agricultural tile radiating like the spokes of a wheel and with a downward slope from the base of the tree to beyond the spread of the branches. Cover the drains with gravel or crushed stone before installing the fill.

GRAFT HYBRIDS. See Chimera, Crataegomespilus, and Laburnocytisus.

GRAFTING. By amateur gardeners one of the least practiced of garden procedures, the art of grafting is an ancient one. About it in the minds of many lies an aura of mystery. It is commonly regarded as something only skilled professionals do. Perhaps those who adopt this view subconsciously relate grafting to operating on the human body and react by feeling it is best left to the doctors. Be that as it may, a vast number of gardeners, who without trepidation and with some confidence of

success, undertake seed sowing and such surgical operations as dividing plants, taking cuttings, and even layering, shy away from grafting. There is no valid reason for this. Grafting is a simple procedure not beyond the competency of the majority of amateur gardeners. Some know-how is of course needed.

Grafting consists of causing the tissues of a piece or a part of a plant to unite and grow together with those of another or those of a different part of the same plant to form a complete and permanent union. Chiefly employed as a means of propagation, under some circumstances it can be used effectively to repair wounds and brace weak limbs. It is sometimes employed to develop specimens (apple trees, for example) with more than one variety on the same tree and to establish on female trees of unisexual species (certain kinds of holly, for example) a branch that will produce male flowers and so ensure pollination and fruiting. Grafting is employed as a means of dwarfing certain fruit trees (most notably apples), and in the case of grapes, for controlling the root louse called phylloxera. In some types of formal training (pleaching, for example) branches are united by grafting.

Grafting as a means of propagation, like other modes of vegetative increase, is chiefly used to multiply plants of which seeds are not available or that do not reproduce true to type from seeds. Since the introduction of mist propagation, rooting hormones, and other sophisticated aids to rooting cuttings, grafting is less used than formerly for the propagation of some plants, particularly rhododendrons, maples, and others once considered difficult from cuttings but that respond to the newer techniques. Grafting as compared with other modes of propagation in many

Ideally, the understock and the scion grafted onto it increase in girth at the same rate, as with this tree

cases saves time and labor by producing good-sized plants one to several years sooner than could be done in other ways.

Disadvantages sometimes occur, as when the selection of inappropriate understocks results in greatly different rates of growth of stock and scion and the consequent development of an ugly bulge at the junction between them. Or again, if understocks are selected unwisely, weak unions may result so that as the head of the tree becomes bigger it is subject to breakage. A not uncommon disadvantage of grafting is the development of sucker

A poorly chosen understock may increase in girth faster or slower than the scion grafted onto it: (a) This golden English oak (*Quercus robur concordia*) has grown faster than its undetermined understock

(b) An ash (*Fraxinus angustifolia lentiscifolia*) grafted on a slower-growing undetermined understock

(c) The understock has grown faster than the weeping elm (*Ulmus carpinifolia pendula*) grafted upon it

shoots from below the point of union, which if not cut out promptly can result in the less worthy ornamental or fruit producer that is the stock taking over from and eventually crowding out the superior sort grafted onto it.

The history of grafting is long. Just when it was first done no one knows. In China the art has been practiced since remote times, especially in its form known as inarching. In ancient Greece grafting was commonplace. The Bible, Romans XI verses 16 to 24, explicitly extols the virtues that result from grafting olive trees. The Roman naturalist Pliny the Elder, in the first century A.D., described the procedure.

Observation of natural grafts undoubtedly led ancient man to attempt the same result artificially. Natural grafts occur much more frequently than is generally realized, between roots as well as branches. A walk through most wooded areas will usually reveal to a keen observer examples of this phenomenon between branches of adjacent trees or between those of the same individual. It is more frequent with thin-barked trees, such as beeches and plane trees, than with sorts with thick, rough bark. It commonly occurs between branches of climbing specimens of English ivy. A study of natural grafts reveals that they occur only where the parts in contact are held so they do not move. This explains why they are most frequent where a branch becomes wedged in a fork formed by the bases of two others. The wounding of two branches caused by the friction of rubbing will not result in a natural graft, but such is likely to occur where one branch rests quietly on another. This perhaps explains why grafts between roots, for instance those of beech trees, are so frequent.

The underlying principles of grafting are few. For practical purposes the procedure is restricted to dicotyledons. Rarely has it been achieved with monocotyledons, this because the stems and roots of the latter are without true cambium layers. The botanical affinity between plants to be grafted must be fairly close. Often they will be varieties of the same species or species of the same genus. Practically always they will be of the same family. Thus apples may be grafted on apples, roses on roses (here plants of the same species or genus are united). Pears are often grafted on quinces

and can be grafted on hawthorns, lilacs on privets (these are examples of plants of different genera, but of the same families being joined). In the cactus family most genera can be grafted with comparative ease upon other genera. The few reliably reported instances of grafting having been successful between plants of different families are mostly with annuals and biennials. Exceptions are the successful unions that have been made between *Didierea* of the family DIDIEREACEAE, and certain species of the cactus family CACTACEAE.

But compatability or congeniality between stock and scion (the first the term for the understock or root portion of the grafted plant, the other for the part joined to it that becomes top or branched part) depends upon more than close botanical affinity. It refers to the readiness, under favorable circumstances, with which stock and scion unite and the satisfactory functioning and persistence of the union. Other than experience, much of which is adequately recorded and published, there is no reliable guide to determining the likelihood of closely related plants forming compatible graft unions.

A further requirement for successful grafting is that the cambium layers of the parts to be united be brought into intimate contact and be held securely until they have grown together. (The cambium of dicotyledons forms a very thin tube or cylinder just beneath the bark around the woody core of each branch and stem.)

Modes of grafting are many. Two, because they are usually considered by gardeners to be different operations, are discussed in this Encyclopedia under the

Natural grafts

separate entries Budding and Inarching or Approach Grafting. Budding is a style of grafting in which a single bud instead of a shoot having few to several buds is employed as the scion. Inarching or approach grafting is a procedure in which both stock and scion are rooted plants.

In selecting the grafting method to be employed, the character of stock and scion must be considered in relation to the type of carpentry to be used in making the cuts. With dormant stocks and scions as thick or somewhat thicker than a pencil and of equal or approximately equal diameter simple splice or whip grafting, whip and tongue grafting, saddle grafting, and wedge grafting are generally appropriate. Side or veneer grafts are often best for young evergreens and for stocks quite a little thicker than the scions. Other methods are employed when, as is the case with a headed-back apple tree or cut-down old camellia, the diameter of stock is much greater than that of the scions. Then the crown or rind graft or the cleft graft are ordinarily favored. Bridge grafting is used to repair large wounds in trees. Minor variations of grafting methods are employed by individual operators and for special purposes.

Of primary importance in all grafting is to have healthy understocks and scions in the right condition. Most grafting is done in winter or spring. In the majority of cases, certainly with woody plants, it is important that the understocks be in slightly active growth, the scions less advanced at the time the operation is done. In greenhouses this is accomplished by forcing potted understocks into somewhat earlier growth than normal by raising the temperature for a period. To achieve the same result with hardy deciduous trees or shrubs to be grafted in the open scions may be cut a month or so before grafting is to be done and buried for two-thirds of their lengths in soil on the north side of a building or other shaded place where their growth will be retarded or, in severe climates, be cut well ahead of grafting time and be stored in a mixture of slightly damp peat moss and sand in a cellar or other place where a temperature of 35 to 40°F can be maintained.

The time to graft indoors depends upon available facilities as well as the kind of plant. Professional nurserymen with greenhouses at their disposal do much of this in winter, some in late summer. If a greenhouse is not available nearly as good results can be had in a carefully managed cold frame, but then the grafting should be done in early spring just before the first urge of spring growth rather than in winter.

The technique of grafting calls for some dexterity. Work as quickly as you easily can so that the cut surfaces do not have time to dry. Make all cuts with a very keen knife or in the case of small herbaceous stocks and scions with a razor blade. This is important. Ragged or bruised cuts made by a blunt tool unite poorly or not at all. Professional propagators prefer a knife with a blade flat on one side, sloped on the other. Make the cuts so that stock and scion fit snugly.

Suitable understocks are important. When grafting is done to change the varieties of old trees or shrubs, to provide bracing for weak limbs, or to repair injury, the understocks will often be of considerable age, but for propagation purposes they will normally be young vigorous specimens of kinds appropriate for the scions and raised specially for the purpose from seeds or cuttings or in other ways. In most cases far the best results are had if the understocks are well established. Grafting on understocks that have been potted or planted less than a year in most cases greatly reduces the chances of success. With some plants, however, such as dogwoods, lilacs, and magnolias, grafting onto bare-root understocks gives good results. With some other plants pieces of roots are satisfactory understocks. Examples are clematises, bignonias, gypsophilas, tree peonies, wisterias, and rhododendrons.

The selection of shoots for scions needs care. With woody plants they should usually be of the previous year's growth and fully mature. Generally the center portions of such shoots are used, the buds on the lower parts commonly not being as well developed and the terminal portions being too immature, thin, and generally less suitable than the part below. The scions most often are made of such lengths that they have two to four buds, but shorter ones are sometimes employed.

For tying scions to stocks either soft string or cloth bands, preferably rubbed with beeswax or soaked in grafting wax, or special rubber bands or adhesive tapes are employed. The latter have the advantage of expanding as the shoots thicken. String or cloth ties must be watched carefully and loosened before injury results. Some gardeners treat the string with copper naphenate to prevent it from rotting before the graft unites.

Sealing the sites of the operations and all exposed cut surfaces including the tips of the scions is usually done, but when grafting soft-stemmed plants in greenhouses it is sometimes omitted. As a sealer special grafting wax obtainable from dealers in nursery and garden supplies is used or sometimes polyethylene plastic film is substituted.

The splice or whip graft is one of the simplest to make. Prepare the stock by removing its top with an upward, slanting cut five to six times as long as the thickness of the shoot. Slice the base of the scion with a downward cut to correspond, place the exposed surfaces together, and tie to prevent movement. Because the parts must be held together while tying this is not a convenient graft to make near ground level. Its use is usually limited to bench grafting. Lilacs are readily united with privet understocks in this way.

The whip and tongue graft, a modification of the last that eliminates the necessity of holding the parts in place while tying, is one of the most popular and practical grafting techniques. To perform it, prepare stock and scion as described for splice grafting then make a short downward cut across the exposed surface of the stock and a corresponding upward one into the scion to provide a flap or tongue. Insert the tongue of the scion into the cut in the stock and press them gently together until they in-

The splice or whip graft using a potted understock: (a) Preparing the understock

(b) The scion, prepared

(c) Tying scion to understock with soft string

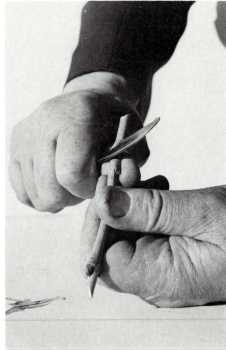

(b) Preparing the scion

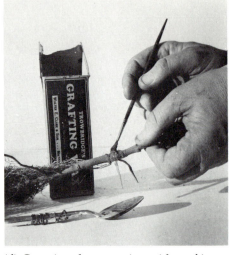

(d) Covering the operation with grafting wax

(d) The job completed

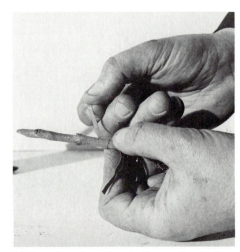

(c) Securing the scion to the understock with a rubber band

Saddle graft: (a) Preparing the understock

(b) Inserting the cleft in the scion over the saddle of the understock

The splice or whip graft using a bare-root understock: (a) Preparing the understock

and tongue grafting, sometimes called double-tongue grafting, two cuts instead of one are made across stock and scion and are fitted together. This method often gives superior results with plants that have shoots with thick piths.

The saddle graft, as its name implies, is one in which the scion is seated in saddle-fashion on the stock. Prepare the latter by making a slanting, upward cut from each side so the bared surfaces form an up-pointing wedge. Cut a notch to correspond in the base of the scion and fit it over the wedge of the stock. Then tie and wax. This graft is often used for such fairly thick-stemmed plants as magnolias and rhododendrons. It and the next are also frequently employed for cactuses. With cactuses the scion is held in place by tying or by pinning it to the stock with long spines of a cactus. Waxing is unnecessary.

terlock. Then both of your hands are freed for tying and waxing. If stock and scion are of slightly different diameters make sure that the cambium layers on at least one side are in contact. In a modification of whip

(c) Tying the graft securely

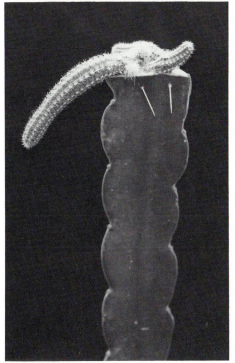

Wedge graft: (a) Peanut cactus (*Chamaecereus sylvestri*) on *Hylocereus,* the scion secured with long cactus spines pushed through stock and scion

(c) Two or three years later

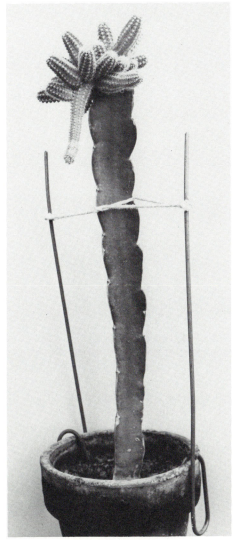

(b) Union completed and, some months later, scion has made appreciable growth

Young wedge grafts of three different cactuses

A crested variety of cactus wedge grafted onto a different understock

Wedge grafts of trumpet vine (*Campsis*): (a) Cutting pieces of root for understocks

Grafted cactuses at the Montreal, Canada, botanical garden

(b) A scion inserted in the roots, and several grafts tied to secure the scions to the understocks

The wedge graft is the reverse of the saddle graft and is made in the same manner except that the notch is cut in top of the stock and the base of the scion is fashioned into a wedge to fit into it. The wedge graft is often used when the understock consists of a piece of root only as, for instance, with trumpet vine. It is often the best method of accomplishing the grafting of plants in the seedling stage as is done with *Clianthus formosus*, and sometimes for experimental purposes. For grafting seedlings use a razor blade.

The crown, rind, or bark graft is employed when the diameter of the stock is much greater than that of the scions. It is a usual method for top-working fruit trees. To effect this graft, pare smooth the sawn ends of the trunk or branches that are to receive the scions. Prepare the latter by cutting their bases on a slant 1 inch to 1½ inches long as is done in splice grafting. Next choose two to four places, depending upon the size of the stock, around its circumference for the insertion of the scions. Select clean spaces free of knots for these. At each location with the point of a knife make a downward cut 1½ to 2 inches long through the bark, but not into the wood beneath. Do not remove any bark, but pry it up slightly along the sides of the cuts. Next gently push the scion down between the bark and wood until the top of its cut

Old apple tree top worked with crown, rind, or bark grafts

surface is even with the top of the stump of the stock. Finish by tying and covering the areas of operation and the top of the stock with grafting wax.

The cleft graft, also used on stocks much greater in diameter than the scions, involves a cruder procedure than the crown graft. Except that the stock is much bigger than the scions it is similar to the wedge

Crown, rind or bark grafts: (a) With
scions inserted and, in this example, the
limb taped around before covering with
grafting wax

Side graft: (a) *Chamaecyparis*, newly tied

(c) Japanese maple

(b) One scion has united with the
understock and started into active
growth, the other has failed to take (grow)

(b) With tie removed

(d) Close-up of graft

graft. The cleft graft is often used to make
over old camellias to a different variety.
Usually two, sometimes four scions are inserted in each trunk or branch of a cleft-
grafted stock. To perform cleft grafting
take a chisel or special cleaver-like grafting
tool and split the end of the stock across
its center. Cut long, wedge-shaped bases
on the scions, and insert one at each end
of the cleft at the circumference of the
stock so that cambiums of stock and scion
are in contact. To make insertion easier,
the cleft may be opened slightly by driving
a wooden wedge into it, the wedge to be
withdrawn when the scions are in place.
To prevent entry of water and disease organisms that may cause rotting, be sure to
cover all grafts of this type, including the
full length of the cleft, with a thick layer
of grafting wax.

The side graft differs from all grafts previously dealt with in that the scion is inserted into the side instead of at the apex
of a cut-off stock. Depending upon the
vigor of the stock, its top is cut off or
partly cut back at grafting time or is removed after union has taken place or,
when a male branch is grafted onto a female tree, it is left without cutting. The
side graft is much in favor for propagating

evergreens in greenhouses. To make this
graft slice downward into the side of the
stock for 1 inch to 1½ inches at an angle
of about 20 degrees, but not cutting into
the stock for more than one-third its diameter. Next, fashion the lower part of the
scion into a wedge by making flat, slanting
cuts on opposite sides of it. Let one cut,
that on the side that will be uppermost
when the scion is inserted, be longer than
the other. This is necessary to permit a
snug and complete fit with all cut surfaces
in contact. Close the flap of the stock
against the scion, tie it into place, and wax
the point of operation.

The veneer graft is a variation of the
side graft. Instead of the lower part of the
scion being fashioned as a wedge, a slant-

To assure high humidity newly made grafts may be: (a) Plunged in a greenhouse propagating case

Veneer graft, holly (*Ilex aquifolium* variety on seedling understock)

(b) Accommodated in a terrarium, this one made of polyethylene plastic, or

A brace graft several years after being made

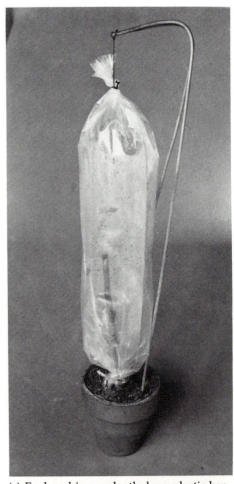

(c) Enclosed in a polyethylene plastic bag

ing cut is made down one side of it, extending at its base nearly to the opposite side, and in place of a slit in the stock a thin slice is removed completely. Make at the bottom of the exposed part of the stock a horizontal cut so that a small sill or ledge results that affords support for the base of the scion cut to fit it.

Bridge grafting is extremely useful for correcting mechanical damage, such as may result from an automobile running into a tree, girdling by deer, or other injury not the result of an uncontrollable disease. To bridge graft begin by cutting away all dead and damaged tissues, shaping the exposed area as an ellipse, and paring its edges smooth. If the damage extends to the ground clear away sufficient soil to expose undamaged bark and replace it after the operation is completed. Next, cut enough scions so that, spaced 1½ to 2 inches apart, they will extend across the exposed area. Make the scions 2 or 3 inches longer than the gap they are to bridge. Bevel one side of each for about 1 inch at each end. Make suitable slits in the bark at the top and bottom of the gap to allow the scions to be pushed under the bark with their beveled sides inward so that their cambium and that of the trunk are in contact. Taking care not to split the scions, secure them in position, bowed slightly outward, by driving a slender nail through both ends of each. Finally cover the points of insertion with grafting wax.

Brace grafting is sometimes done to reduce the danger of narrow crotches between limbs of nearly equal size splitting. To accomplish it, a young shoot must be available on facing sides of each of the branches to be braced and at approximately the same distance, normally from 1 foot to

2 feet, from the crotch. Some little way above the shoots a temporary rope or wire brace is installed between the limbs to establish rigidity by pulling them slightly together. Then the shoots are brought together, parallel to each other and with the tip of each pointing toward the base of the other. They are then twisted around each other and secured with ties to keep them in position. In time, as the new shoots grow together and thicken, their tissues unite so that branches that come in contact naturally sometimes do, and the crotch is immensely strengthened by a brace of living wood between its branches.

Care of plants newly grafted outdoors makes no special demands of the gardener other than they must be examined periodically to make sure the ties are not binding unduly. Plants grafted indoors, often referred to as bench-grafted, because the understocks are not established in permanent beds, but are in pots or are otherwise mobile enough to be brought to the potting shed bench for grafting do need special care following the operation. Most commonly this consists of putting them in a propagating or grafting case in a greenhouse where high humidity is maintained until union has taken place or in a cold frame where approximately the same environment can be provided. A smaller number of plants can be accommodated in a terrarium or by covering them with a plastic bag. A temperature of about 70°F is, with most plants, conducive to good results.

GRAFTING WAX. This is a preparation used to daub over fitted parts of newly made grafts. Its purposes are to exclude disease organisms and air without hindering tissue growth or swelling. Commercial grafting waxes are available or one can be made by melting together in the proportions of one, two, and four, tallow, beeswax, and resin. Stir until thoroughly mixed then pour the preparation into a container of cold water. Before it becomes too hard pull it by stretching and restretching it in the manner of the old fashioned taffy was pulled. It may then be stored indefinitely. Kneading it in the hand will soften it sufficiently for use.

GRAMINEAE—Grass Family. This vast family, the source of such important foods as barley, corn, oats, rice, rye, sesame, sorghum, sugar cane, and wheat and of pasture, lawn, and other practically useful and ornamental grasses including bamboos contains by far the greatest number of individual plants of any family of flowering or seed plants, ferns, and fern allies. Its numbers are exceeded in the vegetable kingdom only perhaps by certain groups of bacteria, algae, and other lowly forms. It contains about 620 genera, approximately 10,000 species.

The grass family, of cosmopolitan provenance and the most widely distributed one of higher plants, is composed of monocotyledons including annuals, deciduous and evergreen herbaceous perennials, and sorts called bamboos with perennial, woody, sometimes climbing stems, sometimes of great height. The group has jointed, mostly hollow stems and generally linear, parallel-veined leaves the lower parts of which form sheaths slit down one side, embracing portions of the stems. The highly specialized, minute flowers are borne singly or several to many in spikelets with two-ranked, overlapping bracts, the basal two without flowers in their axils. The flowers and individual plants may be bisexual or unisexual. Usually there are three, sometimes fewer or more stamens, and one pistil with generally a pair of feathery stigmas. The fruits are usually grains or seeds, rarely nutlets, berries, or utricles. They are sometimes surrounded by persistent bractlike parts.

The genera of grasses presented as separate entries in this Encyclopedia include these: *Agrostis, Alopecurus, Ammophila, Ampelodesma, Arrhenatherum, Arundinaria, Arundo, Avena, Bambusa, Bouteloua, Briza, Bromus, Chasmanthium, Chimonobambusa, Chloris, Coix, Cortaderia, Cymbopogon, Cynodon, Dactylis, Dendrocalamus, Deschampsia, Desmazeria, Eleusine, Elymus, Eragrostis, Eremochloa, Erianthus, Festuca, Gynerium, Helictotrichon, Holcus, Hordeum, Koeleria, Lagurus, Lamarckia, Lolium, Melica, Milium, Miscanthus, Molinia, Neyraudia, Oplismenus, Oryza, Panicum, Paspalum, Pennisetum, Phalaris, Phragmites, Phyllostachys, Poa, Polypogon, Pseudosasa, Rhynchelytrum, Saccharum, Sasa, Semiarundinaria, Setaria, Shibataea, Sorghum, Stenotaphrum, Stipa, Thysanolaena, Uniola, Vetiveria, Zea, Zizania,* and *Zoysia.* For the common names of grasses, together with their botanical equivalents, see the Encyclopedia entries Bamboos; Grasses; and Grasses, Ornamental.

GRAMMATOCYMBIDIUM. This is the name of bigeneric orchids the parents of which are *Cymbidium* and *Grammatophyllum.*

GRAMMATOPHYLLUM (Grammatophýllum)—Giant Orchid or Queen Orchid. An amazing orchid belongs here. Sometimes called giant orchid, *Grammatophyllum speciosum* has the largest pseudobulbs of the orchid family ORCHIDACEAE. They are stemlike and sometimes attain lengths in excess of 25 feet. The genus consists of about ten species, natives of tropical Asia, Indonesia, the Philippine Islands, New Guinea, and other islands of the Pacific. The name, from the Greek *grammata,* letters, and *phyllon,* a leaf, refers to the markings on the flowers of some kinds.

Grammatophyllums are evergreen epiphytes that perch on trees, but take no sustenance from them. There are two types, those with obvious, flat, comparatively short pseudobulbs and those in which the pseudobulbs are in effect tall stems with foliage in two ranks, which continue growing for more than one year. Both kinds have long, strap-shaped leaves. Their splendid erect or arching racemes from the bases of the pseudobulbs bear many large, showy blooms, those low on the raceme frequently more or less abnormal in structure or appearance.

The giant orchid or queen orchid (*G. speciosum* syn. *G. giganteum*), though sometimes attaining dimensions mentioned at the beginning of this entry, in cultivation usually has stemlike pseudobulbs 6 to 10 feet tall and of a maximum diameter of about 3 inches. Its arching, narrowly-strap-shaped leaves, up to 2½ feet long, are along the upper parts of the stems. The thick-stalked, erect racemes of

Grammatophyllum scriptum tigrinum

flowers up to 6 feet tall or taller bear up to 100 long-lasting blooms 4 to 6 inches wide or wider. They have wavy, yellowish or greenish sepals, petals sparsely to thickly spotted with reddish-brown or reddish-purple, and a small white and yellow, three-lobed lip similarly marked.

Variable *G. scriptum* (syns. *G. measuresianum, G. multiflorum*), of the Philippine Islands, has deeply-ribbed, ellipsoid to egg-shaped pseudobulbs up to 1 foot long or sometimes longer. The two to three wavy leaves from near their summits are pointed, strap-shaped, 1 foot to 2 feet long, and up to more than 3 inches wide. Erect, arching, or drooping, the 2- to 4-foot-long racemes may have fifty to one hundred waxy blooms 2 to 3 inches in diameter. They have similar blunt, oblong sepals and petals, prevailingly light greenish-yellow blotched with brown. The lip is deeper yellow with reddish-brown blotches. More intensely spotted flowers fully 3 inches in diameter are characteristic of *G. s. tigrinum.*

Garden Uses and Cultivation. Except in the torrid, humid tropics and in large tropical greenhouses, the giant orchid is almost impossible to grow, and even in those environments it does not prosper and bloom as freely as could be wished. The other species described is less tantalizing, but cannot be accounted easy to cultivate. Both need constant high temperatures and high humidity. They may be accommodated in large, well-drained containers or raised beds in osmunda fiber, tree fern fiber, or other rooting medium suitable for epiphytic orchids. Generous watering and fertilizing is needed during their periods of active growth, somewhat less watering and no fertilizing in winter. Only enough shade to prevent scorching the foliage is advisable. For more information see Orchids.

GRANADILLA. See Passiflora.

GRAPE. In addition to its use for species and varieties of *Vitis* (see discussions un-

Grapefruit

Grapes, a favorite fruit for home gardens

der Grapes and Vitis) the word grape is used as part of the following common names: chicory-grape (*Coccoloba venosa*), grape fern (*Botrychium dissectum*), grape-hyacinth (*Muscari botryoides* and *Synthyris*), grape-ivy (*Cissus rhombifolia*), Oregon-grape (*Mahonia aquifolium*), sea-grape (*Coccoloba uvifera*), and tail-grape (*Artabotrys hexapetalus*).

GRAPEFRUIT. Some doubt surrounds the origin of this popular, delicious fruit, too well known to require description. Its ancestry, like that of all major fruits of the *Citrus* genus, undoubtedly traces back to the Asian tropics, but it has never been found in the wild. It is not inconceivable that somewhere in Asia or nearby islands the grapefruit exists in a natural state, but that is very unlikely. The most probable explanations of its origin is that it appeared as a sport (mutant) or as a seedling variant of a shaddock or pummelo (*Citrus maxima*) in the West Indies or that it is a hybrid between the shaddock and sweet orange (*C. sinensis*).

The known history of grapefruit (*Citrus paradisi*) supports the belief that in 1823 Count Odette Philippe, formerly chief surgeon in the French Navy at the time of Napoleon, established a citrus grove on old Tampa Bay, Florida, and planted grapefruits almost surely obtained from the Bahamas. These and seedlings from them planted in other parts of the state became the basis of the grapefruit-growing industry, but not until between 1880 and 1885 were fruits shipped in commercial quantities to the north.

From the shaddock the grapefruit differs chiefly in being a larger, hardier tree, in its shoots and leaves being hairless, and in having superior, fine-grained fruits. The latter are mostly in bunches, which gives reason for the common name, but those of some varieties, such as 'McCarty', are gen-

erally solitary. The coarse-grained fruits of shaddocks are solitary or in clusters.

In the United States cultivated chiefly in Florida, California, Arizona, and Texas, grapefruits may be grown wherever sweet oranges are hardy, but the production of the highest quality fruits needs higher summer temperatures. Unrestrained by pruning, grapefruit trees eventually attain heights and spreads of more than 50 feet. In groves a common spacing is 30 feet between individuals. Seedling trees are occasionally planted, but the great majority have fruits markedly inferior to those of named varieties. The latter are increased by grafting or budding, chiefly onto seedling understocks of sour orange and rough lemon. Less frequently grapefruit seedlings and seedlings of trifoliate-orange (*Poncirus trifoliata*) are employed as understocks.

Favorite varieties are 'Duncan', an excellent medium- to large-fruited variety more resistant to low temperatures than most and with fruits with pale pulp; 'Marsh', with seedless or nearly seedless, medium-sized, pale-fleshed fruits; 'McCarty', with large fruits with greenish-gray flesh; 'Ruby', with fruits with red-tinged skins and ruby-red pulp. They have none or few seeds. 'Thompson' differs from 'Marsh' only in its fruits being pink-fleshed and ripening slightly earlier. 'Triumph' and similar or perhaps identical 'Imperial' are excellent for home gardens. They have small, juicy fruits.

Cultivation. This does not differ materially from that appropriate for oranges.

GRAPES. Among the most important fruits, grapes are much esteemed and cultivated for eating out of hand, wine making, and drying as currants and raisins. They are varieties of various species of *Vitis* of the grape family VITIDACEAE. Based on their ancestral species three distinct

types of grapes are cultivated in North America. Each has many varieties, is best adapted to specific regions, and is managed differently.

Vinifera grapes, grown in California and other mild-climate areas, are derivatives of *Vitis vinifera*. These are the grapes of antiquity, of the classics, to which reference is made in the Old Testament and the New Testament of the Bible. They are cultivated in vast quantities in all major grape-growing and wine-making regions of the world except eastern North America. They are the grapes of Europe, the Mediterranean region, South Africa, Australia, South America, and western North America.

Cultivated for several thousand years, vinifera or European grapes as they are sometimes called, probably originated in the Transcaucasian region of western Asia. From there they were taken first to Mediterranean lands. Later, as European peoples settled in other parts of the world they took with them grapes.

Early attempts to cultivate vinifera grapes outdoors in eastern North America

Vinifera grapes in a greenhouse at Longwood Gardens, Kennett Square, Pennsylvania

Vinifera grapes in California: (a) Trained along horizontal wires

(b) In fruit

failed miserably as have all later ones. The climate is not suitable. Winters are too cold in the north, summers too wet in the south. Very rarely now, but formerly not infrequently on large estates, grapes of these kinds were grown in greenhouses in eastern North America and in northern Europe.

Introduction of vinifera varieties to California was by Franciscan fathers, who established mission gardens in the latter half of the eighteenth century. The vines prospered in the Mediterranean-like climate and became the basis of the great grape-growing and wine-making industries that flourish in California, Arizona, Oregon, and elsewhere in the West.

Soils for these grapes may vary considerably. Coarse, gravelly loams and clayish loams are often preferred. Sharp drainage is of the utmost importance and a generous admixture of organic matter is advantageous. Throughout the summer the earth must not lie wet for more than a couple of days at a time. Irrigate with this in mind. Do not give water until the leaves remain slightly wilted overnight. In late winter wet soil for longer periods is not injurious.

Phylloxera insects, a kind of root louse, are highly destructive of vinifera grapes on their own roots in many regions. The one way to avoid this is to plant only vines grafted or budded onto phylloxera-resistant understocks. There are many of these, including 'Rupestris St. George', 'Aramon' × 'Rupestris Ganzin No. 1', and 'Mouvedre' × 'Rupestris 1202'. 'Solonis' × 'Othello 1613' has moderate resistance to phylloxera. It is very resistant to root-knot nematode. Consult a Cooperative Extension Agent or other local authority before choosing varieties for planting.

Planting is done in rows 7 to 12 feet apart with about 7 feet between vines in the rows. Trim the roots to 3 to 4 inches and set the plants at the same depth as they previously were, grafted ones with the graft union 4 to 5 inches above the surface. If in contact with the soil, the scion portion is likely to develop roots, inviting the attentions of phylloxera.

Two systems of training are chiefly followed. One to give head-pruned vines, the other horizontal cordons. Head-pruned vines are secured to individual stakes 1 foot to 3 feet high. Each is allowed to de-

Labrusca grape trained to a single stake

Labrusca grapes trained along horizontal wires

velop a single trunk with at its top a circle of short, armlike branches from which grow the fruit-bearing shoots. Cordon-trained vines are tied to a trellis or fence of two wires stretched tautly between uprights spaced at intervals. The lower wire is 2½ feet to 2 feet 10 inches, the upper one 3½ to 4 feet above the ground. The vine is allowed to develop a trunk reaching to the first wire. Along the wire two

Labrusca grapes trained vertically across horizontal wires (a) After pruning

(b) Starting into new growth

(c) In foliage

(d) In fruit

branches stretching in opposite directions are trained. Variations in the branch pattern of cordon systems are sometimes followed for decorative effects. For instance, more than one horizontal branch in each direction may be developed at different levels, a branch or branches may be allowed in one direction only, or the branches may be erect or at an angle from the vertical. Such departures from the typical training pattern are useful when grapes are to clothe arbors and other decorative supports. A disadvantage of vertical cordons and those with their stems trained at angles other than horizontal is that the upper spurs develop vigorously at the expense of the lower ones and after a few years the latter cease to be productive.

Pruning in the early stages is designed to establish the permanent framework of trunk and branches. Do not prune the first year. Let the shoots develop maximum leafage to manufacture food to strengthen the root system. The first winter cut out all except the strongest cane, and shorten it to two or three buds. When in spring shoots from these are 6 to 8 inches long, select the sturdiest and keep it tied loosely in position to form a trunk. Remove other shoots. When the retained shoot has attained a height about 1 foot above where branches are needed to form a head or arms of a cordon, cut it back at one node above the level at which branching is desired. Allow only the number of shoots needed as arms to develop. Pinch side

shoots that come from them at 10 inches. The following winter cut these shortened side shoots of cordons back close to their bases.

Begin pruning for fruit production the third winter after planting and continue in succeeding years. This pruning consists of cutting out all weak and crowding canes and shortening others, those of cordons spaced 6 to 10 inches apart, to two or three buds to form spurs.

Cane pruning is another method sometimes employed. For it the vines are trained as for head pruning except that they are allowed to develop only four branches, these in the plane of the trellis instead of sprouting in all directions from the trunk. Cane pruning for fruit production consists of cutting out in winter all canes that carried the previous season's crop and of replacing them with new canes of the previous year's growth that come from the short permanent armlike branch or from as close to the base of the old fruiting cane as possible. Good judgment is needed to determine the number and lengths of the canes to be retained. The canes retained are shortened, depending upon their vigor, to lengths of from eight to fifteen buds. During summer shoots from as close to the trunk arms as possible are selected for retention as renewal canes to fruit the next year and are tied into position.

Thinning flower clusters and young berries is highly recommended as a way of obtaining superior fruits. Flower cluster

thinning consists of reducing the number of flower clusters by pinching out those considered excessive, especially any loose or poorly formed. Do this early before the blooms open. Berry thinning is the removal of portions of the bunches while the fruits are yet tiny. It consists of cutting out some branches from the clusters or in some cases removing their ends. It is done as soon as the flowers that have failed to set fruits shed. The number of branches left is usually six to eight, enough to carry eighty to one hundred berries. Berry thinning does not materially improve the size of seedless grapes, but with other kinds it does. It also reduces crowding of the berries in the clusters and results in more uniform color when ripe.

Girdling or ringing is yet another method employed to increase berry size and quality, and with 'Black Corinth' to assure satisfactory sets of fruit. The berries of 'Thompson Seedless' and other seedless varieties are greatly improved in size if girdling is done a week or two after blooming. Done with a special double-bladed tool, it consists of removing from completely around the trunk, arm, or cane, while the vines are in bloom, a 3/16-inch-wide ring of bark. When girdling take care to remove only the bark. Do not injure the wood beneath. Make sure that following girdling the vines do not suffer from insufficient water and allow them to carry about only two-thirds the number of bunches that an ungirdled vine of the same size would have.

Other cultural practices include shallow cultivation or mulching to control weeds and on land subject to erosion growing between the rows of vines a winter cover crop such as a mixture of oats or barley and purple vetch. Fertilization designed to supply nitrogen in amounts and at times determined by the vigor and fruitfulness of the vines may be needed.

Labrusca and labruscana grapes, the former derivatives of the native eastern North American fox grape (*Vitis labrusca*) and hybrids of it and other native species, the latter hybrids between it and vinifera varieties, are the chief grapes cultivated in eastern North America. Labruscana hybrids were raised in the early years of the nineteenth century. Following the first fruiting of the pure labrusca variety 'Concord' in 1849, grape growing in the Northeast developed rapidly especially in regions near the Great Lakes and other large bodies of water that moderate the climate by delaying early fall frosts and spring growth until danger from frost has passed.

The best sites and soils for these grapes are elevated land that ensures good air drainage without the danger of freezing that low-lying frost pockets present. Like vinifera varieties, labrusca and labruscana grapes adapt to a wide variety of soils, but deep, fertile, sandy or gravelly loams, with sharp subsurface drainage, suit them best. Grape roots penetrate to depths of 4 to 6 feet. In preparing the land for planting add organic matter in liberal amounts by plowing or spading under manure, compost, or heavy sod that has been growing *in situ* for a few years.

Planting is generally done in spring, but may be carried out in fall if soil is mounded about the young plants to reduce the danger of them being heaved from the ground by alternate freezing and thawing. Rows are commonly spaced 8 to 10 feet apart with 8 to 9 feet allowed between plants in the rows. No fertilizer is needed at planting time. Pruning then consists of cutting the canes back to two buds or leaving only the strongest cane with eight to ten and cutting out all others.

Supports may be trellises of wires stretched between posts of durable wood treated with a preservative (not creosote) to extend their usefulness as long as possible. The end posts of each row must be suitably braced. The most popular training is the single-stem, four-arm Kniffin system. This calls for a trellis of two wires, one at 2½ to 3 feet from the ground, the other about 3 feet higher. Grapes in home gardens are also often grown on arbors.

A grape arbor at the Berkshire Garden Center, Stockbridge, Massachusetts

Training must be orderly. Vines are neither manageable nor fruitful if permitted to grow unsystematically or if they carry too many or too-crowded canes. The chief methods of training provide for the current season's shoots to be tied in place more or less vertically or for them to hang. The hanging plan is generally preferred because vines so trained are less likely to be damaged by wind. Under the single-stem four-arm Kniffin method of training a single trunk reaching to the top wire and tied there is developed. From it four fruiting canes, one to each wire, that is two in each direction, are lead away from the trunk. These sprout the shoots that carry the flowers and fruits. Each winter canes that have fruited are cut out close to their

bases and a new one that developed during the summer from a renewal spur near the trunk is tied in.

Pruning calls for judgment. The objective is to leave enough lengths of fruiting canes, in other words a sufficient number of growth buds, to produce as many bunches as the vine can bring to good quality maturity, but not more. Overbearing and underbearing are to be avoided. Under the Kniffin system the fruiting canes, depending upon their thickness and vigor, are left with from eight to sixteen buds. On arbors they may be rather longer. Some gardeners shorten the leafy shoots, except the ones from the base of the fruiting canes that are to fruit the following year, in summer, but this is harmful rather than helpful to the production of good quality fruit. After ten to fifteen years it is good practice to develop a new trunk. To do this, train in a sucker shoot from the base of the vine and in about three years when the young one attains sensible production, cut out the old trunk at its base.

Summer care requires that weeds be controlled. During the early part of the season this may be done by cultivating the soil shallowly and not oftener than is necessary or by mulching. Grapes resent deep disturbance of the soil and too frequent cultivating results in excessive loss of organic matter and on slopes to exposing the soil to erosion. A plan often followed is to cultivate until late July, then sow rye grass or winter rye as a cover crop or alternatively to mulch with waste hay or any other suitable material. If need for fertilizing is indicated by less than satisfactory vigorous growth of the vines apply a dressing of a 10-10-10 fertilizer or one of some other formulation that supplies a fair amount of nitrogen. Do this in spring or before sowing the cover crop.

Muscadine grapes are varieties of *Vitis rotundifolia* a native from Delaware southward and to Texas. They are better suited for climates characterized by hot, humid summers than vinifera, labrusca, and labruscana varieties and so are the grapes of

Muscadine grapes

the south. Many varieties are selections from wild plants and because they are unisexual females it is necessary to interplant male vines with them to serve as pollinators to ensure fruit. More recently self-fertile varieties have been introduced and these, for home garden purposes at least, are to be preferred.

Soils suitable for other grapes are satisfactory for these. Planting is done in very early spring, or earlier in the far south. One-year-old or sometimes two-year-old plants are set in rows 10 feet apart with, depending upon vigor of the variety, 15 to 20 feet between individuals in the rows.

Muscadine grapes are generally trained in one of two ways. A three-wire vertical trellis is employed with the lowest wire 2 feet, the others 4 feet and 6 feet, respectively, above the ground, and the branches are fanned or trained horizontally along the wires. Alternatively, an overhead horizontal trellis held on stout posts about 7 feet above the ground is erected. On this the about eight branches allowed to develop from the top of the vertical trunk of each vine are spread and tied.

Pruning in the early years is to establish the framework of permanent branches. From then on it consists of cutting back the canes along the arms to three or four buds. As the branches from the top of the trunk age their vigor declines so that eventually they must be removed and replaced. Do this by cutting out the wornout branch near its base and training a strong young shoot in its place. Do not do this with more than one or two of the horizontal branches each year. Let renewal be a gradual program spread over a few years.

Harvest grapes of all kinds as soon as they are fully ripe, but not before. There is no advantage in allowing them to hang on the vines beyond that stage. Neither labrusca nor muscadine grapes keep for long after picking, but vinifera varieties do and so do some of the labruscanas in which vinifera characteristics are strongly evident. The best storage is had by spreading the bunches one layer deep in trays and keeping them where the temperature is as close to just above 32°F as possible. Under such conditions they will keep for two to three months.

Propagation of grapes is done in various ways. All can be raised from hardwood cuttings and this is usual with labrusca and labruscana varieties. Even with these some advantage has sometimes been secured by grafting them onto understocks that are strongly resistant to phylloxera. This latter procedure, or instead of grafting, chip budding onto phylloxera-resistant rootstocks, is the common way with vinifera or European grapes. Cuttings of muscadine grapes root much less readily than those of other kinds, and so it is usual to increase those by layering shoots of the current season's growth about mid-

Rooted cuttings of a labrusca grape

Graptopetalum paraguayense

summer. By fall the layers will have rooted sufficiently to be severed from the mother plant and planted separately.

Varieties of grapes are many. Before you plant ascertain which are most likely to prosper in your locality. Your Cooperative Extension Agent or State Agricultural Experiment Station will gladly advise you or perhaps you can obtain the information from local nurseries or growers of grapes. Give thought, too, to the chief purpose for which you expect to use the fruit, as table grapes, for wine making, for canning, or for drying as raisins. Varieties vary in their suitability for different uses. Descriptions of varieties are given in nursery catalogs and State Experiment Station bulletins.

Vinifera grape varieties for eating out of hand include 'Cardinal', 'Emperor', 'Flame Tokay', 'Malaga', 'Muscat of Alexandria', 'Muscat Hamburg', 'Red Malaga', and 'Ribier'. The chief canning grapes of this kind is 'Thompson Seedless'. Black-fruited vinifera wine grapes are 'Alicante Bouschet', 'Cabernet', 'Carignane', 'Grenache', 'Mataro', 'Mission', 'Petite Sirah', 'Sauvignon', and 'Zinfandel'. White-fruited vinifera wine grapes include 'Burger', 'Franken Riesling', 'Johannisberger Riesling', 'Palomino', 'Sauvignon Blanc', and 'Semillon'. Good raisin grapes are 'Black Corinth', 'Muscat of Alexandria', and 'Thompson Seedless'.

Labrusca and labruscana grapes include such widely planted sorts as 'Buffalo', 'Catawba', 'Concord', 'Delaware', 'Fredonia', 'Sheridan', and 'Worden', among red- and black-fruited varieties. White-fruited kinds of these groups are 'Golden Muscat', 'Himrod', 'Interlaken', 'Niagara', 'Ontario', 'Portland', and 'Seneca'.

Muscadine grape varieties long known in cultivation are 'James', 'Scuppernong', and 'Thomas', the first and last with dark purplish or wine-colored fruits, 'Scuppernong' with green to reddish berries. These have unisexual flowers and so to assure

fruiting must be planted near male plants. Self-fertile, bisexual muscadine grapes include 'Burgaw', 'Duplin', 'Mish', 'Pender', 'Tarheel', 'Wallace', and 'Willard'.

Pests and Diseases. Like all fruits, grapes are subject to a number of pests and diseases that must be combatted successfully if fine produce is to be had. Information about these and latest recommendations for dealing with them may be had from Cooperative Extension Agents and State Agricultural Experiment Stations. Pests include flea beetles and phylloxera. Black rot of the fruits and downy mildew on the foliage are common diseases.

GRAPTOPETALUM (Grapto-pétalum). Once included in *Cotyledon* and closely related to *Sedum*, the genus *Graptopetalum* belongs in the orpine family CRASSULACEAE. It involves ten species, natives from the southern United States to Paraguay. The name, alluding to the markings of the flowers, is from the Greek *graptos*, marked with letters or writing, and *petalon*, a petal. Hybrids between *Graptopetalum* and *Echeveria* are named *Graptoveria*.

Graptopetalums are nonhardy, evergreen herbaceous perennials with much the aspect of *Echeveria*, *Dudleya*, and *Pachyphytum*, but differing in their flowers having petals marked with red dots usually arranged in cross bands, united in their lower parts and spreading from about their middles to form a star-shaped face to the bloom. They are stemless or have thick, fleshy stems. Their undivided, lobeless, toothless, fleshy leaves are alternate, in rosettes, or more loosely arranged. They may be round in cross section or much flatter. The stalks that carry the umbel-like clusters of blooms come from the leaf axils. Each flower has five sepals as long as the corolla tube, five petals, ten stamens, their pollen unpleasantly scented, and five pistils that mature into little podlike fruits.

One of the most handsome and popular graptopetalums, *G. paraguayense* (syns. *Echeveria paraguayense*, *Sedum paraguayense*, *S. weinbergii*) is hairless and up to about 1 foot tall. It has stems with spreading branches ending in loose rosettes of broad, thick, glaucous leaves 2 to 3½ inches in length. They are flat or hollowed above, bluntly-keeled on their undersides. The ½-inch-wide blooms are white, spotted with red. This is a native of Mexico.

Another very attractive kind, *G. amethystinum* (syns. *Echeveria amethystina*, *Pachyphytum amethystinum*), native to Mexico, is a subshrub 6 inches or so tall the stems of which become prostrate with age. Branched from below, they carry at their ends loose rosettes of very thick, blunt or slightly pointed, oblanceolate to ellipticobovate leaves 2 to 3 inches long by onehalf as wide, hollowed on their upper sides. They are bluish-gray to greenish with a beautiful overlay of amethyst-purple. The branched flower stalks, up to about 6 inches long, carry up-facing, pale greenish-yellow to light yellowish-green blooms, their petals with bands of red dots. They are about ½ inch in diameter.

Graptopetalum amethystinum

Graptopetalum macdougallii

Other kinds cultivated include the following: Mexican **G. filiferum** (syn. *Sedum filiferum*) forms clumps of rosettes of spatula-shaped to obovate leaves. The rosettes are up to a little more than 2 inches in diameter. The leaves, ⅓ to ½ inch wide, up to ⅙ inch thick, and bristle-tipped, are lustrous-green with white, winglike edges. Up-facing and ¾ inch across, the flowers are in loose, two- or three-branched, few-leaved clusters. They have red-spotted, white petals. Also native of Mexico, **G. grande** is a bushy species with thick, erect, branched stems up to 1 foot or taller. Its broadly-spatula-shaped, flat, thinnish leaves are slightly glaucous, especially the younger ones, and yellowish. They are thinnish, up to 3½ inches long by 1½ inches wide. The blooms are in panicle-like arrangements with coiled, zigzagged stalks up to 1¼ feet long. They are ¾ inches wide, sulfur-yellow sprinkled with red dots. Stemless **G. macdougallii** is another Mexican. This forms clumps of crowded, very glaucous rosettes of tongue-shaped, bluish leaves nearly 1½ inches long and short-pointed at their apexes. Their upper sides are slightly convex. In many loose, umbel-type to panicle-like clusters, the ¾-inch-wide blooms have whitish-yellowish-green insides with the petals brown-tipped. They are green on their outsides. Native of Arizona, **G. orpetii** is stemless. It has rosettes up to about 3 inches wide that form clumps. The pointed-oblong-lanceolate leaves, somewhat upturned toward their

Graptopetalum pachyphyllum

ends, are ¼ to slightly over ⅓ inch wide, a little hollowed on their olive-green upper sides and rounded and apple-green beneath. Branched or not, the flowering stalks, 2½ to 3½ inches long, carry red-banded, pale yellow blooms approximately ½ inch in diameter. Mexican **G. pachyphyllum** has trailing stems up to 8 inches long that branch from their bases. In rosettes of twenty to fifty, the often red-tipped, blue-glaucous, club-shaped leaves are ½ to ¾ inch long. Bearing similar leaves, the flowering stems carry on each of their few branches five or fewer ½- to ¾-inch-wide, sparsely-dotted flowers. Stemless **G. rusbyi**, native of Arizona and Mexico, has rosettes of up to thirty-five oblanceolate to spatula-shaped, somewhat pustuled leaves ½ inch to 2 inches long by

up to a little over ½ inch wide. The 3- to 5-inch-tall flowering stems bear on each of their two or three branches seven or fewer five- to seven-petaled blooms slightly over ½ inch in diameter. What seems to be a larger variant of *G. rusbyi* is sometimes mistakenly named *G. occidentale*. The species to which that name properly belongs is probably not in cultivation.

Garden and Landscape Uses and Cultivation. These are as for *Echeveria*.

GRAPTOPHYLLUM (Grapto-phýllum)—Caricature Plant. The only known cultivated representative of *Graptophyllum* is admired for its handsomely variegated foliage. The genus, belonging in the acanthus family ACANTHACEAE, ranges in the wild from Polynesia to Australia. Its name is derived from the Greek *grapho*, to write, and *phyllon*, a leaf, and alludes to the markings on the foliage.

Graptophyllums are nonhardy shrubs with opposite, usually lobeless and toothless, generally colored leaves. The reddish to purple, wide-gaping, tubular flowers are in more or less spikelike terminal clusters or come from the leaf axils. They have five sepals and a corolla tube that broadens above and has an upper lip of two short, recurved lobes and a three-lobed lower one. There are two stamens. The fruits are capsules containing two seeds.

Graptophyllum pictum

The kind popular in cultivation is **G. pictum** (syn. *G. hortense*), a native of New Guinea. This 8-foot-tall, rounded shrub is freely planted in the American tropics and in other warm, humid regions. Its ovate or elliptic leaves are up to 6 inches long. They are smooth-edged, green or purplish and most commonly clearly and irregularly blotched with yellow along their centers and have mid-veins and stalks tinged pink. A plain green-leaved form is sometimes seen. The flowers, in short clusters, are about 1½ inches long and have protruding stamens. The fruits are club-shaped. A variety of this plant, cultivated under the misnomer of *Eranthemum* 'Eldorado' has the variegation pattern of its leaves reversed so that the irregular central portion is green, the surrounding areas yellow.

Garden and Landscape Uses. In tropical climates these decorative foliage shrubs can be used effectively to provide accents of color in the landscape. They are seen to best advantage when used in conjunction with green-foliaged plants rather than associated with other brightly colored kinds, such as crotons. They grow well in part-day shade and in full sun if the soil is not excessively dry. They are also useful foliage plants for tropical greenhouses.

Cultivation. The caricature plant does best in fertile, fairly moist soil. It needs no special care and only whatever pruning is deemed desirable to limit its size or keep it shapely. When cut back it renews itself freely from the base. Under greenhouse cultivation it gives the best results when grown in a humid atmosphere where the minimum night temperature in winter is 60 to 65°F. Day temperatures in winter may be five to ten degrees above those maintained at night. In summer both night and day temperatures may with advantage be considerably higher than those maintained in winter. Light shade from strong summer sun is needed. Greenhouse-grown specimens revel in rich, coarse soil kept always moist, but not constantly saturated. When the roots crowd the containers weekly or biweekly applications of dilute liquid fertilizer are helpful. In late winter or early spring old specimens should be pruned to shape and repotted or top dressed. Occasional pinching of the shoots is likely to be needed during the growing season to keep the plants shapely and, in the case of young ones, to promote branching. Propagation is easy by cuttings, which root readily in sand, sand and peat moss, perlite, vermiculite, or other propagating medium, in a highly humid atmosphere and shaded from direct sun.

GRAPTOVERIA (Grapto-vèria). These are hybrids beween *Graptopetalum* and *Echeveria* of the orpine family CRASSULACEAE. Of garden origin, they have characteristics intermediate between those of their parents. Their uses and care are those of the parents. Kinds cultivated are *G. calva*, a hybrid between *Graptopetalum paraguayense* and *Echeveria pulvinata*, and *G. haworthioides*, the result of crossing *Graptopetalum paraguayense* and *Echeveria agavoides*.

GRASSES. All plants, including bamboos, that belong in the grass family GRAMINEAE are technically grasses, but because gardeners and horticulturists usually consider bamboos separately they are so treated in this Encyclopedia. For information about them see Bamboos. Many grasses are of immense economic importance to mankind, notably the cereals barley, corn, oats, rice, rye, sorghum, and wheat and,

in addition, sugar cane. With the exception of corn the cereals are primarily agricultural crop. Neither they nor sugar cane are of much horticultural significance.

Grasses that hold special interest for gardeners are those grown as ornamentals (see Grasses, Ornamental), those used in lawns (see Lawns, Their Making and Renovation), and certain more or less pestiferous weeds such as crab grass. They include Bahia grass (*Daspalum notatum* and variety), basket grass (*Oplismenus compositus*), beach or marram grass (*Ammophila*), beard grass (*Polypogon*), bent grass (*Agrostis*), Bermuda grass (*Cynodon dactylon*), bottle brush grass (*Hystrix patula*), brome grass (*Bromus*), brook grass (*Catabrosa aquatica*), camel grass (*Cymbopogon schoenanthus*), Canada blue grass (*Poa compressa*), Canary grass (*Phalaris canariensis*), centipede grass (*Eremochloa ophiuroides*), citronella grass (*Cymbopogon nardus*), cloud grass (*Agrostis nebulosa*), dune grass (*Elymus arenarius mollis*), esparto grass (*Stipa tenacissima*), European reed sweet grass (*Glyceria maxima*), feather grass (*Stipa pennata*), fern grass (*Catapodium rigida*), finger grass (*Chloris*), fountain grass (*Pennisetum setaceum*), foxtail grass (*Alopecurus*), grama grass (*Bouteloua*), hair grass (*Agrostis hiemalis*, *Aira*, *Deschampsia*, and *Koeleria*), hare's tail or rabbit's tail grass (*Lagurus ovatus*), Japanese or Korean lawn grass (*Zoysia japonica*), Johnson grass (*Sorghum halepense*), Kentucky blue grass (*Poa pratensis*), khus-khus grass (*Vetiveria zizanioides*), kikuyu grass (*Pennisetum clandestinum*), Korean velvet or mascarene grass (*Zoysia tenuifolia*), lemon grass (*Cymbopogon citratus*), love grass (*Eragrostis*), lyme grass (*Elymus*), Manila grass (*Zoysia matrella*), manna grass (*Glyceria*), meadow grass (*Poa*), melic grass (*Melica*), Natal or ruby grass (*Rhynchelytrum repens*), oat grass (*Heliotrichon* and *Arrhenantherum*), orchard grass (*Dactylis glomerata*), palm grass (*Setaria palmifolia*), pampas grass (*Cortaderia selloana*), plume or ravenna grass (*Erianthus ravennae*), purple moor grass (*Molina caerulea*), quake grass (*Bromus brizaeformis*), quaking grass (*Briza*), redtop, whitetop, or fiorin (*Agrostic gigantea*), reed grass (*Calamagrostis* and *Phragmites communis*), reed canary grass (*Phalaris arundinacea*), reed meadow grass (*Glyceria grandis*), reed sweet grass (*Glyceria maxima*), Rhode's grass (*Chloris gayana*), ribbon grass (*Phalaris arundinacea picta*), rough-stalked meadow grass (*Poa trivialis*), rye grass (*Lolium*), St. Augustine grass (*Stenotaphrum secundatum*), silk grass (*Agrostis hiemalis*), silky-bent grass (*Apera interrupta*), spear grass (*Stipa*), spike grass (*Desmazeria sicula*, *Leptochloa fasicularis*, and *Chasmanthium latifolium*), squirrel tail grass (*Hordeum jubatum*), Sudan grass (*Sorghum bicolor*), switch grass (*Panicum virgatum*), uva grass (*Gynerium sagittatum*), velvet grass (*Holcus lanatus*), wild-oats (*Chasmanthium latifolium*), wire grass (*Eleusine indica* and *Poa compressa*), witch grass (*Panicum capillare*),

wood meadow grass (*Poa nemoralis*), yard grass (*Eleusine indica*), and zebra grass (*Miscanthus sinensis zebrinus*).

Plants other than grasses that have the word grass as part of their common names include bear-grass (*Dasylirion texanum* and *Xerophyllum texanum*), blue-eyed-grass (*Sisyrinchium*), China-grass (*Boehmeria nivea candicans*), cotton-grass (*Eriophorum*), curly-grass fern (*Schizaea pusilla*), deer-grass (*Rhexia*), eel- or tape-grass (*Vallisneria*), fish-grass (*Cabomba caroliniana*), golden-eyed-grass (*Sisyrinchium californicum*), grass nut (*Triteleia laxa*), grass-of-Parnassus (*Parnassia*), grass-pea (*Lathyrus sativus*), grass-pink orchid (*Calopogon*), grass-tree (*Xanthorrhoea*), mondo-grass (*Ophiopogon*), pepper-grass (*Lepidium*), scurvy grass (*Cochlearia*), squaw-grass (*Xerophyllum*), star-grass (*Aletris* and *Hypoxis*), viper's-grass (*Scorzonera*), water star-grass (*Zosterella*), wool-grass (*Scirpus cyperinus*), worm-grass (*Spigelia marilandica*), and yellow-eyed-grass (*Xyris*).

GRASSES, ORNAMENTAL. Grasses include all plants of the grass family GRAMINEAE. Here belong cereals, such as barley, corn, oats, rice, rye, and wheat, and sugar cane, sorgham, and bamboos, giant kinds of which sometimes attain 100 feet in height. Gardeners most often omit all or most of these from their consideration of grasses and think only of other kinds ornamental and of some that are weeds. Among the latter crab grass and quack grass are well known.

Grasses of horticultural merit include annuals and perennials. Among the most important are sod-making kinds used in lawns. For information about them see Lawns, Their Making and Renovation. Here we focus on sorts, excluding bamboos, which are dealt with under Bamboos, employed for other decorative purposes. The most impressive include pampas grass (*Cortaderia selloana*), giant-reed (*Arundo donax*), eulalias (*Miscanthus*), and the variegated-leaved variety of corn (*Zea mays*). Were it not for its treacherous take-over propensities common reed-grass (*Phragmites communis*) might well be included. Unfortunately that is much too rampant and difficult to contain or eradicate to be admitted to gardens. There are many ornamental grasses of interest and decorative merit, among them animated oat (*Avena sterilis*), fountain grass (*Pennisetum setaceum*), and Job's tears (*Coix lacryma-jobi*).

The chief employment of ornamental grasses are in beds and borders and for cutting for fresh and dried flower arrangements. Their chief beauty lies not in the individual blooms, which are minute and scarcely recognizable by the nonbotanist as flowers, but in their varied arrangements in spikelike or more feathery and plumelike panicles and the graceful foliage. Some ornamental grasses are dried, sometimes dyed, and sold commercially. Dying is rarely an improvement.

The cultivation of ornamental grasses is simple. They are not choosy as to soil, adapting well to a wide variety of types. Most need full sun for their best development. The perennials, where hardy (not all are in the north), succeed under conditions appropriate for most herbaceous perennials. They are easily propagated by division and seeds. Some, especially if started early indoors and later planted out, make a good showing the first year. Annual sorts grow readily from seeds sown outdoors in spring where the plants are to remain.

Perennial grasses of ornamental merit include blue fescue (*Festuca glauca*), bottle brush grass (*Hystrix patula*), eulalia (*Miscanthus sinensis*), feather grass (*Stipa pennata*), fountain grass (*Pennisetum setaceum*), giant-reed (*Arundo donax*), Job's tears (*Coix lacryma-jobi*), oat grass (*Heliotrichon*), palm grass (*Setaria palmifolia*), pampas grass (*Cortaderia selloana*), plume grass (*Erianthus ravennae*), quaking grass (*Briza media*), ribbon grass or gardener's garters (*Phalaris arundinacea picta*), sea lyme grass (*Elymus arenarius mollis*), spike grass (*Uniola latifolia*), and zebra grass (*Miscanthus sinensis zebrinus*).

Annual grasses grown for ornament include cloud grass (*Agrostis nebulosa*), hare's tail grass (*Lagurus ovatus*), love grass (*Eragrostis japonica, E. tenella,* and *E. mexicana*), Natal or ruby grass (*Rhynchelytrum repens*), quake grass (*Bromus brizaeformis*), quaking grass (*Briza maxima, B. minor*), silky-bent grass (*Apera*), squirrel tail grass (*Hordeum jubatum*), and variegated corn (*Zea mays japonica*).

GRASSHOPPERS. Active jumping insects with bodies usually 1 inch to 2½ inches long and somewhat deeper than wide, long hindlegs, and prominent eyes, grasshoppers are destructive to many kinds of plants, feeding by day in sunny places. Control is chiefly by poison baits.

GRATIOLA (Grat-ìola)—Hedge-Hyssop or Gratiole. Belonging in the figwort family SCROPHULARIACEAE, this group of about twenty species of annual and perennial herbaceous plants is of minor horticultural importance. One, *Gratiola officinalis*, was formerly used officially in medicine and is still employed by herbalists. It has cathartic and emetic properties. Because of these it was formerly called Gratia Dei. The name *Gratiola*, from the Latin *gratia*, thanks or favor, alludes to these medical virtues.

Gratiolas are natives of North America, Europe, temperate Asia, and Australia. They have opposite leaves and, singly on stalks from the leaf axils, small white or yellow flowers with usually two sepal-like bractlets immediately beneath the calyx. There are five, usually unequal-sized se-

Gratiola officinalis

pals, a tubular to narrowly-bell-shaped, indistinctly two-lipped corolla with the upper lip notched or cleft into two and the lower into three lobes, two functional and sometimes two rudimentary stamens, and one style. The fruits are small capsules.

The European hedge-hyssop or gratiole (*G. officinalis*) is native of wet soils throughout much of Europe. A hairless perennial with creeping rhizomes, it is 8 inches to 2 feet tall and has lanceolate leaves, toothed toward their apexes. Its long-stalked blooms are ½ to ¾ inch long. They have lanceolate calyx lobes (sepals) and corollas with yellowish tubes and pink- or purple-tinged spreading lobes (petals). The stamens do not protrude. Golden hedge-hyssop (**G. aurea**) occurs as a native, especially in acid, muddy, and sandy soils, along the coast from Newfoundland and Quebec to Florida, and inland from Ontario and New York to Illinois and South Dakota. This prostrate or creeping perennial, hairless or sometimes shortly-hairy in its upper parts, is up to 1 foot tall and has stalkless, broad-based lanceolate or ovate leaves up to 1 inch long with sometimes just a suggestion of teeth at their edges. The sepals are lanceolate, the corolla bright yellow and ½ inch long or slightly longer.

Garden Uses and Cultivation. The species last described may be grown in bog gardens and in wet soil at watersides, where it helps to prevent washing. The European hedge-hyssop is suitable for inclusion in gardens of plants that have been used medicinally. Both are hardy and grow without trouble in wet soils in sun. They are easily propagated by seeds, division, and cuttings.

GRATIOLE is *Gratiola officinalis*.

GRAYBEARD is *Tillandsia usneoides*.

GREASEWOOD. This is a common name of *Adenostoma fasciculatum* and *Sarcobatus vermiculatus*.

GREATER CELANDINE is *Chelidonium majus*.

GREATER SPEARWORT is *Ranunculus lingua*.

GREATWOODARA. This is the name of hybrid orchids the parents of which include *Ascocentrum*, *Euanthes*, *Renanthera*, and *Vanda*.

GREEK-VALERIAN is *Polemonium caeruleum*.

GREEN. The word green appears as part of the common name of the following plants: green-aloe (*Furcraea foetida*), green dragon (*Arisaema dracontium*), green-gentian (*Frasera*), green hellebore (*Helleborus lividus*), green rose (*Rosa chinensis viridiflora*), green sapote (*Pouteria viride*), green water-rose (*Samolus parviflorus*), and green wattle (*Acacia decurrens*).

GREEN MANURING. This is the practice of growing and turning under cover crops for the special purpose of increasing the organic content, and in some cases, the nutrient value, of soil. Because it requires the ground to be given over for at least several weeks to the growth of the green manure, it is more widely practiced by truck farmers and commercial gardeners than amateurs and home gardeners. Yet there are places and times when the latter can employ green manuring to good purpose. The graded ground around newly built houses is often left in a deplorable state from a gardening viewpoint. If time allows, tremendous improvement can be wrought by raising two or more successive green manure crops and plowing, rototilling, or spading them into the soil. Even one crop so incorporated will effect some improvement. The greatest benefit usually results when green manure plants are turned under shortly before they reach maturity, but for convenience of handling it is often better in gardens to do this before they exceed 8 inches in height. Vegetable gardens afford opportunities to practice green manuring advantageously. Whenever an area is to be left unplanted for sufficient time to raise green manure this should be done. Such opportunity commonly occurs after late summer and fall harvesting. Then winter rye is likely to prove an ideal green manure. If the garden is big enough, it may be divided into sections allotted on a three- or four-year rotation devoted each year to improvement by green manuring.

Green manure crops fall into two types, those such as winter rye and buckwheat that belong to botanical groups other than the pea family (LEGUMINOSAE) and legumes, plants that belong in the pea family. Insofar as nutrients are concerned green manures of the first group add nothing to the soil, although they may serve to conserve elements already there by absorbing them and so checking leaching. After the green manure is turned under such nutrients gradually become available to growing plants. But the chief benefit of green manures of this type is the amount of organic matter they supply. Legumes, in addition to adding substantial amounts of organic matter, nourish the soil. This because they have the peculiar ability, through bacteria inhabiting the nodules on their roots, of fixing the free nitrogen of the air and storing it in forms that after the roots die and rot become available for the use of living plants. The increase in the nitrogren content of the soil that comes from turning under a legume crop is usually of less importance to home gardeners than commercial growers. At relatively small expense the same amounts of nitrogen can be added in the form of fertilizers. The most useful nonlegume green manure crops for gardens are rye grass, winter rye, winter wheat, winter oats, and buckwheat. Legumes include soybeans, cow-peas, hairy vetch, crimson clover, and sweet-clover. The choice of which to use should be based on the geographical region and the season the crop is sown. For fall sowing winter rye, winter wheat, winter oats, and hairy vetch are suitable. These are ready for turning under the following

spring. The other green manures mentioned require a summer season of growth. Because nitrogen is used by microorganisms that effect the decay of turned-under green manure crops the soil may, until the organisms themselves die, be temporarily partially depleted of this element. Therefore, either fairly heavy fertilizing should be done or a reasonable period allowed for the decay of the cover crop before other planting is done. See also Cover Crops.

GREENBIER. See Smilax.

GREENHEART. See Ziziphus.

GREENHOUSE ORTHEZIA. Related to mealybugs and scale insects, the greenhouse orthezia or lantana bug is a pest of many plants in greenhouses and, in warm climates, outdoors. Adult females together with their white, fluted egg sac attached, are ½ inch long and encircled with conspicuous, white, waxy fringes. Juveniles (nymphs) are pinhead-sized, dark green, and clothed with rows of tiny waxy plates. Control is by spraying with a contact insecticide.

GREENHOUSES and CONSERVATORIES. A greenhouse is a walk-in-size structure of chiefly glass or light-admitting plastic (with a necessary supporting framework) designed for the cultivation of plants. Those in which plants are displayed artistically chiefly for aesthetic enjoyment are often called conservatories. From cold frames, hotbeds, and similar garden appurtenances, greenhouses differ in being tall enough to walk into. Pit houses or pits are greenhouses with floors and usually

A pit greenhouse

the benches on which the plants stand, below ground level. This arrangement conserves heat.

Greenhouses are employed extensively by commercial florists and nurserymen. Conservatories are features of most botanic gardens and some public parks, and home greenhouses operated by amateurs are increasingly popular. The principles involved in the establishment and management of the latter are essentially the same as for bigger ones, except for some labor-saving procedures that larger operations make practicable.

The possession of a greenhouse extends the gardener's horizon tremendously. With one, no matter where one lives, one can engage actively in gardening throughout the year as compared with the five or six months that is all that may be practicable without such a convenience. A greenhouse makes possible the production of pot

A cover crop of winter rye

Forking under a cover crop of buckwheat

Conservatories: (a) The Enid A. Haupt Conservatory, The New York Botanical Garden

(b) Climatron, Missouri Botanical Garden

(c) Palm House, Royal Botanic Gardens, Kew, England

(d) Palm House, Botanic Garden, Berlin, Germany

Interiors of conservatories: (a) Succulent House, The New York Botanical Garden in 1942

(b) In the conservatory at The New York Botanical Garden in 1942, *Victoria amazonica*

plants for indoor decoration, of cut flowers and perhaps some salads and vegetables throughout the winter, of raising young plants to furnish the outdoor garden in summer and vegetable plants to set outdoors at appropriate seasons. Groundcovers, shrubs, evergreens, and trees if one so wishes, can be propagated in a greenhouse for later use outdoors. A greenhouse serves wonderfully well as a vacation or recovery place for houseplants that become a little tired of their less-than-ideal environments. One of the chief enjoyments of a greenhouse is that of the hobbiest, who devotes his structure to the cultivation of a particular group of plants, such as begonias, ferns, gesneriads, orchids, or succulents.

(c) Economic plants, The New York Botanical Garden in 1965

(d) Tropical Plants, Longwood Gardens, Kennett Square, Pennsylvania

(e) Calanthe orchids, Longwood Gardens

(g) Royal Gardens, Brussels, Belgium

(f) Landscaped conservatory, Duke Farms, New Jersey

(h) Palmengarten, Frankfurt-am-Main, Germany

Control of the environment, the maintenance inside of a climate favorable to plants when that outside is hostile, is what makes possible the miracles that can be achieved with a greenhouse. And miracles is not too strong a word to employ when we consider the tremendous achievements of greenhouse gardeners today as compared with those who first attempted growing plants in the primitive structures of the Romans some 2,000 years ago or even in those of George Washington and King George III, 1,800 years later.

By the beginning of the twentieth century the construction of greenhouses and the techniques of growing plants in them were so well established that results in most cases equal to the best that can be had today were common. A body of empirical knowledge that served gardeners well had been built up. But it usually took several years apprenticeship under a master gardener to acquire a good grasp of greenhouse skills. Climate control was based entirely upon seven-day-a-week, dawn-to-dusk-and-later, human judgments and implementations involving hand-fired furnaces, hand-manipulated ventilators, hand procedures to supplement humidity, and other demanding and sometimes laborious operations. Greenhouse ownership was practically restricted to those who could afford to employ professional gardeners. That has now all changed.

Modern automatic devices, especially thermostatically controlled heating plants and ventilators, as well as mist systems, watering systems, and even methods of controlling shading and supplying additional light have relieved greenhouse gardeners of the necessity of hour-by-hour attention and made it entirely feasible for the amateur to leave his greenhouse untended throughout the day, over a weekend, or even for longer periods.

The history of greenhouses is long. Wealthy citizens of ancient Rome had their specularia, glazed with sheets of translucent mica and heated by wall flues or water, in which they grew various fruits. They introduced such structures to other places they colonized, but progress beyond these primitive attempts at indoor plant cultivation were slow indeed and presumably ceased after the overthrow of the Roman Empire.

In 1670 Thomas Baskerville described a "fair greenhouse or Conservatory to preserve tender plants and trees from the Injury of hard winter" as being at the Oxford Botanic Garden, England. This masonry and glass building was roofed with stone shingles and heated in cold weather by a four-wheeled fire basket drawn back and forth along the path by a gardener. Similar structures, called orangeries and used to winter to protect orange trees and other near-hardy plants in a semidormant state, subsequently became common in the great gardens of England.

A heating arrangement decidedly superior to the Oxford fire baskets was in operation at Chelsea Physic Garden, England, before 1685. In that year the diarist John Evelyn visited the garden and wrote "What was very ingenious was the subterranean heate conveyed by a stove under the conservatory, which was all vaulted with bricks, so as he [the gardener] had the doores and windows open in the hardest frosts, secluded only from the snow." It was this early use of stoves with flues that conducted the heat through walls and floors that occasioned the use, still not uncommon in England but scarcely known in America, of stove plants and stove houses as names for tropical plants and greenhouses in which they are grown.

In the early part of the eighteenth century, fruit trees trained to masonry walls in England were being given the added protection of glazed sash set in front of them. In time these were developed into lean-to greenhouse-like structures with a slate or tile coping roof and often with heating flues running through the wall.

As early as the second decade of the eighteenth century a great interest in growing exotic plants developed in England, and new kinds were being introduced from many parts of the world. Considerable attention was then given to designing structures better adapted for growing plants than the old orangeries, the chief purpose of which was merely to store them over winter. The first wooden-framed greenhouse was erected at Oxford Botanic Garden in 1734. The greenhouse George Washington built at Mount Vernon has many of the characteristics of this early type. In 1761 a warm greenhouse 110 feet long called the Great Stove and an orangery (still extant) 130 feet long was erected at Kew Gardens, England. The

present Palm House at Kew, surely one of the loveliest greenhouses ever built, was erected in 1841. It encloses, without partitions, 1¼ acres.

The first greenhouse in North America is thought to be one erected at Boston by Andrew Faneuil, who died in 1737. Another early example of which there is record was built for George Beekman, of New York City, in 1764. Like its European contemporaries this was a solid-roofed, glass-sided structure of the orangery type. The Elgin Botanic Garden in New York City, founded in 1801 on the site where Rockefeller Center now stands, had a considerable range of greenhouses.

All of these early attempts were heated, like those abroad, by flues or by fermenting manure or tanbark. The use of steam pipes was first introduced in England about 1820, later into the United States. Not until the early 1830s did heating by hot water become available. As the nineteenth century advanced, the art of greenhouse construction developed rapidly and numerous ranges were built by florists and nurserymen and on private estates. Toward the latter part of the century and early in the next, several notable public conservatories were built, among them those of the Brooklyn Botanic Garden, New York City; Garfield Park Conservatory, Chicago, Illinois; Missouri Botanical Garden, St. Louis, Missouri; the New York Botanical Garden, New York City; and Phelp's Conservatory, Pittsburgh, Pennsylvania; and somewhat later the great range of greenhouses at Longwood Gardens, Kennett Square, Pennsylvania.

These conservatories are all of traditional Victorian design. Later in the twentieth century, both in North America and

abroad, different design concepts made possible by the availability of new materials and new mechanical systems were tried. These resulted in the production of conservatories that in many instances looked very different from their predecessors. Some, notably those of the Montreal Botanic Garden, Canada (this relatively traditional in concept), and the Edinburgh Botanic Garden, Scotland, have worked out very well. Others, for the design of which more reliance was placed on innovators and theorists than experienced cultivators of plants in conservatories, have been less successful in attaining announced expectations for them. Examples are the greenhouses at the Brussels Botanical Garden in Belgium and the Climatron at the Missouri Botanical Garden.

Amateur gardeners who elect to have a greenhouse have many choices. They may opt for an even-span-roofed structure freestanding or joined by one end or a corridor to a house, potting shed, or other building or for a lean-to one side of which is a wall. It may be framed with wood, galvanized steel, or aluminum. In Europe even concrete-framed greenhouses are built. Glass is still much favored for glazing, but fiberglass is gaining in popularity and less long-lasting polyethylene is useful for some purposes. Other plastics including Plexiglas and the polyester plastic Mylar have been used.

Greenhouses may be custom designed and erected by specialist firms, be of standard types offered by such concerns and erected by them, or be prefabricated and come in sections for home assembly. There is great variety in these do-it-yourself offerings. If you consider such, appraise them carefully before making a de-

Free-standing, even-span greenhouse with vertical sides

Free-standing, even-span greenhouse with sloping sides

Even-span greenhouse attached to building

A lean-to greenhouse with exterior wooden roller shade

cision. Useful greenhouses can even be self-designed and erected by one handy at carpentry and similar skills, but here one can easily make serious errors unless well acquainted with what is needed. Proper provision must of course be made for heating and ventilation, also for the conveyance of condensed moisture in proper channels so that it does not drip on the plants and thus become a disease hazard. Other problems may arise. If you plan to design and build your own greenhouse first visit several operating units and talk with those in charge.

Not all of the above choices may apply to all sites. In urban and suburban localities local building regulations may prohibit buildings not attached to the house (such can sometimes be overcome by joining house and greenhouse by a breezeway, pergola, or arbor), or there may be other

restrictions. Be sure to check these before proceeding with your plans.

Choosing a site calls for early decision. Often the placement of the structure will to some extent be dictated by circumstance. The location of the house, garage, or other buildings, the grade of the land, or just convenience may influence choice. Certainly if they are to be near together the architectural relationship of greenhouse to house must be given serious thought. The former should enhance rather than detract from the major building. A complementary feeling may be gained by careful choice of style, dimensions, and materials. A "marrying" effect may be had if the foundation walls of the greenhouse are of the same material as the house walls or of something that blends.

Certain practical matters must receive attention. For the very best results with a

wide variety of plants full-day sun is necessary or desirable. Less than half-day exposure the year around seriously limits the kinds of plants you can grow successfully, if much less than that chiefly to foliage sorts. This means that lean-to houses if possible should face south, southeast, or southwest. Free-standing house unshaded

Lean-to with vertical sides

Lean-to with sloping sides

Three-quarter span, fiber glass greenhouse, Chicago Parks Department: (a) Exterior

Home-built greenhouses: (a) Even-span

A well-sighted greenhouse in an attractive garden: (a) Exterior

(b) Interior

(b) Lean-to

(b) Interior

Greenhouses of polyethylene plastic: (a) A small unit

(c) Built of cold frame sash

(b) A large unit with an interior perforated tube through which air is blown by a fan to maintain interior pressures slightly above the outside atmosphere

Home-built greenhouse, interior

by buildings or trees may be run in any direction. If choice exists orient them with the following thoughts in mind. If they run north and south all parts of the house will be equally lighted, but in northern latitudes less light will be transmitted through the glass than if an east-west orientation is chosen. Plants on the north side of east-west houses will usually receive less light than those on the south side. If you are growing a mixed collection having different light requirements this is likely to be an advantage. Sometimes additional light can be assured by removing a limb or two from a nearby tree or in extreme cases by cutting down the offender. In other instances it may be possible to alleviate lack of natural light by installing fluorescent lights in dull parts of the greenhouse These can only aid, however; they are in no sense complete substitutes for sunlight.

Direction of prevailing winds, especially those of winter, is another matter to consider. An exposed greenhouse is an expensive one to heat. Strategically located buildings, shelter belts of trees or tall hedges, the latter open enough to permit some air to pass through them at a reduced rate rather than merely to be diverted over them and dumped onto the greenhouse, do much to relieve this problem.

Avoid low areas. Besides the drainage problems they may present, cold air flowing from higher land may create frost pockets that in winter add to the heating bill and at all seasons interfere with free air circulation. Ground drainage may be improvable by installing land drains leading to a suitable outlet. Freer air circulation can sometimes be established by creating openings in hedges or shrubbery leading to lower ground.

Foundations for greenhouses, except in climates where little or no freezing occurs, must be carried below the locally recognized frost line. If a greenhouse firm is to erect the structure or if you buy a greenhouse from such a firm to set up yourself, they will supply specifications for the foundation. Below ground it will usually be of reinforced concrete or concrete blocks. Depending upon the type of greenhouse, the foundation may stop at approximately ground level or be carried higher as walls. The first type is used for greenhouses with glass or plastic sides down to the ground. These are best suited for comparatively mild climates. In regions of much winter cold and snow, structures with solid sides carried to a height of about 2½ feet are preferable. They are less expensive to heat.

Walls above ground may be any one of many materials, masonry of various types, wood, fiberglass, or asbestos composition panels, for example. Those are best that assure good insulation and are congruous with nearby architecture.

Wooden-framed greenhouses undoubtedly have certain advantages, notably the lesser heat loss they are subject to and their tendency to retain humidity to a higher degree. Also, their first cost is usually less. They have the grave disadvantages of needing painting periodically and reglazing at intervals of a few years. All in all, the aluminum-framed house is best for amateurs.

The greenhouse framework must be strong enough to support the glass or plastic covering together with any snow load it may have to carry, as well as exposure to considerable wind. So long as it does this adequately, the lighter the framework, the less shadows it casts, and the more light is admitted. The angle of the roof and, if the sides are slanted, the angles of the sides are important. A steep slope shucks accumulations of snow faster than a flatter one and is less likely to cause interior drip during rain storms. But more important is that the closer the surfaces are to being at right angles with the rays received from the sun the greater the amount of light admitted. Ideally the roof in most cases should approximate this angle as it applies in winter when days are shortest, light intensity is comparatively low, and the sun is low in the heavens.

Have drip grooves in the roof bars to convey condensed moisture to the sides. Even so, the roof slope should not be less than 1 foot rise for each 2 feet horizontally.

Glazing with glass is done as tightly as possible. The sheets are set in much the manner of shingles on a house, but with a very much smaller overlap (about ½ inch). They are bedded in glazing compound or putty and held in place with metal sprigs driven into wooden sash bars just beneath and at the sides above each pane or with metal clips. Then a seal of glazing compound or putty is run down the edges of the panes where they contact the bars. Bar caps of aluminum that cover the bars and sealing material may be installed to reduce frequency of painting and reglazing. The latter, a somewhat costly operation, may be needed every ten to twenty years.

Fiberglass and other plastic coverings, because they come in larger sheets and are lighter than glass, are easier to install, but some, polyethylene, for example, have a very much shorter life. The surface of some kinds of fiberglass weather to expose the fibers, which then collect grime that reduces light transmission. This can be prevented by coating the surface with acrylic material at intervals of a few years.

Heating plants are of many types. Sometimes those that service the dwelling can be used, with separate control valves installed. Most practicable for amateurs are those using hot water circulating through finned radiator pipes and those supplying humidified warm air. To generate heat, oil, gas, or where winters are not too cold or costs too high and where supplies are dependable, electricity may be employed. Coal and coke, once standard fuels for greenhouses, are little used. Furnaces must be vented to prevent escape of fumes into the house.

The size of the heating unit should be adequate to supply approximately 10 percent more heat than needed to maintain the lowest temperature acceptable on the coldest winter night. This will permit economical operation without forcing the plant at its fullest capacity. Obviously, you must first decide what this minimum shall be, then consult an experienced greenhouse constructor or heating engineer about how many BTUs per hour your installation must supply to maintain this, and the size and type of the unit best adapted to produce that amount of heat.

Greenhouse temperatures are based on those maintained at night during winter. Depending upon the plants to be grown these are in cool houses 40 to 50°F, in intermediate houses approximately 55°F, and in warm or tropical houses 60 to 70°F. Because even the best heating system is subject to failure it is advisable to install an alarm system fitted with dry cell batteries that rings a bell within the home

should through power failure or other cause the greenhouse temperature fall to a dangerous level on a winter night. It is well to have portable kerosene heaters on hand to take care of any such temporary emergency. The same alarm system should be geared to warn if, through failure of automatic ventilators to open, the interior temperature rises above a predetermined level. As a heat energy conservation measure it has become a fairly common practice in recent years to install thin sheets of plastic on the insides of the roofs and sides of greenhouses. It is important that openings be left in the plastic to allow an exchange of air between the greenhouse and outside. If this is not done the interior atmosphere becomes excessively humid and condensation collects on the plastic. The condensation is likely to cause harm by dripping on the plants.

To conserve heat in winter, this greenhouse is lined inside with polyethylene plastic

Cooling greenhouses in summer is much less common than heating them in winter. It is however very advantageous for such crops as cyclamens, primulas, and certain orchids intolerant of high temperatures. The most effective system, one that works especially well when the outside humidity is low, less so in muggy weather, is called evaporative cooling. This is done by installing in one end of the structure large panels of wire mesh loosely stuffed with excelsior or similar material kept wet by dripping water and at the other end an exhaust fan. The result is that air sucked through the moist excelsior is cooled. As it flows slowly through the greenhouse it absorbs surplus heat that is discharged by the exhaust fan. Another method sometimes employed is to install along the ridge on the outside of the roof a perforated pipe that spreads a film of water that runs down the roof. In addition to cooling, this serves to some extent as shade.

Services beside heating that you will need or find useful are a water supply and electricity for operating ventilators, fans, and perhaps other equipment, as well as lights, and heating cables for a propagating case. Needless to say the wiring should be installed by a licenced electrician. The fitting of a water supply may or may not call for the services of a plumber.

The floor except for the path should be of loose, moisture-holding material. Under the benches spread crushed stone, gravel, or coke over a soil base. This will absorb water and release moisture into the air, thus helping to humidify the atmosphere. The path may be concrete, brick, tile, or other suitable material. An exception to the chiefly loose, porous flooring is appropriate in greenhouses of the conservatory type, attached to dwellings and used essentially as sitting rooms or sunrooms. Their floors may be paved throughout and the humidity kept somewhat lower than in typical growing houses.

This greenhouse is fitted with concrete benches. The wheels at the sides of the benches operate the ventilators

Benches (tables upon which potted plants are stood or are filled with soil in which plants are set) should be of heights convenient to work at. About 2¾ feet is about right. They should not be wider than can be easily reached across. If accessible from both sides 4½ to 5 feet is satisfactory. Side benches should not be more than 3 feet across. They may be supported on metal legs, masonry pillars, or even cinder blocks. For the bottoms and sides of benches a cement-asbestos material called Transite has largely replaced the wood, tiles, slates, and galvanized iron sheets previously popular. If you use lumber select cypress, redwood, or other rot-resistant sort. Metal hardware cloth is used for special purposes. Shallow benches, their edges merely a rim an inch or two high, are satisfactory for pot plants, but those to contain soil must be deeper, 5 to 6 inches as a rule. All except special types to be flooded for automatic watering must have an adequate number of drainage slots or holes.

Cut flower crops in soil-filled benches with Transite sides: (a) Carnations

(b) Snapdragons

Cover solid benches on which pot plants are to stand with gravel, slag, crushed stone, crushed shells, or similar absorbant material. This affords a moist bottom on which to stand pots, flats, and other containers, and like the loose material under the benches, if kept moist contributes humidity to the atmosphere. For most orchids and other epiphytes (tree-perching plants), benches of wood slats with spaces between them or of rigid wire mesh hardware cloth, raised a few inches to a foot or more above the layer of loose material of a solid bench or with only the loose material of the floor beneath, suit. These assure the free circulation of air about them that delights such plants.

Misting nozzles installed under the benches and operated automatically or manually may be used for damping-down to increase humidity. Screens on ventilators are useful to keep out bees and other pollinating insects prone to visit certain flowers, orchids, hyacinths, and narcissuses among others, and cause them to fade more quickly than they otherwise would. A large slow-moving fan (air turbulator) installed horizontally near the peak ridge of the greenhouse and protected by a wire mesh guard ensures ade-

quate air circulation. This does much good especially in hot, humid weather and helps to reduce the incidence of mildew and certain other diseases.

Exterior roller shades that can be raised or lowered at will (it is even possible to arrange for automatic equipment to open and close venetian-shade types) make possible greater control of light than can be had with painted-on or sprayed-on shading. Such shades can be of wood or metal slats or of plastic Saran cloth. It is an advantage (by keeping the greenhouse cooler in hot weather) if the shades operate on a pipe framework that raises them 3 or 4 inches above the greenhouse roof. An unusual method of shading that has been tried with some success consists of a system that uses a pump to circulate dyed water that trickles as a film over the greenhouse roof from a perforated pipe installed along the ridge and is collected in the gutter for recirculation. Arrangement has to be made that the mixture is not diluted by rain or if it is to add more dye.

A greenhouse propagating case

A propagating case will usually be needed. This is a cold-frame-like installation set on a greenhouse bench, used for rooting cuttings, starting seeds, and similar purposes. It makes feasible the maintenance of a more humid atmosphere inside and when needed a higher temperature than that of the open greenhouse, and is easily shaded when plants in other parts of the greenhouse need more light. It is advantageous to have electric heating cables embedded beneath the sand, perlite, or vermiculite in which cuttings are usually planted in propagating cases.

Lights adequate to make possible the enjoyment of the greenhouse, and perhaps on occasion to work in it at night, are an advantage. They are essential if you are to engage in manipulating the flowering seasons of plants by supplying additional illumination. Make sure the outlets are of the outdoor waterproof type so that they will not be subject to shorting as a result of condensed moisture or accidental wetting.

Work space is of course needed. Ideally this is provided by a potting shed or head house attached to the greenhouse where it will not shade it. In a very small unit it is possible to dispense with this and carry out necessary operations in the greenhouse itself, but a potting shed, even if tiny, is highly desirable. In it you may store soils and similar needs, equipment, fertilizers, sprays, etc., as well as records. A solid work bench or potting bench is a must as is a sink and faucet. If you can arrange for hot and cold water so much the better.

Successful management of a greenhouse calls for skill and good judgment, but not more than an interested beginner can acquire fairly easily. If new at the game make a point if possible of visiting other greenhouses and talking to their operators.

You will have decided of course whether yours is to be a cool, intermediate, or warm (tropical) greenhouse, a decision based upon the kinds of plants you intend to grow. In arriving at this, remember that if you really *must* cultivate a greater variety of plants than you have ideal conditions for, two circumstances may favor you. In nearly all greenhouses there are locations slightly warmer and somewhat cooler than the main body of the house. These provide the opportunity to accommodate special plants. Also, many plants are reasonably accommodating and can be grown fairly well if not to the highest perfection under conditions somewhat at variance with the ideal. Nevertheless, the nearer a perfect environment you provide the more certain are the results.

Having established the temperature to be maintained on winter nights, that referred to by gardeners when they speak of a 50 degree house, a 55 degree house, a 65 degree house, and so on, consider desirable variations. Daytime temperatures should ordinarily be higher than night temperatures by five to ten or on occasion fifteen degrees depending upon the brightness of the day. As light intensity increases so may temperature. At times of the year when outdoor temperatures are above those maintained on winter nights daytime temperatures in the greenhouse will normally be higher than night ones. In summer plants benefit from more heat than is best for them in winter, this because days are longer, light more intense. Even cool greenhouse plants, such as carnations, endure tropical temperatures in summer in most parts of North America. Unless the greenhouse is air-conditioned the only relief comes from adequate ventilation, light shading, and damping-down interior surfaces.

Ventilation must be directly related to temperature and humidity. With all except natives of extremely moist regions, such as tropical rain forests, too high humidity works harm and is likely to encourage disease. Too high temperatures can be as damaging as excessively low ones. In addition, air circulation to dissipate pockets of dead air and assure the plants adequate supplies of carbon dioxide is needed. The most beneficial practice is to open ventilators gradually as the day becomes warmer and to close them progressively as the outside temperatures fall and before serious drops. Allowing temperatures to rise much above the optimum and then at once opening the ventilators widely is harmful. The same is true of shutting up at the close of the day, with one exception. With plants that are being forced it is helpful to close the ventilators some little time ahead of what would be normal for plants not being forced and at the same time to damp-down the interior of the greenhouse. This bottling up of heat with a consequent rise of temperature to near maximum together with increased humidity has a decidedly forcing effect. Other occasions when one may permit a somewhat extraordinary rise of temperature are on cold, sunny, and especially windy days in late winter when the admission of much cold air would be more dangerous than a somewhat too high temperature. Here one chooses the lesser of two evils.

Damping-down is done to moisten the atmosphere. Unless water is added to air when its temperature is raised its relative humidity drops. This happens when outside air comes into a greenhouse and is warmed. To restore the balance or to make the air inside more humid than that outside, gardeners wet the floors, walls, and other interior surfaces of their greenhouses. Traditionally this has been done with hose or watering can, but now mist nozzles are often installed beneath the benches to take over the chore. They may be turned on and off at set intervals by a timer or in more sophisticated set-ups whenever needed by a humidistat. Whatever the method used, the importance lies in the amount of surface covered, not in the volume of water used. The frequency of damping-down depends upon the kinds of plants and environmental factors. For instance cactuses and other succulents, carnations, and many other cool-house plants need much lower humidity than most tropical plants. On bright days and when the ventilators are open wide, damping-down is needed more often than in dull weather or when little or no ventilation is being given. Cold, winter days that call for the use of considerable artificial heat make damping-down necessary more often than at times when less heat is called for. In most instances the greenhouse is damped-down first thing in the morning and again in late afternoon with as many dampings in between as circumstances make desirable.

Shading to reduce light intensity and often to moderate temperatures is needed in most parts of North America by the great majority of greenhouse plants in summer, by none in winter. Although for most of them it is not absolutely necessary, even cactuses and other succulents may benefit from slight relief from the fierce rays of high summer's sun. Delicate ferns stand the brightest light midwinter affords. There are plants with all varying requirements between these extremes. Which sorts need shade, how much, and when are largely matters to be settled by experience and judgment. The only general rule is that practically all sorts do best when exposed to the highest light intensity they will take without their foliage on its most exposed parts paling or scorching. This is especially true of flowering plants, notably so of many orchids. Remember that sudden exposure to intense light after a period in duller conditions can do harm that would not occur were exposure more gradual and that young, tender growth is more susceptible to sun scorch than older, tougher parts.

Sprayed-on shade

If painted or sprayed-on shade is used, such as one of the special preparations sold for the purpose, make the first application of the season a very light one and apply more to densify the shade as the year advances. In place of a purchased preparation you may use kerosene, white lead, and linseed oil in the proportions of ½ gallon, 4 pounds, and ⅛ pint, respectively. In the latitude of New York City the first application of shading is likely to be needed by the first of March or perhaps earlier. Do not use lime for shading. It is destructive to aluminum and causes putty to dry out. Remove painted-on or sprayed-on shade if possible in two operations spaced two or three weeks apart, beginning as soon as there is no longer danger of foliage yellowing or scorching, at New York City in September.

A type of shade consisting of thin green plastic sheets squeegeed onto the inside of the greenhouse roof after first wetting it is sometimes used. The method of application perhaps appeals, but green light is generally not advantageous to plants. Better results would be had were the plastic white, gray, brown, or some other color. Another disadvantage of this is that it must usually be put on and taken off in single operations thus eliminating the benefits of gradualism.

Roller lath shade

Adjustable shading that can be given or not as weather makes desirable is ideal. This, made possible by roller shades that can be raised or lowered or by shades that admit of opening and closing, alone makes possible taking fullest advantage of all available light without risking harm. Even in the brightest part of the year the full light of early morning and late afternoon benefits all plants.

Watering is one of the most important phases of greenhouse management, an art to be mastered only by careful observation and attention. It demands the drawing of correct conclusions from many variable signs, not all apparent to the beginner. The old saying of professionals, questionable grammatically and by no means entirely true, that "the man with the hose grows the plants" still makes much practical sense. Excessive watering, by which is meant too frequent applications, not the giving of too much at one time, is a major cause of distress and loss in greenhouses operated by inexperienced and careless growers.

One rule of watering is inviolate, when a plant is in need drench the entire body of soil occupied by the roots then refrain from giving more until the need arises again. Need is dictated by the kind of plant, its growth activity, whether or not its roots are pot-bound, type of soil, drainage, day-to-day weather, and other variables. In mixed collections watering is a selective job. Some plants will need attention when others do not. As many decisions are called for as there are containers. With watering can or hose in hand, especially the latter, it is all too easy for the careless operator to slop

water into the pots of plants that do not need it. Do not do it.

Take care not to wash or disturb surface soil by using too strong a stream. A rose (spray nozzle) attached to the can or a water-breaker to the end of the hose will prevent this. Experienced gardeners often use fingers or thumb to achieve the same result. Except when watering small plants overhead, those in flats for instance, avoid wetting foliage. Hold the end of the hose or watering can spout near the soil so that the water flows onto the beds or benches or into the pots gently without compacting the soil.

Watering: (a) With a can

(b) With a hose

Despite frequent statements to the contrary, except perhaps with a few plants such as African-violets, certain other members of the gesneria family, and others notably sensitive, no harm appears to be done even to tropical plants, by using water considerably colder than air temperature. For kinds known to resent cold douches and for others if you wish, you may temper cold water by mixing with it warm.

When attending to watering give attention also to nonwatering. Many greenhouse occupants, notably bulb plants such as bowieas and hippeastrums, have seasons of complete dormancy when water

must be withheld entirely. Others, and many succulents belong here, have periods during which they are partially dormant and when only enough water is needed to keep their tissues from withering. These resting periods must be respected as must the need for resuming more frequent applications at their conclusions. It is very helpful to put in one place all plants at the time completely dormant. Place them on shelves, lay them with their pots on their sides under the greenhouse benches, or move them to a cold frame or other place where you are not likely to forget them. Semidormant specimens may be stood fairly closely together in one part of the greenhouse. These segregations of dormant and semidormant plants reduces the danger of their being wetted thoughtlessly or accidentally and makes more space available for specimens in active growth.

Simple tests are available to help, but only help, in determining, in cases where there may be doubt, the approximate dryness of the soil. A time-honored one is to rap the pot sharply with a small wooden mallet. You can make such a tool by attaching as a head to a stick a foot or so long a short section of a broomstick or a thread reel. A clear ringing sound suggests the need for water, a dull, heavy one that the soil is moist enough. Another way is to lift the pot and judge according to its weight. A more scientific measure of moisture can be had by using one of the simple tensiometers or moisture meters available that when pushed into the soil indicate its degree of wetness or dryness. With a little practice you will in most cases get along perfectly well with on the spot judgments, mostly made by simple glancing at the soil and at the plant. A subtle change in the appearance of the foliage of many plants is noticeable to experienced growers when water is required. A certain lackluster look that begins before wilting signals need. If the soil of a plant is approaching dryness in the morning it is usually wise to water it, whereas late in the day soil in the same condition would very likely be best left without water until the following morning. So far as possible, especially in dull weather, do most of your watering early in the day, but if there is a clear need soak the soil at any time.

Automatic and semiautomatic watering systems are best adapted for long-time use when considerable numbers of plants with approximately the same needs for water are being grown. They can also be very useful on a temporary basis, as when one is away for a vacation, for a collection of plants of more diverse water requirements. At least they will prevent disaster resulting from soil drying out and if a few specimens get somewhat more water than they actually require over a short period they are not likely to be killed. A practical automatic system for pot plants consists of a plastic hose into which are fitted at regular intervals small-bore subsidiary tubes so that the whole assemblage is sometimes rather facetiously referred to as spaghetti. The end of one, or with large containers sometimes more, of the offshoot tubes is placed on top of the soil of each pot and kept in place by a lead weight. Equivalent systems for watering beds and benches containing soil are available. These consist of a plastic pipe, clamped to the edges of the bed or bench, into which at intervals of about 2½ inches nozzles can be inserted. Both systems can be operated by a valve turned on and off by a time clock or can be manipulated manually.

Capillary watering systems can be highly successful and relieve the amateur greenhouse gardener of much worry. A simple device for vacation or other short-term use consists of a frame, say 6 to 8 feet long by about 2 feet wide, made of 1-inch-thick lumber 2 to 3 inches wide stood on edge and nailed together. A sheet of polyethylene plastic film is draped over the inside so that it forms a shallow, flat-bottomed tray or basin and is stapled or tacked to the upper edges of the sides of the frame. The tray is filled with sand or vermiculite and then with water. The pots, clay or other porous ones, the system does not work well with plastic containers, are stood on and slightly pressed into the sand or vermiculite. Before going away for any length of time try out the plants you intend to leave in this manner. If the bottoms of the pots contain many loose crocks these may interfere with the capillary rise of the water.

More sophisticated capillary systems consist of carefully constructed, perfectly level, waterproof benches with V-shaped bottoms. The V is filled to its top with gravel or slag and over this and the entire bottom of the bench an inch or two of sand is spread. On top of the sand soil is placed or pot plants are stood. A tank with a float valve maintains the water level in the bench almost to the top of the sand layer. From this constant-level reservoir moisture is drawn by capillary attraction into the soil above. Pot plants give the best results if they are without crocks. Fertilizing can be done by periodically adding soluble fertilizers to the water in the tank. With all capillary systems it is important to flood the soil from the top periodically to leach out accumulations of salts before they become so concentrated that roots are harmed.

Syringing, the term recalls the time when the operation was commonly done with a pail of water and a garden hand syringe, means wetting the foliage with a fine spray of water. In small operations it is still carried out with a hand spray, on a larger scale usually with a hose. It calls for nice judgment. Some plants resent overhead wetting. This is particularly true of hairy-leaved sorts. Plants that most benefit are tropical kinds with smooth firm foliage such as dracaenas, ficuses, and palms. The force of the spray must not be so strong that it batters foliage, yet if it is to achieve best results it should fall only just short of this. A forceful, but not destructive spray directed to the underside of the foliage dislodges and discourages mealybugs, red spider mites, and other unwelcome creatures.

When syringing do not use so much water that the soil of plants not in need is soaked. Usually it should not be wetted at all, only the plants. Do not syringe in dull weather or so late in the day that the foliage will not dry before nightfall.

The objectives of syringing are to humidify the air, reduce the incidence of pests, and clean the foliage of grime. Carelessly done at wrong times it can encourage mildews, rots, and other diseases. It is helpful with plants that are being forced. A mild variation called misting consists of applying a very fine and not very forceful spray of water so that it falls on the upper sides of the foliage of cuttings, newly potted plants that have suffered considerable root disturbance, and in other cases where it is desired to reduce transpiration.

Routine matters to which the greenhouse gardener must give timely, but not daily attention include seed sowing and other forms of propagation, shallow cultivation of surface soil, potting and repotting, pruning and tying, and of course pest and disease control. Each must be performed according to the needs of the kinds of plants he grows. Not the least of the puzzlements to the beginner is timing, when to do what to achieve particular results. For such information consult entries under the names of specific plants in this Encyclopedia.

Good sanitation is essential for first-rate results. Once a year, whenever the greenhouse is least crowded with plants or in summer when its occupants can be put temporarily outdoors or elsewhere, wash down all interior framework and glass or plastic substitutes with strong laundry soap and water and before it dries hose it off with clear water. Begin at the highest parts and work downward. At the same time clean the ground under benches and whitewash or paint white wall surfaces to increase their reflectability.

Day to day sanitary measures include keeping all debris off floors and from beneath benches, picking and removing dead, decayed, and fallen leaves and flowers, and pulling any weeds that appear. The good greenhouse grower does not neglect these details until a special clean-up job has to be done. He attends to them each day, perhaps while watering or immediately afterward, or as he notices something that needs attention, such as a few weeds to be pulled or a plant that needs to be staked, as he walks through the greenhouse. His method is that of the housewife who picks up a newspaper, straightens a cushion, or empties an ash tray when it needs doing instead of waiting for a major assault on the task of cleaning the living room.

Accumulations of debris, dead or dying plant parts, old pots, flats, stakes, and similar stuffs left lying about are likely to afford hiding and breeding places for insects and disease-causing organisms. Keep a sharp lookout for the first signs of disease and pest troubles and take appropriate remedial measures promptly, or if none is available discard infected or infested plants. The good grower acts before such troubles become well established.

The choice of plants to grow must be made with regard to the environmental conditions that are to be maintained, most especially to temperatures. If the greenhouse is to be devoted to only one kind of plant, such as carnations, poinsettias, roses, or compatible kinds of orchids, no other selection has to be made and the task is accordingly simplified. Often a succession of plants possibly needing different conditions is grown in the same house, but only one kind at any one time. Fall-flowered chrysanthemums or poinsettias may be followed by Easter lilies and those in turn by spring bedding plants. Houses in which only one crop is grown at a time are easily managed. Amateurs frequently favor a mixed collection of plants, not all of which require perhaps identical environments. Within limits, with some accommodations, and perhaps with some small sacrifice of perfection a surprising lot can be done to make such collections possible and agreeable. One thing to be avoided is serious overcrowding. This, by denying adequate light and making routine care difficult, is often the cause of inferior results, straggly and not infrequently neglected specimens. In mixed houses it is desirable so far as possible to confine inhabitants to plants that need approximately the same environments and to try and locate those that depart from the norm by placing them in parts of the house that are warmer, cooler, sunnier, or shadier according to their known preferences.

A cool greenhouse, one with a winter night temperature of 40 to 50°F affords opportunity to grow a wide selection of beautiful plants. Among the most popular are carnations and chrysanthemums. Such a greenhouse must be ventilated with much greater freedom than one housing more tropical plants. Its atmosphere should never be oppressively humid. In addition to being suitable for growing decorative plants of the kinds here suggested, cool greenhouses provide the opportunity to raise a great variety of annuals and vegetable plants for later transplanting

Some plants for cool greenhouses: (a) Florist's anemones

(b) Calceolarias

(c) Calendulas

(d) Cinerarias

outdoors. Winter and spring displays in such a greenhouse of this type may include a very wide selection of garden annuals raised from fall sowings. Among such are ageratums, annual chrysanthemums, asters (*Callistephus*), butterfly flower (*Schizanthus*), calendulas, clarkias including godetias, forget-me-nots (*Myosotis*), larkspurs (*Consolida*), Mexican tulip-poppies (*Hunnemannia*), nemesias, nicotiana, painted tongue (*Salpiglossis*), snapdragons (*Antirrhinum*), stocks (*Matthiola*), and

sweet-peas (*Lathyrus*). Other annuals and plants grown as annuals popular for cool greenhouse cultivation are calceolarias, cinerarias, and cyclamens and *Primula kewensis*, *P. malacoides*, and *P. obconica*.

Biennials can be lifted from nursery beds in fall, potted and placed in a cold frame for a while, and later brought into bloom ahead of their natural season. Kinds adaptable for this are English daisies (*Bellis*), English wallflowers (*Cheiranthus*), foxgloves (*Digitalis*), pansies, and

sweet williams (*Dianthus*). Other biennials, for later blooming, are *Campanula pyramidalis*, celsias, and incense plant (*Humea*).

Bulb plants in a large variety can be bloomed with great success in a cool greenhouse. They include almost all South African kinds, such as albucas, babianas, calla-lilies (*Zantedeschia*), freesias, gladioluses, ixias, lachenalias, ornithogalums, oxalises, sparaxises, tulbaghias, vallotas, and watsonias. New World natives that succeed in cool greenhouses include bro-

(e) Freesias

(f) Lachenalias

(g) Narcissuses

(h) Ranunculuses

diaeas, calochortuses, ipheions, leucoco-
rynes, and zephyranthes. Dutch bulbs,
hardy kinds suitable for blooming in winter and early spring, succeed splendidly.
Here belong crocuses, daffodils (*Narcissus*), Dutch and Spanish irises, English
and Spanish bluebells (*Endymion*), grape-
hyacinths (*Muscari*), hyacinths, squills
(*Scilla*), striped-squills (*Puschkinia*), and tulips. Florists' anemones, such as the St.
Brigid and DeCaen strains and turban ra-

nunculuses, are other bulb plants appropriate for cool greenhouses.

Hardy perennials that can be gently
forced early in a cool greenhouse include
astilbes, bleeding hearts (*Dicentra*), delphiniums, English and polyanthus primroses (*Primula*), hostas, and lily-of-the-valley (*Convallaria*). Nonhardy perennials are
alstroemerias, blue-lily-of-the-Nile (*Aga-
panthus*), carnations, and clivias. A considerable variety of cactuses and other suc-

culents are suitable for growing in cool
greenhouses.

Shrubby and subshrubby plants and
vines adapted for cool greenhouses include abutilons, acacias, Algerian and
English ivy (*Hedera*), angel's trumpet (*Da-
tura*), *Asparagus densiflorus*, Australian silk-
oak (*Grevillea robusta*), azaleas (*Rhododendron*), bottlebrush (*Callistemon*), *Buddleia
asiatica* and *B. farquhari*, camellias, *Daphne
odora*, *Fatshedera*, fuchsias, *Gardenia florida*,

Some plants for intermediate greenhouses: (a) Achimenes   (b) Begonias

(c) Bouvardias   (d) Clerodendrums

geraniums (*Pelargonium*), heaths (*Erica*), India- and Yeddo-hawthorn (*Rhaphiolepis*), myrtle (*Myrtus*), oleanders (*Nerium*), *Osmanthus fragrans*, pittosporums, and *Plumbago auriculata*.

Intermediate or warm-temperate greenhouses, those in which temperatures on winter nights are maintained at about 55°F, make possible the cultivation of many kinds of flowering and foliage plants and vines. They can be kept gay with bloom throughout the year. In addition to housing permanent occupants it may be used for forcing hardy bulbs and perennials of sorts suggested for cool greenhouses and for raising for planting outdoors later many annuals and other decorative plants and vegetables. The atmosphere in the intermediate house should be pleasantly warm and moderately, but not oppressively, humid. In summer the structure should be ventilated freely and shaded.

Less ventilation is needed in winter and spring than is desirable for a cool greenhouse, and shade is likely to be needed somewhat earlier in the year.

Examples of plants suitable for intermediate greenhouses are these: abutilons, achimenes, African-violets (*Saintpaulia*) and many other kinds of gesneriads, aphelandras, begonias (most kinds), bird-of-paradise (*Strelitzia*), bouvardias, browallias, cactuses and other succulents in

(e) Hippeastrums

(f) Orchids (*Cattleya*)

(g) Passion flower

(h) Rouge plant

great variety, caladiums, calla-lilies (*Zan-tedeschia*), clerodendrums, clivias, coleuses, crown-of-thorns (*Euphorbia*), eupatoriums (some kinds), ferns (many kinds), gloriosas, haemanthuses (some kinds), hippeastrums, hoyas, jacobinias, lantanas, manettias, orchids (many kinds), palms (many kinds) passion flowers (*Passiflora*), patience plants (*Impatiens*), pick-a-back plant (*Tolmiea*), pentases, rouge plant (*Rivina*), spider plant (*Chlorophytum*), streptosolens, and vallotas. There are numer-

ous others including a wide range of foliage plants. See Foliage Plants.

Plants suitable for tropical greenhouses, those in which the winter night temperature is maintained at 60 to 70°F, are very numerous. They include many foliage plants, a wide variety of orchids, and many of the kinds that can also be grown in intermediate house temperatures. A high degree of humidity is necessary in houses of this sort and much less ventilation is needed than with cooler greenhouses. Typ-

ical of kinds that thrive in tropical greenhouses are acalyphas, allamandas, alocasias, Amazon-lily (*Eucharis*), anthuriums, ardisias, banana (*Musa*), begonias (many kinds), bougainvilleas, bromeliads (most kinds), brunfelsias, caladiums, calatheas, *Cissus discolor*, clerodendrums, columneas, crotons (*Codiaeum*), dracaenas, episcias, ferns (many kinds), fittonias, gardenias, hibiscuses, hippeastrums, hymenocallises, ixoras, mandevillas, medinillas, palms (many kinds), pandanuses, peperomias,

Some plants for tropical greenhouses: (a) Allamandas

(b) Anthuriums

(c) Bananas

(d) Bromeliads (*Billbergia*)

philodenrons, pileas, poinsettias, pothoses, *Pycnostachys*, tibouchinas, and wandering jew (*Zebrina*).

GREENOVIA (Green-òvia). Very similar in appearance to *Aeonium*, and, like it, formerly included in *Sempervivum*, the genus *Greenovia* belongs in the orpine family CRASSULACEAE. Its name commemorates a geologist, George Bellas Greenough, who died in 1855. There are four species, natives of the Canary Islands.

Greenovias are low, evergreen, usually hairless and glaucous herbaceous perennials. They have dense, cup-shaped or rounded rosettes of stalkless, undivided, lobeless, toothless leaves with horny, hairy, or glandular-hairy, often slightly eroded edges. From the centers of the rosettes arise the flower stalks, clothed with leaves from the base to where the flowers begin. The blooms garland the upper sides of the spreading branched or branchless stalks and are presented in more or less flat-topped, loose heads or narrow sprays. Always, the yellow, starry blooms face upward. They have bowl-shaped calyxes cleft into from twenty to thirty-two seg-

ments. There are as many narrow petals and twice as many stamens as calyx lobes. The carpels are partly buried in the disks. Considerable variation is exhibited by the species, and as is true of many succulents, environmental conditions have marked effects on their size, coloring, and aspect.

Largest and most handsome, *G. aurea* is stemless or very short-stemmed. In the wild it produces offsets, but cultivated specimens rarely do this. Its glaucous, spatula-shaped leaves, hairless or with very few marginal hairs, are in rosettes 3½ to 10 inches across. Normally the outer

(e) Crotons

(f) Ixoras

(g) Peperomias

(h) Poinsettias

ones are widespread and the inner ones erect, but under drought conditions the outer leaves are raised until the rosettes become urn- or egg-shaped. The numerous flowers, ¾ to 1 inch wide and with usually twenty-five petals or more, are in massive, almost horizontally-branched clusters up to 1½ feet or sometimes more in diameter. Sometimes flowering branches develop lower on the stems than main clusters. An intermediate hybrid between G. aurea and the next species described occurs.

Immediately recognizable by its leaves being clothed with fine glandular hairs, *G. aizoon* is a much-branched, offset-producing kind with flattish rosettes 2 to a little over 3 inches across. Its flowers are few together in flattish-topped clusters that terminate stems 4 or 5 inches tall. Even during droughts the rosettes remain fully expanded. Similar to G. aurea, but never making offsets, **G. diplocycla** has rosettes 3½ to 10 inches across of leaves generally densely fringed with hairs. Characteristically the leaves of its flowering stems, ex-

cept those close to the base, are approximately of equal size, and in this respect differ from those of G. aurea, which are successively smaller from the base upward. The flowers of G. diplocycla are slightly more than ½ inch across and have only about twenty petals.

The rosettes of **G. dodrentalis** are dense and normally not over 2 inches in diameter. From 6 to 10 inches tall, the slender, glandular-hairy flower stems terminate in flat-topped clusters of about twelve blooms. This species produces offsets very freely.

Greenovia aurea

Garden Uses and Cultivation. Greenovias are satisfactory for inclusion in outdoor collections of succulents in mild, frost-free, dry regions, such as parts of the West, and in greenhouses and window gardens. In bloom those with large trusses of flowers are very handsome. Their needs are simple. They prefer richer soil than many succulents. For pot cultivation, one based on good loamy topsoil to which has been added a generous dash of dried cow manure or sheep manure and some bonemeal is satisfactory if it is highly porous. To achieve the latter condition it may be necessary to add to the mixture sensible amounts of coarse sand and brick broken to the size of peas to peanuts.

Repotting is done in spring, in the case of blooming specimens as soon as flowering is through. From spring to fall the soil is watered with fair freedom, so that it never is really dry, but in winter it is maintained more decidedly on the dry side, applications being made only to prevent the plants from suffering from lack of moisture. When in spring the flower stalks begin to push up an occasional application of dilute liquid fertilizer aids their development. Greenovias are extremely easy to

increase. Cuttings root with great ease, seeds germinate readily.

GREENS. Vegetables of which the leaves and leafy stems of immature plants are prepared for eating by boiling are called greens or sometimes pot herbs. There are several kinds, among those cultivated, chard or Swiss chard, collards, corn salad, dandelion, kale, mustard, New Zealand spinach, spinach, whitloof chicory or French endive, and beet and turnip greens. Wild plants, including dandelions, lamb's quarters or pigweed, and marsh-marigolds are sometimes gathered and used as greens.

Christmas greens are branches of various evergreen trees and shrubs as well as some other plants, such as lycopodiums, employed for Christmas decorations. The most traditional are holly and mistletoe. Others are English ivy, galax, mountain-laurel, and smilax.

GREENWOOD. Current year's stems of woody plants that have completed their season's growth but have not yet fully matured or ripened are identified as greenwood shoots. They are frequently ideal material of which to make cuttings.

GREIGIA (Greì-gia). This genus belongs in the pineapple family BROMELIACEAE. Its name commemorates Major General Samuel Alexeivich Greig, president of the Russian Horticultural Society. He died in 1887. Native from Mexico to Andean South America and Juan Fernandez, *Greigia* consists of possibly eighteen species, many natives at high altitudes where they are most frequent in cool cloud forests bathed in mist much of the time.

Greigias are evergreen perennials with rosettes of spiny leaves arranged in the manner of those of a yucca or an agave. Unlike those of most bromeliads, the rosettes do not die after flowering, but continue to produce blooms for many successive years. The stalkless or nearly stalkless heads of bloom, also unlike those of most bromeliads, commonly arise from the leaf axils instead of from the centers of the rosettes and are hidden rather than flaunted. Individual blooms last for but a single day. They have three each sepals and petals and six stamens. The fruits are berries.

Chilean *G. sphacelata* attains heights of 3 feet or more. It has sharp-pointed, sword-shaped leaves up to 6 feet long by about 1¼ inches wide, furnished along their margins with rigid spines. Overlapping each other in crowded heads, the lavender-pink, stalkless flowers are about 3 inches long. The bracts are large and green-tinted. Native of Mexico and Guatemala, *G. steyermarkii* has rosettes of 3-foot-long, spiny, green leaves. The flowers are white. Mexican *G. van-hyningii* has leaves that may exceed 3 feet in length and, in heads of about ten, flowers with deep magenta petals.

Garden Uses and Cultivation. Greigias make little appeal except to keenly interested fanciers of bromeliads. They are not satisfactory where summer temperatures are high. Little experience with growing them is reported. For more information see Bromeliads or Bromels.

GREVILLEA (Grev-íllea)—Silk-Oak or Silky-Oak, Humming Bird Bush. Natives of Australia and New Caledonia, the nearly 200 species of *Grevillea* belong to the protea family PROTEACEAE. Their name commemorates Charles Francis Greville, vice president of the Royal Society of London. A patron of horticulture and botany, he died in 1809.

Grevilleas are nonhardy, evergreen shrubs or less commonly trees admired for their attractive foliage and often showy flowers. From nearly related *Hakea* they differ chiefly in their seeds not terminating in a long wing sometimes extending down the sides, but being wingless, narrowly-winged all around, or having a narrow wing at the end or outer margin, also in the flower clusters being usually terminal, rarely axillary. The leaves of *Grevillea* vary tremendously in size and style according

Grevillea robusta as a street tree in Buenos Aires

Grevillea robusta, a young plant

Grevillea hilliana at Los Angeles State and County Arboretum

Grevillea banksii at Los Angeles State and County Arboretum

Grevillea banksii, pink-flowered, at the Royal Botanic Gardens, Kew, England

to species. They are alternate, lobeless, pinnately- or twice-pinnately-lobed, or pinnately-divided. The flowers are bisexual, in pairs in sometimes umbel-like racemes. Their more or less tubular perianths consist of four petal-like sepals. They are without petals. The sepals are usually ribbed longitudinally and more or less curved toward their apexes. There are four stamens. The long, undivided style protrudes through a slit in the tube formed by the sepals. It is usually the most conspicuous feature of the bloom. The fruits are woody follicles.

The silk-oak or silky-oak (**G. robusta**), native to Queensland and New South Wales, is best known. This impressive species is a tree up to 100 or even 150 feet in height, but more commonly does not exceed 50 or 60 feet. When old it is decidedly picturesque. In youth it is pyramidal and symmetrical. Its yellowish-green to bronzy-green leaves, 6 inches to nearly 1 foot long, are in somewhat fernlike fashion twice lobed into toothed, lanceolate segments

that have rolled-under margins. Their undersides are silky-hairy. The cadmium-orange flowers are in one-sided racemes up to 4 inches long borne on short leafless branchlets. Another big tree, **G. hilliana** is called white silky-oak. Attaining heights of 50 to 60 or occasionally 90 feet, this has leaves lobeless and oblong-elliptic or more or less deeply lobed. They are 6 inches to 1 foot long. The white flowers are crowded into cylindrical racemes up to 8 inches in length. A tall shrub or slender tree 15 to 20 feet tall, **G. banksii** has leaves 6 inches to 1 foot long, pinnate or deeply-pinnately-cleft into five to eleven narrow leaflets or lobes with rolled-under margins and silky hairs on their undersides. The red flowers are crowded in erect, one-sided racemes, solitary or up to three together at the ends of terminal, leafless stalks.

Shrubby **G. thelemanniana** in the wild favors alkaline soils. Known as humming bird bush, this is 3 to 5 feet tall. It has softly-hairy shoots. Its 1- to 2-inch-long

leaves are finely-pinnately-divided into many slender, more or less cylindrical segments, the lower ones usually again divided. Its green-tipped, pink to rich red flowers are in somewhat drooping, one-sided terminal racemes 1½ to 2 inches long and wide. Their sepals recurve. Spreading or procumbent, shrubby **G. obtusifolia** has undivided, lobeless, toothless, narrow-spatula-shaped to oblong-linear, blunt leaves ½ inch to 1¼ inches long, with rusty-hairy undersides and rolled-under margins. The flowers are in short, nearly stalkless, more-or-less recurved, loose, one-sided, terminal racemes 1 inch to 1½ inches long. About 6 feet tall and compact, **G. rosmarinifolia** is nearly as broad as high. Known as the rosemary grevillea, this has dark green, linear to lanceolate leaves with rolled-under margins. Their undersides are silvery with silky hairs. They are 1½ inches long. The red, less often pink or white blooms are in short, stalkless, crowded racemes.

Grevillea punicea

Grevillea juniperina

An elegant shrub about 5 feet tall, **G. punicea** has oblong to elliptic, silky-hairy leaves from ½ inch to 2 inches long and, crowded in very short racemes about 2½ inches across, rich red flowers.

Other kinds cultivated include **G. alpina.** This, one of the hardiest, is up to 4 feet tall and bushy. It has hairy shoots. Its crowded, dark green, narrowly-oblong to linear leaves, ⅓ to 1 inch long by up to ¼ inch wide, are downy above and silky-hairy on their undersides. Their margins are rolled-under. Few together in short, terminal clusters, the flowers are yellow with swollen red bases. A shrub or tree 10 to 15 feet tall, **G. asplenifolia** has slender, pointed, linear-lanceolate to lanceolate leaves 4 inches to 1 foot long, their margins with coarse, triangular teeth. Their undersides are clothed with silvery or yellowish hairs. The reddish-pink blooms are crowded along the undersides of ¾-inch-long, stalkless spikes that come from the leaf axils. Its shoots usually hairy, **G. bipinnatifida** is a shrub, sometimes almost prostrate or 3 to 5 feet tall, with ovate, twice-pinnately-lobed leaves 3 to 5 inches in length, and almost as broad as long. Each has eleven to twenty-one primary divisions. The ultimate ones end in slender spines. In terminal, loose, long-stalked racemes or panicles up to 6 inches in length, the bright scarlet flowers are softly-hairy on their outsides. With crowded, sharp-pointed, almost needle-like leaves ½ to 1 inch long and hairy on their undersides, **G. juniperina** (syn. *G. sulphurea*) is a shrub up to about 6 feet in height. Flushed with pink or red, the soft yellow flowers are in terminal clusters of a dozen or more. This is more resistant to cold than most grevilleas. Gray-green in aspect, **G. lanigera,** the woolly grevillea, is from 1 foot to 3 feet tall, and 6 to 10 feet in diameter. Its shoots are densely-hairy. The crowded, slender, stalkless, heathlike leaves, ½ to 1 inch long, have rolled-under margins. The ter-

Grevillea lanigera at Los Angeles State and County Arboretum

minal racemes of crimson and cream blooms attract humming birds. A compact shrub, often under 8 inches in height, its stems sometimes procumbent, variable **G. lavandulacea** has silky-downy shoots. Its stalkless, pointed, broadly-oblanceolate to narrowly-lanceolate, rigid leaves, silky-hairy on their undersides and with recurved margins, are ½ inch to 1¼ inches long. The bright red, pink, or nearly white flowers, hairy on their outsides and bearded inside, are in short terminal racemes of three to eight at the shoot ends. A bushy shrub 5 feet tall and as wide, or perhaps sometimes larger, **G. vestita** in the wild favors limestone soils. Its wedge-shaped leaves, three-lobed at their apexes, are ¾ inch to 1½ inches long. Produced along the stems in loose racemes, the small flowers are white, flushed with pink when young. Erect and 3 to 5 feet tall, shrubby **G. wilsonii** has short-stalked, rigid, twice- or thrice-pinnate leaves. Their ultimate segments are ½ to 1 inch long, sharp-pointed, and needle-like. The bright scarlet flowers 1½ inches long, in short-stalked, erect, loose racemes or panicles, have the upper parts of their sepals conspicuously curled backward.

Garden and Landscape Uses. Grevilleas include many very fine ornamentals, several cultivated in California and other warm-climate regions. Many others would be worth trying. Most succeed only in dryish climates, even in semidesert and desert regions, but the silk-oak adapts to more humid ones as well. It and *G. banksii* are much planted in Hawaii. The silk-oak is grown in Florida. It is used as an avenue and street tree. Unfortunately it has the disadvantage of its wood being brittle and subject to storm damage.

Shrubby grevilleas are quite useful for fronting shrub beds, in transition zones between manicured areas and more natural ones, and for other purposes where the soil is well-drained and dryish. Even in poor soils most kinds do well. Experience in California indicates most grevilleas are not well adapted for lawn areas. Taller kinds, including the silk-oak, allowed to grow naturally or sheared, are useful as screens and hedges. Lower ones can be used to cover large banks. Young specimens of silk-oak in 4- to 6-inch pots are attractive greenhouse and window plants. In larger containers they are effective for decorating terraces, patios, and similar places. In these sizes their foliage is their claim to beauty. They do not bloom until very much bigger.

Cultivation. In the open grevilleas call for no special care. Excessive watering is harmful to most kinds. When used as hedges or screens periodic shearing or pruning is needed. Propagation is chiefly by seed. It is possible to root cuttings of some kinds, and grafting onto seedlings of silk-oak is in some cases practicable. Seeds must be sown in very well-drained, sandy soil.

To have grevilleas as small decorative pot plants sow the seeds in pots or pans (shallow pots) of sandy soil in late winter or spring. It is a good plan to push the seeds into the soil on edge rather than to allow them to lay flat (this reduces danger of rotting). Then just cover them with soil. Kept moderately moist, but not soaking wet in a temperature of 60 to 70°F, they germinate fairly soon. When large enough to handle transplant the seedlings individually to small pots and to larger ones as growth makes necessary. Use porous, fertile potting soil. Grow the plants in full sun, or with very light shade in summer, in a greenhouse or window. A night temperature of 45 to 55°F in winter suits, with an increase of five to fifteen degrees by day. In summer the plants may be put outdoors. If kept inside, the structure must be freely ventilated. Water to keep the soil evenly moist, but not saturated. After the containers are well filled with roots, give biweekly applications of dilute liquid fertilizer. Prune old specimens to shape and repot them each early spring.

GREWIA (Grèw-ia). Alternate-leaved trees and shrubs restricted in the wild to the Old World, chiefly to warm parts, constitute this genus of the linden family TILI-ACEAE. There are approximately 150 species. The name honors Nehemiah Grew, an English botanist, who died in 1712.

Grewias have few to many stellate (star-shaped) hairs. Their undivided, short-stalked, two-ranked leaves are toothed or toothless and have three to seven chief veins radiating from their bases. The flowers, solitary or in clusters from the leaf axils, have five sepals, usually colored on their insides, five petals each narrowed at its base to a slender portion called a claw, with a small gland or pit at its bottom, many stamens, and one style ending in a shortly two- to four-lobed stigma. The fruits are fleshy or fibrous drupes (fruits plumlike in structure) containing one to four stones.

The only kind hardy in the north, into southern New England, is *Grewia biloba*

parviflora, of China and Korea. This differs from typical G. *biloba,* in its foliage being rough-hairy above and densely clothed with hairs underneath. The species, native of the Himalayas, is perhaps hardy as far north as Virginia. It is a deciduous shrub up to 12 feet in height, with more or less ovate to lanceolate, pointed, irregularly toothed, and sometimes slightly lobed leaves almost hairless on their top sides and with few hairs beneath. They are 2 to 5 inches long by one-half to two-thirds as wide. In densely-hairy, short-stalked umbels of up to eight, the creamy-yellow flowers, from a little under to a little over ½ inch across, are displayed in summer. The usually two-lobed, orange or red fruits are ⅓ inch or a little more in diameter.

Native of South Africa, **G. occidentalis** is a sometimes rather straggling, freely-branched shrub 6 to 18 feet tall. It has thin, broad-elliptic leaves 1 inch to 2¼ inches long, clearly round-toothed, and with three main veins from the base. The flowers, on rigid stalks, have sepals tan on their outsides, pink within. They are as long as the bright purple to mauve petals. The latter are ¼ to ½ inch long. Yellow-orange when ripe, the three- to five-lobed fruits are ½ inch wide by under ½ inch long. This is hardy only in nearly frost-free and frost-free climates.

Garden and Landscape Uses and Cultivation. Of secondary importance horticulturally, grewias are mainly restricted to botanical collections and gardens of those interested in rarer and lesser known shrubs. They grow without special care in ordinary soils and situations, and are increased by seeds and by cuttings.

GREYIA (Grèy-ia)—Natal-Bottle-Brush. Named in honor of Sir George Grey, a Governor of Cape Colony, who died in 1898, *Greyia* is included in the melianthus family MELIANTHACEAE, or by some botanists is segregated as the only representative of the greyia family GREYIACEAE. It includes three species of South African trees and shrubs with alternate, undivided leaves, flowers in axillary racemes, and fruits that are capsules. The only kind ordinarily grown is the beautiful small tree or shrub, *Greyia sutherlandii*, which is planted outdoors in the south and in California and is sometimes grown in greenhouses. Another desirable species, *G. radlkoferi*, taller than the Natal-bottle-brush, has velvety leaves and similar blooms. It is native to the Transvaal.

The Natal-bottle-brush (**G. sutherlandii**) as it occurs in cultivation is a deciduous shrub with alternate, stalked, rounded or somewhat heart-shaped, coarsely- and ir-

Greyia sutherlandii

Grindelia robusta

regularly-toothed, rather leathery leaves up to 4 inches across. They somewhat resemble the leaves of geraniums (*Pelargonium*). Before they drop in fall they assume attractive shades of red. The brilliant red or bright brick-red nodding, bisexual flowers, about ½ inch in length, are borne in tight spikelike clusters that terminate the bare branches just before or about the time the new leaves appear.

Garden Uses and Cultivation. Although it grows fairly quickly and becomes 8 to 10 feet tall, this species blooms freely even as a much smaller specimen, a feature that endears it to the cultivator of unusual greenhouse plants. It is a delightful flowering shrub for beds and borders and for growing in display greenhouses. The Natal-bottle-brush grows freely in any ordinary well-drained soil in full sun and is increased without difficulty by seeds and cuttings, and by detaching rooted suckers and potting or planting them. It will stand a touch of frost and is fairly drought-resistant. Pruning to keep the plant shapely and remove weak shoots is done immediately after blooming.

Under greenhouse cultivation this plant thrives in any good porous potting soil and where the night temperature in winter is about 50°F and daytime temperatures not more than five or ten degrees higher. Full sun and airy conditions are needed. In summer the plants can with advantage be plunged to the rims of their containers in a bed of sand or ashes in a sunny place outdoors. During the winter dormant season only enough water should be given to

keep the stems from shriveling, but from the beginning of new growth in spring until leaf drop in fall the amounts given should be generous and during that time, too, well-rooted specimens should be stimulated by regular applications of dilute liquid fertilizer. Pruning and repotting, when needed, may receive attention as soon as the blooming season is through.

GRINDELIA (Grin-dèlia)—Gum Plant. Grindelias are chiefly herbaceous perennials, more rarely biennials or annuals, of North America. They are prevailingly of coarse appearance, and are of decidedly minor horticultural importance. They belong in the daisy family COMPOSITAE and have a name commemorating David Hieronymus Grindel, a Russian botanist, who died in 1836. There are sixty species.

Grindelias are resinous-sticky. They have alternate leaves and generally medium-sized to quite large, yellow flower heads of the daisy type, with a central eye of disk florets encircled by petal-like ray florets. Rarely the ray florets are wanting. The seedlike fruits are achenes.

One of the more attractive species, but somewhat coarse, *Grindelia robusta* inhabits dry soils, seashores, and borders of salt marshes in California. It has stout stems, usually branched above, and 1½ to 4 feet tall. The toothed or toothless leaves are up to 6 inches long and a little over 1 inch wide. The upper ovate-lanceolate to lanceolate leaves are much smaller than the oblanceolate lower ones and are stem-clasping. From 1¼ to 2 inches wide, the

flower heads have twenty-five to forty-five ray florets approximately ½ inch long.

Garden and Landscape Uses and Cultivation. The species described, as well as some others, may be planted locally in native plant gardens and naturalistic landscapes. They need dry soil and full sun, and are raised from seed. They are not adapted to regions of cold, wet winters.

GRISELINIA (Gris-elínia). In the dogwood family CORNACEAE belongs this genus of six species of trees and shrubs. Its name commemorates Francesco Griselini, an Italian botanist, who died in 1783. In the wild the group occurs in New Zealand and Chile, often near seashores. Its members are not hardy in the north.

Griselinias are often epiphytic in their natural habitats, at least in their young stages. This means that they grow perched on other trees, but do not invade their tissues and absorb nourishment from them as do parasites. Instead, they obtain nutrients from debris that collects in crotches and crevices of the branches of their hosts. As they grow they are likely to send down liana-like roots that enter the ground and take up moisture and nutrients. These roots may be so numerous and heavy that they eventually envelop the trunk of the host and seriously damage or kill it. Griselinias have alternate, thick, glossy, undivided, often oblique leaves, angled or spiny-toothed at their margins, and with inconspicuous veins. The unisexual, minute flowers are in axillary panicles or racemes, the male and female on different plants. The blooms make no effective display. They have five-toothed calyxes, five petals, and, the males, five stamens. The females have three styles. The fleshy fruits are usually one-seeded.

Under favorable conditions 30 feet or sometimes considerably taller, *G. littoralis* has slightly unequal-sided, broad-ovate to ovate-oblong leaves 1¼ to 4½ inches long. Its greenish flowers, both sexes with petals, are in racemes. This, the hardier of the kinds described here, is en-

Griselinia littoralis

demic to New Zealand. It usually begins life in the ground rather than as an epiphyte. Its variety *G. l. variegata* has variegated foliage. The only other New Zealand species, also endemic, is **G. lucida.** From the last this differs in having broadly-ovate to oblong leaves markedly unequal-sided at their bases, and 2¾ to 7 inches long, and greenish flowers in panicles. The female blooms are without petals. In the wild this species commonly begins life as an epiphyte and finally develops into a shrub or tree up to 25 feet tall.

Garden and Landscape Uses. Griselinias are attractive for outdoor planting in California and places with similar climates. Although it does not tolerate the most exposed locations, *G. littoralis* is excellent for seaside planting and should be more freely used.

Cultivation. These trees prosper in ordinary well-drained soils. They are increased by seeds and are easily propagated by cuttings.

GRISLEA. See Combretum.

GROUND. This word is employed as part of the common names of various plants including ground-cedar (*Lycopodium complanatum*), ground cherry (*Prunus fruticosa*), ground-cherry (*Physalis pruinosa* and *P. pubescens*), ground-ivy (*Glechoma hederacea*), ground-pine (*Lycopodium obscurum*), and ground-plum (*Astragalus crassicarpus*).

GROUNDCOVERS. The term groundcover refers to a use to which certain plants are put, not to any natural grouping or relationship. All groundcover plants can be and most on occasion are used in other ways. To serve well, groundcovers must be suitable for clothing considerable expanses with carpets or low, fairly dense masses of greenery. They must be able to get along with minimal attention and generally must not be too expensive.

Except in cultivated areas kept hoed or mulched, it is desirable to keep the surface of the soil covered with some kind of low vegetation. This keeps down weeds, prevents erosion, and protects the roots of trees and shrubs from extremes of heat and cold. If appropriately done, it also adds charm to the garden picture, showing off trees and shrubs and flowering plants to best advantage. Such greenery appears cool in summer and gives relief to the eye from the brighter colors in flower beds and borders.

Lawn, although rarely thought of as such, is the most universally used groundcover. In many places and for many purposes closely mown grass is unsurpassed. Considering that more than one-third of a million different kinds of higher plants exist wild in the world and a large number of others have been developed by man, this is remarkable. It is nevertheless true.

There are many beautiful easy-to-grow, low, groundcovers that carpet the ground effectively, but none stands wear like grass. For a practical lawn to be much walked on or played on grass is a must. Some groundcovers, such as creeping thyme, yarrow, chamomile, and dichondra, are fair substitutes. They stand more wear than most groundcovers, but are not as good as grass.

Because of this some gardeners make the mistake of attempting to solve all their groundcover problems by sowing grass seed. This just does not work. There are places where a lawn is certainly *not* the answer to the groundcover problem. In deep shade, for example, and on steep banks where it is almost impossible to use a lawnmower effectively or where a perpetual battle to maintain grass is required, even if you do succeed in establishing it, and in places where tree roots rob the soil of food and moisture.

In spots such as these try using some other plants. Sweeps of groundcovers are excellent under trees, bordering shrub plantings, on banks and other places where turf is difficult to grow or mow, and where weeds must be kept down or erosion checked. First cost of some kinds is rather high because most must be planted fairly closely, but nearly all can be propagated at home very easily, some by simply dividing up older plantings and replanting the divisions, others by inserting cuttings rather closely together in sandy soil in a shaded cold frame in summer.

In any case do not sacrifice suitability or quality. Better start with fewer plants of kinds you like and believe will grow satisfactorily for you than with a larger number of a less desirable sort. If you cannot or do not feel inclined to purchase all the plants you need buy some. Lay in a stock sufficient to plant part of the area you want to cover. And then begin a program of propagation. Within two to three years your stock will have increased many-fold.

Early spring and early fall are the best times to set out groundcover plants. If you are planting on steeply sloping land the former is decidedly to be preferred, since there is less chance of erosion before the plants take hold. When planting such areas mulch the surface with coarse compost or litter, just as a precaution.

The number of really good, widely adaptable groundcovers is not vast, but is greater than most gardeners suppose. With a little thought and imagination it is not too difficult to come up with something other than the most commonly used. In addition to those suggested here there are a number of ferns, succulents, and other plants suitable for special situations.

The lists that follow are presented as suggestions. They must be culled with care for sorts best suited and most practical for any particular location. Not only

must the hardiness of the plants and whether they are deciduous or evergreen be evaluated, but also their soil preferences, moisture needs, sun or shade requirements, heights, displays of blooms, and other matters of pertinence.

Unless the plants you select will give good accounts of themselves in the environments you can offer they will not be suitable no matter how satisfactory they are elsewhere. Above all else, groundcovers must prosper and grow with fair vigor to do their job and look well. If you are unfamiliar with them or their needs, look them up under their genus in this Encyclopedia before committing yourself to a planting upon which you may expend money and effort only to meet disappointment or failure.

Hardy evergreen groundcovers include these: *Achillea tomentosa*; *Antennaria*, some kinds; *Asarum caudatum*; Baltic ivy (*Hedera helix baltica*); bearberry (*Arctostaphylos uva-ursi*); bergenias, most kinds; box huckleberry (*Gaylussacia brachycera*); cowberry (*Vaccinium vitis-idaea*); creeping-myrtle (*Vinca minor*); creeping thymes (*Thymus serpyllum* varieties); English ivy (*Hedera helix*); European wild-ginger (*Asarum europaeum*); *Galax aphylla*; heather (*Calluna vul-

Some hardy evergreen groundcovers:
(a) Bearberry

(b) Junipers

(c) *Pachysandra terminalis*

Some hardy deciduous groundcovers:
(a) Bugle weed (*Ajuga reptans* 'Jungle Beauty')

(d) Lily-of-the-valley

(d) Purple-leaf wintercreeper

(b) *Ceratostigma plumbaginoides*

(e) Variegated yellow archangel

(e) *Sedum acre*

(c) Crown-vetch

garis, varieties); heaths (*Erica herbacea, E. erigena*); junipers (*Juniperus*, many prostrate and low kinds); *Lonicera henryi*, only partially evergreen where winters are cold; *Mahonia repens; Minuartia verna*; mockstrawberry (*Duchesnea indica*), evergreen in mild climates; moss-pink (*Phlox subulata*); *Muehlenbeckia complexa*, deciduous where winters are cold; *Pachysandra terminalis*; pick-a-back plant (*Tolmiea menziesii*), deciduous in regions of cold winters; *Potentilla*

tridentata; purple-leaf wintercreeper (*Euonymus fortunei colorata*); sedums, many kinds; sempervivums, in variety; *Teucrium chamaedrys;* and thrift (*Armeria maritima*).

Hardy deciduous groundcovers include these: *Akebia quinata*, evergreen in mild climates; beach wormwood (*Artemisia stellariana*); bird's-foot-trefoil (*Lotus corniculatus*); bugle weed (*Ajuga reptans*); camomile (*Chamaemelum nobile*); *Ceratostigma plumbagi-*

noides; climbing hydrangea (*Hydrangea petiolaris*); cotoneasters, several low, spreading sorts; crown-vetch (*Coronilla varia*); Hall's honeysuckle (*Lonicera japonica halliana*), evergreen in mild climates; hostas, most kinds; *Indigofera incarnata alba;* lily-of-the-valley (*Convallaria majalis*); *Mazus reptans;* memorial rose (*Rosa wichuraiana*); *Muehlenbeckia axillaris; Polygonum cuspidatum compactum; Rhus aromatica;* shrub yellow-root (*Xanthorhiza simplicissima*); snow-in-summer (*Cerastium tomentosum*); strawberry (*Fragaria chiloensis*); sweet-fern (*Comptonia peregrina*); sweet woodruff (*Galium odoratum*); *Vancouveria hexandra;* and variegated yellow archangel (*Lamiastrum luteum variegatum*).

Evergreen groundcovers generally suitable only for warm or at least mild climates include these: Algerian ivy (*Hedera canariensis*); *Arundinaria disticha, A. pumila,* and *A. variegata; Baccharis pilularis;* brass buttons (*Cotula coronopifolia*); *Ceanothus,* low, spreading and creeping kinds; *Cephalophyllum,* various kinds; crassulas, some kinds; *Delosperma,* some kinds; *Dichondra micrantha; Drosanthemum,* several kinds; echeverias, some kinds; *Gazania ringens;* Hottentot-fig (*Carpobrotus edulis*); *Hypericum calycinum; Lampranthus,* several kinds; *Lantana montevidensis;* lilyturfs, species and

Some evergreen groundcovers for mild climates: (a) Algerian ivy

(b) *Baccharis pilularis*

(c) Hottentot-fig

(d) *Hypericum calycinum*

(e) Lilyturf (*Ophiopogon*)

varieties of *Liriope* and *Ophiopogon*; *Malephora*, several kinds; *Phyla nodiflora*; salal (*Gaultheria shallon*); *Setcreasea pallida*, and *S. p.* 'Purple Heart'; star-jasmine (*Trachelospermum jasminoides*); *Vinca major*; wandering jew (*Zebrina pendula*); and *Wedelia trilobata*.

GROUNDNUT. This as a common name is used for the potato-bean (*Apios americana*) and for the peanut (*Arachis hypogaea*).

GROUNDSEL. See Senecio. Groundsel bush is *Baccharis halimifolia*.

GROW HARD, TO. This refers to growing plants, especially in greenhouses and cold frames, under conditions that ensure firm shoots and foliage rather than softer tissues. Plants grown hard are more resistant to disease and better able to withstand transfer to relatively unfavorable environments than those raised under softer conditions. Growing hard is the reverse to forcing. It involves the strict avoidance of temperatures higher than necessary, ventilation of the greenhouse or other structure as freely as weather permits, exposure to the maximum light the particular plants will accept without harm, and restraint in watering or fertilizing.

GROW ON, TO. This in gardeners' parlance means to keep growing. It is commonly used in reference to seedlings and other young propagations planted in pots, flats, or cold frames to "grow on" toward maturity. It is also applied to plants that, having completed one blooming season, are repotted or given such other attentions

they need, and are then grown on for another year.

GROWTH RETARDANTS. Chemical growth inhibitors are used by commercial growers of some crops, notably azaleas, chrysanthemums, Easter lilies, gardenias, hydrangeas, poinsettias, and certain bedding plants, including China asters, marigolds, petunias, and salvias. They produce more compact, but not stunted growth, and usually darker green foliage. With azaleas they also promote the formation of flower buds. Their effect is the opposite of that of gibberellic acid.

The most favored growth retardants are B-Nine (*N*-dimethylamino-succinamic acid), used as a foliage spray; Cycocel (2-chloroethyl trimethyl ammonium chloride), applied as a foliar spray or soil drench; and Phosphon (2,4-dichlorobenzyl phosphonium chloride), used as a soil drench. With all it is essential to follow the manufacturer's directions carefully.

GRUBS. These are the larvae of beetles. See Larva, and Beetles.

GRUMICHAMA is *Eugenia brasiliensis*.

GRUMILEA. See Psychotria.

GRUSONIA (Grusòn-ia). The possession of clearly longitudinally ribbed stems separates this genus of the cactus family CACTACEAE from allied *Opuntia* in which some authorities include it. It consists of three Mexican species. The name honors Hermann Gruson, a collector of cactuses. In aspect *Grusonia* more closely resembles an *Echinocactus* or a columnar cactus than *Opuntia*, but a study of its blooms reveals its true relationship.

Forming thickets up to 6 feet or so tall, *G. bradtiana* (syn. *Opuntia bradtiana*) has many grayish-green branches with cylindrical-spindle-shaped joints about 3 inches in diameter. The eight or nine ribs are somewhat tuberculate (lumpy) and have woolly areoles (specialized parts of the stems of cactuses from which spines, hairs, etc., develop), each with a cluster of a dozen or more yellowish-brown to bluish-white radial spines, up to 1¼ inches long, and four to five longer central spines, the stoutest of which, up to 2 inches long, point upward. There are tiny, vestigial leaves on the youngest stems, but these, like the glochids (minute barbed spines from the areoles) are soon shed. The yellow flowers are 1¼ to 1½ inches wide. Much less robust, *G. santamaria* is indigenous to Baja California. It is a spreading plant up to 2 feet in height and has stem joints up to 1½ feet long by 1½ inches wide. They are eight- to nine-ribbed and have ½-inch-long, red-purple spines in clusters of about twenty. The rose-red blooms, with yellow centers, are about 1 inch long. Also indigenous to Baja California, **G. hamiltoniana** has very much smaller spines than the others.

Garden and Landscape Uses and Cultivation. These are the same as for *Opuntia*. Excessive watering is to be avoided at all times and a sunny location outdoors in desert regions, or in a greenhouse, provided. For general suggestions see Cactuses.

GUABA is *Inga vera*.

GUAIACUM (Guaìac-um)—Lignum-Vitae. A notable product of this genus of six New World species of the caltrop family ZYGOPHYLLACEAE, is the wood lignum-vitae, the name of which translates as "wood of life." One of the hardiest and heaviest commercial lumbers (even when dry it mostly sinks in water), it has the very valuable quality of being self-lubricating. Because of this and other reasons it is esteemed for pulley sheaves, bearings, casters, and especially for lining the propeller shafts of ships, as well as for turnery and the manufacture of bowling balls. It is extremely resistant to friction and abrasion. Second only to the wood of common lignum-vitae (*Guaiacum officinale*) in commercial importance and used for similar purposes is the wood of *G. sanctum*. In the past resins and other extracts of lignum-vitae were considered specifics against gout, syphilis, and many other ills. A distillation of the wood is sometimes used in proprietary medicines as an expectorant. In addition to their commercial importance, these trees are greatly esteemed in the tropics and subtropics as ornamentals.

Consisting of evergreen and deciduous trees and shrubs, *Guaiacum* has a name that is a modification of a native one. All of its species are remarkable for their hard, resinous woods. They have opposite, leathery, toothless, pinnate leaves, with an even number of leaflets, and stalked, blue or purple flowers paired or in clusters. Each bloom has four or five sepals, the same number of petals, twice as many stamens, and a usually five-lobed style. The fruits are capsules.

Common lignum-vitae (*G. officinale*) is a short-trunked, round-headed tree sometimes 30 feet or more in height, but often not over one-half that. It has handsome, dark green foliage. Its leaves are usually of four, but sometimes six, stalkless obovate or broadly-elliptic leaflets ¾ inch to 2 inches long, with the upper leaflets bigger than the lower ones. The fragrant, deep to pale blue, slender-stalked, starry flowers are several to many together at the twig ends and in axillary clusters. They are ¾ inch or slightly more in diameter and are minutely-hairy on the outsides of their petals. Their stamens are blue with yellow anthers. As the flowers age they become paler. The flattened, heart-shaped, slightly winged, orange-brown fruits are ¾ inch in

diameter and indented at their apexes. This species is a native of the West Indies and northern South America. From it *G. sanctum*, which ranges from the Florida Keys to Mexico, Central America, northern South America, and the West Indies, differs noticeably in its leaves mostly having six to nine leaflets and its fruits usually having four or five angles or wings and pointed tips.

Garden and Landscape Uses. The species discussed are well worth planting for beauty of bloom and foliage. They stand dry conditions and exposure to sun and wind and are well adapted for planting near the sea. They are useful for hedges and screens and for grouping and as single specimens.

Cultivation. In frost-free or essentially frost-free, warm climates these trees grow without particular care other than, if they are maintained as hedges, periodic shearing. They are propagated by seed. Cuttings afford an alternative means of increase.

GUAJILOTE is *Parmentiera edulis*.

GUAMA is *Inga laurina*.

GUANABANA or SOURSOP is *Annona muricata*.

GUANO. The excreta of sea birds collected from desert islands and coastal regions of Chile, natural guano is a very effective fertilizer. An artificial guano prepared from fish is also used as a fertilizer. See Fertilizers.

GUATEMALAN-HOLLY is *Olmediella betschleriana*.

GUAVA. See Psidium. The Chilean-guava is *Ugni molinae*, the pineapple-guava *Feijoa sellowiana*, the yellow strawberry guava *Psidium littorale*, and the purple strawberry guava *Psidium littorale longpipes*.

GUAYMOCHIL is *Pithecellobium dulce*.

GUAYOTE is *Gonolobus edulis*.

GUAYULE is *Parthenium argentatum*.

GUELDER-ROSE is *Viburnum opulus roseum*.

GUERNSEY-LILY is *Nerine sarniensis*.

GUIANA-PLUM is *Drypetes lateriflora*.

GUILIELMA. See Bactris.

GUINEA. This word forms part of the common names of these plants: Guinea-chestnut (*Pachira aquatica*), Guinea gold vine (*Hibbertia scandens*), guinea hen flower (*Fritillaria meleagris*), and guinea hen weed (*Petiveria alliacea*).

GUIZOTIA (Guiz-òtia). Named in honor of François Pierre Guillaume Guizot, French historian and statesman, who died in 1874, this genus of twelve species of tropical African annuals belongs to the daisy family COMPOSITAE. Ranil oil is expressed from the seeds of the species described below.

Guizotias have chiefly opposite leaves. The upper ones are sometimes alternate. The solitary or clustered, yellow flower heads consist of a center of disk florets (those of the kind that form the eyes of daisies) surrounded by petal-like ray florets three-toothed at their apexes. The seedlike fruits are achenes.

Fairly attractive **Guizotia abyssinica** (syn. *G. oleifera*) is about 6 feet tall. It has toothed, lanceolate, stem-clasping leaves, and golden-yellow flower heads ¾ inch to 2 inches in diameter, each with an involucre (collar) of five bracts.

Garden and Landscape Uses and Cultivation. This is occasionally grown in collections of plants that are sources of useful products. It grows easily in sunny locations in fertile soil and responds to treatment satisfactory for commonly cultivated annuals. Seeds may be sown directly outdoors in spring, or started early indoors to give plants for setting out later.

GUM. This is a common name for kinds of *Eucalyptus*. The word gum is also used as part of the common names of these plants: black or sour gum (*Nyssa sylvatica*), cotton or sour gum (*Nyssa aquatica*), gum-myrtle (*Angophora lanceolate*), gum plant (*Grindelia*), sweet gum (*Liquidamber styraciflua*), and water gum (*Tristania laurina*).

GUMBO or OKRA is *Abelmoschus esculentus*. See Okra or Gumbo. Gumbo limbo is *Bursera simaruba*.

GUMI is *Elaeagnus multiflora*.

GUMMOSIS. The unnatural exudation of gummy sap or latex that collects and dries on the trunks and branches of certain woody plants is called gummosis. A symptom, it may indicate infection with disease organisms such as those that cause bacterial canker and brown rot of fruit trees, insect damage such as that of the peach borer, or sometimes only unsatisfactory environmental conditions such as poorly-drained soil. Control can only be had by determining and eradicating the cause of the trouble.

GUNNERA (Gun-nèra). Visitors to gardens in Great Britain and other parts of Europe often are impressed by waterside plantings of huge rhubarb-like plants with leaves several feet in diameter. These are usually gunneras (although *Peltiphyllum peltatum* also satisfies the description), plants rarely seen in American gardens. The genus *Gunnera* is named after the Norwegian botanist

Gunnera manicata

Gunnera manicata, in bloom

Gunnera chilensis, in bloom

Gunnera hamiltonii

Johan Ernst Gunnerus, who died in 1773. Widespread in the southern hemisphere, it is also represented in the native floras of Malaya and Hawaii. There are fifty species.

Gunneras are herbaceous perennials, some of massive size, others low, small-leaved creepers. They belong in the water milfoil family HALORAGIDACEAE, or by the accounting of some botanists, to a family of their own, the GUNNERACEAE. They have creeping rhizomes, and all-basal, stalked, lobed, lobeless, or toothed leaves. The uni-

sexual and bisexual flowers are in spikes or panicles, individual plants having one or both kinds. The blooms are minute and are with or without sepals or petals. There are one or two stamens and two styles. The fruits are tiny, berry-like drupes.

The largest species, **G. manicata**, a native of southern Brazil, has a massive crown or rootstock from which spread to form a huge dome many handsome leaves with thick, fleshy, reddish-hairy stalks 4 to 8 feet long, and palmately- (in hand-fashion) lobed, slightly kidney-shaped, round

blades 4 to 6 feet in diameter. The leaves are peltate, their stalks are attached to the blades some distance in from the margins. The flowers of this gunnera are in long, thick, clublike spikes that come from the crown of the plant and are largely hidden among the leafstalks. Nearly or quite as big and very similar in appearance to the last species, **G. chilensis** (syns. *G. tinctoria, G. scabra*) has nonpeltate leaves (the stalks join the blades at the top of a basal sinus or bay in the margin). Also, the branches of its flower spikes are thicker, not over 3

Gunnera magellanica   Gurania malacophylla

inches long, and not longer than the bracts. Those of *G. manicata* are up to 6 inches in length, considerably exceed the bracts, and are flexuous.

Native to mountains in Hawaii, strange-looking **G. mauiensis** has thick, creeping stems that turn upward at their ends to heights of about 6 feet and terminate in a crown of rhubarblike leaves with stout, rough stalks 1 foot to 3 feet long, and hairy, round, heart-shaped, or kidney-shaped, shallowly-lobed blades. The numerous, minute, two-petaled, bisexual flowers, in panicles up to 3 feet long, are succeeded by tiny, reddish fruits.

Very different from those discussed above, *G. dentata*, *G. hamiltonii*, and *G. prorepens*, of New Zealand, and *G. magellanica*, of southernmost South America and the Falkland Islands, are low, mat-forming or mounding creepers with underground or above-ground stolons and stalked leaves. The first (**G. dentata**), 1 inch to 3 inches high, has gray-green, sparsely-hairy, irregularly-coarsely-toothed leaves with narrow-ovate to elliptic blades ½ to 1 inch in length. Its flower spikes are l inch to 3 inches long. The triangular-ovate-bladed leaves of **G. hamiltonii** are in rosettes crowded together to form cushions or mounds 1 inch to 3 inches high. Dark gray-green and almost or quite hairless, they have finely-evenly-toothed margins. The flower spikes are up to 2½ inches long. From 2 to 6 inches tall, **G. magellanica** has hairless or hairy, long-stalked leaves with circular to kidney-shaped blades 1 inch to 3 inches across and with finely-round-toothed margins. The panicles of male blooms are longer than the

leaves, the female panicles are shorter. Brownish to purplish, usually long-stalked, thin, ovate leaves with blades, finely-toothed or toothless and ¾ inch to 2 inches across, are characteristic of *G. prorepens*, which has flower spikes up to 2½ inches long or sometimes longer.

Garden and Landscape Uses and Cultivation. Immense-leaved *G. chilensis* and *G. manicata* are magnificent adornments for sunny watersides and, if their crowns and roots are protected over winter with a thick layer of leaves or litter, may be expected to succeed outdoors at Washington, D.C. or perhaps even further north. The small-leaved, creeping kinds are less resistent to cold. They are best suited for rock gardens and similar locations in mild, humid climates such as those of parts of the Pacific Northwest. Gunneras appreciate deep, moist, rich soil well supplied with organic matter. Propagation is by division and by seed sown in earth kept evenly moist.

GURANIA (Gu-rània). This not very well known genus of the gourd family CUCURBITACEAE consists of seventy-five species of vines and shrubs of tropical America. The name *Gurania* is an anagram of *Anguria*, a generic once used for related *Citrullus*.

Guranias have branchless tendrils and undivided leaves, lobed or of three or five separate leaflets. The flowers, usually unisexual, rarely bisexual, are red or orange and yellow. They have five-parted calyxes with scarlet tubes and small, fleshy, five-parted corollas. Female blooms, solitary or in heads, have a style with a pair of two-lobed stigmas. The males, in long-stalked heads, racemes, or otherwise loosely ar-

ranged, have a calyx and corolla similar to those of females and two stamens. The fruits are botanically berry-like developments called pepos.

A vine of the upper Amazon region with stems up to 30 feet long, **G. malacophylla** has hairy, broadly-ovate, more or less deeply three- or five-lobed, finely-toothed leaves. Up to 8 inches long and broad, they have deeply-heart-shaped bases. The quite handsome flowers, about 1½ inches long, have bright orange to red calyxes and yellow petals. The males are spaced several together in very long, slender, drooping, branched panicles. The females are stalked and solitary or two or three together in the leaf axils of young, conspicuously-hairy shoots. The fruits, obovoid to club-shaped, about 2½ inches long by l inch wide are green with greenish-yellow stripes.

Garden and Landscape Uses and Cultivation. In the tropics and in large tropical greenhouses the species described is an imposing vine of interest for its attractive foliage and blooms. It thrives in rich fairly moist soil in part-shade and is readily propagated by seeds and by cuttings.

GUTIERREZIA (Gutier-rèzia) — Matchweed or Snakeweed. The herbaceous perennials and subshrubby plants that constitute this genus of the daisy family COMPOSITAE are of slight horticultural significance. Chiefly natives of western North and South America, they are frequent weeds of overgrazed range lands. There are about twenty-five species. The name honors Pedro Gutierrez, a Spanish nobleman.

Gutierrezias are low plants that from woody bases produce many wandlike stems. They have alternate, undivided, toothless, linear leaves, hairless and besprinkled with resinous glands, and loose or dense terminal clusters of small flower heads, each of a few ray and disk florets. The former, analogous to the spreading, petal-like ones of daisies, are female. The disk florets, those that in daisies form the eye of the flower head, are bisexual or male. The seedlike fruits are achenes.

Matchweed or snakeweed (*Gutierrezia sarothrae*) is a common, aggressive native of desert and semidesert regions in western North America and Mexico. Up to about 1¼ feet in height, from its woody base it produces numerous herbaceous stems. Its very narrow, linear leaves are up to 1½ inches long. The top-shaped flower heads, with usually three to eight ray florets and three to eight disk florets, the latter bisexual, are in congested clusters, and appear in late summer and fall. The flower heads are yellow.

Garden and Landscape Uses and Cultivation. In their native regions gutierrezias occasionally may be introduced to plantings. They need conditions similar to those they know in the wild. They may be propagated by seed.

GUTTA PERCHA TREE is *Palaquium gutta*.

GUTTIFERAE — Garcinia family. Tropical and subtropical in its natural distribution, the garcinia family comprises about 1,000 species of dicotyledons representing forty genera. Trees and shrubs, many of its sorts yield useful lumber, some commercial resins, *Garcinia* the delicious fruit called mangosteen, *Mammea*, the mammee-apple.

Plants of this family have opposite or whorled (in circles of more than two), undivided leaves frequently with tiny translucent dots clearly seen when viewed against the light. In branched clusters or umbels, the symmetrical flowers are frequently unisexual. They exhibit in different species considerable variation in form and size. Male and female blooms may be on the same or separate plants. They have two to six or occasionally more of both sepals and petals, many separate or partly united stamens sometimes in a spherical mass and a style short or long or sometimes absent. The stigma often has radiating lobes. The fruits are berries, drupes, or less commonly capsules. Cultivated genera include *Calophyllum*, *Clusia*, *Cratoxylum*, *Garcinia*, *Mammea*, *Mesua*, and *Rheedia*.

GUZMANIA (Guzmàn-ia). The name of *Guzmania*, of the pineapple family BROMELIACEAE, commemorates the eighteenth-century Spanish naturalist Anastasio Guzman. The genus consists of 125 species extending from southern Florida to the West Indies and Brazil, with the greatest number

Guzmania berteroniana

Guzmania lingulata

of species in the Andean rain forests. In the main they are epiphytes (tree-perchers). A few grow in the ground.

Guzmanias have rosettes of usually lustrous leaves without spines along their margins. In this they resemble some species of *Tillandsia*, but differ in their petals and sometimes their sepals being joined into a tube. From *Vriesia*, some of which resemble guzmanias, they differ in that neither their sepals nor petals have a little tongue or scale at their bases inside. The spike- or conelike, bracted flower heads top short stalks from the centers of the rosettes. Yellow or white, the flowers have three sepals, three petals, six stamens, and

a three-parted style. The fruits are capsules.

Endemic to Puerto Rico and one of the most beautiful bromeliads, *G. berteroniana* has a medium-sized rosette of plain green to wine-red, thin leaves from which thrusts a spindle- or pointed-poker-shaped, long-lasting flower spike clothed with uppointing, tightly-overlapped, bright vermilion bracts from between which peep from below upward yellow flowers in succession. Variety *G. b. rubra* has deep copper-red foliage. Another medium-sized species, with plain green leaves and stiff, elongated flower spikes looser than those of the last and not nearly as long-lasting, is *G. monostachia* (syn. *G. tricolor*), wild from southern Florida to the West Indies and Brazil. The floral bracts of this are green to salmon-red striped with brown. The flowers are white. The apex of the spike may vary from brilliant red to pale orange or almost white. A variety with variegated foliage is reported. Somewhat bigger *G. zahnii* is lovely. Its slender, almost translucent leaves up to a little over 1½ feet long, are green to coppery-green, longitudinally-striped on both sides with red-brown or crimson and sometimes tinged pink at their ends. At flowering time the centers of the rosettes become rosy-pink. Nearly as long as the leaves, the long-lasting flower spikes have bright red bracts and short branches with yellow blooms.

Distinctive *G. lingulata* and its varieties are among the most beautiful and popular bromeliads. Native from the West Indies to northern South America and Brazil, this has rosettes of metallic-green leaves up to 1½ feet long. From the center comes the stalked, flat, star-shaped flower head nestled in a collar of spreading or recurved brilliant red bracts. By the uninitiated the bracts are easily mistaken for the petals of a single splendid large bloom. The smaller, innermost ones are orange-red tipped with yellow. The whitish flowers are concealed by the bracts. Varieties are *G. l.* 'Broadview', an especially fine form of the species; *G. l. cardinalis* (syn. *G. cardinalis*), with purplish leaves and larger heads with very brilliant red bracts; *G. l. flammea* (syn. *G. minor flammea*), in which the red bracts are tipped with white; *G. l. minor* (syn. *G. minor*), more than 1 foot in diameter, its leaves penciled with purple, its flower heads with bracts ranging from scarlet to orange or yellow; and *G. l. splendens* (syn. *G. peacockii*), its rosettes up to 2 feet wide, with bright purplish-red outer leaves, reddish-green inner ones. The purplish-red flower heads have white-tipped, yellowish center bracts.

One of the most strikingly colored species, *G. sanguinea* differs from *G. lingulata* in having flowers up to 3 inches instead of not more than 2 inches long, with petals joined for a short distance at their bases instead of being separate, and in having stalkless flower heads. This native from Costa Rica to northern South America and Trinidad has flattish rosettes of 1-inch wide, thick, scaly-based leaves up to 1 foot long, the outer ones bright green, the inner from their middles to their tips ruby-red and to their bases bright yellow and chartreuse. The straw-colored flowers are not showy, but the brilliance of the leaves and bracts at flowering time make this outstanding.

Handsome-foliaged *G. musaica* under good cultivation has leaves 1½ to 2 feet long by 4 inches wide. They are bright green to slightly brownish, conspicuously, irregularly cross-banded with numerous wavy, dark green lines resembling hieroglyphics, and darker on the purplish undersides of the leaves than above. The pink- or red-bracted flower spike, carried on a red-bracted stalk to a height of 1 foot or more, is of crowded, white, waxy blooms 1 inch to 1½ inches long, bullet-shaped in the bud stage and projecting outward. This is native from Panama to Colombia. A variety with especially rich markings is *G. m. zebrina*. Another with leaves conspicuously cross-banded is *G. lindenii* to be described later. Attractive as a foilage plant, *G. fuerstenbergiana,* of the Ecuadorean Andes, has 1-foot long leaves with longitudinal maroon stripes. Its whitish blooms are in 3-inch-long, cylindrical, red spikes.

Three giants of the genus are *G. danielii, G. gloriosa,* and *G. lindenii.* The first two are tree-perchers, the other grows in the ground. All have leaves approximating 3 feet in length. Reddish-green *G. danielii* is a native of high mountains in Colombia. The foliage of *G. gloriosa,* native at high altitudes in Equador, is green. The erect or ascending leaves of *G. lindenii,* about 3 inches wide, are heavily cross-banded with dark green on their upper sides, red beneath. A native of Peru, this has not especially showy flowers. They are whitish and in long, narrow panicles.

Miniature guzmanias are cultivated. Widely distributed in Central and South America, *G. angustifolia* has ¼-inch-wide leaves about 6 inches long and dense, red-bracted spikes some 5 inches in length, with yellow flowers. There is a red-leaved as well as a green-leaved form of this species, which is considered by many fanciers rather difficult to grow. Spreading, pale green leaves of the same dimensions as those of *G. augustifolia* are characteristic of beautiful *G. dissitiflora,* of Central American and Colombian mountains. This has yellow, up-pointing flowers in red-bracted, 9-inch-tall, open spikes. Much less showy in flower than those just described, somewhat bigger *G. vittata* has narrow, pointed leaves cross-banded with purple on their undersides. The white blooms are in small, spherical heads atop greenish stalks. The bracts are green margined with purple. This is a native of Colombia.

Hybrid and presumed hybrid guzmanias, several of European origin, are in cultivation in North America. Here belong kinds named 'Claudine', 'Cristine', 'Exodus', 'Exotica', 'Fantasia', 'Fleur d'Anjou', *G. insignis, G. intermedia,* 'Memoria', 'Meyers's Favorite', and 'Naranja'.

Garden and Landscape Uses and Cultivation. Guzmanias are among the most beautiful and satisfactory bromeliads for outdoor cultivation in the humid tropics, warm, humid subtropics, and in tropical greenhouses. Some kinds accommodate fairly well as houseplants if the air is not too dry, but all do much better as permanent residents in greenhouses. These are lovers of warmth. Indoors, minimum winter temperatures of 55 to 60°F rising by up to fifteen degrees by day are favorable. Shade from strong sun and plenty of humidity are needed. All kinds succeed in potting mixtures satisfactory for epiphytic bromeliads. For more information on these delightful plants and their cultivation see Bromeliads or Bromels.

GYMLEUCORCHIS. This is the name of orchid hybrids the parents of which are *Gymnadenia* and *Leucorchis.*

GYMNADENIORCHIS. This is the name of bigeneric orchids the parents of which are *Gymnadenia* and *Orchis.*

GYMNANACAMPTIS. This is the name of bigeneric orchid hybrids the parents of which are *Anacamptis* and *Gymnadenia.*

GYMNAPLATANTHERA. This is the name of orchid hybrids the parents of which are *Gymnadenia* and *Platanthera.*

GYMNASTER (Gymn-áster). Native of eastern Asia, *Gymnaster* consists of three species of the daisy family COMPOSITAE, that some botanists include in *Aster.* The name is derived from the Greek *gymnos,* naked, and *Aster.* It alludes to the achenes being without a pappus of bristles, scales, or hairs.

Gymnasters are erect herbaceous perennials with alternate, hairy or hairless leaves and flower heads of the daisy type with disk and ray florets. The fruits are seedlike achenes.

Native of mountain woodlands in Japan, *G. savatieri* has short rhizomes and stems 8 inches to 2 feet tall, branched near their tops. The oblong to obovate leaves, clothed with short hairs, are coarsely-toothed. The long-stalked flower heads, in loose clusters, are 1¼ to 1½ inches wide. The ray florets are blue or white. Variety *G. s. pygmaeus* has long, creeping rhizomes, is 6 to 8 inches tall, and has leaves

Gymnaster savatieri pygmaeus

¾ inch to 1¼ inches long. The flower heads are solitary atop long stalks.

Garden Uses and Cultivation. The species described and especially its variety are attractive for adding interest to plant collections. They thrive in woodland soils in light shade. Propagation is by seed and by division. These plants are hardy.

GYMNIGRITELLA. This is the name of bigeneric orchid hybrids the parents of which are *Gymnadenia* and *Nigritella*.

GYMNOCACTUS (Gýmno-cactus). A dozen Mexican species of the cactus family CACTACEAE, constitue the genus *Gymnocactus*. By some authorities they are included in closely related *Neolloydia*, by others some sorts are referred to *Thelocactus*. The name *Gymnocactus*, derived from the Greek *gymnos*, naked, and cactus, alludes to the flowers and fruits being without scales.

Gymnocactuses are small, spiny cactuses with solitary or clustered stems or plant bodies with tubercled (lumpy) ribs tipped with elongated areoles (areas in cactuses from which spines develop). The funnel-shaped flowers come from near the tops of the plants. They open by day. Their ovaries and perianth tubes, like the fruits, are naked of scales.

Variable *G. beguinii* (syn. *Neolloydia beguinii*) has mostly solitary, pale green, cylindrical stems 4 to 6 inches tall with thirteen to twenty-one lumpy ribs. They are practically hidden by numerous white spines, each cluster of which consists of twelve to twenty dark-tipped radials approximately ½ inch long and one longer, straight, rather weak central. Bright lilac-pink, the flowers are 1¼ to 1½ inches across. Variety *G. b. senilis* has longer, thinner, white spines tipped with brown. In *G. b. smithii* each spine cluster has four brown centrals. The plant bodies of *G. gielsdorfianus* (syn. *Thelocactus gielsdorfianus*) are blue-green to gray-green, 3 inches or slightly more in diameter, at their apexes woolly. In clusters of six to eight, the spines (all radials) are ½ to ¾ inch long, awl-shaped, thin, bent, and brown to grayish-brown tipped with black. The ½-inch-wide blooms are ivory-white to cream-colored. Bluish-green, spherical to short-cylindrical plant bodies with white wool at their apexes and up to about 4½ inches high are characteristic of *G. horripilus* (syns. *Neolloydia horripila, Thelocactus horripilus*). They may branch from their bases and occasionally higher. The spine clusters are of nine or ten black-tipped, white, needle-like radial spines about ½ inch long in each cluster, and often but not always one straight or slightly curved, stouter central. The purple blooms are about 1 inch in diameter. Yellowish-green to dark green, the solitary or clustered plant bodies of *G. knuthianus*, about 2½ inches wide, have thirteen to twenty-one ribs. Its spine clusters are of

sixteen to twenty slender, yellowish-based, spreading, white radials approximately ¼ inch long and one slightly stouter, ½-inch-long central tipped with brown. The light lilac-pink flowers are ¾ to 1 inch in diameter.

A much thickened, turnip-like root is characteristic of *G. mandragora* (syn. *Thelocactus mandragora*). Its spherical, grayish-green plant body, about 2½ inches across, is practically hidden beneath white spines, which are in clusters of about twelve incurved, awl-shaped radials and generally two, erect, brown-tipped centrals approximately ¾ inch long. The 1-inch-wide blooms are white striped with rosy-pink. The solitary or clustered plant bodies of *G. roseanus* (syn. *Thelocactus roseanus*) are about 2 inches high by a little over 1 inch thick. They have eight to thirteen low, lumpy ribs. The spine clusters are of about fifteen radials slightly exceeding ½ inch in length and four to six stouter, ¾-inch long centrals. The blooms are light pink. Similar to the last, *G. aquirreanus* differs in having bigger and squatter, usually solitary, plum-colored plant bodies with orange-tan to plum-colored spines, each cluster with thirteen to sixteen radials and two to six centrals. The flowers are yellowish to reddish-yellow, the outer petals often tipped with reddish-purple and with center streaks of the same color. The green to bluish, more or less globular, 2- to 3-inch-wide plant bodies of *G. viereckii* (syn. *Thelocactus viereckii*) have fifteen to eighteen lumpy ribs. The dark spines are in clusters of about twenty radials less than ½ inch long and four centrals ¾ inch long. The violet flowers are 1 inch in diameter.

Garden Uses and Cultivation. This group is of much interest to collectors of cactuses. Its kinds are generally not difficult to grow in sandy, well-drained, preferably slightly acid soil. They are slow growers that seem to prefer a little shade from strong direct sun. See also Cactuses.

GYMNOCALYCIUM (Gymno-calýcium — Chin Cactus. Some authorities include, probably with sufficient reason, *Weingartia* and *Neowerdermannia* in *Gymnocalycium*, but in this Encyclopedia, in accordance with the prevailing practice of most cactus collectors, they are treated separately. The genus *Gymnocalycium*, of the cactus family CACTACEAE, consists of sixty species, natives of South America. The name, from the Greek *gymnos*, naked, and *kalyx*, a bud, alludes to the flower buds being naked.

These cactuses have small, spherical, solitary or clustered stems. Their well-formed ribs have protrusions or tubercles with more or less well-developed chins from their undersides. The flowers, bell- to shortly-funnel-shaped, have tubes with scales that are without hairs or wool in their axils. The fruits, also scaly, are oblongish and red.

Highly colored variants of *G. mihanovichii* are among cactuses best known to the lay public. They are freely sold as novelties in florists' stores and elsewhere as well as by specialist cactus dealers. The species of which these are variants has somewhat flattened, globose, grayish-green stems approximately 2 inches in diameter. There are eight ribs with spine clusters from small areoles spaced less than ½ inch apart. Each cluster is of six to eight yellowish,

Gymnocalycium mihanovichii

Gymnocalycium mihanovichii 'Pink Cap'

Gymnocalycium baldianum

Gymnocalycium damsii

Gymnocalycium mihanovichii 'Yellow Cap'

spreading spines up to 1¼ inches long. The sometimes red-tinged, green to yellowish-green flowers have brownish-green outer petals. Reddish stems, deciduous spines, and pink flowers distinguish *G. m. friedrichii*. The colored variants of this species named respectively with regard to their hues 'Red Cap', 'Pink Cap', 'Yellow Cap', and 'White Cap' are all devoid of chlorophyll. They are in effect albinos and as such are unable, unlike chlorophyll-containing plants, to manufacture from soil nutrients and air the foods they need. They can only exist as artificial grafts on other green-stemmed cactuses.

Other gymnocalyciums treasured by contemporary cactus collectors include

these: *G. andreae* has clustered stems, less than 2 inches in diameter, with eight ribs, spine clusters with one to three whitish centrals ¼ to ½ inch long, and five to seven radials. The bright sulfur-yellow blooms are 1¼ inches in diameter. *G. anisitsii,* short-cylindrical and about 4 inches tall, has about eleven lumpy ribs with clusters of five to seven slender, yellowish spines up to a little over 2 inches long. The funnel-shaped flowers, approximately 1½ inches long, are white with greenish-white outer petals. *G. asterium* (syn. *G. stellatum*) has spines in clusters of three to five and white to pale pink flowers 2½ inches long by 1½ inches wide. *G. baldianum* (syn *G. venturianum*) has a low, spherical, nine- to eleven-ribbed stem about 3 inches in diameter. In clusters of five, the gray spines, all radials, are about ½ inch long. The flowers, 1½ inches in diameter, are wine-red to purple-red, rarely pink. *G. bodenbenderianum* is allied to *G. platense*. It has a low, disklike, tubercled stem about

3½ inches across, spineless at its middle. There are eleven to fourteen low ribs. The backward-curving spines, all radials, in clusters of three to five, are ⅓ inch long. The 1½-inch-wide, pink-flushed, white flowers have petals with a brownish central stripe. *G. bruchii* (syn. *G. lafaldensis*) has clusters of small stems with twelve low, rounded ribs and clusters of ten to twelve very short, white spines. The funnel-shaped white flowers tinged with pink are 1 inch across. *G. castellanosii* has stems with ten to twelve blunt ribs with clusters of one central and five to seven radial, dark-tipped, white spines ½ to 1 inch long. The white-throated, pink blooms are 1½ inches across. *G. damsii* is variable, much like *G. mihanovichii*. Its flattened-spherical stems have ten to twelve ribs notched into low, slightly-chinned tubercles. The slightly upcurved spines, white to gray, tipped with brown and up to ½ inch long, are in clusters of six to eight. The green-tubed flowers have pure white inner petals, red-edged, white outer ones. *G. deeszianum* has stems with seven or eight ribs and clusters of yellowish, twisted, spines ½ to 1 inch long. The 2-inch-wide blooms are ivory-white with pink throats. *G. denudatum,* up to 4 inches tall and 6 inches in diameter, has five to eight low ribs with poorly developed tubercles. Its spines, all radials, are in clusters of usually five, sometimes up to eight. The blooms are white to light pink. *G. gibbosum* is variable. Several varieties have been named. Its stems, at first globular often becoming cylindrical with age, may be 8 inches tall by 3½ inches wide. They have twelve to nineteen ribs with prominently-chinned tubercles and clusters of seven to ten radial spines up to 1½ inches long and sometimes one or two similar centrals. The white to reddish blooms are about 2¼ inches long. Variety *C. g. nigrum* has black spines. *G. leeanum* is dwarf and

Gymnocalycium denudatum

Gymnocalycium platense

clustering. Its stems are more or less flattened-spherical, the tubercles not regularly arranged. The spine clusters are of about eleven small radials that lie close to the plant body and one ascending central. The comparatively large flowers have pale yellow inner petals, purplish-tinged, green outer ones. *G. leptanthum* much resembles *G. platense*, but its flowers have longer tubes. *G. loricatum* (syn. *G. spegazzinii*) has a flattened-orbicular to short cylindrical stem up to about 4½ inches in diameter with ten to twelve ribs. The clusters of spines are of five to seven all radial, recurved spines up to about 1¼ inches long. The blooms are white, approximately 1½ inches wide. *G. mazanense* is low and rounded. It has ten to twelve ribs. The spine clusters have seven or eight radials and one or two or no central spines up to 1½ inches long. The 2-inch-wide flowers are white to pink. *G. platense*, globular and up to 4 inches in diameter, has eight to twelve broad, low ribs divided into well-chinned tubercles. The spines, about ⅓ inch long and all radials, are in clusters of mostly seven, sometimes fewer. The greenish-white flowers 2 to 2¼ inches in length, have reddish bases to their petals. This close relative of *G. gibbosum* is variable. *G. quehlianum* is by some authorities considered to be a variety of *G. platense*. Its flat-topped stems, not over 2 inches high and up to 6 inches wide, have eight to thirteen ribs with prominently-chinned tubercles and in clusters of five, all-radial spines about ⅓ inch long. The flowers, 2 inches wide or a little wider, have red-based, white inner petals, red-edged, greenish outer ones. *G. saglione* may attain a height of 1 foot and a width of 6 inches. It has up to thirty-two rounded, tubercled ribs and clusters of up to fifteen reddish-brown to

nearly black spines 1 inch to 1½ inches long. The white to pink, bell-shaped flowers are 1 inch in diameter. *G. stuckertii* has a nine- to eleven-ribbed, strongly-tubercled stem up to 3 inches wide or somewhat wider, and clusters of seven to nine 1-inch-long radial spines that spread parallel with the plant body. The white to pink flowers are about 1½ inches long.

Garden and Landscape Uses. These are among the easiest of cactuses to grow and so can be strongly recommended to beginners. Most bloom with considerable enthusiasm and regularity. They are suitable for outdoors in rock gardens and similar places where the climate is warm and dry, for greenhouses, and as window plants. They may be grown in full sun, but tolerate, and some perhaps are better for, a little shade from the strongest light.

Cultivation. As with all cactuses good drainage is absolutely essential. Given that, gymnocalyciums are not choosy about soil.

Gymnocalycium stuckertii

A porous, fertile one that contains only a small amount of organic matter is best. Propagation is by seeds, offsets, and grafting. For more information see Cactuses.

GYMNOCARPIUM (Gymno-cárpium)—Oak Fern. This genus of the aspidium family ASPIDIACEAE was formerly included in *Dryopteris*. Its three or perhaps five species, natives of north-temperate regions, Taiwan, the Philippines, and New Guinea, differ from that genus in their leafstalks having only two conducting bundles and in the veins of their fronds reaching to the margins of the segments. Another difference is that the clusters of spore capsules in *Gymnocarpium* are without coverings (indusia). This last characteristic is responsible for the name, from the Greek *gymnos*, naked, and *karpos*, a fruit.

Gymnocarpiums are deciduous ferns with creeping, branched rhizomes from which spring at intervals erect, membranous fronds. The blades of the fronds, triangular or pentagonal, are twice-pinnate, with the segments, other than perhaps the uppermost, pinnately-lobed. The clusters of spore capsules are round.

The oak fern (*G. dryopteris* syns. *Dryopteris disjuncta*, *D. linnaeana*) occurs wild mostly in cool woodlands from Labrador to Alaska, Virginia, Iowa, and Arizona, and in Europe and temperate Asia. It has dark, slender rhizomes with light brown scales, and glandless or nearly glandless fronds up to 1½ feet in length. They have blades five-sided in outline, up to 8 inches long by up to 10 inches wide. They are twice- or thrice-pinnate, with the segments pinnately-lobed. The two to six pairs of veins of each segment are mostly not forked.

The limestone oak fern, northern oak fern, or scented oak fern (*G. robertianum* syn. *Dryopteris robertiana*) inhabits limestone rocks from Newfoundland to the Yukon, Alaska, Pennsylvania, Iowa, and British Columbia, and occurs also in Europe and temperate Asia. This has black rhizomes with a few pale brown scales. The fronds, a little over 1 foot in length or shorter, have triangular blades up to 6 inches long and slightly wider than their lengths. They are twice-pinnate, with the segments pinnately-lobed. The two to five pairs of veins of each segment are not branched. Like the stalks, the blades of the fronds are covered with small glands.

Garden and Landscape Uses and Cultivation. Gymnocarpiums are grown by native plant specialists and fern fanciers in woodland gardens and similar shaded places. The kinds described above need cool, humid environments approximating those in which they grow as wildlings. Limestone soil is needed by *G. robertianum*. Propagation is by division in early spring and by spores. For further information see Ferns.

GYMNOCEREUS (Gymno-céreus). Two Peruvian species by conservative botanists included in *Browningia,* constitute *Gymnocereus,* of the cactus family CACTACEAE. The name, alluding to the spines shedding from old parts of the stems, comes from the Greek *gymnos,* naked, and the name of the related genus *Cereus.*

Gymnocereuses are treelike cactuses, 12 to 15 feet tall. They have stout, erect, strongly-ribbed stems that branch above in candelabrum fashion and white flowers that open at night and close the next day. The pink or red, spherical to oblongish fruits contain small black seeds.

Not common in cultivation, *G. microspermus* has stems with up to twenty low, rounded ribs and clusters of thirty or more bristly, brown spines ½ inch long. Equally as rare, *G. amstutziae* differs from the last in the eleven or more ribs of its stems being higher and pointed, and in having 1- to 2-inch-long spines, at first brown, later gray to black, in clusters of about fifteen.

Garden and Landscape Uses and Cultivation. These are as for *Browningia.* For more information see Cactuses.

GYMNOCLADUS (Gymnóclad-us)—Kentucky-Coffee Tree. The only American representative of this genus of three deciduous trees, and the hardiest and best known, is the Kentucky-coffee tree. The other kinds are natives of Asia. The group belongs to the pea family LEGUMINOSAE. Its generic name, from the Greek *gymnos,* naked, and *klados,* a branch, refers to the branches having few twigs.

All kinds of *Gymnocladus* have stout branches, and branchlets with thick pith. Their leaves are pinnate or twice-pinnate and toothless. They have five-petaled, ten-stamened, symmetrical (not pea-shaped) flowers in terminal panicles, with the sexes on separate trees or with unisexual and bisexual flowers on the same one. The fruits are thick, pulpy, broad-oblong pods containing few to several large flattened seeds.

The Kentucky-coffee tree (*G. dioica*) is decidedly picturesque, and especially beautiful when in fresh leaf. In the open it develops a broad ovoid or obovoid crown. Under forest conditions it is less spreading and sometimes 100 feet tall. Its loose, rather coarse foliage consists of both once- and twice-pinnate, broad leaves, 2 to 3 feet long. When first they expand in spring they are pinkish. Before they drop in fall they turn clear yellow. The greenish flowers, borne in early summer, have little or no decorative appeal. Fertilized females and bisexuals are succeeded by pods 4 to 10 inches long by 1½ to 2 inches wide that contain a sweet pulp. At maturity the pods are brown. They hang on the trees through most of the winter. It is said that in early colonial days the seeds, about ¾

Gymnocladus dioica: (a) In summer   (b) In winter

Gymnocladus dioica (fruits)

inch in diameter, were used as a substitute for coffee. This accounts for the common name, but if the story be true the colonists contented themselves with a very poor substitute for the fragrant and stimulating product of *Coffea arabica.* The Kentucky-coffee tree is indigenous to rich, low bottom lands from New York to Tennessee, Nebraska, and Oklahoma. It is hardy through most of New England.

Southern Chinese **G. chinensis,** hardy only in warm parts of the United States has smaller leaflets than the American species and they are pubescent on both sides whereas those of the Kentucky-coffee tree are hairy only on the undersides when young. Also, the lilac-purple flowers of the Asian species, which grows to a height of about 60 feet, appear before the foliage. In its homeland the pods of this tree provide a soap substitute for laundry purposes. A superior perfumed soap for personal use is prepared by adding honey,

camphor, musk, sandalwood, and other ingredients. After their black coats are removed by steaming, the seeds are employed in the same manner as wax, to gloss silk threads used for embroidery.

Garden and Landscape Uses. Although perhaps not among the best shade trees, the Kentucky-coffee tree is distinctly worthwhile as a landscape decorative because of its unusually picturesque appearance. This is particularly apparent in winter when it is leafless and its stout, gaunt trunk and branches trace interesting patterns against the sky and the branchlets of fruiting specimens are festooned with conspicuous seed pods. Because it drops pods and large leaves from time to time, some consider it to be a "dirty tree," but surely the effort of an occasional raking up is a small price to pay for the aesthetic charm this native American provides. The tree is remarkably free of pests and serious diseases.

Cultivation. The Kentucky-coffee tree responds best to a deep, rich, moderately moist soil. It transplants satisfactorily and needs no special care in the matter of pruning. It is propagated by seeds and by cuttings.

GYMNOGLOSSUM This is the name of orchid hybrids the parents of which are *Coeloglossum* and *Gymnadenia*.

GYMNOGRAMMA. See Pityrogramma.

GYMNOSPERMS. All plants that belong in the botanical subdivision of the plant world called *Gymnospermae* are gymnosperms. Those best known to gardeners are conifers, cycads, and ephedras. Gymnosperms are seed plants that differ from the other great subdivision of that group, the angiosperms, in being without structures that in any horticultural sense could be called flowers. Instead they produce ovules (representing female flowers) that are not, like those of angiosperms, enclosed in an ovary but that lie naked on the scales of cones or on carpels. Naked pollen-producing organs clustered in various ways represent male flowers. The word gymnosperm is derived from the Greek *gymnos*, naked, and *sperma*, a seed.

GYMNOSPORIA. See Maytenus.

GYMNOSTACHYUM (Gymno-stáchyum). About twenty-five species of the acanthus family ACANTHACEAE constitute *Gymnostachyum*, a native of Ceylon, the East Indies, and Malaya. Its name, alluding to the lack of conspicuous floral bracts present in many other members of the family, comes from the Greek *gymnos*, naked, and *stachys*, a spike.

Evergreen subshrubs or shrubs, the sorts of this genus have usually thin, essentially lobeless, toothless, sometimes variegated leaves, and in erect, spikelike racemes or panicles, little tubular flowers with four scale-like perianth segments, four stamens, and a stigma that sits on top of the ovary without an apparent style. The fruits are capsules.

Native to Ceylon, **G. celanicum** is low and spreading with long-stalked, white-veined, dark green, elliptic leaves and loose racemes 6 inches to 1 foot long of white-anthered, yellow flowers.

Garden Uses and Cultivation. The sort described is an attractive groundcover for gardens in the humid tropics and warm subtropics and is also suitable for greenhouses where night temperature in winter is 55 to 65°F and that by day five to ten degrees higher. Well-drained soil containing a generous proportion of organic matter and kept always moderately moist, suits. Shade from strong sun is needed. Increase is easy by cuttings planted in sand or perlite or in a mixture of either of these and peat moss, and by seeds.

GYMNOTRAUNSTEINERA. This is the name of orchid hybrids the parents of which are *Gymnadenia* and *Traunsteinera*.

GYMPIE NUT or MACADAMIA NUT is *Macadamia ternifolia*.

GYNANDRIRIS (Gynánd-riris). This genus of twenty species of the Mediterranean region and South Africa is closely related to *Iris* with which by some authorities it is combined, and to *Moraea*. It belongs to the iris family IRIDACEAE. The name *Helixyra* was previously used for *Gynandriris*. Its present name presumably derives from the Greek *gyne*, female, *andros*, male, and the name of the genus *Iris*.

The species of *Gynandriris* are deciduous herbaceous perennials with fibrous-coated corms (bulblike organs that are solid rather than composed of concentric or overlapping scales). The longitudinally parallel-veined leaves, chiefly basal, are linear, and unlike those of *Iris* are not folded at their bases so that they envelop each other. The several decidedly iris-like, short-lived blooms arise from the axils of spathes (bracts) at the upper parts of the flower stalks and open in succession. At flowering time the spathes are membrane-like between their rather widely spaced veins. Each bloom has six petal-like segments, not, as are those of irises, joined at their bases into a distinct tube. The upper parts of the outer segments droop, the other segments are erect. There are three stamens each nestled beneath and more or less adhering to one of the three broadly-expanded style branches. Petal-like in color and texture, the style branches are deeply-cleft at their apexes into two lobes. The fruits are papery-walled capsules, at maturity hidden from view by the persistent spathes. Differences between *Gynandriris* and *Moraea* are that at least the inner layers of the outer coverings of the corms of the first are of parallel soft, rather than coarse, woody, fibers and that the floral spathes of *Moraea* are not membranous and do not hide the mature seed capsules.

Native of arid and semiarid areas in the Mediterranean region, **G. sisyrinchium**

Gymnostachyum celanicum

Gynandriris sisyrinchium

(syns. *Helixyra sisyrinchium, Iris sisyrinchium*) is about 1 foot high. It has a small corm and mostly two arching leaves 6 inches to 1 foot long. The lavender-blue to blue-purple flowers, 1 inch to 1½ inches wide, are displayed, solitary or in groups of up to six, in spring. They have three outer segments (the falls) with a central spot of yellow bordered with white. The inner segments are up to ¼ inch long.

Garden Uses and Cultivation. This is a collectors' species of special interest to lovers of rare plants. It needs the same general treatment as bulbous irises, such as Dutch and English kinds, but is hardy only where winters are moderate and summers hot and dry. Wet conditions during its summer dormant period are likely to prove disastrous. At the conclusion of the growing season, when the foliage has died naturally, the corms may be dug and stored in a dry place indoors for replanting in fall. This interesting species can also be grown in pots in greenhouses, given the conditions and care that suit freesias, tritonias, and other bulb plants that need cool conditions and that grow from fall through spring and are dormant in summer.

GYNERIUM (Gy-nérium)—Uva Grass. In gardens the pampas grass (*Cortaderia*) is often mistakenly known as *Gynerium*, which name properly belongs to a related genus of one species, the uva grass. This species differs from *Cortaderia* in its leaves, instead of being all basal, being borne along tall stems. Both genera belong to the grass family GRAMINEAE. The name *Gynerium*, derived from the Greek *gyne*, female, and *erion*, wool, alludes to the hairiness of parts of the female spikelets.

Uva grass (**G. sagittatum**) is perennial and reedlike. Native of wet soils from Mexico to the West Indies and South America, it is 12 to 30 feet tall or taller, and has stems about 1 inch in diameter, with their lower parts thickly clothed with the bases of old leaves. The flat leaf blades, up to 6 feet in length by 1 inch to 4 inches wide, are spaced evenly along the stems, but the lower ones drop early leaving the others in fanlike clusters near the tops of the stems. The plants are individually male or female. They have plumelike panicles 3 feet long or longer, with drooping branches, and numerous several-flowered spikelets, with those of female plants conspicuously silky-hairy.

Garden and Landscape Uses and Cultivation. In the tropics and subtropics, and sometimes in large conservatories, uva grass is occasionally grown for ornament. For its best development it needs fertile, moist soil. In greenhouses it may be accommodated in ground beds, tubs, or large pots. It thrives where the night temperature in winter is 55 to 60°F and by day and at other seasons higher. A sunny location is desirable, and specimens in con-

Gynerium sagittatum

Gynura aurantiaca

tainers benefit from liberal fertilizing. Increase is by division in late winter or early spring, and by seed.

GYNURA (Gy-nùra)—Velvet Plant. Natives of the Old World tropics, the 100 species of *Gynura* belong to the daisy family COMPOSITAE. Cultivated kinds are admired chiefly for their foliage. The name, alluding to the tailed stigmas, comes from the Greek *gyne*, female, and *oura*, a tail.

Herbaceous perennials or subshrubs, erect or more or less vining, gynuras have alternate, lobed or lobeless leaves and flower heads of only disk florets (the kind that form the centers of daisy-type flower heads). The involucres (collars of bracts at the backs of the flower heads) are bell-shaped. The fruits are seedlike achenes.

The common velvet plant (**G. aurantiaca**), of Java, is an erect, branched subshrub 2 to 3 feet in height or with age

Gynura hybrid, purple passion vine

The popular purple passion vine (G. 'Purple Passion') is a hybrid, its parents G. *aurantiaca* and probably *P. procumbens*. This has somewhat vining stems that tend to trail or twine. Its lanceolate to oblong-oblanceolate leaves, up to 4½ inches long and 2 inches wide have shallowly-pinnately-lobed or wavy-toothed margins and are clothed with purple hairs. Their undersides are wine-red. In terminal clusters, the small heads of flowers are orange.

Erect and branched **G. bicolor**, of the Molucca Islands, is 2 or 3 feet tall, has thinnish, slightly-downy, coarsely-toothed or lobed, ovate-lanceolate to oblanceolate leaves 3 to 6 inches long, dullish gray-purple above, rich violet-purple on their undersides, and orange-yellow flower heads. Native to Malaya and the Philippine Islands, nearly hairless **G. procumbens** (syn. *G. sarmentosa*) has stems at first erect, later semitrailing or vining and up to 10 feet long. Its ovate to lanceolate, toothless to distantly toothed leaves with blades up to 5 inches long by one-half as wide are green with a purple midrib. The lower ones are stalked, the upper stalkless. The orange flower heads are in terminal panicles.

Garden Uses and Cultivation. Gynuras are best adapted for outdoor cultivation in the humid tropics and in tropical greenhouses, but some hobbyists succeed with them as houseplants. They thrive where the minimum temperature at night is 55 to 60°F, that by day five to fifteen degrees higher, and require shade from strong sun. For their best contentment they need rich, well-drained soil always kept fairly moist without being constantly saturated. Well-rooted specimens benefit from biweekly applications of dilute liquid fertil-

semivining and much taller. It has thickish stems, their young parts, like the foliage, densely clothed with violet-purple hairs. The soft, coarsely-toothed, purple-veined, ovate leaves 3 to 8 inches long and up to 4½ inches wide have mostly narrowly-winged, short stalks, but the upper leaves are stalkless. The orange to yellow flower heads, ½ to ¾ inch wide, are in erect, loosely-branched, terminal panicles.

Gynura bicolor

Gynura procumbens

izer. Occasional pinching out of the tips of the shoots stimulates branching and the development of young shoots, which normally carry the most highly colored foliage. Gynuras grow readily from seeds, but are more often raised from cuttings. These root as easily as those of geraniums and begonias in sand, vermiculite, or perlite, or in a mixture of peat moss and one of these, in a greenhouse propagating case or elsewhere where the atmosphere is humid and there is shade from sun.

GYPSOPHILA (Gypsóph-ila) — Baby's Breath. Annual and perennial herbaceous plants and subshrubs, the majority satisfactorily hardy, make up this genus of 125 species of the pink family CARYOPHYLLA-CEAE. Several are popular. They are inhabitants of Europe, Asia, and North Africa. Their name comes from the Greek *gypsos*, gypsum, and *philos*, loving, and refers to the liking of some kinds for soils derived from gypsum rocks.

Gypsophilas vary from very low, compact plants to diffuse kinds up to 4 feet in height. Characteristically their flowers are small and numerous, on much-branched, slender stems or in compact clusters. They are white or light pink, and have five-toothed calyxes that are very obviously papery and colorless except for five slender green veins. There are five petals, rounded or notched at their apexes, ten stamens, and two or rarely three styles. The fruits are small, spherical to egg-shaped capsules. As with other members of their family, the leaves are opposite on stems that are swollen at the nodes (joints).

Annual gypsophilas include the popular annual baby's breath (**G. elegans**). Native

Gypsophila elegans

to the Caucasus, this erect, graceful plant has slender, forking stems 1 foot to 1½ feet tall, lanceolate leaves 1 inch to 3 inches long, and white or pink flowers, up to ½ inch or slightly more in diameter, and elegantly displayed in loose panicles. The petals, twice or thrice as long as the calyx, are notched at their ends. Varieties with pink flowers are offered under such designations as *G. e. atrosanguinea*, *G. e. carminea*, and *G. e. rosea*. A smaller annual, **G. muralis**, a native of Europe, is 6 inches to 1 foot high and has linear leaves narrowed at both ends and about 1 inch long. Its slender stems are branched freely and bear loosely arranged, rosy-pink flowers with round-toothed margins to the petals, which are twice as long as the calyx lobes. Variety *G. m. alba* has white flowers. Both *G. elegans*

and *G. muralis* are naturalized in parts of North America.

Perennial baby's breath (**G. paniculata**) is by far the most popular of tall perennial kinds. An old-fashioned garden plant, native to Europe and northern Asia, it is naturalized in parts of North America. It has extensive, deep, forking roots and forms broad, billowy clouds, 3 feet or more in height, of slender, much-branched stems furnished with pointed, linear-lanceolate, leaves and myriads of white flowers about ¹⁄₁₆ inch in diameter. The leaves are ordinarily less than ½ inch broad and usually single-veined. The largest, those toward the base of the plant, may be 3 or 4 inches long and are under one-fourth as wide as long. Variety *G. p. compacta* is dwarfer. In *G. p. flore-pleno* the flowers are double. Those of *G. p. ehrlei*, and *G. p.* 'Bristol Fairy' are double and larger than those of the typical species.

Other tall perennials include **G. acutifolia**, of the Caucasus, which is similar to *G. paniculata*, but less glaucous, and has broader leaves with three or five veins. Its lower leaves are at least four times as long as they are wide. Native to Korea, **G. oldhamiana** is up to 2½ feet tall. Its stems branch only in their upper parts. The leaves are oblong-lanceolate, three- or five-veined, and up to 2½ inches long. Pink, ⅛ inch or slightly more across, the flowers are in dense clusters. Their petals are twice as long as the calyx lobes. The Siberian **G. pacifica** has numerous pale pink to purplish flowers, ¼ inch or slightly more across, in loose, much-branched panicles up to 4 feet tall. The petals are twice as long as the lobes of the calyx. A distinguishing characteristic is that the lower leaves are only about twice

Gypsophila elegans (flowers)

Gypsophila paniculata flore-pleno

Gypsophila repens

as long as they are wide. The leaves are ovate-oblong.

Several attractive low perennial kinds are cultivated. One of the most popular is *G. repens*, a hairless, often slightly glaucous, prostrate or trailing plant, up to 1 foot tall, with bluish-green, linear leaves generally under 1 inch long, and dainty white or pink blooms ⅓ inch in diameter. *G. r. rosea* has pink flowers and ordinarily is not over 6 inches tall. *G. r. fratensis* is very similar to *G. r. rosea*. For a long time the botanical relationship of this kind was in doubt, but as it occasionally reverts to typical *G. repens* there is no doubt that it belongs with that species. A hybrid, *G. bodgeri*, between *G. r. rosea* and a double-flowered variety of *G. paniculata*, attains a height of 1 foot or more and has stems that are prostrate below and double white or pink flowers in loose panicles.

The mouse-ear gypsophila (*G. cerastioides*) differs markedly from those previously described. It is a cushion-like plant, 2 to 4 inches tall, hairy, and with obovate or spatula-shaped leaves ½ inch to 2 inches long, the lower ones long-stalked. Its pink-veined, white flowers, ⅔ inch in diameter, with notched petals, are in loose clusters. This is native in the Himalayas.

Choice rock garden kinds of very low growth include *G. alpigena*, of the Pyre-

Gypsophila aretioides

nees, which is related to *G. repens*, but is only 1 inch to 3 inches tall. Its flowers are often solitary. Forming small, dense, firm, gray-green mats, *G. aretioides*, a native of Iran, has pearly-white flowers. Other dwarf kinds are sometimes listed in catalogs of fanciers. Often they are relatives of *G. repens*. Most are worth trying by dedicated rock gardeners.

Garden and Landscape Uses. These are plants for deep, thoroughly drained soils and full sun. They do not object to dryish conditions. They appreciate, or at least tolerate, limy soils. The taller kinds are excellent for flower beds and borders and for supplying cut flowers to mingle with larger blooms. The lower kinds are splendid rock garden plants and may be used effectively in dry walls, between paving stones, and in rocky places.

Cultivation. Seeds afford a ready means of obtaining plants of most gypsophilas. The perennials can also be raised from cuttings of firm, but not hard and woody shoots. These are planted in summer under mist or in a shaded, humid, cold frame, in sand, sand and peat moss, perlite, or vermiculite. The young plants are potted and carried through the winter in a cold frame or cool greenhouse. Root cuttings can also be employed as a means of increasing the perennials. Because double-flowered varieties cannot ordinarily be propagated by seeds, cuttings are used, or they are grafted onto single-flowered seedlings. Once planted, it is better not to move perennial gypsophilas, but this can be done if necessary. Early spring is the most opportune time and every effort should be made to preserve as intact as possible their long, straggly roots. No special care is needed by established specimens.

Annual gypsophilas are easily grown from seeds sown outdoors in spring, or in regions of fairly mild winters in fall, where the plants are to bloom. Two, three, or more spring sowings at two-week intervals provide a long succession of blooms for cutting. If crowded, the seedlings should be thinned to 3 or 4 inches apart. To have early flowers in greenhouses seeds are sown from October to January. The seedlings are transplanted 2 to 3 inches apart in benches or deep flats in porous, fertile soil. They are grown in full sun in a night temperature of 45 to 50°F and daytime temperatures five to ten degrees higher.

GYPSUM. Also known as sulfate of lime, this is the common name of commercial calcium sulfate. Its horticultural use is as a conditioner to improve salty (black alkali) soils, those that have been flooded with seawater, and clays deflocculated to the extent that they are pasty, sticky, and impervious to water. Unlike lime, also used for this last purpose, gypsum does not lower acidity. Under some circumstances it may increase it. Because of this, it may be used on soils in which acid-soil plants are grown, for which purpose lime and limestone are totally unsuitable. Gypsum supplies the nutrient elements calcium and sulfur. Applications are usually at the rate of 2 to 5 pounds to a 100 square feet, but to relieve very difficult conditions as much as four times the greater of these amounts may be employed.

H

HA-HA. A ha-ha is a boundary wall concealed in a ditch so that it does not intrude upon the view. Much employed by the great nineteenth-century English landscape gardener "Capability" Brown, its original purpose was to make possible uninterrupted views from the lawns and other more neatly cared-for areas surrounding the mansion, of more distant trees, copses, lakes, and meadows grazed by cattle and sheep. The wall is vertical, 6 feet or so high, and supports the side of the ditch nearer the mansion. From its base the ground slopes outward and upward, usually at an angle of about 30°, to the level of the meadow. This makes it possible for livestock that walk into the ditch to return to the meadow, but effectively prevents them coming nearer to the mansion. The name ha-ha derives from the exclamation that a stranger might make upon coming upon such a ditch unexpectedly from the top of the wall. An experience of this kind could, of course, be highly dangerous to the unwary.

HAAGEOCEREUS (Haageo-cèreus). The fifty species of *Haageocereus*, of the cactus family CACTACEAE, are natives of Peru. Closely related to *Borzicactus* and *Trichocereus*, by some authorities they are included in the last. Others employ the name *Binghamia* for them. They are frequently puzzling to identify as to species. The name honors members named Haage of a famous German nursery firm.

Haageocereuses are handsome. They have clustered, cylindrical, many-ribbed, beautifully-spined stems, erect and up to 5 feet in height or more or less sprawling or prostrate. Their flowers are bigger and have longer perianth tubes than those of *Borzicactus*. Borne near the apexes of the stems and opening at night, they have pink, creamy-white, or greenish-white, wide-spreading petals.

Among sorts cultivated are these: *H. acranthus* (syn. *Binghamia acrantha*) has erect stems up to about 3 feet tall and 3 to 3½ inches in diameter with ten to fourteen rather thick, slightly-notched ribs. The twenty to thirty yellowish radial spines of each cluster are up to ½ inch long. There are one or two down-pointing centrals about 1½ inches long. The flowers are greenish-white. *H. chosicensis* (syn. *Binghamia chosicensis*), freely-branched from the base and up to 4½ feet tall, has stems with about nineteen low ribs. The closely-set spine clusters are of approximately thirty thin, bristly radials about ¼ inch long and two to four centrals ¾ inch long. All are dingy to brighter yellow with darker tips. The flowers are lilac-red. *H. decumbens* (syn. *Borzicactus decumbens*) has prostrate to ascending stems about 2 inches thick and with about twenty ribs. Its spine clusters are of about thirty light brown, ¼-inch-long radials and one or two needle-like brown centrals 2 inches long. The flowers are white. *H. dichromus*, about 3 feet tall, has stems 2 to 3½ inches thick with about twenty ribs. The spine clusters are of about eight radials ⅓ inch long and a ¾-inch-long yellow central. The flowers are white inside, and wine-red on their outsides. *H. laredensis* forms clumps of low, erect stems 3 to 3½ inches thick and with about eighteen ribs. Its slender, awl-shaped, golden-yellow spines in clusters of forty to forty-five are about ½ inch long. The blooms are white. *H. pacalaensis* has erect, yellowish-green stems up to about 5 feet tall by 4 to 4½ inches thick, with seventeen to twenty ribs. The spine clusters are of about twenty radials, under ½ inch long, and four to six stiff centrals, ½ inch to 2½ inches long. All, at first yellow, later turn gray. The flowers are white. *H. pseudomelanostele* (syns. *Binghamia pseudomelanostele*, *B. multanagularis*) has 3-foot-tall, thick stems with eighteen to twenty-two ribs and clusters of twenty-five to thirty-five slender, yellow radial spines, one or more grayish centrals 2 to 3½ inches long, and some bristles. The flowers are greenish-white. *H. versicolor* (syn. *Binghamia versicolor*) has slender, erect,

Haageocereus versicolor aureospinus

dark green stems with about sixteen or sometimes more ribs. Its spines, banded with lighter and darker reddish-brown and yellow, are in clusters of twenty-five to thirty ¼-inch-long, thin radials and one or two stiff centrals about 1½ inches long. The flowers are white. The spines of *H. v. aureospinus* are golden-yellow.

Garden Uses and Cultivation. Haageocereuses understandably appeal to collectors of succulents. They prosper in full sun under conditions that suit most desert cactuses and are easily raised from cuttings and seeds. For more information see Cactuses.

HAASTIA (Haást-ia)—Vegetable Sheep. This entirely New Zealand genus of three species belongs in the daisy family COMPOSITAE. Its name commemorates Sir Johann Franz Julius von Haast, nineteenth-century geologist. Herbaceous perennials with stems somewhat woody at their bases, haastias are plants of alpine and subalpine regions.

The vegetable sheep (*Haastia pulvinaris*) forms dense, rounded cushions up to 5 feet in diameter and with branches of such even height and so tightly fitted together that "it is impossible to thrust a pencil point between them." In appearance this kind resembles *Raoulia eximia* which also is called vegetable sheep. Other haastias are less compact. Mostly their stems are hidden by persistent, densely-woolly-hairy, alternate leaves. The flowers of all sorts are in solitary, terminal heads of all disk florets (the type that compose the eyes of daisies); there are no ray florets (the petal-like ones of daisies). Stalkless or nearly so, the heads nestle among the upper leaves. The seedlike fruits are achenes.

Rarely cultivated, *H. recurva* is procumbent, about 4 inches tall, and loosely- to fairly densely-branched with its main branches up to 10 inches long. The bases of the strongly recurving leaves sheathe the stems. The leaves are obovate and up to ¾ inch long. They are thickly covered with long reddish-orange to reddish-brown hairs. The flower heads are ¾ inch across. Variety *H. r. wallii* has white-hairy foliage.

Garden Uses and Cultivation. Very little is known about the cultivation of haastias. It may be presumed that they require the same treatment as raoulias. They are for trial only by skilled cultivators of alpine plants. It is unlikely that they will grow where summers are exceedingly warm or winters excessively cold. Seeds and perhaps cuttings afford the most promising means of propagation.

HABENARIA (Haben-ària)—Rein Orchid or Fringed Orchid. This vast group of orchid species, in number approximating 600 and widely dispersed through tropical, subtropical, and temperate regions of the Old World and the New World, except for a few native sorts sometimes tried in wild gardens, rock gardens, and similar special areas is scarcely known in cultivation. It belongs in the orchid family ORCHIDACEAE and has a name alluding to the strap-shaped lip of the flowers of some kinds, derived from the Latin *habenula*, a narrow strap or rein. A section of *Habenaria* that includes the ones described here is by some botanists segregated as the separate genus *Platanthera*.

Habenarias are mostly ground orchids. A minority of warm-climate species, but not any described here, are adapted to living on rocks and even perched on trees as epiphytes, but these are exceptions. These orchids have rhizomes, tubers, or fibrous rootstocks from which arise branchless, generally leafy stems terminating in a raceme or spike of usually small or smallish blooms. Each flower has three spreading sepals, two similar or sometimes smaller petals, and a lip representing a third petal

that may be plain, three-lobed, toothed, or fringed. The lip is prolonged backward as a short or long spur. The short column very slightly if at all surpasses the lip.

The yellow fringed orchid (*H. ciliaris* syn. *Platanthera ciliaris*) is one of the showiest native American species, wild from Newfoundland to Ontario, Michigan, Florida, Missouri, and Texas. From 9 inches to 3 feet tall, it has thick, fleshy roots, stout stems leafy in their lower parts, and oblong-lanceolate to lanceolate, generally markedly-keeled leaves, their bases sheathing the stem, up to 6 inches long or sometimes longer and about 1½ inches wide. Bright yellow to deep orange, the flowers are many in crowded cylindrical racemes 2 to 6 inches long by about 2 inches wide. The blooms have a deeply-fringed lip with a long, slender spur. This species inhabits a variety of acid-soil habitats including bogs, swamps, and marshes; deep organic soils and moist places in woodlands; and open, drier, grassy places. The golden fringed or crested fringed orchid (*H. cristata* syn. *Platanthera cristata*), native in moist, acid soils from Massachusetts to Florida and Louisiana, is up to 3 feet tall. It has linear-lanceolate leaves up to 8 inches long, and in dense, many-flowered racemes up to 6 inches long, orange flowers about ½ inch across and with a long-fringed, oblong lip. The white fringed orchid (*H. blephariglottis* syn. *Platanthera blephariglottis*), except for its flowers being snow-white and the fringe of the lip being not quite as deep, is similar to *H. ciliaris*. It is native in acid swamps and bogs from Newfoundland to Ontario and Michigan and along the coastal plain to Florida and Mississippi. In the southern part of its range it has looser spikes of larger blooms than in the northern reaches of its

Habenaria cristata

Habenaria psycodes grandiflora

natural distribution. A large-flowered variant is distinguished as *H. b. conspicua*.

The lesser purple fringed or pink fringed orchid (*H. psycodes* syn. *Platanthera psycodes*) and its larger-flowered variety the purple fringed orchid (*H. p. grandiflora* syn. *H. fimbriata*), differ only in the sizes of their racemes and individual blooms, and these intergrade. The first inhabits a wide variety of moist and wet acid-soil habitats from shores of Nova Scotia to Manitoba, Nebraska, Delaware, and Ohio and in the mountains in North Carolina and Tennessee. From 6 inches to 3 feet tall, this kind has tuberous roots and up to five elliptic-oblong to narrowly-lanceolate or oblong-obovate leaves, their bases sheathing the stem, 2 to 10 inches long by up to nearly 3 inches wide. The crowded to rather loose racemes up to 8 inches long by 2 inches in diameter, are of lilac-lavender to pinkish-purple or rarely nearly white flowers with a lip ⅓ inch long or a little longer deeply-cleft into three toothed or fringed lobes. The spur is long, slender, and recurved. The racemes of bloom of the purple fringed orchid may be 1 foot long by usually about 2½ inches wide. The fragrant lilac to white blooms have deeply-three-lobed lips, fringed sometimes to one-half their depth, up to nearly ¾ inch long by 1 inch wide. One of the most lovely native orchids, this favors wet and boggy, acid soils from Quebec to Ohio, West Virginia, and North Carolina.

The ragged fringed or green fringed orchid (*H. lacera* syn. *Platanthera lacera*) is wild in open, sunny, acid swamps or sometimes brackish soils or occasionally drier ones from Newfoundland to Manitoba, South Carolina, Alabama, and Arkansas. It has slender, fleshy roots, stout

Grafted specimens of varieties of *Gymnocalycium mihanovichii*

Gymnocalycium mihanovichii 'Red Cap' a grafted specimen

Gypsophila repens rosea, with gray-leaved salvia

Gymnocalycium, undetermined species

Habenaria blephariglottis

Habenaria ciliaris

Haemanthus natalensis

Haemaria discolor

Hamamelis japonica

HABIT OR HABIT OF GROWTH

Habenaria lacera

Habenaria rhodocheila

stems 9 inches to 2½ feet tall, linear-oblong to linear-lanceolate or oblong-obovate leaves with basal parts sheathing the stems, up to 9 inches long by 2 inches wide. The loose- to dense-flowered raceme is of light yellowish-green to whitish-green blooms with a deeply-three-parted lip with deeply-lacerated margins. The lip is nearly ¾ inch long by approximately as wide. Intermediate hybrids between this and the purple fringed orchids are named *H. andrewsii*.

Tropical and subtropical habenarias include **H. pusilla,** of Indochina. One foot or more tall, this has leaves up to 9 inches long and ½ inch wide. Its flowers, in loose racemes, have green sepals and petals, the upper sepal with the petals forming a hood. The lip is scarlet, its center lobe cleft. By some authorities treated as a variant of the last, **H. rhodocheila,** of south China, Indochina, and Thailand, up to 2 feet tall, has foliage similar to that of *H. pusilla*. Its flowers have usually green sepals and petals, the upper sepal and petals forming a hood. The lateral sepals are spreading and twisted. The very large, deeply-three-lobed lip, its center lobe notched at its apex, may be yellow, orange, salmon-pink, cinnabar-red, or bright scarlet.

Garden Uses and Cultivation. American habenarias are unfortunately not amenable to cultivation. Only if the exacting conditions of soil and other environmental factors under which they grow in the wild are closely duplicated is there even the slightest chance of success with a very few kinds, the yellow- and green-fringed orchids perhaps, but even that is far from

certain. It is better to abstain from attempting these beautiful natives unless perchance you have opportunity of obtaining them from places unquestionably being destroyed as plant habitats as a result of roadmaking or other construction. In the interests of conservation do not dig plants from other areas where they are native and do not purchase from dealers, who certainly obtain their stocks from such sources. The tropical sorts respond to conditions and care appropriate for *Phaius*. For more information see Orchids.

HABERLEA (Habér-lea). One of the few hardy genera of the gesneria family GES-NERIACEAE, the one here considered has two species, natives of the Balkan Peninsula. Closely related and similar to *Ramonda*, *Haberlea* consists of rosette-forming, evergreen, herbaceous perennials. From *Ramonda* it differs in its flowers having long instead of very short corolla tubes. The name *Haberlea* commemorates Karl Konstantin Haberle, a professor of botany at Pesth, who died in 1832.

Haberleas have basal rosettes of hairy, spreading leaves, and leafless flower stalks that support terminal, umbel-like clusters of few more or less pendulous blooms. The flowers have deeply-five-parted calyxes, narrowly-tubular corollas with five spreading lobes (petals) that form a slightly asymmetrical face to the bloom, four stamens, and one style. The fruits are capsules.

Softly-hairy, **H. rhodopensis** has blunt, toothed, obovate or ovate-oblong, spreading leaves up to about 3 inches in length. On stalks 3 to 6 inches tall it carries up to

Haberlea ferdinandi-coburgii

six pale lilac blooms each about 1 inch wide and long. In *H. r. virginalis* the flowers are pure white. Much like the last but larger, **H. ferdinandi-coburgii** has usually not more than four blooms in each cluster. They are pale lilac with the top of the corolla tube deeper colored than its underside, and the white-hairy throat of the flower spotted with yellow.

Garden Uses and Cultivation. These are as for *Ramonda*.

HABIT or HABIT OF GROWTH. These terms allude to the natural forms and growth of plants. Thus the habit may be bushy, spreading, or trailing; low, medium-high, or tall; loose or compact; deciduous or evergreen; aquatic; bulbous; annual, biennial, or perennial; and so on

Habranthus tubispathus

Habranthus brachyandrus

Habranthus brachyandrus (flowers)

for many other characteristics and aspects of growth.

HABITAT. The environments in which plants grow naturally are their habitats. The word has an ecological rather than a geographical significance. It is not correct to refer, as is often done, to the habitat of a plant being, for example, North America or Europe and Asia. The better term to use in such cases is natural distribution. Examples of habitats are bogs, limestone cliffs, prairies, sand dunes, seashores, and woodlands.

HABRANTHUS (Hab-ránthus). Closely related to *Zephyranthes*, and included there by some botanists, *Habranthus*, of the amaryllis family AMARYLLIDACEAE, comprises about twenty species of New World bulb plants that differ from *Zephyranthes* in their flowers being angled outward from the stalks they terminate rather than erect, and in having stamens of four lengths. The name comes from the Greek *habros*, graceful, and *anthos*, a flower.

Habranthuses are low and have narrow, grassy leaves that are more or less evergreen or appear with or after the flowers.

The leafless, hollow flower stalks each carry one bloom with six perianth parts (petals, or more correctly, tepals), six stamens, and a slender three-lobed style. The fruits are capsules.

Commonly cultivated species include *H. tubispathus* and more brightly colored *H. brachyandrus*. Hybrids between these, more closely resembling the former than the latter, have been raised and given garden names such as 'Primo', and 'Sparkman's Beauty'.

Native of Argentina, deciduous, sparsefoliaged *H. tubispathus* (syns. *H. robustus*, *Zephyranthes robusta*) is 6 to 9 inches tall. It has recurved-spreading, linear leaves that develop after the whitish-throated, light pink flowers have faded. The funnel-shaped blooms are about 3 inches long. Stronger-growing *H. brachyandrus* (syn. *Hippeastrum brachyandrum*), up to 1 foot tall, has leaves about as long. Its 3-inch-wide blooms are lavender-pink with their bases deep reddish- to blackish-purple.

Small-flowered *H. texanus* is an endemic of moist soils in Texas, and is closely related to *H. andersonii*, of South America. It has narrowly-linear leaves up to 4 inches long that come after the flowers, and solitary nodding blooms 1½ inches long on stalks up to 1 foot in height. The flowers, 1 inch to 1¼ inches long, are orange-yellow with reddish-copper shadings in their throats and on their outsides.

Other sorts in cultivation include *H. gracilifolius* (syn. *Zephyranthes gracilifolia*), of Uruguay, which has nearly cylindrical leaves up to 1½ feet long and stalks to 8 inches high carrying one or two flowers about 1¼ inches long with green perianth

Habranthus texanus

tubes and pale purple petals. Argentinian *H. juncifolius* has cylindrical leaves up to 2½ feet long. Its short-tubed white flowers blushed with pink are about 2¼ inches long.

Garden and Landscape Uses and Cultivation. Habranthuses, not hardy in the north, are excellent for gardens in the deep south and elsewhere where the bulbs are not subjected to freezing. They may be grown in pots in cool greenhouses and as window plants. Outdoors, they fit well into rock gardens and other detailed landscapes and can be used with good effects at the edges of flower beds and borders. Deep, nutritious, well-drained soil and warm, sunny locations are best to their liking. They multiply by offsets and are easily raised from seeds and from bulb cuttings. Under favorable conditions they self-sow freely.

HACKBERRY. See Celtis.

HACKELIA (Hack-èlia) — Beggar's Lice, Stickseed. About forty American, Asian, and European species comprise *Hackelia*, of the borage family BORAGINACEAE. The name commemorates the Czech botanist Josef Hackel, who died in 1869. This genus of mostly horticulturally uninteresting herbaceous perennials or biennials contains sorts that may be occasionally cultivated,

sometimes under their synonymous name *Lappula*.

Hackelias have alternate, undivided leaves and terminal, usually paired racemes of small blue or white flowers with deeply-five-cleft calyxes and corollas that are narrowly-tubular and have five spreading petals, or funnel-shaped and with a crest in the throat. There are five short stamens and a short style. The fruits consist of four prickly nutlets which give reason for the common names beggar's lice and stickseed.

Native of thickets and woodlands from Minnesota to British Columbia and California, *H. floribunda* (syn. *Lappula floribunda*), 1 foot to 3½ feet tall, has narrowly-oblanceolate leaves progressively reduced in size from the lower ones to the upper. The blue or white flowers are up to ⅓ inch wide. Indigenous from Idaho and Nevada to British Columbia and California, softly-hairy *H. jessicae*, up to 3 feet tall, has oblanceolate basal leaves up to 6 inches long and smaller, stalkless, lanceolate leaves above. The light blue flowers, about ¼ inch wide, have yellow crests.

Garden Uses and Cultivation. The species described and others perhaps occasionally are grown in native plant gardens and flower borders. They thrive with minimum care in ordinary garden soils and are easily raised from seeds.

HACKMATACK is *Latrix laricina*.

HACQUETIA (Hac-quètia). One European mountain plant of the carrot family UMBELLIFERAE is the only representative of this genus, whose name commemorates Balthasar Hacquet, who died in 1815. He authored a book on alpine plants.

From 3 to 6 inches in height, *Hacquetia epipactis* (syn. *Dondia epipactis*) is a tufted hardy perennial with all-basal leaves each with three wedge-shaped, twice- or thrice-cleft, bright green leaflets. The small yellow blooms are in umbels that nestle in collars (involucres) of five or six green leafy bracts longer than the umbels. They are borne in spring and at a casual glance are deceiving, the umbels with their surrounding bracts looking like green anemone flowers with yellow centers.

Garden Uses and Cultivation. Of rather unassuming appearance, this hardy plant is nevertheless worthy of a place in rock gardens. Although it makes no great display, it associates well with other alpines and rock plants and adds interest and variety and provides groundcover. A rather heavy soil is most to its liking and it appreciates part-shade. This plant resents root disturbance. It should not be transplanted unless quite necessary. Propagation is best by seed.

HADRODEMAS (Hadro-dèmas). This genus of one species of the spiderwort family COMMELINACEAE has a somewhat checkered record with regard to its name. For about eighty years after it was first described in 1848 it was accepted as *Tradescantia warszewicziana*. Since, it has been referred, reflecting the opinions of various students of the family, to *Spironema*, *Tripogandra*, *Phyodina*, and *Hadrodemas*. The last of these dispositions was first made in 1962. It is derived from the Greek *hadros*, well developed or bulky, and *demas*, a living body, and alludes to the comparatively large size of the plant.

Handsome in foliage and flower, and a native of Central America, *H. warszewiczianum* is a robust, evergreen, herbaceous perennial, with stems, often branched, that may attain 3 feet in length and over 1 inch in diameter. The fleshy, stalkless, narrowly-ovate leaves are in terminal rosettes. They are arranged spirally, sheathe the stems with their bases, and attain a maximum size of 1 foot long by approximately 3 inches wide, but often are considerably smaller. The flowers are in showy, arching, few-branched, terminal, leafy-bracted panicles that generally develop small plantlets from their lower parts. In the axils of the bracts short branches with flowers or small groups of flowers are borne. Each little bloom has three persistent, fleshy, lilac-purple sepals and the same number of short-lived, ovate, rosy-purple petals, about ¼ inch in length.

Hadrodemas warszewiczianum

Haemanthus albiflos

There are six stamens and a longer style with a headlike stigma. The fruits are capsules enclosed by the persistent sepals and remains of the petals.

Garden and Landscape Uses. With age this quite beautiful species becomes rather massive for other than fairly large greenhouses, but it is attractive and blooms well as a comparatively small specimen in 5- or 6-inch pots and may even be grown as a window plant. In the tropics and warm subtropics it thrives outdoors. One great merit is its exceedingly long period of bloom, which often extends for several months. Though the petals of individual flowers last for only a few hours the other floral parts are colorful for a much longer period, and a long succession is maintained.

Cultivation. Indoors a minimum winter night temperature of 60°F rising five to fifteen degrees by day, and at other seasons higher temperatures, are requisite for *Hadrodemas* to give of its best. A humid atmosphere is most to its liking, but it will tolerate fairly dry conditions. It does well in any coarse, fertile soil that permits the free passage of water and is kept moderately, but not excessively moist. Well-rooted specimens appreciate regular applications of dilute liquid fertilizer. It is necessary, or at least desirable, to stake the stems of pot-grown specimens as they lengthen. Outdoors they may be allowed to more or less sprawl. Plants in cultivation do not seem to set seeds, but increase is easily had by cuttings and by the plantlets that grow on the flower panicles.

HAEMANTHUS (Haem-ánthus) — Blood-Lily. Blood-lilies (*Haemanthus*), of the amaryllis family AMARYLLIDACEAE, include several outstanding and some quite aston-

ishing ornamentals. These are bulb plants suitable for outdoors in the subtropics and tropics, for pots and tubs in greenhouses and window gardens. There are probably not over thirty species, natives of tropical Africa, South Africa, Arabia, and the island of Socotra. The name, alluding to the flower color of some kinds, is from the Greek *haima*, blood, and *anthos*, a flower.

Haemanthuses have usually large bulbs and short, thick stems or none. Their broad, deciduous or evergreen leaves are thick and leathery or less commonly are thinner. The flowers are many together in umbels, often large, spherical or shaped more or less like a paint or a shaving brush. They are white, pink, or red. Individual blooms have tubular perianths of six narrow, often spreading petals (more correctly, tepals), the same number of usually long-protruding stamens, and one style. The fruits are berries. Besides the species here described, some hybrids, usually intermediate between their parents, are cultivated.

Small haemanthuses, easy to grow and well adapted to window gardening, include *H. albiflos*, a very reliable bloomer. This has bulbs 3 to 4 inches in diameter. It rests in summer. In fall it sprouts new foliage and stalks 6 inches to 1 foot tall topped with 2-inch-wide floral paint brushes, white with stamens tipped with yellow anthers. The fleshy, more or less spreading, strap-shaped leaves, in two rows, up to 8 inches long by one-half as wide, are fringed with white hairs. The flowers are succeeded by attractive berries as big as large peas, at first green, ripening bright red, and clus-

Haemanthus albiflos (fruits)

tered above a collar of leafy bracts. Another low grower, *H. puniceus* has bulbs 1½ to 3 inches in diameter and almost evergreen leaves with blades 6 inches to 1 foot long and 2 to 4 inches wide. The leafstalks are one-half as long as the blades. Atop mottled stalks 6 inches to 1 foot tall or taller, this carries paint-brush-shaped umbels of bright red or paler blooms 3 to 4 inches in diameter, surrounded by a collar of thick green bracts.

Somewhat larger *H. coccineus* blooms in fall immediately before its new foliage develops. This kind has compressed bulbs about 3 inches in diameter. The two tongue-shaped leaves produced by each bulb become 1 foot to 2½ feet long and 4 to 8

Haemanthus puniceus

Haemanthus katherinae (flowers)

inches wide. The umbels, 2 to 3 inches across, are of coral-pink blooms with white stamens ending in yellow anthers. The umbels, each cupped in a collar of eight, broad, waxy-red bracts, so that at first glance they look like a large single bloom with red petals, sit atop brown-mottled stalks up to about 1 foot in height. Very similar **H. tigrinus** also has umbels of blooms cupped in an involucre of eight broad, petal-like, red bracts. Without foliage it is virtually impossible to distinguish this from *H. coccineus*. The chief differences between these are that the shorter, narrower leaves of *H. tigrinus* are hairy along their margins. The bases of the leaves of this last, like the flowering stalks, are spotted with red, but such mottling also sometimes occurs in *H. coccineus*. Much like *H. coccineus* except that its leaves, which develop in fall after flowering, are nearly circular, are flat on the ground, and about 8 inches wide is **H. rotundifolius**.

Distinct leafy stems from the bases of which arise the flower stalks are characteristic of *H. katherinae*, *H. multiflorus*, *H. natalensis*, *H. magnificus*, and *H. pole-evansii*. The first (**H. katherinae**) has a stem 6 to 8 inches long with three to six short-stalked leaves that develop with the blooms. They are oblong, 8 inches to 1 foot in length, and one-half or more as wide as long. The flower stalk arises from the bottom of the stem. It is topped by a large, many-flowered, nearly spherical umbel 6 to 10 inches in diameter. The six bracts at the base of the umbel spread widely or droop. The blooms have perianth tubes ¾ inch long and narrow, spreading or reflexed petals 1 inch in length. The stamens are about 1½ inches long, and like the petals, bright

Haemanthus natalensis

salmon-pink or salmon-red. A native of tropical Africa and rather resembling the last, **H. multiflorus** has large, thinnish leaves less conspicuously veined than those of *H. katherinae*. Differing markedly in aspect, **H. natalensis** develops a leafy stem 2 to 3 feet tall, generally overtopping the head of bloom and appearing with the flowers. The several leaves are ascending, lustrous, hairless, and may attain 1 foot in length and 4 inches in width. The basal, bractlike ones are spotted with red-brown. The flower stalk, stout and leafless, ends in a many-flowered, crowded umbel of orange-scarlet to scarlet flowers nestled in a cup formed by the seven or eight, showy, purple-red, erect to spreading bracts. The

Haemanthus natalensis (flowers)

total effect is that of a massive shaving brush. The individual flowers have corolla tubes nearly ½ inch long, petals ½ inch in length, and somewhat longer, yellow-anthered stamens. The fruits are bright red berries. Beautiful **H. magnificus** produces its brilliant, scarlet or pink paint brushes on 1- to 1½-foot-tall stalks with maroon-spotted bases before the new foliage appears in fall. The stamens are topped with golden-yellow anthers. The flower heads are partially encased by an involucre of crimson bracts. The bases of the over 1-foot-long leaves form a false stem about 2 feet high. First discovered in 1962, **H. pole-evansii** is native to the highlands of Rhodesia. Deciduous, this blooms when leafless or just as new foliage is appearing. Its sturdy, reddish-brown, spotted flower stalks are 2 to 4 feet tall. They bear spherical umbels, 6 to 9 inches in diameter, of

Haemanthus pole-evansii

rich salmon-pink flowers. The blooms have contrasting bright green ovaries and are 1½ to 1¾ inches across. The oblanceolate leaves are up to 2 feet long by one-quarter as wide.

Hybrid blood-lilies include beautiful *H.* 'King Albert', the result of a mating of *H. katherinae* and *H. puniceus*. The vigorous offspring has broad leaves, and immense, spherical heads of individually stalked, bright red flowers. Crimson-centered, coral-pink blooms in large, spherical heads, their stamens ending in yellow anthers, are borne by a hybrid between *H. multiflorus* and *H. katherinae*. The leaves of this, spotted brown at their bases and with ivory-white midribs, are present during the flowering period.

Garden and Landscape Uses. Where hardy, haemanthuses are of considerable value for outdoor landscaping. They are also splendid for ground beds in conservatories, and pots in greenhouses and windows. Their placement depends upon their size and growth habits. Low ones, such as *H. albiflos* and *H. rotundifolius*, are appropriate for rock gardens in subtropical regions, and as window plants. Those considerably larger are better in flower borders or grouped casually in less formal landscapes. All need well-drained, nourishing, porous soil, moist when they are in active growth, dry when they are dormant. Light shade from strong sun is needed.

Cultivation. Most haemanthuses have a definite dormant season at the beginning of which the foliage dies completely. Some, such as *H. katherinae*, retain their foliage throughout the year or lose it for a time depending upon conditions. If kept warm and watered they are evergreen. But even these partially rest for a period. The time

of dormancy or semidormancy varies with the species. Some rest in winter, some in summer. Careful observation of when new growth commences and when old foliage begins to show signs of dying must be used as guides to watering. Preferences of different kinds for different temperatures must be respected. Natives of South Africa, such as *H. albiflos*, *H. magnificus*, *H. natalensis*, *H. rotundifolius*, and *H. tigrinus*, need winter night temperatures of about 50°F, with an increase by day of up to about ten degrees. For those that come from more tropical parts, such as *H. katherinae* and *H. multiflorus*, temperatures about ten degrees higher are needed. Again, close observation of the plants will reveal their particular needs and preferences. Root disturbance is resented by haemanthuses. Do not transplant or repot oftener than necessary, then attend to this just before new growth begins. Set the bulbs of most kinds with their tips just below the soil surface, those of *H. albiflos* with most of the bulb above ground. Water most haemanthuses freely from the start of growth until the onset of dormancy, then taper off and finally withhold water completely. Kinds with thick, fleshy leaves, such as *H. albiflos*, and those with few leaves, need watering more circumspectly. Allow the soil to become fairly dry between soakings. Give well-established specimens regular applications of dilute liquid fertilizer when they are in active growth. Thin-leaved haemanthuses, such as *H. katherinae*, need a humid atmosphere, those with thick, fleshy foliage a distinctly drier one. Haemanthuses are easily raised from seeds, the young plants taking three or four years to attain flowering size. They are also multiplied by offset bulbs, and can be increased by bulb cuttings.

HAEMARIA (Haem-ària)—Jewel Orchid. This is one of a few genera of the Orchid family ORCHIDACEAE cultivated chiefly for their foliage, although in this instance the flowers are by no means without beauty. Collectively called jewel orchids, they include *Anoectochilus*, *Macodes*, *Dossinia*, and *Haemaria*. The last, consisting of one highly variable species, is the easiest to grow and is very beautiful. It is wild from southern China to Burma and the islands of Indonesia. This is a ground (terrestrial) orchid. The name, from the Greek *haima*, blood, alludes to the red undersides of the leaves.

An evergreen with a creeping rootstock, **H. discolor** (syn. *Ludisia discolor*) has erect or lax, brittle, succulent stems generally not exceeding 6 inches in length, and reddish or purplish. Near their bases are up to six ovate to elliptic leaves about 3 inches long by one-quarter as wide. Their upper surfaces are dark green, sometimes with silvery streaks, their undersides are bright purple. The erect, short-hairy flower spikes attain heights of up to 1 foot, and

Haemaria discolor dawsoniana

Haemaria discolor nigrescens

have greenish bracts. The white, quite showy flowers, about ¾ inch across, have the lip joined to the column. They present themselves in fall and winter. Very beautiful *H. d. dawsoniana* has leaves up to 3½ inches long and proportionately wide. Their velvety upper sides are red to crimson intricately netted with paler red or yellow veins. In taller spikes than those of *H. discolor*, the flowers are accompanied by usually pink bracts. Other variants have been given horticultural names chiefly in recognition of variations in foliage coloring. One of these, *H. d. nigrescens*, has leaves that are nearly black.

Garden Uses and Cultivation. Admirable for the adornment of tropical greenhouses and terrariums, these sorts grow with less trouble than other jewel orchids.

They need high temperatures, high humidity, and a fair amount of shade. They can be accommodated in well-drained pots or pans (shallow pots) in completely porous soil that contains a great deal of decayed organic matter, such as leaf mold, as well as osmunda or tree fern fiber and coarse sand, and some crushed charcoal. Because they are evergreen they must be watered to keep the soil evenly moist, but not soaking wet, throughout the year. For more information see Orchids.

HAEMATOXYLUM (Haemat-óxylum) — Logwood or Bloodwood Tree or Campeachy Wood. This genus occurs from Mexico to northern South America, the West Indies, and in southwest Africa. It is composed of three species, the most important of which is the logwood, bloodwood tree, or campeachy wood (*Haematoxylum campechianum*). Haematoxylums belong in the pea family LEGUMINOSAE. The name comes from the Greek *haema*, blood, and *xylon*, wood, and refers to the color of the heartwood.

Haematoxylums are evergreen, usually thorny trees with pinnate leaves, the leaflets of which are in opposite pairs without a terminal one. The flowers, in dense racemes, have calyxes of five sepals separate to their bases, five spreading, nearly similar petals, ten stamens, somewhat hairy toward their bases, and a slender style terminated with a small stigma. The fruits are compressed pods.

Commercial logwood was, until the introduction of aniline products, a most important dye material. Spanish ships loaded with logwood were prized prey of British privateers dispatched especially to seize cargoes. During the latter one-half of the nineteenth century exports from Mexico reached enormous tonnages. Logwood is still important although much less so than previously. The peculiar virtues of logwood dye are its intense blackness and extreme permanence. The purplish-red juice extracted from the wood is treated with iron salts to achieve blackness. A related species, the brazilette (*H. brasiletto*), of the Pacific coast of Baja California, Nicaragua, Colombia, and Venezuela, is the source of a bright red dye.

The logwood tree (*H. campechianum*) is broad-headed and 20 to 50 feet tall. It has clustered leaves, about 3 inches long, of two to four pairs of reverse-heart-shaped, bright green leaflets up to 1 inch in length. The young foliage is red. In racemes from the leaf axils the fragrant, bright yellow flowers develop. They have oblong, spreading petals ¼ inch long. The fruits are flattened, papery pods, narrowed at each end and about 1¼ inches long. They usually contain two or sometimes three seeds.

Garden and Landscape Uses. As an ornamental and a shade tree for warm climates the logwood has considerable character. As it ages its usually crooked trunk develops buttresses, and its foliage is abundant and pleasing, as are the masses of blooms. It is attractive as a lawn specimen and for this use is suited because grass grows well beneath it. It can also be used to good purpose in other landscape plantings. It is occasionally cultivated in pots in tropical greenhouses, especially in those devoted to displaying plants useful to man.

Cultivation. No special trouble attends the cultivation of this species in regions suitable to its growth. Ordinary soil of moderate moisture content and a well-lighted location suit it. In greenhouses it needs a minimum winter temperature of 55 to 60°F, a humid atmosphere, and shade from strong sun. Fertile, well-drained soil kept uniformly moist, but not saturated is required. Repotting is done in late winter or spring. Propagation is by seeds, cuttings, and air layering.

HAEMODORACEAE — Bloodwort Family. Botanists are by no means agreed as to the limits of this family, but it may be taken as consisting of seventy-five species of monocotyledons arranged in fourteen genera and represented in the native floras of the Americas, South Africa, and Australia. Its members are herbaceous plants usually spreading by stolons, often with orange or red sap, and with alternate, mostly basal, linear or sword-shaped leaves and usually densely-hairy clusters, in panicles, of symmetrical or slightly asymmetrical flowers. The blooms have tubular six-parted or six-cleft perianths, three or six stamens, and one style. The fruits are capsules. Cultivated genera are *Conostylis*, *Lachnanthes*, *Lophiola*, *Tecophilaea*, and *Wachendorfia*.

HAKEA (Hà-kea). Hakeas are evergreen shrubs and small trees, many astonishingly beautiful in bloom. There are between 130 and 140 species, all natives of continental Australia or Tasmania. Belonging in the protea family PROTEACEAE, they bear a name commemorating a German patron of botany, Baron Christian Ludwig von Hake, who died in 1818. Several kinds are grown in California and places with similar warm, dry climates; others should be tried.

The genus *Hakea* is closely related to *Grevillea*, differing most markedly in its seeds having long terminal wings. Its firm, leathery leaves are alternate and of various shapes; those of young seedlings are often different from those of older plants of the same species. The usually asymmetrical, bisexual blooms are in pairs in the axils of bracts crowded in racemes or clusters in the leaf axils. The perianths are four-lobed with the lobes joined in their lower parts into tubes. There are four stalkless stamens attached to the perianth lobes. The styles,

Hakea, undetermined species

which are dilated at their tips, and in many kinds are very long and conspicuous, in others short and unobtrusive, protrude through slits in the perianths. As fruits hakeas have hard, woody, often large capsules that contain two long-winged seeds. For convenience these plants may be grouped according to whether their leaves are needle-like or are broader and flatter. According to species the needles may be divided (branched) or not.

Needle-leaved species with undivided leaves include the following attractive kinds. With creamy-white to pink flowers in its upper leaf axils *H. gibbosa* is an erect shrub 3 to 9 feet tall. Its younger shoots are densely-hairy. The sharp-pointed leaves, hairy when young, are up to 3 inches long. Very like the last, but its young shoots and leaves nearly or quite hairless, *H. acicularis* (syn. *H. sericea*) differs also in its fruits being rougher and more distinctly beaked. Differing from *H. gibbosa* and *H. acicularis* in the perianths of its small white flowers being pubescent, *H. pugioniformis* (syn. *H. teretifolia*) is tall and often somewhat straggling; its branches tend to be pendulous. Its rigid, sharp-pointed leaves are up to about 2 inches long. Also with creamy flowers from the upper leaf axils, *H. propinqua* differs from the last in having smaller blooms and leaves, the latter not hairy. It attains a height of 6 to 9 feet. Often a rounded shrub not more than 6 feet tall, *H. muellerana* on occasion is considerably taller. Its young shoots and leaves are clothed with yellow hairs, which they lose with age. The sharp-pointed leaves, ¾ inch to 2½ inches long, spread horizontally. The small, white, feathery flowers are abundant and in small clusters from the upper leaf axils.

Bright yellow flowers in great cylindrical clusters, and undivided needle leaves are characteristics of *H. preissii*, which goes by the name of Christmas hakea in its native Western Australia. This beautiful species is 6 to 10 feet tall and has leaves ¾ inch to 1½ inches long. Another yellow-flowered kind of Western Australia, *H. platy-*

sperma, has thick, cylindrical, undivided leaves 3 to 5 inches long.

Kinds with usually branched or forked needle leaves include these good ornamentals. With bright red flowers *H. purpurea* is up to 6 feet in height. Its leaves generally once- or twice-divided into up to seven needle-like segments; sometimes many or most of the leaves are undivided. They are up to about 2½ inches long. A white- to pink-flowered kind, *H. lissocarpha* is 3 to 5 feet tall and broader than wide. Its slender, rigid leaves are of three to five segments and are ½ to 1 inch long. A few flat, oval leaves are often mixed with the more frequently three-forked ones of *H. trifurcata.* A much-branched species attaining heights of up to 10 feet, *H. trifurcata* has white flowers. From it, *H. erinacea,* which is 3 to 6 feet tall, differs in its 1-inch-long leaves being divided into many segments. Pinnately-divided leaves 3 to 4 inches long are characteristic of *H. suaveolens,* which may be 6 feet tall and has sweetly fragrant white blooms. As its name suggests, the leaves of *H. varia* are of different shapes. Up to 2 inches long, they have sharp-pointed segments. The small white flowers are in clusters.

Hakeas with flat leaves include several popular in cultivation as well as lesser known, worthwhile kinds. One of the finest, *H. laurina* (syn. *H. eucalyptoides*), because of the appearance of its globose clusters of crimson blooms, with yellow styles protruding, is called the sea urchin hakea and pincushion plant. Sometimes 30 feet tall, but usually much lower, this has lanceolate to narrow-elliptic leaves 4 to 6 inches long by up to 1 inch wide. It is often considered the most beautiful hakea. Its leaves change to orange and red before they fall. Other kinds with richly colored blooms are *H. multilineata* and *H. francisiana.* An erect to spreading shrub up to 10 feet tall, *H. multilineata* has long narrowly-linear-lanceolate, many-veined leaves and bright pink to red flowers in cylindrical, spikelike racemes 1 inch to 2 inches long. Slender, and 6 to 12 feet in height, *H. francisiana* is variable and has pointed leaves 6 to 8 inches long and up to ⅓ inch wide. The bright pink to red blooms are in cylindrical, spikelike clusters up to 3½ inches long. Cylindrical spikes of orange to red flowers 3 to 4½ inches long decorate *H. bucculenta,* a bushy species 6 to 10 feet tall with extremely slender leaves up to 6 inches long and with one mid-vein. Very different from the sorts already discussed *H. cucullata* ranges from 3 to 10 feet in height and has softly-hairy shoots and stalkless, roundish to kidney-shaped, slightly crinkle-edged, glaucous leaves 2 to 4 inches across, those of the flowering branches strongly concave above and with pink to red flowers nestling in their axils. Somewhat similar, but with leaves margined with short, prickly teeth and having

larger fruits, is *H. conchaefolia.* Also with very broad leaves, although much smaller than those of the last, is red-flowered *H. myrtoides.* It may be low and diffuse or up to 6 feet or more tall. Its stalkless leaves are ½ to ¾ inch long and sharp-pointed. The flowers are in spikes up to 4 inches long.

Flat-leaved species with white or whitish flowers include *H. saligna,* which is grown more for its willow-like foliage than its small and less showy fragrant blooms. This becomes a tall shrub or small tree and has grayish, nearly or quite hairless shoots and leaves, the latter 2 to 4 inches long by not over ½ inch wide. Somewhat similar are *H. salicifolia* and *H. dactyloides,* large shrubs or small trees with lanceolate or oblanceolate leaves 2 to 4 inches long and up to slightly more than ½ inch wide. Those of *H. dactyloides* have three prominent veins not present in those of *H. salicifolia.* The flowers of *H. dactyloides* are cream, those of the other tend to be greenish. Especially attractive because of the beautiful bronze hue of its young foliage, *H. elliptica* is 6 to 15 feet tall and has rounded clusters of white flowers. Its broad to narrowly-elliptic leaves, 2 to 3½ inches long by up to one-half as wide, have wavy margins and five to seven longitudinal veins.

Garden and Landscape Uses. In warm, dryish climates hakeas serve many purposes. Chiefly they are attractive for their evergreen foliage and their pretty and often showy blooms, but the curious, woody fruits of some kinds, which remain on the plants for long periods, are by no means devoid of interest. These shrubs are excellent as single specimens or for grouping, and some, such as *H. dactyloides, H. salicifolia, H. saligna,* and *H. sericea,* stand shearing well and can be used as formal and informal hedges. The stiff-needle-leaved kinds are less likely to suffer from vandalism than many shrubs and are thus of particular value in public places. Most grow satisfactorily in a variety of soils, even somewhat alkaline ones, provided they are well drained, porous, and fairly deep. Mostly resistant to drought and lovers of full sun, they are not averse to part-day shade.

Cultivation. Hakeas may be propagated from cuttings made from firm shoots, but seeds afford the most convenient and dependable method. They must come from fruits that have ripened on the plants for a year or more, and the fruits must be well dried to release the seeds. Germination takes place in three or four weeks, and the young seedlings are potted singly as soon as they are big enough to handle with facility. Later they are transferred to cans or other larger containers in which they are grown until they are planted in their permanent locations. During the summer following planting some watering may be

needed in long spells of drought, but great care must be taken not to overwater established specimens; the kinds cultivated are typically dry region species. The only pruning needed is any desirable to keep the plants shapely. This may receive attention just before the commencement of new growth.

HAKONECHLOA (Hakòne-chloa). In the wild rather rare, and confined to the mountains of central Japan where it favors wet rocky cliffs, the only species of this genus belongs in the grass family GRAMINEAE. Its name is a combination of the Japanese place named Hakone and the Greek *chloa,* a grass.

Spreading by creeping, scaly rhizomes, *Hakonechloa macra* (syn. *Phragmites macra*) has smooth, slender, erect to spreading leafy stems 1 foot to 2½ feet tall. The leaves are glabrous, glaucous on their upper sides, and have pointed blades that narrow to their bases and are 4 inches to 1 foot long and up to ⅓ inch wide. In loose, nodding, narrow- to broadly-ovoid panicles 2 to 6 inches long, the yellowish-green, linear-oblong flower spikelets are borne. They are from about ½ to ¾ inch long. Each contains three to five flowers. Variety *H. m. aureola* has green-lined yellow leaves; in *H. m. albo-aurea* the leaves are variegated with white and yellow; those of *H. m. albo-variegata* are green variegated with white. In Japan these are grown as pot plants as well as in outdoor gardens.

Hakonechloa macra aureola

Garden Uses and Cultivation. By no means common in American gardens, this grass is hardy at least as far north as New York City and is attractive, especially in its variegated forms, for outdoors and for pot cultivation. It grows well in ordinary garden soil enriched with peat moss, compost, or leaf mold, kept fairly moist. It needs light shade. Propagation is usually by division. The green-leaved species may also be raised from seed.

HALESIA (Halès-ia)—Silverbell, Snowdrop Tree. Until 1924 the only silverbells known were three or four species endemic to the southern United States, and their varieties. Then a species was discovered in eastern China, and *Halesia* joined the not inconsiderable list of genera that are natives of eastern North America, eastern Asia, and nowhere else. The genus is named after Stephen Hales, English physiologist, who died in 1761. It belongs in the storax family STYRACACEAE and differs from *Styrax* in its flowers having their parts in fours and multiples of four rather than five.

Halesias are deciduous trees more or less furnished with stellate (star-shaped) hairs, with alternate, undivided, stalked, toothed leaves. Their pendulous, bell-shaped flowers, in axillary clusters or short racemes, on shoots of the previous year's growth, are usually white, rarely delicate pink. They have top-shaped, slightly four-ribbed, persistent calyxes with four minute teeth, joined to the ovaries. The corolla has four lobes (petals). There are eight to sixteen stamens and a slender style. The dry fruits, technically drupes (fruits structured like plums), have prominent longitudinal wings and contain a stone composed of one to three seeds.

Halesia monticola (flowers)

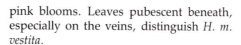
Halesia monticola vestita

Halesia carolina

Halesia monticola

A splendid flowering tree up to 90 feet tall, but often considerably smaller, **H. monticola** is native of the mountains from North Carolina to Tennessee and Georgia. It is hardy in southern New England. Pyramidal when young, it becomes round-topped at maturity. Its pointed, elliptic to oblong-obovate leaves have distantly-spaced teeth and are 3 to 6 inches long. Except from the veins on their undersides they lose all hairs early. Two to five together, the white flowers are ⅝ to 1 inch in length and have stalks ⅓ to 1 inch long. They have shallow corolla lobes that are flaring rather than incurved at their tips. There are ten to sixteen stamens, hairy at their bases. The oblong-obovoid, four-winged fruits are up to 1 inch in length. Variety *H. m. rosea* has delicate

pink blooms. Leaves pubescent beneath, especially on the veins, distinguish *H. m. vestita*.

Not exceeding 40 feet in height and indigenous from West Virginia to Florida and Texas, **H. carolina** (syn. *H. tetraptera*) has flowers about ¾ inch long with corolla lobes incurved at their mouths. This kind is sometimes no more than a large shrub. It has spreading branches and ovate to ovate-oblong, pointed leaves 2 to 4 inches in length, that remain pubescent beneath, but soon become hairless above. The flowers are in twos to fives. They have stalks up to ¾ inch long, shallow corolla lobes, and ten to sixteen hairy-stalked stamens. The oblong to obovate-oblong, four-winged fruits are up to 1½ inches in length. This, the hardiest silverbell or snowdrop tree, survives in Massachusetts. The corollas of *H. c. dialypetala* are cleft nearly to their bases. In *H. c. mollis* the leaves are hairy, densely so on their undersides. Possibly of hybrid origin, *H. c. meehanii* has upright

Halesia carolina meehanii

branches, wrinkled leaves not as big as those of the species, and smaller, cup-shaped, more deeply-lobed flowers with hairless anthers.

Easily distinguished by its fruits having only two large wings, but usually with two very narrow ones alternating with them is

H. diptera, a shrub or tree up to 30 feet in height that inhabits moist soils from South Carolina to Tennessee, Florida, and Texas. Less hardy than the kinds discussed above, it blooms two or three weeks later. It survives about as far north as southern New York and has long-pointed, elliptic to obovate leaves 2½ to 5 inches long. They have tiny, distantly-spaced teeth. At first somewhat hairy, they soon lose the hairs from their upper surfaces, but retain those below, at least on the veins. The white flowers, ¾ to 1 inch long, have corolla tubes deeply cleft into broad elliptic or obovate lobes (petals). The hairy-stalked stamens usually number eight. The fruits are 1½ to 2 inches long.

Uncommon in cultivation and not generally hardy in the north, although success with stock from northern Florida has been reported from Philadelphia, Pennsylvania, *H. parviflora* is a shrub or small tree that differs from *H. carolina* chiefly in having flowers up to ⅓ inch long and club-shaped narrowly-winged fruits. This species is native from Georgia to Florida, Mississippi, and Oklahoma. The Chinese *H. macgregorii* does not seem to be cultivated. It is a tree up to 75 feet tall, with hairless shoots and leaves, the latter short-stalked and with glandular teeth, varying in shape and size, but characteristically elliptic to ovate-elliptic, and 1½ to 3½ inches long. No information is available regarding the flowers. The fruits, solitary, in twos or threes, are from egg-shaped to nearly round and four-winged and about 1½ inches long.

Garden and Landscape Uses. Silverbells or snowdrop trees are charming and elegant for landscaping. They give refined displays of pretty blooms in spring and pleasing fall foliage color. They appreciate fertile, well-drained, moderately moist soil, full sun or light part-day shade, and shelter from wind. They are lovely as single specimens and in groups.

Cultivation. These trees are easily cared for. They transplant readily even when large. No systematic pruning is needed. Propagation of the species can be by seeds, which should be sown as soon as they are ripe or be stratified in slightly damp peat moss until late winter or spring and then sown. If allowed to dry, germination is likely to be delayed for a year. Other means of increase, the only ones practicable with the varieties, are layering, root cuttings, and leafy cuttings under mist or in a cool greenhouse propagating bench. Cuttings made from young shoots of plants forced into early growth give the best results.

HALF-HARDY. Trees, shrubs, vines, and herbaceous perennials that survive outdoors if afforded some winter protection, but without it cannot be relied upon to survive, are said to be half-hardy. For instance figs are half-hardy in the vicinity of New York City, hardy in milder climates. Half-hardy is also applied as a somewhat imprecise term to certain annuals and other plants grown as annuals that because they cannot stand frost, but need a long season of growth, are started early indoors. Seeds of such plants are sown in greenhouses or with other protection and the seedlings grown on in flats or small pots until the weather is warm and settled enough for them to be transplanted outside. There is no distinction between half-hardy and hardy annuals. Many sorts usually considered as belonging to the first group, celosias, for example, give good results, but flower later if sown directly outdoors. Some plants gardeners class as half-hardy annuals are in fact nonhardy perennials that for convenience are grown as annuals. Here belong lobelias, petunias, snapdragons, and verbenas.

HALF-RIPE. This term is used to describe the condition of current season's shoots of trees and shrubs that have attained an intermediate stage between the softness of actively growing young stems and the fully firm, woody stage characteristic of mature ones. Half-ripe shoots are semimature. They are often preferred for making cuttings for propagation.

HALIMIOCISTUS (Halimio-cístus). This name, derived from those of its parent genera, is applied to hybrids between *Halimium* and *Cistus.* In characteristics they are intermediate between their parents. They belong in the rock-rose family CISTACEAE.

One, *H. sahucii,* the offspring of *Halimium umbellatum* and *Cistus salvifolius,* is a nearly prostrate, mat-forming shrub 3 feet or more across and up to 1¼ feet tall. Its linear to linear-lanceolate leaves, conspicuously veined on their undersides and with stellate (starry) hairs, are up to 1¼ inches long by not over ¼ inch wide. In clusters of two to five, the pure white flowers, 1¼ inches across, appear in May or June, and more sparsely later. They have four, five, or, rarely, three sepals. Another kind, *H. wintonensis,* a hybrid raised in an English nursery, reportedly between *Halimium ocymoides* and *Cistus salvifolius,* is a gray-foliaged shrub about 2 feet tall, with ovate-lanceolate, three-veined, woolly leaves ¾ inch to 2 inches long. The white flowers are 2 inches in diameter and have a zone of penciled crimson-maroon markings contrasting with yellow blotches at the bases of the petals. A third hybrid, *H. ingwersenii,* has as parents, it is believed, *Halimium umbellatum* and *Cistus hirsutus.* Originally found in Portugal, this is a spreading shrub 1½ to 2 feet tall with downy leaves ¾ inch to 1¼ inches long and under ¼ inch wide; the panicles of pure white flowers, ¾ to 1 inch across, have white-woolly sepals.

Garden and Landscape Uses and Cultivation. These attractive plants cannot be expected to grow where winters are immoderate. In California, *H. sahucii* has proved a satisfactory and most useful groundcover for sunny locations. Other kinds thrive under similar conditions. They prosper in well-drained soils wherever rock-roses (*Cistus*) do well, and are readily increased by cuttings made from the shoot tips in summer.

HALIMIUM (Hal-ímium). Closely related to and much like sun-roses (*Helianthemum*), halimiums are Old World perennial herbaceous or subshrubby plants belonging in the rock-rose family CISTACEAE. There are fourteen species. None is hardy in the north, but they are satisfactory where winters are fairly mild and summers are warm and dryish. Their name is from *halimos,* the ancient Greek name for *Atriplex halimus,* and refers to the similar aspect of the foliage.

From *Helianthemum* the genus *Halimium* differs in its flowers having very short and straight, instead of long, curved styles. Many of its kinds have only three sepals. Its leaves are opposite, and the flowers have five spreading petals that drop quickly and numerous stamens. The fruits split along three vertical lines to release the seeds.

With beautiful silvery-gray foliage, and flowers like small single roses, *H. atriplexifolium,* of southern Europe and North Africa, is a shrub up to 4 feet tall and spreading. Broadly-ovate and three- or five-veined, its 1- to 2-inch-long leaves are ¾ inch to 1¼ inches broad. The flowers, in clusters of up to eight, and 1½ inches in diameter, are golden-yellow with a brown spot at the base of each petal. There are three sepals. A shrub about 2 feet tall and with gray-downy shoots and leaves, the latter ovate-lanceolate to narrowly-obovate, the lower ones short-stalked, the upper ones stalkless, *H. alyssoides* has bright yellow, spotless flowers 1½ inches in diameter, on hairy stalks and with hairy sepals. It is a native of southwest Europe.

A much-branched shrub, 2 to 4 feet tall, *H. halimifolium* has scaly, downy shoots, and oblong to narrowly-obovate, short-stalked, gray-downy leaves ¾ inch to 2 inches long. In clusters of two to seven, its bright yellow flowers, 1½ inches wide and marked with tiny dark spots at the bases of the petals, are on slender, erect stalks. Their three to five sepals are scaly. This is native to southern Europe and North Africa. Indigenous to Portugal, *H. lasianthum* (syn. *Helianthemum formosum*) is a gray-downy shrub 1½ to 3 feet tall and broader than high, with short-stalked, ovate to lanceolate, three-veined leaves up to 1½ inches long and ½ inch wide. The bright yellow flowers, blotched with crimson-purple at the base of each petal, are 1½ inches across and have three sepals. Variety *H. l. concolor* has blotchless flowers. Another Portuguese, **H. ocymoides** (syn. *Helianthemum ocymoides*), attains a height of 2 to 3 feet and has slender, white-hairy shoots and narrowly-obovate or oblong, three-veined leaves ½ to 1 inch long and up to ¼ inch wide. The leaves of the nonflowering shoots are gray-hairy and stalked; those of the flowering shoots green and stalkless. In loose clusters, the bright yellow flowers, 1 inch to 1½ inches in diameter, are usually purple at the bases of the petals. The three sepals and the flower stalks are sparsely-hairy or hairless.

Flower color is the most obvious difference between *H. commutatum* (syns. *H. libanotis*, *Helianthemum libanotis*) and *H. umbellatum* (syn. *Helianthemum umbellatum*), both of the Mediterranean region. The former may be 2 feet tall, the latter rarely exceeds 1 foot. Both have linear, stalkless leaves, white- or gray-downy on their undersides, and ½ inch to 1½ inches long. Those of **H. umbellatum** are hairy, those of **H. commutatum** hairless or nearly so on their upper sides. The flowers, solitary or in small terminal clusters, of *H. commutatum* are about 1 inch across and pale yellow, those of *H. umbellatum* are white with yellow at the bases of the petals. They are ¾ inch in diameter.

Garden and Landscape Uses and Cultivation. These have similar uses to rock-roses (*Cistus*). In mild, Mediterranean-type climates they are useful for rock gardens, beds, and other places where they have well-drained soil and full sun. Little care beyond, possibly, a light shearing as soon as blooming is through is needed. Propagation is easy by seeds and by summer cuttings. Established specimens do not transplant well. It is advisable to set out young plants from containers.

HALIMODENDRON (Halimo-déndron) — Salt Tree. The common name salt tree and the botanical *Halimodendron*, derived from the Greek *halimos*, maritime, and *dendron*, a tree, seem a little pretentious for a shrub that does not exceed 6 feet in height. Both are applied to the only species of its genus, of the pea family LEGUMINOSAE.

A close relative of *Caragana*, native to windswept salt steppes in central Asia, **H. halodendron** is deciduous and extremely hardy. It has wide-spreading, grayish, spiny branches, silky-hairy when young, and pinnate leaves of one or two pairs of grayish or bluish-green, stalkless, oblanceolate leaflets ¾ inch to 1½ inches long, up to ¼ inch wide, and with very short silky hairs, at least when young. The midrib terminates in a stout spine; when the leaflets fall the spine remains. The fragrant, pale purplish-pink to purple blooms are pea-shaped and a little over ½ inch long. Borne in early summer, they are in short, slender-stalked, drooping racemes of two

Halimodendron halodendron

to four; they originate from short, leafy, lateral branchlets called spurs. The fruits are few-seeded, brownish-yellow, inflated pods ½ to 1 inch long and ¼ to ½ inch wide. In variety *H. h. purpureum* the blooms are rosy-purple.

Garden and Landscape Uses. Although this free-flowering shrub has considerable grace, it is not especially recommended for ordinary gardens with normally fertile soil. There are many shrubs as well or better suited and as decorative for such situations. The salt tree is preeminently a special-purpose plant, ideally adapted for limestone, alkaline, and saline soils. In such, it flourishes as few other shrubs will. It is admirable for seashore plantings.

Cultivation. Once established, the salt tree gives no particular trouble provided its soil is thoroughly well drained and never remains wet for long periods. The difficulty lies in that seedlings on their own roots frequently fail, especially in moist soils and humid climates. The most practical method of propagation is by grafting onto understocks of *Caragana* or *Laburnum*. The salt tree needs full sun. In addition to saline and alkaline soils it does well in extremely sandy ones.

HALORAGIDACEAE—Water Milfoil Family. The plants of this family of dicotyledons vary greatly in form and aspect. Some are submersed or floating aquatics, others land plants. Most are herbaceous, a few subshrubby. They have alternate or opposite leaves, according to kind from small and flimsy to huge and much firmer. The flowers, frequently minute, are usually unisexual with the sexes commonly, but not always on separate plants. Solitary or grouped in various types of axillary clusters, they may have a two- or four-lobed calyx or none, and two, four, or no petals. Generally there are four or eight stamens, one to four styles, and often feathery stigmas. The fruits are nutlets or small drupes. The genus *Hippuris*, by

some authorities treated separately as the family HIPPURIDACEAE, is in this Encyclopedia accepted as belonging to the HALORAGIDACEAE. Other genera cultivated are *Gunnera*, *Myriophyllum*, and *Proserpinaca*.

HAMAMELIDACEAE — Witch-Hazel Family. Many ornamental species are in this dicotyledonous family of deciduous and evergreen trees and shrubs, which is most numerous as to sorts in Asia, but is also native in North America, Africa, Madagascar, and Australia. The group is divided into twenty-two genera and eighty species. Some yield useful lumber. Extract of witch hazel is obtained from *Hamamelis* and *Liquidambar*.

Their leaves and other parts often furnished with stellate (star-shaped) hairs, plants of the witch-hazel family have alternate, undivided, lobeless or palmately-lobed, toothed or toothless leaves and bisexual or unisexual flowers with the sexes on the same or separate plants. The blooms, in spikes or heads from the leaf axils, sometimes have associated with them colored bracts. They have a tubular four- or five-lobed calyx, and may or may not have a corolla of four or five petals. There are two to eight stamens and two each styles and stigmas. The fruits are beaked, woody capsules. Cultivated genera include *Corylopsis*, *Disanthus*, *Distylium*, *Exbucklandia*, *Fortuneria*, *Fothergilla*, *Hamamelis*, *Liquidambar*, *Loropetalum*, *Parrotia*, *Parrotiopsis*, *Rhodoleia*, *Sinowilsonia*, and *Sycopsis*.

HAMAMELIS (Hamam-èlis)—Witch-Hazel. The cultivated witch-hazels are desirable flowering small trees and shrubs. They are especially esteemed because of their unusual seasons of blooming. There are five or six species, of which four, and some hybrids, are commonly grown. The genus *Hamamelis* is confined in the wild to eastern North America, China, and Japan. It belongs in the witch-hazel family HAMAMELIDACEAE. The name is the ancient Greek one for the medlar (*Mespilus*) and was perhaps applied because of a vague similarity in the appearance of the fruits.

Witch-hazels have deciduous, alternate, short-stalked, straight-veined, coarsely-toothed leaves, obliquely-lopsided at their bases and furnished with stellate (star-shaped) hairs. They have a general resemblance to those of hazelnuts (*Corylus*). Their bisexual flowers, quite distinct from those of any other hardy tree or shrub, are similar to those of their more tender evergreen relative *Loropetalum*. The blooms are few together in short-stalked clusters from the axils of the leaves. They have a calyx of four spreading lobes, and four narrow, strap-shaped, crumpled petals. There are four very short stamens, the same number of scalelike staminodes (non-functional stamens), and two short styles. The fruits are capsules with the persistent calyx lobes

Hamamelis virginiana

Hamamelis vernalis

at or below their middles. Each contains two glossy black seeds that are explosively discharged when ripe. The American *H. virginiana* is the source of an extract, which is used as an astringent and to treat inflammation, bruises, and cuts. The Indians used it to heal wounds.

Blooming in fall at about the time its leaves drop, **H. virginiana** is one of the very few hardy woody plants that can be relied upon to flower at that season. Unfortunately its floral display is often hidden to some extent by leaves that have not yet fallen, but have turned yellow. This is a broad shrub or small tree up to 15 feet in height with obovate or elliptic leaves that are rarely hairy beneath except on the veins and that soon lose most or all of the pubescence from their upper surfaces. They are 3 to 6 inches long and obovate or elliptic with blunt or short-pointed apexes and rounded to heart-shaped bases. The leaves have five to seven pairs of veins; they turn bright yellow in fall. The flowers have bright yellow petals, ½ to ¾ inch long, and a calyx that is dull yellow on its inner side. Variety *H. v. rubescens* has reddish petals. This species is indigenous from Nova Scotia to Georgia, Nebraska, and Arkansas.

Another American native, **H. vernalis,** ranges in the wild from Missouri to Louisiana and Oklahoma, but is hardy in southern New England. It is the least showy witch-hazel in bloom, but its flowers are fragrant. This is an upright, suckering shrub, rarely more than 6 feet tall, with obovate to oblong-obovate, blunt leaves 3 to 5 inches long that have usually wedge-shaped bases. There are four to six pairs of veins, which, on the undersides of the leaves, are often pubescent. The blooms

appear from December to March according to climate and weather. Their calyxes are dark red on their insides. The petals are light yellow, often with reddish bases, and about ½ inch long. Variety *H. v. tomentella* has the undersides of its leaves somewhat glaucous and more or less densely-pubes-

cent, and yellow or reddish petals. In *H. v. carnea* the petals are red or reddish.

The finest witch-hazel species in bloom is the Chinese **H. mollis.** This shrub or tree, up to 30 feet in height, is hardy in southern New England. From other kinds it is distinguished by its softly-hairy young shoots

Hamamelis mollis

and undersides of its leaves. It has round-ish-obovate to obovate-oblong, short-pointed leaves, unevenly heart-shaped at their bases and 4 or 5 inches long. The inside of the calyx is brownish-purplish. The petals are golden-yellow with, usually, reddish bases. They are ¾ inch long. This witch-hazel blooms from January to March, depending upon climate and weather. An excellent variety is *H. m. brevipetala*, distinguished by its unusually short, ochre-yellow petals and calyxes that are not brown-purple on their insides. It is very free flowering.

The Japanese witch-hazel (*H. japonica*) is similar in size to *H. mollis*, blooms at the same time, and is about as hardy. It has broad-ovate to nearly round or rarely obovate, blunt or pointed leaves with about five pairs of veins and more or less

Hamamelis japonica

unevenly heart-shaped bases. From 2 to 4 inches in length, the leaves have slightly hairy stalks. The calyx is usually purplered inside. The petals, about ¾ inch long, are generally more slender than those of *H. mollis*, which accounts for the more spidery aspect of the blooms. Variety *H. j. arborea* is treelike. In *H. j. flavo-purpurascens* the petals are reddish, at least in their lower parts. The very beautiful *H. j. zuccariniana* has the inside of the calyx greenish-yellow and petals of clear lemon-yellow. It blooms later than typical *H. japonica*.

Hybrid witch-hazels, the results of crossing *H. mollis* and *H. japonica,* are grouped as **H. intermedia.** Developed in America, Europe, and Japan, several of the best have been given names such as 'Arnold Promise', 'Jelena' (syn. 'Orange Beauty'), 'Ruby Glow', and 'Winter Beauty'. Their characteristics are intermediate between those of their parents, but generally the flowers are held in an upward- or outward-pointing position like those of *H. mollis*, rather than pointing downward as the flowers of *H. japonica* usually do. As a display feature this is an advantage.

Garden and Landscape Uses. Witch-hazels are attractive fall and winter-flowering trees and shrubs the blooms of which withstand the vagaries of northern winters. This never fails to astonish and intrigue those who meet these plants for the first time and, be it admitted, not a few of those who are thoroughly familiar with this gracious habit. All cultivated witch-hazels are hardy at least as far north as Boston, Massachusetts, and the most cold-resistant *H. virginiana* into Canada. They are at their best in fertile, slightly acid, peaty soil. The Asian kinds need full sun, the American kinds prosper in light shade. The Asians do well in drier places than the Americans, but not in really dry soils. For their well-being, native American kinds must have their roots in moist, but not wet, earth.

Cultivation. Species of witch-hazel are most commonly raised from seeds, which do not usually germinate until the second spring from the time of sowing. Selected varieties and hybrids can be propagated by grafting onto seedling understocks of *H. virginiana* in a greenhouse in late winter or spring. All kinds can be increased by layering, and *H. vernalis* by division. Established specimens need no special care or regular pruning, but young plants that are to be encouraged to assume tree form should have their leading shoots tied to supporting stakes and any branches that compete with the leader shortened so that a dominant central shoot is maintained.

HAMATOCACTUS (Hamato-cáctus). Three species of small cactuses of the southwestern United States and northern Mexico constitute *Hamatocactus* of the cactus family CACTACEAE. The name from the Latin *hamatus*, hooked, and *cactus*, alludes to the central spines.

The species of this genus are variable and several varieties of each are recognized by some botanists. They have globular to cylindrical stems with blunt or sharp-edged ribs in more or less spirals around them. The spine clusters have long

Hamamelis japonica (flowers)

Hamamelis japonica zuccariniana

cylindrical or semicylindrical central spines, one at least of which is sharply hooked. The funnel-shaped to nearly tubular blooms are succeeded by small, red, globular fruits containing black seeds.

Common in cultivation, the hedgehog cactus, free-flowering *H. setispinus* (syn. *Echinocactus setispinus*) is spherical to short-cylindrical and bright green. Up to about 4½ inches in diameter, frequently smaller and most often solitary, but sometimes with offsets, this kind has thirteen to fifteen, angled, notched, lumpy ribs. Under ½ inch apart and sprouting from white-woolly are-

Hamatocactus setispinus

oles, the spine clusters are of one to three usually white, in some variants yellow, centrals with hooked apexes and twelve to fifteen shorter needle-shaped white to brown radials generally about 1½ inches in length. Borne from the tops of the plants and 2¾ inches long, the funnel-shaped flowers have wide-spreading petals, the inner ones lustrous golden-yellow with red bases, the outer ones greenish-yellow margined with red. The stamens and style are yellow, the latter with five to eight lobes. The dryish fruits, which split to their bases, are spherical to ellipsoid and have a few scales on their outsides. Dark green, spherical to cylindrical *H. hamatacanthus* (syns. *Echinocactus hamatacanthus, Ferocactus longihamatus*), of Texas, New Mexico, and Mexico, has thirteen to fifteen lumpy, wavy, high ribs. More widely spaced than those of *H. setispinus,* the areoles, from which sprout the spine clusters, have yellowish-white wool. Each cluster is of four semicylindrical centrals straight or slightly hooked except for one that is strongly hooked at its apex and up to 6 inches long. The eight to twelve radial spines, spreading and needle-like, are 2 to 3 inches in length. Funnel-shaped and about 3 inches across, the scaly-tubed

flowers have glossy, bright yellow inner petals, red at their bases and reddish on their undersides, and brownish-green outer petals. The stamens are yellow as is the style and the fifteen- to eighteen-lobed stigma.

Garden and Landscape Uses and Cultivation. These easy-to-grow, attractive cactuses thrive indoors and in warm dry climates outdoors in rock gardens and similar places with minimum care. For more information see Cactuses.

HAMBURG PARSLEY. Also called parsnip-rooted parsley, Hamburg parsley is a variety of *Petroselinum crispum* that is grown for its swollen parsnip-like roots rather than for its leaves. These are used to flavor soups and stews and are boiled and eaten as a vegetable. Because the roots can be stored in the same way as parsnips and carrots, they can be had throughout the winter when fresh leaf parsley is not available. Hamburg parsley is easy to grow. It responds to the soil conditions and care recommended for parsnips.

HAMELIA (Ham-èlia)—Scarlet Bush. Some forty species of *Hamelia,* of the madder family RUBIACEAE, are indigenous from Florida to Mexico, the West Indies, and Paraguay. They are evergreen shrubs. The name commemorates the French botanical author Henri Louis Duhamel du Monceau, who died in 1781.

Hamelias have undivided leaves without lobes or teeth. They are opposite, or more rarely in circles of three or more. In terminal, forking clusters, the red or yellow flowers are short-stalked or stalkless. They have five erect, persistent sepals, a tubular to bell-shaped corolla with five short lobes (petals), five stamens, and a single stigma. The fruits are small, many-seeded, dark red, purple, or black berries that are quite attractive.

The scarlet bush (**H. patens** syns. *H. erecta, H. sphaerocarpa*), of Florida to South America, is 6 to 12 feet tall or sometimes taller. It has stalked, elliptic-ovate to oblongish, pointed leaves, usually in threes, 3 to 8 inches long, and hairless or minutely-hairy. They are bright green or for part of the year tinged purplish, and have prominent mid-veins, with lateral veins curving outward and upward. The narrow, orange-scarlet blooms, about ¾ inch long, and almost without individual stalks, are grouped along the three to five branches of the flower clusters. They are upturned and have protruding stamens. The long-lasting, egg-shaped, dark red to purple berries are ¼ long.

Garden and Landscape Uses and Cultivation. These are attractive shrubs for general landscaping in Florida, Hawaii, and other warm, nearly or quite frost-free places. The scarlet bush makes a brave display of bloom over a long period. Hame-

lias grow well in ordinary soil in sun. They are adaptable for pots in greenhouses. Of easy cultivation outdoors, they need no particular care other than a little pruning to shape, and to thin out the branches if they become overcrowded. In greenhouses conditions and care appropriate for ixoras give good results. Propagation is by seeds, and by cuttings of firm shoots made in summer and planted under mist or in a greenhouse propagating bench.

HANDFLOWER TREE, MEXICAN is *Cheirostemon platanoides*.

HANDKERCHIEF TREE. See Davidia.

HANGING BASKETS, POTS and PLANTERS. Ornamental plants in suspended containers offer possibilities as decorations quite different from plants used in other ways. They make possible, as it were, three-dimensional gardening. Furthermore, some plants can only be displayed to fullest advantage in this manner and some, notably many epiphytes (plants that in their native homes perch on trees), thrive better above the ground. Traditionally, hanging plants have been accommodated in wire baskets, common clay flower pots, or for orchids, baskets or rafts constructed of slabs of wood. There are other possibilities. Decorative containers in considerable variety are sold by garden centers and similar places or can be devised. Sometimes a discarded light fixture can be adapted to the purpose.

Akin to hanging containers in that they serve somewhat similar purposes, are suitable for the same kinds of plants, and need the same care, are containers held in brackets attached to walls.

Where to use plants grown in this way calls for thought. Obviously, they must be where environmental conditions are reasonably suited to their needs, where they will not be in the way or present danger to the unwary, where drip from them will not mar floors or anything else beneath, and where attention can be given to them with fair ease. In greenhouses and lath houses such conditions are usually easily met. In homes and other buildings they can often be contrived in windows, especially if a shallow tray filled with gravel or similar material, such as is often used under potted plants, is positioned below. This not only increases humidity, but also catches any drip from the baskets. Outdoors, in summer where winters are severe, the year around in mild climates, baskets can be shown with excellent effect suspended from wide eaves, at entrances to passageways, from staircases, from porches and balconies, in patios, and in many other locations that will suggest themselves to the imaginative. A single specimen is sometimes most effective. In some locations a row of regularly spaced baskets can be used to emphasize an eave line or a porch. Charming effects can be had by grouping about five hanging containers at different levels and of different sizes to produce something like the effect of a mobile, or more correctly, a stabile.

Containers may be of openwork as are wire and wood slat baskets or have solid sides and bottoms as do pots, bowls, and dishes. If solid, it is important that there be drainage holes for surplus water to escape. If there are none be sure to have some drilled before planting. This can be done in ceramic ware and even glass. Commercial pots designed for suspending are often fitted with saucers to catch drip, an excellent precaution in critical locations. With a little ingenuity it is possible to improvise sightly drip saucers to attach beneath other units.

Planting can be done for permanent or temporary effects. One-season baskets containing annuals or plants commonly grown as annuals, either one kind in a container or in mixture, can be very gay. Favorites for such use include abutilons, annual phlox, black-eyed-Susan vine, browallias, coleuses, English ivy, fuchsias, geraniums, heliotropes, impatiens, lobelias, nasturtiums, Paris-daisies, petunias, sweet alyssum, trailing lantana, variegated ground-ivy, verbenas, vincas, and wax begonias.

(c) *Chlorophytum comosum vittatum*

Some plants for hanging containers:
(a) *Begonia limmingheiana*

(b) *Browallia speciosa major*

(d) *Columnea microphylla*

(e) Ivy-leaved geranium

Baskets to last for more than one season are usually restricted to one kind of plant. Sometimes two kinds, one with arching, the other with pendulous stems are used. Among plants especially suitable for growing permanently in this fashion are *Abutilon megapotamicum*; achimenes; aeschynanthuses; asparagus-ferns; begonias (many kinds); bougainvilleas; Christmas, Easter, and some other cactuses including rhipsalises; *Campanula isophylla*; Caroline jessamine; chlorophytums; columneas; English ivy; episcias; ferns (several kinds); *Ficus pumila*; grape-ivy; *Gynura procumbens*; ivy-arum; ivy-leaved geraniums; Kangaroo vine; *Manettia bicolor*; orchids (many kinds); oxalises; philodendrons; pick-a-back plant; trailing lantana; vincas; and wandering jews.

Care of basket plants is that appropriate for pot plants except that more frequent watering may be needed, but that must be

(f) Orchid (*Coelogyne cristata*)

(c) Setting a center plant in place

(d) The completed basket

adjusted to the rate of drying. If, unhappily, a basket becomes really dry the only satisfactory solution is to take it down and set it in deep water for fifteen minutes or so. Routine watering is done with a watering can, with a pipe extension attached to a hose, or by lowering the basket and soaking it in a pail or other receptable. Plants in baskets filled with roots benefit from regular applications of dilute liquid fertilizer.

Planting is usually best done in spring. If the container is an open-sided basket, first line it with sheet moss, coconut husk fiber, or fine plastic mesh. If it is solid-sided, be sure to provide for drainage by putting a layer of crocks in the bottom. In making up temporary baskets and in some cases permanent ones, it is well to have some plants growing out of their sides as well as tops. Position these, they must be small, as the work of filling the basket proceeds. As with all plants used, make sure that their root balls are thoroughly soaked with water an hour or two before planting. Fill some soil into the basket, tamp it firm, and at intervals push small plants through the sides of the basket so that their tops protrude and their root balls rest on the soil. Put in more soil and repeat as the basket is filled in around the main center plants, which are set vertically. Pack the soil firmly. Leave the upper surface slightly hollowed and rimmed so that it will hold water. After planting, water thoroughly and put the basket out of drafts and in light shade for a couple of weeks. During this time spray its foliage once or twice a day with a fine mist of water. Avoid keeping the soil in a soaked condition, but do not let it dry. The only other attentions likely to be needed are picking off dead leaves and faded blooms, any steps that may be necessary to control

Planting a basket with Boston fern:
(a) Lining the basket with moss

(b) Setting small plants through the sides of the container

pests and diseases, and any trimming necessary to improve shapeliness. In cold baskets must be kept indoors from fall to spring. Refurbish permanent baskets in spring. At that time prick away some of the old surface soil and replace it with fresh, rich earth.

HAPLOPAPPUS (Haplo-páppus). The 150 species of this genus of the daisy family COMPOSITAE are inhabitants of temperate and mountain regions in North and South America. Of very varied appearance and growth habits, they have by botanists who accept relatively small differences as justifying generic recognition, been split into more than a dozen genera, but more conservative views are commonly favored. The name, from the Greek *haploos*, single, and *pappos*, down, alludes to the hairs accompanying the fruits.

Haplopappuses are tap-rooted annuals, biennials, herbaceous perennials, and shrubs. They have alternate, often thickish, sometimes glandular, pinnately-lobed, toothed, or plain-edged leaves and solitary or clustered, yellow or rarely reddish or creamy-white flower heads of the daisy type (with a central eye of disk florets encircled by petal-like ray florets), or consisting of only disk florets. The disk florets are bisexual and usually seed-producing, the ray flowers are female and often sterile. The fruits are seedlike achenes.

Annual or biennial, **Haplopappus ciliatus**, 1½ to 6 feet tall and hairless, has erect stems that, except at their tops, are usually branchless. Its stalkless, stem-clasping leaves are oblong to ovate or elliptic-ovate, and spiny-toothed. They are up to 3½ inches long by 1½ inches wide. The flower heads, few together in clusters, have numerous ray florets and are 1½ to 2 inches in diameter. This species, which looks much like *Grindelia*, inhabits open sites from Missouri to Texas and New Mexico.

Sometimes called camphor-daisy, *H. phyllocephalus* (syns. *Sideranthus phyllocephalus, Machaeranthera phyllocephalus*) is an erect or sprawling, frequently glandular-hairy annual 1 foot to 3 feet tall, and usually branched above. Its slightly stem-clasping leaves are thick, the principal ones ½ inch to 2 inches long, oblong to spatula-shaped, lobed or toothed, and with a bristle at the end of each lobe or tooth. The yellow or rarely reddish, stalkless or nearly stalkless flower heads, up to 2 inches in diameter, are solitary or up to three together at the stem ends. They have fifteen to forty ray florets. This species inhabits sandy beaches and subsaline soils from Louisiana to Texas and Mexico. From it *H. p. annuus* (syn. *Sideranthus annuus*) differs in the leaves for some distance below the yellow flower heads being much smaller than those beneath. The flower heads are in loose clusters of few to many. This occurs from Colorado to Kansas and Texas.

Mock-heather (*H. ericoides* syn. *Ericameria ericoides*) is a compact, broad, sparsely-hairy shrub 1 foot to 3 feet tall or sometimes taller. Its somewhat resinous stems and foliage are rather heathlike in aspect. The slender-cylindrical leaves are numerous, crowded, spreading, and up to ⅓ inch long. In their axils are tufts of shorter leaves. Terminating the many erect, leafy branches, the flower heads, with two to six ray florets, and about ⅓ inch long, are clustered. Mock-heather is a native of coastal sand dunes in California.

Very different from the last, and a native of the California coast and offshore islands, *H. canus* (syn. *Hazardia cana*) is an open-branched shrub 2 to 8 feet tall, with beautiful, heavily white-felted stems and foliage. It has blunt, obovate to oblanceolate, stalked or stalkless, toothed or toothless leaves 2 to 5 inches long and ⅓ inch to 2 inches wide. The many flower heads, about 1 inch wide, which with age turn from yellow to purplish, are in large, rather loose panicles or clusters. They have six to fourteen inconspicuous ray florets. A low herbaceous perennial, *H. lyallii* has a woody rootstock and leafy stems not over 6 inches tall, often much lower. The oblanceolate to spatula-shaped leaves are up to 3 inches long. The flower heads are ¾ inch to 1½ inches in diameter and have ten or more ray florets.

A widely variable perennial that includes several botanical varieties, *H. spinulosus* (syn. *Sideranthus spinulosus*) ranges through much of western North America from Minnesota to Saskatchewan and Mexico. A subshrub up to about 2 feet tall, this has many leafy stems. The leaves are oblong-spatula-shaped to narrower, lobeless, or once- or twice-pinnately-cleft so that they have a ferny appearance, or toothed and slightly stem-clasping at their bases and ¾ inch to a little more than 2 inches long. The flower heads, each with fifteen to fifty ray florets, are clustered and about ½ inch in diameter.

A number of low, yellow-flowered, perennial, mountain species not known to be cultivated seem well worthy of attempting by dedicated rock gardeners. Here belongs *H. armerioides*, of the Rocky Mountain region, 4 to 8 inches in height, with mostly erect, basal, slender leaves and solitary flower heads 1 inch or so wide. Another good possibility, *H. acaulis* has crowded mats of leafy branches and rather rigid flower stalks up to 4 to 6 inches tall, topped by solitary flower heads about 1 inch across. This inhabits mountains in western North America. Usually 4 to 6 inches tall, *H. apargioides* is native to the mountains of California. Mostly 4 to 6 inches high, but sometimes twice that, it has narrowly-oblanceolate, usually toothed leaves and solitary flower heads about 1 inch wide. Native of Argentina and Chile, *H. glutinosus* (syn. *H. coronopifolius*) is a loosely-branched, mat-forming perennial 4 inches to nearly 1 foot tall. Probably not reliably hardy where winters are more severe than those of Washington, D.C., it has thick, coarsely-toothed to more or less pinnately-lobed, spatula-shaped, sticky leaves ½ to 1 inch long. Its golden-yellow flower heads, solitary on longish stalks, are about 1 inch wide. Seldom over 6 inches tall, *H. lanuginosus*, of the mountains of the northwestern United States, has densely-tufted, soft, linear-spatula-shaped leaves up to 4 inches long and solitary flower heads approximately 1 inch across.

Garden and Landscape Uses and Cultivation. The most appropriate use for the more attractive species of this genus is for colonizing in more or less natural areas where the environment is reasonably similar to that which they know in the wild. They are rarely grown outside general geographical regions to which they are natives. They succeed in ordinary soils in sun and are raised from seeds, or the perennials by division at the beginning of the growing season. Because of their taproots they are difficult to transplant.

HAPLOPHYLLUM (Haplo-phýllum). From closely related *Ruta* this genus differs in its

Haplopappus glutinosus

leaves being undivided, or three- or more rarely five-parted, and in its flowers having five each sepals and petals and ten stamens hairy in their lower parts. There are about seventy species, natives from the Mediterranean region to eastern Siberia. They belong to the rue family RUTACEAE. They are herbaceous perennials or subshrubs, with alternate leaves and small yellow flowers in terminal clusters. The name, from the Greek *haploos*, single, and *phyllon*, a leaf, alludes to the foliage of some kinds.

Sometimes cultivated, although common rue (*Ruta graveolens*) is quite often mistakenly grown under its name, *Haplophyllum patavinum* (syn. *Ruta patavina*) is a native of southern Europe, naturalized to some extent in California. From 4 inches to 1¼ feet tall, it has pubescent stems, crowded with lanceolate-oblong to oblong-obovate, hairless leaves ½ to ¾ inch long. The lowermost are undivided, the middle ones, comprising most of the foliage, are of three leaflets, and the uppermost undivided or three-lobed. In compact terminal clusters 1 inch to 2 inches wide, the yellow flowers have a central green rib to each petal.

Garden Uses and Cultivation. The cultivation of this plant is for the most part restricted to herb gardens. It responds to the same conditions and care as rue (*Ruta*).

HARBINGER-OF-SPRING is *Erigenia bulbosa*.

HARBOURIA (Har-boùria). One species of the carrot family UMBELLIFERAE is the only representative of *Harbouria*. Native of the Rocky Mountain region, it has a name commemorating J. P. Harbour, who collected plants in that area. The dates of the birth and death of this nineteenth century botanist are not known.

A deep-rooted, hairless herbaceous perennial, *H. trachypleura* is 1 foot to 2 feet tall and has mostly basal foliage, erect, branching, few-leaved stems, and leaves three or four times divided into nearly threadlike final segments. Its little yellow flowers are in umbels 1½ to 2 inches wide of many smaller umbels that terminate erect, slender stalks. The fruits are dry and seedlike.

Garden Uses and Cultivation. In its native region suitable for including in collections of native plants and of merit for rock gardens, this needs well-drained soil and full sun. It is easily raised from seeds, but because it resents transplanting should be set in its permanent location while quite young.

HARD-WOODED PLANTS. Growers of greenhouse and conservatory plants sometimes group under this name shrubs and trees grown indoors. Less used than formerly, it provides a convenient way of referring to plants with hard, woody stems, which generally require different cultural care from such softer-stemmed kinds as begonias and chrysanthemums. Typical hard-wooded plants include acacias, azaleas, boronias, callistemons, camellias, ericas, and rhododendrons.

HARDENBERGIA (Hardenbérg-ia) — Australian-Sarsaparilla. Closely related to *Kennedia*, from which it differs in technical characters only, Australian *Hardenbergia* consists of two twining evergreen vines suitable for outdoor cultivation in California and similar mild climates and in greenhouses. It is a member of the pea family LEGUMINOSAE. Its name commemorates Franziska, Countess von Hardenberg, of Germany.

Hardenbergias have alternate, toothless leaves, and racemes of pea-like flowers with a somewhat two-lipped, five-lobed calyx, a broad banner or standard petal, and a broad keel shorter than the wings. There are nine united stamens and one free, and one style. The fruits are pods.

Hardenbergia comptoniana

Hardenbergia violacea

Sometimes 20 feet tall, but often lower, *H. comptoniana* has leaves of three or occasionally five narrow-lanceolate to ovate leaflets up to 3½ inches long that spread in finger-like fashion. Its small, violet-blue or blue flowers are strung in twos, threes, or fours along the slender racemes. They are less than ½ inch long and are succeeded by slender, compressed pods up to 2 inches in length. Variety *H. c. alba* has white flowers. From the last species *H. violacea* differs in its leaves normally having only one leaflet up to 4 inches long, narrowly-lanceolate to ovate. Its flowers, under ½ inch in length, are usually violet, but other color forms occur and have been named *H. v. alba*, with white flowers; *H. v. lilacina*, with lilac flowers; and *H. v. rosea*, with pink blooms.

Garden and Landscape Uses. Hardenbergias are attractive for arches, trellises, fences, and growing on walls fitted with wires or other supports around which they can twine. They bloom chiefly in winter and spring depending upon local climate. In greenhouses they may be grown along wires stretched under the roof glass or on other supports or in pots with their stems twined around a framework of stakes or wires.

Cultivation. These plants need a neutral to slightly acid soil, well drained and always moderately moist, but never waterlogged. Some shade from strong summer sun is beneficial, but too much inhibits blooming. As soon as the flowering season is over, prune the vines rather severely to shape them and encourage the development of new shoots to bloom the following season. They succeed in light, airy greenhouses where the winter night temperature is about 50°F and the day temperature just a few degrees higher. Specimens in pots or tubs benefit from being plunged for the summer, sinking them outdoors up to the rims of their containers in a bed of sand or ashes in a lightly shaded spot. Repot in well-drained pots or tubs in peaty, moderately fertile soil when necessary, usually at intervals of two or three years. Do this immediately after blooming. Propagation is mostly by cuttings or by layering. If seeds are used soak them in tepid water for twenty-four hours before sowing. Container-grown hardenbergias are impatient of poor drainage and watering that results in constantly saturated soil. Well-rooted specimens benefit from regular applications of dilute liquid fertilizer from the time new growth begins in spring until fall. Scale insects sometimes attack these plants.

HARDENING OFF. In the language of gardeners this describes the accustoming to outdoor conditions of plants that have been grown in greenhouses, hot beds, cold frames, or elsewhere indoors. It involves gradual rather than sudden change. The last can be very harmful and cause wilting, yellowing, dropping of leaves, and other evidences of a severe check to growth. Ordinarily plants put outside must adjust to lower temperatures, more airy conditions, and light of a different character and often greater intensity than that indoors.

Begin hardening off by ventilating the greenhouse or frame more and more freely, especially in mild weather. After a period of this treatment transfer plants from greenhouses to cold frames ventilated sparingly at first then with increasing freedom or stand them in a sheltered place outdoors for a week to ten days, possibly covering them at nights with polyethylene plastic film, before setting them in the garden. Harden off plants in hotbeds and cold frames similarly by affording additional ventilation for a period and then removing the sash completely for a week to ten days before planting in the garden.

The practice of hardening off is based on the very sound principles of avoiding sudden shock and whenever possible not subjecting plants, at one time, to more than one set of conditions that may check growth. Of necessity the root disturbance incident to transplanting, even the slight amount that accompanies setting plants from pots or other individual containers into the ground, results in a small to more serious check. It is better that it be done after instead of at the same time as the plant is called upon to adjust to other changed conditions.

HARDHACK is *Spiraea tomentosa*.

HARDPAN. Hard, compacted, mineral earth of almost rocklike density that forms a subsurface layer in the ground, especially in clayey and other fine-textured soils, is called hardpan. Roots cannot penetrate such material, and since it is impervious or nearly so to water, the soil above is often poorly drained and wet. A not infrequent cause of hardpan is the leaching downward of salts of iron and lime. These at certain depths combine with the soil and cement its particles into the almost concrete-like layer that is hardpan. Such pans are sometimes less than an inch, or at most are not over a few inches thick. It is important to break them up by deep spading or plowing or in exceptional cases by dynamiting (done of course by an expert) before planting.

HARDY and HARDINESS. These terms, so frequently and often glibly employed by gardeners, and indeed so useful, are not susceptible to precise definition or application. In their broadest meanings they refer to ability to survive under the total year-round climatic conditions of a designated region or place. In the narrower sense, in which they are more commonly used, they allude to capability of persisting through the winter and this of course is closely related to minimum temperatures.

Ability to survive low temperatures is influenced by many factors. There are trees and shrubs that because prevailingly warm summers and dry falls result in their current season's shoots maturing well are winter hardy in northeastern North America, but not in the much milder climate of Great Britain. Kinds that survive in porous, well-drained soils succumb in moister, clayey ones where winters are no colder. A thick covering of snow that lasts through the winter may make possible the persistence of deciduous and low shrubby plants that would be killed where winter temperatures are higher, but the snow cover is less or not continuous.

The duration of low temperatures and when they are experienced may be of determining importance. If in late winter and early spring spells of comparatively warm weather are following by freezing, growth may be stimulated prematurely only to be killed by temperatures considerably higher than would be harmless earlier when the plants were fully dormant.

Exposure is often of critical importance in determining whether or not plants, especially trees and shrubs, survive winters. In regions where they are borderline hardy, rhododendrons and other broad-leaved evergreens are more likely to live if located on land sloping to the north than to the south and against west- to north-facing walls than those otherwise oriented. This because in such places they are less subject to the stresses imposed by maximum exposure to strong sun when the ground is frozen and especially to morning sun following extremely cold nights. Similar considerations affect the winter survival of many alpine plants.

Wind, especially accompanied by low humidity, dehydrates woody plants and especially evergreens. In cold climates this may result in severe winter-killing or death at temperatures considerably higher than would be harmless in less exposed locations. To minimize this danger position plants bordering on tenderness in sheltered places.

Ill-advised cultural practices can serve to reduce resistance to cold and increase the danger of winter-killing. Cultivating the surface soil and fertilizing from mid-August to late September may stimulate growth too soft to survive. Hard pruning in fall with consequent reduction of top growth stored with moisture and food and exposure of parts previously more or less sheltered and shaded can be disastrous to slightly tender shrubs.

Several attempts have been made to classify plants according to their winter hardiness and to relate the classifications to zoned maps. While helpful to a degree, chiefly with trees and shrubs and for limited areas such as the northeastern United States and California, these do not and cannot provide more than approximately reliable information, especially when larger regions of highly diverse climates are considered.

Such zone maps, as they are called, are usually based on temperatures only. With slight variations those who contrive them accept the average minimum of the coldest month as reported by the United States Weather Bureau and the Meteorological Division of the Department of Transportation of the Canadian Government as likely to be indicative of the hardiness of plants. But, as we have seen, many factors other than the intensity of midwinter cold determine whether plants survive. And here one should remember that over long periods extremes rather than averages are decisive. One extremely important element reflected sketchily, if at all, on zone maps is altitude, yet in the eastern United States for each 1,000 feet of elevation winter minimum temperatures are lowered the approximate equivalent of moving 300 miles northward at sea level. Another limitation of zone maps is that in many cases they suggest hardiness based on projections across the continent of known responses of plants in the eastern United States. This because of insufficient recorded experience with the same kinds in other parts of the zones. Only rarely, and then quite inadequately are herbaceous plants calibrated in zone maps.

As used in this Encyclopedia the word hardy without supplementation is applied to plants that, favorably located, survive winters north of the Mason and Dixon line, in most cases to Philadelphia or New York City, with many kinds satisfactory much further north. More explicit suggestions about hardiness such as "hardy in southern New England" or "hardy in southern Canada" are given when reliable information is available. In the final analysis with plants of suspected tenderness and possibly borderline hardiness the only reliable way for gardeners to determine their permanence is to try them under the most favorable conditions they can provide.

HARDY ANNUAL. As used by gardeners this term designates annuals that may be successfully grown by sowing the seeds outdoors in early spring and the seedlings of which withstand low temperatures and, in most cases, even light frosts. Under favorable garden conditions some sorts reproduce freely from self-sown seeds. To achieve early flowering it is common practice to sow certain hardy annuals indoors earlier than outdoor sowing is practicable and to set the seedlings in the garden as sizable young plants. Asters and zinnias are sorts often grown in this way. Other examples of hardy annuals are larkspurs, poppies, sweet-alyssum, and sweet-peas.

HARDY PERENNIAL. As used in gardens this term is restricted to hardy herbaceous perennials, including bulb plants. Technically many deciduous and evergreen trees, shrubs, and vines are hardy perennials, but are excluded from the horticultural meaning of the term. Well-known hardy perennials include all or some sorts of achilleas, anchusas, bleeding hearts, campanulas, chrysanthemums, columbines, crocuses, delphiniums, dianthuses, geums, globe-thistles, hyacinths, irises, lilies, meadow-rues, narcissuses, oriental poppies, peonies, phlox, plantain-lilies, salvias, and veronicas.

HAREBELL is *Campanula rotundifolia*. The harebell-poppy is *Meconopsis*.

HARIOTA. See Hatioria.

HARPEPHYLLUM (Harpephýll-um)—Kafir-Plum. One species constitutes *Harpephyllum*, of the cashew family ANACARDI-ACEAE. The name is derived from the Greek *harpe*, a sickle, and *phyllon*, a leaf. It refers to the shape of the leaflets.

Harpephyllum caffrum

The Kafir-plum (*H. caffrum*) is an evergreen tree of good appearance that in its native South Africa becomes 20 to 50 feet tall. It has rough, dark brown bark and glossy and hairless, rich green, pinnate leaves 6 to 10 inches long, crowded at the ends of the branches. Each leaf has four to seven pairs of pointed-lanceolate or slightly sickle-shaped, leathery, toothless leaflets and a terminal one attached to a slightly-winged midrib. The leaflets are 2 to 3 inches long. Individual leaves turn red and drop when they are about two years old. Male and female flowers are on separate trees. They are small, whitish, and in compact clusters arising from the leaf axils near the branch ends. Each has a four- or five-cleft calyx, and four or five petals. There are nine or ten stamens. The fruits are olive-shaped, dark red at maturity, about 1 inch long by one-half as wide, and contain a sour, edible pulp and a distinctly pitted seed.

In its native land this species is used as a street tree and to form living fence posts. Living branches trimmed to form stakes and set as posts usually take root and eventually develop into short, round-topped trees. The Kafir-plum yields fairly heavy, strong wood that polishes well and is used for furniture, construction material, planking, and other purposes.

Garden Uses and Cultivation. This is a quite attractive evergreen tree for frost-free or nearly frost-free climates, such as those of southern Florida and southern California. It succeeds without special care in any ordinary garden soil and is easily increased by seeds and by cuttings.

HARPULLIA (Har-púllia). Belonging to the soapberry family SAPINDACEAE, the genus *Harpullia* is related to *Xanthoceras*. Its members are thirty-seven species of trees of warm parts of Asia, Pacific islands, and Australia. They have alternate pinnate leaves, the leaflets of which are alternate, lobeless, and toothless. The flowers are small and in panicles of either unisexual or unisexual and bisexual individuals. They have four or five erect sepals, the same number of larger petals, five to eight stamens, and an elongated style with a long, usually more or less twisted stigma. The fruits are inflated, two-lobed, two-celled capsules with one or two seeds in each cell. The name *Harpullia* is based on an Indian one.

Cultivated as a shade and ornamental tree in Florida, California, and other warm regions, *H. arborea* is a splendid ornamental that withstands a few degrees of frost. It attains a height of 35 feet or more, and is densely foliaged with lustrous leaves that have seven to eleven glossy, oblong-elliptic leaflets 3½ to 8 inches long. The inconspicuous, whitish flowers, in drooping panicles from the leaf axils, make no significant show, but the abundant, strongly two-lobed, orange-red fruits, about 1½ inches wide and broader than long, are very decorative. At maturity they split to reveal the large, smooth, black seeds. This is a native of India, Malaya, and the Philippine Islands. Similar *H. cupanoides* differs somewhat in its foliage and in its slightly smaller fruits of a more yellowish hue. It is native from India to southern China and New Guinea.

The Australian tulipwood tree (*H. pendula*) has leaves with four to ten pairs of oblong or narrowly-elliptic leaflets up to 6 inches long by 2 inches wide, but often smaller. The flowers are green-petaled and in panicles. About 1 inch in diameter, the smooth red or orange fruits split when ripe to show their pink interiors and shining,

black seeds. In Australia the wood of this species is esteemed for cabinetmaking.

Garden and Landscape Uses and Cultivation. These are superior warm-climate trees for shade and beautiful displays of fruits. They are easily grown in reasonably good soil, and preferably in full sun. Propagation is usually by seed.

HARRIMANELLA. See Cassiope.

HARRISIA (Har-rísia). Conservative botanists include *Eriocereus* in *Harrisia*. In this Encyclopedia it is treated separately. So interpreted, *Harrisia* comprises thirteen species, native to the West Indies and Florida. From South American *Eriocereus* it differs in its fleshy fruits being yellow, orange, or dull red and not bursting open when ripe, instead of being brighter red or carmine and splitting at maturity. Belonging to the cactus family CACTACEAE the genus *Harrisia* has a name commemorating William Harris, a one-time Superintendent of Public Gardens and Plantations in Jamaica. He died in 1920.

Harrisias have procumbent, clambering, or erect, branched, slender stems with four to twelve prominent ribs or angles, usually very spiny. The flowers, large and long-tubed, open in late afternoon, evening, or at night. Borne near the tops of the stems, they are long-tubed, funnel-shaped, white or pinkish with the outer petals mostly pink to greenish. There are numerous stamens shorter than the petals and a longer style. The generally nearly spherical, fleshy fruits commonly have deciduous scales. Rarely they are spiny. With the exception of *H. aboriginum*, the flowers of all species treated here come from areoles furnished with hairs.

Native to sand dunes in Florida, *H. fragrans* has ten- to twelve-ridged, erect, clambering, or reclining stems up to 15 feet long. They are plentifully furnished with needle-like spines ¾ inch to 1½ inches in length, in clusters spaced ¾ inch to 1½ inches apart, of nine to thirteen. The fragrant, white to pinkish blooms are 5 to 8 inches long. Their petals are not toothed. Dull orange-red and spherical to obovoid, the fruits are a little over 2 inches long. Another Floridian, *H. simpsonii* inhabits the southern part of the mainland and the Keys. This has erect, spreading, or reclining, branched or branchless stems with eight to ten ribs. The clusters of seven to fourteen spines up to 1 inch long are spaced up to ¾ inch apart. The flowers, 5 to 8 inches long, are white. Their petals are toothed. The orange-red, flattened-spherical fruits are up to 2¼ inches in diameter. Yet a third native of Florida, *H. aboriginum* may attain a height of 20 feet. Its stems, erect or sprawling, and sometimes branched, have nine to eleven rounded ribs. The clusters of seven to nine short spines are up to 1¼ inches apart.

The white flowers, from areoles with brown hairs, have toothed petals. The yellow fruits are up to 3 inches in diameter.

Native to Cuba and the Isle of Pines, *H. eriophora* attains a maximum height of about 10 feet. Its approximately 1½-inch-wide stems are prominently eight- or nine-ribbed. Spaced ¾ inch to 1½ inches apart are clusters of six to nine dark-tipped spines, the longest from 1 inch to 1½ inches in length. The flower buds are conspicuously clothed with white hairs. From 4½ to 7 inches long, the blooms have toothless petals, the inner ones pure white, the outer pinkish to greenish. The subspherical fruits are edible, yellow, and somewhat over 2 inches in diameter. Endemic to Jamaica, *H. gracilis*, up to 22 feet in height, has spreading branches. The stems have nine to eleven rather low, rounded ribs with clusters, up to ¾ inch apart, of ten to sixteen black-tipped, whitish spines, the longest ¾ to 1 inch in length. About 8 inches long, the flowers have usually toothed, white inner petals, pale brown outer ones. The yellow fruits are up to 2¾ inches in diameter.

Garden and Landscape Uses and Cultivation. Because of their space requirements and often somewhat graceless, ungainly habits of growth harrisias are not among the most popular of cactuses. In mild climates they are appropriate for outdoor succulent collections and elsewhere for greenhouses where they may be trained up pillars or under the roof glass. They are vigorous, easy to grow, and propagate with ease from cuttings and seeds. For more information see Cactuses.

HARRISIELLA (Harris-iélla). The only species belonging here is closely allied to *Campylocentrum,* and by some authorities is included there. A member of the orchid family ORCHIDACEAE, it is native to Florida, the West Indies, and Mexico. Its name, sometimes spelled *Harrisella,* commemorates William Harris, one-time Superintendent of Public Gardens, Jamaica. He died in 1920.

Tree-perching *Harrisiella porrecta* (syn. *Campylocentrum porrectum*) is an unusual leafless species with clusters of slender, 6-inch-long, white, flexuous, often partially hanging roots and minute stems. On threadlike, zigzagged stalks 1 inch to 2 inches long from the centers of the root clusters are borne in racemes of two or more, not fully expanding, minute yellow-green flowers.

Garden Uses and Cultivation. As a curiosity this species is sometimes attempted by orchid enthusiasts. Unless attached to living trees it is difficult to grow. Removal from the branches of the host tree usually results in death of the orchid. For more information see Orchids.

HARRY LAUDER'S WALKING STICK is *Corylus avellana contorta.*

HARSINGHAR is *Nyctanthes arbor-tristis.*

HARTWEGIA. See Nageliella.

HASELTONIA (Hasel-tònia). The only species of *Haseltonia,* of the cactus family CACTACEAE, is by those who favor concentrating cactus species into comparatively few genera included in *Cephalocereus.* Native of southern Mexico, it has a name honoring Scott Haselton, distinguished American editor of the *Cactus and Succulent Journal.*

Columnar and with affinity to the old man cactus (*Cephalocereus senilis*), although without the very long silvery hairs of that well known sort, *H. columna-trajani* (syns. *H. hoppenstedtii, Cephalocereus hoppenstedtii*), 15 to 30 feet in height, has branchless spindle-shaped, grayish-green stems thickest toward their centers and with about sixteen notched ribs. The spine clusters, from areoles except those near the tops of the stems without wool, are of fifteen to twenty soft, white radials ⅓ inch long or a little longer and five to ten stout, soft centrals up to 3½ inches long. Borne only by old specimens, the 3-inch-long flowers have pink or pink-tipped outer sepals or petals and white or pale yellow inner ones.

Garden and Landscape Uses and Cultivation. This has the same uses as the old man cactus and other sorts of *Cephalocereus* and responds to conditions that suit such sorts. For more information see Cactuses.

HASHISH. See Cannabis.

HAT PLANT. The Chinese hat plant is *Holmskioldia sanguinea,* the Panama hat plant is *Carludovica palmata,* the Puerto Rican hat plant *Sabal causiarum.*

HATCHET-VETCH is *Securigera securidaca.*

HATIORA (Hati-òra). Related to *Rhipsalis,* the four or five species of Brazilian *Hatiora* are spineless plants of the cactus family CACTACEAE. They are epiphytes, perching on trees in the fashion of many orchids and bromeliads, but not taking nourishment from their hosts as do parasitic plants. The name is an anagram of *Hariota* which commemorates Thomas Hariot, a surveyor in Virginia. He died in 1621.

Hatioras have slender, cylindrical, jointed stems that fork repeatedly, at each dividing point giving rise to two or more new branches. The joints are more or less club- or sausage-shaped with the stems much constricted between the segments. At the apex of each joint is a woolly areole (specialized area from which hairs and spines, when present, as well as new branches and blooms, develop on cactuses). The blooms are yellow to salmon-pink and have distinct perianth segments (petals) that spread widely only in sun. The fruits are white and spherical. Some authorities include *Hatiora* in *Rhipsalis.*

Most often grown, *H. salicornioides* (syn. *Rhipsalis salicornioides*) is a freely-branched, erect or somewhat pendent shrub up to 1 foot high, but with stems that may be considerably longer. From its branching points three to five, or sometimes fewer, new stems develop. Their segments are ½ inch to 1¼ inches long, up to ¼ inch thick, and club-shaped. Their areoles sprout short white hairs. Solitary

Hatiora salicornioides

or in twos, the yellowish to yellow, funnel-shaped flowers, with fleshy petals, are under ½ inch long. They have reddish stamens, shorter than the petals, and a white four- or five-lobed stigma. The semitranslucent, white fruits are reddish at their apexes. An erect plant up to 6 feet in height with bamboo-like thicker nodes and longer joints than those of the preceding kind, **H. bambusioides** differs also in having one compound areole at the apex of each branch instead of several along the sides of the upper halves of the branches. The plant grown as *H. cylindrica* probably belongs here. The branched, soon-drooping stems of **H. clavata,** up to 3 feet long, have club-shaped joints with one compound areole at each terminal. The flowers are white, a little over ½ inch long.

Garden Uses and Cultivation. These are the same as for *Rhipsalis*. For additional information see Cactuses.

HAW. See Crataegus. Black-haw is a vernacular name of *Viburnum lentago* and *V. prunifolium*. Southern black-haw or blue-haw is *Viburnum rufidulum*. Possum-haw is a common name of *Ilex decidua, Viburnum acerifolium,* and *V. nudum*. Swamp-haw is a common name of *Viburnum cassinoides* and *V. nudum*.

HAWAIIAN-MAHOGANY is *Acacia koa*.

HAWANE. See Pritchardia.

HAWKESARA. This is the name of hybrid orchids the parents of which include *Cattleya, Cattleyopsis,* and *Epidendrum*.

HAWK'S BEARD. See Crepis.

HAWKWEED. See Hieracium. The name golden-yellow hawkweed is sometimes used for *Tolpis barbata*.

HAWORTHIA (Hawór-thia). Named in honor of Adrian Hardy Haworth, an English botanist interested in succulent plants, who died in 1833, *Haworthia* belongs in the lily family LILIACEAE. Closely related to *Aloe*, it differs most obviously in its kinds being considerably smaller than the vast majority of aloes and in its flowers being white with greenish or pinkish longitudinal stripes, two-lipped, and under 1 inch long. The number of species is estimated as being about 150, but the group is poorly understood botanically and it seems certain that some of the kinds that have been named as species are hybrids of unrecorded garden origin. The group is much in need of botanical study. All Africans, haworthias are succulent perennials.

Haworthias, stemless or short-stemmed, are neat of aspect. They have usually crowded, fleshy leaves, in rosettes, or up-pointing and overlapping in spirals or distinct rows along the stems. Often they are

Haworthia bilineata

decorated with little white, pearl-like tubercles. Sometimes tiny translucent areas serve as windows to admit light to the internal tissues. The leaf margins and apexes may be bristly-hairy. In loose racemes or panicles, the asymmetrical blooms have six nearly equal lobes (petals, or more correctly, tepals), their free parts recurved, six nonprotruding stamens, and one short style. The fruits are capsules.

These haworthias are a selection of the many available: **H. angustifolia** is highly variable, with many varieties. Typically stemless and not much suckering it has rosettes about 2 inches in diameter of about twenty lanceolate, bristle-tipped leaves often marked with longitudinal, yellowish-green lines and with whitish-toothed margins. **H. armstrongii** suckers freely from the bottoms of its up to 5-inch-long, leafy stems. The erect, lanceolate, sharp-pointed leaves, in spirals, are dark green and up to about 1½ inches long. Somewhat channeled above, they have rounded undersides with pale tubercles along the keel. **H. asperula** has few-leaved rosettes about 3 inches across. The green, triangular-ovate leaves have flat upper surfaces with white apexes. **H. attenuata** has numerous varieties. Typically it has rosettes of thirty to forty tapering, oblong-lanceolate leaves 2½ to 3 inches long conspicuously decorated with white tubercles often arranged in cross-bands. *H. a. clariperla* is strikingly so ornamented. **H. batesiana** forms crowded cushions of 2-inch-wide rosettes of tapering, ovate-oblanceolate to oblong, minutely-toothed, plump, bristle-tipped, grayish leaves with a few darker, longitudinal lines connected by cross

Haworthia bilineata (flowers)

lines. **H. bilineata** is stemless and forms tight clumps of rosettes 2 to 3 inches wide of moss-green, bristle-tipped, pointed-obovate to oblong-lanceolate leaves, somewhat translucent along their slightly-toothed margins and near their tips. **H. blackbeardiana** has stemless, many-leaved rosettes about 2 inches wide, their inner leaves markedly incurved. The leaves end in a long bristle, and their margins have large bristly teeth. The leaves are pale grayish-green lined with gray. **H. chal-**

Haworthia chalwinii

winii has erect, leaning, or prostrate stems 4 to 5 inches long, furnished throughout with about 1-inch-long, ovate-triangular, purplish-bronzy-green, overlapping leaves, incurved at their tips and freely bespeckled with rows of tiny pearly-white, wartlike protuberances. *H. coarctata* has stems up to 8 inches tall with sucker shoots produced from their bases. Erect and in spirals, the lanceolate-triangular leaves are 1½ to 2 inches long by, at their bases, one-half as wide. Flat above and rounded on their undersides, they have usually few or no tubercles. *H. cooperi* is stemless. It has rosettes about 2 inches across of mostly spreading, oblong-lanceolate, bristle-tipped, purplish-brown to brownish leaves with semitranslucent apexes and bristle-tipped teeth along the margins. *H. cuspidata* forms clusters of rosettes, stemless and about 2½ inches across, of thirty to forty leaves. The minutely-toothed leaves are ovate-lanceolate to ovate, pale green, translucent toward the apex, and marked with a few darker lines. The undersides are rounded. *H. cymbiformis* is represented by several varieties. In its typical form it has freely-suckering, stemless rosettes, 3 to 4 inches in diameter, of thick, pale gray-green, short-pointed, broad-ovate to obovate, toothless leaves with hollowed upper surfaces, their undersides strongly rounded, and translucent apexes with dark green lines running into them. Those of *H. c. translucens* are translucent throughout, marked with darker longitudinal stripes, with brown-red stripes on their undersides. *H. dekenahii* is stemless. Its rosettes, up to 3½ inches wide, are of about fifteen toothed, light green leaves becoming darker above and with indistinct

whitish-green lines. Variety *H. d. argenteomaculosa* has beautifully variegated leaves. *H. fasciata* comes in several varieties. Typically it has stemless rosettes of many ascending or erect, firm, 1½-inch-long, tapering-triangular leaves, their upper surfaces mostly flat, their backs markedly rounded, and keeled toward the apex. Slightly lustrous-green, they are prominently marked with cross-bands of white tubercles. *H. fouchei* has stemless, spiraled rosettes of 3-inch-long, tapering, long-lanceolate, bristle-tipped somewhat lustrous, green leaves with lighter spots toward their tips and darker lines. It makes few offsets. *H. fulva,* stemmed and about 4 inches tall, produces many sucker shoots from the base. The broad-lanceolate leaves, approximately 1 inch long, nearly as broad at their bases and indistinctly keeled, have convex upper surfaces with prominent greenish-white to white tubercles. *H. greenii* is very variable. Typically it has clumps of branchless stems up to 8 inches tall, erect becoming sprawling. The pointed-lanceolate leaves are erect, olive-green to brownish-green, hollowed on their uppersides, rounded beneath. On both surfaces are white to green tubercles. *H. haageana* has rosettes about 1½ inches in diameter of lanceolate to triangular, up-pointing, pale green to reddish, often mottled leaves with rounded undersides and nearly flat upper ones. This kind makes few offshoots. *H. kewensis* forms clusters of stems with spirally-arranged, pointed-broad-ovate leaves a little over 1 inch long, nearly as wide at their bases, dark green and with tubercles. Flat above, they have rounded, keeled undersides. *H. lepida* has stemless rosettes a little over 2 inches wide

of about forty soft, pointed-ovate leaves with bristle-tipped apexes. They have rounded upper sides, usually with translucent spots and darker lines. *H. limifolia* is represented by a number of varieties. In its typical form it has stemless rosettes about 4½ inches wide of about eighteen sharply-tapered, triangular to lanceolate, greenish to brownish leaves with hollowed upper surfaces. The tubercles form conspicuous cross ridges. *H. longiana* has stemless, few-leaved rosettes of more or less erect, long-tapered leaves with triangular-ovate bases. They are ¾ to 1 inch long by one-half as broad at their bases. Both surfaces have tubercles, often in longitudinal lines. Their upper sides are almost flat. Their undersides are rounded. *H. margaritifera* includes several varieties and hybrids much confused as to their identifications and names. In its typical form it is a robust, stemless kind with rosettes up to 8 inches in diameter. Its tapered, triangular-ovate, firm, fleshy, dark green leaves, at first erect, later are spread. Their upper surfaces are flat or slightly hollowed; underneath they are keeled toward their apexes. Both surfaces are conspicuously decorated with large, creamy-white, rounded tubercles. *H. marginata,* related to the last, has tapered, ovate-lanceolate, short-pointed, smooth leaves without tubercles, except for a few on the keels beneath, in stemless rosettes about 4½ inches wide. They have flat upper surfaces, keeled, rounded undersides, and thin, whitish skins over dark green tissues. *H. maughanii* is stemless, much like *H. truncata.* Its 1-inch-long, erect, semicylindrical, gray-green leaves are in two opposite rows. Their apexes are cut squarely across at right angles to the length of the leaf, thus forming a flat terminal surface that is more or less translucent and admits light to the inner tissues. *H. mirabilis* forms clusters of stemless rosettes about 2 inches wide of about twenty spirally-arranged, toothed, light green, triangular leaves, translucent toward their apexes and with three to five green lines there. The upper sides are rounded toward their bases. The undersides are rounded and keeled. *H. musculina,* up to 8 inches tall, has clusters of leafy stems at first erect, later sprawling. Spreading, the pointed-ovate-lanceolate, light green to bronzy-green leaves, with conspicuous whitish tubercles, are about 1½ inches long by one-half as wide. Flat to slightly rounded above, they have rounded undersides. *H. nigra* is represented by many varieties. Typically it forms stems up to 4½ inches in length. Arranged in about five rows, the pointed-ovate, spreading leaves, at first somewhat hollowed above, later become flat or slightly rounded. Their undersides are rounded and keeled toward their tips. The black-green leaves have many roundish or elongated tubercles. *H.*

Haworthia papillosa

Haworthia planifolia

nitidula has stemless rosettes about 2 inches across that make few or no suckers. The leaves are pointed-lanceolate, under ½ inch wide, rounded beneath, slightly so on their upper surfaces, with little bristly teeth toward the apex. *H. obtusa* is represented by several varieties. Characteristically it is stemless and has rosettes approximately 2 inches wide with many more or less erect, long-ovate leaves thickened at their apexes and ending with a short, bristle-tipped point. One inch long or a little longer, they have somewhat rounded upper surfaces, with undersides keeled in their upper parts. They are grayish-green, translucent, and marked with dark lines near their tips. *H. otzenii* suckers little from its base. Its stemless rosettes a little over 2 inches across are of about fifteen erect or ascending, firm, fat, toothless leaves under ½ inch wide, translucent green toward the apex and with pale green lines. Their rounded undersides, whitish-spotted, are keeled toward their tips. *H. pallida* has clustered, stemless rosettes up to 3 inches wide of erect and ascending, pointed-lanceolate, toothed, graygreen leaves under ½ inch wide. They often have several tubercles and darker longitudinal lines. The upper surfaces are slightly, the lower ones markedly, rounded. *H. papillosa* is very handsome. It has rosettes up to 4 inches across of few longtapering, slender-pointed leaves at first erect, later spreading. Their nearly flat upper surfaces have few tubercles. Beneath, they are markedly rounded and freely sprinkled with large, conspicuous, white tubercles. *H. planifolia* is variable. There are numerous varieties. In its typical form it has stemless rosettes 2 to 4 inches wide

Haworthia reticulata

of dull light green, broad-ovate to ovate, short-pointed leaves with flat upper surfaces, the lower ones rounded and toward their translucent apexes keeled. *H. pygmaea* has rarely suckering rosettes 2 inches wide of about ten oval leaves, translucent dark green toward their apexes and with a few paler lines. Their undersides are rounded and keeled. *H. radula* has clusters of stemless rosettes of leaves 2 to 3 inches long, at their bases

about ¾ inch wide. They are green abundantly sprinkled with tiny white tubercles. Their upper surfaces are flat, their undersides often keeled. *H. reinwardtii* is an erect-stemmed species with numerous varieties. Its typical form is 4 to 6 inches tall by about 2 inches in diameter. Arranged spirally, its tapered, pointed-lanceolate, overlapping leaves are erect to somewhat recurved. About 2 inches long, they have flat upper sides sometimes with a few tubercles and much-rounded lower sides freely and conspicuously dotted with large white tubercles. *H. reticulata* has crowded clusters of stemless rosettes of very thick, oblong-lanceolate leaves that are up to 1¼ inches long, streaked longitudinally with darker lines, and tipped with a long bristle. The upper one-third of the leaves are translucent. The leaves of *H. r. acuminata* are longer than those of the typical species, and tapering. *H. retusa,* of which there are several varieties, characteristically forms clusters of stemless rosettes, each rosette 3 to 4 inches across and of ten to twenty very fat, rigid, ovate-triangular, spreading, pale green, toothed leaves, translucent toward their apexes and clearly marked with pale longitudinal lines. *H. rubrobrunnea* suckers freely. It develops a stem with long-tapered, ovate-lanceolate, reddish-brown leaves spiraled around it. The leaves, a little over 1 inch long by one-third as wide at their bases, have nearly flat upper surfaces, sometimes with a few tubercles, and rounded, blunt-keeled undersides with many, not very conspicuous tubercles. *H. rugosa* is attractive, stemless, and suckers sparingly. Its many spreading, tapered-lanceolate 3- to 4-inch-long leaves, keeled beneath, have slightly rounded upper surfaces. They are dark green, sparingly dotted above and freely dotted below with white tubercles. *H. schuldtiana* has many varieties. Typically it has tightly clustered rosettes about 1½ inches wide of bluish-, brownish-, or reddish-green, stiff, ascending, recurved, fat, sharp-pointed, lanceolate leaves with or without a few light tubercles. Their rounded, keeled undersides are marked with darker lines. The keels and leaf margins are toothed. *H. setata* has several varieties. Characteristically the beautiful, symmetrical, stemless, 2-inch-wide rosettes are of thirty to forty more or less erect, tapered-lanceolate, deep green leaves each tipped with a long bristle and with pure white bristles fringing the margins and keels. *H. subfasciata* has crowded clusters of stemless rosettes of long-tapered, triangular leaves 3 to 5 inches long. They are shiny green above and on their undersides are plentifully sprinkled with small, white, wartlike protuberances. Variety *H. s. kingiana* has similar spots on both surfaces of its leaves. *H. tenera* has crowded rosettes up to a little over 1 inch across, but often smaller, of grayish, narrow-lanceolate to narrow-ovate, leaves that become paler or have pale spots toward their bristle-tipped apexes. Their upper surfaces are slightly rounded, beneath they are much-rounded. The margins are prominently fringed with bristles. *H. tessellata* exists in numerous varieties. Its typical form is a starlike, stemless rosette, somewhat over 2 inches across, of ten to fifteen lustrous, spreading, broad-ovate-triangular, rigid, pointed leaves up to nearly or quite 1 inch wide at their

Haworthia subfasciata kingiana

bases. They are dark green or sometimes reddish. Their upper sides are flat or flattish, lustrous, and are marked with evident longitudinal lines and usually cross lines that produce a pattern of small rectangles. The rounded undersides have small white tubercles. *H. tortuosa* has stems up to 5 inches long, suckering from their bases and with three spiraled rows of overlapping, pointed-ovate-lanceolate leaves about 1½ inches long. They have hollowed upper surfaces and rounded, tubercle-spotted lower ones keeled toward their apexes. *H. triebneriana* has many varieties. Typically stemless, its rosettes are some 2½ inches in diameter. They are of thick, lanceolate to ovate, green leaves translucent toward their recurved apexes, with a center line and two smaller ones, and less than ½ inch wide at their bases. Their flat upper surfaces are rounded and keeled below and sprinkled with pale tubercles. Their margins are lined with white teeth. *H. truncata,* its name aptly means its leaves are truncated or cut off squarely at their tops, is much like *H. maughanii.* It is stemless. Erect, incurved, and in two rows, the dark greenish-brownish leaves, about ¾ inch long, are rough with tubercles. The translucent leaf tips serve as windows to admit light to the interior tissues. There are several varieties. *H. tuberculata* is represented by a few varieties. Typically it forms stemless rosettes of ovate-lanceolate leaves 2½ to 3 inches long by about 1 inch wide at their bases. Their upper sides are flat or slightly rounded, beneath they are rounded and keeled so that they are nearly triangular in cross section. Dark brownish-green, they are studded with

Haworthia turgida

many conspicuous tubercles. *H. turgida* has a few varieties. In its typical expression it forms clusters of almost stemless rosettes, 2 to 3 inches wide, of lustrous, pale green, stiffish, fat, ovate leaves with translucent apexes marked with green lines. Their upper surfaces, flat below, are rounded toward the apexes and obscurely marked with fine lines usually in a pattern of small rectangles. The undersides are rounded and keeled. *H. variegata* has stemless rosettes 1½ inches across of twenty to thirty tapering, narrow-lanceolate, pale-spotted, toothed, brown leaves. Their upper sides are nearly flat and have a conspicuous center line. The undersides are keeled toward their apexes. *H. viscosa* comes in numerous varieties. Typically

Haworthia turgida (flowers)

it forms clumps of stems up to 4 inches long closely furnished with three rows of spreading, finely-rough-surfaced, dull green, sharp-pointed leaves with overlapping bases. The leaves have hollowed upper sides and rounded lower ones, which toward their apexes are sharply-keeled.

Garden and Landscape Uses. Haworthias are among the most charming and easily grown succulent plants. In warm, frostless or essentially frostless desert or semidesert climates, they are admirable for rock gardens and similar places and are splendid for inclusion in greenhouse collections of desert plants. But beyond those obvious uses they also serve well. They are good room plants, thriving with minimum care in pots in windows, and useful for dish gardens. Their miniature proportions are especially appropriate for this last employment.

Cultivation. These plants are easily raised from seeds, but because they hybridize with notable abandon, unless pollination is very carefully controlled seeds collected from species may give rise to hybrid progeny and those from hybrid plants (and some of the so-called species belong here) produce offspring exhibiting considerable variation from the seed parent. All in all it is better to rely on means other than seeds for increasing haworthias. Most kinds make offsets freely. These, easily detached with a few roots attached, can be potted separately. Cuttings of stemmed

kinds root readily. Leaf cuttings can also be employed as a means of increase.

Soil for haworthias should be porous, well-drained, and without too much organic matter. One-third part by bulk may with advantage consist of crushed brick, perlite, or coarse grit. The remainder may be medium loam with the addition of not more than one-tenth part by bulk of leaf mold or peat moss. A dash of crushed limestone is appreciated. Do not plant in pots over-large in relation to the sizes of the plants. Make sure the receptacles are well drained.

Unlike most succulents, haworthias generally appreciate some shade from strong sun. Over-exposure results in red or purplish foliage and poor growth (the same symptoms can indicate destruction of roots by over-wetness or other cause). Shading the plants soon results in the restoration of healthy green if too much sun is the cause of the trouble, not if the roots have rotted. As with all succulents, watering must be done with some care. From mid-summer until early fall haworthias are partially dormant. Then keep them nearly dry. At other times soak the soil thoroughly at intervals, but permit it to become noticeably dryish before doing so. Ordinarily needed at intervals of two, three, or more years only, repotting is done in early fall or early spring. In greenhouses winter night temperatures of 45 to 50°F are adequate. By day increases of five

to fifteen degrees are in order. On all favorable occasions ventilate the greenhouse freely. As houseplants haworthias adapt quite well to higher temperatures if they are in a light window or if they receive supplemental artificial light. They can be grown in artificial light gardens without any natural light. For more information see Succulents.

HAWTHORN. See Crataegus. India-hawthorn is *Raphiolepis indica*. Water-hawthorn is *Aponogeton distachyus*. Yeddo-hawthorn is *Raphiolepis umbellata*.

HAZARDIA CANA is *Haplopappus canus*.

HAZEL. See Corylus and Filbert. The Chile-hazel is *Gevuina avellana*. Winter-hazel is *Corylopsis*, witch-hazel *Hamamelis*.

HAZELNUT. See Corylus and Filbert.

HE-HUCKLEBERRY is *Lyonia ligustrina*.

HEAD. More or less compact clusters of flowers, such as those of agapanthuses, geraniums, and hydrangeas, are often called heads and so are the compact masses of foliage or flower buds of broccoli, cabbage, cauliflower, and lettuce. Another usage of the word is for the tops formed of the branches of standard (tree-form) specimens of such plants as geraniums, heliotropes, and lantanas.

HEAD BACK or HEAD IN. These are terms applied to pruning back all the branches severely.

HEAL-ALL or SELF HEAL is *Prunella vulgaris*.

HEART. This word is used as part of the common names of these plants: bleeding heart (*Dicentra*), heart leaf (*Asarum*), heart-of-flame (*Bromelia balansae*), and heart seed (*Cardiospermum*).

HEARTNUT is *Juglans ailanthifolia cordiformis*.

HEARTSEASE is *Viola tricolor*.

HEARTWOOD. If a trunk or a large branch of a tree is cut across, a central core by reason of its darker color is usually visibly different from the wood that surrounds it. Sometimes the line of demarcation is sharp, sometimes less pronounced, sometimes difficult to detect. In any case the wood of the core is dead tissue no longer functioning in the life processes of the plant. It is the heartwood. The younger, usually lighter colored wood surrounding it, which consists largely of still living cells, is called sapwood. Because of its superior strength, hardness, and resistence to rot as lumber heartwood is much superior to sapwood.

HEATH. This is the common name of all members of the genus *Erica*. In Australia kinds of *Epacris* are called heaths. Other plants that have the word heath as part of their common names are heath-myrtle (*Baeckea*), Irish- or St. Dabeoc's-heath (*Daboecia cantabrica*), sea-heath (*Frankenia laevis*), and spike-heath (*Bruckenthalia spiculifolia*).

HEATH or HEATHER GARDEN. This horticultural feature is more popular in Europe than North America, although not unknown here. A heath or heather garden is an area planted chiefly with species and varieties of *Erica* and *Calluna*, so that a pleasing, satisfying landscape results. Ideally its style should be naturalistic and suggest the wildness of the moors and similar regions where these plants are abundant as natives. But often, especially in small gardens, rather tamer effects are unavoidable. Even so, the rigid formality of sharply defined beds planted with equally discrete patches of various kinds of heaths and heathers is deplorable. Such patchwork planting is more appropriate for perennial borders than heath or heather gardens.

If possible choose an open, exposed site for a garden of this kind. Much is gained if the surface slopes gently or can be contoured into low, undulating hills, or if it is relieved by a few outcropping rocks or well-placed boulders. Informally placed small groups and single specimens, sparsely introduced rather than in too great numbers, of compatible shrubs other than heaths and heathers can be incorporated to relieve flatness. Let such introductions be of kinds that suggest natural moorlands and heathlands. Among those appropriate are dwarf pines, low birches, junipers, brooms (*Cytisus* and related genera), and *Potentilla fruticosa*. Avoid those of strictly formal outline as, for instance, *Picea glauca albertiana* and such exclamation points as *Juniperus chinensis stricta*. Lower plants that associate well with heaths and heathers and can be used to good effect to supplement them and provide variety include the Irish-heath (*Daboecia*), the spike-heath (*Bruckenthalia*), bearberry (*Arctostaphylos*), sand-myrtle (*Leiophyllum*), low huckleberries (*Gaylussacia*), and blueberries (*Vaccinium*).

A meandering path or paths through the garden with natural-type surfaces rather than paved ones, of varying width and with the margins obscure and formed chiefly of the plants themselves rather than sharply defined, adds much to the scene as well as to the convenience of viewing the plants and working the garden. If you will, and traffic is not likely to be too heavy, set here and there casually, as if they were chance seedlings, a few plants of low varieties in the path itself. An occasional rock or stone may show at the path surface but do not let these be high enough to trip the unwary.

Do not be fussy in maintaining the path. It should be of the nature of a sheep track across a moor rather than that of a conventional garden path. Low grasses, creeping thymes, veronicas, potentillas, and other dwarf plants not harmed by stepping on may be planted in the right of way, but not so thickly that its earthy or gravelly surface is obscured. In locating the path avoid stylized serpentine curves. Among heaths and heathers they are ludicrous. Instead, let deviations from the straight be responsive to or apparently responsive to the need to avoid a projecting rock; a massive clump of heath, heather, or other tall plants; or a wet, boggy spot, and to the desire to follow the easiest, most convenient way around or up slopes—in short, assume temporarily the mentality of an intelligent sheep wishing to go from here to there and locate your path accordingly.

Soil for the heath or heather garden should unquestionably be somewhat acid, this even though a few of the tribe will grow in limestone earths. The truth is that most will not and those that do prosper equally as well in acid soils. It is not necessary that the earth be peaty; a sandy, loamy, even gravelly or stony soil containing a fair amount of organic matter suits. It should be well drained. The fine roots of heaths and heathers do not adapt well to cloddy or stiff clayey soils that bake and cake in dry weather.

Planting is best done in early spring. Space the plants irregularly and with some thought to their ultimate size in drifts and clumps of varying sizes and shapes and occasionally as single specimens. Do not define the outlines of the clumps and drifts. It will help the total effect if here and there a plant or two of one kind appears as a stray among a grouping of another. Let casualness be the guiding principle. If after you have finished, observers accept the planting as one developed largely by nature with but a little assistance from you, you have succeeded beyond ordinary expectations. For subsequent care of heaths and heathers see Erica and Calluna.

HEATHER. This is the common name of *Calluna vulgaris*. The word heather is also used as part of the names of these plants: beach-heather (*Hudsonia*), bell-heather (*Erica cinerea*), Christmas-heather (*Erica canaliculata*), mock-heather (*Haplopappus ericoides*), and white-heather (*Cassiope mertensiana*).

HEAVENLY-BAMBOO is *Nandina domestica*.

HEAVING OF THE SOIL. A lifting effect caused by alternate freezing and thawing of the ground can, in winter, loosen the hold young plants and others not securely anchored by deep roots have, even to lifting them out of the soil. This is called heaving. Affected plants are damaged by

their roots being torn and as a result of exposure to drying air and sun.

Precautions against damage by heaving in climates where it is prevalent include not setting small plants out too late in the fall for them to become well established before the onset of severe weather. Covering plants, as soon as the upper inch or so of the soil freezes, with a loose layer of branches of evergreens, salt hay, or similar mulch that shades and so tends to keep the surface frozen instead of alternately thawing and freezing helps to prevent heaving.

If it occurs push affected plants back into the soil promptly to minimize danger of their roots drying. Unless suitable precautions are taken very severe damage can accrue from heaving.

HEAVY SOIL. When applied to soils heavy does not refer to weight, but to the degree of tenaciousness or stickiness caused by a high clay content. Heavy soils are more difficult to work with tools and implements than light (sandy) ones, but are more retentive of nutrients and moisture and properly managed are often fertile and highly productive. Because they warm later in spring than light soils they are generally less well suited for producing early crops.

HEBE (Hè-be). Formerly included in *Veronica* and still sometimes so called by gardeners, *Hebe*, of the figwort family SCROPHULARIACEAE, is most abundant in New Zealand. A few of its more than 100 species occur in Australia, Tasmania, and New Guinea, and two in South America, one of the latter extending to the Falkland Islands. The name, derived from the Greek *hebe*, youth, is not of apparent particular application.

The group differs technically from *Veronica* in the manner in which its seed capsules open, more obviously in being leathery-leaved, evergreen shrubs or small trees with always opposite leaves, rather than herbaceous or subshrubby plants with softer, mostly deciduous leaves, the uppermost usually alternate. Except in small seedlings the leaves of hebes are generally toothless and mostly have only the mid-vein conspicuous. The small flowers are in branched or branchless spikes or racemes from the leaf axils or from the ends of the stems. They have calyxes with usually four lobes, or four lobes and a fifth smaller one. The short- or long-tubed corollas have four spreading lobes (petals). There are two stamens and a long style tipped with a rounded stigma. The fruits are capsules. All species discussed below inhabit New Zealand.

Popular *H. brachysiphon* is frequently misidentified as *H. traversii*, a name which properly belongs to a closely allied species perhaps not in cultivation and differing

Hebe speciosa

Hebe 'La Seduisante'

Hebe 'Alicia Amherst'

summer, originate from leaf axils near the ends of the shoots. The flowers are up to ⅓ inch in diameter and have purple-brown anthers. This is probably the most cold-resistant species.

Highly variable, and hybridizing freely with others, **H. speciosa** in its homeland inhabits sea cliffs. A rounded shrub 3 to 6 feet tall, it has hairless shoots, and thick, glossy, nearly stalkless, broad-elliptic to obovate-oblong leaves 2 to 4 inches long by about one-half as wide. Usually longer than the leaves, and not branched, the spikes of crowded, reddish-purple to violet-purple flowers come from the leaf axils. In its typical form which is rare in cultivation, this species is a parent of several excellent hybrids. Hardier than *H. speciosa*, which it much resembles, handsome and vigorous *H.* 'Alicia Amherst' is 3 to 4 feet tall and has elliptic to elliptic-ovate leaves up to 3½ inches long by 1½ inches wide. Its quite large, deep-violet flowers are crowded in racemes up to 3 inches long or a little longer. Another close ally of *H. speciosa* but less hardy, *H.* 'La Seduisante' has elliptic leaves 2 to 4 inches long and with purple undersides when young. Its dark magenta-purple flowers are in racemes 3 to 4 inches long. Another native of sea coasts, **H. elliptica** (syn. *H. decussata*) is indigenous to southern South America and the Falkland Islands as well as New Zealand. About 6 feet tall and freely branched, or less commonly a tree up to 20 feet tall, it has shoots with short, stiff hairs. Its elliptic to elliptic-oblong or obovate-oblong, somewhat fleshy leaves ½ inch to 1¼ inches long, have hairless stalks, but the margins of the blades are

from *H. brachysiphon* in having flowers with very slender corolla tubes and seed capsules about four times as long instead of only two times as long as the calyx lobes. A dense, rounded, broad shrub up to 6 feet tall or sometimes taller, *H. brachysiphon* has rather slender, erect, hairless or finely-hairy branches that with age become quite smooth. Crowded along the shoots in four longitudinal rows, the overlapping, dullish green leaves are narrowly-oblong to narrowly-elliptic or slightly obovate and ½ to 1 inch long by up to ¼ inch wide. About twice as long as the leaves or somewhat longer, the branchless racemes of white flowers, displayed in late white-hairy. The dense, branchless, erect racemes, from the upper leaf axils, are 1 inch to 1½ inches long and are of fourteen or fewer white or bluish, fragrant blooms up to ⅔ inch across. Showier *H. bollonsii* is a coastal species 3 to 6 feet in height that has finely-hairy shoots and more or less erect, glossy, broad-elliptic leaves 1½ to 3½ inches in length. Its long-stalked, branchless racemes of white, faintly bluish to rich lilac, ⅜ inch wide blooms are two times or more as long as the leaves.

The kind identified as *H. buxifolia* may not be distinct from *H. odora*, a variable species that attains heights up to about 5 feet but apparently is not cultivated. The shoots of *H. buxifolia* carry two lines of hairs and its overlapping, four-ranked, elliptic-ovate leaves, glossy on their upper sides, and with beveled, hairless margins, are mostly ⅓ to ⅔ inch long. The ½- to 1-inch-long, often branched, stalked flower spikes are generally in threes at the branch ends. The blooms, ¼ to ⅓ inch across, are white. This sort withstands cold, heat and drought better than most hebes. A robust form of *H. odora* has been called **H. menziesii**, but according to modern interpretations does not differ sufficiently from *H. odora* to warrant separate specific identification. Its leaves are ¾ to 1 inch in length, the flower spikes are mostly or all lateral, and usually solitary. The flowers are comparatively large.

Hebe diosmifolia

Much-branched **H. diosmifolia,** as known in cultivation 2 to 5 feet tall, is reported to attain up to 20 feet in the wild. It has minutely-downy young shoots and flower stalks, and short-stalked, narrowly-oblong to narrowly-elliptic leaves ½ to 1 inch long by up to ⅙ inch wide. Their up-

per surfaces are dark green, their undersides paler. Borne near the ends of the shoots, the ¼ to ⅓ inch wide, lavender-blue to white flowers are in rounded clusters ¾ to 1 inch in diameter. They have usually a three-lobed calyx. About 3 feet in height, and glaucous, **H. glaucophylla** has slender, hairy shoots, the hairs usually in two lines. The lanceolate to pointed-elliptic leaves are ½ to ¾ inch long. Branchless, the racemes, from the leaf axils, are of white flowers that have ovaries with stiff, scattered hairs; they are 1 inch to 1½ inches long. A mountain species some 4½ feet tall, **H. venustula** (syn. *H. laevis*) has shoots with two lines of hairs, and bright green, elliptic-oblong leaves, with dull undersides, up to ¾ inch long by up to ¼ inch wide. The racemes, about 1½ inches long, of white flowers have one or two pairs of branches or none.

Hebe salicifolia

Hebe salicifolia (flowers)

A variable species much given to hybridizing with others, *H. salicifolia* is a loosely-branched shrub up to 15 feet tall. Its shoots are hairless, its lanceolate leaves, 2 to 6 inches long by up to 1 inch wide, taper from above their middles into long-pointed apexes. Sometimes their margins are minutely-toothed. The slen-

der-cylindrical, branchless flower spikes, up to 6 inches or sometimes longer, are from the leaf axils. The blooms are small and white to pale lilac. This species inhabits southern Chile as well as New Zealand.

Low species include *H. buchananii, H. chathamica, H. epacridea,* and *H. hulkeana.* Much-branched from the base, **H. buchananii** is 6 inches to 1½ feet tall. It has black, rather crooked stems, the younger shoots with two lines of hairs. The crowded, broad-ovate, spreading, dull, stiff leaves are normally not over ¼ inch long by almost as broad as long, but they may be somewhat larger on cultivated specimens. The branchless spikes of white flowers, from the leaf axils, are about ¾ inch long. Prostrate **H. chathamica** grows on cliffs washed by sea spray. It has slender, trailing stems and thickish, elliptic to obovate-oblong leaves ½ inch to 1¼ inches long by ¼ to nearly ½ inch wide. They are disposed more or less in one plane. Its purple flowers are in branchless spikes about 1 inch long and nearly as wide. They come from the leaf axils. Very stiff, rigid leaves are characteristic of much-branded, prostrate **H. epacridea.** In overlapping, opposite pairs, the recurved, dull green leaves, those of each pair united at their bases, are pointed-ovate and about ³⁄₁₆ inch long. The tiny, white, slender-tubed, fragrant flowers are in compact, egg-shaped clusters, ½ inch to 1¼ inches long, that terminate the shoots. Rather uncommon in cultivation, but a very worthwhile ornamental, **H. hulkeana** is up to 1 foot high. It has prostrate stems and is distinct from other kinds described here in having distinctly-toothed leaves. They are oblong-elliptic to nearly round, glossy above, paler beneath, and 1½ to 3 inches long or occasionally longer. The lavender to white flowers are in spikes branched to form broad panicles up to 1 foot in length.

Hebe hulkeana

Hebe ochracea

Hebe andersonii

Whipcord hebes is a group name for a number of species of small shrubs that have stems that suggest cords because their little, stalkless, scalelike leaves overlap to give a braided effect. The flowers are in short, branchless, terminal spikes. Most likely of these curiosities to be cultivated, **H. cupressoides** has much the aspect of some strange conifer. It is a slow-growing, symmetrical, rounded, compact, glaucous bush 3 to 6 feet tall. The branchlets are erect and flexible. The minute, fleshy, narrowly-triangular, scale-like leaves hug the stems. The white to pale blue flowers, ⅛ inch in diameter, are in loose racemes of three to eight. They make no significant display. Usually less than 2 feet tall, loosely-branched **H. ochracea** (syn. *H. armstrongii*) has blackish stems with the ultimate branchlets pointing upward. About ¹⁄₁₆ inch long and closely pressed against the stems, the triangular leaves of this whipcord sort are olive-green, tinged at their tops and margins with yellow. The tiny white flowers are in short, terminal spikes.

Hybrid hebes are numerous and often confusing to identify. One of the most commonly cultivated, and a highly satisfactory garden plant, is **H. andersonii,** the parents of which are *H. salicifolia* and *H. speciosa*. Intermediate between its parents, this has spikes of bloom, white at their bases and rich violet above. Popular variety *H. a. variegata* has foliage beautifully variegated with creamy-white. Attractive **H. cranleighensis** is a hybrid with narrow, willow-like leaves and from the upper leaf axils longish-stalked spikes of flowers. These flowers are light pink at first but become white as they age. The hybrid be-

Hebe cranleighensis

tween *H. speciosa* and *H. elliptica* is **H. franciscana.** The form commonly cultivated is known as *H. f.* 'Blue Gem'. It has been misidentified as *H. decussata,* which is properly a synonym of *H. elliptica*. A hybrid between *H. speciosa* and an undetermined species, **H. carnea** is of rather loose habit. In favorable locations it may be 10 feet tall. It has spikes, smaller than those of *H. speciosa,* of rose-pink flowers. Possibly a hybrid between *H. speciosa* and *H.*

salicifolia, but perhaps only a variant of the first, **H. imperialis** much resembles *H. speciosa*. Of compact habit, this beautiful hebe is 3 to 5 feet tall. It has reddish foliage and long racemes of glowing, reddish-purple or violet-purple flowers. Prostrate *H.* 'Autumn Glory', probably of hybrid origin and a splendid groundcover, has small, dark green foliage and dense spikes of beautiful purplish-blue blooms displayed over a long season.

Garden and Landscape Uses. Hebes are grand shrubs for landscaping in California, the Pacific Northwest, and other regions of mild winters. They are admired for their habits of growth, beautiful foliage, and most kinds for their fine displays of bloom that are attractive for long periods. They do well in a variety of soils that are not too dry and are especially suitable for locations near the sea. Although hebes are singularly free of diseases and pests, neglected specimens may become infested with scale insects.

Cultivation. Few shrubs are easier to handle and maintain than hebes. Watering in dry weather is needed. A moisture-conserving mulch minimizes the need for it. Hebes are naturally shapely, and unless they are to be restricted to smaller size than they grow naturally, pruning is rarely or never needed. They stand pruning well, however, and develop new shoots readily from below the cuts. Neglected examples can be restored to vigor and beauty by sensible use of the knife or pruning shear. Propagation is very easy by cuttings in a greenhouse or cold frame propagating bed, or in flats, which, after the cuttings are planted, are covered with polyethylene plastic film stretched over a frame of wire or wood strips.

In addition to their usefulness as outdoor ornamentals in mild climates, the showier flowered kinds, such as *H. speciosa*, and its hybrids, are good greenhouse pot plants. In containers they are useful decorations for terraces and patios. They succeed in ordinary fertile soil under cool greenhouse conditions. In winter a night temperature of 45 to 50°F is satisfactory, with a few degrees more by day permitted. The soil should always be moderately moist. Regular applications of dilute liquid fertilizer from spring to fall are beneficial.

HEBENSTRETIA (Heben-strètia). This African genus of the figwort family SCROPHULARIACEAE has a name sometimes spelled *Hebenstreitia* that commemorates John Ernst Hebenstreit, professor of medicine at Leipzig, Germany, who died in 1757. It comprises forty species of annuals, herbaceous perennials, and shrubs, with chiefly alternate leaves, but the lower ones sometimes opposite. The flowers, in spikes, have bractlike or spathelike, sometimes minutely-toothed calyxes, sometimes membranous or translucent, and shorter than the true bracts from the axils of which the blooms come. The flowers have slender-tubed corollas, often split for some distance at the front, and with one lip with three, four, or occasionally five small lobes. There are four stamens and a slender style. The fruits are nonsplitting capsules.

An annual or perennial 1 foot to 2 feet tall and native to South Africa, *Hebenstretia dentata* is branched, and has linear to linear-oblanceolate leaves ½ inch to 1½ inches long, toothed toward their apexes. The flower spikes are dense and up to 4 inches long. The blooms have calyxes with two small teeth and white corollas with an orange blotch in the throat. The corolla tubes are split for about one-half their lengths. The central pair of lobes of the lip are longer and narrower than the two side ones.

Also South African, *H. comosa* is a herbaceous perennial 2 to 4 feet tall, with somewhat woody stems, and linear-lanceolate, coarsely-toothed, stalkless leaves 1 inch to 2½ inches long. Its white or yellow blooms, marked with an orange-red blotch, are ½ inch long. They are in dense spikes 2 to 6 inches in length, and at night are fragrant. Another herbaceous perennial of South Africa, *H. integrifolia* is 6 inches to 2 feet tall. It has downy shoots and undivided, smooth or somewhat rough-hairy, threadlike leaves ½ inch to

Hebenstretia integrifolia

1¼ inches long. In cylindrical, terminal spikes, 3 to 6 inches in length, its yellow flowers suffused with red are a little over ½ inch long.

Garden and Landscape Uses and Cultivation. The species described are usually grown as annuals for their profuse displays of mignonette-like spikes of bloom. The flowers do not last when cut. Although less popular than many showier annuals, they are well worth including in flower beds for beauty and variety. Seeds may be sown in spring outdoors and the seedlings thinned out to about 4 inches apart. An alternative procedure, and a better one where the growing season is rather short, is to sow indoors in a temperature of 65 to 70°F some eight weeks before it is safe to transplant the young plants to the garden, which is done as soon as the weather moderates after the last frost, and is settled. The seedlings are transplanted 2 inches apart in flats, or individually to small pots, and are kept in a sunny greenhouse where the night temperature is 50°F and that by day five to fifteen degrees higher, until about ten days before planting out time. Then the flats or pots of young plants are stood in a cold frame or sheltered place outdoors to harden off in preparation for planting. Young plants grown without pinching are spaced about 4 inches apart, but if when they were 3 or 4 inches tall the tips of their stems were taken out they branch, and such plants are set in the garden 6 to 8 inches apart. When the first flush of bloom is over, the plants are cut back to a height of 6 or 8 inches. They then produce new shoots that bloom later. Hebenstretias are not frost hardy.

HECHTIA (Hécht-ia). In aspect similar to nearly related *Dyckia*, the about forty-five species of *Hechtia* belong to the pineapple family BROMELIACEAE. Chiefly natives of desert and semidesert regions in Mexico,

Hechtia argentea at the Royal Botanic Gardens, Kew, England; this specimen was shown in Belgium in 1864, photographed in 1978

but extending to El Salvador and Texas, unlike the majority of the pineapple family they grow in the ground instead of perched as epiphytes on trees. The name commemorates Julius Gottfried Konrad Hecht, a Prussian, who died in 1837. At the Royal Botanic Gardens, Kew, Surrey, England, there is still displayed in flourishing condition a splendid specimen of *H. argentea* that was exhibited at Brussels, Belgium, in 1864.

Hechtias have little floral beauty. Their chief attractions are their habits of growth and foliage. The blooms, small, somewhat dowdy and inconsequential, are in mostly tall, slender or wide-branching panicles. They differ from those of *Dyckia* in that they are unisexual, each individual plant being male or female. Generally the blooms have remnants of the organs of the nonfunctional sex present. The flower stalks of nearly all kinds normally come from one side of the rosette, rarely are they central and terminal. Each flower has a perianth of three each sepals and petals, the latter usually quite separate, six stamens, and a three-parted style. The fruits are capsules.

The Texan hechtias number three species including rare *H. texensis*, a local endemic of dry limestone bluffs, with loosely wide-branched panicles of bloom, and very similar *H. scariosa*, of wider distribution in similar habitats in Texas and Mexico. These have dense rosettes of linear-triangular leaves margined with distantly-spaced spines, and covered thickly on their undersides with white, scurfy scales. The flower panicles are up to 6 feet tall. Those of *H. scariosa* are shorter than those of *H. texensis*, and their flowers are more crowded. Also, the sepals, in both species whitish, are much longer instead of only as long as broad, and have usually one to three chief veins instead of five. Inhabiting gravelly and sandstone soils in Mexico as well as Texas, *H. glomerata* forms rosettes of viciously spiny, lanceolate leaves, closer together than those of other Texan hechtias, and their undersides densely beset with whitish or light brown scales. The panicles of bloom, about 5 feet in height, have flowers with blunt or short-pointed, brown sepals.

Mexican species likely to be met with in the collections of desert plant enthusiasts include *H. argentea,* with recurving leaves about 1 foot long, sharply spined, and to a greater or lesser extent lustrous-silvery on both surfaces; *H. capituligera,* slightly smaller, and with foliage of a translucent light amber hue; *H. ghiesbreghtii,* with recurving leaves about 8 inches long, conspicuously spined, channeled, and marked with red brown above; *H. marnier-lapostollei,* with spiny leaves 5 to 10 inches long, scurfy toward their apexes, and brownish at their bases; *H. podantha* with grayish-green, recurving, spiny leaves, and flower stems up to 6 feet tall; *H. schottii,* with lustrous green leaves with white longitudinal lines on their undersides; *H. stenopetala,* with lanceolate, recurved, big-spined leaves 2 feet long, and flower panicles up to 6 feet tall; and *H. tillandsioides,* which has long, narrow, very small-spined, tapering leaves that tend to curve in many directions and loose flower panicles with long, slender branches.

Garden and Landscape Uses and Cultivation. As components of desert plant collections hechtias have much to recommend them. Most have rosettes 1½ to 2 feet across and so are less appropriate than dyckias for small greenhouses, window gardens, and other places where space is at a premium. They can be displayed with handsome effects in more roomy areas. Hechtias associate well with rocks and are excellent embellishments for desert rock gardens. They love bright sun and high summer temperatures.

Excellently drained, coarse soil suits them. In winter they withstand low temperatures, but should not be subjected to freezing. In greenhouses winter night temperatures of 40 to 50°F are adequate, with a daytime increase of five to fifteen degrees. Water is given in moderate amounts from spring to fall, only just enough to keep the soil from drying completely in winter. Repotting is needed at intervals of several years only. Propagation is by offsets and by seeds. For more information see Bromeliads or Bromels.

HEDEOMA (Hed-eòma) — American-Pennyroyal, Squaw Root. Here belong about twenty-five natives of the western hemisphere. They are strong-scented annuals and perennial herbaceous plants of the mint family LABIATAE. The name derives from the Greek *hedyosmon,* the name of an Old World mint (*Mentha*).

Hedeomas have square stems, small opposite leaves, and little blue or purple, slightly two-lipped, stalked blooms in numerous few-flowered clusters in the leaf axils. The upper lip of the tubular corolla is erect and notched, the lower spreading and three-lobed. There are two stamens about as long as the upper lip and ascending beneath it. Hedeomas are of little or no ornamental value.

American-pennyroyal (*Hedeoma pulegioides*) must not be confused with the pennyroyal of Europe and Asia (*Mentha*

Hechtia texensis

Hechtia marnier-lapostollei

Hedera helix '238th Street'

Hedera helix climbing a tree

Hedera canariensis

Helianthus annuus flore-pleno

Heliopsis helianthoides scabra

Helichrysum angustifolium

Helichrysum bracteatum

pulegium). The flowers of the latter have four stamens. Native to woodlands and roadsides from Quebec and Nova Scotia to Michigan, South Dakota, Alabama, and Arkansas, the American-pennyroyal is an annual with erect, usually much-branched, slender stems 6 inches to 1½ feet tall and finely-pubescent, at least in their upper parts. The lanceolate to elliptic or obovate leaves have short stalks and are sometimes toothed. They are ½ to 1 inch long or slightly longer. The flowers, up to ¼ inch long, have corollas scarcely longer than the calyxes. Bluish-purple, they are borne in summer. Other species of *Hedeoma* may occasionally be brought into gardens but the American-pennyroyal is the one most frequently cultivated.

Garden and Other Uses. American-pennyroyal is primarily a herb garden plant. From it is brewed an excellent tea that has been recommended as an alleviant of colds, fevers, headaches, nausea, and other ills. It is reported to be a mild stimulant. Because it was used to relieve disorders of American Indian women it became known as squaw root. Some Indians believed that regular drinking of the hot tea had a contraceptive effect. The tea is made in the manner of ordinary tea; to boil it destroys its flavor. Rubbed over the skin, fresh leaves and stems of this plant serve as an insect repellent. The dried herb, in sachets, was placed among woolens to discourage moths, and strewn in dog houses to, it was hoped, keep away fleas.

Cultivation. American-pennyroyal is best grown in a lean soil. In earth too rich it does not develop its aromatic qualities to the fullest. An acid, dryish rooting medium and light shade suit it best. Seeds are sown in spring where the plants are to remain and the seedlings thinned to 4 to 6 inches apart. This herb is cut in June or July and dried in a cool, airy place. When quite dry it is stored in tightly sealed jars or other containers.

HEDERA (Héd-era)—Ivy. Ivy, without such adjectival qualification as German, Swedish, or Boston, properly means *Hedera*. Even when preceded by certain geographical indicators, for example English, Baltic, and Algerian, it still alludes to *Hedera*. That is the genus of the classical or true ivies, natives from the Canary Islands, Madeira, North Africa, and Europe to China, Taiwan, and Japan. None is indigenous to the western hemisphere. Some are naturalized there. Botanists differ in their interpretations as to how many species are involved. Four or five are conservative figures. In addition there are many, in the case of English ivy, perhaps a hundred natural and hoticultural varieties. This genus belongs in the aralia family ARALIACEAE. Its name is the ancient Latin one for ivy.

Hederas are, except for some bushy types, artificially maintained as propagations of fruiting parts of vining species, evergreen vines that if given opportunity climb by attaching their stems to tree trunks, cliffs, walls, and similar supports by adventitious rootlets from the stems. Without support they trail and root into the ground. All have two very distinct stages, the juvenile, in which the stems vine and no flowers or fruits are produced, and the adult, in which flowers and fruits are borne abundantly and, characteristically, the stems are neither vining nor rooting (see *H. helix* '238th Street' for an exception to this). The juvenile stage persists for many years, commonly several decades. Indeed unless the plants have opportunity to climb to a considerable height, it remains a stable feature. High-climbing specimens eventually assume adult characteristics, that is, their upper parts do; the lower stems remain vinelike. Not only are flowers and fruits produced, but the leaves of the shrubby adult parts differ in shape and arrangement from those of the vining portions. They are lobeless or scarcely lobed and instead of being two-ranked are borne all around the stems. Excellent examples of tall English ivies with bushy adult upper parts and vining lower stems are to be seen on many trees at Williamsburg, Virginia, and many other places in the south. By propagating from adult shoots horticulturists have developed the so-called tree ivies more commonly seen in Europe than America.

Identifying characteristics of the genus *Hedera* are the alternate, long-stalked, leathery leaves, heart-shaped to angled or more or less deeply-lobed. The young shoots, leaves, and stalks of the flower clusters are furnished with stellate (star-shaped) hairs or scales or both. Borne in stalked umbels that are solitary or in terminal racemes or panicles, the small, yellowish-green flowers of ivies, favorites of

English ivy climbing trees, at Williamsburg, Virginia: (a) The trunk and lower branches of one tree is clothed with ivy

(b) This ivy has ascended a tree; a few feet above the ground it has assumed adult characteristics and developed as a dense bush of foliage

Hedera helix: (a) As a vine

(b) As a groundcover

bees, have five-lobed or five-toothed ca-lyxes, five each spreading petals and sta-mens, and one style with an obscurely five-lobed stigma. The fruits are berry-like drupes (fruits constructed like plums) con-taining four or five seeds. Most commonly black when ripe, they are sometimes yel-low, orange, or cream. Identification of ivies as to species is based chiefly on the characteristics of the minute hairs on the young shoots, undersides of the leaves, and stalks of the flower clusters. These may be stellate, that is radiate like the spokes of a wheel from the tops of very short erect stalks, or be scaly, rest directly on the leaf surface and have flat, more or less united, sometimes forked, radiating arms. A good hand lens is needed for crit-ical examination of the hairs.

English ivy (**H. helix**), variable in the wild, is extremely so in cultivation. The number of horticultural varieties and the confusion of the application of names to many of them is little short of horrendous. Some of the more distinct and popular ones are described below. Others are listed in the catalogs of specialist growers. In its typical form, *H. helix* is a high-climb-ing vine or groundcover with the hairs of its young shoots, leaves, and flowering parts all stellate and with four to six arms or rays. The leaf blades, 1 inch to 2½ inches long and broad, are thick, leathery, dark green, and when mature, have con-spicuous, raised, grayish-white veins. They are mostly five-lobed with the ter-minal lobe about as broad as long. Some-times the two basal lobes are much re-duced in size or are absent. In the adult phase the leaves are without lobes and generally are wedge-shaped or at least not

Hedera helix (fruit)

Hedera helix hibernica on a wall

Hedera helix baltica, the type (original) plant at the Arnold Arboretum, Jamaica Plain, Massachusetts

markedly heart-shaped at their bases. The fruits are black. Much ivy grown in the United States as common English ivy is more properly the Irish ivy (*H. h. hibernica*). Its origin slightly obscure, there seems no doubt that it is a natural variant that originated in southwest Ireland. From typical *H. helix* it differs in its more robust growth and larger foliage. The blades of its leaves are 2 to 6 inches long and wide. Their veins, paler than the body of the leaf, are light green, not grayish-white. The stellate hairs of the shoots have six to eight rays, those of the leaves usually only four. Irish-ivy is a tetraploid, in appearance intermediate between typical English ivy and Algerian ivy. Apparently a variant of the Irish ivy, *H. h. maculata* has white or cream, spotted or streaked foliage without the variegation being in marginal bands. Also similar to Irish ivy, *H. h. lobata-major* differs most obviously in the terminal lobe of its large leaves being considerably bigger and the clefts between it and the side lobes narrower.

Baltic ivy (*H. h. baltica*) is one of the two most cold-resistant cultivated ivies. The other is *H. h.* '238th Street'. From typical English ivy, Baltic ivy is scarcely distinguishable by any observable morphological characteristic. Attempts have been made to separate the two on the basis that the stellate hairs of Baltic ivy are often eight-rayed, but this is by no means always conclusive. For practical purposes, except for its greater hardiness, Baltic ivy and the typical form of English ivy are identical.

238th Street ivy (*H. h.* '238th Street') is a very distinct, exceptionally hardy variety of English ivy. Beyond that it was first observed established in a planting in the

Hedera helix '238th Street', the original plant on a chain-link fence bounding the grounds of a church on 238th Street, the Bronx, New York City

Bronx, New York City, and described by Thomas H. Everett of the New York Botanical Garden, nothing is known of its origin. Its leaves are heart-shaped and without lobes. Even when young it flowers and fruits profusely. Unique among ivies, it produces from the flowering branches long vining shoots. These have leaves smaller than the 2- to 3-inch-wide ones of the flowering shoots. This ivy makes a

splendid groundcover, or with slight support an upright bush.

Many other varieties of English ivy are grown, some primarily as indoor plants, others outdoors. Among kinds favored for indoor cultivation are some, classified as the ramosa group, that naturally produce lateral branches in great abundance and so are distinctly bushy. There are rigidly erect varieties, small and shrublike. There are

Hedera helix '238th Street': (a) Characteristic long vining, root-producing shoots

"tree ivies," shrublike and the stems not producing aerial rootlets. These are obtained by propagating from adult-type shoots..There are varieties with variegated foliage. Differences in habits of growth, shapes and sizes of leaves, patterns and colors of variegation must all be taken into consideration when attempting to identify English ivy varieties. We shall now consider some of the most notable ones. Others are offered in trade lists. New ones appear from time to time.

Vining varieties of English ivy, their foliage not variegated and in all except the first green, include the following varieties: *H. h.* 'Buttercup' (syn. 'Russell Gold') is the finest yellow-foliaged variety. At first rich yellow, the leaves change to yellowish-green as they age. Except that in young leaves the terminal lobe is longer, this except in color resembles typical English ivy. *H. h. crenata* is very like *H. h. digitata,* but has less plentiful aerial roots, stouter shoots, and wavy, less deeply-lobed leaves sometimes with very few blunt teeth. *H. h. deltoidea* is distinct by reason of its heart-shaped leaves, which have overlapping basal lobes and are without other lobing. *H. h. digitata* merges into the typical species.

Hedera helix digitata

(b) Rootless, flowering and fruiting shoots

Its five- to seven-lobed leaves, the lobes alike in size and shape, are without markedly wavy margins and are generally toothless. *H. h. glymii* (syn. *H. cordata*) has rooting stems and essentially lobeless, often somewhat twisted, ovate, lustrous, apple-green leaves up to about 1½ inches long, and usually broader than long. Their basal lobes rarely overlap. *H. h. gracilis,* a spindly kind, has slender, freely-rooting, reddish stems and reddish-stalked, three- to five-lobed, wavy-edged, whitish-veined leaves up to nearly 2 inches long. The terminal lobe is largest. *H. h. helvetica* (syn. *H. h.* 'Leyland') is a very hardy kind much like *H. h. sagittaefolia* from which it differs in its

Distinctive varieties of *Hedera helix:* (a) 'Curlylocks', with roundish, wavy-edged leaves with paler veins

(b) 'Green Spear', with spear-shaped green leaves with paler veins

leaves have purplish stalks and the edges of the blades become reddish in fall.

Bushy, nonvining English ivies include horticultural specimens, sometimes called tree ivies, that have resulted from propagating from adult, flowering and fruiting branches of normally vining kinds. Although these, from a genetical viewpoint do not warrant a varietal name they are often alluded to as *H. h. arborescens.* Much less common in North America than in Europe, they grow slowly, but eventually make dense, rounded shrubs 8 feet or so high and as much through. They flower and fruit freely. Slow-growing *H. h. conglomerata* makes a dome 1 foot or so high of rigid, at first erect, later sprawling, often contorted stems that have abundant aerial roots. Its more or less two-ranked leaves have dull, three- to five-lobed,

veins of its leaves being whiter and the hairs usually having four to six rays. *H. h. minima* is a name not applied to any well-defined variant, but is most properly a kind similar to *H. h. pedata.* But it is more variable than that variety in the size and lobe characteristics of its leaves. It belies its name by not infrequently having its generally deeply-, three- to five-lobed, usually bronzy-green leaves ¾ inch to 5 inches long. Their terminal lobes may range from narrowly-lanceolate to fairly broad-triangular. Their bases are heart-shaped. *H. h. pedata* (syn. *H. h. caenwoodiana*) is akin to *H. h. minima.* Its bright green, mostly deeply five-lobed leaves often have a few marginal teeth. *H. h. poetica*, native from the Balkan Peninsula to the Caucasus, and sometimes called Italian ivy, has shallowly-lobed or nearly lobeless, triangular to ovate leaves, the juvenile

ones glossier than those of typical English ivy. In winter the foliage often assumes a bright coppery-bronze hue. The fruits are larger than those of the species and are yellow. *H. h. sagittaefolia* (syn. *H. h. taurica*) has hairy, more or less arrow-shaped, dull leaves, the basal lobes spreading or pointing backward, the terminal lobe much longer than the others. Some or many of the hairs are eight-rayed. *H. h. scutifolia* is a variable kind with small, reddish-stalked, heart-shaped, dark green leaves with distinctly pale veins.

English ivy varieties with variegated foliage include these as well as others listed in the catalogs of specialists: *H. h. aureovariegata*, has cream to deepish yellow variegation confined to the leaf margins or consisting of blotches and streaks throughout. Sometimes plain green leaves are produced. *H. h. 'California Gold'* is freely-branched and bushy. Its roundish, shallowly-lobed leaves, especially the younger ones, are marbled with yellow. *H. h. cavendishii* (syn. *H. marginata*) has small, triangular to ovate to five-lobed leaves up to 2½ inches long, margined, often narrowly, with white or ivory-white. The midrib is raised. *H. h. discolor* (syn. *H. h. marmorata*) differs from the typical species in at least some of its foliage being more or less flecked or sometimes blotched with white or yellow. *H. h. 'Glacier'* is similar to the form of *H. h. cavendishii* often identified as *H. h. marginata.* Its leaves are pink-edged and variegated with pale gray-green and ivory-white. *H. h. 'Gold Heart'* is slender-stemmed. Its small, red-stalked, three- or five-lobed leaves have golden-yellow and cream centers. *H. h. palmato-aurea* has leaves similar to those of *H. h. digitata*, but, especially the younger ones, blotched, streaked, or margined with yellow. *H. h. tricolor* is very like *H. h. cavendishii* except that its

Hedera arborescens, of gardens: (a) Typical shrublike specimen

(b) Young plant in bloom

wavy or cupped blades ½ inch to 1½ inches long. Variety *H. h. erecta* (syn. *H. h. conglomerata-erecta*) differs from the last in that its stems, rarely contorted, remain erect and its more obviously longitudinally-channeled leaves have sharper-

Hedera helix pedata

Hedera helix conglomerata

Hedera canariensis

pointed, shallower lobes and are usually more definitely two-ranked. This presumably is the kind offered as *H. c. congesta*.

Other bushy ivies, low, dense, and characterized by the very abundant production of branches from the leaf axils, are grouped as ramosa or self-branching ivies. The varieties that belong here are not always clearly distinct, and some tend to revert to types from which they have sported (mutated). Notable among ramosa varieties is *H. h.* 'Pittsburgh', the first of the complex. This apparently originated between 1915 and 1920 probably as a sport of *H. h. hibernica*. Its side branches are especially numerous on the lower halves of the shoots and often they branch again. The leaves, up to 1½ inches long and mostly five-lobed, are lighter green than those of typical English ivy. Variety *H. h.* 'Albany' (syn. *H. h. dankeri*) resembles in foliage *H. h. hibernica*. Stout-stemmed and with few or no aerial roots, this has five- or occasionally three-lobed leaves ¾ inch to 3 inches long. Often the shoots are flattened and broadened (fasciated). Other ramosa varieties, all or most derived directly or indirectly from *H. h.* 'Pittsburgh', include 'Green Quartz', 'Hahn's Self-Branching', 'Lee Silver', 'Maple Queen', *H. h. meagheri* (syn. 'Green Feather'), 'Merion Beauty', 'Needlepoint', and 'Sylvanian'.

Algerian ivy (*H. canariensis* syn. *H. helix canariensis*) not only inhabits, as its botanical name implies, the Canary Islands, but also the Azores, Madeira, northwest Africa, and Portugal. It apparently intergrades in some

parts of its range with English ivy and some botanists treat it as a variety of that. As known in cultivation, however, it is distinct. It differs from English ivy in having mostly bigger leaves in the juvenile phase, up to 6 or even 8 inches in diameter, heart-shaped at their bases and shallowly three- or five-lobed, in the adult form lobeless and with rounded bases. The leafstalks are usually burgundy-red. A more critical determining feature is that the stellate hairs generally have twelve to sixteen branches or rays fused for one-quarter of their length from their bases. Most commonly cultivated is *H. c. azorica*. The young shoots and foliage of this are clothed with tawny, felted hairs. The comparatively bright green leaves, 3 to 6 inches wide, have in the juvenile phase five or seven blunt, ovate lobes. Its mostly ovate leaves, irregularly marked and blotched with green, gray-green, and creamy-white, *H. c. variegata* (syn. *H. c.* 'Gloire de Marengo') is a handsome ivy with reddish-purple stems. Much like this, *H. c. margine-maculata* has the cream-colored marginal areas of the leaves more or less flecked and marbled with dull green. Others with variegated foliage are *H. c.* 'Canary Cream', which has leaves variegated with ivory-white or sometimes completely so colored, and *H. c. striata*, which has leaves with dark green margins and middle portions streaked with ivory-

Hedera canariensis variegata

white or pale green. Known as variegated ghost tree, an erect, bushy, nonvining variety of *H. canariensis* that has ovate, lobeless green, gray, and cream variegated leaves is a tree ivy that originated by propagating from adult type shoots.

Hedera helix 'Merion Beauty'

Hedera canariensis margine-masculata

Hedera colchica dentata-variegata

Its huge leaves a distinctive feature, **H. colchica** is native to Asia Minor and the region of the Caucasus. From other ivies this differs in the scales forming a scurfy covering of its young shoots and flower stalks having fifteen to twenty-five rays or arms, united except for their tips. The leaves of the adult parts differ from juvenile leaves less markedly than is the case with most ivies. They are narrower and less lobed. Juvenile leaves have blades up to 10 inches long by 7 inches wide. Shallowly-lobed or lobeless, and strongly heart-shaped at their bases, they sometimes have a few sharp teeth. The fruits of *H. colchica* are black. Its leaf blades, up to 1 foot in length, lobed or not and with little teeth, *H. c. amurensis* is dubbed with a misleading varietal name. Its origin is unknown, but it surely is not the Amur River region of northern Asia. Because it does not cling well this variety is best as a groundcover. If it is to clothe supports it must usually be tied to them. Commonly cultivated *H. c.*

Hedera colchica dentata

dentata has distantly-small-toothed, dullish, comparatively light-colored leaves. A variant of the last with creamy-edged leaves with an interior zone of gray-green is *H. c. dentata-variegata*. Himalayan **H. nepalensis** has the yellowish-brown scales of its young shoots and flower stalks with twelve to fifteen rays or branches. The taper-pointed juvenile leaves of this, 2 to nearly 5 inches long by approximately one-half as wide, are triangular-ovate to ovate-lanceolate. They are grayish-green with paler veins. Not infrequently they have bluntish teeth and a pair of blunt basal lobes. The adult-type leaves are ovate-lanceolate, lobeless and toothless, and one-half to two-thirds as wide as long. The fruits of this kind are yellow.

Japan and Korea are the native lands of **H. rhombea,** a kind with scales with fifteen to twenty rays on its young shoots and flower stalks. Triangular to ovate and mostly slightly three-lobed, on juvenile shoots the dark green leaves have blades up to about 2 inches long, generally with heart-shaped bases. The leaves of adult branches are mostly ovate with somewhat angular margins and broadly-wedge-shaped or rounded bases. The fruits are black. The leaves of *H. r. variegata* exhibit narrow marginal variegation.

Garden and Landscape Uses. Ivies are much esteemed outdoors and in. They are used to decorate greenhouses and homes as well as gardens. For these purposes they are admirable. Their chief, in most cases only, attraction is their evergreen foliage. The hardiest varieties of English ivy (*H. helix baltica* and *H. h.* '238th Street') live as climbers in sheltered places outdoors at Boston, Massachusetts and other varieties of that species similarly at New York, although in exposed places and in severe winters they are harmed or killed there. As groundcovers, varieties of English ivy survive, especially where there is a good snow blanket in much colder climates than they will tolerate as climbers. Other ivy species are generally less hardy, although *H. colchica* is very satisfactory as a groundcover in sheltered locations in the vicinity of New York City. In milder climates ivies thrive and exhibit great vitality, often climbing to the tops of tall trees and flowering and fruiting there. Contrary to opinions sometimes expressed, ivy clothing the trunks and bare branches of trees does no appreciable harm. Only if it invades the leafy portion of the crown and so interferes with light and air circulation does serious damage result. In California and other warm dryish climates the Algerian ivy is superior to the English for use in some locations because it stands exposure to sun better. As a group ivies prefer partial shade, but if they do not lack for moisture they stand considerable sun. Fertile ground with a fairly high organic content is best to their liking.

The chief outdoor uses of ivies are as self-clinging climbers to adorn masonry, tree trunks, and tree stumps and as

English ivy embellishing a chimney

English ivy clothing balustrades in Italy

A slope covered with English ivy

In Dallas, Texas: (a) Building landscaped with "ropes" of English ivy

English ivy on a north-facing wall

(b) The "ropes," trained to wires

English ivy varieties make attractive pot plants

groundcovers. In the latter capacity they are splendid under trees and for holding banks. Where winters are not too severe they may be used to clothe chain link fences. They stand city conditions well and so are reliable for town gardens. As indoor plants ivies do very well, and as long as the air is not too arid, adapt to cool and warm rooms. They get along well in light of low intensity. Cut branches are decorative and will live for many months and often root in water. Ivies can be trained to wire frames in almost any form the imagination can conceive. Small-leaved varieties are particularly well adapted for this use.

Cultivation. Trimming to keep outdoor ivies shapely and to check them from spilling into space not allotted to them, or to prevent the growth becoming so great that its own weight tears it away from its supports, is the chief care needed. Spring or summer are the best times to do this cutting or shearing. Vigorous growth is encouraged by spring fertilization and possibly by another application after midsummer. If the weather is dry for long periods watering is very helpful. In fall careful raking may be needed to prevent heavy accumulations of fallen leaves remaining on the ivy for long periods. Indoor ivies need regular watering and occasional applications of dilute liquid fertilizer; also their foliage should be sponged from time to time to remove dust and grime and possibly scale insects, mealybugs, or red spider mites. They are staked, tied, and trimmed to keep them shapely.

Propagation of ivies is chiefly by cuttings, which root readily, and more quickly if planted in a propagating bench with a little bottom heat. Shade is necessary and the rooting medium must be kept moist. Pot the rooted cuttings individually and grow the young plants in pots until they are set in their permanent locations. It is quite practicable to transplant field-grown ivies, but pot-grown specimens usually establish themselves more quickly. Layering is another easy means of increasing ivies. Grafting is sometimes resorted to for multiplying arborescent or tree ivies, the understocks used being young juvenile-type ivies. If the plants are not destined for outdoors in cold climates, *Fatshedera* and probably *Fatsia* should prove good understocks. Umbrella-headed (standard) specimens of ivy can be had by grafting shoots onto single-stemmed fatshederas at 3 to 4 feet above the ground. The fatshedera forms the "trunk" of the finished specimen, the ivy the head.

Pests and Diseases. Pests of ivies are aphids, mealybugs, red spider mites, and scale insects. The chief diseases are fungus

English ivy grafted onto *Fatshedera*

and bacterial leaf spots. A less common one is powdery mildew. The leaf spots can be checked by picking infected leaves and the bacterial condition by avoiding excessively high indoor temperatures and wetting the foliage unnecessarily, the fungus by spraying with a copper fungicide.

HEDGE. The word hedge is employed as part of the names of these plants: hedge-hyssop (*Gratiola*), hedge-nettle (*Stachys*), and hedge-thorn (*Carissa bispinosa*).

HEDGEHOG. This word forms part of the common names of these plants: hedge-hog-broom (*Erinacea pungens*), hedgehog cactus (*Hamatocactus setispinus*), hedgehog gourd (*Cucumis dipsaceus*), hedgehog holly (*Ilex aquifolium ferox*), and hedgehog prickly-poppy (*Argemone platyceras hispida*).

HEDGES. As dividers, screens, backgrounds, definitions for vistas, windbreaks, and protection from intruders, hedges are often regarded with greater favor than fences or walls, yet they serve essentially the same purposes and in effect are walls of living greenery. Hedges form strong horizontal lines that can be used effectively as architectural elements to prolong those of buildings, to tie buildings to the ground and in other ways to establish unity, and to provide enclosures.

Before planting, consider the chief purpose or purposes of the installation. If it is to discourage trespass, a dense, possibly thorny hedge, such as hawthorn, barberry, or trifoliate-orange, may be best. To be effective as a screen throughout the year a hedge must be evergreen. Perhaps arbor-vitae, boxwood, cypress, false-cypress, hemlock, holly, evergreen privet, or yews will do.

Then one must decide upon the height and width the hedge is to attain and whether it is to be strictly sheared or allowed to grow informally. These decisions will to a considerable extent dictate the choice of plants, as too, of course, will climate. Only plants surely hardy should generally be planted as hedges and it is well to remember that hedges kept closely sheared are likely to be more susceptible to extreme cold than specimens of the same plants growing naturally without clipping. This was well illustrated in the vicinity of New York City in the severe winter of 1933–34 when all privet hedges were killed to the ground and free-standing, unsheared privets were unharmed.

Informal hedges or screens can be of acacias, crape-myrtle, camellias, lilacs, mock-oranges, rose-of-Sharon, shrub roses, and many other plants not well suited to formal shearing. If a strictly formal hedge is desired, such favorites as hemlocks, hornbeams, privets, or yews may be the choice. As windscreens select from among plants known to withstand exposure well;

arbor-vitaes, hawthorns, osage-orange, or Russian-olive may do.

There are many possibilities other than those just mentioned for hedges of different kinds and various needs and locations. Ponder all carefully before deciding. Cost is often an important consideration. Let it be emphasized, it is usually better to save expense by starting with smaller plants of a desirable kind than to settle for a less satisfactory sort in a larger size. As a general rule space should be allowed at planting time for the hedge to develop if necessary a base equal in width to its height. Not all hedges will do this, but many, especially if grown informally, will and it is always advisable to allow for the possibility. For hedges that must be considerably narrower than their heights select plants, such as hawthorn, hornbeam, and privet, that are known to stand close shearing well, or columnar, naturally slender sorts, such as *Berberis thunbergii erecta*, *Cryptomeria japonica lobbii*, *Cupressus sempervirens*, *Juniperus scopulorum*, *Thuja occidentalis*, and *Taxus media hicksii*.

Planting calls for special attention. Of necessity hedge plants are crowded against competitive neighbors, all seeking moisture and nutrients. It pays therefore to do the best job possible in preparation for planting. The most satisfactory way is to excavate a trench or ditch at least 1½ feet wide and not less than 1 foot deep, more is better and indeed is essential if the plants are large. Do not skimp here. Break up the bottom of the trench with a fork and mix in compost, humus, or manure. Then fill back good soil mixed with the same materials until the bottom of the trench after treading it moderately firm is at a depth suitable to accommodate the roots.

Spacing is dependent upon plant size and how quickly a closed effect is desired. With decidous sorts such as privets, good results can be had if the plants are 1 foot to 1½ feet apart. It is more usual, partly because of their generally higher cost, to allow, depending upon their size, 1½ to 3 feet between evergreens. Such spacings may not at first keep dogs out. If this is an objective it is helpful to run a temporary fence of chicken wire through the center of the hedge or along one side of it.

When planting, set the plants slightly deeper than they were previously. If bare-rooted, as deciduous hedge plants usually are, spread the roots in a natural manner and work good soil among and around them and pack it firmly. Unless very small, evergreen hedge plants should not be bare-rooted. They should have good, unbroken balls of soil. Set these a little deeper than they have previously been, work good soil around them and pack it firmly. In all cases it is well to leave a shallow depression along the base of the hedge to encourage water to flow there.

Pruning at planting time is important. Unless deciduous hedge plants have abundant branches 1 foot from the ground, it is strongly advisable to cut them back to a height of from 6 inches to 1 foot. To the inexperienced this is likely to seem a wasteful, ridiculous procedure. To reduce 2 to 3 feet or taller plants as severely as that looks like butchery, a denial of the planter's objective of securing a barrier or screen as quickly as possible. It does of course lower the hedge temporarily, but it stimulates the production of an abundance of strong shoots from close to the ground. These produce a well-furnished, dense bottom to the hedge instead of an open, gappy one.

Planting-time pruning of evergreen hedges should rarely be as severe. Many evergreens react badly to such treatment, and with most others recovery would be disappointingly slow. Exceptionally, straggly specimens of kinds known to sprout freely from old wood, such as evergreen privets or yews, might be so treated, but in the main the evergreens used as hedges need only be sheared fairly severely at planting time, not drastically cut back.

Shaping formally trimmed hedges calls for some consideration. For satisfactory results, from the beginning prune or shear to the shape you wish. One cardinal rule, of particular importance with evergreen hedges, is that the sides should slope slightly inward from base to top, never the reverse. This assures that lower parts receive sufficient light to encourage the putting forth of new shoots essential to maintaining a dense growth and preventing dieback. Privets and a few other deciduous hedge plants, and among evergreens yews, can be maintained with vertical sides if their bases are not shaded by plantings in front of them, but with all, sloped sides are preferable. The tops of hedges may be pointed or ridged, rounded, or flat. In regions of heavy snows flat-topped examples may, because they perhaps shed snow less readily, be more subject to breakage than those with ridged or rounded tops.

Informal hedges not shaped as strict, neat walls, but allowed to retain something of the natural habit of the plants, are pruned differently. They are not sheared, but projecting branches are cut back as seems necessary to encourage enough side branches to develop to keep the hedge decently thick.

Maintaining established hedges calls for more or less regular attention according to their kind. Informal ones need pruning to shape annually or less often. Prune flowering kinds that bloom before June as soon as they are through flowering, late-bloomers at the end of winter or in spring.

Most formal hedges need shearing once a year, but some quick-growers, such as privet, honey-locust, and osage-orange, require attention more often. Experience

Formal hedges need shearing regularly; string strung between stakes is used to guide cutting: (a) Sides cut with hand shears

(b) Top cut with hand shears

shows that in the north annual shearing is best done early enough in the growing season, not later than the end of June or early July, to allow the new shoots to mature sufficiently by fall that they will not be unduly susceptible to winterkill, or that it be delayed until the end of the growing season so that new shoots do not come until the next spring.

With hedges that have not reached the size they are to be, at each shearing reduce the shoots of the last growth period to from one-third to two-thirds their lengths. It is a mistake to allow a too rapid gain in height. To do so will most likely result in the sacrifice of desirable density and compactness. Shear mature hedges to within an inch or less of the bases of the latest shoots. Even this tight clipping allows for a gradual, if slow increase in size, and eventually it may seem desirable to do a more drastic job by cutting into older wood and thus reducing height and width. Be wary about doing this. Not all hedge plants respond. Some may be killed or at least severely damaged by hard pruning. Others that sprout freely from older wood, such as privets, honey-locusts, and hibiscuses, may be so treated.

Other maintenance involves keeping the bottom of the hedge free of weeds and accumulations of trash. Unless growth is patently inadequate, fertilizing is usually unnecessary. Certainly it should not be done to the extent that over-vigorous shoot growth is stimulated. Nevertheless, old hedges and especially evergreen ones often are improved by fertilizing in spring.

English boxwood, one of the choicest evergreen hedge plants, can be used in many ways: (a) Informally, without shearing

(b) Trimmed formally at an entrance

(c) Closely sheared, two specimens of topiary enclosed by a hedge

(d) Closely sheared in a knot garden

Hedge of *Pittosporum tobira* at San Francisco, California

This handsome, tall hedge is of cherry-laurel (*Prunus laurocerasus*)

It is also often advantageous to keep the ground near them mulched. Pests and diseases must be looked for and controlled before they do serious harm.

Mild-climate evergreens for hedges of low to medium height include these: *Abelia grandiflora* (loses its foliage where winters are cold), African-box (*Myrsine africana*), *Diosma ericoides*, English boxwood (*Buxus sempervirens*), *Euonymus japonicus* varieties, evergreen privets (*Ligustrum japonicum ro-*

Hedge of evergreen privet (*Ligustrum lucidum*) at Virginia Beach, Virginia

tundifolium and *L. lucidum*), *Gardenia* (in variety), *Hakea* (in variety), *Hebe* (in variety), India-hawthorn (*Raphiolepis indica*), lavender (*Lavandula spica*), lavender-cotton (*Santolina chamaecyparissus*), *Lonicera nitida*, myrtle (*Myrtus communis* varieties), Natal-plum (*Carissa grandiflora*), *Paxistima myrsinites*, *Pittosporum tobira*, and rosemary (*Rosmarinus officinalis*).

Mild-climate plants for medium-sized to tall hedges, evergreen unless otherwise noted, include these: *Acacia longifolia*, American holly (*Ilex opaca*), Australian-pine (*Casuarina equisetifolia*), California bayberry (*Myrica californica*), *Camellia* (in variety), *Ceanothus* (in variety), *Chamaecyparis lawsoniana*, cherry-laurel (*Prunus caroliniana* and *P. laurocerasus*), *Cocculus laurifolius*, *Cotoneaster* (in variety), *Cryptomeria* (in variety), *Cupressocyparis leylandii*, *Duranta repens*, dwarf pomegranate (*Punica granatum nana*) (deciduous), *Elaeagnus pungens*, English holly (*Ilex aquifolium* and *I. altaclarensis* varieties), *Erica arborea*, *Escallonia* (in variety), *Euonymus japonicus* varieties, evergreen-huckleberry (*Vaccinium ovatum*), flowering quince (*Chaenomeles japonica*) (deciduous), Guatemalan-holly

One of the fastest-growing evergreen hedges, *Cupressocyparis leylandii*

English holly as a hedge

(*Olmediella betschleriana*), *Hebe* (in variety), incense cedar (*Calocedrus decurrens*), India-hawthorn (*Raphiolepis indica*), *Itea ilicifolia*, laurel (*Laurus nobilis*), laurestinus (*Viburnum tinus*), *Leptospermum* (in variety), Mexican-orange (*Choisya ternata*), mirror shrub (*Coprosma repens*), *Murraya paniculata*, myrtle (*Myrtus communis* varieties), oleander (*Nerium oleander* in variety), Oregon-grape (*Mahonia aquifolium*), *Osmanthus* (in variety), *Photinia* (in variety), *Pieris ja-*

Round-topped hedge of *Lonicera nitida*

American holly makes a dense, impenetrable, evergreen hedge

ponica, pineapple-guava (*Feijoa sellowiana*), *Pittosporum* (in variety), plum-yew (*Cephalotaxus harringtonia*), *Podocarpus* (in variety), redwood (*Sequoia sempervirens*), *Rhamnus alaternus* (sometimes only partially evergreen), *Severinia buxifolia*, strawberry guava (*Psidium cattleianum*), *Syzygium paniculatim*, *Tamarix* (in variety), *Teucrium fruticans*, yaupon (*Ilex vomitoria*), and yellow-oleander (*Thevetia peruviana*).

(b) As a round-topped hedge

Japanese holly lightly trimmed

The erect variety of the plum-yew (*Cephalotaxus harringtonia fastigiata*) as a nicely textured hedge in Maplewood, New Jersey

Hardy, low to medium-height, evergreen hedges can be formed from these: arbor-vitae (*Thuja occidentalis* varieties), *Berberis buxifolia nana* and *B. julianae*, *Chamaecyparis obtusa compacta*, *C. pisifera* varieties, edging box (*Buxus sempervirens suffruticosa*) (may need protection north of Maryland), *Euonymus fortunei carrierei*, Japanese holly (*Ilex crenata* varieties), Japanese yew (*Taxus cuspidata* varieties), Korean boxwood (*Buxus microphylla koreana*), red-cedar (*Juniperus virginiana* varieties), Swiss stone pine (*Pinus cembra*), and yew (*Taxus media* varieties).

Hedges of yew

Japanese holly closely sheared: (a) As a flat-topped hedge

Hardy, tall evergreen hedge plants include these: arbor-vitaes (*Thuja occidentalis* and *T. orientalis*), Douglas-fir (*Pseudotsuga menziesii*), false-cypresses (*Chamaecyparis pisifera* in variety), hemlock (*Tsuga canadensis*), Japanese holly (*Ilex crenata* varieties), *Juniperus scopulorum* varieties, red-cedar (*Juniperus virginiana*), spruces (*Picea abies* and *P. glauca*), and white pine (*Pinus strobus*).

Hardy deciduous plants for low to medium-height hedges include these: alpine currant (*Ribes alpinum*), Amur privet (*Ligustrum amurense*), *Berberis mentorensis* (partially evergreen), California privet (*Ligustrum ovalifolium*), *Deutzia gracilis* and *D. lemoinei*, *Euonymus alatus compactus*, five-leaf-aralia (*Acanthopanax sieboldianus*), Japanese barberry (*Berberis thunbergii*), Japanese-quince (*Chaenomeles speciosa*), ninebark (*Physocarpus monogynus*), *Potentilla fruticosa*, Regal's privet (*Ligustrum obtusifolium regelianum*), *Rhamnus frangula*, sea-buckthorn (*Hippophae rhamnoides*), shrub roses (*Rosa* in variety), *Spiraea bumalda* 'Anthony Waterer', *S. japonica ovalifolia*, *S. thunbergii*, *Stephanandra incisa*, and *Viburnum opulus nanum*.

Arbor-vitae (*Thuja occidentalis*): (a) Closely sheared

(b) As a tall screening hedge

A hemlock hedge (*Tsuga canadensis*)

White pine is satisfactory as a tall hedge

A well-maintained spruce hedge

California privet thrive in: (a) Sun

(b) Partial shade

Japanese barberry hedge fronting a bank of English ivy

Hardy deciduous plants for medium-height to tall hedges include these: bayberry (*Myrica pensylvanica*), *Caragana arborescens*, cockspur thorn (*Crataegus crusgalli*), cork-winged euonymus (*Euonymus alatus*), European beech (*Fagus sylvatica*), European hornbeam (*Carpinus betulus*), trifoliate-orange (*Poncirus trifoliata*), hedge maple (*Acer campestre*), rose-of-Sharon (*Hibiscus syriacus*), Russian-olive (*Elaeagnus angustifolia*), *Salix purpurea*, shingle oak (*Quercus imbricaria*), *Spiraea vanhouttei*, *Syringa josikaea*, and wayfaring tree (*Viburnum lantana*).

Bayberry does well lightly trimmed

European hornbeam closely trimmed: (a) In summer

The lilac *Syringia josikaea* is effective lightly pruned to form a tall screen

(b) As a tall screen, in winter

A few other unusual and interesting hedges: (a) Sea-grape (*Coccoloba uvifera*)

(b) Cornelian-cherry (*Cornus mas*)

(c) Monterey cypress (*Cupressus macrocarpa*)

(d) Chinese holly (*Ilex cornuta burfordii*)

(e) Cactus (*Opuntia*)

(f) *Ixora coccinea*

(g) Firethorn (*Pyracantha*)

(h) Mountain-laurel (*Kalmia latifolia*)

(i) *Rhododendron mucronatum*

HEDRAEANTHUS. See Edraianthus.

HEDYCARYA (Hedy-cárya)—Pigeon Wood. Chiefly native of New Caledonia and Polynesia, *Hedycarya*, of the monimia family MONIMIACEAE, has one species of its approximately twenty endemic to New Zealand. This is sometimes planted in California. The name derives from the Greek *hedys*, sweet, and *karya*, the walnut.

Hedycaryas are opposite-leaved trees or shrubs, the leaves toothed or not, with flowers unisexual, or unisexual and bisexual on the same plant. The blooms are small and in axillary clusters or racemes. They have cup-shaped perianths of five to ten segments (petals). The males have many stamens, the females conical styles. The fruits are technically drupes; they are structured like plums.

The pigeon wood (*H. arborea*), 20 to 40 feet high, has evergreen, short-stalked, leathery leaves, two types on the same tree, one elliptic-obovate, bluntish, distantly-toothed, and 2 to 4½ inches long by 1 inch to 2 inches wide, the other oblanceolate to lanceolate, usually pointed, distantly-toothed to nearly toothless, and ¾ inch to 1¼ inches in width. The flowers are in branched clusters shorter than the leaves. The females are about ¼ inch in diameter, the males slightly larger. The fruits are clusters of about ten egg-shaped, orange-red, ½-inch-long drupes attached to a disklike receptacle or stalk end.

Garden and Landscape Uses and Cultivation. This is an interesting general purpose evergreen for mild climates. It succeeds in ordinary soil and is usually propagated by seed.

HEDYCHIUM (Hedých-ium) — Ginger-Lily. This group of vigorous, tropical, perennial herbaceous plants consists, except for one species indigenous to Madagascar, of natives of warm parts of Asia. The fifty species of *Hedychium* belong in the ginger family ZINGIBERACEAE. The name is from the Greek *hedys*, sweet, and *chion*, snow. The reference is to the fragrant, snow-white flowers of some species.

Hedychiums have more or less tuberous or rhizomatous rootstocks from which arise many reedlike, leafy stems along which lanceolate or linear-lanceolate leaves are arranged in two ranks. The stems terminate in showy spikes or heads of handsome flowers accompanied by large bracts. These plants resemble *Curcuma* in that they have well-developed lateral staminodes (abortive petal-like stamens), but differ in that the filament of the fertile stamen is long and slender, as well as in other botanical details. In true ginger (*Zingiber*) the lateral staminodes are not petal-like. The fruits of hedychiums are capsules.

The best known kinds are the white ginger-lily or garland flower (*H. coronarium*), the yellow ginger-lily (*H. flavescens*), and the kahili ginger-lily (*H. gardneranum*). Native to India, Burma, and Ceylon, **H. coronarium** has become naturalized in parts of tropical America. It has green, canna-like leaves up to 2 feet long by 5 inches wide on stems 4 to 6 feet in height. They are hairless above, but hairy on their undersides. The flowers, up to 4 inches across, heavily fragrant, and pure white except for sometimes a green stain on the lip, are in spikes up to 1 foot long or longer. Sometimes classed as a variety of *H. coronarium*, and a native of India and the Mascarene Islands, **H. flavescens** is naturalized in Hawaii and some other tropical places. Growing to a height of 5 to 6 feet, it has foliage like that of the white ginger-lily. Its heavily-perfumed, creamy-yellow flowers, about 4 inches across, like those of the white ginger-lily, are in compact spikes. They are deeper and brighter yellow toward their centers.

The kahili ginger-lily (**H. gardneranum**) has leaves about 2 feet long and 6 inches wide on stems up to 6 feet tall. The undersides of young ones are powdery-white. The flowers, in slender, loose inflorescences up to 1½ feet long, are light yellow with a protruding bright red stamen considerably longer than any of the other flower parts. The flowers are smaller than those of the white and the yellow ginger-lilies. This, a native of the Himalayas, is one of the hardiest of the genus.

Sometimes regarded as varieties of the white ginger-lily, which they resemble, *H. maximum* and *H. chrysoleucum*, are attractive. Indian **H. maximum** has broader leaves than the white ginger-lily and larger flowers with lateral staminodes often with a central lobe or tongue, and a pinkish filament to the stamen. The bases of the lip and the lateral staminodes of the deliciously scented flowers of **H. chrysoleucum**, native to India, are deep orange, otherwise they resemble those of *H. flavescens*. They are about 3½ inches across. The flower spikes of **H. greenei**, of India, are about 5 inches long. The blooms, not more than 2 inches wide, are perhaps the most brilliantly colored of any ginger-lily. They are rich fiery-red and have a red stamen. This kind attains a height of about 6 feet and has leaves, somewhat hairy beneath, up to 10 inches long by 2 inches wide. About the time its flowers fade young plantlets develop among the bracts.

Approximately the same height as *H. greenei* but with 2-inch-wide leaves up to 1½ feet in length, **H. coccineum**, of India, has red flowers with the stamen filament pink. They are in spikes up to 10 inches in length. Variety **H. c. angustifolium** is distinguished by its shorter leaves and brick- or salmon-red flowers in spikes up to over 1 foot long. Larger (up to 3 inches wide) pink flowers with dark spots on the lip are borne by **H. c. carneum**. Native to the eastern Himalayas, **H. densiflorum** is about 4 feet tall and has narrow-cylindrical spikes 6 to 8 inches in length of tangerine or deep coral-pink flowers and with stamens of the same color. Madagascan **H. peregrinum** is about 3 feet tall. It has leaves, softly-hairy beneath, about 1¼ feet long by 3 inches wide and white flowers with orange filaments.

Hedychium densiflorum

Hedychium coronarium

Hedychium densiflorum (flowers)

There are a number of good hybrid ginger-lilies. Among the best is **H. pradhanii**, a vigorous plant with leaves up to 1½ feet long by 2 or 3 inches broad, and delightfully fragrant flowers 2½ to 3 inches wide that open white with pink stainings and change to pale yellow the second day. The stamen has a deep pink filament and a yellow anther. With large, white-and-yellow flowers that turn yellow the second day, in tight, conelike spikes, **H. chandrabiranum** is another hybrid of merit. Its stamens are brilliant orange. This kind is 3½ to 4½ feet in height and has dark green leaves 8 inches long by 1½ inches wide. A pretty hybrid with compact flower spikes of cream-white blooms and bright yellow buds is the hybrid **H. ghalii**. Its leaves are about 1 foot long by 1½ inches wide. Yet another excellent hybrid is **H. kewense**, which is 6 to 7 feet in height and has fragrant, bright tangerine flowers with long protruding stamens in open spikes about 10 inches long. The parents of this fine ginger-lily are *H. coccineum angustifolium* and *H. gardneranum*.

Hedychium kewense

Other ginger-lilies cultivated include these, all natives of India. **H. aurantiacum**, up to 10 feet tall, has about 1-inch-wide leaves up to 1½ feet long. Its orange flowers in spikes 4 to 6 inches long have a corolla tube ¾ inch long, 1-inch-long petals, and a bright red stamen. **H. aureum** is low and has pointed-lanceolate leaves up to 9 inches long and ¾-inch-long, golden-yellow flowers in crowded spikes approximately 2 inches long. **H. elatum**, which may exceed 12 feet in height, has leaves up to 2 feet long and 2½ inches wide. Its yellowish-white flowers have 1-inch-long corolla tubes, petals three-quarters as long, and a pink stamen. **H. ellipticum**, 4 to 6 feet tall, has slender-pointed leaves up to 1¼ feet long and 5 inches wide and, in crowded 4-inch-long spikes, yellowish-white flowers with a 3-inch-long corolla tube, 1-inch-long petals, and a purple stamen. **H. flavum**, about 5 feet tall, has oblong to lanceolate leaves up to 1¼ feet long and 2 inches wide. Its flowers, including the stamen, are yellow to orange-yellow, in spikes up to 6 inches long. **H. glaucum** (syn. *H. gracile glaucum*), about 5 feet tall, has leaves up to nearly 1 foot long by 3 inches wide. Its white flowers have a 1-inch-long corolla tube, petals about 1½ inches long, and a red stamen. **H. gracile**, 1½ to 2 feet in height, has leaves about 5 inches long by 1½ inches wide, with glaucous undersides. Greenish-white, the flowers have a corolla tube about 1 inch long, petals about three-quarters as long, and a red stamen. **H. spicatum**, 3 feet tall, has leaves more or less hairy on their undersides, up to 1¼ feet long by 4 inches wide. Its yellow flowers in rather loose spikes up to 8 inches in length have a corolla tube about 3 inches long, petals about 1 inch long, and a reddish stamen. Variety *H. s. acuminatum* has leaves hairy on their undersides and flowers with purple petals. **H. thyrsiforme**, 5 to 6 feet high or sometimes

Hedychium thyrsiforme

higher, has leaves up to 1¼ feet long and 5 inches broad. The white flowers, in dense spikes up to nearly 5 inches long, have a corolla tube and petals each about 1 inch long and a whitish stamen. **H. villosum**, is 7 to 9 feet tall, has leaves up to 1 foot long and 4 to 5 inches wide. The white flowers with the corolla tube 2 to 2½ inches long and a purple stamen are in loose spikes up to 10 inches long.

Garden and Landscape Uses. Hedychiums are magnificent for outdoor cultivation in warm moist climates. They thrive in Hawaii and southern Florida and are splendid for grouping in borders and foundation plantings. They seem to prosper particularly on the north sides of buildings and are seen to excellent advantage when planted near pools. In addition, they are good container plants to embellish terraces and patios and handsome furnishings for large greenhouses and conservatories. Their spikes of bloom, with well-foliaged stems, are splendid for bold flower arrangements.

Cultivation. In the moist tropics ginger-lilies thrive without trouble in any fertile soil where their roots have access to adequate moisture. They stand part-shade or full sun. In southern Florida many kinds grow well and respond to generous fertilizing and to watering well during dry weather. They benefit from being rested for a month or two in winter. This may be encouraged by withholding water at that time, but in constantly wet climates they are likely to be evergreen. Ginger-lilies are highly susceptible to frost. In regions where more than a few degrees are likely to be experienced they should be dug in fall and the roots be stored, like those of cannas, in slightly moist soil in a temperature of 35 to 45°F until planting time in spring. Treated in this way they can be grown successfully in many parts of the south.

In containers ginger-lilies need ample root room and rich, coarse, well-drained soil that has mixed with it an abundance of organic matter. They are suitable for tubs or large pots. They should be planted in early spring and liberally watered throughout the growing season. It is advantageous if the containers stand with their bases in water so the soil is kept constantly moist by capillarity. Once the containers are filled with healthy roots, weekly or semiweekly applications of dilute liquid fertilizer should be the rule. In fall, when flowering is through, the old spikes may be cut off and the plants rested by keeping the soil somewhat drier, but it is advisable not to cut the leafy stems down until the new growth is well advanced in spring, for the leaves of the old shoots aid the growth of the young ones by supplying sustenance. A warm-temperate greenhouse, lightly shaded in summer, with a minimum winter temperature of 50 to 55°F affords ideal conditions for these plants. Too much shade and excessively high winter temperatures inhibit blooming. Propagation is by division in late winter or early spring, by seed, and, in some cases, by plantlets that develop from the flower spikes.

Pests. Ginger-lilies are little subject to pests. Occasionally they may become prey to scales and red spider mites.

HEDYOTIS (Hedy-òtis)—Quaker Ladies or Bluets, Creeping Bluets. The genus *Hedyotis*, of the madder family RUBIACEAE, consists of possibly 400 species of herbaceous plants and shrubs, chiefly tropical and subtropical, and less often natives of temperate regions. A few of the latter, formerly segregated as *Houstonia*, are the only ones ordinarily grown in North America. The name, from the Greek *hedys*, pleasant or charming, and *otos*, having the quality of, is self-explanatory.

Hedyotises have opposite, stalked or stalkless leaves, and terminal, solitary or clustered, generally small flowers. The blooms have usually four sepals and tubular, funnel- or salver-shaped corollas with four lobes (petals) often hairy on their insides. There are four stamens, and a slender style with two stigmas. In some flowers the stamens are longer than the style, in the others the reverse is true. The fruits are capsules.

Quaker ladies or bluets (*H. caerulea* syn. *Houstonia caerulea*), is perennial and hairless. It has slender rhizomes and is native of meadows and moist soils from Nova Scotia and Quebec to Wisconsin, Georgia, and Arkansas. Its stems, branched or not, are 2 to 8 inches tall. The lower leaves have obovate to spatula-shaped blades ¼ to ½ inch long and stalks of about the same length. The upper leaves are almost stalkless and linear to oblong-spatula-shaped. From the tips of the stems and from the upper leaf axils the solitary, yellow-eyed, pale to deep blue flowers up to ½ inch wide are carried on slender, erect stalks. Variety *H. c. alba* has white blooms.

Hedyotis michauxii

Creeping bluets (*H. michauxii* syn. *H. serpyllifolia*), a perennial of moist mountain soils from Pennsylvania to Georgia, is mat-forming. It has completely prostrate, creeping, rooting stems 4 to 8 inches long. Its short-stalked leaves have ovate to almost circular blades up to ¼ inch long. Terminal, or from the upper leaf axils of short branches, the solitary blue to violet-blue blooms on stalks up to 1½ inches long are ⅓ to ½ inch wide.

Other perennial kinds are sometimes brought into gardens. These may include *H. purpurea, H. p. longifolia,* and *H. p. tenuifolia,* all less decorative then the kinds described above. Native from southern New England to Michigan, Missouri, Alabama, and Texas, variable **H. purpurea** is up to 1½ feet tall, but often lower. It has stalkless, ovate to ovate-lanceolate leaves up to 2 inches long. The many purplish to white flowers, about ⅓ inch long, are in up-facing, loose or dense clusters. Longer-stalked, smaller flowers, and narrower leaves are the most obvious differences between *H. purpurea* and its varieties *H. p. longifolia* and *H. p. tenuifolia*.

Hedyotis caerulea

Hedyotis purpurea

Garden and Landscape Uses and Cultivation. Rock gardens, open woodlands, shaded paths, and similar places where the soil is cool and dampish are to be considered as possible sites for bluets and creeping bluets. The first also succeeds in sunny locations where the soil is moist. The other kinds described above prosper in drier soils in light shade. Sometimes bluets and creeping bluets accept environments chosen for them with grace, sometimes they linger or pine and die without apparent cause. Or again, they may completely reject sites carefully selected and prepared and transfer by self-sown seedlings to areas that to the gardener appear less likely to content them. Perhaps soil acidity has something to do with this. These species need at least moderately acid soils. Be that as it may, it is worth some trial and error planting to please these attractive natives, and unless one gardens on limestone, with a little effort places agreeable to them are likely to be found. Once established little care is needed. A shallow mulch of leaf mold or other organic material applied each fall is beneficial, and in dry weather watering may be needed. Propagation is by division, in spring or fall, and by seed.

HEDYSARUM (Hedyś-arum) — French-Honeysuckle. Hedysarums are hardy herbaceous perennials, subshrubs, or rarely shrubs of the pea family LEGUMINOSAE. They have alternate leaves with an uneven number of toothless leaflets and pea-shaped blooms in racemes or heads from the leaf axils. They are natives of all continents of the northern hemisphere. The name is from *hedysaron,* an ancient Greek name for some unidentified plant. There are 150 species.

The flowers of hedysarums are purple, red, white, or occasionally yellow. Their calyxes have five slightly unequal teeth. The banner or standard petal is obovate to reverse-heart-shaped and longer than the oblong wing petals, which are shorter than the keel. Nine of the ten stamens are united, one is free. The fruits are compressed, usually jointed pods.

French-honeysuckle (**Hedysarum coronarium**), a native of the Mediterranean re-

Hedysarum coronarium

gion, is a good-looking herbaceous perennial, 2 to 4 feet tall, with erect, branched stems. Its leaves, somewhat hairy on their undersides, have seven to fifteen elliptic to roundish leaflets. Deep red and fragrant, the blooms are in dense spikes or racemes of ten to thirty-five. In *H. c. album* the flowers are white.

Another attractive herbaceous perennial, **H. hedysaroides** (syn. *H. obscurum*) is 8 inches to 1¼ feet tall and hairless or sparingly-hairy. Its leaves have six to twenty blunt leaflets up to 1 inch long by approximately one-half as wide. The reddish-violet or rarely white blooms, ½ to 1 inch long, are in racemes of fifteen to forty or occasionally more. This is a native of the mountains of southcentral Europe, northern Asia, and Japan. Pale-yellow-flowered **H. grandiflorum,** of the Balkan Peninsula, is a herbaceous perennial 8 inches to somewhat over 1 foot tall. Its leaves, clothed with silvery hairs or nearly hairless, have five to eleven elliptic to ovate leaflets ½ inch to 1½ inches long. The blooms are ¾ to 1 inch in length.

Other Asian sorts include **H. multijugum** of Mongolia. A deciduous shrub 2 to 5 feet tall, this has leaves of twenty-one to forty-one broad-elliptic to ovate leaflets and erect, long-stalked, loose racemes 6 inches to 1½ feet in length of magenta-purple blooms ½ to ¾ inch long. The one- or two-seeded pods are nearly circular. Variety *H. m. apiculatum* differs in its leaves having seventeen to twenty-seven leaflets. Not over about 6 inches tall, herbaceous perennial **H. sikkimense,** a native of the high Himalayas, has leaves with twenty-one to twenty-seven ovate-lanceolate leaflets up to ½ inch long. The flowers of this are bright red. Indigenous in Japan and from Korea to Siberia, **H. vicioides** (syn. *H. esculentum*) is a more or less hairy, tufted herbaceous perennial 1 foot to 3 feet tall. From 3 to 6 inches long, its leaves have eleven to twenty-five narrow-ovate to broadly-lanceolate leaflets. The long-stalked, one-sided racemes of many ½- to ¾-inch-long, creamy-yellow flowers are 3 to 4 inches long.

Several North American species, mostly mountain plants, are worthy of cultivation. Wild in the Pacific Northwest, **H. occidentale** has a woody rootstock from which come several stems 1¼ feet long to twice that, and usually branched above. The leaves are of nine to twenty-one leaflets up to slightly over 1 inch long. In racemes of twenty to eighty, the nearly 1-inch-long, pendent blooms are reddish to purplish. Similar to the last, rather smaller-flowered **H. boreale** (syn. *H. pabulare*) is an astragalus-like plant that occurs wild in moist soils through much of subarctic and northern North America.

Garden and Landscape Uses and Cultivation. Herbaceous perennial hedysarums are suitable for flower beds and borders,

Hedysarum vicioides

and the American ones in their home regions for native plant gardens. Most commonly grown and one of the most ornamental, the French-honeysuckle is useful for cut flowers. Hedysarums are generally easy to grow. They respond to ordinary, reasonably fertile, well-drained soil, and open, sunny locations. They root deeply and once established it is best to leave them undisturbed. Propagation is by seed, or the herbaceous kinds by careful division in spring.

The shrub species, *H. multijugum,* described above is of interest because it makes a good display in summer after most shrubs have finished flowering. Unfortunately, the magenta color of its flowers is less pleasing than could be wished. With age this shrub tends to become straggly. To overcome this, peg the branches to the ground. This induces the production of new shoots from the center of the bush. Pruning consists of thinning out old and crowded shoots and shortening long ones. Do this each spring. Propagation is by layering, summer cuttings made of side shoots, and seeds.

HEDYSCEPE (Hedyscè-pe)—Umbrella Palm. Like the more familiar howeias, the only member of *Hedyscepe,* of the palm family PALMAE is endemic to Lord Howe Island, almost 500 miles northeast of Sydney, Australia. At home it occupies higher territory than the howeias, occurring at altitudes of from about 1,400 feet upward, but not plentifully until the 2,000 feet contour is reached. Its name is derived from the Greek *hedys,* pleasant, and *skepe,* shade.

The umbrella palm (**H. canterburyana** syn. *Kentia canterburyana*) is a beautiful, unisexual, feather-leaved tree that attains a height of about 40 feet and is much like *Howeia.* It differs in having flower clusters with many flexuose branches and in other technical details. Its fruits, about 2 inches long, are larger than those of *Howeia.* The leaves of the umbrella palm arch gracefully. They have numerous narrow leaflets, green on both sides.

Garden and Landscape Uses and Cultivation. The landscape uses of this tree are the same as those of howeias and, like them, when young, it is an attractive and easy-to-grow plant in pots and tubs. It thrives outdoors and indoors under conditions favorable to howeias, but grows more slowly. Because it occurs naturally at higher altitudes one may assume that it is likely to be somewhat more cold-resistant than *Howeia*, especially than *H. forsteriana*, which as a native is not found much above sea level, but little information is available as to how much cold it withstands. For more information see Palms.

HEEL. A small piece of older wood consisting of a longitudinal sliver of the branch from which a side shoot used as a cutting was taken, and which remains attached to the cutting, is called a heel. Cuttings made with such attachments are heel cuttings. These, especially if made from soft shoots, often root with greater facility than cuttings without heels.

Cuttings with a heel attached

HEELING IN. This is a procedure designed to keep alive and in the best possible condition bare-root plants dug for transplanting that cannot be planted immediately. Delay may result from need to prepare the planting site, construction work in progress, unsuitable weather, or other cause. The plants to be heeled in may be lifted from your own garden or may be from stock received by mail or other means from a nursery or elsewhere.

Heeling in consists of planting temporarily. It is done by digging a trench or ditch of sufficient size to accommodate the roots of plants laid as closely together as practicable without breaking, or bunching the roots to the extent that soil filled in will not be in contact with them.

Position the plants in the trench with their tops sloped toward the south at an angle of about 45 degrees. This minimizes exposure to the sun. Before the roots have time to dry shovel soil over them and with the ball of the foot, not the heel as the name of the procedure suggests, make the soil firm. Take care not to break the roots in doing so. There is no need to work the soil among the roots as is done when planting. Covering to the extent that none is exposed is enough.

If a considerable number of plants are to be heeled in put them in closely spaced parallel trenches. Their tops then afford shelter and shade to each other. Soil taken to form the second trench is used to cover the roots of plants in the first, soil from

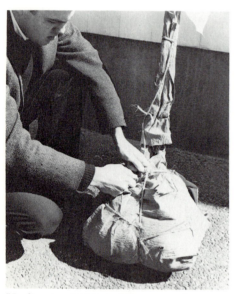

Heeling in: (a) Unpacking young bare-root trees received from nursery

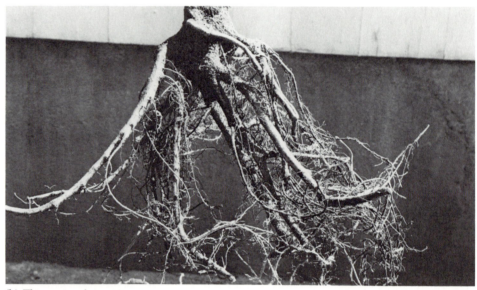

(b) The roots of one tree

(c) Trees set in trench, soil being shoveled over roots

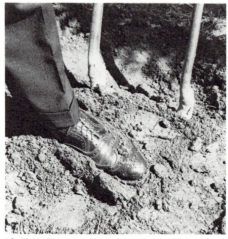

(d) Treading to eliminate air pockets about the roots and to firm the soil

(e) The finished job, trunks slanted at a 45 degree angle

the third to cover the roots of those in the second, and so on.

Locations for heeling in, where choice exists, should be sheltered and lightly shaded. Should the soil be dry, water it as soon as the operation is completed. If the plants are to be pruned do this before heeling them in. This reduces the tops and hence minimizes loss of moisture.

Heeled-in plants may remain for a week or two or more or even through a winter, but not after new growth begins in spring. See that they are taken up and planted before then. For short-time keeping, instead of being conventionally heeled-in, plants may be stood on the ground in a sheltered, lightly shaded spot with their roots well covered with peat moss, sawdust, sand, or some other loose, moisture-retaining material.

HEERIA. See Heterocentron.

HEIMERLIODENDRON. See Pisonia.

HEIMIA (Heìm-ia). Named after Dr. Ernst Ludwig Heim, a German physician, who died in 1834, the genus *Heimia* consists of two or three New World species. It belongs in the loosestrife family LYTHRACEAE.

Heimias are deciduous shrubs, not hardy in the north, with slender, wandlike branches and leaves opposite, partly alternate, or in threes. The solitary, short-stalked, axillary flowers are yellow. They

have bell-shaped calyxes with hornlike appendages between the lobes. There are five to seven spreading petals, ten to eighteen stamens one-half the length of the petals, and a slender style longer than stamens. The fruits are capsules containing numerous small seeds.

The most familiar species is *H. salicifolia,* native from Mexico to Argentina. Attaining a height of 10 feet, this hairless shrub has slightly winged stems and narrowly-oblong to linear-lanceolate, pointed leaves up to 2 inches long; the upper ones are often alternate, the lower ones opposite or in threes. The flowers, about ¾ inch across, have broad-ovate petals that soon fall. Variety *H. s. grandiflora* has blooms 1 inch or more in diameter. In Mexico *H. salicifolia* is used medicinally. Another kind, *H. myrtifolia,* of Brazil, is 3 feet tall and has linear to lanceolate leaves up to 2 inches long. Its flowers are very much smaller than those of *H. salicifolia.*

Garden and Landscape Uses and Cultivation. Heimias bloom over a long period in summer and are useful general purpose shrubs for mild climates, such as that of southern California. They succeed in ordinary garden soil in sunny locations and are easily increased by seeds and cuttings. Occasional thinning out of older branches to check overcrowding is the only pruning ordinarily needed, but if the necessity arises and they must be cut hard back they soon renew themselves from their bases.

HELENIUM (Helèn-ium)—Sneezeweed. The unattractive colloquial name of this genus is unwarranted. Its flowers do not trigger sneezing. Nor is its botanical one apt. It is an ancient Greek name given to a plant in honor of Helen of Troy. Whatever the plant known to the Greeks was, it certainly was not what we now call *Helenium* for that genus is native only in the New World. Consisting of about forty species of annuals, and mostly coarse, deciduous herbaceous perennials of the daisy family COMPOSITAE, it occurs in both North and South America. The commonly cultivated kinds are North American species and derivatives of them.

Heleniums have erect stems and alternate, toothed or toothless leaves speckled with tiny dark dots. Often the bases of the leaves are continued down the stems as wings. The yellow, yellow and partly purple, or brownish flower heads are solitary or clustered. Each has a collar of leafy bracts (involucre) at its base, spreading or reflexed, and consisting of two or three rows. Usually they have both disk and ray florets. A few kinds have disk florets only. The ray florets, often somewhat drooping, are wedge-shaped, and three- to five-toothed, and are female or sterile. The disk florets (those that form the center of the flower head) are bisexual. The fruits are seedlike achenes.

The most important species horticulturally is *H. autumnale.* It has produced several admirable varieties. A fibrous-rooted perennial that inhabits moist soils from Quebec to British Columbia, Florida, and Arizona, this species is somewhat variable in the wild. From 2 to 5 feet tall, it may be hairless or hairy. The numerous toothed leaves, the upper ones as large as those below, are lanceolate-linear to narrowly-obovate. They narrow at their bases into wings that flank the stems, and are 2 to 6 inches long. The 1- to 2-inch-wide flower heads are several to many together in leafy clusters. Their high centers are subglobose and yellow. There are ten to twenty yellow, somewhat drooping, three-lobed ray florets. Varieties of *H. autumnale* are *H. a. grandicephalum,* with flower heads larger than those of the typical species; *H. a. minor,* low-growing and with yellow and reddish flower heads; *H. a. montanum* (syn. *H. montanum*), from 1 foot to 3 feet tall, with finely-toothed or toothless leaves, and flower heads up to 1¾ inches across and yellow; *H. a. nanum praecox,* which is low-growing and blooms earlier than other forms of the species; *H. a. pumilum,* up to 2 feet in height; *H. a. rubrum,* with deep brown-red flower heads; *H. a. striatum,* with red-striped ray florets; and *H. a. superbum,* with extra-large flower heads. Varieties of special merit that bear fancy garden variety names are described in catalogs of dealers in hardy perennials.

Helenium autumnale variety

Other heleniums likely to be cultivated include perennial *H. bigelovii.* This, a native of moist meadows in California and Oregon and up to about 4 feet tall, has lanceolate leaves 4 to 10 inches long that are continued down the stems as wings. The yellow-rayed flower heads have yellow or reddish-purple centers and are about 2½ inches in diameter. They are long-stalked and mostly solitary, more rarely they are in twos or threes. Quite popular is *H. hoopesii,* a stout perennial 1½ to 3 feet tall and native of moist soils from the Rocky Mountains to California and Oregon. Its leaves do not run down the stems as wings. They are toothless and up to 10 inches long or sometimes longer. The handsome, golden-yellow flower heads, 3 inches in diameter, are solitary or clustered. Their rays droop only slightly. This species is poisonous to sheep and has caused much trouble in the Rocky Mountains. Perennial *H. flexuosum* (syn. *H. nudiflorum*), indigenous in moist ground from Massachusetts to Florida and Texas and 1½ to 3 feet tall, has lanceolate to linear-lanceolate leaves up to 6 inches long and scarcely toothed, that are continued as wings to the stems. Its clustered, short-stalked flower heads have drooping, yellow ray florets, sometimes tinged at their bases with brownish-purple. They are 1 inch to 2 inches across. The central disk is purple or brownish-purple.

An attractive annual, *H. amarum* (syn. *H. tenuifolium*) is native chiefly of sandy soils from Virginia to Florida, Missouri, Kansas, and Texas. It is naturalized in other parts of the United States. This sort has branched or branchless stems 8 inches to 1½ feet tall and numerous very slender or threadlike, pale green leaves ¾ inch to 3 inches long. The many short-stalked flower heads, about 1 inch across, are clustered. In the typical species both rays and disk are yellow, but there is a variety, *H. a. badium,* in which the latter is purple.

Garden and Landscape Uses. Sneezeweeds are useful for late summer and fall bloom in beds and borders and for less formal places where they can be planted more casually. They are appropriate in native plant gardens in areas where they are indigenous, and provide good cut flowers. Primarily plants for moistish soils, they do not withstand dry conditions well. They appreciate full sun, but will stand a little part-day shade.

Cultivation. The annual species is easily grown from seeds sown in spring where the plants are to bloom. The young plants are thinned to 6 inches apart and kept free of weeds. Usually they require staking. With the perennials it is important to divide and replant the clumps fairly frequently, say every second or even every year. In this way they are kept vigorous and less likely to shed their lower foliage early, retaining it even while in bloom. Be-

fore planting, the soil should be spaded deeply and made nourishing by the liberal admixture of compost, rotted manure, or other decayed organic matter together with a generous lacing of bone meal and, if nutrients are low, a dressing of a complete general purpose fertilizer. Planting may be done in spring or early fall, setting smallish divisions or young plants about 1 foot apart.

Routine care of established plants is not exacting. A spring application of a complete fertilizer is in order. If an excessive number of shoots start from the base they may be thinned out while small to allow more light and air to reach those left. Staking should be done before the stems topple. Tall kinds can be reduced in height by pinching out the ends of the shoots in early July. In cold climates a light winter covering of branches of evergreens, salt hay, or other suitable protection may with advantage be placed over the plants after the ground has frozen to a depth of an inch or two.

HELIABRAVOA (Helia-bravòa). Conservative botanists include the only species of *Heliabravoa,* of the cactus family CACTACEAE, in *Lemaireocereus.* Native to Mexico, it has a name honoring the twentieth-century Mexican botanist Helia Bravo-Hollis.

Massive, much-branched, treelike, 10 to 30 feet tall, and often as broad or broader than high, *H. chende* (syn. *Lemaireocereus chende*) has a short, thick trunk and

Heliabravoa chende

crowded, erect branches, their younger parts bright green, their older parts grayish. They have seven to eleven ribs and clusters of three to six black-tipped, needlelike, gray spines ¾ inch to 1½ inches long. The very beautiful flowers, white or perhaps sometimes pink, have short scaly and bristly perianth tubes. The fruits are red and spiny.

Garden and Landscape Uses and Cultivation. This is a striking cactus for planting outdoors in warm, dry regions and for inclusion in greenhouse collections. It grows readily in well-drained, reasonably fertile soil and appreciates full sun. Propagation is by seeds and by cuttings. For more information see Cactuses.

HELIAMPHORA (Heliám-phora). Botanists recognize six species from the mountains of northern South America as belonging to this genus. They are related to the North American pitcher plants *Sarracenia* and *Darlingtonia,* and with them constitute the sarracenia family SARRACENIACEAE. The name *Heliamphora* is derived from the Greek *helios,* the sun, and *amphora,* a pitcher, and relates to the form of the leaves.

From other genera of its family *Heliamphora* differs in having flowers in racemes instead of solitary. Its erect leaves are all basal, tubular, pitcher-shaped, winged down their fronts, with open, flaring mouths, with sometimes rudimentary lids at the ends of the midribs.

Only one species of *Heliamphora* is known to be cultivated, and that, but rarely. Acknowledged to be one of the most challenging of tender plants to grow successfully, *H. nutans* is rarely attempted in botanical gardens and other special plant collections. This, the first species known to science, is less imposing than others, some of which have broad-petaled blooms 4½ inches in diameter, but none of which, alas, is known to have been cultivated. Nodding white or delicate pink blooms, few together on slender, erect stalks up to 1 foot in length, are produced by *H. nutans.* The perianth is of four to six pointed-ovate parts (petals). There are several stamens and a straight style. The fruits are capsules.

Heliamphora nutans

Garden Uses and Cultivation. This is a collectors' item adapted for growing under cool greenhouse conditions such as suit the orchids *Coelogyne* and *Disa*. In many parts of North America it is probable that success can be had only in greenhouses air-cooled in summer. A rooting medium of chiefly sphagnum moss with the admixture of some peat and coarse sand, is satisfactory; it must be kept always moist with nonalkaline water. This is best achieved by standing the pots or pans (shallow pots) in which the heliamphoras are growing in saucers kept filled with water. A highly humid atmosphere is needed. This may be ensured by keeping the plants in terrariums or under bell jars. Needed repotting is done in spring. Propagation is by careful division of the rhizomes and by seed sown on sphagnum moss.

HELIANTHELLA (Heli-anthélla). Of secondary horticultural importance, *Helianthella*, of the daisy family COMPOSITAE, consists of about ten species of usually hairy, hardy herbaceous perennials of the western United States, adjacent Canada, and Mexico. Its name is a diminutive of the related genus *Helianthus*, from which it differs in its seedlike fruits being flattened.

Helianthellas have branchless or sparingly-branched stems, and alternate or opposite, lanceolate to ovate, undivided, smooth-edged, stalkless leaves. Their long-stalked, medium to large flower heads consist of a central eye of bisexual disk florets encircled by a single row of few to many sterile, petal-like ray florets. Those of most kinds are solitary or have only a few smaller heads accompanying the main terminal one. The seedlike fruits are achenes.

Native to the Rocky Mountain region, sunflower-like *H. quinquenervis* is sparsely-hairy to nearly hairless, and 1½ to 5 feet tall. Its basal leaves may be 1 foot long or longer. Its stem ones, opposite, shiny, and five-veined, are smaller, and ovate- to elliptic-lanceolate. The flower heads, which because their stems bend are held vertically rather than facing upward, are 3 to 4 inches across. They have yellow centers and pale yellow ray florets. They may be solitary or the terminal head may have a few smaller ones below it. From the last, *H. uniflora,* native from Montana to Wyoming and Colorado, differs in lacking large basal leaves and in those on the stems having only three veins. Also, its flower heads face upward. Variety *H. u. douglasii* (syn. *H. douglasii*) is distinguished by its somewhat larger flower heads, and its greater hairiness. Ordinarily not more than 1 foot tall, *H. parryi* has many long-stalked basal leaves and on its stems only one or two pairs of much smaller leaves. Its side-facing flower heads are yellow and about 2 inches in diameter. This is native from Colorado to New Mexico and Arizona.

Garden and Landscape Uses and Cultivation. Helianthellas are most likely to be used in semiwild and naturalistic landscapes in regions where they are native. They may also be planted in mixed flower borders. They succeed in ordinary, reasonably moist soil in sunny locations. Seeds and division afford means of propagation.

HELIANTHEMUM (Heliánth-emum)—Sun-Rose, Frostweed. Approximately 110 species constitute this genus of the rock-rose family CISTACEAE. They are natives from Europe to central Asia and of North and South America. American sorts are sometimes treated separately as *Crocanthemum*.

From related *Cistus* the genus *Helianthemum* differs in its fruits opening by three instead of five, six, or ten valves. The name is derived from the Greek *helios*, the sun, and *anthemon*, a flower. It alludes to the sun-loving proclivity of the genus.

Sun-roses are mostly low, evergreen shrubs and subshrubs. A few are annuals. Usually the leaves are opposite, undivided, lobeless, and without teeth. According to kind, they may or may not have appendages (stipules) at the bases of their leafstalks. The yellow, orange, pink, red, or white flowers are sometimes solitary, more frequently in terminal clusters or sprays, often raceme-like, and sometimes branched. They have five sepals, the outer two smaller and generally narrower than the others, five petals or some flowers with none, numerous stamens, and in the shrubby and subshrubby kinds a long, slender style, which serves to distinguish this group from *Halimium* in which the style is short or wanting. The annual species have short styles or none. The fruits are capsules. The plant sometimes called *H. procumbens* is *Fumana procumbens*, the one previously named *H. tuberaria* is *Tuberaria lignosa*.

Extremely variable **H. nummularium** (syn. *H. vulgare*), not over 1 foot tall, is often lower. It has procumbent stems, erect or ascending branches. Its oblong to ovate or lanceolate leaves, ¼ to 1 inch long by up to ¼ inch wide, are flat. They are green and more or less hairy above. Their undersides are clothed with white or grayish hairs or in some variants are green. They have leaf-like, lanceolate to linear-lanceolate stipules longer than the leafstalks. The flowers have calyxes hairy at least at their margins and along the chief veins. Typically they are yellow or rarely white, but those of *H. n. pyrenaicum* and *H. n. berterianum* are pink.

Helianthemum nummularium variety

Helianthemum nummularium variety (flowers)

The golden- or orange-yellow blooms of *H. n. grandiflorum* are up to 1½ inches in diameter. Larger than normal leaves, and flowers up to 1¼ inches across, characterize *H. n. tomentosum*.

Closely allied **H. apenninum,** of Europe, differs from *H. nummularium* in that the stipules at the bottoms of its leafstalks are linear and not leaflike. This kind branches freely to form a spreading shrub up to 1½ feet tall. Most often its stems and foliage are covered with white, star-shaped hairs that give a mealy appearance, but sometimes the leaves have green upper surfaces. Their margins are slightly to conspicuously rolled back. One inch wide or a little wider, the pure white flowers, stained with yellow on the claws (shafts) of their petals, are in terminal clusters. The sepals are white-hairy, the two outer ones very small and linear, the others much bigger and ovate. Variety *H. a. roseum* (syns. *H. a. rhodanthum, H. rhodanthum*), a native of Italy and the Balearic Islands, has foliage green on its upper surfaces and pink flowers. This, which once was named *H. rhodanthum carneum*, must not be confused with the garden hybrid cultivated under that name. The latter is very similar to and perhaps identical with the hybrid variety 'Wisely Pink'.

Helianthemum oelandicum

Helianthemum apenninum

Another closely related to *H. nummularium*, but with the upper surfaces of its leaves nearly white and the edges of its leaves often slightly or markedly rolled under, **H. croceum** (syns. *H. glaucum, H. g. croceum*) is a shrub up to about 1 foot tall. Native of the western Mediterranean region, this has thick, roundish to linear leaves, the upper ones of the latter type, ¼ to ¾ inch long by up to slightly over ¼ inch wide. Their stipules are large and leaflike. The orange-yellow, bright yellow, or white flowers are up to ¾ inch across.

Variable and divided into five subspecies or varieties, **H. oelandicum,** native in one or other of its phases through much of Europe, is represented in cultivation by one or two of these. Most commonly encountered in gardens is quite lovely *H. o. alpestre* (syn. *H. alpestre*), of the mountains of central and southern Europe. From 3 to 5 inches tall, this forms a cushion of spreading stems and densely-minutely-hairy branches. Its leaves are without stipules. They are narrowly-oblong to oblong-elliptic or elliptic-lanceolate, sparsely-hairy, green on both surfaces, and ¼ to ½ inch long by up to ⅛ inch wide or slightly wider. In raceme-like arrangements of

Helianthemum oelandicum alpestre

three to six or sometimes more, the bright yellow flowers, without blotches, are ½ to ¾ inch wide. Their sepals are hairy. Of looser growth and with racemes, sometimes branched, of up to twenty ½-inch-wide blooms, *H. o. italicum* inhabits the Mediterranean region.

Dwarf compact shrubs from 4 to 6 inches high or occasionally taller and broader than high, *H. canum* and *H. lunulatum* are tufted or cushion-like. The first is widely distributed in the wild from much of Europe to Asia Minor and the Caucasus, the other is limited to the Maritime Alps of Italy. Extremely variable, **H. canum** is divided by botanists into several not very clearly differentiated varieties. It has elliptic, obovate, lanceolate, or linear leaves, green or gray-hairy on their upper surfaces, gray-hairy beneath, without basal stipules. Solitary or in dense or loose clusters of as many as five, the flowers are bright yellow and ½ inch in diameter and have hairy sepals, the two outer ones very small. The ½-inch-wide, bright yellow flowers with an orange spot at the bottom of each petal of **H. lunulatum** are solitary or few at the ends of leafy shoots. This species has twisted, subspiny stems, downy shoots, and short-stalked, elliptic-lanceolate to obovate, green, slightly-hairy leaves a little more or less than ½ inch long and up to ³⁄₁₆ inch wide. The lower ones are without, the upper ones sometimes with, stipules.

The frostweed (*H. canadense* syn. *Crocanthemum canadense*) is a hoary-pubescent, 1- to 2-foot-tall native from Maine to North Carolina and Missouri. It has one to few slender, sometimes few-branched stems and linear-oblong to oblanceolate or narrowly-elliptic leaves from a little less to a little more than 1 inch long, and grayish on their undersides. Its flowers are of two kinds; those borne early in the blooming season, solitary or sometimes in twos, ¾ to 1 inch across, with yellow petals; and those produced later, several together, much smaller, and without petals. The flowers are soon overtopped by the branches and then appear as if growing from the sides of the stems. Similar, but with more petalled flowers in loose terminal racemes, and more petal-less ones crowded on short branches, *H. bicknellii* (syn. *Crocanthemum bicknellii*) is native from Maine to Colorado, North Carolina, and Texas.

Hybrid sun-roses, some of natural, others of garden origin, are plentiful and handsome. They are derivatives chiefly of *H. apenninum*, *H. croceum*, and *H. nummularium* and generally exhibit characteristics intermediate between those of these species. Some horticultural varieties may be selections of variants of the last named rather than hybrids. The available kinds of this group are named and described in the catalogs of nurserymen, especially those who cater to rock gardeners. They include single- and double-flowered varieties. Among the first are 'Butterpat', yellow; 'Dazzler', bright crimson; 'Flame', flame-pink; 'Goldilocks', with silvery foliage and yellow blooms; and 'Peach', with apricot flowers. Among double-flowered varieties are 'Boule de Feu', crimson; 'Snowball', white; and 'Sun Fleck', bright golden-yellow.

Garden and Landscape Uses. Sun-roses are splendid furnishings for rock gardens, rocky edgings to flower beds, banks and other places where they can spread or cascade to display their great wealths of fugitive blooms to advantage, each day's crop ended and their petals dropped before evening, in some cases by midday, to be followed on the morrow and for many morrows by equally as floriferous offerings. Sun is a must for sun-roses. In shade or part-shade they sulk or die, or at best open their blooms tardily. Plant them in well-drained places. They do well in sandy, gravelly and stony soils that are dryish, but not excessively so, and succeed in earths of a limestone character. Some kinds, not quite as hardy as one would wish, suffer somewhat in severe winters in the vicinity of New York City, but most do not.

Cultivation. Sun-roses respond badly to root disturbance. Instead of attempting to transplant older specimens set out young ones from small pots. This is best done in spring. Keep them watered in dry weather until new roots have spread into the soil around the root ball. Routine care of established plants consists of shearing old flowering stalks and other straggling shoots as soon as blooming is through and, in severe climates, of placing over them after the ground freezes in fall a covering of branches of pines or other evergreens, salt hay, or similar suitable material. Propagation is by seeds, and by summer cuttings planted under mist or in a cold frame or greenhouse propagating bench. The cutting method is the only practicable one for hybrids and garden varieties.

HELIANTHOCEREUS (Heliantho-cèreus). Thirteen species of cactuses, native to Argentina and Bolivia, constitute *Helianthocereus* of the cactus family CACTACEAE. They are closely related to and by some authorities are included in *Trichocereus*. The name comes from the Greek *helios*, the sun, *anthos*, a flower, and cactus.

The species of this genus range from treelike kinds up to 30 feet tall to clustering sorts scarcely exceeding 1 foot in height. They have prominently ribbed stems and needle- to awl-shaped spines. Their large, trumpet-shaped blooms, open by day, have perianth tubes and ovaries that, like the fruits, are scaly and hairy.

Sometimes 30 feet tall, but frequently lower, *H. pasacana* (syn. *Trichocereus pasacana*) has solitary or branched stems 1½ to 3 feet in diameter with fifteen to thirty or a few more ribs. The spines are yellow, awl-shaped, up to 5 inches long, in clusters of many. The flowers are white and about 4½ inches long. The roundish fruits, about 1½ inches thick, are edible. From 3 to 12 feet in height, *H. poco* (syn. *Trichocereus poco*) has solitary or branched stems that may attain 2 feet in diameter and that have about twenty-five prominent ribs with clusters of up to fifty mostly yellowish to whitish, slender spines, the radials up to 1½ inches long. There are usually six to nine centrals, up to 3 inches in length, and yellowish to reddish-brown. The purplish-pink to red blooms are about 5 inches long.

Much lower *H. huascha* (syn. *Trichocereus huascha*) has clustered stems about 4 inches in diameter with twelve to eighteen low, notched ribs, clusters of ten to fifteen ½-inch-long radial spines, and four to six stouter centrals up to 2¼ inches long. The yellow flowers are about 3 inches wide. Those of *H. h. rubriflorus* are slightly smaller and blood-red, those of *H. h. auricolor* are fiery-red. From 1 foot to 1½ feet tall and much-branched, *H. grandiflorus* has stems approximately 2 inches thick. Its slender, needlelike, pale yellow spines are in closely spaced clusters of eight to twelve about ½-inch-long laterals and one central. Brilliant red, the blooms are some 3½ inches wide.

Garden and Landscape Uses and Cultivation. Generally easy to manage, plants of this genus are well adapted for outdoor cultivation in dry climates where little or no frost occurs and for inclusion in greenhouse collections of succulents. They respond to reasonably nourishing, very well-drained, slightly acid soil and full sun. They appreciate more moisture than most desert cactuses and are relatively cold resistant. For more information see Cactuses.

HELIANTHUS (Heli-ánthus)—Sunflower, Jerusalem Artichoke. The somewhat coarse, but often showy annual and perennial herbaceous plants that constitute *Helianthus* number more than sixty species, mostly natives of North America, but with a few in temperate South America. They belong to the daisy family COMPOSITAE. Because of variability and tendency to hybridize sunflowers are not always easy to identify as to species. The name, alluding to the form of their flower heads, is from the Greek *helios*, sun, and *anthos*, a flower. Most kinds are hardy.

Sunflowers have undivided, often toothed leaves, the lower ones opposite, those above often alternate. The flower heads, of the daisy pattern, are solitary or clustered. They have a central disk of bisexual, yellow florets, and surrounding it, a circle of yellow, sterile, petal-like ray florets. The seedlike fruits are achenes.

One *Helianthus*, the Jerusalem artichoke, is cultivated for its edible tubers, which are cooked as a vegetable, pickled, or sometimes eaten raw. This was one of the few crops cultivated by the American Indians. In Europe it is frequently grown as a food crop, but rarely in America. Because the tubers contain no starch and very little sugar they have been advocated as food for diabetics. The Jerusalem artichoke is not related to the common artichoke. The name is a corruption of its Italian name girasole. The common sunflower is esteemed for its seeds which, especially in Russia and adjacent lands, are eaten much as Americans eat peanuts. They are favorites of parrots and other birds, and after the oil they contain has been expressed from them the residue oil cake is fed to livestock and poultry.

Common sunflower (*H. annuus*), in its cultivated varieties, has much bigger flower heads, often 1 foot or more in diameter, than those of its wild progenitor. These huge, flat-centered "suns" are carried at the tops of stout, erect stems that may be 10 to 15 feet tall. They have brownish, purple, or sometimes yellow centers, and generally yellow rays, but there are variants. In *H. a. purpureus* the rays are magenta, in *H. a. citrinus* primrose-yellow. Variety *H. a. florepleno* has double flower heads of mostly ray-type florets. Variegated foliage characterizes *H. a. variegatus*. Extremely vigorous *H. a. giganteus* is taller than the typical species, and *H. a. nanus* dwarfer, and with double

Helianthus annuus

hairy, especially on their younger parts. The leaves are ovate, toothless or sightly toothed and have blades 4 to 8 inches long. The purple-centered, yellow-rayed flower heads, with densely-silky involucres (collars of bracts at their rears) are 3 inches or more across.

Another annual, *H. debilis* ranges in the wild as a variable species from Florida to Texas. Most likely to be cultivated are the cucumber-leaf sunflower (*H. d. cucumerifolius*) and garden varieties of it. These are sturdier and have more erect stems, usually conspicuously mottled with purple, than *H. debilis*. The cucumber-leaf sunflower is 3 to 7 feet tall, and has alternate, long-stalked, toothed, rough-hairy leaves with triangular-ovate, slightly-wavy margined blades 2 to 4 inches long, and heart-shaped at their bases. The flower heads, with brownish-purple centers and yellow rays, are 2 to 3 inches in diameter. There are horticultural varieties with the rays of the flower heads chestnut-red tipped with yellow, zoned with chestnut-red and yellow, and almost white, as well as double-flowered ones.

Perennial sunflowers are numerous as to species and locally many kinds are likely to be introduced to gardens. Thin-leaf sunflower (*H. decapetalus*) is about 5 feet tall. It has hairless stems, and toothed, ovate to ovate-lanceolate, more or less rough-hairy leaves up to 8 inches long, and a plentitude of 3-inch-wide flower heads with usually yellowish centers. It is native from Quebec to Georgia and Missouri. Double-flowered *H. d. flore-pleno* and *H. d. grandiflorus* are grown. Larger flower heads with pointed ray florets characterize *H. d. maximus*.

flowers. Variety *H. a.* 'Russian Giant' has solitary flower heads of huge size. Excellent garden varieties with chestnut-red blooms have been raised. As it occurs in the wild in dry soils and prairies throughout much of the United States, the common sunflower is a coarse, branching, rough-hairy annual generally 3 to 10 feet tall. Except for the lower ones its long-stalked, usually toothed, broad-ovate to heart-shaped leaves are mostly alternate and have blades up to 1 foot long. The flower heads are generally several to many, and mostly 3 to 6 inches across. Very similar to the wild common sunflower, but seldom exceeding 3 feet in height and with narrower leaves with rarely heart-shaped bases, the prairie sunflower (*H. petiolaris*) is native throughout much of the United States. It is an annual with flower heads up to 3 inches across.

Silverleaf sunflower (*H. argophyllus*), probably originally confined to Texas, is now spontaneous in other parts of the southern United States. An annual 3 to 6 feet tall, its stems branch freely above, and like both sides of the mostly alternate, stalked leaves, are densely-silky-white-

Helianthus annuus, garden variety

Helianthus annuus flore-pleno

Helianthus decapetalus grandiflorus

A horticultural variety with semidouble flower heads with quilled ray florets is *H. d.* 'Soleil d'Or'.

Native to wet soils from New York to Florida and Texas, the swamp sunflower (*H. angustifolius*) is a perennial or biennial 2 to 7 feet tall with rough-hairy stems, and stalkless, linear, toothless, mostly alternate leaves up to 7 inches long and, except sometimes for the lowermost, not over one-tenth as wide as long. The purple-centered flower heads, 2 to 3 inches across are solitary or few together. Their ray florets are bright yellow.

Also with linear leaves, perennial *H. salicifolius* (syn. *H. orgyalis*) is native from Missouri to Colorado and Texas. From 8 to 10 feet tall, its essentially hairless stems are without branches except in their upper, flowering parts. They are very leafy throughout. The leaves are drooping, mostly alternate, very narrow-linear to lanceolate, and 6 inches to more than 1 foot long. The lower ones are stalked, those above stalkless. Numerous, the 2-inch-wide flower heads have brown or purplish centers and lemon-yellow ray florets.

Because of its hoary-pubescent stems and foliage called ashy sunflower, *H. mollis* is a perennial 3 to 5 feet tall, that has mostly opposite, toothed, ovate to lanceolate leaves up to 5 inches long, the lower ones heart-shaped and stem-clasping. The flower heads, solitary or few together, have yellowish centers and are 2 to 3 inches across. This kind occurs in dryish soils from Massachusetts to Illinois, Georgia, and Texas.

Dark-eye sunflower (*H. atrorubens* syn. *H. sparsifolius*) is a rough-hairy perennial up to 5 feet tall. It has opposite, toothed, ovate to oblong-lanceolate leaves with winged stalks and blades up to 10 inches long. The dark-purple-centered flower heads, about 2 inches wide, are loosely clustered. This is native from Virginia to Florida and Louisiana. The variety *H. a.* 'Monarch' has larger blooms.

Called giant sunflower, perennial *H. giganteus* is less massive than annual *H. annuus*. A native of wet soils from Maine to Alberta, Colorado, and Florida and 3 to 10 feet in height, it has thick roots and stems with hairs at right angles to the surface. Its pointed-lanceolate, short-stalked, rough-hairy leaves are up to 7 inches long and are more or less strongly-toothed. Sometimes all the leaves are opposite, more often those above are alternate. The several to many flower heads, 1½ to 3 inches across, have yellowish centers and pale yellow rays.

Grayish-green, conspicuously short-hairy foliage, and flower heads with yellow centers and deep yellow rays are typical of *H. maximiliani.* This native of moistish soils from Minnesota to Texas has rough-hairy stems, mostly branchless and 3 to 12 feet high. Its narrow-lanceolate, slightly toothed or toothless leaves, are 3 to 7 inches long or sometimes longer. Nearly all are alternate. The short-stalked flower heads are few together or rarely solitary. They are 2 to 3 inches in diameter and have bright yellow rays.

Helianthus maximiliani

Showy sunflower (*H. laetiflorus*) chiefly inhabits dry prairies and plains from Minnesota and Indiana to Montana, Missouri, and New Mexico. A perennial with stout rhizomes, it is 2 to 6 feet tall and rough-hairy to nearly hairless. Its stems are usually branched only in their upper parts. Its essentially stalkless leaves are firm-textured and nearly all opposite. They are chiefly lanceolate to narrow-ovate, pointed and toothed or toothless. Their blades are 2 to 10 inches long. The flower heads, their centers usually yellow, rarely brownish to purple, have yellow rays and are 2 to 4 inches across. Much like the last, *H. rigidus* (syn. *H. laetiflorus rigidus*) ranges from Manitoba and Wisconsin to Georgia and Texas. Up to 6 feet tall or sometimes taller it has usually red stems sparingly- to densely-rough-hairy. Its leaves are broader than those of *H. laetiflorus* and very rough-hairy. The flower heads, up to 4 inches across, have yellow to deep red centers.

An interesting horticultural hybrid, *H. multiflorus*, its parents annual *H. annuus* and perennial *H. decapetalus*, is a perennial up to 6 feet tall; slightly bristly-hairy, it has mostly alternate, pointed-ovate, toothed leaves up to 10 inches long. Its golden-yellow flower heads 3½ to 5 inches in diameter are single, semidouble, or fully double.

Helianthus multiflorus: (a) Single-flowered

(b) Double-flowered

Jerusalem artichoke or girasole (*H. tuberosus*) is a vigorous, stout-stemmed, branching perennial 3 to 10 feet tall. It usually bears on underground stems edible, somewhat potato-like tubers that in cultivated varieties may be 3 to 4 inches long and 2 to 3 inches in diameter, but these may not develop if conditions are not favorable. The stems and leaves are generally rough-hairy. The latter are opposite on the lower parts of the stems, alternate above. They are ovate to broadly-ovate-lanceolate, pointed, and toothed. The leafstalks are winged, the leaf blades 4 to 8 inches long. The several to many flower heads, 2 to 3½ inches across, have yellow centers and light yellow rays. This species is indigenous through much of North America.

Garden and Landscape Uses. The Jerusalem artichoke is cultivated for its edible tubers, the common sunflower for its seeds. These and others discussed here are also grown as ornamentals and for cut flowers. None is difficult. Most need full sun and succeed in ordinary, well-drained soil, but some, notably *H. atrorubens*, stand partial shade, and *H. angustifolius, H. giganteus*, and *H. maximiliani* are partial to moist or wet soils. All sunflowers are best displayed in groups rather than as single plants.

Garden varieties of the common sunflower are so distinctive that they form prominent accents wherever they are placed. There is a certain homey quality and old-fashioned rural character about them that makes them suitable for locating near outbuildings, along fences, or where their huge flower heads may be viewed overtopping walls. For large flower beds only are these sometimes appropriate; then they should be placed at the rear. Less monster-flowered annual kinds are well suited for flower borders and, especially the cucumber-leaf sunflower and its varieties, as cut blooms.

Perennial sunflowers are vigorous growers likely to crowd out more delicate neighbors. Because of this, they should be located with some care in flower borders or be set naturalistically in less formal surroundings. They are gross feeders and for best results should be dug up, divided, and replanted in newly spaded and fertilized ground every second year. This is especially necessary with double-flowered kinds. If not done, the flower heads produced tend to be single or semidouble rather than fuller.

Cultivation. Annual sunflowers are raised with great ease from seeds sown outdoors in spring, or by sowing indoors three or four weeks before the expected date of the latest frost, and transplanting to the garden later. The young plants are grown in the interim in full sun where the night temperature is about 50°F and that by day five to ten degrees higher. Plants in the garden should be 1 foot to 2 feet apart.

Perennial sunflowers, except those double-flowered kinds that are usually seedless, are easily had from sowings made outdoors or in a cold frame in May, the young plants being transplanted to nursery beds to complete their first season's growth and from these, in fall or spring, to their flowering stations. But a more common means of increase is by division in early fall or spring. Strong outside pieces of the root clumps are selected for replanting. Cuttings taken in early summer root readily in a cold frame or under similar conditions, and make good young plants by fall. Seasonal care of perennial sunflowers makes little demand of the gardener. A spring application of a complete fertilizer is helpful. If so many young shoots develop that crowding seems likely they should be thinned out early. Staking to prevent storm damage is likely to be needed. Watering regularly and generously in dry weather does much to maintain health and vigor. Unless seeds are needed, faded blooms should be removed promptly, and after the first killing frost the tops are cut down and cleared away. For cultivation of Jerusalem artichoke see Artichoke, Jerusalem.

HELIAPORUS. A hybrid between *Aporocactus flagelliformis* and *Heliocereus speciosus* is named *Heliaporus smithii*. See Aporocactus.

HELICHRYSUM (Heli-chrỳsum)—Everlasting, Strawflower, Curry Plant, Immortelle. The name *Helichrysum*, derived from the Greek *helios*, the sun, and *chrysos*, golden, alludes to the form and color of the flower heads of some of the 500 species of this genus of the daisy family COMPOSITAE. The group consists of annuals, herbaceous perennials, and subshrubs, widely distributed as natives throughout most of the world, but absent from the western hemisphere. Some kinds are called everlastings or immortelles, names also applied to other genera including *Ammobium, Anaphalis, Antennaria, Helipterum*, and *Xeranthemum*.

Helichrysum have mostly alternate, generally downy or woolly leaves ranging, according to species, from large to tiny. Rarely, the lower leaves are opposite. The flower heads, solitary or clustered, are of all disk florets, the equivalent of those of the central eyes of daisies. There are no ray florets corresponding to the petal-like ones of daisies, but often the inner bracts of the involucre (collar behind the flower head) are enlarged, colorful, and more or less petal-like. These are the showy parts of the flower heads of strawflowers, and as is usual in *Helichrysum*, they are membranous, papery, and retain their form and color after the flower heads are dried, thus accounting for their everlasting qualities. The fruits of helichrysums are seed-like achenes.

Strawflower (*H. bracteatum*) is a popular, stout-stemmed, branched annual 1½

Helichrysum bracteatum

Helichrysum angustifolium

Helichrysum angustifolium, trained as a standard

to 3 feet tall. Its oblong-lanceolate, short-stalked, hairless or nearly hairless leaves are 2 to 5 inches in length. Solitary at the stem and branch ends, the flower heads are 1 inch to 2 inches in diameter. The inner rows of involucral bracts are much elongated and petal-like. They are bright yellow, orange or copper, crimson, or white, greenish at their bases. Strawflowers are natives of Australia. Variety *H. b. monstrosum* has larger flower heads with many more colorful bracts that give the effect of a double flower.

The curry plant (*H. angustifolium*) has a vernacular name that alludes to the curry-like odor of its foliage when lightly brushed against. A nonhardy woody-based subshrub of the Mediterranean region, 1 foot high or a little higher, it has slender-linear white- or gray-hairy leaves ½ inch to 1½ inches long, with rolled-under margins. On the lower part of the plant these are densely crowded. The yellow flower heads up to ¼ inch wide are in clusters 1 inch to 2 inches wide terminating long, sparsely-foliaged, erect stems.

Cultivated as an ornamental foliage plant, *H. petiolatum* (syn. *Gnaphalium lanatum*) is a beautiful nonhardy subshrub. Native of South Africa, about 2 feet tall, it has stems and foliage densely clothed with a flannel-like felt of whitish to yellowish hairs. The stalked leaves have broad-ovate to nearly circular, about 1-inch-long blades that narrow abruptly to squarish bases. In tight clusters 1 inch to 2 inches in diameter, the ⅛-inch-wide flower heads have creamy-white involucral bracts, but often they are not produced on cultivated specimens.

Very different *H. bellidioides* is a choice, dwarf subshrub of New Zealand, perhaps hardy as far north as Philadelphia. Its

Helichrysum petiolatum

slender, prostrate, much-branched, rooting stems carry spatula-shaped to obovate leaves ¼ to ½ inch long. Green above and with white-woolly undersides, they have stem-clasping bases. The mostly solitary

Helichrysum bellidioides

flower heads ¾ inch to 1¼ inches wide and with white involucral bracts are on slender, erect stalks 1 inch to 5 inches long. In *H. b. prostratum* the stalks of the flower heads are very short. Subshrubby *H. orientale*, of southern Europe, attains a height of 6 to 9 inches. It has very woolly,

Helichrysum orientale

grayish-white, long-obovate leaves and clusters of light yellow to white, satiny flower heads terminating erect, densely-felted stalks. Lovely *H. milfordiae*, of southern Africa, has low, compact cushions of small, tapering, ovate leaves clothed with silvery hairs and comparatively large, white, solitary flower heads

Helichrysum milfordiae

reminiscent of little English daisies. The ends of the undersides of the bracts are crimson or brown. This kind is perennial.

Choice but very difficult to grow, **H. frigidum** tests the skill of even the most accomplished grower of alpines. Native of high warm places in Corsica and Sardinia, this "miffy beauty," as the great English rock gardener Reginald Farrer describes it, perhaps may be persuaded to prosper in parts of the Pacific Northwest and where winters are not excessively cold and wet nor summers too humid. A compact gem, in bloom scarcely 2 inches tall, this sort forms a tuft or cushion of crowded shoots clothed with tiny leaves. The silvery-white flower heads, about ½ inch wide, have the everlasting characteristic of their larger relatives. For this species Farrer prescribes planting on a sloping site in light, nourishing, stony soil. Propagation, he says, can be achieved by taking cuttings in August.

Helichrysum frigidum

Garden and Landscape Uses. Strawflowers are popular for garden decoration and for cutting and drying for use in arrangments. In mild, dryish climates *H. angustifolium* and *H. petiolatum* may be grown permanently outdoors at the fronts of flower beds and borders, in rock gardens, and similar locations. They can be also grown from cuttings each year for summer foliage effect in flower gardens, window boxes, urns, and other containers. In cold climates young plants of these are overwintered in greenhouses or cold frames. The New Zealand species described and *H. milfordiae* are choice for rock gardens in mild, cool climates and for growing in pans (shallow pots) in alpine greenhouses.

Cultivation. The helichrysums described here are lovers of sun and freely drained soils. Sow seeds of strawflowers directly outdoors in spring where the plants are to remain and thin out the seedlings to 6 to 8 inches apart, or sow earlier indoors in a temperature of about 60°F, transplant in flats or small pots, and plant outdoors when there is no longer danger of frost. Summer care consists of weeding and, in very dry weather, watering. To harvest blooms for drying, cut them just before they are fully open, tie them in bundles, and hang them upside down in a dry, airy, shady place.

Gray-foliaged *H. angustifolium* and *H. petiolatum* need no particular care beyond any trimming to keep them shapely and the shearing of faded flower heads. They are easily propagated by cuttings. Excessive moisture is their chief enemy. Warmth, sunshine, and dryish to rather arid environments are to their liking. The three other kinds described above are plants for mild-region rock gardens and for alpine greenhouses. They need gritty soil and a sunny location. When accommodated in greenhouses or frames they are best in pans (shallow pots). Increase is by seeds, cuttings, and careful division.

HELICODICEROS (Helicod-íceros)—Twist-Arum. In bloom one of the most foul-smelling of plants, the only species of this genus is offered by bulb dealers and is grown in limited quantities as a curiosity and conversation piece. Native of Corsica, Sardinia, and the Balearic Islands, it belongs in the arum family ARACEAE, an assemblage that includes such notable stinkers as devil's tongue (*Hydrosme*), voodoo-lily (*Sauromatum*), immense *Amorphophallus titanum*, and the, by comparison, mildly odorous skunk-cabbage (*Symplocarpus*), as well as such well-known flowering and foliage ornamentals as anthuriums, calla-lilies, philodendrons, ivy-arums, and monsteras. The name *Helicodiceros* derives from the Greek *helix*, spiral, *dis*, twice, and *keras*, a horn, and alludes to the basal divisions of the leaf twisting and standing erect in the manner of horns.

The twist-arum (**H. muscivorus** syns. *Arum crinitum, Dracunculus crinitus*) is a deciduous tuberous plant, 1½ to 2 feet tall, that flowers in spring along with its foliage. The latter consists of leaves divided in finger-like fashion. What is usually called the flower is really an inflorescence (assemblage of flowers and attendant parts) that consists of a spadix (spike that carries the true small flowers) and from its base a spathe (petal-like bract). In the twist-arum, as in the calla-lily, the trumpet-shaded spathe envelops the tail-like spadix, which protrudes from its mouth, but in the twist-arum, unlike the calla-lily, the trumpet is bent sharply at right angles at about its middle, and the tail-like end of the spadix is conspicuously hairy. The

Helicodiceros muscivorus

spathe is dark purple-brown and is hairy inside. The spadix is shorter than the spathe, and there is a distinct region with only rudimentary flowers between the male blooms that occupy the upper part of the spadix and the females below.

The twist-arum is pollinated by flies, which are attracted to its ripe blooms in such enormous numbers that they often become packed inside and when the spathe withers and closes are entrapped. From its close relative *Arum* the twist-arum differs in technical details of its ovules and in its leaves being divided, and from its ally *Dracunculus* in there being a sterile portion of spadix between the male and female flowers.

Garden Uses and Cultivation. Those who can stand the disgusting odor of the blooms of this plant, or take pleasure in astonishing their friends with it, plant the tubers in fall, in partial shade, in fertile, well-drained soil that does not lack for moisture during the spring and early summer. Decent regard for the sensitivities of others suggests that this species be located away from habitations and where no one is likely to be subjected unwillingly to its foul scent. Following planting a mulch of leaf mold or peat moss is appropriate. Not hardy in regions where its tubers are subject to freezing, the twist-arum is occasionally, again as a curiosity, grown in greenhouses. It is potted in fall in well-drained containers of fertile soil and is placed in a cold frame or cool greenhouse. If in a cold frame the pots are brought indoors before there is danger of them freezing. Winter night temperatures of about 50°F are satisfactory with some little rise by day permitted. Watering is moderate at first, freely done after growth is well started. Following flowering, water, and occasionally applications of dilute liquid fertilizer, are supplied until the foliage begins to die naturally, then fertilizing ceases and watering is gradually reduced, finally stopped, and the soil is maintained in a dry condition until repotting time in fall. Propagation is by division and by seed.

HELICONIA (Heli-cònia)—Wild-Plantain, Lobster Claw. Named without apparent reason after Mount Helicon, seat of the Muses, *Heliconia*, of the banana family Mu-SACEAE, contains eighty mostly botanically poorly understood species. They are chiefly natives of tropical America, with some inhabiting islands of the Pacific. A few in common cultivation in the tropics are grown and admired for their handsome foliage and in some cases for their strikingly beautiful flowers.

Heliconias produce from the ground many long-stalked, undivided, two-ranked, more or less paddle-shaped leaves. The flowers are in erect or drooping spikes, few to several in the axils of usually two-ranked, folded or boat-shaped, often

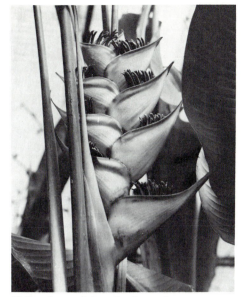
Heliconia, undetermined species

highly colored and showy bracts. They have three each sepals and petals, the latter united to form a short tube and sometimes of very unequal size. There are five or six fertile stamens or five fertile stamens and a staminode (sterile stamen). The style is slender, the stigma sometimes shallowly-three-lobed. The fruits, usually blue, are capsules that separate into three somewhat fleshy, berry-like parts.

The wild-plantain (*H. bihai*) is a vigorous, banana-like species up to 20 feet tall, native

Heliconia bihai

from Mexico to Peru, Brazil, and parts of the West Indies and naturalized in some Pacific Islands. Its long-stalked, oblong leaves are 3 to 4 feet long and 8 inches to 1 foot wide. The colorful flower spikes are erect and have stout stalks 6 inches to 1½ feet long hidden by the bases of long-pointed, ovate to ovate-lanceolate, essentially hairless bracts. The latter are reddish with yellowish to chartreuse or apple-green edges, or sometimes are entirely greenish or reddish. Both at flowering and fruiting time their pointed ends are up-turned. The greenish blooms are 1½ to 2¼ inches long, the oblongish fruits a little over ½ inch

long. From the last, **H. caribaea** differs but slightly if at all botanically. Its leaves are described as having more rounded bases. Its erect flower spikes have fleshy, pointed bracts, the broad bases of which slightly overlap. They are golden-yellow with greenish keels and apexes or are crimson briefly edged with yellow. Plants with bracts of this last coloring are sometimes distinguished as *H. c. purpurea*.

The lobster claw (**H. humilis**), indigenous in South America and Trinidad and akin to *H. bihai*, has more glossy foliage and flower spikes with smaller, boat-shaped, vivid salmon-red bracts that approximate in color a boiled lobster and merge to green. They are clawlike, up to 5 inches long, and alternate in two ranks.

Heliconia humilis

The flowers they enclose are yellowish-white. Also called lobster claw, the plant known in cultivation as **H. jacquinii**, a name without botanical standing, is believed to be a native of the Fiji Islands. Tall and banana-like, its flower spikes have showy, distinctly alternate, boat-shaped, salmon to bright red bracts tipped and edged with green.

Heliconia jacquinii

One of the finest heliconias is robust *H. mariae*, of lowland forests from Nicaragua to Colombia. This banana-like species attains heights of over 15 feet, and has broadly-oblong, bluish-green, round-based leaves with blades, green on their undersides, 3½ to 4 feet long, and stalks of equal length. The pendent, stout-stalked flower spikes, 1 foot long or longer, have densely-crowded, overlapping, rhombic-ovate, blunt to pointed, rosy-red to deep crimson bracts, usually piped with white, widest above their bases, and almost as broad as long. The flowers are deep pink to red, the subspherical fruits dark purple and ⅕ inch thick. Others with hanging flower spikes are *H. pendula* (syn. *H. collinsiana*), of Guatemala, and *H. platystachys*, of Guatemala and Colombia. Characterized by fishpole-like stems 6 to 8 feet tall and paddle-shaped leaves, *H. pendula* has waxy-powdered flower spikes with widely spaced, narrow, long-pointed, pinkish red bracts and rather conspicuous yellow blooms. A big, banana-like species, *H. platystachys* has large leaves, green on both surfaces. Its flower spikes have wavy stalks and well-separated, folded, slender bracts, pubescent near their bases, and up to 7 inches long with those near the apex of the spike shorter than those below. They are bright red margined with green or yellow.

Canna-like *H. psittacorum* is a variable native of mostly lowland forests from Mexico to Brazil, Peru, and the West Indies. From 3 to 10 feet tall, its slender stems have round-based, pointed-oblong-lanceolate leaves 6 inches to 1 foot long by one-half as wide. The slender-stalked flower spikes are erect and may or may not be minutely-hairy. The long-pointed, narrowly-lanceolate, thin bracts, up to 1 foot long, point upward when the flowers are expanded, but later are spreading. They are green, yellow, or red, or are frequently variegated with these colors. The green-tipped, yellow or white flowers, ¾ inch long, are succeeded by dark purple-blue, broadly-egg-shaped fruits under ½ inch in length. Another slender species, about 10 feet tall, *H. metallica,* of Colombia, has red stems and oblong, velvety emerald-green leaves with purplish undersides and pearly-white center ribs. The erect flower spikes have widely spaced, boat-shaped, green-tipped, rose-red bracts.

Unlike those of many heliconias, the showy flower spikes of *H. latispatha,* of Central America and northern South America, are above the foliage. They have widely spaced, narrow, rich orange-yellow bracts, lacquered with red at their apexes and 6 inches long. Sometimes the bracts are uniformly yellow or red or have the colors reversed. The flowers are greenish. The leaves have broadly-oblong blades 3 feet long by one-third as wide.

Low heliconias include Brazilian *H. bicolor* (syn. *H. angustifolia*), 3 to 5 feet tall.

It has leaves with 2-foot-long, leathery blades and erect flower spikes with orange-red, boat-shaped bracts and creamy-white flowers. The bracts deepen in color as they age. With reedlike stems some 3 feet long, Guatemalan *H. choconiana* has thinnish, linear-oblong leaves and stalkless flower spikes with orange-scarlet bracts and well displayed, buff-yellow-tipped, creamy-yellow flowers. Native to southern Mexico, *H. aurantiaca* is 2½ to 3 feet tall. It has reedy stems, oblong leaves, and showy, upright flower spikes with the lower bracts orange tipped with green, the upper ones yellowish-red. The flowers are greenish-red. A compact sort known in cultivation as *H. velutina,* but not recognized botanically, has satiny, pointed, short, green leaves with rich glossy under surfaces.

Kinds grown for their foliage, that rarely or never bloom, and the botanical positions of which are in some doubt, are varieties of *H. illustris* (syn. *H. indica*). These are *H. i. edwardus-rex*, with foliage richly suffused, especially on the under surfaces, with deep coppery-red; *H. i. rubricaulis*, which has green leaves with red undersides, red stalks, very distinct rose-pink midribs, and pink side veins; and *H. i. spectabilis*, which has bronzy-green leaves, wine-red on their under surfaces, red-stalked, and with brown-red midribs. The deeply-boat-shaped floral bracts are reddish and overlapping.

Garden and Landscape Uses and Cultivation. Heliconias can be used with dramatic effects as bold clumps in tropical gardens and are useful sources of cut flowers. They are suitable for outdoor cultivation in warm, humid climates and for large greenhouses. Their needs are simple. A lightly shaded location sheltered from wind, where the soil is deep, fertile, and fairly moist, is all that is needed. Propagation is usually by division, but also by seed.

HELICTOTRICHON (Helicto-trìchon). Some sixty species of the grass family GRAMINEAE compose *Helictotrichon*, the name of which, from the Greek *helictos*, twisted, and *trichos*, a hair, alludes to the twisted bases of the awns of the flowering parts. The genus, native of the northern hemisphere and South Africa, is closely related to *Avena*.

Helictotrichons are perennials forming tufts of slender stems and generally narrow, flat, folded or rolled leaf blades. The flowers are in graceful, erect or nodding panicles of large spikelets.

An attractive ornamental, *H. sempervirens* (syn. *Avena candida*), of southwest Europe, 1 foot to 4 feet tall, forms dense clumps of erect stems and gracefully arching, fine-pointed, tightly-rolled, stiff, blue-green leaves 6 inches to 1½ feet long, not more than ⅛ inch wide when unrolled, and with the lower leaf sheaths hairless or nearly so. The loose panicles 2 to 7 inches

Helictotrichon sempervirens

Helipterum roseum

Hemerocallis, three garden varieties

Heliotrope and gray-leaved *Senecio cineraria*

Hesperis matronalis

Hesperocallis undulata

Hermannia verticillata

Hepatica americana

in length are of purple-stained, yellowish to brownish, two- to three-flowered, oblong spikelets that approximate ½ inch in length.

Garden and Landscape Uses and Cultivation. The species described here can be used effectively in flower beds and borders, especially where gray foliage is desired. It thrives in full sun in any ordinary well-drained soil. In climates harsher than that of Washington, D.C. it should be afforded a sheltered location and be protected over winter. Increase is easy by division and by seed.

HELIOCEREUS (Helio-cèreus). Mexican and Central American, mostly clambering or procumbent, terrestrial or epiphytic (tree-perching) cactuses probably numbering not more than three or four species belong here. The name comes from the Greek *helios,* sun, and *Cereus,* the name of a related genus. These plants belong to the cactus family CACTACEAE.

Heliocereuses have usually weak, but in cultivation often erect, stems with usually three or four, more rarely up to seven, strongly-defined ribs or angles, and from the areoles (spine-producing areas) clusters of all-similar spines. The large, solitary, day-opening, terminal or lateral, scarlet or more rarely white, funnel-shaped flowers have short perianth tubes, spreading perianth segments (petals), and numerous, protruding, down-sweeping stamens. The ovoid or globose, spiny fruits are fleshy. This genus, particularly *Heliocereus speciosus,* has played an important role as parent in the development of horticultural varieties of the hybrid *Epiphyllum* complex.

With clambering or pendulous stems, reddish in their younger parts, elsewhere green, and having three to five conspicuously-scalloped ribs, **H. speciosus** looks rather like a spiny *Epiphyllum.* It is abundantly wild from near Mexico City southward. The areoles are 1 inch to 2 inches or a little more apart. They sprout several to many needle-like, yellow to brownish spines up to ½ inch long or a little longer. The carmine-red blooms with a steel-blue luster are 5 to 7 inches in length and as wide. The style is slightly longer than the stamens. Each flower lasts for two to four days. Variety *H. s. amecamensis* (syn. *H. amecamensis*) has white flowers, greenish on their outsides. Similar to *H. speciosus,* and perhaps derived from it, **H. superbus** has thicker stems bright red in their young parts, and shorter, more slender spines. Its blooms are cinnabar-red.

Others are **H. coccineus** (syn. *H. elegantissimus*), with red flowers with stamens not longer than the style; **H. cinnabarinus,** which is similar but has thinner stems; and **H. schrankii,** which has scarlet to maroon-red blooms with styles decidedly longer than the stamens.

Garden and Landscape Uses and Cultivation. These plants may be grown outdoors in warm, semidesert and desert regions or in greenhouses. They require conditions that suit other sun-loving cactuses, but do not always bloom well indoors. The suggestion has been made that greenhouse specimens summered outdoors bloom more freely than if kept permanently inside. For additional information see Cactuses.

HELIOCHIA. See Epiphyllum and Nopalxochia.

HELIOPHILA (Helióph-ila). Very few of the seventy-five species of South African annuals, biennials, and herbaceous perennials that constitute *Heliophila,* of the mustard family CRUCIFERAE, are known to gardeners. The well-chosen generic name comes from the Greek *helios,* sun, and *philein,* to love.

Heliophilas have blue, purple, pink, yellow, or white, four-petaled flowers in leafless racemes. As is usual for the family, each has four sepals, four petals displayed as a cross, six stamens two of which are shorter than the others, one style, and podlike fruits. In *Heliophila* the pods are slender and contain a single row of seeds. Usually they are constricted between the seeds.

The species most commonly cultivated are *H. leptophylla* and *H. linearifolia,* both with clear blue flowers about ½ inch across with yellow bases to their petals. Compact, bushy, and 1 foot to 1½ feet in height, **H. leptophylla** has slender, erect stems, almost threadlike, glaucous, blue-green leaves, and pendulous seed pods markedly constricted between the seeds. With narrow, pointed leaves, **H. linearifolia** is 1 foot to 3 feet tall. Its seed pods are erect, markedly

Heliophila linearifolia

three-veined, and not narrowed between the seeds. Other kinds occasionally grown as annuals are **H. amplexicaulis,** 1 foot to 2 feet tall and with lanceolate leaves, sometimes slightly hairy, and white, yellow, or purple blooms; **H. coronopifolia,** which attains a height of 1 foot or more and has leaves deeply divided into pointed, narrow segments so that they have a ferny appearance, and white, pink or lilac, often purple-spotted blooms; and **H. pilosa,** an erect or somewhat sprawling kind, 6 inches to 2 feet tall, with narrowly-oblong, pointed leaves and blue or lilac flowers with yellow centers.

Garden Uses. The cultivated heliophilas are delightful where summers are not oppressively hot and humid in flower beds and rock gardens. Where torrid summers prevail they are useful outdoors only for early summer blooming. With the arrival of hot weather they quickly pass out of bloom. Even in regions where summers are to their liking they do not flower for a long period, and two or three successional sowings should be made to be certain of a display throughout the season. Heliophilas are splendid and elegant for growing in pots to decorate greenhouses and conservatories in late winter and spring.

Cultivation. Given well-drained, fertile soil and an open, sunny location no particular difficulties face the grower of these charming plants. Sow the seeds in early spring outdoors where the plants are to bloom or, for an early display, indoors in a temperature of 60 to 65°F about eight weeks before you expect to set the plants in the garden. Outdoors, simply rake the seeds shallowly into the ground and later thin the seedlings so the young plants stand 4 to 6 inches apart.

Transplant seedlings from indoor sowings as soon as they are big enough to handle, 2 inches apart in flats of porous soil. Grow the young plants in a sunny greenhouse in a night temperature of 50 to 55°F and day temperatures five to ten degrees higher. Water with care. Excessive wetness of the soil for long periods is likely to be disastrous. Before the plants are transplanted to the garden harden them for a week or two by standing them in a cold frame or sheltered place outdoors. Take care when transplanting. The young plants are rather frail and easily damaged. Space them 5 to 6 inches apart. A little twiggy brushwood pushed into the ground among them affords all necessary support.

Heliophilas as pot plants are grown from seeds sown from September to January, the earliest sowings producing the largest and earliest-flowering plants. For success, full sun and a night temperature of 50°F, rising to 55 or 60°F by day, is necessary. The soil must be well drained, porous, and moderately fertile. As soon as they are big enough to handle, carefully transplant the seedlings three to 5-inch, or five to 6-inch pots or deep pans. Water sparingly at first, more generously after the roots have permeated the soil, but never with abandon. Keep the atmosphere on the dryish side and the greenhouse ventilated on all favorable occasions. Light staking may be needed.

HELIOPSIS (Helióp-sis). About six species of sunflower-like, deciduous herbaceous perennials or rarely annuals, all natives of the New World, belong in *Heliopsis*, of the daisy family COMPOSITAE. The name is from the Greek *helios*, the sun, and *opsis*, resembling. From sunflowers (*Helianthus*) heliopsises differ in that when the ray florets of their flower heads wither they remain attached to the fruits or achenes (commonly called seeds) instead of separating from them. All species have flower heads with fertile or more rarely sterile, yellow female ray florets, and bisexual, fertile disk florets that form the usually golden-brown central eye of the flower head. The involucre (collar of leafy bracts at the back of the flower head) consists of one or two rows of bracts.

Heliopsises are erect, loosely-branched, and have opposite, stalked, coarsely-toothed leaves with three main veins. Horticultural varieties with double or semidouble flower heads, that is with the flower heads composed entirely or mostly of ray florets, are commonly grown.

The only species of garden significance is **H. helianthoides.** From it and its botanical variety *H. h. scabra* (syn. *H. scabra*) the commonly grown horticultural varieties have been developed. This inhabits dry, open woodlands, prairies, and waste places from Quebec to British Columbia, Georgia, and New Mexico. A rather coarse, gaunt plant in its wild form, *H. helianthoides* grows 3 to 5 feet tall and is hairless or nearly so. It has

Heliopsis helianthoides variety

pointed, ovate to lanceolate-ovate, thinnish, toothed leaves, 3 to 6 inches long, and many broad-rayed flower heads, 1½ to 2½ inches in diameter. The ray florets, pale to brassy yellow, are about 1 inch long and

often slightly toothed at their ends. The achenes are quadrangular. From the species the variety *H. h. scabra* differs chiefly in being rough-hairy throughout and in having leaves of rather firmer texture.

Heliopsis helianthoides scabra

Garden varieties of *Heliopsis* include a number of very attractive plants. Commonly they are mostly lower, more compact and more refined than the wild plants. One of the older ones is *H. h. pitcheriana*, which has deep yellow flowers. In *H. h. zinniaeflora* the flower heads are fully double. Those of *H. h. incomparabilis* are double or semi-double, rich golden-yellow, and 3 to 3½ inches in diameter. Nearly double chrome-yellow flower heads are produced by *H. h. excelsa*. More modern varieties include 'Gold Greenheart', with double yellow flower heads with attractive green centers; 'Golden Plume', a good double-flowered variety of neat habit; 'Light of Loddon', a free-bloomer with deep lemon-chrome-yellow blooms; and 'Summer Gold', which has brilliant golden flower heads 3 inches in diameter. Other varieties may be expected to be developed.

Garden and Landscape Uses. Plant breeders have done a good job with *Heliopsis* and the end is not yet in sight. The better varieties well deserve places in perennial borders and their blooms supply useful cut flowers. These plants can also be used in clumps to fill gaps at the fronts of shrub beds, and in informal parts of the garden.

Cultivation. Some botanical texts describe *H. helianthoides* as a short-lived perennial, but limited life is not a characteristic of garden varieties; they persist as well as most perennials. Gardeners must not be led astray either by the fact that in the wild these plants often occupy dry, comparatively infertile soils. Under cultivation they respond most favorably to fer-

tile earth that does not suffer excessively from drought. In order to maintain maximum vitality it is well to divide and replant the sorts of *Heliopsis* in newly spaded soil, enriched with compost or other decayed organic matter and fertilizer, every three or four years. This should be done in spring or early fall. Divisions may be spaced about 2 feet apart, and staking to provide some support will usually be needed. The prompt removal of faded blooms encourages prolonged flowering. In years when dividing is not done a spring application of a complete garden fertilizer should be given. In dry periods watering is highly beneficial. Propagation of garden varieties should always be by division or early summer cuttings. Plants raised from seed tend to revert to the wild type.

HELIOTROPE. See Heliotropium. Garden-heliotrope is *Valeriana officinalis*, the heliotrope-tree is *Ehretia acuminata*, the tree-heliotrope is *Messerschmidia argentea*, winter-heliotrope is *Petasites fragrans*.

HELIOTROPIUM (Helio-tròpium)—Heliotrope or Cherry Pie. Old-fashioned heliotrope or cherry pie of flower gardens, as well as a few other cultivated species, belong in *Heliotropium*, of the borage family BORAGINACEAE. The name is derived from the Greek *helios*, the sun, and *trope*, turning. It refers to an old mistaken belief that the blooms turn to follow the sun.

There are annual and herbaceous perennial heliotropiums as well as the more familiar shrubby ones. Botanists recognize about 250 species, natives of the warmer parts of the Old World and the New World including several species indigenous in the United States, many of them weeds of no imaginable interest to gardeners. There are some attractive kinds not known to be in cultivation including the low *H. limbatum*, of Mexico and the southeastern United States, and silvery-foliaged *H. anomalum*, of Hawaii and other Pacific islands.

Heliotropiums are mostly more or less hairy and have usually alternate, rarely nearly opposite, generally undivided, stalked leaves, and flowers ordinarily in coiled, terminal or axillary, spikelike or raceme-like, branched sprays of the type botanists call scorpioid cymes. Each small bloom has a five-toothed or five-lobed calyx and a tubular five-lobed corolla with a short funnel-shaped tube. The corolla lobes may spread or not and range from white through lavender to deep purple, and yellow. The fruits consist of four seed-like nutlets.

Common heliotrope (**H. arborescens** syns. *H. corymbosum, H. peruvianum*) is by far the best known. A perennial, it is a leafy shrub up to about 4 feet in height. Native of Peru, its alternate, ovate to ob-

Heliotropium arborescens, garden variety

long-lanceolate leaves with very definitely marked veins are 1 inch to 3 inches long. The small deep purple, violet, lavender, or white flowers are about ¼ inch long and are clustered in dense heads with coiling branches. Typically, they are sweetly fragrant, but some horticultural varieties, including, interestingly enough, one called 'Royal Fragrance' have scentless or nearly scentless blooms. Common heliotrope is grown in selected horticultural varieties to which names have been given and which are described in catalogs of dealers, and as unnamed seedlings. The named varieties have been selected for their large flower heads, particular shades of flower color, and compactness of plant growth.

A perennial kind naturalized in parts of California and in Hawaii is the deep-rooting *H. amplexicaule* (syn. *H. anchusaefolium*), a native of Argentina. It has prostrate stems 1 foot to 2 feet long and lanceolate-oblong, toothed leaves up to 2½ inches long. The flower heads, at first dense, but later loose, are of forked, coiled branches. The flowers are lilac-purple.

Annual heliotropes sometimes cultivated are *H. convolvulaceum* (syn. *Euploca convolvulacea*), of Washington to California, and New Mexico, and the European *H. europaeum.* The former is the more attractive. The European kind is somewhat weedy-looking; naturalized in North America it is scarcely attractive enough to merit cultivation. Very different in appearance from other cultivated heliotropes is *H. convolvulaceum.* As its specific name suggests, its flowers have the aspect of small convolvuluses. This is a showy annual up to 2 feet tall with ovate, lanceolate, or sometimes linear, short-stalked leaves and angular-lobed, fragrant, white flowers that open only at night and are about ½ inch in diameter.

Garden Uses. Annual heliotropes are appropriate for the fronts of flower borders and for rock gardens. Common heliotrope is an excellent summer bedding plant and is useful for vases, jardinieres, and other containers used to decorate patios, terraces, and suchlike places. It may be grown in bush form or in tree fashion, as standards as gardeners call plants trained as "trees."

Heliotrope trained as a standard

Its flowers are delightful for cutting and, if immediately plunged to their necks with the stems deep in water and kept for a few hours in a cool, dark place before being displayed, last well without wilting. The more prostrate *H. amplexicaule* may be treated in much the same way as common heliotrope, but is less well suited for formal bedding.

Cultivation. The cultivation of annual heliotropes is simple. Seeds are sown in spring where the plants are to remain in agreeable, porous soil, neither excessively rich nor so lacking in fertility that the plants must struggle to survive. The site must be sunny. The seedlings are thinned to about 6 inches apart and subsequently are kept free of weeds and watered quite thoroughly at intervals should the weather be excessively dry. An alternative plan calls for sowing the seeds some eight to ten weeks before planting out time (which is a little later than it is safe to plant tomatoes) in a greenhouse in a temperature of about 60°F and to transplant the seedlings 2 inches apart in flats and grow them in a sunny greenhouse with a night temperature of 50 to 55°F and day temperatures five to ten degrees higher until ten days or two weeks before they are to be set in the garden. In preparation for that move they are hardened by being placed in a cold frame or sheltered, sunny place outdoors.

Common heliotrope and other perennial kinds can be raised from seeds sown early indoors as recommended above for annual heliotropes, the only difference being that it is well to sow about twelve weeks in advance of planting out in the garden, to pinch the young plants once or twice to induce bushiness, and, if fairly large plants are needed for bedding, to transfer them from flats to 3½- or 4-inch pots as soon as they begin to crowd each other. When raised from seeds common heliotrope is likely to vary quite a little in flower color and other characteristics. Especially attractive plants may be selected for propagating by cuttings.

Raised from cuttings, perennial heliotropes give plants of uniform appearance excellent for summer beds and borders. To have plants in 3½- or 4-inch pots in bloom and ready for planting out in May, cuttings are inserted in a propagating bench in a greenhouse with an air temperature of 60 to 65°F in February. The temperature of the propagating medium should be maintained by bottom heat at about 70°F. It is important that the cuttings be planted immediately after they are taken from the stock plants and not be allowed to wilt or be floated in water to prevent them from wilting. This last treatment usually results in the cuttings turning black and dying. The stock plants from which the cuttings are taken are carried through the winter in a 55°F greenhouse. Because heliotropes do not lift well from outdoor beds it is better that the stock plants be grown in pots during the summer (those left over from early summer bedding operations are suitable) than that plants dug from the garden in fall be potted. Alternatively, cuttings may be rooted in August and the tops of the resulting plants be taken as February cuttings. Older stock plants are cut back a little in early January, top dressed with rich soil or watered occasionally with dilute fertilizer, and sprayed lightly with water on sunny days to encourage strong new shoots that will make good cuttings.

The planting distance for common heliotrope may be 8 to 10 inches for plants from 3½- or 4-inch pots, that for *H. amplexicaule* may be 1 foot to 2 feet. If the ground is quite rich there may be a tendency for the common heliotrope to make enormous shoot and foliage growth and to produce too few flowers. This can be obviated by planting them without removing them from their pots. The basal drainage holes

Heliotropium europaeum

in the latter are enlarged to 1 inch to 1½ inches in diameter and the pots are buried in the ground with the root balls; this serves to restrict wild growth and promote abundant bloom. Plants so treated must be kept well watered for the first month after they are planted.

Tree or standard heliotropes are plants of common heliotrope trained so that they have a branchless stem 2 to 3 feet tall topped by a more or less spherical head of branches, foliage, and flowers. Such specimens can be kept for many years as is commonly done with lantanas, fuchsias, and some other plants trained in this fashion, but many gardeners prefer to raise new ones each year and discard the old ones at the end of the summer. Standard plants are raised by rooting cuttings in August and keeping the resulting plants growing without check throughout fall, winter, and spring. To do this necessitates accommodation in a sunny greenhouse with a night temperature of 55 to 60°F and a fairly humid atmosphere. It is most important that growth is not checked by low temperatures, failure to repot when the roots become crowded, excessive dryness of the soil, insect infestation, or other cause. A fertile, well-drained potting soil is used. From the propagating bench the rooted cuttings are transferred individually to 3-inch pots and are repotted successively as root growth makes necessary until they occupy containers 8 or 9 inches in diameter. In their young stages all side shoots are pinched out as soon as they are big enough to be taken between forefinger and thumb. The main stem is kept neatly tied to a stake and when it is 2 to 3 feet tall its tip is pinched out and branches allowed to develop from near its top. When 5 or 6 inches long these are pinched as are succeeding branches whenever they are 4 to 6 inches long. In this way a well-shaped head is developed. From April or May onward no further pinching is done. Then, flowers are encouraged to develop.

HELIPTERUM (Helíp-terum)—Everlasting. Represented in the natural floras of Australia and South Africa, *Helipterum*, of the daisy family COMPOSITAE, includes a few favorite "everlasting" flowers. From nearly related *Helichrysum* it differs in the bristles that accompany its ovaries and seeds being feathery along their entire lengths instead of at their tips only. This is believed to have inspired the name, derived from the Greek *helios*, sun, and *pteron*, a feather. There are almost fifty species, the majority Australian. They include annuals, herbaceous perennials, and a few shrubs and subshrubs. Plants previously known as *Acroclinium* and *Rhodanthe* are included.

Helipterums have undivided, lobeless, toothless, generally alternate leaves that, with the stems, are often more or less white-woolly, but in some kinds are nearly or quite hairless. As is usual in the daisy family, the apparent flowers are really heads or groups of little florets. The heads may be clustered or not. In *Helipterum* the florets of each flower head are surrounded by several circles of often highly colored, showy parts that look like petals and that remain attractive long after the flowers are dead and dried. These are the bracts of the involucre (a collar behind the flower heads of daisies and similar flowers). The florets, at the centers of the flower heads of helipterums, are yellow and few to many. They are tubular, usually bisexual and five-toothed, but a few of the outer ones may be female and three- or four-toothed and a few inner ones may be sterile. The seedlike fruits are achenes.

The only helipterums commonly cultivated are annuals or kinds grown as such. Shrubby and subshrubby kinds have proven difficult to nearly impossible to manage when it was attempted, chiefly in Europe, to grow them in greenhouses. It is possible that they would succeed outdoors in desert or semidesert conditions in California and other parts of the West. Some are extraordinarily beautiful.

One of the most popular, western Australian *H. roseum* (syn. *Acroclinium roseum*) is a hairless annual 1 foot to 2 feet tall, with many slender, erect branches from low down, furnished with small, linear to spatula-shaped or lanceolate leaves. The flower heads are solitary on slender bractless or nearly bractless stalks from the ends of the branches. They are 1 inch to 2 inches across and have bright pink inner petal-like bracts and outer ones with brownish tips. In *H. r. album* the bracts are white. The flower heads of *H. r. grandiflorum* are larger than those of the species, those of *H. r. plenum* have more than the usual number of bracts, giving the effect of double flowers.

Helipterum roseum (flowers)

Swan River everlasting (*H. manglesii* syn. *Rhodanthe manglesii*) is a much-branched, western Australian, hairless annual, 1 foot to 1½ feet tall. From *H. roseum* it differs in having broad-elliptic to ovate, stem-clasping leaves 1 inch to 4 inches long, and solitary flower heads on slender, branching stalks. The flower heads are 1 inch to 1½ inches across, solitary or in loose clusters, and have pink, purplish, red, or white bracts. Double-flowered varieties with heads with more than the usual number of bracts are grown.

Erect and freely-branched, *H. corymbiflorum,* of southern and eastern Australia, is a white-woolly annual, 8 inches to 1 foot tall or slightly taller, with partly stem-clasping, lanceolate to linear leaves, and top-shaped, nearly 1-inch-wide, white flower heads in loose clusters. The bracts of the flower heads spread widely, the outer ones are tipped with golden-brown. The largest flowered annual species, *H. splendidum* of western Australia, has mostly basal foliage and erect, slender stalks 1 foot to 2 feet tall topped by solitary pale yellow or white flower heads 2 to 2¼ inches across.

Very different from the kinds described above is *H. humboldtianum* (syn. *H. sand-*

Helipterum roseum

Helipterum humboldtianum

fordii), of western Australia. It is erect, or has the lower parts of its stems horizontal, and is 1 foot to 1½ feet tall. When young, and sometimes later, it is clothed with white hairs. It has linear to narrowly-reverse-lanceolate, somewhat stem-clasping leaves 1½ to 3 inches long by up to ¼ inch wide. The numerous yellow flower heads, up to ⅓ inch in diameter, are in crowded terminal clusters 3 to 4 inches across. Their outer bracts are brownish.

Garden and Landscape Uses and Cultivation. The cultivated helipterums are charming and useful garden annuals for display in beds and borders and for cut flowers to be used fresh or dried. They are easily grown, prospering in full sun in thoroughly well-drained soil; soils of a sandy character are better than clayey ones. The plants succeed remarkably well in earth that is dryish and relatively poor in fertility. Seeds may be sown in early spring where the plants are to remain or be started earlier indoors in a temperature of about 60°F, and the seedlings transplanted to flats or small pots and grown in these until all danger of frost is past. Sowing indoors is done about eight weeks before the plants are to be set in the garden. The young plants are grown in full sun in a night temperature of about 50°F and day temperatures five to fifteen degrees higher, depending upon the brightness of the day. Outdoors the plants may be in rows 1 foot to 1½ feet apart with 4 to 6 inches between individuals, or in groups with individuals spaced, according to kind, 6 inches to 1 foot apart. Sowing directly outdoors is usually preferred because helipterums resent root disturbance, and in this way transplanting is avoided. If the blooms are to be dried for winter use they should be cut before they are fully expanded, tied in bundles, and hung upside down in a shaded, airy place until they are thoroughly dry.

As greenhouse plants helipterums may be grown for spring blooming from seeds sown in September in well-drained porous soil. The seeds are sown thinly in 5-inch pots and the seedlings thinned to leave three to five in each pot. They are grown without repotting in a night temperature of 50°F, and a few degrees more by day. Watering is done somewhat sparingly, and after the containers are filled with roots mild applications of dilute liquid fertilizer are given.

HELLEBORE. See Helleborus. For white-hellebore see Veratrum.

HELLEBORINE is *Epipactis helleborine*, giant helleborine *E. gigantea*.

HELLEBORUS (Helléb-orus) — Hellebore, Christmas-Rose, Lenten-Rose, Bear's Foot. Of the twenty-one species of this attractive genus twenty inhabit Europe and western

Asia, one eastern Asia. They belong in the buttercup family RANUNCULACEAE. The name is a modification of *helleboros*, the Greek name of *H. orientalis*. In addition to the natural species there are numerous hybrids. The roots of the Christmas-rose, known as black hellebore, are violently purgative. All parts of this and probably of most or all hellebores are poisonous if eaten. The bruised leaves of the Christmas-rose and some other kinds cause severe dermatitis in susceptible individuals. For other plants sometimes called hellebore, but more properly called false-hellebore, see *Veratrum*.

Hellebores are low, evergreen and deciduous herbaceous perennials with thick, fibrous roots. They have rhizomes, and nonwoody stems that last for one season, or are without rhizomes and have somewhat woody, permanent, erect stems. They have long-stalked, usually palmately- or pedately-divided (except for the upper bractlike ones) leaves, those of most species all basal, but some with their major leaves all on the stems. The large flowers, solitary or in clusters of few, have five or more rarely six, big petal-like, persistent sepals, the same number of inconspicuous, small tubular petals, and numerous stamens usually longer than the petals. There are three to ten stalkless pistils that become the leathery podlike follicles that are the fruits.

The Christmas-rose (**Helleborus niger**), an old and much-loved inhabitant of gardens, is somewhat naturalized in parts of North America. Native to woods and thickets in the European Alps and Apennines, this is a rhizomatous kind with nonwoody flower-bearing stems that persist for only one season and evergreen, leathery, hairless basal leaves often overtopping the flowers. These leaves are

deeply divided into seven or nine oblong to narrowly-obovate, toothed leaflets. The much smaller, pale green bractlike leaves of the branching or branchless stems are ovate and undivided. The somewhat nodding, white or pink-tinged flowers with broad-ovate sepals, in twos or threes, are 1½ to 2½ inches in diameter. Variety *H. n. macranthus* (syns. *H. n. altifolius*, *H. macranthus*), of Italy and Yugoslavia, is larger and more robust. It has longer-stalked, subspiny-toothed leaves with broadly-lanceolate as opposed to oblong-wedge-shaped segments. Its rarely pink-tinged blooms are larger than those of *H. niger*, up to 4 inches wide or sometimes wider, and have narrower sepals overlapping only to their middles.

Evergreen kinds with their major leaves all basal, that differ from *H. niger* in the bracts of their flower-bearing stems being leafy and divided, include several. Here belongs the Lenten-rose (**H. orientalis**), a hairy or hairless native of Greece and Asia

Helleborus orientalis

Minor. This has much-branched rhizomes and leathery, long-stalked leaves almost 1½ feet across, with five to eleven double-toothed, broad-elliptic leaflets. The saucer-shaped blooms, three or four together on stalks usually shorter than the leaves, are up to 2¼ inches across. At first greenish-cream, they fade to brownish-yellow-green or occasionally purplish. Those of *H. o. albus* are white, those of *H. o. atropurpureus*, purplish.

Helleborus niger

Helleborus orientalis albus

The usually solitary leaves of fragrant-flowered *H. odorus* are of five to eleven ovate-lanceolate, lobeless or slightly lobed, leathery, broad-lanceolate leaflets, dull green on their upper sides, paler, lustrous, and with prominent veins beneath. Exceeding the foliage and up to 2 feet tall, the stems carry two or three slightly nodding, clear yellowish-green blooms 2 to 2½ inches in diameter, with yellowish-white stamens. Variety *H. o. laxus* has leaves of five to seven usually lobed leaflets and stems with sometimes four or five blooms. From the last species and its variety, variable *H. multifidus* (syn. *H. odorus multifidus*), of the Balkan Peninsula, differs in its distinctly nodding flowers being not over 1½ inches in width and having narrower petals. Its leaves, hairy on their undersides, are of nine to fifteen toothed leaflets cleft nearly to their bases into three to twelve linear lobes. The plant sometimes identified as *H. odorus istriacus* is *H. multifidus istriacus*. It differs from *H. multifidus* in its usually finely-toothed leaf segments being without lobes or lobed only to their middles.

Evergreen hellebores endemic to the region of the Caucasus include *H. abchasicus* and closely related *H. guttatus*. Their leathery, hairless leaves are about 1 foot across and of five to seven, double-toothed, ovate-lanceolate leaflets. On stems taller than the foliage, *H. abchasicus* has nodding flowers, purple on their outsides, purple or green within, 2½ to 3 inches across and usually four or five on each stem. Variety *H. a. coccineus* has maroon-crimson blooms. Variety *H. a. venosus* has distinctly veined, rose-purple flowers. From *H. abchasicus* and its varieties, *H. guttatus* is distinguishable by its densely-red-spotted, white flowers and its paler green foliage.

Evergreen kinds without basal foliage, all leaves being on the stems, and without rhizomes, are bear's foot or stinking hellebore (*H. foetidus*) and, also called bear's foot or sometimes green hellebore (*H. lividus*). Native from the British Isles to Italy and southwest Europe, *H. foetidus* has stout, leafy, perennial stems 9 inches to 2½ feet tall. Its leaves are pedate, of seven to eleven toothed, narrowly-lanceolate leaflets. The many bell-shaped flowers, from under ½ inch to 1¼ inches in diameter, nod. They are green, usually edged with purple. From this, *H. lividus*, of Mediterranean islands, differs in its leaves never having more than three leaflets, toothless or with small, distantly-spaced teeth, and its pale green flowers being flat. Variety *H. l. corsicus* (syn. *H. corsicus*), native of Corsica and Sardinia, differs in having leaf margins with close, spiny teeth.

Kinds that lose their foliage in winter include *H. viridis*, a variable native from Ireland to central and southern Europe, naturalized in parts of North America. Its slightly pedate, dull green leaves, about 10

Helleborus lividus corsicus (foliage)

inches across and prominently veined and pubescent on their paler undersides, are of seven to thirteen toothed leaflets. The two to four blooms on each stem are 1¾ to 2 inches across. They have yellow-green, spreading sepals. The leaves of *H. v. occidentalis* have broader, more coarsely toothed leaflets with hairless under surfaces. The flowers of this are smaller than those of the typical species. Closely similar to the evergreen Lenten-rose (*H. orientalis*), but deciduous and having yellow-green, scented flowers, is *H. cyclophyllus*, of the Balkan Peninsula. The pedate, thin, deciduous leaves of *H. dumetorum* are completely hairless and without prominent veins on their undersides. They have seven to eleven leaflets. This native of eastcentral Europe is up to 1½ feet tall. From 1½ to nearly 2 inches in diameter, the blooms, two to three together, have spreading, violet or green sepals. Variety *H. d. atrorubens* (syn. *H. atrorubens*) has usually bigger leaves, and stems generally taller, with flowers dull purple on their outsides and greenish-purple within and 1½ to 2¼ inches in diameter. Often confused with the last variety, *H. purpurascens*, an eastcentral European species, differs in its up to 1-foot-wide deciduous leaves of usually five, broadly-wedge-shaped, not distinctly pedate segments lobed to their middles being hairy, at least on the veins of their undersides. The purplish-violet flowers, up to three together, 2 to 2½ inches wide, have spreading sepals and whitish-green stamens.

Hybrid hellebores usually grouped as Lenten-roses, include natural ones that

have occurred in the wild and numerous kinds raised as the result of chance or deliberate crossings in gardens. The Christmas-rose (*H. niger*) does not hybridize easily with other kinds, but in the late 1920s it was successfully crossed in England with *H. lividus corsicus* to produce the very fine *H. nigricors*. Many other hybrids grown in European gardens are little known in North America.

Garden and Landscape Uses. Hellebores are well suited for planting singly, in small groups, or in drifts to cover larger areas in lightly shaded places, such as along the fringes of woodlands, shrub borders, and foundation plantings and in open woodlands and rock gardens. Their flowers are suitable for use in small arrangements. They thrive in rich, moist, but not wet, loamy soil that contains a liberal proportion of organic matter. They do not object to limy soils, but seem to prosper equally as well in slightly acid ones. Because most kinds bloom in winter and early spring it is important that they be in sheltered locations where damaging winds are less likely to harm the flowers. To assure the most perfect blooms, unmarred by inclement weather, Christmas-roses are grown in cold frames, or specimens may be dug carefully in fall and potted to be brought indoors to flower later.

Cultivation. Once established and doing well, hellebores prosper best if left undisturbed. They benefit greatly from an annual mulching with old, rotted manure, rich compost, leaf mold, or other organic material applied in fall and left to rot. In severe climates it is well to lay over evergreen kinds, after the ground freezes, a light covering of branches of pine or other evergreen. In dry weather deep soaking with water at about weekly intervals is needed. A spring application of a complete garden fertilizer, preferably one with its nitrogen content organic, encourages sturdy growth. Weed carefully and do not cultivate close to hellebores. If the ground is undisturbed it is not unusual for volunteer seedlings to appear. Propagation is by careful division of the clumps done immediately flowering is through. Plants can also be raised from seeds, but hybrids do not, of course, come true to the parent type when propagated in this way and at best it is a slow process. Sow the seeds as soon as ripe in well-drained, sandy peaty soil in a shaded cold frame and make sure that the seed bed is kept evenly moist, but not saturated. Hellebores take a few years to flower from seeds.

Self-sown seedlings near *Helleborus niger*

HELMINTHOSTACHYS (Helmintho-stáchys). A single species constitutes *Helminthostachys*, of the adder's tongue family OPHIOGLOSSACEAE. Its name, from the Greek *helmintho*, a worm, and *stachys*, a spike, alludes to the appearance of the fertile portion of the frond.

A fern of variable size and leaf dissection, and of unusual appearance, *H. zeylanica* is found wild from India to Taiwan and New Caledonia. It has creeping rhizomes from which arise each growing season a single leaf (frond). The leaves, curiously, have somewhat the aspect of those of certain hellebores (*Helleborus*), but are of thinner texture. Their stalks, 6 inches to over 1 foot long, are erect, and have at their tops a sterile (non-spore-bearing) blade deeply-palmately (in hand-fashion) -cleft into three major divisions fingered or forked into several long-elliptic to lanceolate, toothed or toothless lobes. The fertile (spore-bearing) portion of the frond arises from the base of the barren part. Slender, spikelike, and erect, it looks much like the fruiting spike of a plantain (*Plantago*). Its spore cases are clustered on extremely short side branches along the upper portion. The lower part of the frond is stalk-like.

Garden Uses and Cultivation. This collectors' item is suitable for growing under the humid, shaded, warm conditions that most tropical, terrestrial (ground-rooting) ferns appreciate. It is increased by division and spores. For further information see Ferns.

HELONIAS (Helòn-ias)—Swamp-Pink. The only member of this genus of the lily family LILIACEAE inhabits bogs and swamps from southern New York to North Carolina. One of the lesser known and most charming American wildflowers, it accommodates readily to gardens and deserves wider cultivation. Its name comes from the Greek *helos*, a swamp, and alludes to its preferred habitat.

The swamp-pink (*Helonias bullata*) is a tuberous-rooted herbaceous perennial with basal foliage usually evergreen, but deciduous in severe climates. The several strap-shaped leaves, up to 1 foot long or a little longer by up to 2 inches wide, are in rosette-like clusters. The erect flower stalks are hollow, 1 foot to 2 feet tall, and are furnished with short, bractlike leaves, densely toward their bases, more sparsely above. The fragrant, pink flowers, each rather less than ½ inch wide, are densely arranged in cylindrical-ovoid, terminal heads 1½ to 4 inches long by over 1 inch wide. They come in spring. There are six petals (properly tepals) that are persistent and surround the three-lobed, obovoid seed capsules. The six stamens, tipped with blue anthers, are about as long as the petals. There are three styles.

Garden and Landscape Uses and Cultivation. No difficulty attends the cultivation of the swamp-pink. It is admirable for planting by watersides either in sun or partial shade and succeeds in wet, fertile soils, and in drier ones provided they are watered well in dry weather. Propagation is easy by division in spring. Seed may also be used, but is not commonly produced in cultivation. The swamp-pink is excellent for forcing for early bloom in cool greenhouses. To do this, the plants are potted in spring and grown with their containers buried to their rims in a bed of sand or peat moss, either outdoors or in a cold frame. Early the following year they are brought into a greenhouse where the night temperature is about 50°F with daytime temperatures five to fifteen degrees higher. Under these conditions they soon develop their attractive blooms. Throughout, their soil is kept moist and during the summer they are supplied with dilute liquid fertilizer.

Helonias bullata

Helonias bullata (flowers)

HELONIOPSIS (Heloni-ópsis). Four species of Japan, Sakhalin Island, Korea, and Taiwan make up this genus, a close relative of the North American *Helonias*, but differing in having looser clusters of blooms with comparatively long, branchless styles. Their name emphasizes this relationship. It is derived from that of its sister genus and the Greek *opsis*, resembling. These plants belong to the lily family LILIACEAE. They are herbaceous perennials of undetermined hardiness, but perhaps capable of wintering outdoors in southern New York.

Growing from short, thick, horizontal rhizomes the all-basal, evergreen leaves of *Heloniopsis* are hairless and narrowly-oblong to oblanceolate. From the centers of the plants arise branchless flower stalks with rarely one, usually few, nodding blooms in generally short, rather umbel-like racemes. The flowers have six persistent, spreading, blunt, oblong petals (properly tepals), pinkish, purplish, or white, gradually changing to greenish as the seed pods develop. There are six slender-stalked, purple-blue stamens, one style, and a knob-shaped, purple stigma. The fruits are three-lobed capsules.

Native to Japan, Korea, and Sakhalin Island, *H. orientalis* has somewhat lustrous, spreading leaves 3 to 6 inches long and up to 1½ inches wide, with pointed apexes and narrowing gradually toward their bases. At blooming time 4 inches to 1 foot tall, the flower stems lengthen later. They are furnished with small, up-pointing, lanceolate leaves and have up to ten rose-purple flowers with petals almost or quite ¾ inch long, and somewhat longer styles. Variety *H. o. flavida* is more slender and has thinner foliage with wavy margins and white flowers. In *H. o. breviscapa* (syn. *H. breviscapa*) the white to pale pink petals are shorter than those of the species. The fruits are reddish or yellowish-green.

Garden Uses and Cultivation. Primarily of interest to rock gardeners and collectors of the rare and unusual, *Heloniopsis* affords opportunity for experiment. It is likely that its hardiness depends to some extent upon the latitude and altitude of the provenance of the wild plants brought into cultivation, those from more northern locations and higher elevations being likely to withstand severer winters. They succeed in soil that is well-drained and fairly moist, and are propagated by division and by seed. A gardener who grew *H. o. breviscapa* in Connecticut reports that it proved hardy and prospered without special care. He observed that in fall small plantlets developed at the ends of the leaves, and he used these to multiply his stock.

HELWINGIA (Helwíng-ia). A botanical novelty, one species of this genus of four or five that inhabits the region extending from Japan to Taiwan and the Himalayas, is occasionally cultivated. The group, named after G. A. Helwing, a German clergyman and botanical author, who died in 1748, consists of deciduous shrubs of the dogwood family CORNACEAE.

Helwingias have alternate, undivided, stalked, toothed leaves and tiny unisexual flowers that are unusual in that they appear to arise from the midribs of the leaf blades; actually the stalks of the flower clusters are joined to and run along the midribs; they are, as botanists say, adnate to the midribs. The flowers are without calyx lobes. They have generally four, but sometimes three or five petals. The males have three to five thick-stalked stamens and sometimes a vestigial ovary. The females have three to five united styles and are without sterile stamens. The berry-like fruits, containing one to three stones, are technically drupes.

Bushy, broad, 2 to 6 feet in height, and with hairless, slender green branches, *Helwingia japonica* (syn. *H. rusciflora*) inhabits woods and thickets in Japan and the Ryukyu Islands. It has ovate to elliptic, pointed leaves 1 inch to 4 inches long and ¾ inch to 1½ inches broad. The flowers are pale green and up to ⅕ inch wide, the females solitary or in twos or threes, the males in larger clusters. The black spherical fruits are about ⅓ inch in diameter.

Garden Uses and Cultivation. No great merit as a landscape component lies with this plant. Interest generated by the curious placement of its flowers is about all it has to recommend it, consequently it is unlikely to attract much attention other than from maintainers of botanical collections. It is hardy in very sheltered locations as far north as New York City and grows satisfactorily in ordinary soils. Pruning to thin out old crowded shoots may be done in late winter. Multiplication is by seeds, and by cuttings made from short side shoots planted under mist or in a greenhouse or cold frame propagating bed in summer.

HELXINE. See Soleirolia.

HEMEROCALLIS (Hemero-cállis)—Day-Lily. Probably nowhere in the world are day-lilies esteemed to the extent they are in the United States. The reasons are clear. These tolerant, hardy herbaceous perennials can endure extremes of climate, the fierce heat of summer and severe winter cold, characteristic of vast areas of the North American continent and American plant breeders have been in the forefront in the development of spectacularly beautiful varieties. Modern day-lilies are as advanced over their wild ancestors as are modern chrysanthemums and roses over theirs, more so in the opinion of some day-lily fans. The genus *Hemerocallis*, the name comes from the Greek *hemera*, day, and *kallos*, beauty, consists of twenty species of the lily family LILIACEAE. It is a native of temperate Asia, particularly Japan, and Europe. Day-lilies are closely related to *Hosta*, but despite attempts that have been made the two genera have never been successfully hybridized.

Day-lilies are deciduous and evergreen, or in cold climates partially evergreen, hardy perennials with ample more-or-less fleshy roots and an abundance of basal and near-basal foliage. They vary in height from 1 foot to 7 feet. The spreading to arching and ascending leaves are strap-shaped, in their lower parts channeled on their upper sides, keeled beneath. Generally much taller than the foliage mass, the erect, branched, flowering stalks carry several to many broadly-funnel- to nearly bell-shaped flowers with six spreading, recurved or sometimes nearly erect perianth segments (petals, or more correctly, tepals). There are six stamens and a long slender style ending in a small stigma. The fruits, those of many kinds rarely produced, are capsules. In China the nutritious flower buds of some day-lilies are cooked with meat and in soups and are eaten raw in salads. Dried, they are called kim choi (golden cabbage), sometimes rendered gum tsoy, and are employed for flavoring foods. In the past, in England, the foliage of day-lilies was used to a considerable extent as fodder for cattle.

The history of hybrid day-lilies is not a particularly long one. Although the common orange and common yellow day-lilies were known to Europeans as early as the sixteenth century and the former was introduced to England from about 1600 and undoubtedly was brought to America by the early colonists, it was not until the nineteenth century was well advanced that attempts at hybridization began. The pioneer was George Yeld, an English schoolmaster and amateur gardener, who began his work in 1877 and continued to raise new day-lilies for almost half a century. A benchmark was established when in 1892 he announced the first published hybrid, the result of a cross between *H. lilioasphodelus* and *H. middendorffi* to which he gave the name 'Apricot'. Amos Perry of England, other plant breeders there and some in Italy, France, Holland, and Germany gradually entered the field with very encouraging results. The year 1899 saw the first day-lily hybrid of which we have record produced in the United States. Named 'Florham', this was raised in New Jersey by Arthur Herrington. In the twentieth century American breeders became increasingly involved and soon led the field in the production of new varieties, a preeminence they still hold.

About 1921 the distinguished geneticist and plant breeder Dr. A. B. Stout began assembling from all over the world at The New York Botanical Garden all procurable varieties and species of *Hemerocallis*. For more than thirty years he systematically engaged in hybridizing, breeding, and promoting the use of day-lilies in gardens. The magnificent array of varieties we now enjoy is very largely the result of the labors of the inspired and dedicated group of American breeders. The end is by no means yet. Among newer innovations are tetraploids, kinds with twice the normal number of chromosomes. The first of these came in the late 1940s, but it was nearly twenty years later before they assumed any considerable prominence. By 1967 more than eighty such varieties were registered with the American Hemerocallis Society, an organization founded in 1946 that has had a tremendous influence in furthering interest in day-lilies.

Modern day-lilies are procurable in hundreds of varieties (in the present century thousands have been raised, but many have been discarded or at least are not presently available). A glance through the catalog of any day-lily specialist will reveal selections of kinds in a bewildering variety of heights, flower forms and colors, and other particulars such as seasons of bloom. Most varieties make a good display for about a month, but by making appropriate selections a succession of bloom can be had from late spring until frost. In subtropical and tropical regions such as Hawaii, flowers of some kinds are produced throughout the year.

Hemerocallis in a garden

Hybrid day-lilies

Flower colors include cream-white, clear lemon-yellows and rich golden-yellows, tones of orange, and many tawny hues. There are kinds with lavender to vinous-purple flowers, others with blooms of pink and red. The flowers of many are parti-colored, shaded or lightened in their throats or with striped petals. There are self-colored and bicolored varieties. Flower forms range from simple and lily-like to semi-double, double, and more fancy types with ruffled or twisted petals. Heights vary according to variety from about 1½ to more than 4 feet.

A list of varieties if presented here would serve no useful purpose. New ones are introduced yearly and some older ones are dropped from commerce. Selections must be based on individual preferences. Do not make the mistake of assuming that new, usually higher priced varieties are superior. Older ones retained in dealers' catalogs are likely to be those that have proven their garden worth under a wide variety of conditions. They are the stand-bys nonspecialist growers should to a large extent rely upon. One generalization may be made. For Florida and other parts with warm winters kinds with evergreen foliage are to be preferred, those with deciduous leafage are better adapted to regions of hard winters.

The common orange day-lily, or fulvous day-lily as it is sometimes called (*H. fulva*), is of uncertain origin, but almost surely was originally Asian. Whether that is so or not it now occurs spontaneously from Europe to Siberia and is naturalized in North America. The leaves of this are up to 2 feet long or longer by approximately 1 inch broad. The stalks carrying the blooms are longer. The flowers, six to twelve to each branched stalk, are orange-red, up to 5 inches long, and 3½ inches in diameter. Their perianth tubes are slender, not over 1 inch long, and their three outer petals are up to ¾ inch wide. The broader inner ones have somewhat wavy margins. All spread widely. The blooms are not fragrant. Variety *H. f.* 'Europa' does not set seeds, but produces fertile pollen, which has been used successfully in producing garden varieties. Variety *H. f.* 'Kwanso', spontaneous in Japan, has longer-lasting, sterile, double flowers. The larger blooms of *H. f. maculata* are variously marked inside with red-purple. Those of Chinese *H. f. rosea* are rose-red. Bright orange instead of reddish flowers are characteristic of *H. aurantiaca*, of China. This has leaves 2 to 3 feet long by 1 inch wide or somewhat wider. About as long as the leaves, the erect flowering stalks each have up to eight 3- to 4-inch-long, fragrant flowers with perianth tubes approximately ¾ inch long and petals about 1 inch wide, those of the typical species not opening widely, but those of the more frequently grown *H. a. major* bigger and with wider-spreading petals. Formerly named *H. a. lit-*

torea, but now accepted as a separate species under the name *H. littorea* is a kind endemic to locations near seashores in Japan. From *H. aurantiaca* it differs chiefly in having thicker leaves and tufts of leaves among the flowers.

The common yellow day-lily (*H. lilioasphodelus* syn. *H. flava*), native from Japan to Siberia, blooms early. Its 1- to 2-foot-long leaves up to ¾ inch wide, are exceeded in length by the flowering stalks each with up to nine fragrant, yellow blooms 3 to 4 inches long with perianth tubes ½ to over 1 inch long. Taller, later-blooming, paler-flowered *H. l. major* is perhaps of hybrid origin. From *H. lilioasphodelus* Japanese *H. thunbergii* differs in blooming considerably later and in its roots being scarcely swollen. Its leaves and flowering stalks are approximately the same length, up to about 2 feet. The lemon-yellow flowers, about 3 inches long, have perianth tubes approximately 1 inch long. There may be as many as fifteen on each flowering stalk. Their outer petals are about ½ inch, the inner approaching 1 inch, in width. Broader leaves and bigger blooms are characteristic of *H. t. major*. The plant known as *H. luteola*, which has golden-yellow blooms on flowering stalks about 3 feet tall and leaves only a little shorter, is a hybrid between *H. thunbergii* and *H. aurantiaca major*. The kind grown as *H. ochroleuca*, which has fragrant, sulfur-yellow blooms that open in the evening, is reportedly a hybrid between *H. thunbergii* and *H. citrina*. Somewhat belying the name day-lily, midsummer-blooming *H. citrina* has fragrant, lemon-yellow blooms that open fully only toward nightfall. Chinese, this robust grower has leaves up to 3½ feet long by more than 1 inch broad and flowering stalks about 4 feet tall. The blooms, with perianth tubes up to 1½ inches long, are 5 to 6 inches long. The petals are from a little less to somewhat more than ½ inch broad. Free-flowering *H. multiflora* is a Chinese species with leaves up to 2½ feet long by ¾ inch wide forming a foliage mass generally not over 1½ feet tall. The slender flowering stalks, about 3 feet tall, are repeatedly branched and may carry as many as 100 orange or cadmium-yellow blooms, about 3 inches wide and with ½-inch-long perianth tubes, tinged red on their outsides. This sort blooms in late summer and fall.

Three dwarfer species, all natives of Siberia, the first two also of Manchuria, Korea, China, and Japan, are *H. dumortieri*, *H. middendorffii*, and *H. minor*. Its flowering stalks not longer and often shorter than the leaves, which attain 1 foot to 1½ feet in length and up to ¾ inch in width, *H. dumortieri* has fragrant, yellow blooms up to 2½ inches long with perianth tubes not longer than ¼ inch, two or three on each flowering stalk. The petals do not spread widely. The outer ones, under ½

inch wide, like the somewhat broader inner ones, taper to their apexes. From the last, *H. middendorffii* differs in its flowering stalks being longer than its 1- to 1½-foot-long leaves, in the latter being ½ to ¾ inch wide and in the blooms, up to four on each flowering stalk, having broad-spatula-shaped petals. The fragrant, yellow flowers have perianth tubes about ½ inch long, outer petals ½ to ¾ inch wide, the inner ones somewhat broader. Smallest of the species described here, *H. minor* has leaves not over ¼ inch in width by 1 foot to a little more than 1½ feet long. The flowering stalks each carry up to six fragrant, yellow blooms up to 4 inches long with perianth tubes ½ to 1 inch long. Their outer petals are under ½ inch wide, the inner somewhat wider. Similar *H. gracilis* is a hybrid with rather larger, lemon-yellow to light orange flowers.

Garden and Landscape Uses. Day-lilies are high on the list of easy-to-grow, completely satisfactory, hardy herbaceous perennials for American gardens. The wide diversity of plant sizes and flower colors in which they come, chiefly as the result of the work of American breeders, make it a simple task to select kinds for a wide variety of uses. The boldest and most magnificent can with good conscience be used to bring beauty to flower beds and borders. Many less highly bred sorts are splendid for naturalizing in groups or great drifts in informal or semiformal landscapes. They look well on high ground near watersides, at the fringes of woodlands, and as soil-binders to control erosion as well as to beautify slopes and banks. The dwarfs make good edgings and are useful in rock gardens. Such is the adaptability of day-lilies that they serve well in numerous places, and best of all, do so with minimum care. Generally they do best in full sun, but will stand a little afternoon shade. In the south they are probably better for it.

As cut flowers day-lilies have the fault that their individual blooms usually last for but one day. But if well-budded stems are cut and stood in water a succession of buds will open over a period of a few days, not ideal perhaps for arrangers who depend for their effects on precisely positioned blooms, but very acceptable for more informal displays.

Cultivation. Among the most grateful of garden plants, day-lilies ask little from gardeners. They may remain undisturbed for years. Only when their centers become obviously crowded and somewhat elevated, and the production of blooms begins to diminish, is it necessary to dig them up, divide them, and replant. This can be done at any time when the ground is not frozen, even in high summer, but early spring and early fall are the preferred times. To divide, dig the clumps, shake them free of soil, cut the roots back to

Dividing day-lilies: (a) Digging up a clump

(b) Divisions suitable for planting

about one-half their lengths and the foliage to a length of 2 or 3 inches. Then with a sharp, heavy knife or other such implement cut the clumps into sizable portions. But it is better that they not be too big. Pieces consisting of four to six shoots are generally satisfactory. If more rapid multiplication is desired, the divisions may consist of single growths with roots attached, but such small segments take longer to attain respectable flowering size specimens and may need a little more initial care. Space the transplants according to the vigor or the variety. From 2 to 3 feet is about right between individuals of the bigger kinds, closer spacing is appropriate for dwarf, compact day-lilies. Raising day-lilies from seeds is very easy, but is only likely to be done by breeders of new varieties. Seedlings usually bloom in their second year. The seeds may be sown outdoors in spring or fall.

Routine care is as nearly minimal as can be. Unless the ground is decidedly poor avoid fertilizing. A too-rich diet encourages gross foliage, often at the expense of bloom. The same is true of watering. If the soil is really lacking in nutrients or dries abnormally a spring application of fertilizer and watering deeply at intervals in dry weather promote good growth and health. The prompt removal of faded blooms makes for tidiness. This is likely to be of greater importance in flower borders than in naturalistic plantings. The fall clean-up involves cutting back dead foliage, or in regions of severe winters, this may be left until spring and done just before new shoots appear. The retained foliage affords winter protection for the roots. North of New York City varieties with evergreen foliage and those with *H. aurantiaca* in their line of ancestors are likely to benefit from the additional winter protection of a covering of salt hay or similar material. Pests and diseases that may affect day-lilies are fairly numerous, but most sorts are not too troubled by these. They include aphids, nematodes, red spider mites, slugs, snails, tarnished plant bug, thrips, and crown rot.

HEMIANDRA (Hemi-ándra). Native to Australia, *Hemiandra* is a genus of seven shrubs or subshrubs of the mint family LABIATAE. Its name comes from the Greek *hemi*, half, and *andros*, male, and alludes to the one-celled anthers.

Hemiandras have stiff, narrow, opposite leaves and from the leaf axils solitary, white or pink, tubular, asymmetrical, two-lipped flowers. The upper lip is two-lobed, the lower three-lobed with the center lobe often again lobed. There are four stamens and a short, two-lobed style. The fruits consist of four seedlike nutlets.

Probably the only species cultivated, *H. pungens* is an evergreen shrub 1 foot to 2 feet in height, of spreading habit, and hairless or sparingly-hairy. Its stalkless, sharp-pointed, linear or linear-lanceolate leaves are up to 1 inch long by up to ¼ inch wide. The pink, lilac, or white corollas are usually a little over ½ inch in length, about ¾ inch across their mouths, and are commonly dotted with red.

Garden Uses and Cultivation. For rock gardens and other outdoor places where low shrubs are appropriate, the species described is suitable in climates such as that of California. This plant may also be accommodated in greenhouses in which the winter night temperature is about 50°F. On all favorable occasions the greenhouse must be ventilated freely. Good growth is made in fertile, well-drained, ordinary soil that does not become excessively dry. Full sun is desirable. Increase is easy by seeds, and by cuttings planted in a greenhouse propagating bed or under mist.

HEMICYCLIA. See Drypetes.

HEMIEVA. See Suksdorfia.

HEMIGRAPHIS (Hemí-graphis). Of the more than sixty species of *Hemigraphis*, only one or two are cultivated. The genus, of warm parts of southern China and southeastern Asia, belong in the acanthus family ACANTHACEAE. The name comes from the Greek *hemi*, half, and *graphos*,

written, and alludes to markings on the foliage of some species.

This genus consists of subshrubs, herbaceous perennials, and annuals with opposite, toothed or smooth-edged leaves and bracted spikes of single or sometimes paired small flowers. The blooms have a five-lobed or five-parted calyx. The corolla is tubular, slender below, expanding above, and with five spreading lobes (petals). There are four nonprotruding stamens and one style. The fruits are capsules.

Of uncertain nativity, *H. alternata* (syn. *H. colorata*) is a prostrate, stem-rooting pe-

Hemigraphis alternata

rennial. Its attractive metallic-purplish, toothed leaves have a puckered surface of the type botanists call bullate. Their undersides are solid purple. The purple-lined white flowers, about ¾ inch long, have but slight decorative appeal. They are in spikes about 1 inch long. Another kind, introduced from New Guinea and cultivated under the name *H.* 'Exotica', is a vigorous trailer with reddish stems and broad-elliptic to ovate leaves about 3 inches long. They are metallic-purplish-green above and have wine-red undersides. They are even more conspicuously puckered than those of *H. alternata*.

Hemigraphis 'Exotica'

Quite different *H. repanda* is of uncertain nativity. A low, prostrate, stem-rooting groundcover, it has coarsely-toothed linear leaves up to about 2½ inches long, purplish-green on their upper surfaces, rich purple beneath. The flowers are white, ½ to ¾ inch long.

Hemigraphis repanda

Garden Uses and Cultivation. These are plants to be used as groundcovers and in pots and hanging baskets in humid tropical greenhouses and outdoors in hot moist climates. They are also useful in terrariums. Their attractions are their colored foliage and trailing growth habits. Provided the soil is neither dry nor excessively wet and is reasonably fertile no trouble is likely to be encountered in growing these plants. Shade from bright sun is needed. They root with the greatest of ease from cuttings. In greenhouses a minimum temperature of 60 to 70°F is satisfactory. Pans (shallow pots) rather than standard pots are the most suitable containers for *Hemigraphis*. If four or five rooted cuttings are planted in a receptacle 6 or 7 inches in diameter and pinched once to induce branching they very soon develop into decorative specimens.

HEMIONITIS (Hemion-ìtis) — Strawberry Fern. This genus of ferns has the unusual natural distribution of seven species confined to northern tropical America, and the only other ranging from India to the Philippines. It belongs in the pteris family PTERIDACEAE. The name, Greek, was used by Dioscorides. It is derived from *hemionos*, a mule, hence barren, and was applied because the plants, erroneously, were thought to be sterile. These are small to medium-sized and have short rhizomes and clustered, dark-stalked fronds (leaves) with rounded, heart-shaped, or triangular blades never divided into separate leaflets, but sometimes shallowly- or deeply-lobed. The fertile fronds are somewhat different from the barren ones and have clusters of spore capsules along their veins.

Strawberry fern (*Hemionitis palmata*) is indigenous from Mexico to northern South America, and in the West Indies. Its fronds have pubescent blades 2 to 6 inches across, and deeply-palmately (in hand-fashion) -cleft into five lanceolate to triangular, toothed lobes. The stalks of barren fronds are up to about 4 inches, those of fertile ones 6 inches to 1 foot, long. Asian *H. arifolia* differs in having smooth-margined, lobeless or scarcely lobed fronds with blades 6 to 9 inches long by 1 inch to nearly 3 inches broad. They are heart- to arrow-shaped, triangular-ovate or oblong-lanceolate. The sterile fronds have stalks 2 to 4 inches long, those of the spore-producing ones are up to 1 foot long. This species develops young plants from buds on its leaves.

Garden Uses and Cultivation. Distinctive and attractive, these easily grown ferns are of interest as greenhouse decoratives, and in humid, frostless climates for outdoor cultivation in shaded rock gardens and other moist-soil locations. Be-

Hemionitis arifolia

cause of their sizes they are particularly appropriate for terrariums. Like most ferns they appreciate soil generously laced with leaf mold, peat moss, or other decayed organic material and containing sufficient coarse sand to keep it porous. It should always be moderately moist, but free of stagnant water; compact earth kept constantly wet is disastrous. For pot-grown specimens it is important not to use containers much larger than their comparatively small root masses. These ferns have rather delicate root systems and are likely to sulk instead of growing satisfactorily if overpotted. Excessive fertilizing must be avoided, but watering strongly rooted specimens occasionally with dilute liquid fertilizer is helpful. Greenhouses and terrariums with minimum winter night temperatures of about 60°F are suitable environments for these ferns. Humidity must be medium to high, and shade from strong sun is needed. Propagation is by spores and by plantlets that form on the leaves of *H. arifolia*. Additional information is given under Ferns.

A groundcover of *Hemigraphis alternata*

Hemionitis palmata

HEMIPTELEA (Hemi-ptèlea). One shrubby, much-branched, deciduous tree, native of northeastern Asia, constitutes *Hemiptelea*, of the elm family ULMACEAE. It is hardy in southern New England. Its name, derived from the Greek *hemi*, half, and *ptelea*, an ancient name of the elm, alludes to the shape of the wings of the seeds.

Up to about 15 feet in height, **H. davidii** (syn. *Zelkova davidii*) has branches, that especially when young are thorny, and alternate, very short-stalked, elliptic to oblong, coarsely-toothed leaves ¾ inch to 2¼ inches long, with eight to twelve pairs of parallel veins angling from their midribs. The flowers, in clusters in the axils of the young leaves, are insignificant. There are bisexual and unisexual blooms on the same plant. The fruits differ from those of related *Zelkova* in being stalked. They are conical, two-edged, and obliquely winged in their upper halves.

Garden and Landscape Uses and Cultivation. In the Orient this species is favored for hedges and can be successfully so used elsewhere. It is also interesting as an untrimmed specimen. Propagation is by seeds sown as soon as they are ripe, by summer cuttings under mist or in a greenhouse propagating bed, by layering, and by grafting onto seedling elms.

HEMLOCK. See Tsuga. Ground-hemlock is *Taxus canadensis*, poison-hemlock *Conium maculatum*, water-hemlock *Cicuta*.

HEMP is the common name of *Cannabis sativa*. The word is also used as part of the common names of these plants: African-hemp (*Sparmannia africana*), bowstring-hemp (*Sansevieria*), Cuban-hemp (*Furcraea hexapetala*), hemp-agrimony (*Eupatorium cannabinum*), hemp tree (*Vitex agnus-castus*), Indian-hemp (*Apocynum cannabinum*), Manila-hemp (*Musa textilis*), Mauritius-hemp (*Furcraea foetida*), sisal-hemp (*Agave sisalana*), and sunn-hemp (*Crotalaria juncea*).

HEMPWEED, CLIMBING is *Mikania scandens*.

HEN-AND-CHICKENS. See Sempervivum, Echeveria, and Bellis.

HENBANE is *Hyoscyamus niger*.

HENEQUEN is *Agave fourcroydes*.

HENNA is *Lawsonia inermis*.

HEPATICA (Hep-ática) — Liverleaf. From closely related *Anemone* this North American, European, and temperate Asian genus of ten species is distinguished by the presence of a calyx-like involucre (collar) of three undivided, stalkless, sessile leaves immediately beneath the flower. It belongs in the buttercup family RANUNCULACEAE. Its name, from the Latin *hepar*, liver, was given because of a fancied similarity of the leaf shape to that of the liver. Because of this, in accordance with the doctrine of signatures, hepaticas were thought to cure diseases of the liver.

Hepaticas are low, woodland, herbaceous perennials with basal tufts of thick, evergreen, three-, five-, or occasionally seven-lobed leaves, often with purplish undersides, from among which in spring come slender, naked stalks each carrying a solitary bloom. What appears to be the calyx is the involucre. The true calyx consists of five to twelve showy petal-like parts. There are no petals. The stamens are numerous, the style short. The fruits are achenes.

Preferring limy soil, **H. acutiloba** inhabits upland woods from Quebec to Minnesota, Georgia, Alabama, and Missouri. Usually three-, occasionally five- or seven-lobed, its leaves are deeply-heart-shaped at their bases. Their lobes are pointed, and about two-thirds the depth of the blade. Hairy, and 2 to 6 inches long, the flower stalks are topped by blue-lavender, pink, or white blooms ½ to 1 inch wide. From the last, **H. americana** (syn. *H. triloba*), a native of acid woodlands from Nova Scotia to Minnesota, Missouri, Georgia, and Tennessee, differs in its smaller leaves having three rounded lobes extending to about one-half the depth of the blade, the middle one often wider than long. The blooms are similar to those of *H. acutiloba*. European **H. nobilis** differs so slightly from *H. americana* that it scarcely deserves status as a separate species. Color forms and some with double flowers are recognized as horticultural varieties. Confined in the wild to Romania, **H. transsilvanica** (syn. *H. angulosa*) differs from *H. nobilis* in having toothed leaf lobes and flowers 1 inch to 1½ inches in diameter. A hybrid between the last two species is **H. media.** All the above kinds are hardy and are 4 to 6 inches tall or a little taller.

Garden and Landscape Uses and Cultivation. Hepaticas are pleasant adornments for woodland gardens, rock gardens, and other partly shaded places. They are easy to satisfy. All except *H. americana* prefer limy soil. All are grateful for fertile earth containing an abundance of leaf mold or other decayed organic debris. Once established, very little care is needed. Self-sown seedlings often appear. Hepaticas are easily increased by division in spring and by seeds sown in soil kept moist, but not wet in a shaded cold frame, or outdoors where they are safe from disturbance. Strong plants potted in 4-inch pots in early fall and then put in a cold frame or buried to the rims of their containers in a bed of sand, peat moss, or similar material outdoors are pretty when forced into bloom in late winter in a greenhouse, or in a window in a cool room. They force readily.

Hepatica americana

HERACLEUM (Herac-lèum) — Cow-Parsnip. Cow-parsnips are less commonly met with in gardens than in the wild. Their large size renders them unsuitable for small properties and in more spacious landscapes they are generally adaptable only for wet soil areas. Because of this, few of the seventy species, natives of north temperate regions and mountains in the tropics, are cultivated, and then only occasionally. The name *Heracleum*, that of a genus of the carrot family UMBELLIFERAE, commemorates the Greek demigod Herakles, better known perhaps as Hercules, who was said to have been the first to use these plants medicinally.

Cow-parsnips include deciduous perennial and biennial herbaceous plants, mostly tall, with stout, erect stems and large, broad, lobed, or pinnately-divided leaves. They are of bold, somewhat coarse appearance and in summer have large compound umbels of numerous, small purplish or white, usually asymmetrical flowers. The outer flowers of the umbels are commonly larger than the inner and are often cleft so that they form rays. From the poisonous water-hemlock (*Cicuta*) and the poison-hemlock (*Conium*) the cow-parsnip is readily distinguished by its fruits (commonly called seeds) being markedly compressed and having their lateral ribs extended as broad, thin wings.

The American cow-parsnip (*H. sphondylium montanum* syn. *H. lanatum*) inhabits moist rich soils from Labrador to Alaska, Georgia, and Arizona, and occurs also in eastern Asia. Often it grows in light shade. From 3 to 10 feet in height and more or less hairy, it has very stout stems. The main leaves are rounded in outline and ½ to 1 foot long. They are divided into three

Heracleum sphondylium montanum

broad-ovate to nearly round leaflets, up to 4 inches long, lobed and coarsely-toothed. The very much broadened leafstalks sheath the stems. The terminal umbel of flowers, ordinarily larger than the secondary ones, is 4 to 8 inches in diameter. Very similar to its variety but with undivided, lobed, or pinnate leaves, *H. sphondylium*, a native of Europe and Asia, is naturalized in parts of North America.

Natives to the Caucasus, **H. laciniatum** (syn. *H. giganteum*) and **H. mantegazzianum** are also impressive. The first is 8 to 12 feet tall, has undivided, but deeply-cleft and irregularly-toothed leaves, gray- or white-hairy on their undersides. The white flowers are in large umbels. Reported to be naturalized locally in New York, **H. mantegazzianum,** 8 to 10 feet tall, has stems and leafstalks flecked with red. Its leaves, green on their undersides and up to 3 feet long, are thrice-divided into large, deeply-lobed leaflets. The umbels of white flowers are displayed in compound inflorescences 3 to 4 feet across.

Heracleum mantegazzianum

Garden and Landscape Uses and Cultivation. These stately, almost gigantic herbaceous plants can sometimes be used effectively as single specimens or in groups in parks and similar broad landscapes, especially along lake or river banks and elsewhere where they are assured ample moisture. Their roots strike deeply. Unless controlled, self-sown seeds can give rise to unwanted seedlings, the removal of which can be arduous. To eliminate this possible nuisance it is necessary to cut off faded flower heads before they mature and disperse their seeds. Cow-parsnips are at their best in fertile earth that has a generous organic content. They are easily raised from seed sown in fall or spring where the plants are to remain, or sown elsewhere and the plants transplanted to their permanent places later, but before they are very big. If carefully done, specimens can

be dug from the wild in early spring and transplanted. Small plants should, if possible, be selected for this. Spacing of about 3 feet between individuals is satisfactory.

HERALD'S TRUMPET is *Beaumontia grandiflora*.

HERB. This word has two distinct meanings important for gardeners to know and differentiate. In its botanical sense a herb (or herbaceous plant) is any that does not develop wood in its tissues, thus, that is without a permanent woody stem. It is used in contrast to woody plant, the term applicable to kinds with enduring woody stems (trees and shrubs). Herbs comprise annuals, which live for only one season, biennials, which live for two, and perennials, of longer duration. The last, identified as herbaceous perennials to distinguish them from woody perennials (trees and shrubs), include deciduous kinds that die to the ground each year and evergreens that retain their foliage throughout the year. Examples of the former are delphiniums, lilies-of-the-valley, and primulas. Evergreen herbaceous perennials include many sedums, thrifts, ophiopogons, and Kentucky blue grass. No sharp distinction exists between herbs and woody plants. Intermediates occur, for example, carnations, many other kinds of *Dianthus*, and evergreen candytuft (*Iberis sempervirens*), the stems of which are retained from year to year and the lower parts at least of which contain some woody tissue. Such plants are said to be subshrubby.

The other usage of herb accounts for plants that are or have been employed for flavoring foods and beverages, or medicinally, and is often extended to cover those employed in perfumery and sometimes dyeing. It particularly applies to those of temperate and warm-temperate regions. Certain tropical and subtropical sorts used similarly are called spices. Herbs in this sense may or may not be herbs botanically. Basil, borage, mint, and parsley are, but lavender, sage, and thyme are subshrubs, damask rose is a shrub, and bay leaves are obtained from a tree. Culinary herbs differ from vegetables in that they are used chiefly to flavor and add piquancy to foods rather than as prime sources of nourishment and major components of meals. Yet some straddle this somewhat artificial fence; angelica, celery, fennel, and onions, for example, are employed as flavorings and also as main vegetable dishes. In the one use they are herbs in the other vegetables.

HERB. The word herb appears as part of the common names of these plants: cow herb (*Vaccaria pyramidata*), herb Christopher (*Actaea spicata*), herb mercury (*Mercurialis*), herb of grace (*Ruta graveolens*), herb paris (*Paris quadrifolia*), and herb patience (*Rumex patientia*).

HERB GARDENS. Aside from their uses as foods, one of mankind's earliest interests in plants centered around their employment in healing. Later the frequent use of some as spices and flavorings to make more palatable the often dismal, not infrequently tainted foods of the times became important. Selected sorts were cherished for their fragrance when dried, others for their use as dyes.

At first reliance was upon plants collected from the wild, but as tribes became less nomadic and the arts of cultivation and husbandry developed, the practicability and convenience of having needed plants growing close at hand became apparent. Herb and medicinal gardens came into being. Such plantings were made by Romans, Greeks, Persians, Chinese, and other ancient peoples.

In Europe in the Middle Ages and during the Renaissance the cultivation of gardens devoted to herbs or simples developed as a considerable art. Such features were maintained at monasteries and by physicians. Great houses had their herb gardens, frequently elaborate and artistic. Lesser folks grew a few herbs in home plots. All put great faith in their healing properties and other virtues.

An outcome of early herb gardens was the development of apothecary gardens and physic gardens in which as many kinds of plants as possible of merit or supposed merit for healing and other practical uses were gathered, cultivated, studied, and written about. The writings were known as herbals, their authors as herbalists. Out of the labors of the herbalists slowly developed the concept of the modern botanic garden.

Early settlers brought to America seeds and plants of treasured herbs. Soon they learned of native plants to which the Indians ascribed healing virtues and some of these were brought from the wild and planted along with more familiar kinds. American housewives were no less alert than their European sisters to the importance of their patches of herbs.

Herb gardens today play a less prominent part in healing, but remain as important, delightful, and appealing expressions of the art of horticulture and as adjuncts to the culinary arts. Well planned and cared for, they are decidedly educational. Examples are to be seen in many botanic gardens and similar horticultural establishments and are favorite developments in home gardens. The Herb Society of America and other specialist groups have done much to stimulate interest in this phase of gardening, to investigate historical aspects of its art and practice, and to publish on these as well as more modern aspects of herb gardening.

Herb gardens, simple or elaborate, appropriate in all parts of North America, can be developed on tiny plots or as parts of more elaborate landscapes. They are fitting in cities and suburbs as in country districts. They do splendidly by the sea. They can even be on roofs. In addition, container-grown herbs can be accommodated on balconies, window sills, and indoors in kitchen windows and suchlike places.

Styles of herb gardens include those of traditional Old World design, often featuring elaborate-patterned knots of little, variously-shaped beds enclosed by miniature hedges of boxwood, germander, lavender-cotton, or other suitable dwarf shrubs or shrublets, more informal gardens, less prim and precise, and examples frankly modern in concept in which the preciousness of imitating the past is abjured without sacrificing the charm of the geometrical. It is fitting that American gardeners address themselves to such developments. Let us consider the rationale.

Traditionally colonial American herb gardens were located near the kitchen door, easy of access to the busy housewife, who was gardener as well as cook. So placed, the garden was handy for picking and tending. It was not large or of intricate formal design as were many European gardens. Rather it reflected the casualness of a practical housewife, who planted herbs for use rather than display. Such gardens had the charm of the functional, natural rather than contrived beauty.

An attractive informal door yard herb garden

A pretty door yard herb garden edged with dwarf boxwood

It is appropriate that contemporary herb gardens in America be in this tradition. This does not mean that they should be slavish imitations of those of the past, only that they should draw inspiration from them.

Other factors must be weighed. America, a big country, has many parts with landscapes and climates totally unlike those of New England, Virginia, or Europe. Life-styles have changed since colonial days. The housewife spends less time in her kitchen. Terraces, patios, and other sitting areas have become important centers of family life. Modern Americans are busy. They have limited time to spend on horticultural activities and hired help is rarely available. Also, Americans like change and are fond of variety.

Taking these and other factors into consideration, a very logical location for a contemporary herb garden is one associated with a sitting area, terrace, or patio. There, herbs can be usefully employed as decorations and can be constantly enjoyed as such, and for their fragrances, as well has being available for picking, and serving as conversation pieces. There, too, there are usually sunny areas, needed by most herbs, and shaded ones preferred by a few native American kinds.

An herb garden of informally planted beds, the Berkshire Garden Center, Stockbridge, Massachusetts

A small suburban herb garden

Herb garden at The New York Botanical Garden

Herb garden, with center knot, at Brooklyn Botanic Garden

Planting may be done in beds level with the ground or terrace floor or raised a few inches or more. The site, personal taste, and ingenuity dictate the design, traditional or modern. The possibilities are nearly endless. The formal and informal can be combined with a knot as the center feature and paths separating it from borders less primly planted in the fashion of a typical perennial bed or border.

One other possibility. Instead of planting in ground beds, grow herbs in containers. The advantages are many. Containers can be arranged and grouped in decorative patterns appropriate to any landscape and congruous with any style of architecture from the ultratraditional to modern or even modernistic. And herbs grow well in containers and are easily cared for. Mints and other rampant spreaders have no opportunity to cause trouble by invading the territory of their neighbors. When replanting is needed a few kinds can be given that attention without disturbing others, and in regions of severe winters it is easy to move into a cool, light cellar or other suitable place kinds, such as rosemary and sweet bay, that would not survive outdoors. Finally, the containers can be moved about as desired to provide changes in garden design.

Containers should be simple rather than elaborate. They can be bottomless or if they are to be moved from time to time be fitted with bottoms. Suitable for the purpose are sections of terra-cotta liners for chimneys or sections of large cylindrical drain pipes. Similar containers can be fashioned from concrete or can be made of such moisture-resistant woods as cypress or redwood. They may be 1 foot high, or variety may be had by having some taller.

A bed of herbs at the Berkshire Garden Center

A border of herbs at the Wave Hill gardens, New York City

Such containers lend themselves to grouping attractively.

Cultural needs of herbs vary to some extent according to kind and this needs consideration when planning plantings. But the vast majority succeed under similar conditions. With comparatively few exceptions they need full sun and well-drained, moderately-fertile, not over-rich soil. Some grow satisfactorily in poor, even stony soils. Too rich a diet can result in gross growth, less beautiful foliage colors, and with those esteemed for their fragrances, such as lavender, rosemary, sage, and thyme, poorer concentrations of volatile oils responsible for such delights.

Many herbs of Mediterranean origin and some others are drought-resisters that prosper best in dryish soils. Some few, as angelica, loveage, the mints, sweet cicely, and sweet woodruff, prefer damper root runs.

Care of herb gardens makes no strenuous demands of the gardener, but does call for regular attention mostly of a housekeeping nature. This involves suppression of weeds, shallow cultivation, pinching, shearing, and otherwise regulating growth, and the pleasant task of harvesting. There is also, in some cases, drying or otherwise preserving the products. Seeds of annual and biennial sorts must be sown each year, an activity that brings pleasure second only to harvesting, or perhaps greater for it holds forth promise as contrasted with marking accomplishment. And in cold climates the few nonhardy kinds, such as rosemary, lemon-verbena, scented geraniums, and sweet bay, must be taken indoors before killing frost.

Culinary and flavoring herbs include ambrosia, angelica, anise, balm, basil, betony, borage, burnet, camomile, caraway, catnip, chervil, chives, clary, coriander, costmary, cumin, dandelion, dill, fennel, fennel-flower, feverfew, garlic, germander, hops, horehound, horse-radish, lemon-verbena, loveage, pot marigold, marjorams, mints, mustards, nasturtiums, origanums, parsley, pennyroyals, peppers, rosemary, roses (some kinds), rue, sage, savory, scented geraniums, sesame, sweet cicely, sweet woodruff, tarragon, thyme, and wintergreen.

Herbs with aromatic foliage, in addition to some of the above, include artemisias, bergamot, feverfew, lavender-cotton, myrtle (*Myrtus*), and sweet bay.

(b) Sage (*Salvia officinalis*)

Some flavoring and culinary herbs:
(a) Sweet woodruff (*Galium odoratum*)

(c) Rosemary (*Rosmarinus officinalis*)

(d) Feverfew (*Chrysanthemum parthenium*)

(e) Costmary (*Chrysanthemum balsamita*)

(f) Borage (*Borago officinalis*)

(g) Chives (*Allium schoenoprasum*)

Medicinal values, real or supposed, have been ascribed to numerous plants. Many of these are appropriate in herb gardens, chiefly for their interest and beauty rather than as home-grown usable aids to relieving and healing bodily ills. In addition to some of the kinds listed in the two previous paragraphs, here is a selection of medicinal herbs: aconite, alkanet, arnica, belladonna, castor-bean, comfrey, foxglove, goldenseal, hellebore, licorice, lungwort, may-apple, saffron crocus, tansy, thorn-apple, and wild-ginger. Some kinds are poisonous if eaten. Examples of herbs employed in dyeing are false-indigo, indigo, saffron crocus, and woad.

HERBA BARONA is *Thymus herba-barona*.

HERBACEOUS. Herbaceous means not woody. Any plant, annual, biennial, or perennial, hardy or nonhardy, deciduous or evergreen, without woody tissues in its stems is herbaceous. Such sorts contrast with woody plants, with trees and shrubs. The line is not always sharply drawn, however, and some plants that tend to be intermediate in this respect are said to be

Medicinal herbs: (a) Aconite (*Aconitum napellus*)

(b) Foxglove (*Digitalis purpurea*)

(c) Comfrey (*Symphytum officinale*)

(d) Arnica (*Arnica*)

(e) May-apple (*Podophyllum peltatum*)

(f) Tansy (*Tanacetum vulgare*)

semiherbaceous or semiwoody or the term subshrub is applied to them. Less properly, gardeners frequently restrict herbaceous to apply only to hardy herbaceous perennials. This is the sense in which it is commonly used in the term herbaceous border.

HERBACEOUS BORDER. This is chiefly a British term for what in North America is more commonly called a perennial border. See Flower Beds and Borders.

HERBARIUM. A herbarium is a collection of pressed and dried plants and plant parts maintained for study, research, and record. Usually the plant specimens are mounted on sheets of stiffish paper and labeled with pertinent data such as name, family, and place and date of collection. For convenience and safety they are generally kept in closed cases and are fumigated or otherwise treated from time to time to prevent damage by insects. The size of the sheets of paper in American herbariums is usually 16½ by 11½ inches. A herbarium is an integral feature of all botanic gardens, and botanical departments of universities and colleges often maintain one. Unfortunately few herbariums feature cultivated plants prominently. The leading one that does is the Bailey Hortorum of Cornell University, Ithaca, New York. Amateur botanists and gardeners can gain much pleasure and greatly enhance their knowledge of plants by forming a private herbarium of kinds in which they are interested.

HERBERTARA. This is the name of hybrid orchids the parents of which include *Cattleya*, *Laelia*, *Schomburgkia*, and *Sophronitis*.

HERBERTIA. See Alophia.

HERBICIDES or WEED-KILLERS. These are chemicals used to kill weeds and occasionally other unwanted plants. Until World War II few were available, and they played a relatively minor part in gardening practice. Since then, many new ones have been marketed and their employment as aids in the continuous battle gardeners must wage against weeds has greatly increased. Herbicides are widely used in commercial operations, less frequently by home gardeners except for the control of lawn weeds and to a lesser extent for killing weeds in paths. The reasons for this are that home gardens often contain in small areas a variety of plants that have different tolerances to particular herbicides and that many herbicides used in larger-scale operations have not been available in conveniently small packages.

Herbicides fall into four chief groups: soil sterilants, soil fumigants, preemergent herbicides, and postemergent herbicides. The first two kill all vegetation and sterilize the ground against development of

any plant growth for a period of several weeks or months. They are useful only on areas where plants are not wanted, such as paths and other paved places and around buildings where growths of tall weeds may be a fire hazard. Weed-kill by soil fumigants is normally incidental to their employment for freeing the soil of insects, nematodes, and other animal pests.

Preemergent and postemergent herbicides are most widely used on cropped and planted land. The first kill the weeds as they germinate and before they emerge from the soil. They must be applied before germination. Postemergent herbicides are applied after the plants emerge from the ground and have developed a certain amount of foliage. The action of certain of these is to kill rapidly on contact. Others, the so-called hormone types, effect the destruction of the weeds more slowly by, after they are absorbed by the leaves and stems, disrupting the plants' metabolic processes. These last are often sufficiently selective that in carefully proportioned amounts they can be used to eliminate broad-leaved weeds such as dandelions and plantains from lawns without seriously affecting the grasses.

Success with herbicides depends upon selecting kinds suitable for the particular purposes for which they are to be used and strictly following the manufacturer's directions about amounts and conditions under which they are to be applied. Great care must be taken that they do not come in contact with desirable plants. It is especially important, particularly with hormone-type herbicides, that fine spray is not carried by wind drift onto ornamentals or other wanted vegetation. In amounts very much smaller than is needed to kill, these can cause serious distortion of young shoots and leaves.

Precautions to take in the use of herbicides include purchasing them in small quantities and storing them in a locked cabinet outside the house where they are not accessible to children, using them as sprays only when there is no wind and with a low pressure sprayer that produces large droplets less likely to drift than fine mist. Use an oil can to spot-treat individual weeds. Use separate equipment for herbicides from that used for fungicides, insecticides, or foliar fertilizers.

HERCULES' CLUB. This is the common name of *Aralia spinosa* and *Zanthoxylum clava-herculis*. For hercules' club gourd see Lagenaria.

HEREDITY. As with all organisms that multiply as a result of a sexual process, heredity is an important factor in determining the characteristics and mode of development of plants. It is the chromosomal genes or determiners passing from one generation to the next that are responsible for the plant's inherited characteristics.

Heredity and environmental factors combined settle how each plant develops and the characteristics it displays. A sound knowledge of the principles governing heredity is of tremendous aid to plant breeders. Recognition of its importance impels gardeners to strive to obtain the best possible seeds. The science of genetics, based on the original work of the Austrian monk Gregor Mendel, who died in 1884, is concerned with heredity.

HEREROA (Herer-òa). Named in recognition of the Herero, a tribe or nation of natives of South Africa, *Hereroa* belongs in the carpetweed family AIZOACEAE. It comprises twenty-eight species, all endemic to South Africa. None is hardy.

Hereroas are low, perennial succulents of the *Mesembryanthemum* relationship. They are tufted and cushiony or sometimes are small shrublets with prostrate stems. Their opposite, soft leaves are in pairs, usually set at right angles to the pairs below and above. Occasionally solitary, more commonly two or three on a stalk, the flowers are yellow changing to pink, orange, or rarely white. Sometimes fragrant, they are daisy-like in appearance, but differ greatly from daisies in structure. Each is a single flower, not as with daisies, a head of florets. The fruits are capsules. Unlike most plants of the *Mesembryanthemum* complex, some kinds are night-bloomers.

Free-flowering **H. granulata** (syn. *Bergeranthus granulatus*) has dark green, slightly rough-surfaced leaves with many translucent dots. At first spreading, they tend to turn inward as they age. They are up to a little over 2 inches long by ¼ inch wide, and semicylindrical. Their apexes are keeled and short-pointed. The 1-inch-wide flowers are light yellow. From this species **H. herrei** differs only in technical details of its seed capsules.

Golden-yellow blooms about 1¼ inches wide, on ½-inch-long stalks, are borne by **H. hesperantha**. The gray-green leaves, clothed with tiny dark dots, are about 1½ inches long by ⅓ inch wide, and approximately one-half as deep. They have rounded margins and keels and are slightly compressed toward their tips. A cushiony plant, **H. gracilis** has shoots each of four crowded, erect or spreading, tapering leaves, that deepen toward their whitish apexes. About 1½ inches long, they are conspicuously thickly covered with small dots. The yellow flowers are 1 inch in diameter. The blooms of **H. puttkammeriana** (syn. *Bergeranthus puttkammerianus*) are orange. Its semicylindrical, bluntly-three-angled, gray-green leaves, 2¼ to 2¾ inches long, and about ¼ inch in diameter, curve inward, then toward their often reddish apexes, outward. They are sprinkled with conspicuous dark dots, particularly on their undersides.

Other kinds cultivated include **H. carinans**, a matting species with short stems and pairs of semicylindrical, blunt-angled, conspicuously dotted, gray-green leaves. They are 1 inch to 1½ inches long, approximately ¼ inch wide, and one of each pair is longer than the other. The flowers are yellow, about 1¼ inches across. Up to about 3 inches tall, *H. muirii* has shoots crowded with two or three pairs of spreading, semicylindrical, round-keeled leaves with small shoots in their axils. They are finely-warty-surfaced and about 2 inches long by ⅓ inch wide. The yellow flowers are on 1-inch-long stalks. Sickle-shaped, green leaves covered with small transparent warts are characteristic of *H. nelii*. They are 1 inch long or a little longer, under ¼ inch wide, and about twice as deep as their widths. Their undersides have rounded keels, above they are flat. The flowers are yellow. Incurved to erect leaves are very densely crowded on the short branches of *H. stanfordiae*. They are 1 inch to 1½ inches long, under ¼ inch wide, deeper than wide, and have compressed, serrated keels. They are glaucous and more or less dotted. The 1¼-inch-wide flowers are yellow. Night-blooming *H. incurva* is a spreading kind with pointed, incurved, glaucous or slightly reddish leaves, flat to somewhat hollowed on their upper sides, and thickly covered with small dots. They are about 1½ inches long by scarcely over ¼ inch wide and thick. The solitary, golden-yellow flowers, on 2-inch-long stalks, are approximately 1½ inches wide.

Garden Uses and Cultivation. Hereroas are pleasing in succulent collections. In warm desert and semidesert regions they can be used to ornament rock gardens and similar places. They are also adapted for greenhouse and window sill cultivation. They succeed in well-drained, porous soil in full sun, and demand little of the gardener other than abstention from excessive watering. Their growing season is summer. Then, they are watered moderately. In winter they are kept much drier. Propagation is easy by cuttings and by seeds.

HERMANNIA (Her-mánnia) — Honey Bell. Adherence to correct botanical naming procedures requires that the plant long known to gardeners as *Mahernia verticillata* be relabeled *Hermannia verticillata*. It is the only species of more than 300 of *Hermannia* at all well known in cultivation. Native to warm parts of South America, Africa, Arabia, and Australia, this genus belongs to the sterculia family STERCULIACEAE and is composed of herbaceous and subshrubby plants or shrublets. They have alternate leaves and generally stellate (star-shaped) hairs. The yellow or red blooms have five sepals joined at their bases, five erect or rarely spreading petals that in the bud stage are twisted spirally, the same number of flat-stalked stamens, and a single style. The fruits are five-ridged capsules. A Dutch botanist, Paul Hermann, who died in 1695, is commemorated by the name *Hermannia*.

Honey bell (**H. verticillata** syns. *H. ciliaris*, *Mahernia verticillata*), of sandy flats in South Africa, has slender prostrate, straggling, or drooping stems, woody at their bases, rough-hairy, up to 3 feet long, and with many erect branches up to 1 foot tall. The leaves are linear, often three-lobed, and ⅓ to 1 inch long. At their bases they have persistent leaflike appendages (stipules). In pairs, the honey-scented, bell-shaped, red-veined, yellow flowers are pendulous on slender, bracted stalks ½ inch to 1½ inches long. Up to ¾ inch long, they have hair-fringed calyx lobes and petals ⅓ inch long that spread outward somewhat at their tops. Above their bases the stalks of the stamens are conspicuously enlarged, which was the basis on which the plant now named *H. verticillata* was previously segregated as *Mahernia*.

Less commonly grown than the last, **H. candicans** is a shrub 2 to 3 feet tall with downy shoots. Its ovate, elliptic, or oblong, shallowly-toothed leaves are ½ inch to 1½ inches long by up to 1 inch wide. Green above, they have under surfaces gray with soft down. Bright yellow and nodding, the flowers, in terminal racemes or panicles 3 to 6 inches long or sometimes longer, are up to ½ inch long.

Garden and Landscape Uses and Cultivation. The chief horticultural employment of the honey bell is as an easily grown pot and hanging basket plant for greenhouses and window gardens. In mild, dryish climates, such as that of California, it can be used in rock gardens, on slopes, and in other sunny locations where the soil is well drained and not excessively dry. Once established it does not

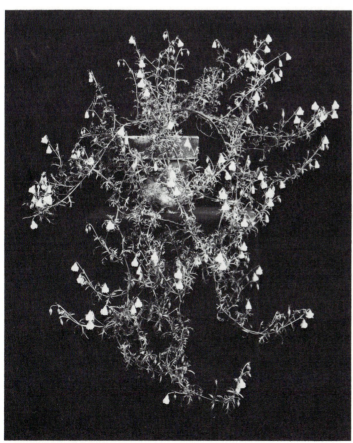

Hermannia verticillata

Hermannia candicans

transplant well. It thrives in any fairly good, sandy soil that is neither excessively dry nor remains wet for long periods, and does well where it has light shade from very strong sun. If the plants tend to become straggly they can be restored to shape and vigor by pruning them moderately in late winter or spring just before new growth begins. Then, too, is the time to attend to needed repotting. Propagation is extremely easy by cuttings, and plants can be raised from seed. Propagated similarly, the other species described here is adapted for outdoor cultivation in mild, dryish climates such as that of California.

HERMINORCHIS. This is the name of orchid hybrids the parents of which are *Herminium* and *Leucorchis*.

HERMODACTYLUS (Hermo-dáctylus) — Snake's-Head-Iris. The snake's-head-iris (*Hermodactylus tuberosus*) is the only species of its genus. It belongs in the iris family IRIDACEAE, and is very closely related to the genus *Iris*, but differs in having a one-celled rather than a three-celled ovary. The snake's-head-iris is native from southern France to Greece, Arabia, and North Africa, and has been naturalized for more than 200 years in a few places in southwestern England and County Cork, Ireland. In its original homelands it commonly grows on rocky, open hills in well-drained, somewhat alkaline soils, usually semiarid or parched, and baked by a merciless sun throughout the summer. The name is derived from that of the Greek god Hermes, and the Greek *dactylos*, a finger; it alludes to the form of the rootstock.

The snake's-head-iris (*H. tuberosus*) is an evergreen, clump-forming, herbaceous perennial with underground tubers smooth and finger-like, and quite different from those of any iris. Its slender, grasslike leaves are glaucous blue-green and four-sided with each of the angles drawn out as a narrow wing. They are erect and 1½ to 2 feet tall. The hollow flower stems are not over 1 foot in height. Each bears a solitary bloom, about 2 inches in diameter, that resembles an iris. The flowers are scarcely showy, but are interesting and attractive because of their peculiar coloring. The falls (the three outer petal-like sepals) are rich velvety black-purple in their upper parts and greenish-yellow below. The true petals or standards are short, pea-green, and contained within the flower. More obvious are the three prominent, forked style branches, which stand erect from the center of the bloom and are yellowish-green feathered with bluish-green. Beneath each and close against it is a single stamen. A variety, *H. t. longifolius*, with leaves 3 to 4 feet long, occurs in southern Italy.

Hermodactylus tuberosus

Garden Uses. This something-of-a-rarity is surprisingly hardy even in upper New York State where it survives winters outdoors without protection and with no more damage than some browning of the ends of the leaves. It is suitable for planting at the fronts of perennial borders and blooms in early spring. The snake's-head-iris is satisfactory for growing in pots for winter bloom in greenhouses and even in cool sunrooms and window gardens; it cannot be expected to thrive at high temperatures.

Cultivation. Provided the soil is very well drained and the plant is exposed to full sun, the snake's-head-iris gives the gardener no trouble. Tubers may be planted in early fall or early spring. Occasionally, when the clumps become too large or crowded, they should be taken up, divided, and replanted. Propagation can also be effected by sowing seeds in sandy soil in a cold frame or in pots or pans in a cool greenhouse. For blooming indoors tubers should be planted fairly closely together in pots of fertile, porous earth in early fall. The planted containers are set outdoors and buried to their rims in sand, ashes, peat moss, or other suitable material that will prevent excessive drying. At first, watering should be done with some caution, with only enough given to keep the soil just moist. Before severe freezing weather the containers are brought indoors to a sunny location where the temperature at night is about 50°F and by day not more than about five degrees higher. Flowers may be expected toward the end of January. If plants so forced are kept growing in the same environment and are fertilized weekly with dilute liquid fertilizer they will be ready for repotting in spring and then may be plunged (buried to the rims of their pots) outdoors to complete their summer growth. They can then be forced again the following winter. Alternatively, forced specimens can be planted in the garden and new stock potted the following fall for forcing.

HERNANDIA (Hern-ándia). This genus, little known horticulturally, typifies the hernandia family HERNANDIACEAE, a group allied to the laurel family LAURACEAE. It is indigenous from Central America and northern South America to West Africa, Zanzibar, Indomalaysia, and islands of the Pacific, mostly in coastal regions. There are twenty species. The name *Hernandia* honors Dr. Francisco Hernandez, a sixteenth/seventeenth-century Spanish physician.

Hernandias are evergreen trees with alternate, undivided, long-stalked leaves and panicles of small, yellowish to greenish-white unisexual flowers. Within the panicles the blooms are in threes, each group with a collar of four or five bracts and consisting of a stalkless female between a pair of stalked males. The flowers have no petals. The males have six, rarely eight calyx segments in two circles, and as many stamens. The females have eight, rarely ten calyx segments in two rings, four or five nonfunctional stamens (staminodes), and a short style with a dilated, toothed or lobed stigma. The hard, ribbed nuts (commonly thought of as seeds) are each enclosed in an enlarged, fleshy body called an involucre, with an aperture at its end through which the nut is visible.

Cultivated in Hawaii and other essentially tropical regions, *H. ovigera* (syn. *H. peltata*) is widely distributed in the tropics. The tree cultivated as *H. sonora* probably belongs here. It is up to 60 feet tall or sometimes taller and has an irregularly rounded, open crown. Its leaves are peltate, the long leafstalks being attached to the blades in from their margins, although often very slightly, without an opening from the edge of the blade to the stalk. They have short-pointed, broadly-ovate blades from 4½ inches to almost 1 foot long. The flower panicles are erect and from 4 inches to 1 foot long. The flowers are about ⅓ inch across and yellowish. In fruit the panicles become pendulous. The fruits have eight or ten longitudinal ridges and resemble tiny pale green to whitish pumpkins each with a hole at its top. They are 1 inch to 1½ inches long and contain a black, longitudinally ridged, oily nut. The soft, light wood of this tree takes fire readily and makes good tinder. The leaves and bark are cathartic and are employed medicinally in Asia. The juice is an effective and painless depilatory.

Garden and Landscape Uses and Cultivation. In nature hernandias are often coastal. They are well suited for locations near the sea, grow in ordinary soil, and may be propagated by seeds and probably by cuttings.

HERNANDIACEAE — Hernandia Family. Two tropical genera containing fifty species of trees, shrubs, and occasionally woody vines belong in this family of dicotyledons. They have large alternate leaves undivided or with leaflets arranged palmately. The bisexual or unisexual flowers have perianths of two circles of four to eight sepal-like segments. There are three to five stamens or in female flowers staminodes (nonfertile stamens), one style, and one stigma. The fruits are achenes or samaras. Only *Hernandia* is cultivated.

HERNIARIA (Hern-iària)—Herniary, Rupturewort. By some botanists those members of the pink family CARYOPHYLLACEAE, such as *Herniaria*, that have one-seeded fruits and are without petals are segregated as the knotwort family ILLECEBRACEAE. But the modern tendency is to include the ILLECEBRACEAE in the CARYOPHYLLACEAE. Native from the Mediterranean region and the Canary Islands to Af-

ghanistan, and with one species in South Africa, *Herniaria* derives both its botanical and common names from virtues it was once believed to possess for treating hernias. The generic name comes from the Latin *hernia*, a rupture. There are about thirty-five species.

Ruptureworts are low, trailing, often mat-forming annual and perennial herbaceous plants with stalkless leaves and minute blooms in clusters in the leaf axils. They are closely related to, and in genera resemble, *Paronychia*, but their greenish flowers make no show, and some kinds have four instead of five sepals. There are as many stamens as sepals, and two styles that may be partly joined. The fruits are tiny capsules.

Perennial or annual, *H. glabra*, native throughout Europe except in the extreme north, and quite hardy, forms dense mats several inches wide and 1 inch to 3 inches high. Its very slender, swollen-jointed stems bear elliptic-ovate, lustrous green leaves about ¼ inch long, hairless or sometimes fringed with hairs. The flowers have five sepals. A perennial phase of this variable species, with slightly woody bases to its stems and leaves fringed with hairs, is sometimes distinguished as *H. g. nebrodensis*.

Herniaria glabra

From the last the annual *H. hirsuta* differs in its leaves, and in the five sepals being markedly hairy. Mostly its branches are alternate. The leaves are elliptic to oblanceolate. The flowers are up to ¹⁄₁₅ inch wide. This is chiefly a native of southern and central Europe. The kind known as *H. cinerea* cannot be clearly distinguished from *H. hirsuta*, the two intergrade. In its extreme form, the sepals of the kind called *H. cinerea* have stout long hairs that produce a grayish-white appearance. An allied, perennial species with a woody rootstock, and flowers with five hairy sepals, *H. incana* has leaves ⅓ inch long and not over one-third as broad. They are densely

covered with stiff white hairs. This is native from southern and eastern Europe northward into Russia.

Garden Uses and Cultivation. These lowly, generally hardy plants are cultivated only for their foliage effects. In rock gardens they may be used as carpetings for deciduous bulbs, and in alpine lawns. They are also appropriate for setting in the crevices of flagstone and other paths. They grow with little or no attention in any ordinary soil, being especially partial to those of a sandy character. They are easily increased by seed and, the perennial kinds, by division and by cuttings. Self-sown seedlings often serve to maintain and increase the stocks.

HERNIARY. See Herniaria.

HERONSBILL. See Erodium.

HERREA (Hér-rea). Named in honor of Hans Herre, curator of the botanic garden, Stellenbosch, South Africa, this genus, which differs from *Conicosia* in technical details of its fruits, comprises about two dozen species, all native to South Africa. It belongs in the *Mesembryanthemum* complex of the carpetweed family AIZOACEAE. One kind, *Herrea elongata*, is naturalized in parts of California.

Herreas are succulent, herbaceous perennials with tuberous rootstocks and annual stems furnished with alternate or opposite leaves, more or less rounded in section. The yellow to rarely white, many-petaled flowers are daisy-like in apparent form, but they do not agree with daisies in structure; each is a single bloom, not an assemblage of many florets, as are the flower heads of daisies. The flowers open in afternoons and close before nightfall. The fruits are capsules.

From a large, turnip-shaped tuber *H. elongata* (syns. *Conicosia elongata*, *Mesembryanthemum elongatum*) sends procumbent stems 1 foot or more in length. Its alternate, green or gray-green, slender, curving, spreading leaves, 4 to 6 inches long, are slightly grooved on their upper sides. Solitary, on stalks 3½ to 5 inches long from the ends of the shoots or leaf axils, the sulfur-yellow flowers are 3 to 4½ inches or sometimes more in diameter.

Garden Uses and Cultivation. These are plants for outdoors in warm, semidesert regions and for inclusion in greenhouse collections of succulents. They require full sun and very well-drained, sandy soil. In greenhouses they should be kept dry in winter and watered sparingly to moderately at other seasons. Good ventilation is necessary and a dryish atmosphere. A winter night temperature of 40 to 50°F is adequate, with a few degrees increase by day permitted. Propagation is by seeds and by cuttings. See Succulents for additional information.

HERREANTHUS (Her-reánthus). Named in honor of Hans Herre, one-time curator of the botanical garden at Stellenbosch, South Africa, and bearing a name derived from his and the Greek *anthos*, a flower, this genus consists of one species. It belongs in the carpetweed family AIZOACEAE and is allied to *Mesembryanthemum*.

Inhabiting desert regions in South Africa, where it grows among rocks it resembles in aspect, **Herreanthus meyeri** is a good-looking, nonhardy succulent that forms low tufts of very fleshy, three-angled, bluish-green, slightly spotted leaves up to 1¾ inches long by about one-half as broad, and joined at their bases. The solitary, terminal, almost stalkless, fragrant, white flowers are about 1 inch across and have sepals and petals united at their bases into tubes. They arise from between a pair of bracts, which, together with the white flowers, distinguishes them from otherwise rather similar species of *Schwantesia*. At first the blooms expand only in sunshine, but as they age they remain open day and night and are attractive for about ten days. They have six-lobed calyxes, many petals, and six slender stigmas. Their fruits are capsules containing smooth seeds.

Garden Uses and Cultivation. Under conditions that suit *Lithops* and similar very fleshy "stone plants" of the *Mesembryanthemum* tribe, *Herreanthus* thrives with comparative ease. It makes its new growth in fall and then should be watered moderately. At other seasons keep it drier. This species may be multiplied by cuttings and seeds. For further information see Succulents.

HERTIA (Hèr-tia). Closely related to *Othonna* and by some authorities included there, the genus *Hertia*, of the daisy family COMPOSITAE, consists of a dozen species, which occur natively in South Africa and from North Africa to Baluchistan.

More or less succulent, hairless sub-shrubs, hertias have alternate, stalkless leaves and at the ends of the branches or in short, leafy panicles, small to medium-sized, solitary flower heads with or without ray florets. The fruits are seedlike achenes.

A subshrub of North Africa, **H. cheirifolia** has prostrate branches, up-turned at their ends, and alternate, somewhat fleshy, oblanceolate, lobeless, essentially toothless, sometimes purple-flushed, green leaves up to 2 inches long. The flower heads, of about a dozen ray florets, are about 1 inch wide.

Garden and Landscape Uses and Cultivation. These are as for *Carpobrotus*.

HERTRICHOCEREUS (Hertricho-cèreus). Named after William Hertrich, a director of the Huntington Botanic Garden, San Marino, California, who died in 1966, and the related genus *Cereus*, Hertrichocereus, of

Hertia cheirifolia

the cactus family CACTACEAE, is by conservative botanists included in *Lemaireocereus*. Considered as a separate genus, it consists of a single species.

Native to Mexico, **H. beneckei** (syns. *Lemaireocereus beneckei*, *Cereus beneckei*) is 3 to 5 feet tall and much-branched with some branches sprawling or clambering, others erect. The stems, 2½ to 3 inches in diameter, have seven to nine lumpy ribs and are brownish-green with a whitish, waxy coating. The spines are in clusters of up to seven, the radials brown and 1 inch long, the one stouter, red, brown, or black, stiff central 2½ inches long and awl-shaped. About 3 inches long and 1½ inches in diameter, the rather dirty-white blooms open at night. Their perianth tubes and ovaries are naked of spines. The spiny fruits are about 2 inches long by a little over one-half as wide.

Garden and Landscape Uses and Cultivation. Chiefly of interest to collectors of cactuses, this may be grown outdoors in warm dry climates, such as that of southern California, and in greenhouses. It succeeds under conditions that suit the majority of desert cactuses. For additional information see Cactuses.

HESPERALOE (Hesper-áloe). Three species of yucca-like plants of the lily family LILIACEAE constitute *Hesperaloe*, a native of Texas and Mexico. The name, from the Greek *hesperos*, western, and *Aloe*, the name of an Old World group of succulent plants, refers to the plants' native abode and their resemblance to *Aloe*. From *Yucca* they are distinguishable by their reddish blooms.

Hesperaloes are without stems. Their tough, leathery leaves, in grasslike clumps and with fibrous or threadlike frayings at their margins, are narrow-linear and grooved. The branchless or branched flower stalks bear nodding, aloe-like blooms with six petals, or more properly tepals, six stamens, and one style. The fruits are capsules containing large, thin, black seeds.

Endemic to Texas, **H. parviflora** (syn. *H. yuccaefolia*) has pinkish to dark red blooms 1 inch to 1¼ inches long. It has arching, spreading leaves up to 4 feet long and 1¼ inches wide with very fine marginal frayings. The more bell-shaped blooms of *H. p. engelmannii* are about 1 inch long. From the last, Mexican **H. funifera** differs in having its up to 6-foot-long leaves margined with much coarser frayings and its up to 8-foot-tall flowering stalks having purple-tinged, green blooms about 1 inch long.

Night-blooming **H. nocturna** (syn. *Nolina microcarpa*), of Mexico, forms big clumps of linear leaves ½ inch or scarcely more wide at their bases, narrower above, and up to 5 feet long. The flowering stalks, branched or branchless and up to 8 feet tall, bear clusters of 1-inch-long flowers, their outsides greenish suffused with pink or lavender, their insides whitish.

Garden and Landscape Uses and Cultivation. These are less showy plants than most yuccas, but have the same general uses and require the same conditions and management.

HESPERANTHA (Hesper-ántha). The name of *Hesperantha*, that of a genus of the iris family IRIDACEAE, directs attention to the sweetly-scented blooms of most kinds not opening until late afternoon. It is derived from the Greek *hesperos*, evening, and *anthos*, a flower. There are fifty species, mostly South African, and a few natives of tropical Africa. They differ from closely allied *Geissorhiza* in having styles not longer than the perianth tubes. None is hardy in the north.

Hesperanthas have small corms, underground food-storage organs that look like bulbs, but differ in being solid instead of like onions built of concentric layers, or lily bulbs of overlapping scales. The stems are usually without branches, and at their bases are sheathed by fans of a few narrow leaves, the lowermost often sickle-shaped. The flowers, in usually one-sided spikes with green bracts, are symmetrical. They have straight or curved, short perianth tubes and nearly equal, spreading perianth lobes (petals, or more correctly, tepals). There are three evenly-spaced stamens and a style with three spreading branches. The fruits are small, obconical capsules.

One of the most desirable species, **H. metelerkampiae**, of South Africa, has usually three lanceolate to somewhat sickle-shaped basal leaves about 4 inches long and hairless stems with a single leaf at the base of the flower spike. The spikes generally have three brilliant golden-yellow and dark purple blooms about 2 inches across. The stamens have yellow anthers, the style deep purple branches.

From the last, **H. inflexa stanfordiae** (syn. *H. stanfordiae*) differs in having brilliant yellow, fragrant blooms with 1-inch-long petals, two to four on each spike. This va-

Hesperantha inflexa stanfordiae

riety, 1 foot to 1½ feet tall, has three sickle-shaped basal leaves 2 to 3 inches long. The one stem leaf, in the axil of which a flowering branch arises, is about 4 inches in length. The blooms face upward and are open from noon to sunset. They are about 2 inches across and have short-stalked stamens with protruding yellow anthers. The species *H. inflexa* has somewhat bigger flowers with dull yellow outer petals and bright yellow inner ones blotched with purple near their apexes.

Bright rose-red flowers about 1¼ inches across are borne on stems up to 2 feet tall by *H. bauri*. The usually three basal leaves are about 1 foot long by ¼ inch wide. The flowers have corolla lobes (petals) about as long as the corolla tube. Cup-shaped flowers, about 1¼ inches wide, four to eight in each loose spike, that open from noon onward and last well are featured by *H. buhri*. They are white, with the outsides of the outer petals cerise-pink. The short stamens have yellow anthers.

Garden and Landscape Uses and Cultivation. With few exceptions, including the sorts described above, hesperanthas are not among the most showy of South African irids. Some are worth considering only for their scented, evening flowers. They respond to cultivation and environments that satisfy *Ixia*.

HESPERETHUSA (Hespere-thùsa)—Naibel. Its name that of one of the Hesperides, the only species of this genus of the rue family RUTACEAE is a native of India and Ceylon, where it grows in dry, hilly country.

A citrus relative, the naibel (*Hesperethusa crenulata* syn. *Limonia crenulata*) is a slender, evergreen shrub or small tree. It has sharp spines, and pinnate leaves up to 4 inches long, with five, seven, or nine widely-spaced, round-toothed leaflets attached to an axis that like the stalk has wide, leaflike wings. The fragrant flowers are small and white. They have four each sepals and petals and eight stamens. Containing up to four seeds embedded in bitter pulp, the spherical, dark-colored fruits are up to ½ inch in diameter. They are structured like oranges.

Garden and Landscape Uses and Cultivation. As an unusual ornamental the naibel is worth using outdoors. It prospers under conditions that suit oranges and other citrus fruits. Not hardy in cold climates, it may be grown in greenhouses and makes a quite decorative pot or tub specimen. It may be propagated by seeds and by grafting onto seedling plants of *Citrus*.

HESPERIS (Hés-peris)—Sweet Rocket or Dame's-Violet. Belonging to the mustard family CRUCIFERAE, the genus *Hesperis* consists of thirty species. It inhabits the Mediterranean region and temperate Asia. The name, from the Greek *hespera*, evening, calls attention to the fragrance of the flowers of some kinds being strongest after nightfall.

These are erect, hairless or hairy biennials and herbaceous perennials with generally undivided, toothed or toothless leaves. In usually showy, loose, terminal racemes or panicles, the blooms are purple, rosy-purple, or white. Each has four erect sepals, four petals that spread to form a cross, six stamens of which two are shorter than the others, and a style tipped with a two-lobed stigma, the lobes, blunt, erect, and parallel. The fruits are slender, spreading pods.

Sweet Rocket or dame's-violet (*H. matronalis*), a biennial or perennial 1 foot to 3 feet tall, native to Europe and Asia, is naturalized in North America, most commonly near old gardens. Usually, but not always more or less hairy, this has stalkless or short-stalked, pointed, lanceolate to lanceolate-ovate, toothed leaves up to about 4 inches long. About ¾ inch long and wide, the sweetly-fragrant purple to lilac-purple flowers are in showy terminal racemes. In *H. m. alba* the flowers are white. Those of *H. m. purpurea* are purple. Double purple blooms are borne by *H. m. flore-pleno*, double white ones by *H. m. alba-plena*.

Hesperis matronalis

Hesperis matronalis (flowers)

Less commonly cultivated *H. tristis,* of central and eastern Europe, is a biennial or perennial up to 1½ feet tall, hairless or sparingly-hairy. It has pointed, ovate-lanceolate, toothless leaves up to 2 inches long. One inch or more long, the yellowish-green flowers are veined with rose-violet.

Garden and Landscape Uses and Cultivation. Single-flowered dame's-violets are pleasant additions to semiwild and naturalistic areas where the soil is slightly damp and there is a little shade. There they will maintain themselves and reproduce with practically no attention. They associate well with ferns. Double-flowered varieties are more demanding and are a good deal rarer. They are best suited for grouping in perennial beds and at the margins of woodlands and shrub borders. A well-drained, but not dry sandy loam enriched with organic matter is to their liking. The double kinds must be increased by division or cuttings. The single-flowered come readily from seeds sown in May in a cold frame or outdoors. The other species described above has similar uses and responds to the same care. All of these sorts are hardy.

HESPEROCALLIS (Hespero-cállis)—Desert-Lily. One species, native of the deserts of California and Arizona, is the only member of this genus. It belongs in the lily family LILIACEAE. Its name is from the Greek, *hesperos,* western, and *kallos,* beautiful.

Flowering in spring, *Hesperocallis undulata* has a deeply-located, solid, ovoid bulb about 2 inches long, from which develops a stout, erect, branchless stem 1 foot to 6 feet tall and fleshy, linear, arching, wavy-edged, mostly basal, blue-green leaves 6 inches to 1½ feet long and up to ¾ inch wide. There are a few, smaller, stem leaves. The funnel-shaped flowers, 1½ to 2½ inches long, form racemes 4 inches to 1 foot in length, each bloom on a stalk under ½ inch long. They are very fragrant, slightly greenish or waxy white, and have six perianth parts (commonly called petals) united below their middles into a tube. Each petal has a green stripe on its underside. There are six stamens with golden-yellow anthers, and a white style. The fruits are somewhat globose capsules containing numerous flat, black seeds. The onion-flavored bulbs were eaten by the desert Indians and early Spanish explorers. An interesting fact about this plant is that in its desert home the bulbs may remain dormant, producing neither leaves nor flowers through one to several dry years.

Garden Uses and Cultivation. Sometimes planted in gardens in warm dry climates, this species is of interest to collectors of uncommon plants. It is acknowledgedly difficult to grow. It may be accommodated in rock gardens and similar places in deep, sandy, well-drained soil in full sun. The bulb should be about 6 inches below the surface. Propagation is by seed.

HESPEROCHIRON (Hespero-chíron). There are only two species in this genus of the water leaf family HYDROPHYLLACEAE. Both are stemless perennial herbaceous plants of western North America. Their name is derived from the Greek *hesperos,* western, and *Chiron,* a centaur with medical skills. These plants have short, thick roots and basal rosettes of stalked, toothless, ovate to spoon-shaped leaves. The solitary blooms are on stems naked of foliage that rise from the leaf axils. They are white to bluish-white, with pinkish veins. They have a five-lobed calyx and five-lobed corolla. Neither the five stamens nor the one style protrude from the corolla tube. The former are often of unequal length, the latter is cleft in two at its apex. The fruits are more or less ovoid capsules containing many dark brown, angular seeds.

Ranging in the wild from California to Washington and Utah, *Hesperochiron californicus* in bloom is 2 to 3 inches high. It has many, more or less gray-hairy, narrowly-oblong to ovate leaves up to 1½ inches long, and funnel- or narrowly-bell-shaped flowers with short hairs on their insides. The flowers are ⅓ to 1 inch long and nearly as broad. This species inhabits moist, subsaline soils above 4,000 feet.

Native at elevations above 1,200 feet in California, Idaho, Nevada, and Arizona, *H. pumilus* differs from the last in having saucer-shaped blooms, ½ inch to 1¼ inches across, densely-long-hairy on their insides. There are usually fewer than ten and sometimes only two hairless or nearly hairless leaves, oblong to oblanceolate, and 1 inch to 2 inches long. This plant in bloom is 1½ to 2 inches tall. It inhabits moist, often somewhat alkaline soils.

Garden Uses and Cultivation. Not a great deal of information is available about the cultivation of these plants outside their native regions. Such experience as is recorded indicates that they are not difficult to grow in well-drained soils in full sun. They have a long period of dormancy. It may be presumed that conditions akin to those they know in the wild would be most suitable. They may be short-lived, possibly behaving as biennials. These plants are appropriate for rock gardens and similar places. Both species vary considerably, plants with large flowers of desirable color should be sought and propagated. Propagation is by seed.

HESPEROYUCCA. See *Yucca whipplei.*

HETERANTHERA (Heter-ánthera) — Mud-Plantain. The genus of the pickerel weed family PONTEDERIACEAE that bears the unlovely common name mud-plantain consists of ten species. It is wild from southern New England to tropical America and in Africa. Its name is from the Greek *heteros,* different, and *anthera,* an anther, in allusion to the two types of anthers the flowers of some of its sorts, but not those of *H. dubia,* possess.

Heterantheras grow in mud, above water or completely submersed, or sometimes float. They have branched stems, round, kidney-shaped or lanceolate leaves, and small white, blue, or violet flowers that are tubular and have six wide-spreading, narrow perianth lobes. They are solitary, paired, or several together in spikes. A sheathing spathe (leaflike organ) is wrapped around the flower stalk and has a single regular leaf below it. The flowers have three stamens and one style. The fruits are many-seeded capsules.

Native of still waters from Quebec to Washington, North Carolina, Arkansas, and New Mexico, the water-star-grass (*H. dubia* syn. *Zosterella dubia*) has thin, trailing, branching stems, the upper parts of which sometimes float and which root from the nodes. The leaves are stalkless, linear, up to 6 inches long, and about ⅙ inch broad. The nearly stalkless flowers are yellow and from ½ to ¾ inch wide by up to 2¼ inches long.

An attractive species with solitary flowers, *H. limosa,* of the central United States, West Indies, and Central and South America, has lanceolate to obovate leaves with stalks up to 9 inches in length. Its flowers are blue with a white spot near the base, or sometimes all white. They are 1 inch to 1½ inches long. Quite different *H. reniformis,* a kind with broadly-heart- to kidney-shaped leaves and 2- to 8-flowered spikes of bloom, is native from southern New England to Nebraska, Florida, and Texas, also in tropical America. The white to pale blue blooms are about ⅓ inch across. Similar to *H. reniformis* is *H. peduncularis,* which is indigenous in Kansas, Missouri, and Mexico. The most easily recognized difference is that in *H. reniformis* there is an obvious space separating the spathe from the leaf below it; in *H. peduncularis* they are adjacent. An excellent kind for tropical aquariums is *H. zosteraefolia,* of Brazil and Bolivia. A very ornamental underwater species, it has long stems and ribbon-shaped, pointed-oval, or spatula-shaped, fragile leaves up to 1½ inches long, some of which float, and solitary or paired bright blue above-water flowers ⅓ to ½ inch wide.

Garden Uses and Cultivation. Heterantheras are grown in aquariums and in pools, ponds, and bog gardens. For the first-named conditions *H. zosteraefolia* is best adapted. It thrives in neutral to alkaline water with its roots in mud or in sand with a mud content. The water temperature should be 65 to 80°F. The others may be grown in unheated tanks and outdoor pools. Propagation is by cuttings, division, and by seeds sown in wet soil. The seeds must not be allowed to dry from the time of gathering to that of sowing.

HETEROCENTRON (Hetero-céntron). Spanish Shawl. About two dozen species, natives of the mountains of Mexico and Central America, constitute *Heterocentron*, of the melastoma family MELASTOMATACEAE. The name from the Greek *heteros*, variable, and *kentron*, a spur, alludes to the anthers.

Subshrubs or herbaceous perennials, erect or creeping, heterocentrons have opposite, lanceolate to ovate-lanceolate leaves. Their white, pink, purplish, or carmine-red blooms are in terminal panicles, or are solitary. They have four-lobed or four-toothed calyxes, four spreading petals, and eight stamens of two sizes. The four larger are furnished with long, cleft appendages. The fruits are capsules.

From 1 foot to 3 feet in height, *H. macrostachyum* (syns. *H. roseum*, *Heeria rosea*), which is sometimes misidentified as *Heterocentron mexicanum*, is an erect subshrub with four-angled stems and moderately long-stalked, sparsely-rough-hairy, elliptic leaves 2 to 4 inches long, that in sun have a tendency to turn reddish. Profuse and in ample panicles, the bright rose-pink flowers come in fall and early winter. Almost 1 inch in diameter, they have slightly concave petals.

Spanish shawl (*H. elegans* syns. *Schizocentron elegans*, *Heeria elegans*), an evergreen, perennial, vigorous creeper that forms dense carpets of slender, rooting stems clothed with short-stalked, slightly-hairy leaves with ovate blades ½ to ¾ inch long with obscurely-toothed edges, is a native of Mexico, Guatemala, and Honduras. On slender stalks ½ inch long, its numerous brilliant carmine blooms are borne. Each has four spreading, broadly-ovate petals from slightly less to slightly more than ½ inch long and nearly as broad.

Heterocentron elegans

Erect, sparingly-branched and up to 6 feet tall, Mexican *H. subtriplinervium* is naturalized in Hawaii and elsewhere in the tropics. Its often green-winged stems have reddish-brown hairs. The pointed, elliptic to ovate, short-stalked, hairy leaves are up to 4 inches long. About ¾ inch across, the white flowers are in panicles. A pink-flowered varient, most common in cultivation, is sometimes misnamed *H. roseum*. The plant cultivated as *H. roseum album* is probably *H. subtriplinervium*.

Garden and Landscape Uses and Cultivation. Only in frostless, dryish climates are these plants successful outdoors, but *H. macrostachyum* and the sort called *H. roseum album* can be used elsewhere to add end-of-summer and early fall color to garden beds, after which the plants are taken up and wintered in a well-protected cold frame or greenhouse. For flowering in greenhouses these plants are grown in pots kept indoors throughout, or in summer plunged (buried to their rims) in a bed of sand, peat moss, or other material outdoors and brought into a greenhouse to bloom. They are easy to manage. Seeds can be sown to raise new plants, but more commonly cuttings are taken in spring or early summer. These root with great ease and are then potted individually in small pots, and successively into bigger ones. The last shift, given in August, is to containers 5 to 8 inches in diameter, depending upon how early the cuttings were taken and the amount of growth the plants have made. The tips of the shoots are pinched out once or twice to stimulate branching, but if this is done too often or too late in the season short shoots of inferior blooming quality result. Fertile soil, well drained and loamy, suits. It must be porous and kept moist, but not wet. After the final pots are filled with roots weekly applications of dilute liquid fertilizer are helpful. Full sun is needed throughout, and indoors a temperature at night of 50 to 55°F, and by day about five to ten degrees higher.

Spanish shawl in essentially frostless, dry climates is very useful as a groundcover and for rock gardens. In greenhouses it is admirable for clothing the surface soil around large palms, succulents, and other plants in tubs, and is excellent for hanging baskets. No special difficulties attend its cultivation. It succeeds in ordinary well-drained soil kept moderately moist, but not saturated, where it receives some shade from the strongest sun. Indoor temperatures in winter of about 50°F at night and a few degrees higher by day suit it. Increase is by division, cuttings, and seeds.

HETEROMELES (Heter-omèles) — Christmas-Berry or Toyon or California-Holly. No native shrub of California is more beloved than the Christmas-berry or toyon

(*Heteromeles arbutifolia*). It is the only representative of its genus and in the wild is restricted to California and Baja California. Very closely related to *Photinia*, it belongs in the rose family ROSACEAE. Its name, derived from the Greek *heteros*, different, and *malus*, the apple, emphasizes its dissimilarity to the related genus *Malus*. The Christmas-berry is also called California-holly, not because its foliage is holly-like, but because its berries are reminiscent of those of the traditional Christmas evergreen and are used in California in great quantities for holiday decorations. Before Christmas florists' windows are well stocked with them, and they are sold by street vendors, often mixed with branches of live oak, the prickly leaves of which suggest the foliage of holly.

The Christmas-berry (*H. arbutifolia*) is an evergreen shrub or small tree of the chaparral, 6 to 30 feet tall, and without spines. Its young shoots are pubescent. El-

Heteromeles arbutifolia

liptic to oblong or lanceolate-oblong, the short-stalked, sharply-toothed, thick leaves are 2 to 4 inches long. They are glossy on their upper sides and are usually without hairs, but sometimes are sparsely-hairy. About ¼ inch across, the white flowers are in large terminal clusters. They have five persistent sepals, five spreading, ovate, saucered petals, five pairs of stamens, and two or three separate styles. The fruits are pomes (fruits structured like those of apples and mountain-ashes). They are berry-like, broadly-egg-shaped, up to ¼ inch long, and at their ends have incurved, thickened sepals. They are in loose clusters of considerable size and typically are bright red, more rarely yellow. They ripen in fall and make a fine display for many weeks. Horticulturally superior to the species, *H. a. macrocarpa* has berries about ⅓ inch long that seem to be less attractive to birds. Its ten rather than twenty stamens readily distinguish *Heteromeles* from *Photinia*.

Garden and Landscape Uses. The Christmas-berry is not hardy in the north. In California and other places with climates as mild, it is greatly appreciated as a shrub for gardens and other landscapes and is much planted. It makes a splendid winter display of berries and at all seasons is a handsome evergreen suitable for planting as a free-standing specimen or in groups of its kind or with other shrubs. It is not choosy about soil, flourishing in any well-drained one of reasonable fertility. It withstands dryish conditions well and needs full sun.

Cultivation. No special care is required. Pruning, as needed, is done in late winter or spring to control size or shape. Propagation is by seeds and by cuttings.

HETEROPAPPUS (Hetero-páppus). About a dozen species of eastern Asian biennials and herbaceous perennials constitute *Heteropappus*, of the daisy family COMPOSITAE. The name, which alludes to the hairs or scales that accompany the ovaries and fruits of the disk florets being different from those of the ray florets, comes from the Greek *heteros*, various, and *pappus*, down. This feature distinguishes *Heteropappus* from closely related *Aster*.

Erect, with alternate, undivided, coarsely-toothed or toothless leaves, heteropappuses have hairy or hairless stems and foliage. Their daisy-like flower heads, in loose clusters, have a central eye of yellow disk florets, and a surrounding circle of blue-purple to white, petal-like ray florets; both are fertile. The seedlike fruits are achenes.

Most often cultivated, *H. hispidus* (syn. *Aster hispidus*) is a variable native of Japan, China, Manchuria, and Taiwan. Japanese botanists recognize four varieties. This has very leafy, coarsely-hairy stems 1 foot to 3 feet tall, branched in their upper parts. The basal leaves, 3 to nearly 6 inches long by up to 1¼ inches broad, are oblanceo-late. Stem leaves are linear, and up to 3 inches long by not over ¾ inch wide. The foliage is more or less hairy and often coarsely-toothed. From 1¼ to 2 inches in diameter, the flower heads have blue-purple to white ray florets. Native from Iran to the Himalayas, *H. altaicus* (syn. *Aster altaicus*) is up to about 1½ feet tall and rough-hairy. Its stem leaves, the basal ones absent at maturity, are linear-lanceolate to spatula-shaped, and generally not over 2 inches long, but the lower ones are sometimes up to 4 inches long. The ray florets of the 2-inch-wide flower heads are purple to white.

Garden and Landscape Uses and Cultivation. These are as for perennial asters. The species described, hardy and of easy cultivation, are propagated by seed and division.

HETEROPTERYS (Heteróp-terys). Previously spelled *Heteropteris*, the name *Heteropterys* comes from the Greek *heteros*, varied, and *pteron*, a wing. The allusion is to the fruits having wings of various shapes. Belonging in the malpighia family MALPIGHIACEAE, this genus of about 100 species is predominantly American, but one species occurs in West Africa.

Plants that belong here are shrubs and woody climbers with opposite, usually undivided, short-stalked leaves, with glandular dots on their undersides, and small yellow or purple flowers mostly in panicles or racemes. The calyx is five-parted. There are five distinctly-clawed petals, sharply narrowed at their bases, ten stamens of unequal size, and three styles. The fruits, like those of maples and ashes, are samaras, that is to say they are winged and do not open to discharge their seeds.

Native to Brazil, *H. chrysophylla* is a climbing evergreen shrub with long stems and opposite, short-stalked, broad-elliptic to ovate-oblong, leathery leaves, dark green and hairless above and clothed with yellow, silky hairs beneath. These have several glands near the leaf margins and two near the end of the leafstalk. The flowers, yellow to orange, and about ½ inch in diameter, are in terminal and lateral panicles. The calyxes are clothed with rusty hairs. The petals are roundish.

The sorbach (*H. beecheyana*), native from Mexico to Bolivia, is another climber. It has pointed, ovate to oblong leaves, up to 3 inches long and downy on their undersides, and large panicles of 1-inch-wide, lilac blooms. The reddish fruits have one to three wings and are about 1½ inches long.

Garden Uses and Cultivation. Plants of this genus are quite handsome climbers for outdoors in the tropics and subtropics, and for greenhouses. They grow in any ordinary soil in sun or part-day shade. If allowed to grow with little or no restraint, they need support, but may be kept shrublike by repeated pruning; when so treated they bloom regularly. Pruning is done at the beginning of the season of new growth. In greenhouses they thrive where a minimum night temperature of 55 to 60°F is maintained, in pots, tubs, or ground beds. They need good light. Propagation is by cuttings and by seeds.

HETEROSPATHE (Heterospà-the). Eighteen species of the Philippine Islands, New Guinea, Solomon Islands, and other islands of the Pacific are included in *Heterospathe*, of the palm family PALMAE. They are feather-leaved, unisexual trees. The name is derived from the Greek *heteros*, various, and *spathe*, an appendage of the flower cluster. It refers to the unequal sizes of the spathes. Only one species is much cultivated, *H. elata*, of the Philippine Islands, Palau, and perhaps the Moluccas. The Palau plant differs slightly in botanical details from that native of the Philippine Islands and possibly from that of the Moluccas.

A graceful palm 45 to 60 feet tall, *H. elata* has a trunk that widens at its base and is ringed with leaf scars. Its arching leaves 10 feet long or longer have numerous, narrow, drooping leaflets 2 to 3 feet long. The bases of the stalks of the leaves do not form a crownshaft. The flower clusters are among the leaves. The outer spathe is 1 foot to 1¼ feet in length, the inner almost twice as long. The flowers are usually in threes, rarely in twos, the males with six stamens. The white subglobose fruits are about ¼ inch in diameter.

Garden and Landscape Uses and Cultivation. This palm is not commonly cultivated in the United States and is adaptable only for moist, tropical climates such as those of Hawaii and southern Florida. It can also be grown in warm, humid greenhouses. In its home islands it occurs in limestone and limestone soils. It has the same cultural requirements as *Verschaffeltia*. For more information see Palms.

Heteropterys chrysophylla

HETEROSPERMA (Heterospérm-a). Belonging to the daisy family COMPOSITAE, the genus *Heterosperma* consists of ten species. It is indigenous from the southwestern United States to South America. The generic name, sometimes spelled *Heterospermum*, is derived from the Greek *heteros*, variable, and *sperma*, a seed.

Heterospermas are low, slender, branched annuals with opposite leaves once- or twice-cleft into linear lobes. The small, terminal, daisy-type flower heads are yellow. Both disk and ray florets are fertile. The fruits are seedlike achenes.

One species, *H. pinnatum*, of Texas, Arizona, and Mexico, is sometimes cultivated. Up to 1 foot tall, this has leaves with narrow, pointed segments. Its bright yellow flower heads are up to ½ inch across.

Garden Uses and Cultivation. A virtue of this not very showy annual is its ability to prosper in comparatively poor, dry soil. Because of this it can be used to clothe medium slopes and other difficult places where more demanding plants would be likely to fail. It is useful in rock gardens and seaside gardens. Choose a sunny location and sow seeds in spring where the plants are to remain. Thin the seedlings to about 4 inches apart. Alternatively, you may sow indoors in a temperature of 60 to 65°F eight weeks before the young plants are to be transplanted to the garden, which may be done as soon as the weather is warm and settled. If you sow indoors transplant the seedlings as soon as they can be handled easily to flats, spacing them 2 inches apart. Grow them in a sunny greenhouse with a night temperature of 50 to 55°F and day temperatures five to ten degrees higher. Allow 4 to 5 inches between flat-grown plants when they are transplanted to the garden.

HETEROTHECA (Hetero-thèca) — Golden-Aster. Some half dozen species of North American annuals and biennials of the daisy family COMPOSITAE compose *Heterotheca*. Their name, derived from the Greek *heteros*, different, and *theke*, a case, calls attention to the fact that the seedlike fruits or achenes of the ray florets are unlike those of the disk florets.

Heterothecas are hairy plants with alternate, usually toothed leaves. They have several to many medium-sized shallowly-bell-shaped to hemispherical flower heads with involucres (collars behind the heads) of several rows of bracts. Both disk and ray florets are yellow. The former are succeeded by flattened, hairy achenes, each with a conspicuous tuft of hairs at one end. The ray florets, those that look like petals, produce thick, usually three-angled, hairless or nearly hairless achenes without tufts.

Of little horticultural merit, the golden-aster (*H. subaxillaris*) is occasionally cultivated, chiefly in areas devoted to native wild flowers and similar places. In the wild it favors dryish, often sandy soil, and occurs from Delaware to Florida, Kansas, Arizona, and Mexico. A glandular-hairy annual or biennial up to about 3 feet tall, it has usually pointed, ovate to oblong, toothed or nearly toothless leaves about 3 inches long. The lowermost have stalks, those above are without and often clasp the stems with their bases. Up to 1 inch across, the flower heads are carried in loose terminal clusters. They come in summer and fall.

Heterotheca subaxillaris

Garden and Landscape Uses and Cultivation. The rather limited uses of the species described have been mentioned. It is easily grown in porous, well-drained soil in open locations, from seeds sown in fall or early spring. The seedlings are thinned sufficiently to prevent undue crowding.

HETEROTOMA (Hetero-tòma) — Bird Plant. Eleven species comprise the horticulturally little known genus *Heterotoma*, of the bellflower family CAMPANULACEAE. They are natives of Mexico and Central America. The name, from the Greek *heteros*, variable, and *tome*, cut, refers to the corollas of the flowers being unequally cut.

Heterotomas are annuals and herbaceous perennials with alternate, stalked leaves. In terminal racemes, the blooms have calyxes of five sepals. The corollas, like those of lobelias slit to their bases down their backs, are tubular with their bases and two of the sepals forming a spur. They are three-lobed beyond their middles. There are five stamens and one style. The fruits are capsules.

The bird plant (*H. lobelioides*) is indigenous to mountain regions in Mexico and Central America. A herbaceous perennial 1½ to 3 feet tall, this has hairy stems, woody toward their bases. Its leaves are long-stalked, pointed-ovate-lanceolate, and toothed. Their blades are 3 to 4 inches long by up to nearly 3 inches wide. The unusual showy flowers are birdlike in aspect (which accounts for the vernacular name of this species). Many together in loose, long-stalked racemes, they are 1¼ to 2 inches long. Each has a slender, 1- to 2-inch-long stalk. The conspicuously-spurred corolla, curved like a sickle, is much wider at its middle than at the ends. The flowers are stalked and solitary from the leaf axils. Their corolla tubes are red and as long as the column of stamens. The three lobes (petals) are bright yellow.

Garden Uses and Cultivation. The species described is suitable for outdoor cultivation in mild, dryish climates, such as that of California, and may be grown as a curiosity in greenhouses. It requires the same care as *Lobelia laxiflora*. Propagation is by seed and by division.

HEUCHERA (Heuch-èra) — Alum Root, Coral Bells. Botanists recognize about fifty species of *Heuchera*, all natives of North America. Few are sufficiently attractive to have horticultural merit and those for the most part are eclipsed by modern hybrids, derivatives of very few species. The group belongs in the saxifrage family SAXIFRAGACEAE. Its name commemorates the German botanist and Professor of Medicine, Johann Heinrich von Heucher, who died in 1747. Alum roots are kin of the pick-a-back plant (*Tolmiea*) and false mitrewort (*Tiarella*). With the latter they have been crossed to produce bigeneric hybrids to which the name *Heucherella* is applied.

Heuchera (with *Rodgersia* behind)

Alum roots have semi-woody, often branching rootstocks. Their long-stalked leaves, variously lobed or toothed, arise mostly from the base of the plant. The flower stalks, with a few leaves or leafy bracts, are slender and erect. They carry many small blooms in racemes or panicles.

The flowers are bell-, urn-, or saucer-shaped. In many species they are greenish or whitish, in some purplish, but those that appeal most to gardeners have bright red or pink blooms. The showy part of the flower is a five-lobed calyx. The five small petals are joined to the calyx and are often shorter than its lobes. There are five stamens, attached to the petals, and two slender styles. The name coral bells is generally restricted to *H. sanguinea* and its hybrids, the mostly greenish flowered kinds are called alum roots.

The best known species, the coral bells (**H. sanguinea**), native from Arizona to Mexico, is 10 inches to 1½ feet tall or slightly taller and glandular-hairy. It has nearly round to kidney-shaped leaves 1 inch to 2 inches or more across, on stalks up to 5 inches long. Its bell-shaped flowers, in airy panicles, are red, pink, or white, and ¼ to ½ inch long. The petals and stamens are shorter than the sepals. Many variations of this species have been named including *H. s. alba*, with white flowers; *H. s. gracillima*, with slender panicles; *H. s. maxima*, with flowers darker colored and larger than normal; *H. s. rosea*, with pink blooms; and *H. s. splendens*, with deep crimson flowers.

Hybrid coral bells are so superior to the wild kinds and even to the selected varieties of *H. sanguinea* that they are the only ones worthy of general cultivation in flower beds and borders. One of the older hybrids, between *H. sanguinea* and *H. micrantha*, is *H.* 'Rosamundi'. Still worth growing, it has 2- to 3-foot-long, sparingly-branched dense spikes of terra-cotta-pink blooms. Probably of the same parentage is **H. brizoides**, with looser, more freely-branched clusters of pink flowers about ⅛ inch long. This kind, which is up to 2½ feet in height and which flowers with great freedom, has been confused with *Heucherella tiarelloides*. It differs in its flowers having only five stamens.

Another hybrid, **H. convallaria** has as parents *H. sanguinea* and *H. pubescens*. Its small greenish, pink-tipped flowers are in slender panicles that have scattered, glandular hairs. There are several forms of this hybrid, varying in flower color, height, and degree of hairiness. More recently much showier garden varieties have resulted from the efforts of European plant breeders in crossing *H. sanguinea* with *H. brizoides*. Among these developments are the varieties 'Coral Mist', with loose panicles of small pink flowers; 'Garnet', with marbled foliage and dark pink blooms; 'Pluie de Feu', 1 foot tall and with scarlet flowers; and 'Snowflakes', which attains a height of 2½ feet and is one of the best white-flowered varieties. Others undoubtedly are yet to come; catalogs of dealers in herbaceous perennials should be consulted.

Other species sometimes cultivated include **H. americana,** native from Ontario to Louisiana, Michigan, Illinois, and Missouri, and 1½ to 3 feet tall. It grows chiefly in dry woodlands. Its leaves, roughly five-sided in outline and shallowly-lobed and -toothed, are mottled when young but become plain green later. Its flowers are greenish-white to purplish and have protruding stamens at least twice as long as the sepals. Indigenous to Oregon, Idaho, and Montana, **H. cylindrica,** is 1 foot to 3 feet tall. It has heart-shaped to round, deeply-lobed, somewhat bristly-hairy, toothed leaves, and yellowish-green to cream flowers in spikelike clusters. A native of Colorado, **H. hallii** has neat basal tufts of longish-stalked, rounded, heart-shaped to kidney-shaped, slightly five- to seven-lobed, round-toothed leaves ½ to 1 inch wide and slender, erect flowering stalks 4 to 8 inches high that are naked of leaves but sometimes bear a few small bracts. They terminate in narrow spikelike panicles of small, sometimes greenish-white flowers that may be tinged with red. Another Westerner, **H. micrantha,** ranges as a native from Oregon to Washington and Idaho. It has obscurely-lobed, usually somewhat bristly, heart-shaped to nearly round, toothed leaves, and whitish or red-tinged flowers, not over ⅛ inch long, with petals twice as long as the sepals. In **H. pubescens** the petals of the purplish-green to whitish flowers are two-thirds as long as the sepals, and the stamens protrude. The flower stalks are 1 foot to 2½ feet in

Heuchera sanguinea

Heuchera hallii

height. This native from Pennsylvania to Virginia, has shallowly-lobed leaves hairy beneath and with upper surfaces at first hairy, but later smooth. Variety *H. p. brachyandra*, which differs in its stamens not protruding from the flowers, ranges from Maryland to Kentucky and North Carolina.

Garden and Landscape Uses. The popular *H. sanguinea* and its hybrids, which have red, pink, or sometimes white blooms and are collectively known as coral bells, are quite delightful for flower borders and beds, edgings, and, the lower-growing varieties, for rock gardens. The flowers are useful for cutting and including in arrangements. The plants can be potted and easily forced into early bloom in greenhouses. These coral bells stand some part-day shade, but are primarily subjects for sunny locations and garden soil of ordinary quality that drains freely without lying wet for long periods. For the best results the soil should contain a fairly high proportion of organic matter, such as compost, leaf mold, peat moss, or humus. So far as bloom is concerned other heucheras occasionally cultivated are a dowdy lot. Yet they are attractive in habit and have quite decorative foliage. These redeeming qualities earn for them consideration for possible inclusion in woodland gardens and other shaded areas and, where geographically appropriate, native plant gardens. Kinds should be allotted dryish or dampish locations according to the known preferences of the species.

Cultivation. Coral bells may be planted in spring or early fall; spring is usually preferred. The young plants or divisions are set with their crowns (rhizomes) about 1 inch beneath the surface and are spaced 10 inches to 1 foot apart. The second or third year will come before they reach their full beauty and not until the fourth or fifth season from the time of planting will it be necessary to divide and replant them. The time is signaled by sparser blooming, shorter flower stalks, smaller, less luxuriant foliage, and a crowded, woody condition of the crowns. Spring is the best time to divide. Routine care is not too demanding of time or effort. An annual application of a complete fertilizer in spring promotes good growth. The prompt removal of spent flower stalks favors successional blooming. In dry weather copious watering at about weekly intervals forestalls the ill effects of drought. Coral bells are shallow rooters and where winters are characterized by alternate freezing and thawing are very likely to be partially heaved out of the ground. Inspection in early spring accompanied by pushing back into place disturbed plants is a wise procedure. As a precaution against winter heaving in cold climates, the plants may with advantage be covered, after the ground is frozen to a depth of an inch or two, with branches of evergreens, salt hay,

or other loose material that permits air circulation.

Propagation is easily accomplished by splitting the clumps in spring into short pieces of rhizome (stem) each with a few roots attached. They are also very easily multiplied from cuttings made from terminal pieces of stem planted in a mixture of sand and peat moss or in sandy soil in a shaded cold frame or under mist in summer. More rapid increase can be obtained by leaf-cuttings taken in summer and planted under similar conditions. Heucheras also come readily from seeds, but hybrid kinds do not breed true when so raised. Seeds sown in sandy, peaty soil in spring germinate well, and plants from them usually bloom in their second year.

Woodland alum roots respond to the cultivation recommended above for coral bells, except that they need shade, and if at all favorably located, need even less attention. Winter protection may be afforded by natural leaf drop from trees and, because they are not exposed to sun, watering may not be required, or if it is, at rarer intervals. The decayed leaves and other woodland debris allowed to accumulate without becoming so deep that it smothers the plants will supply most nutrients needed. If these plants are grown in parts of the garden where tidy "housekeeping" is practiced and they do not have the advantage of natural forest accumulations, a mulch of compost or peat moss and an annual spring dressing of a complete fertilizer will prove acceptable substitutes.

As greenhouse plants for spring bloom coral bells are easily handled. The procedure is to pot well-rooted, vigorous young clumps in 5- to 6-inch pots or pans (shallow pots), in porous, fertile soil in September. They are then plunged (buried to the rims of their containers) in sand, ashes, or peat moss in a cold frame. There they remain until January or February. Then they are brought into a cool, sunny greenhouse where the night temperature is about 50°F, and day temperatures are 55 to 60°F. The plants are watered moderately at first, more freely as growth develops. An occasional application of dilute liquid fertilizer helps. Too high temperatures produce poor results. Specimens grown under cool conditions are sturdy and remain in bloom for a long time. After they are through blooming and all danger of frost is passed, they may be taken from their containers and planted in the open ground.

HEUCHERELLA (Heucher-élla). This name belongs to a bigeneric hybrid between *Heuchera sanguinea* and *Tiarella cordifolia*, of the saxifrage family SAXIFRAGACEAE. It resembles *H. sanguinea* in growth, type of flower cluster, and color of flowers, but its blooms have seven or eight stamens instead of the five of *Heuchera* or ten of *Tiarella*. Sometimes called *Heuchera tiarelloides* and

H. sanguinea tiarelloides, the correct name of this plant is *Heucherella tiarelloides.* In addition to the typical pink- or red-flowered kind there is a variant with white flowers distinguished as *H. t. alba.* Heucherellas require the same conditions and care as *Heuchera sanguinea* and its other hybrids, and may be propagated in the same ways by division and by cuttings. They do not produce seeds and are hardy.

HEVEA (Hè-vea)—Rubber Tree. This genus of the spurge family EUPHORBIACEAE is chiefly known for one species, the source of nearly all commercial natural rubber. It must not be confused with another plant popularly called rubber plant and rubber tree, the Asian *Ficus elastica*. The two are not at all similar, the last mentioned differing most obviously from *Hevea* in having large leathery, undivided, evergreen leaves. There are about a dozen species of *Hevea*. Natives of tropical America, they are large, milky-juiced trees with alternate, long-stalked leaves each with three, toothless leaflets. The flowers, insignificant decoratively, are without petals. They have five-lobed or five-toothed calyxes and five to ten stamens, the stalks of which are joined to form a column. The fruits are large, three-seeded capsules. The name *Hevea* is an adaptation of a native Brazilian one.

The history of rubber and of the tree that is its chief source is fascinating. Long before the discovery of America Indians exploited the rubber tree for its sap, and made from it crude shoes, bottles, balls, and other articles. Word of balls that bounced much better than any known in Europe reached that continent as early as the seventeenth century, but it was not until about 1770 that rubber began to be used outside its homeland. Then small pieces were sold at remarkably high prices for use as erasers to rub out pencil marks, hence the name rubber. Early in the nineteenth century the Scot Charles Mackintosh devised a means of waterproofing cloth by treating it with a solution of rubber. From this he made raincoats (these garments are still called mackintoshes in Great Britain). Mackintosh's product had the grave disadvantages of becoming sticky in hot weather and hard and brittle in cold. This was corrected when Charles Goodyear in America invented vulcanization, which consists of heating rubber with sulfur. The result was a very much more stable product than Mackintosh's. By 1867 solid tires were being made of rubber and in 1888 another Scot, John Boyd Dunlap, made the first pneumatic tires, for bicycles. Before the end of the century the first automobile tires were produced and the rapid development in the use of that vehicle in the twentieth century sparked a vast and rapidly increasing demand for natural rubber, which continued until, during and after World War II, synthetic rubber to

He

Hib

Hibiscus rosa-sinensis variety

Hybrid hippeastrums with white- and pink-flowered *Primula obconica*

Hexisea bidentata

Hibbertia scandens

Hibbertia cuneiformis

HIBBERTIA (Hib-bértia) — Guinea Gold Vine. Few of the 100 species of *Hibbertia*, of the dillenia family DILLENIACEAE, are known to gardeners. Those that are are attractive for outdoors in warm, frostless and nearly frostless regions, and as greenhouse decoratives. The name commemorates the English patron of botany George Hibbert, who died in 1838. The majority of hibbertias are endemic to Australia, a few natives of New Guinea, New Caledonia, Fiji, and Madagascar.

Hibbertias include vines, trailers, shrubs, and sorts that are almost herbaceous. They have generally small, often heathlike leaves with one pronounced vein or midrib. The blooms, solitary at the branch ends, are sometimes arranged as though clustered. They have five persistent sepals, five yellow or rarely orange or white, deciduous, spreading petals, and from four to 150 stamens and sometimes a few nonfertile stamens (staminodes). There are two to five carpels with slender styles. The sorts described here are all Australian.

Certainly one of the loveliest kinds, *H. dentata* is a vine or trailer with stalked, dark bronze-green, lightly-toothed, oblongish leaves up to 2½ inches long, that when young are almost crimson. The deep yellow flowers, 1½ to 2 inches wide and with many stamens some of which are sterile, are produced in quantity over a very long season.

Hibbertia dentata

Guinea gold vine (*H. scandens* syn. *H. volubilis*) is a handsome, fast-growing, generously-foliaged, free-flowering climber 8 to 10 feet tall or taller. Its waxy, dark green, stem-clasping, lanceolate leaves 2 to 3 inches long by up to 1 inch wide, are hairy on their undersides. The showy yellow blooms, that look much like those of a single rose, are about 2 inches in diameter. All their stamens are fertile.

A shrub up to 6 feet tall with a tendency to trail or vine, *H. cuneiformis* (syn. *Candollea cuneiformis*) is one of the more spectacular species. It has oblong to obovate leaves 1 inch to 1½ inches long with

toothed apexes. The rich, golden-yellow, stalkless flowers are 1½ inches wide. They have notched petals. Easily distinguishable from the others described here by the bases of its leaves completely encircling the stem so that the stem appears to pierce the leaf, *H. perfoliata* is an erect or sometimes trailing, hairless shrub with ovate, sparingly-toothed leaves 1 inch to 2½ inches long. Its solitary, bright yellow flowers on stalks 1 inch to 2 inches long are about 1½ inches across.

H. tetrandra is a shrub up to 7 feet tall. Its leaves are short-pointed, elliptic-lanceolate to oblanceolate, ¾ inch to 2 inches long by ¼ to ¾ inch wide, with stem-clasping stalks and with the upper parts of their margins toothed. The bright yellow flowers, 1½ to 2 inches across, have reverse-heart-shaped petals.

Garden and Landscape Uses and Cultivation. The hibbertias described here are splendid ornamentals that adapt well to cultivation and give little trouble. The vines may be used effectively for clothing supports of various types, draping walls, and as groundcovers. Shrubby *H. cuneiformis* makes an attractive free-standing bush. None is hardy, although all endure a few degrees of frost for brief periods. They thrive in California and other regions of mild winters and warm, preferably dry, summers, and accommodate to a variety of soils, in sun or part-shade. As greenhouse plants hibbertias are easy to handle. They succeed where the night temperature in winter is 50 to 55°F, and by day five to ten degrees higher. Fertile, well-drained soil kept evenly moist from spring through fall, somewhat drier in winter, is appreciated. Pot-specimens benefit from being stood outside in summer, but this is not essential. Spring-to-fall periodic applications of dilute liquid fertilizer are helpful. Trimming to shape and repotting is done in late winter or early spring. Hibbertias propagate readily from cuttings planted in sand or perlite mixed with some peat moss, and by layering. Seeds are often difficult to germinate.

HIBISCADELPHUS (Hibisca-délphus). This endemic Hawaiian genus, of the mallow family MALVACEAE, included four species. One is extinct, two have been almost exterminated by grazing animals, and the one discussed here is uncommon. By some botanists *Hibiscadelphus* is included in *Hibiscus*. The name is derived from that of related *Hibiscus* and the Greek *adelphos*, a brother.

An erect *Hibiscus*-like tree 15 to 20 feet in height, **H. hualalaiensis** has long-stalked, broadly-heart-shaped or three- or five-angled, nearly round leaves that are furnished with yellowish, stellate (star-shaped) hairs. They are 4 to 8 inches in diameter. The curved, red, yellow and green, 1- to 2-inch-long, asymmetrical flowers, singly or in pairs, open only sufficiently to form a slight aperture at their ends, through which protrude the column of stamens and the five-branched style. The calyx is three- to six-lobed, the two lower petals recurve at their apexes. The fruits are capsules consisting of five segments or carpels.

Garden and Landscape Uses and Cultivation. Because of its interest, and to provide variety, this tree is occasionally planted in Hawaiian gardens and elsewhere. It responds to conditions that suit tropical hibiscuses. It is raised from seeds, and perhaps from cuttings.

HIBISCUS (Hi-bíscus)—Rose-of-Sharon or Shrub-Althea, Confederate-Rose, Flower-of-an-Hour, Roselle. Cultivated species and varieties of *Hibiscus* are known to gardeners in the north as well as those who pursue the art in warmer climes, but the number of sorts that can be grown outdoors in regions of severe winters is very much more restricted than in the tropics and subtropics. Kinds most familiar to northerners are rose-of-Sharon, rose-mallow, and flower-of-an-hour. The genus, which belongs in the mallow family MALVACEAE, is variously estimated to consist of 250 to 300 species. Its name is the ancient Greek and Latin one for the mallow.

Hibiscuses include trees, shrubs, herbaceous perennials, and annuals. Widely distributed as natives throughout many parts of the world, chiefly in warm regions, they have generally hairy young shoots, the hairs stellate (branched in starlike manner) or an admixture of stellate and branchless and sometimes glandular hairs. The leaves are alternate, often lobed in palmate (hand-like) fashion, more rarely palmately-divided into separate leaflets. The flowers come singly or in clusters from the upper leaf axils or are in racemes or less often panicles. They have a shallowly- or deeply-five-lobed, usually more or less bell-shaped or tubular calyx. The usually showy corolla is of five petals (more in double-flowered varieties) that narrow to their bases. They may be white, pink, purplish, red, or yellow and are often marked on their lower parts with a spot of deeper hue. The stamens cohere into a tubular column around the pistil. The top of this is usually five-pointed, sometimes ends evenly. The anthers are borne below its apex. The style has five slender branches each tipped with a disklike stigma or less commonly is without branches and terminates in a five-branched or five-lobed stigma. The fruits are capsules. Previously included in *Hibiscus*, okra or gumbo is now *Abelmoschus esculentus* and plants once named *H. abelmoschus* and *H. manihot* are *A. moschatus* and *A. manihot*, respectively.

Rose-of-Sharon (**H. syriacus**) is often called shrub-althea because at one time it

Hibiscus syriacus

was included in the genus *Althaea* (now *Alcea*). So closely related to *H. syriacus* that it is scarcely distinguishable, Chinese **H. sinosyriacus** has somewhat broader leaves and wider involucral bracts. Its white flowers have deep crimson centers. Native to eastern Asia, *H. syriacus* is a stiffly-erect, branched, deciduous shrub or tree up to 20 feet tall, and hardy in southern New England. It is esteemed for its showy single, semidouble, or double blooms that come in a wide range of hues and are dis-

Hibiscus sinosyriacus

Hibiscus syriacus, single-flowered variety

Hibiscus syriacus, double-flowered variety

played over a long period in late summer and fall. They are shallowly-bell-shaped and 2 to 3 inches across. The more or less triangular-ovate, three-lobed leaves are 2 to 3 inches long. They have toothed margins. The blooms of double-flowered varieties tend to be smaller than single ones and have an unfortunate tendency to fail to develop properly, particularly at their centers, and especially during dull, wet periods.

Single-bloomed varieties include *H. s. albus*, white; 'Bluebird', blue; *H. s. coelestis* (syn. 'Celestial Blue'), light violet with reddish streaks; 'Mauve Queen', mauve; *H. s. meehanii*, foliage variegated, flowers purplish; *H. s. monstrosus*, white with purplish centers; *H. s. roseus* (syns. *H. s. rubis*, *H. s. rubrus*), pink to reddish; *H. s. totusalbus* (syn. 'Snowdrift'), white; 'Woodbridge', rose-pink to reddish; and 'W. R. Smith', white.

Semidouble-flowered varieties include these: *H. s. ardens*, light purple, flowers sometimes double; *H. s. bicolor*, white to light purplish-pink; *H. s. coeruleus*, pale purple; 'Comte de Haimont', white blotched with bluish-pink; *H. s. elegantissimus*, light purplish-pink blotched and streaked with deeper pink and red; 'Jeanne d'Arc', white; 'Lady Stanley' (syn. 'Lady Alice Stanley'), similar to 'Comte de Haimont', but with broader, less pointed petals; *H. s. paeoniflorus*, white with pink centers, sometimes double and pinkish; *H. s. purpureus-semiplenus*, purple; 'Souvenir de Charles Breton', purple; and *H. s. speciosus-plenus*, deep pink.

Double-flowered varieties include these: 'Admiral Dewey', white; *H. s. amplissimus*, purple-red to pink; *H. s. anemonaeflorus*, white with a dark red center; 'Banner', white with a red center; *H. s.* 'Boule de Feu', purplish-red; 'Duc de Brabant', deep purplish-pink with paler center; *H. s. florepleno*, white; 'Lucy', bright red or pink; 'Pompon Rouge', reddish-purple; *H. s. pulcherrimus*, white suffused with pink; *H. s. purpureus-flore-pleno*, purple; *H. s. speciosus-rubus*, red; and *H. s. variegatus*, dark wine-purple, foliage handsomely variegated with creamy-yellow.

Chinese hibiscus, Hawaiian hibiscus, and rose-of-China are names applied to *H. rosa-sinensis* and to hybrids of it and Hawaiian species and *H. schizopetalus*. This and its hybrids are the most widely grown tropical kinds. Although unknown in the wild, **H. rosa-sinensis** is thought to have originated in tropical Asia. Among the most showy of tropical flowering shrubs,

the varieties of this complex attain heights of 4 to 15 feet or are sometimes taller and treelike. They have evergreen, pointed, ovate to broadly-ovate, lobeless, usually coarsely-toothed leaves ¾ inch to 4½ inches long, and solitary flowers from the axils of the upper leaves. The blooms, 4 to 6 inches across and with flaring petals, are bright red, crimson, orange, yellow, or

Hibiscus syriacus variegatus (foliage)

Hibiscus rosa-sinensis, varieties

white. They have a long-protruding column of stamens. There are single- and double-flowered varieties, with more than 1,000 having been named. As may be imagined, with shrubs so popular and so widely planted for ornament in warm regions, much confusion exists over the application of the names. Often more than one kind is known in different places by the same name. The same kind in different regions is not infrequently known by more than one name. Distinctive *H. r. cooperi* has irregular, narrow leaves variously variegated with pink and white and smallish, sometimes distorted, red blooms.

Deeply-fringed petals are an attractive, identifying feature of the flowers of tropical East African **H. schizopetalus** (syn. *H. rosa-sinensis schizopetalus*), a species with somewhat the aspect of the Chinese hibiscus, but its branches generally more slender and more inclined to droop. This has leaves ¾ inch to 4½ inches long, pointed-ovate-elliptic, and coarsely-toothed. Solitary from the upper leaf axils, the blooms are pendulous. The long-protruding column of stamens is pink toward its base, reddish near its apex. Hybrids between this species and the Chinese hibiscus and between it and native Hawaiian species generally have their petals fringed, but not so deeply as those of *H. schizopetalus.*

Hibiscus rosa-sinensis cooperi

Hibiscus schizopetalus

A Hawaiian medley of four variable evergreen shrubs or small trees of horticultural interest includes **H. arnottianus.** Endemic to Oahu, this large shrub or tree, up to 30 feet tall, has leathery, ovate-elliptic to broad-ovate leaves 2½ to 6 inches long or sometimes longer, toothless or with slight indications of teeth near their tips. The solitary flowers, from the upper leaf axils, are white fading to pinkish. Approximately 5 to 6 inches in diameter, they have a conspicuously-protruded column of red to reddish stamens. Varieties include 'Nuuanu White', 'Punaluu White', 'Tantalus White', and 'Waianae White', all of which except the last have been hybridized with the Chinese hibiscus to produce varieties generally listed as *H. rosa-sinensis* hybrids. Another Hawaiian endemic that in its homeland exhibits considerable variation and like the last has been hybridized with the Chinese hibiscus to give varieties commonly called *H. rosa-sinensis* hybrids, is **H. kokio.** From *H. arnottianus* this differs in having fewer and much smaller orange-red to deep red blooms with narrower, linear-oblong to obovate petals. Varieties of this are 'Hakalau Red', 'Kawai-hapai Red', 'Kipu Red', 'Molokai Red', and 'Oahu Red'. These have been hybridized with the Chinese hibiscus to give offspring usually called varieties of the latter. Very similar to *H. arnottianus* and possibly not specifically distinct from it, **H. waimeae** is endemic on the island of Kauai. This differs from *H. arnottianus* chiefly in having more foliage that is velvety-hairy on the undersides of the leaves, and flowers with longer calyxes. Varieties are 'Knudsen White', 'Lydgate White', and 'Rice White'. This species and its varieties hybridized with the Chinese hibiscus have also produced offspring usually identified as varieties of *H. rosa-sinensis*. The last of the four Hawaiian endemics treated here, **H. brackenridgei** differs from the others in having yellow flowers with or without a maroon spot at the bottom of each petal, and with the stamen column shorter than the petals. A variable, somewhat sprawling to erect shrub or tree up to 30 feet tall, this has thin, long-stalked, toothed, maple-like leaves, rounded in outline and up to 6 inches in diameter, with usually five or seven deep lobes. The blooms, 3 to 8 inches wide, are solitary in the leaf axils or are in short racemes.

Native of the tropics of both hemispheres the mahoe (**H. tiliaceus**) is indigenous in southern Florida and Hawaii. An

Hibiscus tiliaceus

evergreen shrub or small tree, it rarely attains 40 feet in height. Its leathery, lobeless, toothless or round-toothed leaves, whitish-hairy on their undersides, green and nearly hairless or hairless above, are ovate to nearly round, with usually heart-shaped bases. They are mostly 3½ to 8 inches long. In clusters near the branch ends or solitary from the leaf axils, the blooms are 3½ to 7 inches across, have overlapping yellow or whitish petals with or without a brown or reddish spot at the bottom of each. They are longer than the column of stamens. Each lasts one day, gradually fading through orange-yellow to dark-red. This species was formerly and to some extent still is of importance in the tropics as a source, from its inner bark, of fiber for use in making ropes, cordage, nets, and coarse fabrics. Its wood is used for floats and other purposes. Called Cuban bast and mountain mahoe, **H. elatus,** of Cuba and Jamaica, a tree up to 75 feet tall, much resembles *H. tiliaceus*, but differs in the calyxes of its flowers being decid-

uous rather than persistent in fruit and in other botanical details. Also of the *H. tiliaceus* relationship, but differing in its leaves not exceeding 3 inches in length and being sharp- instead of round-toothed is **H. hamabo**, of Japan and Korea. A shrub up to 15 feet tall, this is probably not hardy in the north. Varieties of *H. syriacus* are sometimes misnamed *H. hamabo*.

Called desert-rose, **H. farragei** has broad-heart-shaped, lobeless, but sometimes angled, toothed leaves up to 4 inches in diameter, green above, whitish on their undersides. Usually in clusters of two or three or forming short terminal clusters, the 2-inch-long flowers have purplish petals longer than the column of stamens. This sort is native to Australia. Another Australian species called desert-rose, and previously named *H. huegelii*, is now correctly identified as *Alyogyne huegelii*.

The Confederate-rose or cotton-rose (**H. mutabilis**) is a shrub up to 15 feet tall that where occasional freezes happen behaves more like a herbaceous perennial, sending flowering shoots each year from a brief trunk or woody base. Its young shoots, leafstalks, flower stalks, involucres, and calyxes are thickly clothed with yellowish hairs. The long-stalked, coarsely-toothed leaves 4 to 8 inches across have three to seven shallow-triangular lobes. They are hairy on their lower surfaces, less so above. Solitary from leaf axils and crowded near the branch ends, the white to pink blooms 3 to 4 inches in diameter change to deep red as they age. Their petals are longer than the column of stamens. A double-flowered variant known as *H. m. flore-pleno* occurs. The Confederate-rose is believed to be native of southern China, perhaps also of Taiwan and Japan. A closely similar species, **H. indicus**, probably native of Asia, differs only in recondite botanical details. Hybrids between *H. mutabilis* and *H. moscheutos* are reported.

Rose-mallows are a group of wetland and marsh species, natives of the United States, and horticultural hybrids derived from them. They have erect stems 3 to 6 feet or sometimes more tall, large leaves and big, showy blooms. With the exception of *H. coccineus* the species are a little too coarse for most garden uses, but are well suited for display in native plant gardens and large-scale naturalistic plantings. For most purposes the hybrids are superior.

The species of wild rose-mallows include **H. cocineus,** native in coastal areas from Georgia to Florida, and hardy about as far north as Maryland. Hairless and somewhat glaucous, this has long-stalked leaves cleft or divided into three to seven linear-lanceolate, distantly-toothed lobes or leaflets. The deep red blooms, 4½ to 8 inches in diameter, come from the upper leaf axils. Sometimes called soldier and sweating weed, **H. militaris** is also hair-

less. From the last it differs in its lower leaves being heart-shaped-ovate and three-lobed, its upper one broadly- to narrowly-triangular, often three-, sometimes five-lobed. The blooms, pale pink to almost white and with crimson centers have petals 2½ to 3½ inches long. This is native from Pennsylvania to Minnesota, Florida, and Texas.

Hibiscus militaris

Other native rose-mallows, distinguished from *H. coccineus* and *H. militaris* by their leaves being hairy at least on their undersides, are *H. moscheutos* (syn. *H. oculiroseus*) and *H. lasiocarpus*. Native from Virginia to Ohio, Indiana, Georgia, and perhaps Florida, **H. moscheutos,** as well as being called rose-mallow, is known as mallow-rose and wild-cotton. Its lanceolate to broadly-ovate, saw-toothed leaves, lobeless or three- to five-angled, are clothed on their undersides with white hairs. Their up-

Hibiscus moscheutos

per sides are green and hairless or nearly so. The white, creamy-white, pink or rose-pink blooms, usually with red or purple centers, are 4 to 8 inches in diameter. Except along the seams which open when the seeds are ripe, the seed capsules are hairless. In this they differ from those of *H. m. palustris* (syn. *H. palustris*), which are hairy all over. The variety in general has a more

Hybrid rose-mallow

Hibiscus moscheutos palustris

northern range than the typical species. It occurs from Massachusetts to Indiana and Virginia with intermediates between it and the species found from New Jersey to Virginia. This is called rose-mallow, mallow-rose, sea-hollyhock, and sometimes marsh-mallow, although the last designation is more commonly reserved for *Althaea officinalis*. Similar to *H. moscheutos*, but with the upper surfaces of their leaves permanently hairy are *H. lasiocarpus* (syn. *H. californicus*) and *H. grandiflorus*. Native from Illinois to Missouri, Florida, and Texas, and in California, *H. lasiocarpus* differs from *H. moscheutos* in having densely-hairy seed pods. Confined in the wild from Georgia to Mississippi and Florida, *H. grandiflorus* has very large (up to more than 1 foot in diameter) often deeply-3- or 5-lobed leaves of more or less circular outline. From 8 to 10 inches in diameter, the blooms are whitish, pink, or purplish-pink, frequently with a crimson center. Plants grown in gardens as *H. grandiflorus* are frequently forms or hybrids of *H. moscheutos*.

Hybrid rose-mallows have probably the largest and surely among the showiest blooms of all hardy herbaceous perennials. It is not uncommon for them to measure 8 to 10 inches in diameter. They come

in white and a wide range of lovely colors from pale pink to deep red, often with a central eye and are displayed to fine advantage throughout late summer and fall. The earliest of this hybrid swarm were raised at Philadelphia at the beginning of the twentieth century and were first offered for sale about 1908 under the name 'Meehan's Mallow Marvels'. These originated from the only plant of a population of seedlings that resulted from crossing *H. coccineus* and *H. militaris* with *H. moscheutos* that survived a winter at Philadelphia. A later breeding program based in California and using the same three parents was initiated about 1927. This gave similar results. Yet a third effort, carried out in New Jersey, using *H. coccineus* and *H. militaris* as parents gave rise to a group named 'Avalon Hybrids'. Named varieties are offered in nursery catalogs and are not infrequently illustrated there.

Only a few annual hibiscuses are cultivated. They include the roselle or Jamaica-sorrel (*H. sabdariffa*), a native of the Old World tropics cultivated in warm climates for its edible parts, which are used for jams, jellies, sauces, and beverages. For more about this see Roselle or Jamaica-sorrel. The sort sometimes offered as bronze hibiscus and as *H. eetveldeanus* is the maroon-foliaged phase of *H. acetosella,* an annual or perennial native of warm parts of Africa. Up to about 4½ feet in height, this has ovate to nearly round, mostly conspicuously

three- to five-lobed, but sometimes only shallowly-lobed or lobeless leaves that are hairless or nearly so. The flowers, often not produced because frost comes before they develop, are yellow or purplish-red with deep purple-red centers. They are 2½ to 4 inches across. Kenaf (*H. cannabinus*) is an Old World tropical species cultivated as a source of fiber. Not of great horticultural importance, it may sometimes be included among exhibits of plants useful to man. From 3 to 10 feet tall or taller, this has minutely-spiny stems. The leaves are long-stalked, the lower ones not lobed, those above cleft-palmately (in hand-fashion) into narrow lobes. Yellow or purplish-red, with crimson centers, the flowers are 3 to 6 inches across. Flower-of-an-hour (*H. trionum*), a native of central Africa and now a weed in parts of North America, is sometimes included among plantings of ornamental annuals. From 1 foot to 2 feet in height, and with some of its branches more or less sprawling or prostrate, this has coarsely-toothed leaves of three lobes or three to five leaflets, the center one much bigger than the others. Its fleeting, dark-centered, white or yellow, solitary blooms are 2 to 3 inches wide.

Garden and Landscape Uses. Among the showiest of ornamentals, hibiscuses can be displayed to good purpose in numerous ways. Kinds must of course be selected with reference to climate. For northern gardens rose-of-Sharon, rose-mallows, and annual hibiscuses are well suited. The rose-of-Sharon is stiff-branched and somewhat ungainly when without foliage and even in leaf is scarcely graceful. Because of this, it is usually better accommodated in mixed shrub plantings than as free-standing specimens. It serves well for screens and informal hedges. Rose-mallows, especially the hybrids, are magnificent at watersides, in beds, and as single specimens. Although they grow natively in swamps, in cultivation they prosper in any good garden soil that does not dry unduly. Bog conditions are not necessary. Like the rose-of-Sharon they need sunny locations.

Tropical hibiscuses are excellent general-purpose shrubs and trees for warm, humid climates and some, notably *H. rosasinensis* varieties and hybrids and *H. schizopetalus*, for greenhouses as well. These also make good tub specimens for patios and similar places. They supply long seasons of highly colorful displays of bloom and *H. rosa-sinensis cooperi* is admired for its beautifully colored foliage. The varieties of *H. rosa-sinensis* can be sheared to form excellent hedges. For warm, dry climates, such as that of southern California, *H. huegelii* and *H. farragei* are eminently suitable. Annual kinds of decorative merit are satisfactory in flower beds and borders.

A hedge of *Hibiscus rosa-sinensis* in Puerto Rico

Cultivation. In cold climates newly transplanted specimens of rose-of-Sharon and young ones making vigorous growth may suffer winter injury at temperatures that do not harm older, well-established ones. Because of this, spring planting is recommended and some special protection during the first two or three winters may be desirable. The only pruning often given is any necessitated by shoots becoming crowded. If this occurs, enough of the weaker ones are cut out in spring to assure more air and light for those that remain. Larger flowers can be had by pruning back in spring all of the previous season's shoots to within two or three buds of their bases

and cutting out completely enough shoots to prevent crowding. Propagation is by summer cuttings in a greenhouse, cold frame, or under mist, or by grafting onto seedlings or other young stock in spring.

Tropical shrub and tree sorts are raised from cuttings or seeds. These kinds may be grown with little or no pruning except any needed to shape them, or they may be contained to size by cutting back the shoots annually after they are through blooming. In greenhouses they succeed in a winter night temperature of 45 to 50°F, but from spring to fall it should be ten degrees higher. Day temperatures five to fifteen degrees higher than those maintained at night are in order. A humid atmosphere suits most, but *H. huegelii* and *H. farragei* prefer drier conditions. The soil for hibiscuses grown indoors must be reasonably moist at all seasons, but drier in winter than at other times. Repotting is done in late winter or spring. Specimens that have filled their containers with roots benefit from weekly applications of dilute liquid fertilizer.

Rose-mallows respond to generous fertilizing. Apply a dressing each spring and if it conveniently can be done keep the ground around them mulched in summer. Never allow the earth in which they grow to become dry. Before wilting foliage indicates this, soak the ground deeply and repeat as often as necessary to keep the soil moist. Prune these by cutting all the shoots back almost to the ground in fall or spring. Propagation is by seeds or, choice named kinds, by division in spring or by cuttings.

Annual hibiscuses are raised from seeds sown early indoors or directly outdoors in spring. The first procedure is the better one in the north.

HICKORY. See Carya.

HICKSBEACHIA (Hicks-bèachia)—Monkey Nut. The only two species of *Hicksbeachia*, of the protea family PROTEACEAE, are natives of Australia. The name commemorates Sir Michael Edward Hicks Beach, British statesman and Member of Parliament, who died in 1916.

Hicksbeachias are trees with alternate, stalkless, pinnately-veined leaves, sharply-toothed or deeply-pinnately-lobed. The flowers, in spikelike racemes, are without petals and have four sepals, four stamens, three not functional, and one style. The fruits are leathery follicles.

Rarely cultivated *H. pinnatifolia*, approximately 30 feet tall, has harsh-textured, deeply-pinnately-lobed, prominently-veined, light green leaves about 2 feet or reportedly sometimes up to 5 feet long. They are clustered at the ends of the stems and have usually eighteen to twenty toothed lobes 5 to 9 inches in length by 1 inch to 2 inches wide. The yellowish flow-

ers are in racemes 7 inches to about 1 foot long. They have sepals about ½ inch long, silky-hairy on their outsides and soon curled backward. The edible, but insipid fruits are ovate to nearly spherical, brilliant orange-red, and 1½ inches long.

Garden and Landscape Uses and Cultivation. As an unusual ornamental this is appropriate for California and other places with warm, dry climates. It needs fertile, well-drained soil and a sunny location. Propagation is by seeds and perhaps cuttings.

HIDALGOA (Hidal-gòa)—Climbing-Dahlia. Of the four species of *Hidalgoa*, two are sometimes cultivated. The group belongs in the daisy family COMPOSITAE and consists of Mexican, and Central and South American robust vines that attach themselves to supports by twining the lower parts of their leafstalks around them in tendril fashion.

Hidalgoas are perennials with opposite leaves divided into three or more leaflets. They are allied to *Dahlia* and *Coreopsis*, but differ markedly in being vines and having flower heads in which the disk florets are sterile. The fruits are achenes. The name commemorates the Mexican naturalist Señor Hidalgo.

Native of southern Mexico, Guatemala, Ecuador, and Peru, **H. ternata** in the wild sometimes climbs trees to a height of 75 feet, but often is not over 15 to 20 feet tall. Its leaves have slender stalks up to 2 inches in length, and three ovate, coarsely-toothed leaflets, the center one often larger than the others and up to 3 inches long. The terminal or axillary flower heads, 2 inches or somewhat more across, and solitary or in clusters of few, have yellow centers and five orange ray florets, three-toothed at their apexes.

Hidalgoa ternata

The other kind cultivated, *H. wercklei,* a native of Costa Rica, is tall and has long-stalked leaves, very slightly hairy on their upper sides and coarsely-toothed. They are deeply-three-lobed with the central leaflet often again deeply three-cleft; they have blades about 2½ inches long. The flower heads, solitary from the leaf axils, are 2½ inches across and have about ten three-toothed scarlet ray florets with dirty yellow undersides. The central disk is yellow.

Garden and Landscape Uses and Cultivation. These vines grow with little trouble in ordinary soil in sun. They may be used outdoors for screening and other purposes in regions of mild winters and are probably hardy about as far north as Virginia. They are occasionally grown in greenhouses, more particularly large conservatories, and are attractive foliage vines for windows in cool rooms, but can scarcely be expected to bloom there because of the necessity of limiting them to a convenient size. They are very easily grown from seeds and cuttings. Indoors, during the cool season of the year, temperatures by night of 40 to 50°F, and a few degrees more by day, are adequate.

HIERACIUM (Hier-àcium) — Hawkweed. This botanically complex genus of the daisy family COMPOSITAE has few members attractive to gardeners. Some, notably the orange hawkweed or devil's paintbrush (*Hieracium aurantiacum*), which if its invasive bad habits could be overlooked would be worth growing for its pretty brilliant red-orange flower heads, are pestiferous weeds. The group is native of most temperate parts of the world except Australasia, and of mountains in the tropics. Its name is from the Greek, *hierax,* a hawk, in allusion to an ancient belief that hawks used the plant to improve their sight. The number of species is variously estimated at from 200 to 300 to over 5,000. Perhaps 1,000 is a fair, middle-of-the-road figure to accept. The chief reason for such wide differences of opinion is that many hawkweeds produce viable seeds without any sexual process and seedlings duplicate the parents as truly as do cuttings and other forms of vegetative propagation. In this way minute variants are perpetuated and multiplied.

Hawkweeds are milky-juiced herbaceous perennials, often hairy, with rosettes of basal foliage, and branched or less commonly branchless, usually leafy stems. The leaves are generally toothed, but not deeply incised or lobed. The yellow, orange, or orange-red flower heads, like those of dandelions, are of all strap-shaped, petal-like, florets, closely-spaced. From nearly related *Crepis* hawkweeds differ in their seedlike fruits (achenes) narrowing abruptly at their apexes and in the hairs (pappus) that accompany them being of stiff, usually brownish bristles.

Shaggy hawkweed (*H. villosum*), in bloom 1 foot to 2 feet tall, is spreading and has elliptic to elliptic-oblong, slightly-toothed, silvery-gray leaves with long white hairs. The stem leaves are partially clasping. The bright yellow flower heads, 1½ to 2 inches in diameter and deliciously fragrant, are on stalks 6 inches to 1 foot high. This is a native of central Europe.

Hieracium villosum

Attractive gray-hairy foliage is characteristic of *H. lanatum* and *H. waldsteinii.* Native to southern Europe, and 9 inches to 1½ feet tall, *H. lanatum* has lanceolate to ovate, essentially lobeless and toothless

Hieracium lanatum

basal and stem leaves. Its clustered, yellow flower heads are about 1 inch across. Native to the Balkan Peninsula, *H. waldsteinii* has a basal rosette of elliptic to broadly-obovate leaves and leafy stems 9 inches to 1½ feet tall bearing loose panicles of yellow flowers.

Rather rare in cultivation, *H. gymnocephalum* of the Balkan Peninsula is an attractive species 1½ to 3 feet tall. Its hairy leaves, usually stalkless and spaced along the stems, are pointed-elliptic to oblong and 2 to 8 inches long. The numerous, up-facing yellow flower heads 1 inch to 1¼ inches across are in loose panicles. A Eu-

Hieracium waldsteinii

Hieracium gymnocephalum

ropean, naturalized in northeastern North America, **H. murorum** attains a height of 2 to 2½ feet. Its leaves, mostly in a basal rosette but usually one or two on the flowering stalks, are elliptic, more or less toothed, and 1 to 2 inches long. They have hairy stalks. The up-facing yellow flower heads, about 1 inch across, are abundantly produced in loose panicles.

Hieracium murorum

Garden Uses and Cultivation. Hardy, occasionally grown in rock gardens and in perennial borders, the hawkweeds are easily raised by division and some kinds from seeds. They do best in poorish, well-drained, dryish soil, in full sun.

HIGHBUSH-CRANBERRY is *Viburnum trilobum*.

HILDEWINTERA—(Hildewín-tera). The only species of *Hildewintera*, of the cactus family CACTACEAE, is a native of Bolivia. Its name is commemorative.

The arching, prostrate, or pendulous stems of *H. aureispina* (syns. *Winteria aureispina, Winterocereus aureispina*) are 1½ to 2 inches thick, have sixteen or seventeen ribs and in closely-set clusters of about thirty, yellow spines ¼ to ½ inch long. Apricot-pink, the flowers are approximately 1½ inches long by almost 2 inches wide. The fruits are green and nearly ½ inch wide.

Hildewintera aureispina

Hildewintera aureispina (flower)

Garden Uses and Cultivation. Of chief interest to collectors of succulents, this species is well suited for hanging baskets and pans (shallow pots). It prospers under conditions that suit most desert cactuses and is easily increased by cuttings and by seeds. For further information see Cactuses.

HILL. When gardeners speak of sowing in hills they allude to the practice of setting small clusters of seeds at fairly wide and regular intervals as contrasted with sprinkling them regularly along drills or broadcasting them evenly over the entire surface of the seed bed. Stations where clusters of seeds are set may or may not be raised above the general surface of the ground, the plants may or may not have the soil hilled up to them later. Plants commonly sown in hills include corn, pole beans, cucumbers, melons, and squash. The term hill is also sometimes used for individual, fairly widely-spaced plants as, for instance, a hill of dahlias and a hill of potatoes.

HILL-GOOSEBERRY is *Rhodomyrtus tomentosa*.

HILLEBRANDIA (Hillebránd-ia). Few gardeners are acquainted with any of the five genera of the begonia family BEGONIACEAE, other than diverse, vast, well-known, and much-grown *Begonia*. The subject of this entry belongs in the same family, and consists of a single species. Native of all the Hawaiian Islands except Hawaii, *Hillebrandia sandwicensis*, inhabits wet ravines in rainforests above 3,000 feet. Its name commemorates William Hillebrand, author of a flora of Hawaii, who died in 1887.

To the casual observer *Hillebrandia* looks very much like a begonia, but to botanists it differs sufficiently in its floral structure to warrant segregation. The chief distinctions are that the upper one-third of the ovary is free and extends above the perianth, the ovary is partly superior as botanists say, whereas in *Begonia* the entire ovary, being inferior, is behind or below the perianth.

A hairless, sparsely-hairy, or moderately-hairy herbaceous perennial 2 to 5 feet in height, with a tuberous rhizome and somewhat fleshy stems and foliage, *H. sandwicensis* has long-stalked, broadly-ovate leaves, slightly unevenly lobed at their bases, and with shallowly- five- to nine-lobed, toothed margins. They are 4 to 10 inches across. The white or pinkish flowers are in laxly-forking, panicle-like clusters 4 inches to 1 foot long, from the upper leaf axils. There are conspicuous bracts, pink at their bases and paler or white above. The panicles have flowers of both sexes. The males are without even vestigial ovaries and have five, rarely four, sepals about ¼ inch long, the same number of minute petals, and many yellow stamens. The females have five calyx lobes, about ¼ inch long, five minute petals, five two-branched styles, and a wingless, spherical ovary. The fruits are capsules containing minute seeds.

Garden Uses and Cultivation. Although less beautiful than the best begonias this rare species is well worthwhile including in collections of those plants for its ap-

pearance as well as for interest. It thrives under similar conditions to begonias. A greenhouse in which a minimum night temperature of 55°F in winter, and day temperatures five to fifteen degrees higher are maintained, is satisfactory. The atmosphere must at all times be moderately humid. Shade from strong summer sun is required. Fertile, porous soil, containing a generous proportion of organic matter gives the best results. It should be kept always moderately moist. Propagation is by seeds, cuttings, and division.

HILLING UP. Sometimes, especially in Great Britain, called earthing up, this is the practice of mounding soil, usually to a height of several inches, about the bases of some plants. It is done for a variety of reasons, with corn and pole beans to protect surface roots and encourage new ones from the stems; with cauliflowers, kale, brussels sprouts, and the like to provide some support for the stems; with celery and leeks to blanch the leafstalks; and with roses and certain other shrubby plants to prevent or minimize winter-killing. Hilling up is done with a hoe, cultivator, spade, or plow.

Hilling up pole beans

HIMALAYA BERRY. See Blackberry.

HIMALAYA-HONEYSUCKLE is *Leycesteria formosa*.

HIPPEASTRUM (Hipp-eástrum)—Amaryllis. Most gardeners know the plants of this genus of the amaryllis family AMARYLLIDACEAE by the name *Amaryllis*, and some botanists and the American Amaryllis Society use that name for them, but the consensus of botanical thought is that as a generic name *Amaryllis* should be reserved for a related, but different South African species and that the western hemisphere plants considered here should be named

Hippeastrum. That disposition is accepted here, with amaryllis retained as a vernacular name for hippeastrums. As so interpreted, *Hippeastrum* comprises seventy-five species of nonhardy bulb plants and in addition many hybrids. They are favorites for indoor cultivation in pots and in tropical and warm subtropical climates for outdoors. The species sometimes segregated as *Rhodophiala* are here retained in *Hippeastrum*. The name is presumably from the Greek *hippos*, a horse, or *hippeus*, a rider, and *astrum*, a star, but the application is not clear.

Hippeastrums have all-basal, linear to strap-shaped leaves and, in cultivated kinds, large, horizontal to drooping, trumpet-shaped, lily-like flowers in umbels atop leafless, erect, hollow stalks. The blooms are white, pink, or orange-red to deep crimson, or are striped combinations of these. There are six corolla segments (petals, or more correctly, tepals) of which the inner three are sometimes narrower than the others. There are six stamens and one headlike or three-lobed style. The fruits are capsules containing usually flattened seeds.

The history of hippeastrums in cultivation began with the introduction into Europe in the latter half of the seventeenth century of *H. puniceum*, *H. reginae*, *H. striatum*, *H. reticulatum*, and *H. vittatum* in that sequence. The first hybrid produced, reportedly between *H. reginae* and *H. vittatum*, was recorded in 1799 as having been raised at Preston, Lancashire, England by an amateur gardener, a watchmaker by trade. This was soon followed by others and the raising of hybrids at various places during different periods has continued to the present day, in the nineteenth century and early twentieth century principally in England, Holland, and Belgium, but also in Australia, South Africa, Brazil, India, and the United States. Throughout, breeders and growers in Holland have played prominent parts in hybridizing and growing hippeastrums.

The first introduction of hippeastrums to the United States is not documented, but it undoubtedly occurred early. The bulbs are easily transported and considerable interest in growing exotic and unusual plants developed by the year 1800. From the 1880s on several American breeders engaged in developing distinctive strains, in Illinois, Texas, Washington, D.C., California, and Florida. World War I seriously disrupted hippeastrum growing and breeding in Europe. The introduction in 1919 of plant quarantines in the United States severely limited importations there. These circumstances gave fresh impetus to breeding and growing hippeastrums in North America, with the result that many new strains were developed including one with double flowers. The American Amaryllis Society was founded in 1933. This focused and strengthened interest in hippeastrums. The

Hybrid hippeastrums, with ferns, at Longwood Gardens, Kennett Square, Pennsylvania

organization has been and is very active in supporting explorations to bring into cultivation species not available, in stimulating breeding programs, in promoting research, and in publishing information about hippeastrums.

Hybrid hippeastrums are much more widely cultivated than natural species. By the American Amaryllis Society they are classified into eight divisions based on characteristics that indicate or are thought to indicate the species from which they have been derived. Because of the complicated, often unrecorded parentage of many hybrids the classification is flexible rather than precise, yet it is a convenience.

The most familiar divisions are the Belladonna-type, the Reginae-type, and the Leopoldii-type hybrids. Less commonly grown are the double-flowered, small-flowered miniature, long-trumpet, and orchid-flowered hybrids.

Seedling hybrids, as is to be expected of plants with such complex ancestry, generally show considerable variation. Selected strains in which variation is minimized, but by no means eliminated are propagated commercially in considerable quantities. These for the most part constitute the less expensive bulbs marketed. Lesser quantities, but their numbers in proportion to the whole gradually increasing, of choice named varieties raised from vegetative propagations are also sold commercially. These are uniform within the variety. They are named, described, and sometimes illustrated in catalogs of specialist dealers.

The St.-Joseph's-lily, of Louisiana and other parts of the lower south, is usually identified as *H. johnsonii*, but some doubt exists as to whether it is indeed a lineal descendant by vegetative propagation of the first hybrid hippeastrum (to which that name most properly belongs). Some believe that it represents a seedling of the original hybrid or possibly is a species in its own right. Whatever its ancestry, it is a beautiful spring-bloomer that seems best satisfied with moistish, clayish soil and in-

creases rather slowly. Its horizontally-held, wide-gaping flowers are bright crimson boldly striped part way down the center of each petal with white. A fairly common hybrid, *H. ackermannii,* presumably a hybrid of *H. aulicum*, which it rather closely resembles, has large crimson or crimson and green blooms.

Hippeastrum advena

Species of *Hippeastrum* more or less commonly cultivated include these: *H. advena* (syns. *Amaryllis advena*, *Rhodophiala advena*), of Chile, has bulbs about 1½ inches in diameter and glaucous-green, linear leaves approximately 1 foot long. The flowers, held approximately horizontally in umbels of up to six, are red, orange-red or pale yellow, with the bases of the petals pale green. From 1½ to 2 inches long, they have a three-cleft stigma. *H. aglaiae,* of Argentina, is evergreen and has blackish bulbs about 2 inches in diameter and slightly-channeled leaves 10 inches to over 1 foot long and nearly 1 inch wide. The two- to six-flowered umbels are on stalks up to nearly 2 feet long. The blooms, greenish-yellow below, have light yellow petals. The petals are about 3 inches long, the three inner narrower than the others. The stigma is three-cleft. *H. argentinum* (syns. *H. candidum, Amaryllis candida, A. immaculata*), of

Argentina, has dark purple, globose bulbs about 3 inches in diameter and produced after the blooms, up to seven somewhat glaucous, strap-shaped leaves tapered toward their bases and up to over 1 foot long by ¾ to 1 inch wide. Atop stalks up to 2½ feet tall, the slender-tubed, fragrant flowers, more or less drooping and about 8 inches long, are in umbels of five or six. They are pure white with green bases to the crisped petals. The stigma is three-cleft. **H. aulicum** (syns. *H. robustum, Amaryllis aulica*), sometimes called lily-of-the-palace, is native from Brazil to Paraguay. This has ovoid bulbs about 3 inches in diameter and six to eight blunt leaves about 1½ feet long, 2 inches wide, and not glaucous. The flower stalks, up to 2 feet tall, bear usually two green-throated, rich crimson blooms 5 to 6 inches long. The two upper petals are wider than the others. The stamens, much shorter than the petals, have red stalks. The stigma is three-cleft. Variety *H. a. platypetalum* is a vigorous variant with broader petals. **H. bifidum** (syns. *Amaryllis bifida, Rhodophiala bifida*), of Argentina and Uruguay, is sometimes misidentified as *H. advena*. It has linear, somewhat glaucous leaves and in umbels of three to six, bright

Hippeastrum chilense

Hippeastrum bifidum spathaceum

red, 2-inch-long, very short-tubed flowers. The stigma is three-cleft. Variety *H. b. spathaceum* (syns. *H. spathaceum, Rhodophiala bifida spathacea*) has light raspberry-pink flowers with slightly darker veins in umbels of four to six with the spathe at the base of the umbel split on one side to its base. **H. blumenavia** is a beautiful native of southeastern Brazil that has globose or subglobose bulbs up to 1¾ inches in diameter and up to seven leaves one or two of which are evident at flowering time. The leaves are short-stalked, lanceolate-elliptic to oblong-ovate, up to 5 inches long by ¾ inch to 2½ inches wide. The flowering

stalk, 8 to 10 inches tall, has somewhat drooping, funnel-shaped blooms 2½ to 3 inches long by approximately as wide across their faces. They are white marked with longitudinal lines and bands of mauve-crimson. The petals have wavy margins. The stigma is three-lobed. **H. calyptratum** (syn. *Amaryllis calyptrata*), a Brazilian of peculiar aspect, has long-necked bulbs somewhat over 2 inches in diameter. There are five to nine pointed-oblanceolate, evergreen leaves 1½ to 2 feet long by at their widest 2 inches broad. The flower stalks 1 foot to 2 feet tall carry greenish to pale yellow blooms netted with deeper green veins. Their petals are 3 to 4 inches long. **H. chilense** (syn. *Rhodophiala chilensis*), of Chile, has narrow leaves 8 to 10 inches long. Appearing before or with the

Hippeastrum elegans

leaves and 6 to 10 inches tall, the flowering stalks carry one or two 2-inch-long, red or primrose-yellow, flaring-trumpet-shaped blooms with stamens shorter than the perianth and a three-lobed stigma. **H. correiense** (syns. *H. organense, Amaryllis organensis*) has wide glaucous leaves and flowering stalks with two 6-inch-long, short tubed blooms with crimson petals and a deeply-three-lobed stigma. **H. elegans** (syns. *H. solandriflorum, Amaryllis elegans*), native of Brazil, Colombia, Guiana, and Venezuela, has bulbs 4 inches in diameter, leaves that develop along with the flowers approximately 1½ feet long by 1 inch wide, and atop stalks up to 2 feet tall, two to four funnel-shaped, greenish-white blooms 7 to 10 inches long and with a head-like stigma. Variety *H. e. divifrancisci* has longer-necked bulbs and flowers with definitely three-lobed stigmas. **H. evansiae** (syn. *Amaryllis evansiae*), of Bolivia, differs from *H. puniceum* in its flowers being held horizontally. At first chartreuse-green, they become lighter or pale yellow as they age. **H. maracasum** (syn. *Amaryllis mara-*

Hippeastrum evansiae

Hippeastrum psittacinum

casa), of Brazil, has medium-sized bulbs and seven or fewer leaves, like the flowering stalk covered with a whitish bloom. The latter up to 2 feet tall or taller, carries brick-red flowers veined with deeper red and with a green star in the throat. Not opening widely, they are approximately 5 inches long by about 4 inches wide across their faces. **H. oconequense** (syn. *Amaryllis oconequensis*), of Peru, has short-necked bulbs about 3 inches in diameter, and up to eight evergreen leaves nearly 1½ feet long by a little over 2 inches broad at their widest. About 4 inches long and approximately as wide across the face, the blooms are pink and green. **H. pardinum** (syn. *Amaryllis pardina*), of Bolivia and Peru, has a short-necked, globose bulb 2 to 3 inches in diameter and five to seven strap-shaped leaves that mostly develop after the flowers and eventually become 2 feet long. They are 2 inches wide above their middles, narrower below. The cream-colored, 6-inch-wide or wider blooms are minutely dotted all over with crimson. The stamens are slightly shorter than the petals. **H. psittacinum** (syn. *Amaryllis psittacina*) is indigenous to southern Brazil. It has long-necked bulbs, up to 4 inches in diameter, and six to eight slightly glaucous, strap-shaped leaves 1 foot to 1½ feet long by 1 inch to 1½ inches broad. The blooms, on flowering stalks 2 to 3 feet tall, have green-keeled, crimson-margined and crimson-striped, greenish-white petals 4 to 5 inches long. Stamens and style are shorter than the petals. The stigma is three-lobed. **H. puniceum** (syn. *H. equestre*) is the *Amaryllis belladonna* of those who prefer *Amaryllis* as the generic name of *Hippeastrum,* but it is distinct from *A. belladonna* as *Amaryllis* as interpreted in this Encyclopedia. Native from Mexico to Chile, Bolivia, Brazil, and the West Indies,

Hippeastrum puniceum

H. puniceum has globose bulbs up to 2 inches in diameter. The normally six to eight strap-shaped leaves, coming after the flowers, are 1 foot to 1½ feet long by up to nearly 2 inches wide. From 1½ to 2 feet tall, the flowering stalk carries blooms 4 to 5 inches long by 4 inches wide. They are bright red, scarlet, or occasionally pink with yellowish-green throats. The stamens

are shorter than the petals. Variety *H. p. major,* with larger, more erect leaves and bigger bright scarlet flowers, is naturalized in Florida. Variety *H. p. plena* has semidouble or double scarlet flowers. **H. reginae** (syn. *Amaryllis reginae*) has the distinction of being the only *Hippeastrum* native elsewhere than in the Americas. It is indigenous to an island in West Africa as well as Mexico to Brazil, Peru, and the West Indies. This kind has bulbs 2 to 3 inches in diameter and leaves, not fully developed until after blooming, up to 2 feet long by 1½ inches wide, tapering to their bases. **H. reticulatum** (syn. *Amaryllis reticulata*), of southern Brazil, has a short-necked, subglobose bulb and four to six thinnish, oblanceolate leaves up to 1 foot long by 2 inches wide above their middles, but tapering below. The 3-inch-wide blooms, on flowering stalks about 1 foot tall, have petals up to 4 inches long, bright red with crossbars of a deeper hue. The stamens are shorter than the petals. Variety *H. r. striatifolium* has broader leaves with conspicuous white or pinkish keels and a clear white stripe down the center. Its flowers are almost without crossbars. **H. striatum** (syns. *H. rutilum, Amaryllis striata*), of Brazil, is a variable species of which several varieties have been named. It has played an impor-

Hippeastrum striatum

tant part in hybridizing and is a very satisfactory garden kind. Its short-necked, light-colored bulbs, 2 to 3 inches in diameter, have six to eight strap-shaped, bright green leaves about 1 foot long by 1 inch wide. The flowers, 3 to 4 inches long, have bright crimson petals, their lower halves with green keels. The red-stalked stamens are shorter than the petals. The stigma is three-lobed. *H. s. crocatum* (syns. *H. crocatum, Amaryllis striata crocata*) has pale pink flowers with wavy petals. *H. s. fulgidum* (syns. *H. fulgidum, Amaryllis striata fulgida*) is a superior, vigorous variety with bulbs up to 4 inches in diameter and broader leaves than typical *H. striatum.* The flowers

Hippeastrum striatum crocatum

based on fertile, loamy topsoil, preferably turfy, mixed with approximately equal amounts of good compost or peat moss, and with sufficient sand or perlite to assure porosity. It is well to add one-tenth part by bulk of dried cow manure, and bonemeal at the rate of a pint to each bushel or a heaping tablespoonful to each 6-inch pot of the mix. Let the major ingredients be coarse rather than fine. Do not sift them.

The time to pot or repot is winter or early spring just before new growth begins. Make sure the containers are clean, well drained, and not too big. A space of 1 inch between the outsides of new bulbs without roots and the insides of their pots is sufficient. Set the bulbs so that only about their lower third is beneath the finished level of the soil. Pack the soil beneath the bulb fairly firmly and that around it firmer, but not rock-hard. Use a potting stick to do this.

After potting, water very thoroughly with a fine spray and set the plants where

Potting hippeastrums: (a) Make ready a clean pot by crocking and covering the crocks with prepared soil pressed firm with the fingers. Note the bulb, newly purchased and without roots

(b) If the bulb to be repotted is an old one with roots, remove it from the pot, take out old crocks and, with a pointed stick, prick away as much old soil as is easily possible

are bright red, the lower parts of the petals with green keels. Under good cultivation this blooms several times each season. *H. traubii* (syn. *Amaryllis traubii*), of Peru, has bulbs about 1½ inches in diameter and up to six evergreen, thickish, strap-shaped leaves. About 2 feet tall, the flowering stalk carries flowers with petals about 3 inches long. They are carmine-rose with greenish-white bases. *H. vittatum* (syn. *Amaryllis vittata*), of Brazil and Peru, has a globose bulb 2 to 3 inches wide and six to eight strap-shaped leaves 1½ to 3 feet in length. The two- to six-bloomed flowering stalks are 2 to 2½ feet tall. The flowers vary considerably in size. They commonly are 3 to 4½ inches in width. Their petals are white, longitudinally distinctly or sometimes rather obscurely striped with mauve-red. The stamens are shorter than the petals, and the stigma is deeply-three-lobed. This species is a parent of many hybrids.

Garden and Landscape Uses. Hippeastrums are highly esteemed for pots in greenhouses and windows and in warm regions where little or no frost is experienced as outdoor flower garden bulbs. They tolerate sunny locations, but do better where afforded a little shade. Deep, fertile soil, moist during the time of the year when they are in foliage, dry or nearly dry when they are dormant, is to their liking. They can be displayed to excellent advantage in groups in flower borders, at the fringes of shrub beds, and, the smaller ones, in rock gardens.

Cultivation. No extraordinary skill is required to flower hippeastrums satisfactorily in pots. If dormant bulbs are purchased the chief challenge comes during the first season. It is to persuade them to become reestablished, to put forth plenty of strong new roots. Beginners often overlook this. They are overjoyed when their new acquisition produces a magnificent cluster of blooms, devastated when there is none the following year. Initial success reflects little credit on the new owner. The first flowers were in the bulb at the time of purchase. Warmth and moisture brought them forth. But succeeding years' flowering or non-flowering reflect subsequent care. If it is adequate, hippeastrums normally bloom every year with the exception that newly purchased bulbs often skip the year following their purchase. Here is why. Hippeastrums have permanent roots. Unlike tulips, hyacinths, and certain other bulb plants their roots do not die every year to be replaced by new the next. Yet when you buy hippeastrum bulbs they nearly always are as rootless as hyacinth bulbs. This is because the grower cut off the roots after harvesting the bulbs for sale. And so during its first season after purchase the energies of the plant go largely into renewing the root system of which it has been deprived instead of into nourishing the bulb to the extent that flowering the succeeding season is practically certain.

Soil requirements for hippeastrums are not demanding. Outdoors, they succeed best in fertile loams neither very sandy nor markedly clayey and well supplied with organic matter. The most satisfactory pH is between 6 and 7 or even slightly higher. Hippeastrums are not well suited for saline earths. For potted plants supply a rich mix

(c) Center bulb in pot, taking care, if roots are present, to work soil among them

(d) Pack the soil medium-firm with a potting stick

Following the dormant period the appearance of a flower bud (left) or new leaves (right) signals the beginning of a new period of active growth

Unless seed is needed, cut off the faded flowers

the temperature at night is 60 to 70°F, somewhat warmer by day. Keep them out of direct sun, but in good light. A humid atmosphere is needed, but guard against overwatering. Constantly soggy soil inhibits new root development. It is better that it become dryish, but not dry before water is given, and when it is, the soil must be drenched.

When repotting established bulbs, an attention usually needed only every three or four years, after removing them from their pots, prick away with a pointed stick as much old soil as you can without unduly disturbing the roots. Return the plant to the next size bigger pot and pack the soil around the root ball as advised with new bulbs. In years when repotting is deemed unnecessary, just prick away a little of the surface soil and top-dress by replacing it with a new rich mix.

Except for a few evergreen species hippeastrums are dormant from October to January or February. During this period keep them quite dry where the temperature is about 55°F. Through the remainder of the year they are in active growth and success in flowering the following year depends upon the care they receive then. At

the conclusion of the resting period, when they naturally start into new growth as evidenced by the tip of a flower bud or the ends of leaves peeping from the apex of the bulb, provide encouraging growing conditions. Soak the soil thoroughly with water and top-dress or repot the bulbs according to their needs. Put them in a sunny place where the temperature by night is 65 to 70°F and by day five to ten degrees higher. Maintain fairly high humidity. Water moderately at first, with increasing frequency as foliage develops. After the foliage is half grown begin weekly or biweekly applications of dilute liquid fertilizer to all except newly potted or repotted bulbs. Continue this until late summer. During the summer they may be stood in a shaded cold frame, outdoors in partial shade, or they may at that period be kept indoors or on a porch slightly shaded from strong direct sunshine. Unless you plan to save seeds for propagation, cut off the flower stalks as soon as the blooms fade but do not remove any foliage then.

In preparation for winter rest, in September or earlier if the foliage begins to die naturally, start to reduce water supplies to all except a few less commonly grown evergreen species. Do this by gradually lengthening the periods between applications, allowing the soil to become quite dry between. Finally, withhold water com-

pletely and store the bulbs in their pots of soil under a greenhouse bench (turned on their sides so that drip from the bench will not wet the soil), in a cellar, attic, or other place where the temperature is about 55°F.

Hippeastrums can be increased by offsets taken from the sides of older bulbs. Some sorts develop these fairly freely, others much less often or rarely. Allow offset bulbs, which are to be taken off and potted separately, to become fairly big before

Propagating by bulb cuttings: (a) Slicing the bulb into small sections

(b) The cuttings planted in a mixture of peat moss and perlite

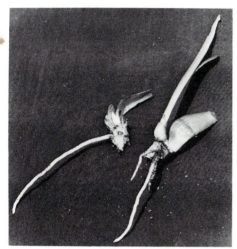

(c) Kept slightly moist, at 75 to 85°F, the cuttings sprout roots, develop young bulbs which

(d) When big enough are potted individually

Flat of seedling hippeastrums

removing them from the mother plant. Another very successful method of propagation, one that results in much more rapid multiplication, is by bulb cuttings. For details of this procedure consult the entry Cuttings, Propagation By.

Seeds also afford a ready means of raising hippeastrums, but seedlings of hybrids are likely to vary considerably. Fresh seeds germinate quickly. Sow them in late winter or early spring in pots or flats in sandy peaty soil kept moderately and uniformly moist, but not constantly saturated, in a temperature of 70 to 80°F. When the young plants are about one month old, transplant them 2 inches apart into pans (shallow pots) or deep flats. From then on grow them in a tropical greenhouse or under approximately similar conditions without allowing them to rest or go dormant until they bloom for the first time, which will be when they are one and one-half to two and one-half years old. During this period minimum

temperatures of 60 to 65°F at night, and five to ten degrees more by day, are appropriate.

When the young plants begin to crowd in the pans or flats pot them individually or preferably plant them in a greenhouse bed or bench at a spacing of 5 to 6 inches apart. Use coarse, fertile, loamy, porous

soil. Light shade from strong sun is needed and the atmosphere must be fairly humid. The winter following their first blooming dry the bulbs off and rest them. From then on treat them as mature bulbs.

Pests and Diseases. Hippeastrum bulbs are attractive to narcissus bulb flies the larvae of which feed on their interiors. These plants may also fall prey to aphids, blister beetles, bulb scale mites, cutworms, nematodes, and thrips. Among diseases they may be infected with a leaf scorch, which causes distortion and red spots and lines on the bulbs, foliage, and flowering parts (bruising is often responsible for a similar reddening). Botrytis blight sometimes appears. Virus infections that cause yellow discolorations are incurable. Destroy virus-infected bulbs promptly.

HIPPOBROMA (Hippo-bròma). The only species of *Hippobroma*, of the bellflower family CAMPANULACEAE, is widely distributed in the tropics, including the West Indies and Hawaii, as a native or naturalized plant. The name, alluding to poisonous properties, said to drive horses mad, comes from the Greek *hippos*, a horse, and *bromos*, rage.

A fairly attractive, nonhardy herbaceous perennial 1 foot to 2 feet tall and usually not branched, **H. longiflora** (syns. *Isotoma longiflora*, *Laurentia longiflora*) has ovate-lanceolate, jagged-toothed leaves up to 8 inches long. The white blooms come from the upper leaf axils and are carried erectly. They have five sepals, a corolla with a very long slender tube, and five spreading lobes (petals). There are five stamens, the two shorter with dense tufts of hair, and one style. The fruits are capsules.

Because the milky sap of this species is extremely poisonous (a single drop in contact with the eye can result in blindness), it is important not to include it in garden plantings and to avoid it in the wild.

Hippobroma longiflora

HIPPOCASTANACEAE — Horse-chestnut Family. Only one of the two or three genera that constitute this family of dicotyledons is known to be cultivated. It is *Aesculus*, which contains the horse-chestnuts and buckeyes.

Native of the northern hemisphere and South America, the horse-chestnut family consists of trees or more rarely shrubs. Its sorts have opposite leaves of three to nine leaflets that spread palmately (in finger-fashion) from the tops of the leafstalks. The flowers are in mostly large, showy, pyramidal, branched clusters from the shoot ends. They have five sepals, those of horse-chestnuts and buckeyes united at their bases, four or five unequal petals with narrow shafts or claws, five to nine stamens, and one style and stigma. The fruits are leathery capsules, sometimes spiny, that contain generally one large seed and when ripe split into three segments.

HIPPOCREPIS (Hippo-crèpis) — Horse-shoe-Vetch. Belonging in the pea family LEGUMINOSAE, and including twenty species of annuals, herbaceous perennials, subshrubs, and rarely low shrubs, *Hippocrepis* is indigenous chiefly to the Mediterranean region and the Canary Islands, but is represented in native floras as far north as the British Isles. Its name is from the

Greek *hippos*, a horse, and *krepis*, a shoe. It alludes to the curved seed pods.

Horseshoe-vetches have pinnate leaves with an uneven number of toothless leaflets, and stalked clusters of nodding, yellow, pea-like flowers followed by flattened, horseshoe-shaped seed pods several times constricted or jointed. The blooms have a shortly-bell-shaped, five-lobed calyx. The wing petals are bent. The keel is beaked. There are nine stamens united and one free.

Perennial *H. comosa* is an attractive native of southern and central Europe, 8 inches to 1 foot tall, with more or less prostrate stems. Its leaves have seven to fifteen blunt, oblong to linear leaflets. Its flowers, about ½ inch long, are in tight clusters of four to twelve. An annual of some merit is quick-growing *H. multisiliquosa*, native of the Mediterranean region. Slender-stemmed, this is up to 1 foot tall. It has pale green foliage and small, bright yellow flowers in short spikes.

Garden Uses. Hardy *H. comosa* is well suited for rock gardens and dry wall gardens, *H. multisiliquosa*, although it makes no great show, for adding variety to flower borders and beds.

Cultivation. Horseshoe-vetches are most satisfactory in porous, well-drained, not excessively fertile soil in full sun. The perennial described here thrives in limestone

soils. It is easily propagated by seeds and by carefully dividing plants in early spring. The annual is reproduced from seeds sown in early spring or, in regions of mild winters, in fall, where the plants are to bloom. The seedlings are thinned to about 3 inches apart.

HIPPOPHAE (Hippó-phae) — Sea-Buck-thorn. Two or three species of spiny, deciduous shrubs or small trees of the oleaster family ELAEAGNACEAE constitute this European and temperate Asian genus. The name is a modification of *hippophaes*, used by the ancient Greeks for a spiny plant, not necessarily one of these.

Hippophaes have their young shoots and their foliage clothed with silvery scales or star-shaped hairs. Their leaves are alternate, short-stalked, narrow, and suggest those of willows. From the flowers of related *Elaeagnus* those of *Hippophae* differ in being shortly-tubular and having two instead of four yellow sepals. There are no petals. Males and females are on separate plants. They appear before the foliage and are small and of no decorative merit. The males have four short stamens, the females a slender style. The one-seeded fleshy fruits are berry-like.

Sea-buckthorn (**H. rhamnoides**), a native of Europe and Asia, is a shrub or tree sometimes 30 to 40 feet in height, usually with spine-tipped twigs. Its very short-stalked leaves, linear to linear-lanceolate and silvery-scaly on both sides, are ¾ inch to 2½ inches long. The highly attractive and profuse fruits produced by female trees, if a male is nearby to pollinate them, last well into the winter. They are nearly spherical to egg-shaped, almost or quite ⅓ inch long, and bright orange-yellow. This is hardy in southern Canada. Variety *H. r. procera*, of China, becomes much taller and has hairy young shoots. It is not thought to be hardy in the north. Also less hardy, but satisfactorily so about as far north as New York City, **H. salicifolia**, which is

Hippophae rhamnoides

less spiny than *H. rhamnoides*, has pendulous branches and light yellow fruits. This native of the Himalayas is up to about 45 feet tall. Its linear-oblong leaves, 1 inch to 3 inches in length, are felty beneath, but not silvery. As an ornamental, this species is inferior to the sea-buckthorn.

Garden and Landscape Uses. The sea-buckthorn is so handsome in foliage and fruit that it surely deserves more attention from gardeners. It must be remembered that to have fruit it is necessary for a male tree to be close by the female. A proportion of one male to six or fewer females is satisfactory. Sea-buckthorn thrives inland as well as near the sea.

Cultivation. Except that they do not transplant as easily as many shrubs and trees, hippophaes give little trouble to gardeners. To meet that difficulty it is advisable to set them in their permanent locations while they are young and small. No regular scheduled pruning is needed. Any done to improve their shape or limit them to size may be attended to in spring. Seeds may be sown in a cold frame or outdoors in fall, or stored and then before sowing be stratified for three months at 40°F. Root cuttings and layering are satisfactory vegetative means of increase and are advisable when specimens of predetermined sex are to be raised.

HIPPURIS (Hip-pùris)—Mare's Tail. Most botanists recognize only one species of *Hippuris*, others divide the genus into two or three species. Whichever view is accepted, the common mare's tail is a deciduous aquatic herbaceous perennial that belongs to the water milfoil family HALORAGIDACEAE. It is sometimes cultivated in bog gardens, water gardens, and aquariums. The generic name is an ancient Greek one used by Dioscorides and derives from *hippos,* a horse, and *oura,* a tail, in allusion to the appearance of the leafy stems.

The mare's tail (**H. vulgaris**), broadly interpreted, is native throughout the colder parts of the northern hemisphere. Commonly it inhabits still waters, occasionally marshes. It has a creeping rhizome and erect, branchless, hollow stems, which in the normal form rise well out of the water and are up to 3 feet in length. They have many tiers of usually six to twelve stalkless, horizontally-spreading, linear leaves up to 1¼ inches long. The underwater leaves are slender and hairlike or may be represented by scales. The minute flowers, female or bisexual, are in the upper leaf axils and form long terminal spikes. They have neither sepals nor petals. A completely submersed variety, *H. v. fluviatilis* has lax stems and longer leaves. A

variety that grows in salt marshes and has leaves in tiers of four is *H. v. maritima.*

Garden Uses and Cultivation. Mare's tail is interesting for shallow-water pools and bog gardens and is sometimes cultivated in unheated aquariums. It thrives in mud, or in aquariums in unwashed river sand mixed with some clay and organic debris. It requires good light. Propagation is by division.

HIPS. The fruits of roses are called hips. They are very rich in vitamin C and were used in Great Britain as an important source of this in World War II.

HISTIOPTERIS (Histió-pteris). Native from the tropics to New Zealand, Tasmania, South Africa, and other parts of the southern hemisphere, *Histiopteris,* of the pteris family PTERIDACEAE, comprises seven species. The meaning of the name is not obvious.

These are robust ferns with long, creeping rhizomes and large to immense, hairless, frequently glaucous, twice- or thrice-pinnate fronds (leaves) of indefinite growth and with opposite or nearly opposite, stalkless leaflets. The clusters of spore capsules, which form a continuous row along the frond margins, are covered by the modified reflexed edges of the leaflets.

Widely distributed as a native practically throughout the range of the genus, *H. incisa* has more or less glaucous fronds with blades 1 foot to 4 feet long or longer and approximately one-half as wide. They are twice-pinnate with the final segments lobed or toothed, or thrice-pinnate.

Garden and Landscape Uses and Cultivation. These are as for *Pteris.* For more information see Ferns.

HOARHOUND is *Marrubium vulgare,* black-hoarhound *Ballota nigra,* water-hoarhound *Lycopus.*

HOBBLEBUSH is *Viburnum alnifolium.*

HOES and HOEING. Among basic garden tools hoes rank high. Of great importance for eliminating weeds, they serve usefully in other ways, notably for cultivating to create and maintain a soil or dust mulch to conserve moisture (see Cultivation). They are also used to draw drills (make shallow furrows) in which to sow seeds and to hill up (mound) soil around the bases of corn and other plants that benefit from this. There are several types of hoes. The wheel hoe or wheel cultivator is described under Cultivators. Hand hoes, fitted with broom-handle-like shafts, are of two chief types. Pull or chop hoes have blades set at approximately right angles to the handle. When used for cultivating these are operated by lifting the blade end well up from the ground and with a forward chopping action striking the soil repeatedly at inter-

Hippuris vulgaris

Hoes: (a) Chop hoe

(b) Scuffle hoe

vals of 2 or 3 inches to break the surface and cut off or dislodge weeds. Hoes of this type, one with a triangular blade is called a Warren hoe, are used to make drills by pulling in such a way that a corner of the blade slides along a line stretched taut across the ground surface. Scuffle hoes, among the best kinds are those known as the English scuffle hoe and the Dutch hoe, have a blade set at much less than right angles to the handle. The correct way of using these is by resting the blade on the ground and pushing the handle with a series of short to longish forward and backward strokes so that the blade slides an inch or slightly more below the surface, cutting off all weeds and breaking up the surface crust. A great advantage of scuffle hoes is that the operator works backwards and does not step on the newly loosened soil.

HOFFMANNIA (Hoffmán-nia). Of the 100 species of *Hoffmannia* of the madder family RUBIACEAE, few are cultivated. Those that are are beautiful tropical foliage plants. In the wild ranging from Mexico to Argentina, the genus consists of woody and her-

baceous perennial plants. Its name honors Georg Franz Hoffmann, a Swedish professor of botany, who died in 1826.

Hoffmannias have undivided leaves, opposite or whorled (in circles of more than two) and mostly of colors other than plain green. Their small flowers, white, yellow, or red, are in clusters. They have four-lobed calyxes and funnel- to nearly wheel-shaped corollas with usually four, rarely five blunt lobes (petals). Generally there are four stamens. The fruits are oblongish berries containing many seeds. A name at one time used for these plants was *Campylobotrys*.

Hoffmannia ghiesbreghtii

Hoffmannia ghiesbreghtii (flowers)

A handsome bushy species up to about 4 feet tall, **H. ghiesbreghtii,** a native of Mexico and Guatemala, is grown in choice collections of tropical plants. Almost hairless, it has squarish, erect stems with their angles narrowly-winged. The pointed, oblong-lanceolate, velvety leaves are up to 1 foot long and up to 3½ inches broad. They have short stalks, with wings continuing

down the stems, and are bronzy-green to moss-green with prominent silvery-green and pink veins, the lateral ones parallel to each other and curving outward and upward from the midrib. The under leaf surfaces are red. Borne from the leaf axils, sometime after the leaves have fallen, and in close clusters, the small yellow flowers each have a red spot. Variety *H. g. variegata* has foliage remarkably and beautifully marbled with green, cream, pinkish-gray, and bronze. Its under leaf surfaces are red.

Hoffmania ghiesbreghtii variegata

Hoffmannia refulgens

A plant of great charm, beautiful **H. refulgens** is 1 foot tall or a little taller. Its red stems are hidden by closely set, thickish leaves up to 6 inches long, and obovate. They have a quilted appearance and are rich coppery-purplish or olive-green, velvety and iridescent, with red-haired, red margins. Their veins, the lateral ones depressed and curving upward and outward from the midribs, are pale green or gray-green. The under leaf surfaces are reddish-purple. The blooms are light red and ¾

Hoffmannia refulgens vittata

Hoffmannia roezlii

inch in diameter. An especially lovely variety, *H. r. vittata* is distinguished by having the veins, margins and marginal hairs of the decidedly coppery olive-green or purplish maroon leaves silvery-gray. The leaves are proportionately longer than those of *H. refulgens*.

The Mexican *H. roezlii* is similar to *H. refulgens* but has broader, rounder, satiny, sparsely-hairy leaves 4 to 8 inches long. They have much puckered or quilted surfaces and are green and pinkish-purple with purple-red centers. The under leaf surfaces are purple, the flowers dark red.

A hybrid between *H. ghiesbreghtii* and *H. roezlii* is *H.* 'Fantasia'. Although not as tall as *H. ghiesbreghtii* it has many of its characteristics. A vigorous grower, its leaves are obovate and lustrous coppery-olive-green with paler veins.

Garden Uses. In the humid tropics hoffmannias may be planted outdoors in shaded locations, preferably where the soil contains an abundance of organic matter and does not suffer from extreme dryness. The lower kinds are appropriate in rock gardens and similar places where their foliage is not likely to be damaged or splashed with mud. The taller *H. ghiesbreghtii* and its variety and hybrid are suitable for beds and fronts of shrub borders. These are also ideal for inclusion in greenhouse collections of tropical foliage plants. They may be grown in ground beds or containers and often do surprisingly well planted under greenhouse benches.

Cultivation. Heat, humidity, and fertile soil are the chief requirements of hoffmannias. Given these, together with shade from strong sun and enough water to keep the earth evenly moist but not constantly saturated, success is practically assured. They must also be kept free of mealybugs, thrips, and other pests. To retain their good looks, care must be used not to break

or otherwise damage their long-lasting leaves. In greenhouses a minimum winter night temperature of 60°F is best. By day an increase of ten to fifteen degrees is permissible and in summer temperatures up to 90°F and higher are agreeable. Well-established plants benefit from applications of dilute liquid fertilizer. Hoffmannias propagate with great ease from cuttings planted in a propagating bench in a tropical greenhouse or under similar conditions of high temperatures, humidity, and shade. Young plants of the taller growers, but not of the low ones, should have the tips of their stems pinched out once or twice to encourage branching. Repotting is done in late winter or spring, and at that time the taller kinds are pruned to size and shape.

HOG. This word is used as part of the common names of these plants: hog-peanut (*Amphicarpaea bracteata*), hog plum (*Prunus reverchonii*), hog-plum (*Spondias mombin* and *Ximenia americana*), and Queensland hog-plum (*Pleiogynium cerasiferum*).

HOHENBERGIA (Hohen-bérgia). Of the thirty-five species of this genus of the pineapple family BROMELIACEAE, few are cultivated. This is understandable if we reflect that compared with more popular bromeliads they are excessively large and their flowers and foliage colors are often much less brilliant than those of many members of related groups. Nevertheless, where space is available *Hohenbergia* is certainly worthy of representation in bromeliad collections. From *Aechmea* to which it is closely related, it differs in its flowers being in small cones in branched panicles. Natives of Brazil, Guatemala, Venezuela, and the West Indies, these plants are especially numerous as to species in Brazil,

which has sixteen natives, and in Jamaica, which has an indigenous population of fifteen species. The name of the group commemorates a Herr Hohenberg who lived in the early part of the nineteenth century.

Hohenbergias are mostly terrestrial; they usually grow in the ground not like most bromeliads perched on trees. Evergreen perennials, they have rosettes of usually broad, spiny-edged, generally spine-tipped leaves. The small, compact, conelike spikes of stalkless blooms accompanied by evident bracts are in tall panicles. The little flowers have three each nearly or quite separate sepals and petals, the latter with a pair of scales on their inner surfaces, six stamens shorter than the petals, and one style. The ovaries, below the petals and sepals, change little as they develop into fruits.

Native to Brazil and Trinidad, *H. stellata* has vase-shaped rosettes of recurved, broadly-linear, yellow-green leaves 3 to 5 feet long by about 3 inches wide. Its showy panicles of bloom have short, rather distantly-spaced branches. The bristly cones of blue-petaled blooms that compose the panicles have brilliant red bracts. In its homelands this occurs as an epiphyte (perching on trees) as well as a terrestrial. Less beautiful in flower, *H. penduliflora* (syn. *Pitcairnia penduliflora*) is sometimes grown under the botanically unacceptable name *H. simpsonii*. An old garden plant, it was introduced to Europe in 1843, to Florida in 1882. Its bluish-green leaves are up to 2 feet long. The flowers are light greenish. Brazilian *H. ridleyi* is one of the giants of the bromeliad clan. Its rosettes may spread 3½ feet. The arching, spiny, strap-shaped, channeled leaves are of a bronzy-yellow hue when bloom time approaches, green-gold at other times. Its small flowers are in long, rangy, loosely-branched, white-woolly panicles, the pinkish stalks of which have purplish bracts. The flowers have lobed sepals, washed-out lavender petals. This species is of much greater interest for its bold rosettes than for its blooms.

Other sorts cultivated include these: *H. blanchetii,* of Brazil, has broadly-linear leaves 2 to 4 inches wide or sometimes wider and 1-foot-long panicles of spikes of flowers with ¼-inch-long blue and white or blue petals. *H. catingae,* of Brazil, has leaves up to 1½ feet long and about 1½ inches broad. The purple flowers in sparingly-woolly-hairy spikes have petals about ½ inch long. *H. distans,* a native of Jamaica, has narrowly-minutely-toothed or toothless, strap-shaped leaves, 2 to 2½ feet in length, and pendulous panicles up to 2 feet long. The white to greenish flowers are about ¾ inch in length. *H. urbaniana* has brown-toothed leaves up to 3 feet long, their undersides clothed with powdery-gray scales. The small cone-shaped spikes of yellow flowers are densely clustered at the ends of erect stalks shorter than the leaves. It is native to Jamaica.

Garden and Landscape Uses and Cultivation. Hohenbergias can be grown in the ground outdoors in warm, frost-free climates and in beds or in large containers in greenhouses and elsewhere indoors where suitable conditions can be had. They are too big to use as window plants or generally as room plants, but can be effective on patios and in similar places. They respond to environments agreeable to aechmeas and need soil suitable for terrestrial bromeliads. For details of cultivation see Bromeliads or Bromels.

HOHERIA (Hoh-èria)—Ribbonwood. Outdoor cultivation of New Zealand flora in the United States, because of climatic necessity, is pretty much confined to the West Coast. This is true of hoherias, more's the pity. Were they hardier to winter cold and more tolerant of summer heat, these attractive small trees would make welcome additions to gardens elsewhere. The genus *Hoheria,* of the mallow family MALVACEAE, occurs natively only in New Zealand. There are four or five species. Its botanical name is a corruption of a Maori one. In their homeland hoherias are known as ribbonwoods, a name also used for the closely related *Plagianthus.* Elsewhere they are sometimes called New Zealand lacebarks. Both appellations allude to the tough inner bark, which is characteristically perforated and pitted.

Hoherias have firm-textured, toothed, alternate, undivided leaves, and small to medium-sized flowers, usually in clusters, but occasionally solitary in the leaf axils. Like those of so many New Zealand plants they are white. The blooms have five sepals, five spreading petals, and many stamens united partway down into a tube that surrounds the six or more styles, but with their lowest parts separated into

groups of five or six. The fruits are dry and contain pendulous seeds.

Native chiefly in the North Island *H. populnea* is evergreen and 10 to 40 feet tall. It has downy shoots, foliage, and flower stalks. The bright green leaves, 3 to 5 inches long and approximately one-half as wide, are irregularly- and sharply-toothed. Pure white, ¾ to 1 inch across, and in axillary clusters, the blooms are produced in great profusion in fall. The handsome variety *H. p. variegata* has its foliage beautifully marked with creamy-white. In most leaves this appears as irregular creamy margins to a central green part of the leaf, but leaves vary from almost entirely green to completely white. Another good variety is *H. p. osbornii,* distinguished by the purplish veins of its leaves and its flowers having slightly lilac petals and purple stamens. Sometimes regarded as another variety of *H. populnea,* the slender, evergreen *H. angustifolia* has linear-oblong to oblong leaves, rarely over 2 inches long and sharply-toothed. Its ½-inch-wide, pure white blooms, in clusters of 2 to 4, appear before those of *H. populnea.*

Hoheria sexstylosa

Differing from *H. populnea* in its much narrower leaves, and its flowers with pink styles, is *H. sexstylosa* (syn. *H. populnea lanceolata*). The evergreen leaves of this kind are ovate-lanceolate to lanceolate, 2 to 4 inches long, pointed, and sharply-toothed. Its blooms, except for the styles, are pure white and ¾ to 1 inch wide. This species occurs in both islands of its homeland.

The deciduous *H. lyallii* (syn. *Gaya lyallii*), from the mountains of both the North and the South Island, is a shrub or small tree with coarsely-toothed, pointed, heart-shaped leaves, like the shoots, more or less covered with starry (stellate) hairs. The hardiest species, in bloom it is somewhat suggestive of a flowering cherry. The

flowers are pure white with overlapping petals and contrasting yellow anthers. They are 1½ inches in diameter and in clusters of two to five. Variety *H. l. glabrata* soon loses its downy hairs, has flowers more cupped, and is less sturdy than the typical species. The leaves of *H. l. ribifolia* are less slender-pointed and more hairy than those of the typical species and are deeply-lobed or toothed.

Garden and Landscape Uses. Wherever white-flowered, small trees or tall shrubs can be used to advantage, either singly or grouped, hoherias suggest themselves for consideration where climate permits. They are deep-rooted and respond to any ordinary, fertile, well-drained soil in sun or part-day shade.

Cultivation. No special care attends the cultivation of hoherias. Ordinarily they need no pruning. They come readily from seeds, often developing with some abandon from self-sown ones, and may also be increased by cuttings and layers.

HOLBOELLIA (Holbo-éllia). Ten Himalayan, Chinese, and Indochinese species of vining shrubs closely related to *Stauntonia* constitute *Holboellia,* of the lardizabala family LARDIZABALACEAE. Their name perpetuates that of Frederik Ludvig Holboell, a superintendent of the botanic garden in Copenhagen, Denmark. He died in 1829.

Rapid-growing, nonhardy, twining, evergreen vines, holboellias have foliage reminiscent of that of their more widely grown relative *Akebia quinata,* but their blooms are distinctly different. Their long-stalked leaves have blades of three to nine stalked, toothless leaflets. The unisexual flowers are in racemes or clusters of usually one sex only. They are white to greenish-white or purplish. They have six fleshy, petal-like sepals and six small nectaries sometimes identified as petals. The males have six separate stamens and rudimentary ovaries, the females three erect styles and small staminodes (nonfunctional stamens). The fruits are large, oblongish, purple pods containing many black seeds. The separate rather than partially united stamens distinguish this genus from *Stauntonia.*

Robust and with stems up to 20 feet tall or taller, *H. coriacea* is a native of China. Its leaves are leathery and have three ovate to oblong-lanceolate or narrowly-oblong leaflets 2½ to 6 inches long, 1 inch to 3 inches wide, the center one biggest and longest-stalked. The male flowers, purplish and fragrant, have 1-inch-long stalks, and are in clusters 3 inches long and 4 inches wide. The stalks of the females are twice as long as those of the males. The females are in clusters of three or four from the lower leaf axils of young shoots. They are paler than male blooms. The fruits are purple, about 2 inches long. From the last, western Chinese *H. gran-*

Holboellia coriacea

diflora differs in having leaves of three to seven oblong to lanceolate leaflets 1 inch to 1¼ inches in length, and grayish-green on the undersides. The 1-inch-long or larger fragrant flowers are waxy-white. The edible purple fruits are 3 to 5 inches long. Native of the Himalayas, *H. latifolia* has leathery leaves of three to seven oblong to obovate leaflets up to 6 inches long. Greenish-white males and purple females intermixed in the same clusters, the flowers are fragrant. The fruits are purple, edible, and about 3 inches long.

Garden and Landscape Uses and Cultivation. Holboellias are attractive ornamentals worthy of more attention from gardeners in regions where they are hardy. They succeed in a variety of soils preferring those reasonably fertile. Increase is by seeds, cuttings, and layering.

HOLCUS (Hól-cus)—Velvet Grass. Eight species of annual and perennial grasses make up this genus of the grass family GRAMINEAE. All are natives of temperate parts of the Old World. Some are naturalized in North America. Their name is the Latin one for some bristly-eared grass, possibly barley. In *Holcus* the two-flowered, flattened spikelets are in dense or loose panicles. The leaf blades are linear and flat.

Velvet grass (*H. lanatus*) is 1 foot to 3 feet tall and has stems that are hairy on their lower parts. It is without rhizomes. Its leaves, including the sheaths that enclose their stems, are covered with soft grayish or whitish hairs. Their blades are up to 6 inches long by ½ inch broad. The narrowly-ovoid-cylindrical flower panicles, 2 to 6 inches in length, are whitish to pale purplish. This European perennial is naturalized in North America. Also perennial and differing from the last chiefly in that it has vigorous slender rhizomes and in that its stems, but not other parts, are hairless, *H. mollis* is a European native naturalized in the United States. Its variety *H. m. albo-variegatus*, sometimes mistak-

enly identified as *H. lanatus albo-variegatus*, has leaves attractively longitudinally striped with white.

Garden Uses and Cultivation. Although rarely cultivated the kinds described are pleasing plants best suited for informal areas and naturalistic plantings. They grow best in sun in moist, but not wet, fertile soils. Propagation of the variegated variety is by division, of the others by division or by seed.

HOLLY. See Ilex. African-holly is *Solanum giganteum*, California-holly *Heteromeles arbutifolia*, desert-holly *Atriplex hymenelytra*, Guatemalan-holly *Olmediella betschlerana*. The name holly fern applies to kinds of *Cyrtomium* and *Polystichum*. The East Indian holly fern is *Arachniodes aristata*. Mountain-holly is *Nemopanthus mucronata* and *Prunus ilicifolia*. Sea-holly is *Eryngium maritimum*, summer-holly *Comarostaphylis diversifolia*.

HOLLYHOCK. This is the common name of the plants dealt with in the next entry. The desert-hollyhock is *Sphaeralcea ambigua*, the sea-hollyhock *Hibiscus moscheutos palustris*.

HOLLYHOCK. Old-fashioned hardy herbaceous perennials, hollyhocks are stately and easy to grow. They add strong, vertical accents and majesty to summer flower beds and borders. Belonging to the genus *Alcea*, of the mallow family MALVACEAE, and formerly included in *Althaea*, the com-

mon hollyhock is *A. rosea*. It originated in China, presumably in cultivation because it has never been found wild. Possibly it is of hybrid derivation. The fig-leaved hollyhock (*A. ficifolia*) is a Siberian species of which varieties in several flower colors are available. It has deeply-lobed leaves and responds to the same care as the common hollyhock.

Modern seed strains of the common hollyhock are superior to those available fifty years or more ago and give plants remarkably true to type. Their flower colors range from white and creamy-whites through a wide range of yellows and pinks to reds, deep crimsons, and nearly black-maroons. There are single- and double-flowered sorts.

Hollyhocks are perennials, of which an early-flowering strain of the common sort that blooms the first year and is called annual is offered. It is not nearly as fine as the older and more familiar perennial kinds. For the best results, in most localities the most satisfactory procedure is to treat the perennials as biennials, to sow seeds one year to give plants to flower the next and then be discarded. The great advantage of this is that plants so grown are free of the troublesome fungus disease called rust, which mars the foliage, reduces vigor, and adversely affects the quality of the flowers.

Soil for hollyhocks is most satisfactory if fertile, deep, and well-drained. Ground capable of growing good vegetables and a variety of common herbaceous perennials will give good results. Full sun for all or most of each day is required.

Sow seeds in a cold frame or nicely prepared bed outdoors in May. As soon as the young plants have their second pair of leaves and are big enough to handle with ease transplant them to a nursery bed 9 or 10 inches apart in rows about 1½ feet asunder. Aftercare consists of keeping the beds free of weeds and watering during dry spells.

Hollyhock: (a) Single-flowered

(b) Double-flowered

Transplant to their blooming locations in early fall or spring. If the soil is at all clayey or inclined to be wet, spring transplanting is to be preferred. Set the plants in groups of three or more in beds and borders or near houses, barns, or other buildings. They are also effective along fence rows and as backgrounds and temporary screens. Distances of 1½ to 2 feet between individuals will be about right.

Perennial hollyhocks can be bloomed the first summer from seeds sown in January in a greenhouse in a temperature of 60 to 65°F. The young plants are transplanted 2½ to 3 inches apart in flats and are grown indoors where the night temperature is 50 to 55°F, that by day several degrees higher, until all danger of frost is over. Then they are planted where they are to bloom. The flower spikes of plants handled in this way come much later and are shorter and less massive than those of two-year or older specimens.

If you grow hollyhocks as perennials, that is, if you keep the plants after their first blooming for flowering in future years, be ever alert for the appearance of small, rusty-yellow spots on the undersides of the leaves. These signal the presence of rust disease. Because the causal fungus lives in the interior tissues and the spots represent only its spore-bearing parts, spraying or dusting is not effective. About all you can do is to pick off and burn affected leaves at the first appearance of the spots.

Annual hollyhocks are raised by sowing outdoors as early in spring as the ground is workable or, in the north, better by sowing indoors some six weeks earlier, transplanting to flats, and growing the plants in a sunny location where the night temperature is 50 to 55°F, daytime temperatures five to ten degrees higher, until they are ready for setting in the garden after all danger of frost is passed.

HOLMSKIOLDIA (Holms-kióldia). The genus *Holmskioldia*, of the vervain family VERBENACEAE, has an interesting natural distribution. One species is native at low elevations in the Himalayas, three in East Africa, and one in Madagascar. Only the first seems to be cultivated in America, although at least some of the others, such as the pink-flowered African *H. tettensis* (syn. *H. speciosa*), have promise as ornamentals. The name of the group commemorates the Danish botanist Theodor Holmskiold, who died in 1794.

Holmskioldias are shrubs with opposite, undivided leaves, and axillary or terminal clusters or racemes of flowers that have conspicuous, sometimes obscurely-five-lobed, saucer-like, colored calyxes that earn for the species in Africa the common name cups and saucers and for the more commonly cultivated Himalayan *H. sanguinea* the vernacular designation Chinese

Holmskioldia sanguinea

hat plant. This because the shape of its calyx suggests the traditional headgear worn by Chinese peasants. The corollas have curved tubes and five short lobes (petals). There are four stamens in pairs of two different lengths. Like the style, they protrude somewhat beyond the throat of the bloom. The fleshy, four-lobed fruits are included in the persistent calyx.

The Chinese hat plant (**H. sanguinea**) is a loose-growing, evergreen shrub from 10 to 30 feet tall, with stalked, ovate leaves 2 to 4 inches long that may be toothed. The flowers have showy orange to brick-red calyxes shaped like shallow, inverted cones with indefinitely lobed margins, and are up to 1 inch across. The corollas are darker and have slender trumpet-shaped tubes about 1 inch long. The fruits are not over ⅓ inch long. In variety *H. s. citrina* the flowers are yellow.

Garden and Landscape Uses and Cultivation. The Chinese hat plant needs humid tropical or warm subtropical conditions. It grows without difficulty in fertile, moderately moist soil. The only routine care needed is occasional pruning to keep it shapely. In greenhouses it thrives where the minimum night temperature is about 60°F. Repotting is done in late winter or spring, and at that same time the plants may be pruned to shape. Light shade in summer may be beneficial, but too much inhibits flowering. Propagation is easy by cuttings inserted in a greenhouse propagating bench provided with mild bottom heat, and by seeds.

HOLOCHLAMYS (Holo-chlámys). The genus *Holochlamys* of the arum family ARACEAE is endemic to New Guinea and consists of five species. Its name, from the Greek *holos*, whole or entire, and *chlamys*, a mantle or garment, probably alludes to the spathes.

Botanically closely related to *Spathiphyllum*, the sorts of this genus are stemless, evergreen, herbaceous perennials with short rhizomes and oblong to oblong-lanceolate leaves. As is usual in the arum family, the tiny flowers of *Holochlamys* are crowded on a spikelike organ called a spadix at the base of which is a bract called a spathe. They are bisexual. The fruits are berries.

From 1½ to 2 feet tall, **H. guineensis** has thinnish, long-stalked, *Maranta*-like leaves

Holochlamys guineensis

with plain green, oblong-elliptic blades 8 inches to 1 foot long, about 3 inches wide, and with many fairly prominent veins angling outward and upward from the midrib. The spadix, atop a short stalk, cylindrical and about 2 inches long, is almost completely encircled by a spathe of approximately the same length.

Garden and Landscape Uses and Cultivation. Unlike many spathiphyllums, the species described above makes no significant floral display. It must be appreciated only for its abundant and handsome foliage. It responds to environments and care appropriate for spathiphyllums.

HOLODISCUS (Holo-díscus) — Rock-Spirea or Ocean Spray or Cream Bush. Belonging to the rose family ROSACEAE and ranging in the wild from western North America to Colombia, *Holodiscus* comprises eight species of deciduous shrubs. Its name derives from the Greek *holos*, entire, and *diskos*, a disk, and refers to the lobeless, disklike structures to which the flower parts are attached.

Holodiscuses have alternate, toothed, usually pubescent leaves and terminal panicles, or more rarely racemes, of small white to creamy flowers with five each sepals and petals, fifteen to twenty stamens, and five pistils. Technically achenes, the tiny fruits are hairy and are enclosed within the calyxes.

The rock-spirea, ocean spray, cream bush, or Idaho plume (*H. discolor* syn. *Spiraea discolor*) is best known horticulturally. It is a spreading shrub, usually 6 to 12, but sometimes 20 feet in height, with slender, arching branches and yellowish, hairy young shoots. Its ovate to ovate-oblong, stalked leaves, 1¾ to 4 inches long, have along each side three or four deep teeth that are again toothed. Their upper surfaces are green and sparingly-hairy or hairless; beneath, the leaves are hairy. The numerous tiny blooms, pinkish in bud, open to creamy-yellow and fade to light brown. In graceful, airy panicles 3 to 10 inches long, they provide an attractive display for several summer weeks. Variety *H. d. franciscanus* has leaves under 1¾ inches long, with two to four teeth, again toothed, on each side. In *H. d. delnortensis* the leaves are under 1¾ inches long, gray-pubescent above, and their teeth are not again toothed. Variety *H. d. ariaefolius* has leaves with grayish-green instead of white pubescence on their undersides. Closely related *H. dumosus* (syn. *Spiraea dumosa*), a native from Wyoming to Utah, New Mexico, and Mexico, up to 15 feet tall, has obovate, coarsely-toothed leaves, pubescent above and white-hairy on their lower surfaces, and up to 2 inches long, and narrow flower panicles 2 to 8 inches long.

Two other species sometimes cultivated are *H. boursieri* and *H. microphyllus*. Native from California to Nevada, *H. boursieri* is

about 3 feet tall and compact. It has usually angled, hairy young shoots, and roundish or ovate, very short-stalked leaves not over 1¾ inches long, almost as wide as long, and with three or four shallow teeth on each side. The leaves are hairy above, and gray-hairy or white-hairy and often glandular on their undersides. The pubescent panicles of bloom are up to 3½ inches long and as wide. Indigenous from California to Colorado and Arizona, *H. microphyllus* is spreading, from 8 inches to 6 feet in height, and has reddish, glandular to long-pubescent young shoots, and very short-stalked, obovate to spatula-shaped leaves finely-toothed only above their middles, ¼ to ¾ inch long, lightly to densely hairy above, and hairy beneath. The flower panicles are ½ inch to 1¼ inches long and as wide. Variety *H. m. sericeus* is more densely-hairy, variety *H. m. glabrescens* less so, than the species.

Garden and Landscape Uses. The kinds described are hardy in southern New England. They succeed in ordinary soil in sun or part-day shade and are satisfactory for massing in beds and borders and informally. The most commonly grown kinds, *H. discolor* and *H. d. ariaefolius*, have much the aspect of, and the same landscape values as *Sorbaria arborea*, from which they are easily distinguished by their leaves not being pinnate and mountain-ashlike. They present graceful, foamy, highly attractive displays of bloom in early summer and when in bloom associate well with other garden flowers. Because of this and their heights, they can be used effectively at the rears of perennial borders.

Cultivation. No special care is needed. Pruning, consisting of removing old, worn-out, and crowded shoots and shortening others, is done as soon as flowering is through. Propagation is easily achieved by seeds and by cuttings.

HOLOPTELEA (Holo-ptèlea). This genus of two species, native to tropical Asia and Africa, belongs to the elm family ULMACEAE. From elms *Holoptelea* differs in its leaves not being toothed and in technical characteristics of its flowers and fruits. The name comes from the Greek *holos*, whole, and *ptelea*, the elm. It probably alludes to the fruits.

Holopteleas are deciduous trees with alternate, two-ranked leaves. Their flowers, not showy, and in clusters from the leaf axils, have four- or eight-parted perianths, four or eight stamens, and a two-branched style. The fruits, technically samaras, are flat with an encircling, thin, more or less circular wing.

A small to medium-sized tree, *H. integrifolia*, of India, has downy shoots and broad-elliptic to ovate or obovate leaves 3 to 6 inches long by 1½ to 2½ inches wide. The greenish-purple flowers, which appear while the tree is leafless, are not quite

¼ inch across. About 1 inch in diameter, the fruits have a wing with a cleft at the apex. When crushed, twigs and bark give off an offensive odor.

Garden and Landscape Uses and Cultivation. This is occasionally planted for ornament in the subtropics and tropics. Little is reported about its cultural needs. Presumably it succeeds in ordinary soils and locations. Propagation is by seed.

HOLTTUMARA. This name is given to trigeneric orchid hybrids the parents of which include *Arachnis*, *Renanthera*, and *Vanda*.

HOLY. As part of common plant names the word holy belongs in these: holy basil (*Ocimum sanctum*), holy-clover (*Onobrychis viciaefolia*), Holy Ghost flower (*Peristeria elata*), and holy-thistle (*Cnicus benedictus* and *Silybum marianum*).

HOMALANTHUS (Homal-ánthus) — Queensland-Poplar. One of the thirty-five species of this genus of the spurge family EUPHORBIACEAE is planted in California and other warm-temperate, subtropical, and tropical regions for ornament. The group is native to Malaya, Ceylon, Australia, and islands of the Pacific. It is closely related to *Sapium*. Its name, derived from the Greek *homalos*, smooth, and *anthos*, a flower, alludes to the blooms.

Homalanthuses are milky-juiced trees and shrubs with undivided, lobeless and toothless, long-stalked, leaves. Their inconspicuous flowers are unisexual and in panicles, with the basal blooms nearly always female, and those above male. They are without petals. The males have one or two sepals and five to fifty stamens. The fruits are fleshy capsules.

The Queensland-poplar (*Homalanthus populifolius*) is a spreading tree up to 40 feet tall, but often not more than one-half that height. It has bluish-green, evergreen or semievergreen foliage. The leaves are triangular-ovate and 3 to 6 inches long. In California, following cold spells, nearly all drop. Before they fall they turn yellow and then bright red. The new leaves are coppery. The flowers, in drooping, terminal, catkin-like panicles about 4 inches long, are green, and without ornamental significance. The females produce fruits less than ½ inch wide, each with two black seeds. These self-sow and give rise to numerous spontaneous seedlings.

Garden and Landscape Uses and Cultivation. Although a little ungainly and slightly weedy, this species has uses where a small evergreen or near-evergreen tree suffices. It is very free of pests and diseases, and fairly drought-resistant. Ordinary soils and situations are satisfactory. Propagation is easy by seed.

HOMALOCEPHALA (Homalo-céphala) — Horse Crippler or Manco Caballo or

Devil's Head. The only species of *Homalocephala*, of the cactus family CACTACEAE, is by conservative botanists included in *Echinocactus*. Those who segregate it do so on the bases of small differences in the fruits. The name, alluding to the flattened plant body, is derived from the Greek *homalos*, level, and *kephale*, a head.

The sinister colloquial names horse crippler, manco caballo, and devil's head are applied to **H. texensis** (syn. *Echinocactus texensis*). They allude to the brutal, tough, viciously spiny character of this native of Texas, Oklahoma, New Mexico, and Mexico. Often half buried in the earth this cactus, which is indeed capable of crippling a running horse that steps upon it, is understandably abhorred by ranchers. From 2 to 8 inches high and flat-topped or domed, the horse crippler sometimes is 1 foot in diameter. Its stems usually solitary, if injured they are likely to develop a cluster of small branches. They have usually thirteen or fourteen, less commonly up to twenty-seven prominent ribs. The center of the plant is conspicuously woolly. The very strong, rigid spines are in clusters of six or seven straight or curved radials from under ½ inch to 2 inches long and one even stouter, straight, curved, or sometimes slightly hooked central spine from ¾ inch to 2¾ inches long. The varicolored,

bell-shaped, slightly fragrant blooms are 1 inch to 2¼ inches long and wide.

Garden Uses and Cultivation. This is for cactus fanciers. It is easy to grow outdoors in warm dry climates and in greenhouses either in full sun or with slight shade. For more information see Cactuses.

HOMALOCLADIUM (Homaloclà-dium)—Ribbon Bush or Centipede Plant. An evergreen shrub of peculiar aspect, this native of New Caledonia is the only representative of *Homalocladium*, of the buckwheat family POLYGONACEAE. Its generic name, of obvious application, comes from the Greek *homalus*, flat, and *klados*, a branch.

The ribbon bush or centipede plant (**H. platycladum** syn. *Muehlenbeckia platyclada*) is commonly 2 to 4 feet tall, but in the tropics sometimes attains heights of 10 to 12 feet. Hairless, it has many erect, jointed, flat, ribbon-like, longitudinally-ribbed branched stems that look like and serve the purposes of leaves. True leaves, lance- or arrow-shaped and ½ inch to 2½ inches long, are often absent or may be present only on young stems. The small whitish or greenish, unisexual flowers clustered at the joints along the edges of the branches are without decorative merit. They have a five-parted perianth, usually eight sta-

mens, one style, and a three-lobed stigma. The fruits are red or purple-red and berrylike.

Garden Uses and Cultivation. Grown chiefly as a curiosity, outdoors in warm climates where little or no frost is experienced and in greenhouses, this plant has considerable ornamental value. Succeeding in any fertile, porous soil kept fairly moist, it withstands some shade. In greenhouses a minimum temperature of 55 to 60°F is satisfactory. The atmosphere should be fairly humid. Propagation is chiefly by division and cuttings.

HOMALOMENA (Homalo-mèna). This is a genus of tropical, evergreen foliage plants of about 140 species, chiefly natives of Asia and Malaysia, but with a few in South America. It belongs to the arum family ARACEAE. The name may come from the Greek *homalos*, flat, and *nema*, a thread, in allusion to the stamens. It is sometimes spelled *Homalonema*.

Homalomenas are similar in aspect to dieffenbachias, but are without aboveground stems or have only short ones. The American species, at one time segregated as *Curmeria*, differ from those of the Old World in having more distinctly tubular spathes more or less narrowed near their middles and in their leafstalks and sometimes blades of the leaves being in some kinds hairy. Old World homalomenas are never hairy and have less obviously tubular spathes.

The leaves of homalomenas are prevailingly heart- to arrow-shaped, with stalks in most species longer, but in some shorter, than the blades. The inflorescences or "flowers," as they are usually termed, consist of a spadix (spike) studded with tiny flowers. From the base of the spadix grows a usually greenish, persistent spathe (leaf-like or petal-like bract), open above, but with its lower part enveloping the spadix. The flowers on the lower one-half of the spadix, not separated by a constricted barren portion of spadix from the male flowers above, are females. They have pistils with spherical ovaries and stalkless stigmas. The male flowers that form the upper one-half of the spadix have two to four, rarely six, stamens. The fruits are blackish-brown, many-seeded berries.

Only two American homalomenas have hairless foliage, *Homalomena wallisii* and *H. roezlii*. The most commonly cultivated and handsomest species, **H. wallisii** much resembles a low dieffenbachia. Native to Colombia, it has leathery, broadly-oblong-elliptic, spreading or somewhat recurved leaves with blades about 5 inches long. They are beautifully marbled with creamy-white or silvery-gray-green and have stalks much shorter than the blades. Variety *H. w.* 'Mauro' is even more abundantly variegated with gray to pale chartreuse-green. Introduced to cultivation from

Homalocladium platycladum

Homalomena sulcata

Homalomena pygmaea

Colombia prior to 1874, **H. roezlii** was subsequently lost and not available to gardeners until after its rediscovery in Costa Rica in 1957. Since then it has been found in Panama. It is a short, densely-foliaged plant with ovate, elliptic, or oblongish, thickish, but not rigid leaves with stalks slightly shorter than the blades. The latter are variegated with irregular patches of green paler than the main body of the leaf.

Other American species are H. crinipes (syn. H. wendlandii), of Costa Rica and Panama, and H. picturata, of Colombia. Robust **H. crinipes** has reddish-margined, dark green, arrow- to heart-arrow-shaped leaves with pale mid-veins. Their blades, up to 10 inches long by two-thirds as broad, are pubescent on their undersides, at least on the veins. The leafstalks, up to 10 inches in length, and the flower stalks are densely clothed with short hairs. Very lovely **H. picturata** is small and has ovate-heart-shaped, dark green leaves with rounded basal lobes. They are boldly marked down their centers with a broad band of silvery-white.

Among Old World species **H. rubescens**, native from Sikkim to Java, is noteworthy. This develops a thick above-ground stem 3 or 4 inches long, and reddish-green, reddish-veined leaves, with slender stalks longer than their up to 1-foot-long, broadly-heart-shaped blades. The spathes are red. From it **H. cordata**, of the Celebes Islands and neighboring islands, differs in having larger, longer-stalked leaves with smaller, green blades. Distinctly narrower, slender-stalked, bronzy-green leaves with blades up to 5 inches long are borne by much smaller, low-growing **H. sulcata**, of Borneo. Native of New Guinea, **H. novaguineensis** has leaves with stalks nearly as long as the oblong-lanceolate to oblong blades, which are up to 5 inches in length by 2 inches wide. They have about twelve

main veins on each side of the midrib. The spathes are about 1 inch long. In cultivation often misidentified as H. humilis, variable **H. pygmaea**, of Malaysia, Indonesia, and the Philippine Islands, has short-stalked, dark green, narrow- to broad-elliptic-lanceolate leaves with wavy blades 2 to 6 inches long, purplish on their undersides. The spathes are yellowish-green to green.

Garden and Landscape Uses and Cultivation. These are as for dieffenbachias.

HOMERIA (Ho-mèria)—Cape-Tulip or Tulp. Among the many beautiful bulb plants native to South Africa homerias rank highly. They are members of the iris family IRIDACEAE and in the wild are found only in southern Africa, where they are called tulp and Cape-tulip, names also sometimes used for Moraea. The name Homeria is derived from the Greek homereo, I meet together. It alludes to the stalks of the stamens being united into a tube that surrounds the style. There are nearly forty species.

Homerias have underground food storage organs called corms. These differ from true bulbs in being solid instead of consisting of concentric layers like onions or of overlapping scales like lily bulbs. The very few basal leaves of homerias are long and slender, those above are shorter and clasp the stems with their bases. The flowers are in loose, fairly ample clusters. Individuals last for only one day, but several to many are open at once, and a succession is maintained for a fairly extended period. The perianth, tubeless or nearly so, is of six petals (properly tepals) that at first are curved upward to form a cupped bloom, but later spread or become recurved. The inner three are narrower than to nearly as broad as the others. There are three stamens. The slender style has three

more or less flattened, bilobed branches, each usually with two small crests. The fruits are capsules. Some species of Homeria are poisonous to livestock. Because of this H. breyniana, which has become naturalized in Australia, is in that country accounted a pest.

One of the best known species, **H. breyniana** (syn. H. collina) is 1½ to 2 feet tall. It has a branched or branchless stem, and two to four long, channeled, almost whip-like, arching leaves up to ½ inch wide, the lowermost originating well up from the bottom of the stem and up to 2 feet long. The upper leaves are shorter. The sweetly fragrant blooms, usually salmon-pink to yellow, but sometimes creamy-white or red, may be 2¼ inches across. A variant with soft coral-pink blooms with a lanceolate blotch of lemon-yellow in the center of the lower one-half of each petal is distinguished as H. b. aurantiaca (syn. H. collina aurantiaca). Up to 2½ feet tall, **H. ochroleuca** has three or four leaves 2 to 3 feet long and branched stems with 2- to 2½-inch-wide, ill-scented flowers, their

Homeria breyniana aurantiaca

Homeria ochroleuca

Homeria lilacina

petals golden-yellow suffused with orange toward their bases or salmon-pink and yellow.

Most fascinating of cultivated homerias, **H. elegans** has 2-inch-wide blooms, basically bright yellow, but variously, attractively patterned or variegated with orange or green. Clear lilac flowers about 1½ inches in diameter are borne at the ends of slender stems by **H. lilacina,** which is up to 1 foot tall and has slender, arching leaves. The blooms do not open until early afternoon, and close at dusk.

Garden and Landscape Uses and Cultivation. Except that their short duration makes the blooms not practicable as cut flowers, homerias have much the same uses as ixias, and respond to the same conditions and care. For the best effects, the bulbs, especially those of *H. lilacina,* which should be spaced about 2 inches apart, should be set quite closely together.

HOMOGLOSSUM (Homo-glóssum). Of the twenty species constituting this South African genus only one is generally available to gardeners. The group belongs in the iris family IRIDACEAE and like so many of its South African kin has deciduous foliage and underground storage organs called corms. These differ from bulbs in being solid throughout instead of consisting of concentric layers like onions or of overlapping scales like the bulbs of lilies. The genus *Homoglossum* is related to *Freesia, Ixia,* and *Sparaxis* and at one time was included in *Antholyza.* Its name derives from the Greek *omoios,* similar, and *glossa,* a tongue, and alludes to the shape and color of the petals of some kinds.

Homoglossums have few usually linear leaves and branchless flower stems with loose spikes of one to about eight asymmetrical blooms. The flowers have six nearly equal perianth segments (petals) and three stamens. The slender style has three branches flattened at their tips. The fruits are capsules containing flattened, winged seeds.

Called red Afrikaner in South Africa, **H. priori** (syn. *Antholyza priori*) has stems 1¼ to 2 feet tall, and four or five leaves with stem-sheathing bases. The flower spikes have one to four blooms, scarlet or with scarlet upper petals and the lower ones yellow streaked with scarlet. The perianth tube is 1½ inches long, the pointed petals about 1 inch long with the uppermost slightly longer and wider than the others.

The most commonly cultivated kind, **H. salteri** (syn. *H. priori salteri*) has stems up to 2 feet tall and a few slender, stem-

Homoglossum salteri

sheathing leaves. In spikes of one, two, or perhaps sometimes more, the watsonia-like flowers are rich brick-red with yellowish throats. They are 2 inches long and wide and have dark anthers.

Garden and Landscape Uses and Cultivation. The uses and cultivation needs of homoglossums are identical with those of *Watsonia* except that it is usual to plant the corms closer together than those of taller-growing watsonias. For indoor cultivation as many as seven or eight corms can be comfortably accommodated in a 6-inch pot or pan (shallow pot).

HOMOGYNE (Homó-gyne). The mountains of central Europe have many much better plants to offer than these rather squalid-flowered relatives of coltsfoot (*Tussilago*). Nevertheless every once in a while enthusiastic collectors of mountain floras introduce one or other of the three species of this woodland clan into their gardens. It belongs to the daisy family COMPOSITAE and bears a name derived from the Greek *homos,* similar, and *gyne,* female, that refers to the likeness of the male and female florets.

From *Tussilago* these plants differ in having smaller, more densely-woolly, evergreen or deciduous leaves and somewhat dingy white to purple flower heads usually without ray florets.

About 6 inches tall, **H. alpina** has lobeless, toothed, roundish to kidney-shaped leaves 1 inch to 3 inches across and sparsely-hairy on their undersides. Similar, but with the lower leaf surfaces silvery hairy, is **H. discolor.** From both **H. sylvestris** differs in having lobed leaves.

Garden Uses and Cultivation. A not too prominent place in moistish soil in partial shade is right for these hardy herbaceous perennials. Their foliage is not unattractive. They increase readily by division and by seed.

HONCKENYA. See Clappertonia.

HONESTY is *Lunaria annua.*

HONEY. This word forms part of the common names of these plants: honey bell (*Hermannia verticillata*), honey bush (*Melianthus*), and honey-locust (*Gleditsia triacanthos*).

HONEYDEW. This is a sweet, sticky, fluid secretion of aphids, scales, and some other insects, produced most abundantly in hot, dry weather. From heavily infested trees it may drip in quantities sufficient to stain and mar garden furniture, automobiles, and other objects beneath. It coats foliage with a tacky glaze over the surface of which a black growth of sooty mold fungus is likely to spread. The fungus harms the plant by shutting off light.

Certain ants and some other insects that esteem honeydew as food are often numerous where it is to be found. Some ants "domesticate" aphids and "milk" them for their honeydew. Such insects are a nuisance to gardeners because they distribute aphids by carrying them from plant to plant. Control of honeydew production is dependent upon preventing or cleaning up infestations of the insects that produce it.

HONEYSUCKLE. See Lonicera. In Australia lambertias are called honeysuckles. The name Australian-honeysuckle is applied to *Banksia.* Other plants than *Lonicera* with common names of which the word honeysuckle is part are bush-honeysuckle (*Diervilla*), Cape-honeysuckle (*Tecomaria capensis*), desert-honeysuckle (*Anisacanthus thurberi*), French-honeysuckle (*Hedysarum coronarium*), Himalaya-honeysuckle (*Leycesteria formosa*), Jamaica-honeysuckle (*Passiflora laurifolia*), New-Zealand-honeysuckle (*Knightia excelsa*), and swamp-honeysuckle (*Rhododendron viscosum*).

HONEYWORT. See Cerinthe.

HOODIA (Hoòd-ia). Belonging in the milkweed family ASCLEPIADACEAE, the genus *Hoodia* is endemic to South Africa. It consists of a group of 10 species first named in 1830 and by the author of the genus dedicated to "Mr. Hood, a cultivator of succulent plants." Of the gentleman so honored no more is known. The genus is related to *Stapelia.*

Hoodias are leafless perennials with branched, fleshy, cylindrical stems with many spine- or bristle-toothed, lumpy, longitudinal ridges. From their upper parts, arising in the grooves between the angles, the flowers develop, solitary or more often in groups of up to five. The blooms are remarkable. For the size of the plant they are large and showy. They have five sepals and a flat, saucer-like or cup-shaped corolla, circular in outline, scarcely or shallowly four- or five-lobed, each lobe ending in an awl-shaped, short point. The five stamens form a column from which arises a double corona or crown, the outer of five spreading, concave, notched or cleft lobes, the inner of the same number of linear lobes.

Among kinds sometimes found in choice collections of succulents are the following. *H. bainii,* with clustered, twelve- to fifteen-ridged stems up to 8 inches tall by 1 inch to 1½ inches thick, has hairless, scarcely-lobed flowers, solitary or paired, bowl-shaped, and 2½ to 3 inches across. They are light yellow or light buff-yellow, sometimes tinged with pink or delicate purple. The corona is black. The slender fruits are 4 to 5 inches long. *H. burkei,* up to over 1 foot tall, resembles *H. gordonii* in growth. Its nearly flat flowers, however, are without minute red pimples at their centers. They much resemble those of *H. bainii,* but are shallower and more conspicuously notched. *H. currori* has stems 1½ to 2 feet tall by 2 to 2½ inches thick, with thirteen or more ridges. From 3½ to 5 inches in diameter, its saucer-shaped flowers are scarcely lobed. Brownish and with long, violet hairs on their insides, they are brownish-red with darker spots and hairless without. This is the most beautiful hairy-flowered species, possibly the finest of the genus. *H. gordonii,* exceptionally fine, has stems 1 foot to 1½ feet tall by about 2 inches in diameter, with erect branches. The spines are brown. The slightly saucer-shaped blooms, pale purple with greenish-yellow stripes, and 3 to 4 inches across, are shallowly-five-lobed. Their centers are thickly sprinkled with minute red protrusions. The corona is purple-black. The spindle-shaped hairless seed pods are 2½ to 3 inches long.

Garden Uses and Cultivation. Hoodias are quite amazing additions to collections of choice succulents, interesting in growth and thrilling to bloom. This because, unless conditions are quite to their liking, they are distinctly shy about producing flowers. One more generous in this respect than most is *H. gordonii.* They need the same general conditions and care as stapelias, generous watering from spring to fall and much drier soil in winter. Because individuals tend not to live for many years in cultivation a need for rather frequent propagation is indicated. Fresh seeds germinate readily. Cuttings may be rooted, but not too surely. Grafting on seedling hoodias or on tubers of *Ceropegia woodii* is recommended. For more information see Succulents.

HOODIOPSIS (Hoodi-ópsis). The only species of *Hoodiopsis* is a rare succulent relative of *Stapelia* first discovered about 1932. Native of South West Africa, it belongs to the milkweed family ASCLEPIADACEAE, or according to those who take narrower views of family limits, to the stapelia family STAPELIACEAE. The name, calling attention of the similarity of this plant to *Hoodia,* is derived from the name of that genus and the Greek *opsis,* resembling.

Forming clumps up to 1 foot across of erect, fleshy, leafless, purple-streaked, green stems 4½ to 7 inches long by a little more than 1 inch thick, and branched from their bases, *H. triebneri* has solitary, starfish-shaped blooms. The stems have seven to nine longitudinal, lumpy ridges, each prominent lump ending in a sharp, horny spine. Short-stalked and arising from the middles of the stems, the flowers have five sepals, a nearly flat five-lobed corolla 4 to 4½ inches across, on its inside deep wine-red and covered with tiny pimples, outside green or pale pink. The lobes, pointed and with recurved edges, extend about half-way to the center of the bloom. The corona or small crown in the center of the flower is double and purple-black. The fruits are paired podlike follicles. From *Hoodia* this plant differs in its stems having fewer ridges and in its flowers being much more deeply lobed.

Garden Uses and Cultivation. These are as for *Stapelia.* For more information see Stapelia and Succulents.

HOOF AND HORN MEAL. This is a slow-acting organic fertilizer akin to bonemeal in its action. See Fertilizers.

HOOP-PINE is *Araucaria cunninghamii.*

HOP or HOPS. See Humulus. The word hop also appears in the common names of these plants: hop bush (*Dodonaea*), hop-hornbeam (*Ostrya*), and hop-tree (*Ptelea trifoliata*).

HORDEUM (Hórd-eum)—Barley, Squirrel Tail Grass. The most important species of this genus, barley (*Hordeum vulgare*), is of direct concern to the agriculturist rather than to the gardener. It is an annual of Old World origin. Hordeums are annuals and perennials of the grass family GRAMINEAE. They are natives of temperate regions and number about twenty species. The generic name is the ancient Latin one for barley. In *Hordeum* the one- or rarely two-flowered spikelets are in threes, often only the central spikelet of each triad is fertile.

The only kind cultivated as a decorative is the squirrel tail grass (*H. jubatum*). This native of North America, Europe, and Asia is sometimes a troublesome weed. It is abundant throughout much of North America, occurring in dry soils in fields, meadows, and roadsides. A tufted bien-

Hordeum jubatum

nial or perennial, the squirrel tail grass is usually grown as an annual. It attains a height of 1 foot to 2 feet and has slender branchless stems, erect, but sometimes with horizontal bases. The leaves are flat, short, narrow, and rough. The gracefully arching, feathery, silvery-green or brownish flower spikes, 2 to 4 inches long, are slender except for their bristles, which spread; 1 inch to 3 inches long, they produce the "squirrel tail" effect.

Garden Uses. The squirrel tail grass is an attractive ornamental for the fronts of flower borders and for cutting. When dried it is useful for winter bouquets. Drying is accomplished by tying the cut stems in small bundles and hanging them upside down in a dry, shady, airy place. For this purpose cutting should be done just before the flower buds are fully mature and they should remain suspended until they are completely dry.

Cultivation. Any ordinary well-drained, dryish soil in full sun is agreeable to this grass. Seeds are sown in early spring where the plants are to remain and the resulting seedlings thinned to about 1 foot apart.

HOREHOUND is *Marrubium vulgare*.

HORKELIA (Hork-èlia). The German physiologist J. Horkel is commemorated by the name of this genus of the rose family ROSACEAE. It consists of seventeen or perhaps more species of perennial herbaceous plants of western North America. From closely related *Potentilla* it differs in having only ten instead of commonly twenty or more stamens, and these have usually dilated stalks.

Horkelias have woody rootstocks and pinnate leaves with crowded, cleft or toothed leaflets. White or sometimes cream or pink, the flowers, in clusters or panicles, have five each sepals and petals, the latter rounded to spatula-shaped, and numerous pistils. The seedlike fruits are achenes.

Inhabiting dry slopes at elevations above 2,000 feet in California and Baja California, *Horkelia truncata* is glandular-pubescent, and 9 inches to 2 feet tall. Its leaves, up to 5 inches in length, have one to three pairs of stalkless leaflets up to 1¼ inches long, and a larger, terminal, stalked one. They are oblongish, and at their apexes usually toothed. The flowers are in somewhat crowded clusters. They are about ½ inch wide and have white petals. Endemic to California, *H. frondosa,* erect to decumbent, 1 foot to 2½ feet in height, and glandular-pubescent has leaves with ovate to oblong, toothed to almost lobed leaflets 1 inch to 2½ inches long. The flowers have petals ¼ inch long or scarcely longer.

Garden Uses and Cultivation. In California *H. truncata* is occasionally included in collections of native plants. It may be grown in dryish soils in full sun there and in similar climatic regions. It is of minor horticultural importance. Propagation is by seed.

HORMINUM (Hormì-num). One species of the mountains of southern Europe is the only member of *Horminum*, of the mint family LABIATAE. Its name is derived from the Greek *horminon*, a kind of sage (*Salvia*), in allusion to some similarity.

A low, herbaceous perennial, *H. pyrenaicum* has clusters of rosettes of stalked, ovate to broad-elliptic, blunt-toothed, mostly basal leaves up to 2½ inches long, and erect flower spikes 3 to 10 inches tall. The spikes, except for a few bracts, are essentially leafless. The nodding, tubular, deeply two-lipped flowers, the upper lip scarcely toothed, the lower three-lobed, are arranged chiefly along one side of the stalk. Dark purple or purple-blue and rather dowdy, they have a deeply two-lipped calyx, four stamens, and one style. The fruits are four seedlike nutlets. The blooming season is late spring and early summer. There is a white-flowered variety named *H. p. album*.

Garden Uses and Cultivation. Hardy and adaptable for rock gardens, but of no great merit, this plant is easily raised from seed and by division in early fall or spring. It requires well-drained, medium-fertile soil that preferably contains lime and does not lie wet for long periods, and full sun.

Horminum pyrenaicum

Horminum pyrenaicum album

HORMONES. These are substances that in extremely minute amounts profoundly affect growth. Akin to vitamins and in plants not always clearly distinguished from them, hormones are usually differentiated because they are migratory within the plant and their effects in the main are confined to particular parts of the organism rather than influencing its entirety. An embracing term for hormones and vitamins is growth-regulating substances.

Green plants, that is, those that contain chlorophyll, manufacture hormones, not in specialized glands as do animals, but in tissues that have other functions.

There are a good number of plant hormones. Perhaps the most familiar and important are the auxins, the chief of which is indole-3-acetic acid, and the gibberellins, of which the best known is gibberellic acid.

Horticultural employments of hormones, usually of synthetic origin and closely similar to indole-3-acetic acid and other natural ones, but for the purposes for which they are used often more effective, include stimulating root development on cuttings and, by initiating abnormal, uncontrolled growth, killing weeds.

Other uses of such substances are to cause the formation of fruits without previous pollination of the flowers, to prevent fruits from dropping prematurely, to delay blooming, and to encourage flowering and fruiting.

When using hormones the almost unbelievable small amounts needed must be measured very accurately. In practice gardeners purchase commercial preparations containing hormones and use them according to the manufacturer's directions.

HORNBEAM. See Carpinus. The hop-hornbeam is *Ostrya virginiana*.

HORNED-POPPY. See Glaucium.

HORNED-RAMPION. See Phyteuma.

HORNWORMS. The larvae of hawk, hummingbird, or sphinx moths are big caterpillars called hornworms, recognizable by the prominent horn that projects from their rears. Best known as garden pests are the tobacco and tomato hornworms. Much alike, these feed hungrily on plants of the solanum family including eggplants, nicotianas, peppers, potatoes, and tomatoes. Hand picking usually gives satisfactory control and so do preparations of the bacterium *Bacillus thuringensis*. Do not disturb hornworms that have spindle-shaped white objects sticking to their bodies. These are eggs of a type of parasitic wasp. If left, larvae will hatch from the eggs, kill the hornworm by feeding on it, then change to new wasps that in turn will lay eggs on other hornworms.

HORNWORT is *Ceratophyllum demersum*.

HORRIDOCACTUS (Horrido-cáctus). More than twenty species of this Chilean genus have been described, but few are cultivated. Belonging to the cactus family CACTACEAE, they are closely related to *Neoporteria*. The name comes from the Latin *horridus*, bristly or prickly, and cactus.

Small, spherical, and with well-defined ribs and many spines the kinds of *Horridocactus* bear their funnel-shaped, day-opening blooms from near the tops of the plant bodies. The fruits are small.

Dark green and up to 8 inches in diameter, **H. tuberisulcatus** (syn. *Malacocarpus tuberisulcatus*) has solitary or clustered plant bodies with fourteen to twenty markedly notched ribs. The spine clusters are of ten to twelve straight, awl-shaped, yellowish-brown radials about ½ inch long and four or five stout centrals of the same hue and about twice as long. The red-striped, yellowish flowers are 1 inch to 2 inches in diameter. This plant is sometimes listed as *Pyrrhocactus tuberisulcatus*.

Garden Uses and Cultivation. Horridocactuses appeal to collectors and grow satisfactorily under conditions that suit most desert cactuses. They appreciate fairly fertile soil, moderate watering, and when young, light shade from the strongest sun. For further information see Cactuses.

HORSE. The word horse appears as part of the common names of these plants: horse-balm (*Collinsonia*), horse-bean (*Canavalia ensiformis*, *Parkinsonia aculeata*, and *Vicia faba*), horse-chestnut (*Aesculus*), horse crippler (*Homalocephala*), horse-gentian (*Triosteum*), horse-mint (*Monarda*), horse-parsley (*Smyrnium olusatrum*), horse-radish (*Armoracia rusticana*), horse-radish-tree (*Moringa oleifera*), and horse sugar (*Symplocos tinctoria*).

HORSE-RADISH. Cultivated for its thick, pungent roots, used as a popular condiment, horse-radish (*Armoracia rusticana*) belongs in the mustard family CRUCIFERAE. A robust, deciduous, herbaceous perennial, native to Europe, it is well established as a naturalized immigrant in parts of North America. In some places it has become a troublesome weed. A few plants are usually sufficient to meet the needs of the home gardener.

Horse-radish succeeds best in temperate regions. Except at high altitudes it does not flourish in the south. Not finicky about soil so long as it is not shallow, infertile, or dry, it grows best in deep, rich loam, well supplied with organic matter and fairly moist. A sunny location is best. To grow straight, thick, tender roots most suitable for the kitchen, plant horse-radish each year as an annual crop. Old plants yield comparatively small, ill-shaped, stringy, tough roots.

Before planting, spade, rototill, or plow the soil deeply, turning under or mixing

Horse-radish

in generous amounts of well-decayed compost or other organic material, but not fresh or partly fresh manure, and a dressing of a complete garden fertilizer. Rankish manure used before planting is likely to cause excessive top growth and forked roots. Heavy manuring for a previous crop such as cabbage, broccoli, beans, or peas leaves residuary benefits for the horse-radish.

Plant root cuttings (sets) in early spring 1 foot to 2 feet apart in rows 2½ feet apart, setting them vertically or at an angle of about 45 degrees. If angled, make sure that the tops point along the rows in the same direction. This facilitates cultivating. Cover the sets with 2 to 3 inches of soil.

Planting root cuttings of horse-radish

Subsequent care includes sufficiently frequent shallow surface cultivations or mulching to keep down weeds. In dry weather deep soakings with water at about weekly intervals are highly beneficial. To assure a high grade crop, lift and strip the roots twice, first when the biggest leaves are 8 to 10 inches long and again about six weeks later. To lift and strip, carefully remove the soil from around the upper ends of the main roots. Raise their top ends and remove all leafy shoots except the main one. Rub off all small roots from the crown and sides of the main root, leaving the branch roots undisturbed only at its lower end. Push the root back to its former position and fill soil around it.

Harvesting is not done until late autumn. This because the roots make their greatest growth in the latter part of summer and fall. They may be lifted and stored or left in the ground and, weather permitting, dug as needed. Take care not to injure the roots at digging time. After lifting, trim off all lateral roots. Save those 8 inches long or longer, of a thickness between that of a pencil and a man's small finger, as planting stock for the next spring. Cut them squarely across at the top, sloping at the bottom (this to more easily distinguish which end to set up at planting time), tie them in small bundles, and keep them until spring under conditions appropriate for the usable crop. Horse-radish can be stored in outdoor pits or trenches lined with straw or dry leaves, the roots piled and covered with 6 inches of the same material and then with a layer of the same thickness of soil. Alternatively, they can be stored in a root cellar or barn kept as cool as possible but above 32°F. The roots must not be exposed to light; otherwise they become green.

Two varieties are grown, common horse-radish, which has broad, crinkled leaves and 'Bohemian', with narrower, smooth leaves. The latter is somewhat inferior in quality, but more resistant to some diseases. Diseases include root rots and, in some areas a virus called curly top, spread by leaf hoppers. The most serious pest is the horse-radish flea beetle. For information about the control of such troubles consult your Cooperative Extension Agent. Do not plant diseased stock and do not plant on land that has borne a diseased crop.

HORSEBRIER is *Smilax rotundifolia*.

HORSESHOE-VETCH. See Hippocrepis.

HORSETAIL. See Equisetum. The horsetail tree is *Casuarina equisetifolia*.

HORTENSIA. This is sometimes used as a common name for varieties of *Hydrangea macrophylla*.

HORTICULTURAL SOCIETIES. Groups of people with a common interest in horticulture, or one or more of its aspects, organized as societies to meet and exchange ideas and information and to promote interest in their fields have long existed. They are to be found in all advanced countries. The most influential is the Royal Horticultural Society of England, which in 1980 had almost 90,000 members. It was founded in 1804.

American societies of this kind are particularly numerous. They are of two groups, those that entertain a catholic interest in horticulture and those that have a concentrated interest in a particular plant or group of plants or in special modes of cultivation or uses of plants. These last are the more numerous.

Certain of these societies maintain permanent quarters with professional staffs and in some cases extensive libraries and other facilities. All hold meetings and many issue bulletins or other publications. Most conduct flower shows. Some operate with amateur staffs elected from their membership and are without permanent headquarters, the address of the President, Secretary, and other officials changing from time to time as individuals succeed each other in these offices.

In the listing here, addresses are given for some of the societies believed to be most permanently located. For addresses of others write to The American Horticultural Society, the Massachusetts Horticultural Society, or the Pennsylvania Horticultural Society, the addresses of which are given under the listing of general interest societies presented below, or to a State Agricultural Experiment Station or a major botanic garden.

Special interest horticultural societies include among others: African Violet Society of America, Inc., American Begonia Society, Inc., American Fern Society, American Gourd Society, American Hemerocallis Society, American Penstemon Society, American Peony Society, American Rhododendron Society, American Rock Garden Society, American Rose Society, Bonsai Clubs International, Bonsai Society of Texas, Bromeliad Society, Cactus and Succulent Society of America, Inc., California National Fuchsia Society, Cymbidium Society of America, Inc., Dwarf Iris Society, Epiphyllum Society of America, International Geranium Society, Inc., Los Angeles International Fern Society, National Chrysanthemum Society, Inc., National Oleander Society, North American Gladiolus Council, North American Lily Society, Inc., Northern Nut Growers Association, Inc., Saintpaulia International, Society for Louisiana Irises, The American Bonsai Society, The American Boxwood Society, The American Camellia Society, The American Daffodil Society, Inc., The American Dahlia Society, Inc., The American Fuchsia Society, The American Gesneria Society, The American Gloxinia Society, and Gesneriad Society, Inc., The American Hibiscus Society, The American Hosta Society, The American Iris Society, The American Magnolia Society, The American Orchid Society, The American Plant Life Society with The American Amaryllis Society, The American Primrose Society, The Bonsai Society of Greater New York, Inc., The Greater New York Orchid Society, Inc., The Herb Society of America, the Holly Society of America, Inc., The Indoor Light Gardening Society of America, Inc., and The Palm Society.

General interest societies are: Albany Horticultural Society, Albany, New York; The American Horticultural Society, Mount Vernon, Virginia; Arkansas State Horticultural Society, Fayetteville; Blue Mountain Horticultural Society, Oregon; California Horticultural Society, Golden Gate Park, San Francisco; Chicago Horticultural Society and Botanic Garden, Illinois; Connecticut Horticultural Society; Edmonton Horticultural Society, Alberta, Canada; Florida State Horticultural Society; Garden Center of Greater Cleveland, 11030 East Boulevard, Cleveland, Ohio; Garden State Horticultural Association, New Brunswick, New Jersey; Georgia Horticultural Society, Inc.; Hampton Roads Horticultural Society, Virginia; Horticultural Society of Maryland; Horticultural Society of New York; Idaho State Horticultural Society; Illinois State Horticultural Society; Indiana Horticultural Society, Lafayette; Iowa State Horticultural Society, State House, Des Moines; Kansas State Horticultural Society; Kentucky State Horticultural Society; Louisiana Horticulture Society; Manitoba Horticultural Association, Canada; Massachusetts Horticultural Society, 300 Massachusetts Avenue, Boston; Michigan Horticultural Society, Dearborn; Minnesota State Horticultural Society, St. Paul; Missouri State Horticultural Society; Nebraska Horticultural Society; New Brunswick Horticultural Society, Canada; Newfoundland Horticultural Society, Canada; New Hampshire Horticultural Society; New Jersey State Horticultural Society, New Brunswick; New York State Horticultural Society; Norfolk Botanical Garden Society, Airport Road, Norfolk, Virginia; North Dakota State Horticultural Society, Fargo; North Shore Horticultural Society of Long Island, New York; Ohio State Horticultural Society; Ontario Horticultural Association, Toronto, Canada; Oregon Horticultural Society, Corvallis; Pennsylvania Horticultural Society, Inc., Independence National Historical Park, 325 Walnut Street, Philadelphia; Queens Botanical Garden Society, Inc., New York; Rio Grande Valley Horticultural Society, Texas; South Dakota State Horticultural Society; Vermont State Horticultural Society, Burlington; Washington State Horticultural Association; Western Colorado Horticultural Society; West Virginia State Horticultural Society; and Worcester County Horticultural Society, Massachusetts.

HORTICULTURE. Basically horticulture is synonymous with gardening. The word derives from the Latin *hortus*, a garden and *cultura*, culture. Horticulture differs from agriculture or farming, although there are areas, such as truck gardening, fruit growing, and nursery production, where the two may overlap to the extent that the distinction is not always clear, in being carried out more intensively and usually on a smaller scale and generally in having concern with purely ornamental plantings as well as the production of food and some other crop plants.

Horticulture is an art, craft, and science. Sometimes the term is used to indicate a greater emphasis on understanding the scientific principles of plant growing, and gardening is employed to describe the art and craft procedures, but the distinction is not valid and it is better to recognize the words as interchangeable.

The chief subdivisions of horticulture are floriculture (the growing of flowers), olericulture (the growing of vegetables), pomology (fruit culture), and ornamental horticulture (the cultivation of trees, shrubs, lawns, etc., for decorative purposes). Landscape gardening and landscape architecture belong with ornamental horticulture, and floriculture is sometimes included with it.

HOSACKIA. See Lotus.

HOSE-IN-HOSE. Tubular and bell-shaped flowers that seem to have two corollas, one inside the other, are called hose-in-hose blooms. Often this form results from the calyx being colored and corolla-like. Examples of hose-in-hose flowers are varieties of canterbury bells, Kurume azaleas, and polyanthus primroses.

HOST or HOST PLANT. A living plant on which other plants, insects, mites, or other organisms live and depend wholly or partly upon for food is called a host. Most plants may serve as hosts to a few or many pests and diseases. Mistletoes and dodders live on host plants.

HOSTA (Hò-sta) — Plantain-Lily, Funkia. Any one familiar with the weed called broad-leaved plantain (*Plantago major*) and lilies will see reason for the common name of this group. Its foliage, at least that of some species, is somewhat plantain-like and its blooms are mildly like lilies. The name *Hosta* commemorates the Austrian physician and botanist Nicolaus Thomas Host, who died in 1834. At one time the genus was named *Funkia* and this is still sometimes used as a common name. In the group are many handsome and useful garden plants that thrive under a wide variety of conditions, with little trouble.

The genus *Hosta*, of the lily family LILI-ACEAE, is found in the wild only in eastern Asia. The number of species it contains is not well established but may be taken to be about forty, the vast majority natives of Japan. In addition, there are numerous hybrids and horticultural varieties. Despite various studies the proper disposition of this botanically complex group is still much clouded, and probably will re-

main so. The chaos, in part at least, is because cultivated plants include species collected in the wild, plants that came to Europe from Japanese and Chinese gardens a century or more ago and have not been found in the wild, and kinds raised in Europe and more recently in America from those brought from the Orient.

Hostas are hardy, deciduous herbaceous perennials with heavy, short-branched rootstocks from which descend thick, cord-like roots, and from which sprout stalked, often slightly fleshy, undivided, strongly-veined leaves and branchless, flowering stalks. The main leaves are all basal; the flowering stalks have only small, sometimes leaflike bracts. Individual blooms are short-stalked and hang downward or are horizontal when fully open. They usually have long perianth tubes with expanded throats, and six nearly erect or spreading perianth lobes (petals). There are six curved stamens as long or slightly longer than the perianth and a slender style tipped with a small, usually protruding, stigma. The fruits are capsules.

The most beautiful flowers are those of *H. plantaginea* (syn. *Funkia subcordata*). They are also the largest. Pure waxy white, deliciously fragrant, and 4 to 6 inches long by 2 to 3 inches across, they resemble the trumpets of true lilies. They are carried horizontally and open in the evening and close about dusk the following day. This easily identifiable native of China, long cultivated in Japan, blooms in August. It has stout rhizomes and forms

2-foot-high, broad mounds of glossy, heart-shaped, yellowish-green leaves with blades 1 foot long by two-thirds as wide, with eight or nine pairs of lateral veins. Up to 2½ feet tall, the flowering stalks have each a single leaflike bract, more rarely two to four, below the blooms, which are in crowded terminal racemes. Each bloom has one, or more usually two unequal-sized, green bracts at its junction with the main stalk. Variety *H. p. grandiflora* (syn. *H. grandiflora*) has longer leaves and longer, narrower flowers.

Sometimes called seersucker plant *H. sieboldii* (syns. *H. albomarginata*, *H. lancifolia albomarginata*), of Japan, in bloom is 2 to 3 feet tall. It has leaves with elliptic-lanceolate, elliptic, or elliptic-ovate blades up to 6 inches long, with four to six veins on either side of the midrib, and with a narrow marginal band of white or yellowish-white. The flowers funnel-shaped, in erect racemes of up to thirty, are 1½ to 2 inches long and violet with darker streaks. Their anthers are pale yellow. Variety *H. s. alba* has plain green leaves and white flowers.

American-raised *H.* 'Honeybells', a hybrid between *H. plantaginea* and *H. sieboldii*, blooms in August. Like those of its first-mentioned parent its flowers are fragrant. Individuals open in the morning and close about twenty-four hours later. This variety has green leaves nearly 1 foot long and somewhat more than one-half as broad, with about ten pairs of veins. The white flowers, 2 inches long by 1½ inches wide and marked with violet lines, are in

Hosta plantaginea

Hosta sieboldiana

racemes of up to sixty on stalks that have two leaflike bracts and may attain a height of 4 feet.

A noble species distinguished by its handsome foliage, **H. sieboldiana** (syn. *H. glauca*) as known in gardens is always gray- or bluish-green because of a light coating of wax that rubs off readily, but in the wild in Japan green- as well as glaucous-leaved plants occur. The spreading leaves, elliptic to ovate-elliptic, have blades up to 1¼ feet in length by 1 foot wide and are paler beneath than on their upper sides. There are twelve to fourteen veins on each side of the midrib. The flowering stalks of the typical species are from as long to up to twice the length of the leaves, and up to 2 feet tall; those of *H. s. hypophylla* are proportionately much shorter. They have lanceolate, spreading, greenish, purplish, or white bracts 1 inch to 2¼ inches long. The flowers of *H. sieboldiana*, which appear in late June and early July, are 2 inches long or slightly longer and white; those of *H. s. hypophylla* are pale lilac.

Conspicuous blue-glaucous foliage is characteristic of **H. tokudama** (syn. *Funkia sieboldiana condensata*), which is closely akin to *H. sieboldiana* and may be identical with the plant sometimes identified as *H. sieboldiana fortunei* (not to be confused with the group of garden hybrids named *H. fortunei*). This kind has leaves with erect stalks and spreading, broadly-heart-shaped, short-pointed, wrinkled blades, mostly turned upward at their rims and with fourteen pairs of lateral veins. As long or slightly longer than the leaves, the crowded, short, one-sided flower racemes together with their stalks are 1 foot to 1½ feet long. The blooms, white to pale purple, come in June or July and are about 1¾ inches long. This species, commonly cultivated in Japan, is reported to be native there as are varieties of it with leaves variously variegated with pale green.

The complex of varieties that constitute **H. fortunei**, of gardens, is probably of hybrid origin with *H. sieboldiana* very likely one parent. These plants are quite different from *H. sieboldiana fortunei* (which may be identical with *H. tokudama*). Vigorous and with flowering stalks much taller than the foliage and up to 2 feet high or higher, they have leaves with ovate blades up to about 5 inches long with eight to ten veins on each side of the midrib and somewhat glaucous undersides. The pale-lilac to violet, funnel-shaped flowers, displayed in late spring and early summer, have purplish anthers and are about 1½ inches long. Varieties include *H. f. aurea*, with leaves of thinnish texture, at first yellow, becoming light green later; *H. f. aureomaculata* (syn. *H. f. albopicta*), which has thin leaves that when young are predominantly yellowish or yellowish-white edged with a narrow band of green and that commonly become green throughout in the summer. The sort grown as *H. f. marginata-alba* (syn. *H. f. albomarginata*), which has leaves with blades up to 1 foot long broadly edged with white, is probably *H. crispula*.

The plant once named *H. fortunei gigantea* is impressively large **H. elata** (syn. *H. montana*). Native to Japan, it blooms in June and July on stalks, many raised well above the foliage, although some may not exceed it. The flowers are white to pale purple, in loose racemes of about forty blooms, with each bloom about 2 inches long by 1¼ inches wide. The glossy, deep green leaves, with paler undersides, are narrowly-ovate to heart-shaped and have eight to thirteen pairs of side veins.

The narrow-leaved plantain-lily (**H. lancifolia** syns. *H. japonica*, *Funkia lanceolata*), of Japan, has leaves with ovate-lanceolate blades 5 to 7 inches long by under one-half as broad and with four to six veins from each side of the midrib. The masses of foliage, about 1½ feet high, are topped in late summer by flowering stalks 2 to 2½ feet tall carrying fifteen to thirty, well-spaced, often whitish-streaked, violet, bell-shaped blooms 1½ to 2 inches long and about 1 inch wide.

Hosta fortunei

Hosta lancifolia

Hosta lancifolia (flowers)

veins. Up to 3 or 4 feet tall, the flowering stalks have two to five leaflike bracts and in July carry about thirty bell-shaped, white blooms flushed and lined with violet. The flowers are 2½ inches long.

Native of China and common in cultivation, **H. ventricosa** (syns. *H. coerulea, H. ovata*) forms broad clumps of ample foliage. Its leaves have channelled stalks and spreading, broadly-ovate or heart-shaped blades up to 8 inches across, slightly lustrous above, glossy beneath, and often with a little twist at their tips, dark green on both sides, and with seven to nine

Hosta ventricosa

Each flowering stalk has two to five green bracts. Variety *H. l. variegata* has leaves variegated with white.

Probably of hybrid origin, **H. undulata** (syn. *Funkia undulata*) is often sold as *H. variegata*. Neither it nor its varieties produce seeds. Its wavy-edged, ovate leaves, with blades 5 inches long by one-half as broad, have about ten pairs of veins and are distinguished by their broad white centers and marginal areas of two shades of green, the deeper color along the edges

of the leaf. About 2 inches long and light purple, the blooms are about ten together on stalks 2 feet tall. This blooms in July. Variety *H. u. univittata* has smaller, less wavy leaves with narrower white centers. Its leaves plain green, *H. u. erromena* (syn. *H. erromena*) is more robust than *H. undulata*. It may have originated as a sport of *H. u. univittata*, which sometimes produces tufts of green foliage. The leaves of *H. u. erromena* are about 8 inches by 5 inches and have about ten pairs of lateral

pairs of side veins. Up to 3 feet tall and lifting the blooms much above the foliage, the flowering stalks are sturdy and carry a long raceme of flowers, dark violet-purple with darker stripes. The flowers are 1½ to 2 inches long. Very noticeably and abruptly the corolla tubes broaden in their upper parts into bell-shaped portions and erect lobes (petals).

Hosta undulata

Hosta undulata univittata

Hosta decorata

Hosta decorata normalis

Kinds with white-margined leaves, in addition to *H. sieboldii* and *H. fortunei marginata-alba*, previously discussed, are *H. decorata* and *H. crispula*. The leaves of **H. decorata** are long-stalked, blunt-elliptic, dark green, and up to 7 inches long by 4 inches wide. They have five or six lateral veins on each side of the midrib. Their undersides are paler than their upper surfaces and the leaves have clear, irregular white margins. Rising well above the 1-foot-tall foliage, to a height of 2 feet, the flowering stalks have about twenty-four violet blooms 2 inches long by three-quarters as wide, which are displayed in August. The flowers have corolla tubes slender below and broadening abruptly into a bell-shaped portion. An all-green-leaved variety (that genetically is probably the species) is *H. d. normalis*. This occurs wild in Japan and the variegated-leaved kind sometimes produces shoots that revert to

Hosta crispula

it. Vigorous **H. crispula** has wavy-edged, gradually tapered, dark green leaves, dull above and lustrous on their undersides, and with irregular, pure white margins broader than those of *H. decorata*. Its leaf blades are 8 to 10 inches long by 4½ to 6 inches wide. They have seven to nine pairs of side veins. The flower stalks, 2 to 3 feet tall or sometimes taller, have up to forty funnel-shaped blooms 1¾ inches long by 1 inch wide, white flushed with purple. This flowers in June and July.

Minature-leaved plantain-lilies include *H. gracillima*, *H. minor*, *H. nakaiana*, *H. venusta*, *H. tardiflora*, and *H. tortifrons*. Spreading, stalked, lanceolate to ovate-lanceolate leaves 1 inch to 2½ inches in length by up to ¾ inch wide, with three or four pairs of veins and flat or crisped edges characterize **H. gracillima**. Its slender flowering stalks, 8 to 10 inches tall, carry about ten, light purple blooms 1 inch to 1¼ inches long, distantly-spaced along one side of the stalk. A native of Korea and perhaps Japan, imperfectly known **H. minor** has broad-ovate to roundish leaves, and on stalks much longer than the leaves, purplish to white flowers up to 2¼ inches long. Japanese **H. nakaiana** has long-stalked, pointed-oblong-ovate leaves with blades up to 3 inches long and with five to seven pairs of veins on each side of the midrib. The purple flowers, on stalks up to 1½ feet tall, are bell-shaped and 1½ to 2 inches long. Ovate or ovate-elliptic, stalked leaves with blades under 2 inches long and not an inch wide and angled upward are characteristic of **H. venusta**. They have three or four pairs of veins. The flowers, borne in summer, are pale purple and 1 inch long or rather longer. They are on

Hosta nakaiana

stalks about 8 inches tall. Flowering in September and October, **H. tardiflora** (syns. *H. sparsa*, *H. lancifolia tardiflora*) is a compact plant with deep green, glossy leaves, with blades 4 to 6 inches long by 1½ to 2½ inches wide, that have five to seven veins on each side of the midrib. About 1½ feet tall, the flowering stalks have two leaflike bracts and crowded racemes of about twenty-four pale violet to whitish blooms 1½ inches long and wide. Known only as a cultivated plant, **H. tortifrons** is very much like *H. tardiflora*, but its leaves are smaller, shorter, and wavy.

Garden and Landscape Uses. Like many natives of eastern Asia, hostas adapt themselves splendidly to cultivation in many parts of North America. Because of this, their very real merits are sometimes overlooked by gardeners who affect to be

Hosta tardiflora

Hostas as groundcover in light woodland

wearied by, or even to despise, the commonplace. Yet, like Lincoln's common man, hostas must be loved, or at least appreciated, otherwise they would be less plentiful. And there are good reasons for holding them in high regard. They not only are easy to grow and propagate, but can be used to produce quite striking effects in gardens and other landscapes. Few hardy plants have such bold foliage. Their flowers supply additional dividends; those of some kinds are indeed lovely.

Once planted, plantain-lilies are likely to live for decades with little care and without transplanting. They appreciate partial shade, succeeding better where strong sun is moderated by a light overhead canopy of foliage or by shade from buildings than in the open, although they will stand full sun if the ground is fairly moist. Hostas are among the comparatively few garden plants that bloom in summer in shade. They show to especially good advantage in informal and semiformal landscapes and are excellent for watersides where the soil is not boggy. The minature-leaved kinds are especially appropriate in rock gardens.

Cultivation. Planting is done in early fall, or in spring before new leaves unfold. Spacing is adjusted to the vigor and needs of particular species and varieties and is likely to be in the range of from 1 foot to 2 feet between individuals. If smallish divisions or plants are set out they may take two or three seasons to become sufficiently established and of sizes to do themselves full justice. The least happy, and unfortunately all too frequent, way of displaying them is in ribbon edgings along paths and borders. This can be especially atrocious if one of the variegated-leaved

kinds is chosen. Plantain-lilies are not choosy about soils, but appreciate those that contain abundant organic matter and do not lack moisture. Propagation is very easy by division in early spring or fall, and seeds germinate readily. Self-sown seedlings sometimes appear.

For forcing in greenhouses as an attractive foliage plant variegated *H. undulata* is excellent. Plants are potted in fall in 5- or 6-inch containers. These are buried to their rims in a bed of sand, peat moss, or similar material in a cold frame or outdoors. From January to March they are brought indoors and watered to keep the soil always moist. In a temperature of 55 to 65°F they soon start growing and develop new, beautiful, fresh-looking foliage. It is well to keep forced hostas standing in saucers filled with water. After they have served as indoor

ornamentals they may be planted in the garden where they soon recover and become permanently established.

HOTBEDS. A hotbed is simply a garden frame containing a bed of soil or other material warmed from below. Its chief use is to gain a start on the season by raising earlier than could be done without extra heat young plants for setting outdoors. Kinds that may with advantage be had in this way include cabbages, cauliflowers, onions, asters, dahlias, salvias, snapdragons, stocks, and many others. Also in hotbeds early crops of lettuce, radishes, and other quick-growing plants can be grown to harvesting size, and cuttings can be rooted.

Traditionally, hotbeds were warmed by setting the frames on thick, compacted beds of fermenting strawy horse manure

An electric-heated hotbed; cables in place ready for being covered with soil

or manure mixed with leaves. Because of the scarcity of such "makings" and the very considerable labor involved that method is now rarely used.

Electric heating cables and hot water pipes are now the commonest means of warming the beds. They are positioned in gridiron pattern on the floor of the frame and covered with 5 to 7 inches of soil in which the seeds are sown, or sand and peat moss or perlite in which to root cuttings. Because of their comparative low cost and ease of installation and operation electric hotbeds are generally best suited to the needs of amateurs. Thermostatically controlled units are available from dealers in garden supplies. They are commonly installed with the wires spaced about 1 foot apart with possibly an additional line about 6 inches from the main grid run near the interior walls of the frame to counteract the colder conditions that prevail there. Management of hotbeds is as for heated frames. See Garden Frames.

HOTCAPS. This is a generic term for small tentlike devices of paper or plastic used to protect young plants from cold winds and late frosts. A proprietary brand named Hotkaps is perhaps best known.

HOTHOUSE. Sometimes used as the equivalent of greenhouse, hothouse most correctly refers to a greenhouse in which conditions suitable for the cultivation of

Hotcaps protecting young tomato plants

tropical plants are maintained, where the minimum night temperature in winter is 60 to 65°F and the atmosphere is highly humid.

HOTTENTOT-FIG is *Carpobrotus edulis.*

HOTTENTOT'S BREAD is *Dioscorea elephantipes.*

HOTTONIA (Hot-tònia) — Water-Violet. Featherfoil. Belonging to the primrose family PRIMULACEAE and native in North America, Europe, and northern Asia, *Hottonia* consists of two species of aquatic plants. The name commemorates Peter Hotton, a Dutch physician and botanist, who died in 1709.

Hottonias are floating, branched herbaceous perennials with finely-divided, pinnate, submerged leaves scattered along the stems in whorls (circles of more than two) or crowded at the bases of clusters of hollow-flowering stalks. The white to lilac flowers are in spikelike racemes raised above the water. They have a five-toothed calyx, a corolla with a tubular base and five petals, five stamens, and one style. The fruits are many-seeded capsules. In fall the plants develop winter resting buds that sink to the bottom, there to remain until spring when they again surface.

Native of Europe and Asia pretty *H. palustris* is most commonly cultivated. This has branches 6 inches to 1 foot long from

which silvery roots descend into the water. In crowded tufts, its submersed, comblike leaves are 1 inch to 4 inches long. The yellow-eyed, white to lilac, primrose-like flowers, with wide-spreading petals, are in spikes consisting of whorls of four to eight blooms lifted 6 to 10 inches above the surface. Less showy in bloom, *H. inflata,* native in shallow waters from Maine to Indiana, Florida, Louisiana, and Texas, has submersed stems up to 1½ feet long, and feathery, oblong leaves. Its partly submersed flowering stalks are conspicuously, almost grotesquely swollen between their several joints. From each constriction comes a whorl of three to ten blooms with linear sepals and shorter, white petals.

Garden Uses and Cultivation. Hottonias are excellent oxygenators for shallow waters in which ornamental fish and other aquatic "livestock" are maintained and are interesting and attractive additions to collections of water plants and for use in aquariums. They are sometimes temperamental, however, and for reasons not always easy to account for, fail. Propagation is by division and by seed. When dividing be sure each piece taken to become a new plant has roots attached. Sow seeds, that have been kept moist, in mud in spring.

HOULLETIA (Houl-lètia). A rather varied dozen species, of the orchid family ORCHIDACEAE, belong here. In the wild restricted to Central and tropical South America, *Houlletia* bears a name commemorating Monsieur B. Houllet, of the Jardin des Plantes, Paris, France, who discovered the first known species *H. brocklehurstiana* near Rio de Janeiro. Houllet died in 1890.

Houlletias are epiphytes (tree-perchers) or sometimes rock-perchers, or they may be terrestrial and root into the ground. Mostly strong growers, they have one-leaved pseudobulbs. The ribbed leaves are stalked, leathery, and often large. The racemes of blooms spring from the bottoms of the pseudobulbs and are erect or strongly pendulous. They bear few to many attractively colored, fleshy blooms with somewhat similar, more or less spreading sepals and petals and a strangely formed lip that is divided into two parts by a slender waist and at its base narrows into a claw. In structure the flowers are quite like those of *Stanhopea,* but are much more symmetrical.

Handsome *H. odoratissima* has clusters of pseudobulbs 2 to 4 inches tall that become furrowed as they age. Its leaves have stalks up to 1 foot long or longer and pointed-elliptic blades 1½ to 2 feet long and approximately one-quarter as broad. The erect, stout-stalked racemes of blooms may attain heights of 1½ feet or more. The well-spaced, long-lasting, fragrant flowers are 3 inches or more in diameter. They come in summer. Except for the lip, which is marked with white, they are bright reddish-brown or chocolate-brown. The petals are considerably narrower than the sepals. The lower part of the large lip has two hornlike appendages that bend backward, the pointed-shield-shaped upper part of the lip has a pair of basal lobes extended as two short horns. This sort is native to Colombia and Panama. Similar, but with reddish-brown sepals and petals, streaked with yellow, and their lower parts usually spotted or suffused with blood-red, *H. brocklehurstiana* is a native of Brazil. The lips of its flowers are shorter than the sepals and petals, and are conspicuously strewn with black warts. Their lower portions are basically white, and the outer trowel-shaped part has yellowish to orange veining. The blooms are produced in summer.

The pseudobulbs of *H. lansbergii* are about 1 inch tall. The leaves are up to 1 foot long by one-third as broad, and elliptic. Two to four together on thick, drooping stems approximately 4 inches in length, the flowers are fragrant, waxy, and about 2½ inches long, but not as wide. They have darker-spotted, reddish-orange sepals and petals, the latter of a deeper hue than the former, and a white lip with its basal part cross-banded with red and its upper portion warted with violet-purple. The yellow column is marked with red. Its pseudobulbs about 3 inches long, *H. picta*, of Colombia, has elliptic-lanceolate leaves and six- to ten-flowered racemes of flowers up to 3½ inches wide. The blooms are cinnamon-brown, checkered with yellow toward the lower parts of the sepals and petals. Shorter than the petals, the lip is pale yellow barred with red-purple. Brazilian *H. vittata* has ovoid,

Houlletia vittata

ribbed pseudobulbs each with a large elliptic leaf. Its flowers, in erect or arching racemes and 2 to 2½ inches wide, have chocolate-brown sepals, petals narrowly margined with yellow, and a yellowish lip striped with chocolate-brown.

Garden Uses and Cultivation. These very desirable additions to collections of orchids do well in intermediate- to warm-temperate greenhouses, and may be grown without a well-marked period of annual rest, although some growers recommend one. *H. odoratissima, H. brocklehurstiana,* and *H. vittata* require the attention recommended for *Phaius.* The other sort described above is best accommodated in hanging baskets like *Stanhopea.* For more information see Orchids.

HOUND'S TONGUE. See Cynoglossum.

HOUSELEEK. See Sempervivum.

HOUSEPLANTS or INDOOR PLANTS. Houseplants or indoor plants, the terms are interchangeable yet neither satisfactorily describes the group it indicates for sorts included are grown not only in dwellings, but also in stores, offices, restaurants, schoolrooms, and other indoor locations, and many plants cultivated in greenhouses, which surely are indoors, do not belong to this category. To be acceptable as such, plants must generally be kinds able to accommodate permanently or at least for long periods to the usually less-than-ideal environments afforded by dwellings and similar places. Exceptions perhaps are plants sold by florists chiefly for the temporary decoration of homes and for use as gifts. For the care of these see Gift Plants.

The discussion that follows is a detailed consideration of most environmental needs of houseplants and of techniques of their care and management. Other aspects of houseplant cultivation including soils and soil substitutes, potting and repotting, and propagation are discussed fully under other entries in this Encyclopedia. Consult Potting Soils and Potting Mixes; Potting and Repotting; Air Layering; Cuttings, Propagation By; and Seeds, Propagation By.

If you want to grow houseplants you can. Perhaps not all the kinds you would like to have will thrive, but certainly some will. The varieties you can cultivate and the success you have will depend upon the locations you provide and the amount of intelligent care you give. The word "intelligent" is emphasized because mere care—even loving care—is not enough; unless it is based on an understanding of the plants' need it may do more harm than

Houseplants grouped effectively in windows: (a) Azaleas in a sunroom

(b) A variety of plants in a window with good light, no direct sun

(c) In a north-facing window: *Fatshedera, Rhoeo,* and *Syngonium*

(d) In a light, but not sunny window; *Echeveria,* African-violets, and *Syngonium*

(e) In a window with bright light, but no strong sun; African-violets, *Impatiens,Cryptanthus,* and a geranium

Houseplants grouped on stands including: (a) Pick-a-back (*Tolmiea*), *Syngonium,* begonias, and *Pteris* fern, appropriate for partial shade

good. Witnesses to this are the many plants that are killed each year by the common mistake of overwatering. The environmental conditions you can supply are of first importance. Give consideration to these in selecting kinds to grow and caring for them afterward.

Light is needed by all houseplants, but not all require the same amount. Bromeliads, palms, philodendrons, sansevierias, rex-cultorum begonias, and most foliage plants get along perfectly well in subdued light and usually respond unfavorably to strong sunshine. A few highly colored foliage plants, such as crotons, coleuses, and most gray-leaved plants, need full sun. Sun-lovers, too, are most cactuses, other succulents, and many flowering plants such as geraniums, abutilons, agapanthuses, and wax begonias. Between the extremes of the cactus that needs full sun and the maranta that thrives better without any direct sunshine are a variety of plants from which kinds can be chosen for all intermediate conditions.

When considering light requirements for your plants, bear in mind the following points. Many that need shade in summer prefer full sun in winter. Light in cities is often more subdued than country light because of smoke and dust particles in the air. Light indoors is much less intense than outdoors and rapidly diminishes as one retreats from the window. Curtains and draperies cut down light very markedly.

South-facing windows afford plants the maximum amount of light, north-facing windows the least. This holds true, of course, only if the light is unimpeded. A south window with a tree growing outside it or with a nearby wall facing it may let in less light than an unshadowed east, west,

(b) Begonias, African-violets, *Cyperus*, and *Spathiphyllum*, appropriate for partial shade

(c) Coleuses and geraniums, appropriate for sun

Combinations of two or more compatible kinds in the same container can be effective: (a) *Dracaena* and *Philodendron*

(b) *Dieffenbachia* and *Philodendron*

(c) Spider plant (*Chlorophytum*) and *Cissus*

(d) *Episcia* and maidenhair fern (*Adiantum*)

Hanging containers are attractive when suitably planted: (a) Spider plant (*Chlorophytum*)

(b) *Pandanus* and *Philodendron*

(c) Wandering Jew (*Tradescantia*)

(c) Corn-plant (*Dracaena*)

(f) *Sansevieria*

Plants that stand considerable shade include: (a) *Philodendron*

(d) Rubber plant (*Ficus*)

(g) *Spathiphyllum*

(b) *Aspidistra*

(e) Chinese evergreen (*Aglaeonema*)

Plants needing good light with shade from strong sun include: (a) Azaleas

(b) Cane begonias

(c) Rex-cultorum begonias

(d) Tuberous begonias

(e) Boston fern

(f) African-violets

(g) Gloxinias

Plants for sunny locations include: (a) Geraniums

(b) Scented geraniums

(g) *Oxalis*

(c) Panda plant (*Kalanchoe*)

(e) Burro's tail (*Sedum*)

(d) Coleuses

(f) Aloe

(h) Wax begonias

A "window greenhouse" is ideal for many kinds of houseplants

Artificial light can be used to supplement natural light

or north window. East and west windows are sunny enough for a great variety of plants.

Bay windows and corner windows are usually particularly good locations for plants because they receive light from more than one side. Sunrooms or solariums and sun porches, too, are lighter than ordinary rooms and hence are well suited for plant growth. The most difficult places in which to persuade plants to grow are locations away from windows in comparatively dark areas of the room, on mantel shelves for example. Only the toughest subjects, such as snake plants, aspidistras, fatshederas, and English ivy can be expected to live with so little light and even they may not succeed indefinitely. It may be necessary to discard and replace them from time to time or to arrange a rotation system whereby they stay two, three, or four weeks in the dark location and then are removed to a window where they remain for a like period.

Of one thing you must be careful, never move a plant from a dark location to a bright, sunny place directly. If you do it will react much as a person does who has been much indoors and then is exposed to strong sunshine. It will suffer from sunburn. In plants this manifests itself either

by scalded areas (which dry, turn brown, and die) appearing on the leaves wherever the maximum sun strikes them, or by an all-over yellowing of the foliage except where it is shaded by other leaves. To avoid this, shade the plants moved from dark locations to sunny ones by throwing a layer or two of cheesecloth over them or use some other way wherever the sun is bright. Do this for a week or two after making the move.

Often natural light can, with advantage, be supplemented by artificial illumination. Some plants, notably African violets, geraniums, and begonias, respond well to light from fluorescent and from incandescent bulbs if they are not so near that the heat from the latter is damaging. For more about this see Indoor Light Gardening.

Inadequate light is usually proclaimed by the plant producing pale anemic-looking leaves, that are smaller than normal. Their leafstalks and stems become weak and stretch toward the light. The distances between leaves on the stem increases and the whole plant takes on a lankier appearance. Plants that become "drawn" in this way are much more likely to become diseased than are sturdier specimens grown with ample illumination. This is particularly true of young seedlings. Damping-off

disease can wipe out great numbers of these in the space of a very few hours. Weakening and "drawing" of the seedlings because of poor light is one of the commonest predisposing conditions to damping-off infections.

Temperature needs vary with different kinds of plants. Some like considerable warmth, others need cooler conditions. The same plant may require different temperatures at different stages of its growth as do, for example, daffodils, hyacinths, and tulips, which thrive best if kept cool until plenty of roots have grown from their bulbs, and then respond to more heat.

Excessive temperatures produced artificially do more harm than the same temperatures resulting from sun heat. This is because artificial heating lowers the relative humidity of the air to where it is often quite difficult to compensate for, and because at the time of the year when the furnace is running, days are shorter and light intensities are lower than during the warmer season. Under these conditions plants naturally need to be kept cooler than during the summer.

As an illustration consider camellias. In summertime, out of doors they thrive where day temperatures of 80 to 90°F and higher are fairly common and where night temperatures do not drop much below daytime levels. Yet it is fatal to attempt to grow them in winter in a living room where the thermometer registers 70 to 72°F. The air is too dry and, for that time of year, the temperature too high. In winter indoor camellias need the shelter only of a light porch or similar place where the temperature is kept between 40 and 50°F and where the air is normally moist.

This matter of seasonal variation in the temperature needs of plants must be taken into account. It varies with different kinds. Those that are natives of low elevations in the tropics, such as dumb canes, snake plants, philodendrons, and the like, get along perfectly well with no marked change from season to season, but plants that have their natural homes in more northerly or more southerly latitudes or that come from high elevations in the tropics ordinarily need comparatively low temperatures during our fall and winter. Here belong azaleas, Norfolk-Island-pine, Kenilworth-ivy, English ivy, leopard plant, and asparagus-ferns.

The plants mentioned above are all evergreen. There are others that lose their leaves during a part of each year—some, including gloxinias, tuberous begonias, and amaryllises in winter, others such as poinsettias and calla-lilies in summer. When they are without foliage these plants rest. While resting they need to be kept fairly cool. Too high temperatures during the dormant season may cause shriveling of the bulbs, excite premature growth, and prevent the plants from blooming the following season.

All plants grow better when nights are cooler than days. That is how it is in nature, that is how it works best with cultivated specimens. A good general rule is to have the temperature at night five to ten degrees below that of normal days. On very sunny days a rise of fifteen degrees above normal is permissible for plants growing in direct sunshine.

Greenhouse men carefully adjust their day and night temperatures to suit the needs of their plants. In the home it is not easy to do this. We heat our houses to suit our own needs and comfort, the requirements of plants take second place. Yet much can be done.

In the first place study the different locations in the home. Some rooms are certainly cooler than others, and equally important, locations in the same room may vary tremendously in temperature. Positions close to radiators and other sources of dry heat are particularly distressing to plants.

But excessive heat is not all that you must guard against. Cold can be quite as

Chinese evergreen (*Aglaeonema*) damaged by near-freezing temperatures

harmful. Do not fool yourself because a thermometer hanging on an inside wall indicates a comfortable 70°F that a plant close to a window in the same room is living at that temperature. When it is cold outdoors the indoor temperature near the glass may be twenty degrees or more lower than in other parts of the room. The only sure way of learning just what temperatures prevail where your plants are or where you consider placing them is to put a thermometer there and watch it at different times of the day and night over a period. The results may surprise you.

No houseplants suffer from cold if the temperature does not drop below 60°F. A few, such as African violets, poinsettias, and florists' gardenias, show ill effects then, but a great many others grow better between 50 and 60°F than at higher temperatures. For most plants our homes are apt to be too warm rather than too cold

except in locations near windows in very cold weather. To prevent danger from this on cold nights, pull down the window shades and if necessary supplement this protection by slipping a few sheets of brown paper or newspaper between the glass and the plants. Alternatively move the plants away from the window to a warmer part of the room. Careful watering, pruning, and soil care are wasted if cold kills your plants.

Excessive heat, especially if accompanied by too much shade, causes plants to become spindly and weak and makes their stems lengthen unduly and the distances between the leaves on the stems become longer than usual. Low temperatures check growth, often cause a yellowing (or in the case of red-leaved plants, a blueing) of the foliage followed by dropping of the leaves beginning with those lowest on the stem.

Air is as necessary to the life of plants as it is to animals, but they do not need it in nearly such great volumes. It is not necessary that the air in rooms in which they grow be changed frequently. Plants will thrive for years in a nearly airtight terrarium or even in a large bottle. Do not open windows or otherwise ventilate merely to give your plants fresh air. Do so on mild days or if you want to reduce the indoor temperature or create sufficient circulation to dry soil or foliage that seems to remain wet too long after watering.

Plants resent drafts. Those with large, soft leaves, such as cinerarias, poinsettias and geraniums, quickly show ill effects by their foliage drooping, dropping off, or yellowing, but even such tough subjects as aspidistras and snake plants are harmed by being constantly exposed to air cur-

Protection from cold by: (a) Pulling the shade at night

(b) Placing newspaper between the plants and the glass

rents, although they may show no immediate effects. If long exposed they deteriorate and may eventually die. When choosing locations for your plants consider carefully whether or not they will be subject to drafts. Situations between doors or windows where cross currents are likely to occur are usually bad, so, too, are locations in empty fireplaces unless care is taken to close the flue while the plants are in position.

Of great importance is the relative humidity of the air. About this it is important to remember that relative humidity varies with changing temperatures. A volume of air, a roomful for instance, contains a certain amount of water vapor, enough, let us say, so when the temperature is 50°F the relative humidity is sixty per cent (a satisfactory level for many plants). Now if the temperature is raised to 70°F the roomful of air contains exactly the same *amount* of water vapor as before but its relative humidity is reduced to less than thirty per cent, a level far too low for the well being of all except desert plants. The only way to bring the relative humidity back to its previous level is to add water vapor to the air or to reduce the temperature.

During that period of the year when our homes are heated, we constantly draw in outside air and raise its temperature. Consequently we lower its relative humidity. That is one of the chief reasons why it is difficult to grow plants in houses. That is why many houseplants thrive all summer and then drop leaves and otherwise fail after the heat is turned on. That is why plants are more difficult to keep in good condition in overheated rooms than where more moderate temperatures are maintained.

Fortunately steps can be taken to humidify the indoor air, at least to a modest extent, if not throughout the entire room then at least in the vicinity of the plants. Let us see what can be done.

First, foliage as well as damp soil and pots gives off moisture; therefore if plants are grown together in groups—many in a window rather than a single specimen, for instance—the air in their immediate vicinity is likely to be moister. A little local climate, more humid than that of the rest of the room, is created. This condition can be accentuated by spraying the foliage on suitable occasions with a fine mist of clear water, wetting it quite thoroughly, but not drenching it.

Just which are suitable occasions? That depends somewhat on the plant. A few hairy-leaved kinds, such as African violets, gloxinias, and gynuras, resent having their leaves wetted. There are really no suitable occasions for spraying them. Other hairy-leaved and soft-leaved plants, such as primroses, begonias, and the pick-a-back plant, may be sprayed once or twice a day whenever you expect that the

moisture applied will dry within an hour or two. This means on the mornings and early afternoons of bright days when air circulation is good. It does not mean on dull days or so late in the day that it will be dark before the leaves are dry.

When spraying such plants as primroses, and pick-a-backs that have their leaves all arising from near the ground, be careful not to get too much water into the centers of the plants—otherwise rotting may result.

Plants with hard leathery foliage, such as palms, screw-pines, bromeliads, aspidistras, and dracaenas, as well as aroids and most other smooth-leaved plants, may be sprayed more freely and more frequently.

Two or three applications a day will ordinarily be beneficial, but even these plants will be better without spraying if the leaves are likely to remain wet for several hours.

An excellent method of adding to the moisture content of the air in the vicinity of your plants is to stand them on broad shallow trays filled with moss, gravel, perlite, or sand that is kept always wet. Evaporation from the trays will effectively moisten the air. Make the trays of zinc, copper, wood, plastic, or other suitable material. It is sufficient if they are about two inches deep and of any suitable length and width.

Terrariums are splendid devices. They make it possible to provide plants with atmospheres that have adequate relative humidity. Terrariums are containers—usually somewhat box-like—built largely of glass or transparent plastic. In effect they are little greenhouses that retain moist air about the plants grown in them. They are provided with adjustable means of ventilation so that the humidity can be controlled. Plants in them are grown either in pots or in a bed of soil or other rooting medium placed in the bottom of the terrarium.

These are some means by which you can increase the humidity about your plants. In addition, more general and decidedly beneficial humidification can be achieved by placing evaporating pans on all radiators and keeping them filled with water, and by making sure that humidifying devices attached to hot air furnaces are always operating satisfactorily. A reasonably humid air results in benefits to you as well as to your plants. You save heat because you feel comfortably warm at lower temperatures than you would in an arid atmosphere. And you probably will be less subject to at least some respiratory ailments.

One more point, do not overlook the fact that in almost every habitation there are rooms and positions in rooms that are naturally moister, and other rooms and positions in rooms that are naturally drier. The kitchen, because of its steaming kettles, pans, and pots, and the bathroom for equally obvious reasons are likely to be

somewhat humid. Locations near radiators and other sources of dry heat are disastrously arid. Consider these factors carefully when locating your plants.

Pollution of the air may cause distress to houseplants. One of the commonest causes of pollution is escaped gas from stoves and furnaces. Traces in the atmosphere too minute to smell may harm plants. Remember that it is *escaped* gas that causes trouble not *consumed* gas.

Heating by gas and cooking by gas are not harmful provided there are no leaks. Be sure that stoves and furnaces are in good order. Ignite jets immediately after they are turned on and be careful that pilot lights do not blow out. Be sure that flues are adequate to carry off incompletely burnt gases.

Common effects of gas poisoning are a rather rapid yellowing or dropping of foliage and a general unhappy appearance within a few hours of exposure. When gas is present African violets do not bloom and Christmas cherries drop their fruits (these happenings can, of course, be due also to other causes).

Two plants most sensitive to gas are tomatoes and carnations. Young plants of the former bend their leaves down sharply after twenty-four hours or less in air containing extremely dilute amounts of gas. Carnations, freshly cut and placed in water, curl their petals inward and "go to sleep" within a few hours. If you suspect gas poisoning set some carnations or potted tomato plants in your rooms as a test. Natural gas is much less harmful than gas manufactured from coal or oil. In any house where gas is burnt, be sure to ventilate the rooms as freely as possible consistent with maintaining comfortable temperatures, but above all have cooking and heating equipment checked occasionally to make sure that there are no leaks.

Plants best able to withstand small amounts of gas without noticeable harm include amaryllises, anthuriums, ardisias, *Begonia heracleifolia*, bromeliads, cactuses and succulents, *Campanula isophylla*, clivias, *Dracaena godseffiana*, *Dracaena sanderana*, English-ivy, gardenias, holly-fern, lantanas, maricas, *Nephthytis afzelii*, patience plants, philodendrons, pick-a-back plant, *Podocarpus neriifolia*, poinsettias, rubber plants, scindapsuses, screw-pines, *Selaginella brownii*, wandering Jews (*Tradescantia* and *Zebrina*), and wax plants (*Hoya*).

Pollution of the atmosphere near industrial plants and in cities is not uncommon. Damage to plants may be caused by the presence of small amounts of sulfur dioxide, hydrogen fluoride, hydrogen chloride, hydrogen sulfide, ammonia, chlorine, mercury vapor, and other gases, as well as by the presence of smog—that curious smoke or smoke-fog combination that is familiar to residents of the Los Angeles area and of some other parts of the country. Pollutions of these kinds may result in retarded growth, leaf drop, yellowing or bleaching of the foliage to an ivory color in patches at the tips or near the margins (or in some kinds the changing of similar patches to a brown or red color). If you live in a constantly polluted area you may find by experiment and observation which kinds are most tolerant to your particular atmosphere. If you are in an area that suffers from pollution only occasionally, as for instance when an unusual change of wind brings the fumes of an industrial plant in your direction or when an occasional smog lies heavy around you, be careful not to overwater, not to wet foliage at such times, and to keep temperatures as low as reasonably possible during the periods of affliction.

It is chiefly gases in the air that cause damage to plants, but accumulations of dust and grime on foliage may cause some harm, particularly by cutting down the amount of light the leaves receive. To remove grime sponge smooth-leaved sorts, such as rubber plants and dracaenas, with soap-sudsy water and rinse immediately with clear water. Most plants that cannot be conveniently sponged may be freed of dirt by washing them thoroughly with a fairly forceful jet of water from a hose or syringe. Plants that are injured by washing or syringing (as African violets may be) are unsuited for cultivation in places where the air contains much dirt. Dust may be removed from them by brushing each leaf with a soft-bristle brush.

Watering, poorly done, sounds the death knell for all too many houseplants. How often shall I water this or that plant is the question most asked of professionals by amateur plant growers. None is less susceptible of a stock answer. The great American horticulturist Dr. Liberty Hyde Bailey emphasized that plants should be watered only when they *need* it, not whenever they will stand it. This is first class advice. The trick is to know when they need watering.

First put aside all thoughts that plants should be watered at *regular* intervals, in the way that a dog is fed once or a husband thrice a day. Plants are not like that. They do not drink at stated times. They absorb moisture continuously.

Therefore, the soil should be always moist (except during the resting seasons of those plants that go completely dormant as do gloxinias, tuberous begonias, and amaryllises. But it should not be constantly saturated (soils of aquatic and bog plants, such as the umbrella plant, are exceptions). The soil for most plants should be always moist throughout, but not so wet that if it were squeezed water would run from it. When as wet as that it contains insufficient air for the well-being of the roots and they rot. The soil is soured. To keep the soil of houseplants sufficiently moist requires that they be watered at intervals. The length of time between waterings depends upon a great many factors such as the kind of plant, its stage of growth, its size in relation to its pot, the character of its soil, the condition of its roots, and such variable environmental factors as light and temperature.

Obviously soil in a pot filled with healthy roots, all absorbing moisture, dries more rapidly than that of a newly potted specimen that has not yet filled its container with roots. Clearly when the temperature is high, the sun strong, and the humidity low, drying will be more rapid than in cool, dull, and moist weather. The frequency with which water should be given varies then, according to conditions.

A leafy hydrangea, primula, or cineraria in a pot well filled with roots may require soaking two or three times a day in sunny, warm weather, whereas a pruned-back geranium, a newly potted amaryllis, or a succulent cactus may not need such attention more often than once a week, particularly if the weather is dull.

To judge whether or not the soil of a plant has reached the stage where water is needed examine its surface. If it looks moist and feels moist it is likely wet enough, although if previous waterings have been skimpy it is possible that the surface is wet and the soil beneath dry. If you suspect this turn the plant out of its pot and inspect its soil ball. You can easily judge by its appearance whether the earth is dry or wet. The weight of the pot and its contents is often a good indication of the degree of moistness of the soil. Wet earth is heavier than dry. With a little practice you will be able to judge by lifting the pot just how wet its contents are. Another time-honored test is to rap the pot with a thick wooden stick or small wooden mallet. A dull heavy sound indicates wetness, a clear ringing sound dryness. If the leaves wilt, suspect dryness. Remember, however, that wilting can be caused also by excessive sunshine, drafts, stem injuries, damage to the roots caused by transplanting, overstrong fertilizers, or even by excessive watering. Make quite sure that the wilting is caused by dryness before you attempt to remedy it by applying water. Actually you should never permit plants to get so dry that their leaves droop unless you are purposely drying them off in preparation for a period of rest. Wilting is harmful to growing plants.

One watering rule is inviolable; when a plant needs water give it plenty, enough to saturate its entire body of soil, not a parsimonious dribble that wets only the surface. This applies whether you are dealing with a bog plant or a desert cactus, a newly planted seedling or an old established, pot-bound specimen. A good way to be sure that you saturate the soil is to immerse the pot to one-half its depth in water and keep it there until moisture seeping from below wets the surface soil. Do not leave it immersed for long after the soil is thoroughly wet. Most plants are harmed if they are left standing in water for lengthy periods. This immersion method is particularly useful for seedlings and newly planted specimens where disturbance of the surface soil may result from top watering. It is good, too, for plants that have filled their containers with a tight mass of roots and that are difficult to water thoroughly from above. It is excellent for any plant that is not too heavy to lift in and out of water.

Popular opinion to the contrary, there are no plants that *must* be watered from below (that is, by the immersion method). It is just a sure means of soaking the soil completely and a method that does not wet the foliage, as careless surface water-

Careful watering is important

ing may, of plants that need to have their leaves kept dry.

Surface watering, properly done, is just as effective as watering from beneath. Properly done simply means that the soil is soaked through and that foliage is not wet if not desirable.

Ordinarily the surface soil of a potted plant is some little distance below the rim of its container. Under the best circumstances the space that is left will hold sufficient water to soak the soil beneath. When this is so, watering consists of filling this space once with water. But due to growth of roots or other causes, the space above the soil is sometimes not sufficient to hold water enough to soak the whole ball of earth. In such cases it is necessary to fill it two, three, or more times at each watering—as many as are needed to make sure that all the soil is saturated and that surplus water runs out of the hole in the bottom of the pot. When, as sometimes happens with plants that have occupied the same containers for a long time and with plants that have been very dry, the soil ball shrinks from the pot leaving a space between the pot and its contents, the fact that water runs out through the bottom of the container does not necessarily indicate that the soil mass is soaked through. In such cases make doubly sure that soaking is accomplished.

Semiautomatic watering by using wicks of glass fiber or capillary mats is possible. Wick watering is most successful with plants in pots 4 to 7 inches in diameter and with fine-rooted kinds such as African-violets, and pick-a-back plants. It is less satisfactory for specimens in quite small or quite large pots and for coarse-rooted subjects such as palms and snake plants. The glass wick is inserted through the hole in the bottom of the pot, the upper end is unravelled and spread and is brought into intimate contact with the soil, the lower end is immersed in a container of water. The wick is put into position when the plant is potted. No drainage is used in the pot. Capillary mats (see the Encyclopedia entry Capillary Mats) may be used successfully with plants in pots from 2½ to 6 inches in diameter.

Unless you use good sense in watering you will not be successful with your houseplants. If you follow the suggestions made and see that the soil is thoroughly saturated when it is watered and then is not wet again until it verges on dryness, but is not yet completely dry, you will go far to becoming a good waterer. But there are refinements to the practice that you should know if you are to do best by your plants. First you must understand that when gardeners speak of this plant needing a lot of water and that plant needing little they do not refer to the *amount* of water that should be given at each application. This must always be sufficient to saturate the soil. They refer rather to the degree of dryness the soil should be allowed to attain before water is applied. Plants that need little water, such as fat cactuses and other succulents, are not watered until their soil is *almost completely* dry. Plants that need a lot of water, such as ferns, hydrangeas in full leaf, and pot-bound cinerarias, are watered as soon as the soil *begins to be dry*. In their needs for water the great majority of houseplants fall between these extremes.

Plants need more water when they are growing actively and are developing new leaves than they do when they are semi-dormant. Specimens that have ample foliage in comparison to the size of the pot they occupy need more water than those that are sparser of leaf. For this reason individuals that have been pruned back or have had their foliage seriously damaged by insects, disease, frost, or other cause should be kept "on the dry side."

Plants that have filled their containers with healthy roots need more water than newly transplanted and freshly potted specimens the roots of which have not yet permeated the available soil. Plants in very porous soils need more water than those in more retentive earths and those accommodated in porous clay pots need more than those in plastic or other nonporous containers.

In dull weather do whatever watering is needed early in the day if you can. Despite this rule, if a plant is evidently suffering from lack of moisture apply it at any time. Many gardeners prefer to use water at room temperature. If you have hard, alkaline water it will bring death to azaleas, heaths, camellias, gardenias, and other acid-soil plants. Use rain water or at least nonalkaline water for such kinds. Rain water, as a matter of fact, is excellent for all plants.

When plants growing in porous clay pots dry out too quickly, thus necessitating very frequent watering, relief may be had by sinking the pot to its rim in a larger pot or other container and packing the space between with peat moss, sand, vermiculite, or sphagnum moss and keeping

Fertilize only plants that have filled their containers with roots

this constantly moist. This is much to be preferred to watering every few hours.

Fertilizing is often uppermost in the mind of amateur growers of houseplants, yet it usually has less bearing on success than most suppose. Of course plants can be starved for lack of nutrients, and you must take care that this does not happen. Periodical applications of dilute liquid fertilizer or the availability of nutrients from slow-release pellets scattered on the soil surface promote growth if other factors are favorable. But a plant distressed by a totally unsuitable environment, by faulty drainage or excessive compaction of its soil, by serious overwatering or underwatering, or any other cause than insufficient supply of nutrients will not be helped by fertilizing.

When you fertilize it is usually wisest and most convenient to use one of the many excellent complete formulations prepared and sold especially for houseplants. Do not overdo fertilizing. Better dilute to half the strength recommended by the manufacturer and perhaps make more frequent applications than the reverse. Houseplants needs for nutrients are generally less than those of the same plants in greenhouses. This is because light intensity is commonly lower. Also, it is often undesirable to encourage exuberant growth. You may not want your specimens to increase greatly in size, but more importantly you may cause the development of more foliage than the roots can supply with moisture, with the result that lower leaves are likely to be shed.

Tailor fertilizing to the needs of individual plants. Here are some guide lines. Only fertilize plants that have filled their containers with healthy roots. Do not fertilize plants that are dormant or semidormant with the exception that the latter if they are evergreen and if their containers are very crowded with roots may be fertilized at intervals three or four times as long as in their active growing seasons, say once a month. Do not fertilize if the soil is very dry. Water thoroughly first and fertilize an hour or two later.

A summer vacation outdoors benefits many houseplants, but is by no means essential. Do not put your charges outside unless you have spots where conditions are favorable. If you have such places, as soon as the weather is warm and settled and there is no longer danger from cold nights, look the situation over. Examine your plants with a critical eye. Perhaps there are some that you really should discard, some that have grown too big or that are in such poor condition that they cannot be expected to recuperate or that for other reasons have outlived their usefulness. Get rid of them. Do not hang on to liabilities.

Of those that you decide to keep, there may be some that go naturally to rest during the summer that would be better off in a cool cellar than outdoors. Such plants include calla-lilies, cape-cowslips, and some kinds of oxalis. Plants with very hairy leaves, such as African-violets, gloxinias, and gynuras, are happier indoors or on a porch where they are protected from rain than in the open.

Most of the others will need some attention before they are set outdoors. Pick off all dead stems and leaves. Prune those that are straggly or that you believe will benefit from this treatment. If any are in-fested with insects, take vigorous measures to eliminate the pests. Pot any that need repotting at least two or three weeks before they are put outdoors. Others may need top dressing.

In rare cases only is it advisable to remove a houseplant from its pot and plant it directly in the soil of the outdoor garden. Not that plants fail to flourish when this is done. Most will take hold and grow well. The trouble comes when they have to be dug up and planted in pots again. Then, because their roots are necessarily cut and disturbed by the digging operation they lose their foliage and are set back to such an extent that the value of their summer vacation is completely lost. Plants, such as poinsettias, that form long straggly roots suffer much more from this disturbance than do those that form compact root systems, such as chrysanthemums and Christmas cherries. Most kinds should remain in their containers.

Specimens in big clay pots that are intended for summer decoration of porch, patio, or terrace thrive best if they are stood inside larger pots or tubs. These shade the pots in which the plants are growing and so prevent their roots from becoming too hot and the soil from drying too rapidly. The outer pots can be decorative.

Other plants that you put outdoors for the summer should also be accommodated in such a way that their soil stays cool and evenly moist. This is best accomplished by sinking their pots to within an inch or two of their rims in a bed of sand, peat moss, sawdust, or soil.

Where you locate them should depend upon their kinds. Sun-lovers, such as geraniums and crotons, need an open, sunny spot. Shade-lovers, such as philodendrons, aspidistras, and ferns, a place where they get good light, but not strong direct sunshine. A great majority, of which fuchsias, clivias, and begonias are good examples, will be grateful for the dappled shade of a tree that lets a little sunlight filter through its foliage or for a position near a building or wall that gets early morning or late afternoon and evening sun only.

Even those plants that appreciate full sun should be protected from its greatest intensities at first. If they are not, their foliage is likely to suffer from sunburn.

You may accustom such plants to the outdoor light either by keeping them in a place that is naturally lightly shaded for a couple of weeks before moving them to their summer location or by putting them directly in the sunny location where they are to stay and rigging a cheesecloth shade that can be kept over them for the first two weeks.

When selecting summer vacation sites for houseplants, avoid very exposed likely-to-be-windy places. Do try and have them not too far away from a water supply

Many houseplants benefit from being summered outdoors

and from the end of a hose so that you can give those that need it a daily spray with plain water.

Take precautions against the admission of earthworms to the pots, against the drainage of the pots becoming clogged, and against the roots of the plants growing into the plunging bed. A 3- or 4-inch layer of gravel beneath each pot with a flat piece of slate or tile on top of this and immediately beneath the hole in the pot's bottom will usually be sufficient to achieve these ends.

Do not, under any circumstances, sink the rim of the pot beneath the level of the plunging bed. If you do the plant is likely to root over its edge into the surrounding sand or earth. Space the plants sufficiently apart so that they have a little room to grow and so that light can get down and air circulate between them.

Care of plants "on vacation" is not markedly different from when they are indoors. Watering, fertilizing, and spraying are the chief attentions. Some staking and tying may be desirable. Fast-growing individuals may benefit from an additional repotting during the summer. Plunged specimens need less frequent watering than those above ground. If the summer is wet, there may be long periods when little or no artificial watering is needed. Even so, check your plants occasionally to be sure that all is well. A daily light spraying with clear water benefits practically all plants while they are outside.

Winter is the most difficult season for most houseplants indoors. Then the days are shortest, the sunlight weakest, and the atmosphere most lacking humidity. Prepare your plants for these trying conditions early.

Plants brought in at least three or four weeks before the furnace is started have a chance to become acclimated to their new environment gradually. The change from outdoors to indoors or from moist greenhouse to living room is not then so great as it would be later when the house is heated.

A few may need repotting, but do not pot at this season unless you are quite sure the specimens need this treatment. In particular avoid overpotting, transplanting into containers that are too large. Very well-rooted fatshederas, Boston ferns, English ivy, and other kinds that make new growth during winter are the ones most likely to require potting. Specimens not in need of repotting may benefit from top dressing with new rich soil.

If the plant pots have been buried to their rims check their drainage to make sure that surplus water can escape readily. Wash the outsides of the pots. Pick off all dead and damaged leaves. Stake and secure with ties plants that seem in need of these aids. Do any pruning that is necessary. Wash the foliage to remove spatterings of dirt and make sure that the plants are free of diseases and pests before you bring them indoors.

Certain plants not in pots that are growing in the outside garden or in window boxes may be dug up and potted for winter use indoors. These include geraniums, fuchsias, lantanas, ageratums, heliotropes, begonias, ivies, vincas, and small plants of such annuals as marigolds, sweet alyssums, and verbenas.

In all cases soak the ground thoroughly with water a few hours before you lift the plants. If possible choose a dull, moist day for digging. Have at hand a supply of sandy fertile soil and crocked pots of requisite sizes. These should be just big enough to accommodate the roots without cramming. Use a fork rather than a spade or trowel for digging; you will not then slice off so many roots. Preserve all the roots you can and keep plenty of soil attached to them. Do not let the roots dry.

It is *very* important to prune large plants that are dug and potted. This restores a balance between the amount of roots and amount of top growth, for no matter *how* careful you are, you are bound to cut off some roots in the lifting operation. Ordinarily you should reduce large plants by one-half or two-thirds. This does not mean that you should simply shear off the top one-half or two-thirds. Remove, rather, all weak, damaged and crowded stems and shorten moderately those that remain.

Small plants that are dug and repotted, such as young annuals and summer-rooted cuttings, will need no pruning if you lift them with good balls of earth and retain all their roots.

In most cases the prunings can be made into cuttings. These, as well as slips of many other houseplants, root readily in late summer and early fall. Among the kinds that can be inserted with advantage at this time are begonias, blood leaf, cigar flower, coleuses, English ivy, fatshedera, fuchsias, geraniums, grape-ivy, heliotropes, Paris-daisies, patience plants, shrimp plant, and wandering Jews.

Certain bulbs need a gradual drying off in preparation for their winter's rest. As soon as their foliage begins to die naturally, gradually lengthen the periods between waterings and finally withhold all water. Achimenes, amaryllises, and tuberous begonias are examples of plants that need this treatment. There are other bulbs that start into new growth in fall and that need repotting then. Here belong freesias, babianas, lachenalias, nerines, tritonias, and a number of others that are native south of the equator and that experience the spring urge to grow in our fall.

Plants that have been indoors all summer should be inspected critically before fall frosts. If there are any you do not intend to keep, discard them. Wash or spray the others to clean them of dust and pests. Top dress and repot any that need these attentions. Do everything possible to put them into good shape for the winter.

Diseases, other than rots resulting from poor drainage and overwatering, are not common on houseplants because the atmosphere is usually too dry to support the growth of funguses. Insects and other small creatures are more often troublesome. Chief among these are aphids, mealybugs, mites, scale insects, thrips, and whiteflies. Springtails may jump about on the soil surface, but do no appreciable harm. Ants crawling over plants usually indicate the presence of aphids, mealybugs, or scale insects. Earthworms in houseplant containers do harm by disturbing the roots. Do not tolerate them.

Eternal vigilance based on frequent close inspection is the best security against serious troubles. At the first suspicion of infection or infestation take prompt remedial measures. Success depends upon early detection, correct diagnosis, and suitable action. Do not mistake such normal seasonal variation as signals the beginning of a dormant period for disease or pest, or changes caused by faulty watering, exposure to drafts, or cold, or other harmful environmental circumstances.

The sorts of houseplants are drawn from a great many genera. Excluding numerous cactuses and a few orchids and palms, which contain numerous kinds favored by houseplant fans (such are among those listed at the conclusions of the Encyclopedia entries Cactuses, Orchids, and Palms) here are a selection of the chief genera that contain favorite houseplants:

Abutilon, Acalypha, Achimenes, Adiantum, Aechmea, Aeonium, Aeschynanthus, Agave, Aglaeonema, Allamanda, Aloe, Ananas, Anthurium, Aphelandra, Araucaria, Ardisia, Aristolochia, Asparagus, Aspidistra, Asplenium, Aucuba, Azalea (Rhododendron), Begonia, Billbergia, Bougainvillea, Caladium, Calathea, Ceropegia, Cestrum, Chlorophytum, Cissus, Citrus, Clerodendrum, Clivia, Codiaeum, Coffea, Coleus, Columnea, Cordyline, Cotyledon, Crassula, Cryptanthus, Cyanotis, Cycas, Cyperus, Cyrtomium, Davallia, Dieffenbachia, Dizygotheca, Dracaena, Dyckia, Echeveria, Episcia, Eucomis, Euphorbia, Fatshedera, Fatsia, Ficus, Fittonia, Fortunella, Fuchsia, Gardenia, Gasteria, Gloriosa, Graptopetalum, Grevillea, Guzmania, Gynura, Haemanthus, Haworthia, Hedera, Hibiscus, Hippeastrum, Holmskioldia, Hoya, Hyacinthus, Hydrangea, Impatiens, Ixora, Jasminum, Kalanchoe, Kohleria, Ligularia, Malpighia, Manettia, Monstera, Myrsine, Narcissus, Nautilocalyx, Neomarica, Neoregelia, Nephrolepis, Nephthytis, Nerium, Nidularium, Nolina, Osmanthus, Oxalis, Passiflora, Pedilanthus, Pelargonium, Pellionia, Pentas, Peperomia, Philodendron, Pilea, Piper, Pittosporum, Plectranthus, Podocarpus, Polyscias, Polystichum, Pothos, Pteris, Punica, Rhoeo, Rivina, Russelia, Saintpaulia, Sansevieria,

Schefflera, Scilla, Scindapsus, Sedum, Selaginella, Setcreasea, Sinningia, Smithiantha, Spathiphyllum, Sprekelia, Stapelia, Stephanotis, Streptocarpus, Syngonium, Thunbergia, Tibouchina, Tillandsia, Trachelospermum, Tradescantia, Tulip, Vallota, Veltheimia, Vriesia, and *Zebrina.*

HOUSTONIA. See Hedyotis.

HOUTTUYNIA (Houttuỳn-ia). A single species of the lizard's tail family SAURURACEAE, with a natural range extending from Japan to the Himalayas, Taiwan, and Java, belongs here. The name of the genus honors Martin Houttuyn, a native of the Netherlands, who wrote on natural history and died in 1798.

A perennial, deciduous, herbaceous species, *Houttuynia cordata* varies in height, depending upon the richness of soil and availability of moisture, from 6 inches to 2 feet or sometimes more. It spreads, under favorable conditions quite rapidly, by slender rhizomes from which arise numerous thin, erect stems bearing alternate, unlobed, sometimes angular, five-veined, heart-shaped leaves up to 3 inches long by almost as wide. The minute flowers are in short, erect spikes. From the base of each spike the four petal-like parts of a persistent white bract spread horizontally to produce the effect of a small flowering dogwood inflorescence with a taller than usual center and almost or quite 2 inches across. They are borne over a long period in summer. A variegated-leaved variety is grown in Japan.

Garden Uses and Cultivation. This interesting, attractive plant is hardy at least as far north as New York City. Except for the fact that its new growth starts late in spring, it is a useful and unusual groundcover that makes sufficiently dense growth to keep down weeds and grows to a uniform height so that it is of neat appearance. Its foliage pattern is pretty and its blooms decorative. Because of its invasive, spreading habit it should not be planted near choice, small plants. Although a lover of moist and wet soils and tolerant of shade, it is usually more attractive and not so likely to get out of bounds in drier, but not dry, soil in full sun. Excessive fertilization, like abundant moisture and shade, encourages tall, loose, undesirable growth. Propagation is very easily accomplished by division in spring and by summer cuttings. Ripe seeds are sown while fresh in moist, sandy peaty soil.

HOVEA (Hò-vea). A dozen species of evergreen shrubs of Australia and Tasmania constitute *Hovea*, of the pea family LEGUMINOSAE. They are suitable for outdoor cultivation in warm, Mediterranean-type climates, such as that of California, and can be grown in greenhouses. Their name commemorates the Polish botanical collector, Anthony P. Hove, who died in 1798.

Hoveas have alternate, undivided, prickly-toothed or smooth-edged leaves, pea-shaped, blue or deep purple flowers in clusters or short racemes from the leaf axils, and inflated seed pods. The stamens are joined, without one, as often is true of flowers of the pea family, being separate.

From 5 to 10 feet tall, *H. elliptica* (syn. *H. celsii*), of Western Australia, has downy shoots and elliptic to lanceolate or oblanceolate, smooth-edged leaves 1 inch to 3½ inches long. In groups of two to four, on lateral, leafy shoots, the blue flowers, ½ inch in length and with a banner or standard petal as long, are borne profusely.

Also Western Australian, *H. pungens* and *H. trisperma* are much lower. The 2- to 3-foot-tall *H. pungens* has rigid, linear or lanceolate, sharp-pointed leaves ½ to a little over 1 inch long, with strongly rolled-under margins. In allusion to these, the name devil's pins is applied in its homeland to this species. The flowers, solitary, in pairs, or in threes, from the leaf axils, are dark violet-blue and about ½ inch wide. Up to 2 feet tall, loosely-trailing *H. trisperma* has linear to ovate leaves up to 3 inches in length, pubescent beneath, and sometimes with toothed margins. Its fairly large flowers are violet to pale lilac or white.

Native to eastern and northern Australia, *H. longifolia* (syn. *H. purpurea*), up to 10 feet tall, has leathery oblong-lanceolate to broad-linear leaves ¾ inch to 2¼ inches long, rusty-hairy on their undersides, and with rolled-under margins. The blue flowers are in clusters from the leaf axils.

Garden and Landscape Uses and Cultivation. Hoveas are quite charming for general outdoor planting in sunny places in frost-free, dryish climates and for growing in cool greenhouses. They succeed under conditions and treatment favorable to acacias, leptospermums, callistemons, and similar warm-temperate region trees and shrubs in reasonably fertile, well-drained soil that contains a fair amount of peat moss or other decayed organic matter.

Houttuynia cordata

Houttuynia cordata (flower)

Any pruning needed to shape the plants or limit their sizes is done as soon as flowering is through. Because older specimens do not transplant well it is advisable to set out young plants from containers. Propagation is by seeds and by cuttings.

HOVENIA (Hovèn-ia) — Japanese Raisin Tree. The popular name of the only cultivated member of this genus does not of course identify it as the source of raisins. It is not, for raisins are dried grapes. But the flower stalks of *Hovenia dulcis* swell, become fleshy, sweet, and edible after the petals fall, and are thought to have something of the flavor of raisins. There are five species of *Hovenia*, a genus native from Japan to the Himalayas that belongs to the buckthorn family RHAMNACEAE. The name honors David ten Hoven, a senator of Amsterdam and commissioner in Japan, who died in 1787.

Hovenias are deciduous trees, unlike many members of the buckthorn family, without spines. They have alternate, long-stalked, ovate to nearly round leaves with three chief veins from their bases. The flowers are bisexual, small, purplish, and without ornamental merit. In axillary and terminal clusters, they have five each sepals, petals, and stamens and a three-branched style. The fruits are slightly three-lobed, three-seeded, berry-like drupes (fruits of the plum type).

Hovenia dulcis

The Japanese raisin tree (**H. dulcis**), usually 30 to 35 feet in height, is often much taller in the wild, and round-topped. Its coarsely-toothed, pointed, ovate to heart-shaped leaves, 4 to 7 inches long by 3 to 6 inches wide, are nearly hairless above, but are downy on their undersides especially along the veins. The ¼-inch-wide greenish or yellowish flowers are in clusters 2 to 3 inches wide. Grayish or brownish, the fruits, at the ends of enlarged, fleshy, red stalks, and often partly embedded in them, are ⅓ inch in diameter.

Garden and Landscape Uses. Although rare in North America the Japanese raisin tree is a worthy ornamental, attractive chiefly because of its large, handsome foliage and, to a minor degree, for its edible flower stalks. It serves well wherever a tree of moderate size suits, and is hardy in southern New England. Ordinary fertile soil, and locations in sun are to its liking.

Cultivation. No special attention is needed by established specimens. Increase may be had by summer cuttings under mist or in a greenhouse or cold frame propagating bed, by root cuttings, and by seeds. It is recommended that the latter be treated before sowing by soaking them for fifteen minutes in concentrated sulfuric acid and then washing thoroughly with water.

HOWEA (Hòw-ea). The genus *Howea*, one of the best known of the palm family PAL-MAE, includes only two species, both natives of a tiny speck of land 480 miles northeast of Sydney, Australia, called Lord Howe Island. The genus is named after its home island, the name of which commemorates Richard Howe, Admiral of the British fleet that played an important part in the American Revolution.

Gardeners have long known howeas as kentias, although the name *Kentia* properly belongs to another group of palms. As kentias they were once grown by the millions in Europe and America to supply the enormous demand for potted palms. They graced hotel lobbies, public buildings, private conservatories, and funeral parlors and were employed as decorations at banquets, weddings, and other festive occasions. Although less popular than they once were, howeas are still important as florists' decorative plants and are raised in considerable numbers for this use. They are planted outdoors in the tropics and near tropics. The name is sometimes spelled *Howeia*.

Howeas are among the most graceful of feather-leaved palms. They have solitary, erect, slender, ringed trunks up to 8 inches in diameter and ordinarily 30 to 35 feet tall, and beautiful crowns of spreading leaves with many regularly arranged, long, pointed leaflets that bend downward. The flowers, in slender branchless spikes from the leaf axils, are sunk into the stalks of the spikes in groups of three, each consisting of one female flanked by two males. Male flowers have thirty to seventy or sometimes more stamens. The reddish, egg-shaped fruits, about 2 inches long, contain a solitary seed.

The commercial collection of seeds of *Howea* was once the chief industry of Lord Howe Island and the keystone of the island economy, but that activity is now of less economic importance than is catering to vacationers and tourists, chiefly from Australia. Even so, essentially all the seeds

of howeas supplied to florists and growers throughout the world are obtained from the palms on Lord Howe Island.

Of the two species, *H. forsterana* predominates at low elevations along sandy shores and in lowland forests, whereas *H. belmoreana* is chiefly a plant of upland forest slopes, abundant up to an altitude of about 1,400 feet. The taller **H. forsterana**

Howea forsterana

Howea belmoreana: (a) The Palmengarten, Frankfurt-am-Main, Germany

(b) A young plant

Hoya carnosa

Hoya carnosa (flowers)

Hoya carnosa compacta

Hoya carnosa exotica

has leaves that are not as strongly arched as those of *H. belmoreana*, but that spread at angles varying from upright to horizontal. The leaflets are less crowded than those of the other species and tend to point downward from the rachis (central stalk of the leaf) rather than arch upward first and then turn downward, as do those of **H. belmoreana.**

Garden and Landscape Uses. Among the most beautiful of palms, these are planted outdoors in California, Hawaii, and to a lesser extent in southern Florida, as well as in many other warm parts of the world. Elegant as single specimens and in small groups, they are at their best where they receive some shade from the fiercest summer sun. They prosper in any well-drained, ordinary garden soil that is reasonably moist. In pots and tubs they are grown as single specimens or are often planted three or more together in containers to form what florists call combinations.

Cultivation. Wherever howeas are planted outdoors in the continental United States they should be given protected locations because they are easily damaged by frosts and high winds. Indoors they last long under quite adverse conditions, but for their well-being should be afforded a minimum temperature of 60°F, good light with shade from strong sun, a fairly moist atmosphere, and fertile, well-drained soil that is never completely dry nor for long periods excessively wet. Specimens that have filled their containers with roots benefit from biweekly applications of dilute liquid fertilizer from spring through fall. Propagation is by freshly imported seeds sown in sandy, peaty soil in a temperature of 80°F. For additional information see Palms.

HOYA (Hoy̆-a)—Wax Plant. As wildlings occurring from eastern Asia to Australia, the about 200 species of *Hoya* belong in the milkweed family ASCLEPIADACEAE. Their name commemorates Thomas Hoy, an eighteenth-century gardener to the English Duke of Northumberland.

Hoyas are nonhardy, evergreen, perennial twining vines and slender-stemmed small shrubs. They have opposite, fleshy or thick, leathery, undivided leaves. Their flowers, also fleshy, are in stalked or stalkless umbel-like clusters from the leaf axils. Each has a calyx of five small sepals, a deeply-five-lobed corolla with the lobes (petals) spreading or pointing backward, a star-shaped crown or corona of five scales, five stamens united into a short tube and with their anthers joined above the short stigma. The fruits are paired, podlike, hairless follicles.

Common wax plant (**H. carnosa**) is an old-time favorite. Native from China to Australia, this stem-rooting vine attains heights of 6 to 8 feet or more. Its short-stalked, toothless, pointed-ovate-oblong, smooth leaves are 2 to 4 inches long. The wheel-shaped, slightly pink-tinged white flowers have decidedly convex, soft pink, star-shaped coronas. About ½ inch in diameter and fragrant, they are in nearly stalkless clusters. Horticultural varieties include *H. c. alba*, with white flowers; *H. c. compacta*, with leaves closer together than those of the typical species; *H. c. exotica* (syn. *H. c. marmorata*), its leaves mar-

Hoya carnosa variegata

Hoya australis

Hoya bella

Hoya bella (flowers)

bled with two tones of green and their centers yellow and pinkish-cream; *H. c.* 'Krinkle Kurl', called Hindu rope plant, which has overlapping leaves, folded inward lengthwise and curiously contorted; *H. c.* 'Mauna Loa', similar to the last except that its leaves have yellow centers or yellow-green or gold margins; *H. c. latifolia*, with broader leaves than those of the typical species; *H. c. tricolor*, the leaves of which have green centers and white, cream, pink, or red margins; and *H. c. variegata*, the green or bluish-green leaves of

which are broadly margined with creamy-white and sometimes pink.

Much like the common wax plant, but more robust and with considerably broader, short-pointed, ovate to nearly circular leaves sometimes sprinkled with silvery dots, *H. australis* is a native of Australia. Hairless, it has white flowers with purplish markings at the base of the corona.

Native of Borneo, *H. imperialis* is a tall climber with downy stems, slightly-hairy, elliptic to linear-oblong leaves 4½ to 9 inches long and approximately one-half as

wide. The flowers, 3 to 3½ inches in diameter, are in clusters about 10 inches across of seven to ten individuals. Slightly-scented, they are deep magenta with a light yellow corona. Chinese *H. pottsii* (syn. *H. obscurinervia*) has slender-pointed, three-veined, ovate to elliptic leaves paler beneath than on their rather rusty-colored upper surfaces. In spherical clusters, the delightfully fragrant flowers are white with yellow coronas.

Very different *H. bella* is exquisite and deliciously fragrant in bloom. A low

Hoya bandaensis

Hoya lacunosa

Hoya darwinii

shrub, it has branches, when young erect, soon drooping, up to about 1½ feet long. Its small, pointed-ovate thick leaves are dark green banded along the midrib with brown. The blooms, many together in flat umbels, are as precisely perfect as if made by a master jeweler. They are white with a rose-crimson to purple corona.

Other hoyas likely to be cultivated include the following: *H. angustifolia* is Chinese. A slender, sparingly-hairy vine, it has linear-lanceolate leaves up to 6 inches long, and in clusters of few, ¾-inch-wide, white flowers with purple at the centers of

their coronas. *H. bandaensis,* of the Molucca Islands, is a hairless vine with rather fleshy, broad-elliptic leaves 3 to 8 inches long by up to 5 inches wide. In clusters of many, the triangular-petaled flowers ⅝ inch across are white, maturing to creamy-white. *H. cinnamomifolia,* of Java, is hairless and has pointed-ovate leaves 3 to 5 inches long with very thick, short stalks and three prominent chief veins. The yellow-green to yellow flowers have a purple-red corona and are in crowded, spherical clusters of many. *H. coronaria* is Javanese. It has short-hairy, thick stems and short-pointed, oblongish to roundish leaves up to 6 inches long and with a conspicuous midrib. Smooth above, they have hairy undersides. The open-bell-shaped flowers 1 inch to 1¼ inches across and white to yellowish spotted with red or purple around the yellow corona, are in umbels of many. *H. darwinii,* an endemic of the Philippine Islands, is a hairless vine with oblong to obovate, prominently-veined leaves up to 3½ inches long. Its upward-facing flowers in loose umbels of rather few, have ½-inch-long, backward-pointing, whitish to rose-pink petals with purple bases. *H. englerana,* of Thailand, has very short-stalked, linear-lanceolate to lanceolate or ovate-lanceolate leaves ½ inch to 1½ inches long. The flowers, a little over ½ inch across and white to pinkish with a pink corona, are mostly in clusters of four. *H. gigas,* of New Guinea, is a high climber. Its broad-elliptic to ovate leaves, up to 5 inches long, have hairy under surfaces. The starry, cupped flowers, 1½ to 2½ inches in diameter, are reddish-brown with paler apexes to the petals. *H.*

globulosa, of the Himalayan region, is a slender vine with thick, slender-pointed, oblong, more or less hairy leaves. In spherical clusters, the flowers are cream-colored with the center of the corona brownish-red. The petals curve inward. *H. kerri,* of Thailand, Indochina, and Fiji, is a vigorous vine with dull, broad, reverse-heart-shaped to nearly round, about 5-inch-long leaves, notched at their apexes and softly-hairy on their undersides. About ½ inch in diameter and densely-hairy on their insides, the flowers are creamy-white with a rose-purple corona. *H. keysii* is Australian. A thick-stemmed creeper with rather closely set leaves, this has light-gray-felted, short-pointed, obovate leaves. *H. lacunosa,* native of Malaysia, is a slender-stemmed, tall vine. It has slender-pointed, elliptic-lanceolate leathery leaves up to 2 inches long by about ½ inch wide, and many-flowered, flattish umbels of fragrant, greenish-yellow, wheel-shaped, ¼-inch-wide blooms, velvety-hairy on their insides and with reflexed petals. *H. latifolia,* of Malaya, has purplish-stalked, broad-ovate, fleshy, lustrous leaves with three clearly defined pale longitudinal veins. Its young foliage is coppery. *H. linearis,* of the Himalayas, has slender stems and short-stalked, rather pointed, cylindrical leaves 1 inch to 2 inches long by about ⅛ inch wide, deeply-grooved beneath. The waxy-white, fragrant flowers have a purple corona and are in loose, stalkless terminal clusters. *H. longifolia,* of the Himalayan region, is a hairless vine with very fleshy, oblanceolate leaves up to 8 inches long and 1½ inches wide and with a sharp downward bend at the top of the stalk. On stalks up to 1¾ inches long the clusters of reddish-centered, white or blush-pink, ¾- to 1½-inch-wide flowers are borne. *H. l. shepherdii* (syn. *H. shepherdii*), of Sikkim, is a thin-stemmed vine with narrow-linear leaves, rounded on their undersides, channeled above. The small white or pinkish blooms in umbels about 2 inches wide have pink-centered coronas. *H. macrophylla*, of Java, nearly hairless, has oblong-lanceolate, prominently-veined, leathery leaves 6 to 10 inches long. Its ½-inch-wide flowers, red on their outsides and thickly-white-hairy on their faces, have white or pink coronas. *H. multiflora*, native of Malacca, is a robust, hairless vine with short-pointed, elliptic leaves. Its flowers, silky-hairy on their insides and in umbels of many, are straw-colored with brown centers. *H. purpureo-fusca*, of Java, resembles *H. cinnamomifolia*, differing most obviously in the color of its blooms; it has been known in cultivation as *H.* 'Silver Pink'. This vine has red-stalked, short-pointed, elliptic to ovate leaves with raised, irregular, pinkish-silvery mottlings on the blades. In large, tight, rounded umbels, the ashy-brown to rusty-red, white-hairy blooms have pinkish coronas. *H. rubida*, of New Guinea, is a vine with fleshy, lustrous, elliptic to obovate leaves about 4 inches long. The glossy, 1-inch-wide, maroon-red blooms have red coronas. *H. sikkimensis*, of the Himalaya region, is a low shrub much like *H. bella*. It has diamond-shaped leaves. Its white flowers have pink coronas, their lobes tipped with purple.

Garden and Landscape Uses. Hoyas are admirable for planting permanently outdoors in warm, humid, frostless climates. They are also admired as greenhouse and window garden ornamentals. The vining kinds are at their best when grown against a moisture-retaining support, such as a damp tree trunk, wall, or pillar or post wrapped with osmunda fiber or some similar material into which their stems can root. They can also be grown trained to stakes or wires without moisture-holding qualities, but are less likely to be outstanding then. Such nonvining kinds as *H. bella* are displayed to best advantage in hanging baskets.

Cultivation. Hoyas need a loose, well-drained soil that contains a fair proportion of coarse organic matter, such as compost, peat moss or leaf mold, together with sufficient coarse sand or perlite to keep it porous. A scattering of charcoal broken into peanut-size pieces and a dash of dried cow manure are helpful additions to the soil for pot specimens. Indoors, a winter night temperature of 50 to 55°F is adequate for some hoyas, including the common wax plant, but those that inhabit the warm tropics, such as *H. bella* and many others, appreciate temperatures about ten degrees higher. By day, for all kinds temperatures five to ten degrees above those maintained

at night are adequate. From spring to fall warmer conditions both night and day are in order. With reference to light the best advice is to expose the plants to the highest intensities they will take without the foliage yellowing or being scorched. A humid, but not dank, atmosphere and watering to keep the soil evenly moist are necessary from spring to fall. Then, too, well-rooted specimens may be given monthly applications of dilute liquid fertilizer. In winter soil and atmosphere should be kept considerably drier and fertilizing is discontinued. A peculiarity of the common wax plant and some other kinds is that the stalks of its flower clusters produce blooms for more than one year. Therefore they should not be removed after flowering is through, but only the faded blooms picked off. Propagation is usually easy by cuttings set in a propagating bed, preferably with mild bottom heat, in a shaded greenhouse, and by layering. Kinds of rather weak growth, such as *H. bella*, and rare species can be increased by grafting on the common wax plant. Mealybugs are the chief insect pest.

HUACO is *Manfreda variegata*.

HUAMUCHIL is *Pithecellobium dulce*.

HUCKLEBERRY. See Gaylussacia. The garden-huckleberry is *Solanum melanocerasum*, the hairy-huckleberry *Vaccinium hirsutum*, the he-huckleberry *Lyonia ligustrina*.

HUDSONIA (Hud-sònia)—Beach-Heather. The common name of this genus alludes to its heathlike aspect. Its botanical designation commemorates the English botanist William Hudson, who died in 1793. Comprising three eastern North American species, *Hudsonia* belongs to the rock-rose family CISTACEAE.

Low, hardy evergreen shrubs, hudsonias have alternate, scalelike or linear leaves and multitudes of small yellow flowers, each solitary at the end of a short, leafy branchlet. The blooms have three sepals, five elliptic petals that soon drop, ten to thirty stamens, and a long, slender style tipped with a minute stigma. The fruits are capsules enclosed by the persistent sepals.

An inhabitant of beaches and dunes near the sea, *H. ericoides* is native from Newfoundland to Virginia. It forms mounds about 7 inches tall and has linear leaves up to ⅓ inch long, up-pointing, but not overlapping. They are hairy, but not to the extent that the green leaf surface is hidden. The blooms are ⅓ inch wide or a little wider. The seed capsules are hairless.

Differing from the last in having ovate-lanceolate leaves up to ⅓ inch long that hug the stems closely and overlap and that are hoary-pubescent to the extent that the green leaf surfaces are scarcely or not visible, *H. tomentosa* grows on beaches, sand

dunes, and sandy prairies from Quebec to North Carolina along the coast, inland to the Great Lakes, Indiana, Illinois, North Dakota, and West Virginia. Its flowers are similar to those of *H. ericoides*. The seed capsules are hairy at their tips. Variety *H. t. intermedia* is probably a hybrid between *H. tomentosa* and *H. ericoides* that occurs in New England and eastern Canada. Confined in the wild to high mountains in North Carolina, *H. montana* has awl-shaped, slightly hairy, green leaves ¼ inch long, and blooms a little over ⅓ inch wide.

Garden and Landscape Uses and Cultivation. If it were not for the difficulties of establishing and growing them, hudsonias would be splendid for seaside gardens, rock gardens, and as groundcovers. Unfortunately, they are very difficult to transplant and under cultivation are usually not long-lived. They need acid, sandy, damp soil and full sun. Attempts at transplanting should be confined to little seedlings from the wild. Plants raised from seeds or cuttings and grown in pots are likely to give better results that transplants. But no sure methods of taming beach-heathers have yet been devised. They are for trial only by patient gardeners who crave the unusual and find pleasure in accepting challenges to their skills as cultivators.

HUERNIA (Huér-nia). A mistake in original spelling is responsible for the present spelling of the name of this genus, which honors Justin Heurnius (the latinized form of van Heurn), a Dutch collector of South African plants. Belonging to the milkweed family ASCLEPIADACEAE and inhabiting tropical Africa, South Africa, and Arabia, *Huernia* comprises thirty or more species of succulent, herbaceous perennials related to *Stapelia*.

Low, leafless, and to observers who lack a sense of the botanical, cactus-like, huernias have gray-green, often reddish, hairless, four- to seven-angled stems with teeth, sometimes bristle-pointed, along the angles. The flowers, solitary or in clusters of few from near the bases or middles of young stems, have a five-cleft calyx and a corolla with five lobes (petals). The corolla is bell-shaped or has a bell-shaped center and spreading petals. Five usually small teeth alternate with the petals, which feature is very characteristic of this genus. There is usually a double corona or crown at the center of the bloom, rarely a single one. The fruits are paired, podlike follicles.

Here in alphabetical sequence are descriptions of a selection of species in cultivation. Others are likely to be grown by specialists. *H. barbata* has many gray-green, upright stems, sharply four- or five-angled and sharp-toothed, up to 2½ inches tall by ¾ inch wide. The flowers, in clusters of several from the bases of the young shoots, and about 2 inches across, have corolla tubes ½ to ¾ inch long. Broadly-bell-shaped, they have red-spotted, light yellow corollas with long, tapering petals. Sulfur-yellow to tannish-colored, they are marked with blood-red spots. *H. hallii* has erect, hairless stems about 1½ inches tall, with four, five, or rarely six blunt, toothed angles. The flowers, ¾ to 1 inch wide and with spotted, spreading, pink petals, are creamy-white on their outsides, white, spotted near the bottom of the corolla tube inside. *H. hystrix* has more or less trailing stems and erect, five-angled branches 2 to 4½ inches high, about ⅓ inch thick, and gray and with large, spreading teeth. From 1¼ to 1½ inches wide, the cupped flowers have pointed-triangular, somewhat re-curved corolla lobes, on their insides yellow and freely adorned with short, red transverse lines. *H. kirkii* has five-angled, hair-

less stems prostrate at their bases, 1 inch to 2 inches high by ½ to ¾ inch thick. They have five sharp-toothed angles. Solitary or up to four together, the flowers, cupped at their centers, 1½ to 1¾ inches across, are

light buff-colored abundantly spotted with crimson. The corolla lobes taper to long points. *H. macrocarpa* is a variable native of Ethiopia, Eritrea, and the Sudan. Its stems are five- to seven-angled, toothed,

Huernia kirkii

Huernia hystrix

Huernia macrocarpa penzigii

Huernia striata

An attractive display of houseplants

An effective planting of hyacinths and pansies

Hydrangea macrophylla, varieties: (a) Pink-flowered   (b) Blue-flowered

(c) Lacecap

erect, and 3 or 4½ inches tall. Coming from near the bottoms of the young stems, the bell-shaped flowers, solitary or up to four together, are ¾ inch across by about one-half as long, greenish-yellow outside, yellowish inside marked with concentric brown stripes. The insides of the blooms of *H. m. arabica*, of Arabia are cherry-red. In *H. m. flavicoronata* they are maroon and pale yellow. *H. m. penzigii* has slightly nodding flowers ¾ inch long by 1 inch wide, evenly dark purple-maroon on their insides, greenish-yellow without. **H. pillansii** has densely-tufted, 1¼- to 1½-inch-tall, green to dull purplish stems up to ¾ inch thick and when young subspherical. They are thickly clothed with recurved, bristle-pointed tubercles (protrusions) arranged in long spirals. In twos or threes from the bottoms of the stems, the bell-shaped flowers have petals that spread in starfish manner. They are pale yellow sprinkled with small red pustules. **H. primulina** has clustered, erect, reddish-spotted, grayish-green leaves 1¼ to 3½ inches in height, less than ½ inch thick, and toothed at the angles. The flowers, up to as many as ten together from the bottoms of the young stems, have very short, bell-shaped corolla tubes and spreading, triangular petals. They are yellowish-white to bright yellow, reddish-spotted near their centers. **H. schneiderana,** grown under dry conditions in the open, forms broad mats of erect stems up to 2 inches tall and, except for six or seven blunt angles, furnished with distantly spaced teeth, cylindrical in section. Indoors under more humid conditions the stems elongate remarkably, sometimes to almost 2 feet in length, and may remain erect, bend, or even become pendulous. The about 1-inch-wide, bell-shaped flowers are nearly black inside and have wide-spreading, short-triangular, light rosy-brown petals. They come from the bases of the stems. **H. somalica** is tufted and has stems up to 2 inches long by ½ to ¾ inch thick. Gray-green, they have five blunt angles furnished with large, spreading teeth. The flowers, from the bases of the young stems, are 1½ to nearly 2 inches wide. They have shallow, bell-shaped centers encircled by a thickened ring. Their outsides are pale, the insides red-brown and glossy to the bottoms of the petals. **H. striata** has crowded, erect stems 1 inch to 2 inches tall with four or rarely up to six angles with very short, triangular teeth. Mostly in clusters of three to five, the flowers, cupped at their centers, are 1 inch or slightly more wide. The spreading, triangular corolla lobes have pale green or reddish outsides, are on their faces light yellow with thin, transverse, purple lines. **H. thuretii** has crowded, erect, gray-green, five-angled stems 1¼ to 4 inches tall, with very short, sharp teeth. Solitary or in clusters of up to four from the bottoms of the stems, the flowers have a corolla with a hemispherical-bell-shaped tube about ⅓ inch

Huernia thuretii

long and wide-spreading, sharp-pointed, triangular lobes forming a face to the flower ¾ inch across. The blooms are dullish yellow, reddish-flushed on their outsides, and freely spotted with blood red. **H. volkartii** has clusters of slender, spreading to ascending, four- or five-angled, dull-purplish stems with small teeth along the angles. From near the bases of the stems the flowers, solitary or in twos or threes and about ¾ inch wide, come. They have corollas with somewhat urn-shaped tubes, warted or rough on their outsides, and short-triangular, spreading, lurid-purple petals thickly covered with red-tipped, tiny white pimples, and with recurved apexes. The inside of the cupped portion of the corolla is dull creamy-white banded with dull crimson.

Garden Uses and Cultivation.   These interesting plants have the same uses and respond to the same care as stapelias. For further information see Succulents.

HUERNIOPSIS (Huerni-ópsis). Species of this genus are low, perennial, herbaceous succulents of the *Stapelia* relationship of the milkweed family ASCLEPIADACEAE. Natives of South Africa, they differ from *Huernia* in their flowers being without projections or intermediate lobes between the five main ones of the corolla. Their name, from *Huernia* and the Greek *opsis*, similar to, has obvious application. There are four species.

The stems of these plants are thick and four- or five-angled. There are no leaves. The comparatively large blooms are bell-shaped and come from the bottoms, cen-

ters, or tops of the stems. They have five spreading or recurved lobes (petals). A five-lobed crown or corona arises from the column of stamens and occupies the center of the bloom. The fruits are paired follicles (pods).

Blooming freely in summer, *Huerniopsis decipiens* has decumbent, more or less club-shaped, dull green or purplish stems up to 3 inches long and from a little under to a little over ½ inch in diameter. Their rounded ridges have spreading teeth with two smaller teeth at their bases. From the middles or toward the tops of young stems, solitary or in twos, threes, or fours, the short-stalked flowers develop, and open in succession, each lasting for several days. About 1 inch in diameter, they have pointed, broad, brownish-red or brownish-crimson petals mottled with yellow, and on their undersides are grayish-green spotted with purple. There are a few purple hairs at their bases within.

The blooms of **H. atrosanguinea** are shorter lived than those of *H. decipiens*. The life-span of individuals is not more than two days. This species has stems 2 to 3 inches in length, toothed at the angles and similar to those of *H. decipiens*. The very short-stalked blooms, about 1¾ inches in diameter, come in twos or threes from the middles of the younger stems. They are without spots and are rich blackish-crimson with the outsides of the sharp-pointed petals grayish-green with purplish mottlings.

Much like *H. decipiens*, but distinguished by the faces of its petals being covered with numerous white hairs swollen at their bases, and with a few purple hairs fringing the bases of the petals, *H. papillata* has glaucous-green stems up to 2 inches long, and flowers about 1¾ inches wide, mottled reddish-purple on a nearly white background. Another species, *H. gibbosa* has more or less procumbent stems about 2 inches long, conspicuously lumpy, and with sharp, white teeth. From near the tops of the stems the three or four short-stalked flowers come. About 2 inches wide, they have pointed-ovate petals rough with tiny warts, greenish-yellow above and dark purple below.

Garden and Landscape Uses and Cultivation. These plants are chiefly for collectors of succulents. They are hardy outdoors only in warm, semidesert climates, such as that of southern California, and are satisfactory for cultivating in greenhouses and window gardens. They need the same conditions and care as stapelias. For further information see Succulents.

HUISACHE is *Acacia farnesiana*.

HULSEA (Húl-sea). Named after G. W. Hulse, American army surgeon and botanical collector, this genus of about eight species of the daisy family COMPOSITAE is restricted in the wild to the western United States. It consists of aromatic, taprooted annuals, biennials, and herbaceous perennials, with sticky, rather fleshy foliage and flower heads constructed like those of daisies, with a central eye of disk florets and spreading petal-like ray florets. The leaves are usually numerous, the basal ones with broad stalks, the stem ones stalkless. They may be undivided or deeply-pinnately-lobed. The involucres (collars of bracts below the flower heads) are persistent and turn backward with age. The ray florets are numerous, yellow or purple, and female. The yellow disk florets are bisexual. The fruits are achenes.

An alpine native at elevations from 8,000 to 10,500 feet in mountains from northern California to Washington, *Hulsea nana* is a perennial, up to 6 inches tall, with a short, branching stem, and pinnately-lobed, oblanceolate leaves in crowded rosettes. They are 1 inch to 3 inches long, and when young are green or are more or less white-woolly. The flower heads, about 1½ inches across, have fifteen to twenty-five yellow rays. From the last *H. algida* differs chiefly in being more robust in all its parts. Its branchless stems are 4 inches to 1¼ feet tall, and its leaves, not woolly, may attain, with their stalks, a length of 6 inches. At home in rocky sites at elevations above 10,000 feet, from California to Nevada, Montana, Oregon, and Idaho, this kind has solitary flower heads about 2 inches in diameter, with twenty-five to fifty rays.

Garden Uses and Cultivation. These high elevation plants are appropriate for alpine gardens where summers are cool. They do not tolerate hot, humid weather. They need gritty, sharply-drained, not-too-rich, adequately moist soil and a sunny location. Propagation is by seed.

HUMATA (Hum-àta)—Bear's Foot Fern. This group of about fifty species of small ferns is so similar to *Davallia* that some authorities believe it should be included there. Its separation is based on technical differences of the indusia (coverings of the groups of spore clusters). This genus belongs in the davallia family DAVALLIACEAE, and ranges in the wild from tropical Asia to Madagascar and islands of the Pacific. The name is believed to be derived from the Latin *humatus*, a cover of earth, and alludes to the rhizomes being buried.

Epiphytes, that is plants growing on trees and similar places without taking nourishment from their hosts, humatas have creeping rhizomes and scattered, leathery, pinnately-divided or undivided, triangular to oblong leaves. The round to kidney-shaped clusters of spore capsules are at the ends of the veins near the leaf margins.

Bear's foot fern (*Humata tyermannii*) is so called because its rhizomes are densely shaggy with white scales. It is a native of warm parts of China. Slow-growing and evergreen, this has leaves at intervals of 2 to 3 inches along the rhizomes. They are triangular, about 6 inches long, and three- or four-times-pinnately-divided.

Humata tyermannii

Native to the Himalayas, *H. griffithiana* (syn. *Davallia griffithiana*) has long, creeping rhizomes densely clothed with white scales. Its evergreen fronds, about 1½ feet long, have three- or four-times-pinnate, triangular blades with the lowermost leaflets up to 9 inches long, the ultimate segments deeply toothed. One of the smallest species, *H. repens* (syn. *Davallia repens*) is native from Taiwan and China, to India, some Pacific islands, and Australia. This has creeping, wiry rhizomes and once-pinnate, evergreen leaves with stalks and blades each rarely more than 4 inches long. Their leaflets are up to 1 inch long and about one-half as wide.

Garden Uses and Cultivation. Only in practically frost-free climates are these ferns likely to live outdoors. They are usually grown in greenhouses, sometimes in terrariums. Shallow pots called pans are better suited for them than deeper containers. They must be very well drained. Loose, porous, humusy soil, such as can be had by mixing together shredded fir bark, peat moss, perlite, sphagnum moss, and crushed charcoal with one-quarter or less of the total bulk of fibrous, turfy topsoil will do, as will rooting mixtures favorable to bromeliads, orchids, and other epiphytes. It is important that the mixture be kept moist, but not constantly saturated, and that the atmosphere be fairly humid. Shade from strong sun is needed, but not too much. Well-rooted specimens benefit from regular applications of dilute liquid fertilizer. Winter temperatures of 50 to 55°F at night are satisfactory, by day an increase of five to ten degrees is appropriate. Propagation is by division and by spores. For further information see Ferns.

HUMEA (Hùm-ea) — Incense Plant. Australia is not only the home of an egg-laying mammal and other strange animals, it is the native land of some quite extraordinary plants including, for instance, orchids that live completely underground (*Cryptantemis* and *Rhizanthella*). Among the unusual flora is the genus *Humea*, of which there are seven species. This group is confined to Australia and Madagascar. One handsome, biennial, Australian species is sometimes cultivated. It is difficult to imagine a more un-daisy-like member of the daisy family COMPOSITAE than this, yet that is where botanists assure us *Humea* belongs. The foliage of *H. elegans* roughly resembles that of a tobacco plant, and its flowers look like those of a giant, graceful grass. Other members of the genus are herbaceous plants and shrubs of somewhat more ordinary aspect. The genus was named in honor of Lady Hume, of England.

The parts of the flower clusters of the incense plant (*H. elegans*) that look like spikelets of a grass are really flower heads (clusters of florets) analogous to the much larger flower heads of a daisy or even of a giant sunflower, but they are tiny and each consists of one to four florets surrounded by thin, nonspreading bracts. There are no ray florets. The fruits are achenes.

Well-grown specimens of *H. elegans* are 6 to 8 feet tall. They have a strong, erect, central stem and many ascending branches gracefully disposed. Stem and branches are clothed with stem-clasping, ovate-lanceolate to oblong-lanceolate, pointed, rather wrinkled, alternate leaves. The lower leaves are largest, above they gradually diminish in size until the uppermost

Humea elegans

Humea elegans (flowers)

are represented by heart-shaped bracts. Foliage and stems are clammy-hairy and have a pervasive balsamic odor that one old book describes as resembling a mixture of the scents of red-cedar wood and haut-boy strawberries. The myriad tiny flower heads are disposed in long, loose panicles. They are warm brownish-red and in sunshine a plant in full bloom looks like a shower of burnished copper. They remain attractive for several weeks.

Garden Uses. For summer display in flower beds and borders and for decorating terraces, patios, and similar places, few plants are as graceful as *H. elegans*. It may be used effectively in groups, or singly, and has the great merit of remaining attractive and unchanged over a long summer period. Not the least of its merits is its pleasant odor. Its feathery flower sprays,

when cut, are useful for combining with other blooms in arrangements.

Cultivation. It requires some skill and attention to grow the incense plant well. If neglected, it loses its lower leaves, becomes straggly, and does not develop as vigorous branches or such large and handsome sprays of bloom as it should. If it is watered carelessly, so that water remains on the leaves for long periods, they become brown-spotted. Strong winds may seriously damage specimens that are not well staked.

The incense plant is a biennial and is discarded after flowering. It is raised from seeds sown in July or August in well-drained containers of light sandy peaty soil. The young seedlings are carefully transplanted to flats or individually to small pots and are kept growing actively in a cool, airy greenhouse or cold frame in full sun. As soon as they are large enough they are transferred to 5-inch pots in rich porous soil where they remain until early in the new year. With the onset of winter, growth slows and less watering is needed, but at no time must the soil dry to the extent that the foliage wilts, and even in winter occasional applications of dilute liquid fertilizer benefit specimens that are fairly well rooted. Cool, airy atmospheric conditions are essential. A night temperature at this season of 50°F is adequate and day temperatures should be only five to fifteen degrees, depending upon weather, higher. An environment congenial to carnations is appropriate for *Humea elegans*. Before the roots become really matted and pot bound the plants should be repotted into larger pots and this is repeated until they occupy receptacles 8 to 10 inches in diameter. It is better to give more than one small shift than to move them from a comparatively small pot to a very much larger one in one operation. Great care must be taken not to break the root ball when repotting; that is fatal. Rich, porous soil should be used.

Humeas are gross feeders and as soon as their final pots or tubs are fairly filled with healthy roots a program of regular feeding with dilute liquid fertilizer should be instituted. Weekly or semiweekly applications are not too frequent. Great care must be taken that the soil never becomes too dry. If that happens the leaves yellow almost immediately and irreparable damage is done. When the plants are watered the foliage should not be wetted, nor should this be done when the benches, floors, and other surfaces of the greenhouse are damped down (sprayed with water). Plants raised in this way may be planted in the garden, again taking great care not to break their root balls, when the weather is warm and settled, about the time that it is safe to plant out geraniums and other tender summer bedding plants. No information seems to be recorded regarding growing this plant in mild cli-

mates outdoors from start to finish, but this would seem to be a distinct possibility in parts of California, the Southwest, and elsewhere where locations free from frost are available. It is worth trying.

HUMIDITY, ATMOSPHERIC. The relative humidity of the atmosphere is very important to the growth of plants and various garden practices are designed to influence it. Note the reference is to relative humidity, not humidity. The latter term is often used, as it is throughout this Encyclopedia, as a substitute and to mean the same as the more precise term relative humidity.

Relative humidity is a measure, expressed as a percentage of the maximum amount of water vapor the air is capable of holding at any specified temperature. It does not allude to the amount of water vapor in a particular volume of air.

If there is no moisture in the air, an unlikely possibility except in a kiln or some such place, the relative humidity at any temperature is zero. Air saturated with moisture so that it can hold no more has a relative humidity of 100 percent. But the *amount* of water vapor needed to produce 100 percent, or any other percent of humidity, in any particular volume of air, varies with the temperature. The warmer it is the more moisture air can absorb, and the more is needed to achieve any particular degree of relative humidity. Unless additional moisture is supplied the relative humidity of the atmosphere decreases as temperature is raised. It increases as it is lowered. It is relative humidity that affects plants and so is important to gardeners and others who cultivate them.

To illustrate, air at 40°F and relative humidity of 75 percent contains in each volume equivalent to a cube with sides of approximately 15 feet long one pound of water. If the temperature is raised to 80°F, four times as much water is required to achieve the same relative humidity. If the same temperature increase occurs without additional water being supplied the relative humidity of the air drops to under 20 percent.

Decreases in relative humidity of this nature occur in apartments and homes during the heating season and are largely responsible for the discomfort of plants grown in them. In greenhouses relative humidity is increased by periodically wetting floors, benches, and other surfaces, by the use of fog nozzles, and by spraying foliage with water. It is decreased when necessary by manipulating the heating system and ventilators, aided sometimes by fans.

HUMMING BIRD BUSH is *Grevillea thele-manniana*.

HUMMING BIRD'S TRUMPET. See Zauschneria.

HUMULUS (Húm-ulus)—Hop. There are two or, according to some botanists, three or four species of *Humulus*, of the mulberry family MORACEAE. Called hops, they are twining perennial vines, natives of north temperate regions. One, the source of the hops used in brewing, is esteemed for the bitter principle chiefly concentrated in the fruiting catkins or "hops." The genus name is an ancient one of unknown significance.

These vines have rough stems and generally lobed, broad, opposite leaves. They are unisexual. The flowers, from the leaf axils, have five sepals. The blooms of male plants are numerous and in panicles. They have five stamens. Those of female plants are paired and are in short spikes, with overlapping bracts. As the spikes pass into fruit, they become the conelike or catkin-like "hops" and contain within their persistent calyxes seedlike fruits called achenes.

Common hop (*H. lupulus*) is a native of Europe, Asia, and North America. The indigenous American population, which has the terminal lobe of the leaf usually at least twice as long as wide, as distinguished from European and Asian phases in which the end lobe is not more than one and one-half times as long as its breadth, is sometimes segregated as *H. americanus.* It is native from Nova Scotia to Florida and Arizona. The European type also occurs in North America as a naturalized introduction. The common hop has stems up to 30 feet long. Its leaves have stalks usually shorter than their blades and, other than those in the flowering parts, which are often without lobes, are usually three-lobed often to below their middles, more rarely five- or seven-lobed and coarsely-toothed. The "hops" are straw-colored and 1¼ to 2½ inches long. Variety *H. l. aureus* has yellow foliage.

Japanese hop (*H. japonicus* syn. *H. scandens*) inhabits Japan, China, the Ryukyu Islands, and Taiwan. Its stems are conspicuously rougher than those of the preceding kind. Its leaves are longer-stalked, the stalks ordinarily exceeding the length of the blades. The main leaves are five- to seven-the upper ones three- to five-lobed. At maturity the "hops" are dull green. This species is naturalized in parts of North America. Variety *H. j. variegatus* has foliage irregularly blotched with white.

Garden and Landscape Uses. Both the common hop and more often the Japanese hop are cultivated as ornamentals, the latter frequently as an annual. They grow very rapidly and form useful and interesting screens and covers for pergolas, porches, trellis, and other places where suitable supports for their twining stems are available. They succeed in sun or part-shade and in any ordinary, reasonably fertile, well-drained soil.

Cultivation. The common hop is grown as a hardy perennial. It is easily propagated by cuttings. Seeds may also be used, but these do not truly reproduce varieties cultivated commercially. The Japanese hop has no value as a source of hops for beer. When grown as an annual its seeds are sown outdoors in spring, or earlier indoors and the young plants are carried in pots for six to eight weeks before they are planted in the open, which is not done until the weather is warm and settled. Indoor sowing is in porous soil in a temperature of 60 to 65°F. The young plants are grown at somewhat lower temperatures, in full sun, until planted outdoors.

HUMUS. Not infrequently mucks and peats sold as soil conditioners are called humus. Usually they are fine-textured, dark brown or black, and consist to a very large extent of organic matter. These are not in the true meaning of the word humus. More correctly they are humus-forming materials as are peat moss, compost, leaf mold, manure, and other organic debris.

Commercial products sold as humus have not completely reached the state of decay characteristic of true humus. Under ordinary conditions they gradually do so after they are mixed with the soil. For convenience they may be called commercial humus.

In its strictest sense humus is organic matter in the last stage of decomposition before conversion into such end products as carbonic acid, ammonia, and water.

Humulus lupulus

Humulus lupulus (foliage and female flowers)

Humulus japonicus (male flowers)

Commercial humus

Plant and animal remains are attacked by a series of decay-causing bacteria. In the absence of air, as when decomposition takes place under water, vegetation is converted into peats and mucks, but the acids formed in this process finally inhibit bacterial action and further decay is suspended before the whole is converted to humus. In the presence of air the breaking-down action by bacteria continues and true humus is formed.

Humus is responsible for the characteristic dark color of surface soil as compared with subsoil. It is amorphous, showing no structure of the tissues from which it is formed. Physically the most important fraction of the soil humus is a colloid that, like colloidal clay, serves as a weak cement to hold larger soil particles together and when in a flocculated condition promotes a desirable crumb structure. Humus helps to prevent leaching of nutrients from soil and serves as a buffering or compensating agent, slowing down what may be the ill effects of excessive available amounts of nutrient salts and other chemical constituents of soils. Other favorable properties of humus are its spongelike ability to hold moisture, especially important in sandy and gravelly soils, and its part in providing the food and energy needed by favorable soil bacteria.

Except in acid bogs and swamps, the destruction by bacterial action in the soil of humus is continuous, occurring more rapidly at high temperatures than lower ones. In the process, nitrogen and to a lesser extent other nutrient elements needed by plants are released and made available to them. The presence of lime in the soil stimulates this activity.

Replenishment of humus lost in this way and the maintenance of a satisfactory proportion in the soil is a major objective of soil management. It is done by adding manure, compost, peat moss, leaf mold, and commercial humus and in some cases other vegetable debris such as sawdust, wood chips, spent hops, bagasse, and the like, and by, in the technique of green

Hunnemannia fumariaefolia

manuring, turning under crops of living plants.

HUNNEMANNIA (Hunnemánn-ia)—Mexican Tulip-Poppy. The only species of this genus is very like the California-poppy (*Eschscholzia*). It differs in the sepals of its flowers being separate instead of completely united to form a cap. Endemic to Mexico, *Hunnemannia* belongs in the poppy family PAPAVERACEAE. Its name commemorates John Hunneman, an English bookseller, who acted as agent for the sale of herbarium specimens and introduced plants. He died in 1839.

Mexican tulip-poppy (*H. fumariaefolia*), although often cultivated as an annual, is a nonhardy herbaceous perennial. In frostless and nearly frostless climates it survives from year to year. Bushy and erect, 1 foot to 2 feet tall, it has finely-dissected, bluish-gray, glabrous leaves and long-stalked, poppy-like, clear yellow flowers with two sepals, four petals, and numerous orange stamens. The blooms are 2 to 3 inches in diameter. They are produced in unbroken succession for several months in summer and fall. The fruits are capsules. A variety with double flowers is cultivated.

Garden Uses. The Mexican tulip-poppy is one of the most reliable plants for summer displays of colorful bloom in flower beds and borders, window and porch

boxes, and suchlike places. Its flowers are useful for cutting and last better in water than those of many other members of the poppy family. This plant may also be grown in greenhouses to provide flowers for winter use. Indoors or out, it must be exposed to maximum sun. It will not thrive in shade.

Cultivation. Any ordinary well-drained garden soil is satisfactory for hunnemannias, but they will not stand wet soil. Sow the seeds, which take a rather long time to germinate, directly where the plants are to flower, as early in spring as the soil can be worked into a suitable condition. Thin the young plants to stand 6 inches apart, but do not attempt to transplant the seedlings. They rarely recover satisfactorily after their roots are disturbed. Alternatively, sow in a greenhouse in a temperature of 55 to 60°F about February to obtain plants to set in the garden soon after all danger of frost has passed. For this indoor sowing fill 2½-inch pots with sandy soil and put four or five seeds in each. As soon as the seedlings are well established, thin them to two or three in each pot and when the pots are filled with roots repot them, without disturbing the roots and still two or three together, into 4-inch pots, using a fertile, porous potting mix and making sure the pots are adequately crocked. Keep the plants in full sun in a greenhouse where the night temperature is 50 to 55°F, and day temperatures are five to ten degrees higher. When the weather is sufficiently warm and settled, transplant the plants to their flowering quarters, spacing them about 8 inches apart, and taking great care not to break the root balls.

Seeds sown in pots in August or September give plants suitable for setting in benches or beds in greenhouses for the production of winter bloom. Hunnemannias do well in a winter night temperature of 50°F, and daytime temperatures a few degrees higher. Ventilate the greenhouse freely whenever weather permits. Take care to keep the atmosphere dryish rather than excessively humid. Water moderately, not excessively.

HUNON-PINE is *Dacrydium franklinii.*

HUNTARA. This is the name of orchid hybrids the parents of which include *Arachnis, Euanthe, Renanthera, Vanda,* and *Vandopsis.*

HUNTLEANTHES. This is the name of orchid hybrids the parents of which are *Cochleanthes* and *Huntleya.*

HUNTLEYA (Húnt-leya). Having much the aspect of *Zygopetalum* and *Batemannia,* and native of Central America and tropical South America, *Huntleya,* of the orchid family ORCHIDACEAE, consists of ten evergreen, epiphytic (tree-perching) species. Its name commemorates an early nineteenth-century fancier of orchids, the Reverend J. H. Huntley.

Huntleyas are without pseudobulbs. Usually they grow in tufts, but sometimes have long rhizomes with leaves spaced at intervals along them. Their more or less strap-shaped, two-ranked leaves are in fans from near the bases of which come slender-stalked, often large, solitary blooms. The flowers have spreading, similar sepals and petals and a lip narrowed below, flaring above and with a fringed crest on its callus. The apex of the column is winged.

Its pointed, linear-lanceolate to elliptic-lanceolate leaves 6 inches to 1 foot long or longer and 1½ to 2 inches wide, *H. meleagris* (syn. *H. burtii*) has blooms on stalks about 6 inches tall. The waxy, fragrant, long-lasting, starry flowers, 3 to 5 inches in diameter and with broad sepals and petals, on stalks about 6 inches long, vary much in color. Commonly their broad, spreading, petal-like sepals and petals are white or yellowish at their bases and shiny, yellow-spotted, reddish-brown in their upper two-thirds. In addition, the bottoms of the petals may be marked with purple. The lip, sharply narrowed and yellowish-white below, is rich reddish- or purplish-brown in its upper part. This species enjoys a natural range from Costa Rica to Brazil.

Huntleya meleagris

Garden Uses and Cultivation. Unfortunately most gardeners find huntleyas difficult to grow well. Fairly cool conditions, such as suit miltonias and high mountain odontoglossums, and high humidity and moderate shade are recommended. They are most likely to succeed in very well-drained pots in a mixture of osmunda or tree fern fiber and chopped sphagnum moss, topped with live sphagnum moss. To prevent rotting it is important to have the base of the plant raised slightly above the compost. Abundant watering throughout the year and regular fertilizing from spring to fall are recommended. For additional information see Orchids.

HUNTSMAN'S CUP. See Sarracenia.

HURA (Hù-ra)—Sandbox Tree. Like several members of the spurge family EUPHORBIACEAE, the genus *Hura* contains a caustic, poisonous, milky or watery sap irritating to the skin and dangerous to the eyes. Native to tropical America and the West Indies, it consists of two species with undivided, rather glossy leaves and petalless flowers. Its generic name is its South American one. The common name sandbox tree refers to a use formerly made of its remarkable fruits. Before the days of absorbent paper these were hollowed and filled with sand for blotting ink. The fruits, 2½ to 3½ inches in diameter, are flattened with a depression at the apex. They are hard-shelled and corrugated by fifteen to twenty deep grooves, and resemble miniature pumpkins. When ripe and dry the fruits explode violently with a loud, startling sound, and split into one-seeded segments that are thrown a considerable distance.

The sandbox tree (*Hura crepitans*) is handsome. It attains a maximum height of about 100 feet and has a globular crown. Usually its trunk and branches are furnished with blackish spines partly surrounded by bark and up to ¾ inch long. The long-stalked, white-veined leaves are heart-shaped, have blades that curve upward from the midrib, and are 5 to 8 inches long by about two-thirds as broad. They may or may not be toothed and are deciduous or nearly evergreen according to climate. Male and female flowers are on the same tree, the former many together in dense terminal spikes an inch or two long and located at the ends of stalks 2½ to 4 inches long, the latter solitary near the ends of the shoots. They are dark red and have cuplike calyxes. The females are ¼ inch long and broad and have a single pistil with a large parasol-shaped stigma. The males are slightly longer and narrower than the females and have eight to twenty stamens in two or three circles on a central column. The other species, *H. polyandra,* native from Mexico to Costa Rica, has white male flowers with more stamens than those of the sandbox tree; the stamens are in a column.

Garden and Landscape Uses. In warm regions, including southern Florida, the West Indies, and southern California, the sandbox tree is sometimes planted for ornament and shade, but this should not be done without full awareness of its disadvantages and even dangers. It is easily damaged by windstorms. Its seeds are toxic to humans and some animals and if pruning or other cutting has to be done adequate precautions must be taken that the juice does not come in contact with the skin or, especially, the eyes of the operator. The sandbox tree is common along roadsides in Puerto Rico and some other parts of its natural range. It is better not to plant it in home grounds, parks, and other public places.

Cultivation. The sandbox tree grows in most ordinary soils, preferring sandy loam. It requires plenty of light, especially when young. Propagation is by seed.

HUSK-TOMATO, STRAWBERRY-TOMATO, GROUND-CHERRY. Neither tomato nor cherry, but by virtue of belonging to the nightshade family SOLANACEAE, more closely related to the former than the latter, the husk-tomato, strawberry-tomato, or ground-cherry is *Physalis pruinosa*, a native of North America.

A vigorous, low annual, *P. pruinosa* is cultivated to a minor extent for its edible fruits. These are cherry-sized, greenish-yellow berries surrounded by large, conspicuous calyxes and containing many small seeds. Very similar *P. pubescens* is probably also grown under the same vernacular names. The Cape-gooseberry (*P. peruviana*) is closely related.

Cultivation. Ordinary, well-drained garden soil suits these plants. A sunny location is needed. Sow seeds outdoors where the plants are to remain or indoors earlier to give plants to set out at tomato-planting time. Allow 2 to 3 feet between individuals.

HUTCHINSIA (Hutchín-sia). This genus of annual, biennial, and perennial herbaceous plants, of Europe and southwest Asia, consists of three or perhaps more species. It belongs in the mustard family CRUCIFERAE and is principally of interest to rock gardeners. Its name commemorates the Irish botanist Ellen Hutchins, who died in 1815. Hutchinsias are low plants with pinnately-lobed or lobeless leaves and small white, four-petaled flowers in terminal racemes. A characteristic that differentiates them from the allied genera *Aethionema*, *Ionopsidium*, and *Cochlearia* is the possession of mostly forked or branched hairs on their leaves. From *Iberis* they differ in having four petals of approximately equal size.

The most commonly cultivated species, *H. alpina* is native of European mountains. Up to 4 inches in height, it has leaves, mostly basal, up to 1 inch long and pinnately one- to four-lobed. Its rather crowded racemes are composed of white flowers under ¼ inch in diameter. The fruits are erect pods up to ⅜ inch in length. Very similar *H. a. brevicaulis*, of the Pyrenees, is smaller and more compact and has pinnate leaves. Biennial *H. stylosa* of Italy has almost lobeless leaves.

Garden Uses and Cultivation. Unpretentious *H. alpina* and its relatives are worthy of places in rock gardens. They form low mats of feathery foliage and bloom for a long while in spring, producing their small flowers in abundance. Hutchinsias

Hutchinsia alpina brevicaulis

are easily raised from seed and, the perennial kinds, by division. They succeed in porous, gritty, well-drained soil in sun, but prefer a cool location such as is provided by a north-facing slope, to more torrid conditions. At New York City they have proved reliable and worthwhile.

HYACINTH. See Hyacinthus. The word hyacinth forms part of the common names of some other plants including these: feather-hyacinth (*Muscari comosum monstrosum*), grape-hyacinth (*Muscari* and *Synthyris*), hyacinth-bean (*Dolichos lablab*), hyacinth orchid (*Arpophyllum*), star-hyacinth (*Scilla amoena*), starch-hyacinth (*Muscari neglectum*), summer-hyacinth (*Galtonia candicans*), tassel-hyacinth (*Muscari comosum*), water-hyacinth (*Eichhornia crassipes*), wild-hyacinth (*Camassia scilloides*, *Dichelostemma pulchellum*, and *Endymion nonscriptus*).

HYACINTHELLA (Hyacinth-élla). This genus of the lily family LILIACEAE consists of about ten species of hardy bulb plants of the Mediterranean region, southeast Europe, and western Asia. It differs from *Hyacinthus* chiefly in a technical difference in its seeds and in the perianth lobes (petal-like parts of the flowers) being much shorter than the corolla tubes. The name *Hyacinthella* means little hyacinth.

Hyacinthellas produce from each bulb usually two, less often one or three, narrow leaves commonly with raised veins. Their small horizontal or up-facing, but never nodding, bell- to funnel-shaped flowers are in cylindrical, spikelike racemes. Blue, violet, or rarely white, they

have six petals (more correctly tepals), six stamens, and one style. The fruits are capsules containing black seeds.

The only commonly cultivated sort, **H. dalmatica** (syn. *Hyacinthus dalmaticus*), of Dalmatia, is 3 to 4 inches tall and has a pair of thickish, linear-lanceolate leaves 2 to 3 inches long and pale blue tubular flowers under ¼ inch long.

Garden Uses and Cultivation. These are as for grape-hyacinths (*Muscari*).

HYACINTHUS (Hyacínth-us) — Hyacinth. The genus *Hyacinthus*, of the lily family LILIACEAE, as now interpreted consists of a single species native of the Mediterranean region, Asia Minor, and Syria. Its name is its ancient Greek one. It is best known to gardeners for its magnificent horticultural varieties, the sources of the massive, obese spikes of heavily-scented blooms that stood stiffly to attention in serried rows in old-fashioned spring flower beds in parks and private gardens of the past. The decline of interest in formal bedding as well as its high costs have sharply reduced the number of such displays, but the same fat hyacinths—Dutch hyacinths as they are called—are still favorites for forcing into bloom as Easter pot plants and for planting in gardens, although less lavishly than formerly. The Roman hyacinth, a variety of the common species, was also popular for forcing in greenhouses. It is more graceful than its Dutch relatives, but tenderer. Other plants previously included in *Hyacinthus* are treated in the genera *Bellevalia*, *Brimeura*, *Hyacinthella*, and *Muscari*. The summer-hyacinth is *Galtonia candicans*.

Hyacinthus orientalis, wild species

Hyacinthus orientalis, garden variety

From nearly related grape-hyacinths (*Muscari*) hyacinths (*Hyacinthus*) differ in having open-mouthed, bell-shaped flowers with spreading perianth lobes. The blooms of grape-hyacinths are pucker-mouthed, urn-shaped or cylindrical, with just a suggestion of perianth lobes. Hyacinths have all basal leaves and erect stems with spikelike racemes of blooms that may be white, pink, red, blue, purple, or yellowish. They have normally six petals (or, more correctly, tepals) that are spreading or reflexed, six short stamens attached to the inside of the corolla, and a solitary pistil. The fruits are three-angled or three-lobed dry capsules.

The common hyacinth (**H. orientalis**) is native from Greece to Syria and Asia Minor. Little known in its wild form, as such it is more graceful than its garden varieties. Its bulbs are large and approximately globular, its leaves fleshy, strap-shaped, and 1 inch wide or wider. Its hollow stalks carry many nodding or horizontally-held, sweetly scented blooms that come in a variety of colors and are about 1 inch long. Pictures of horticultural varieties of this hyacinth confront us in brilliant color from the pages of catalogs of spring bulbs. It was varieties of this that the Empress Josephine cherished in the garden at Malmaison.

Garden varieties of the common hyacinth are so well known it would waste space to list and detail the characteristics of the named entities here, suffice it to say that they may be had in all the colors mentioned earlier and in many shades and tones of each. There are double- as well as single-flowered kinds. Those sold as cyn-

thella or miniature hyacinths produce smaller, more open, less massive spikes of bloom than the others, but differ not in kind. They are merely smaller, younger bulbs not grown by their Dutch raisers to a size where they are capable of producing the gigantic spikes of "exhibition size bulbs," or even of "bedding hyacinths," to use catalog terms. Hyacinth bulbs that have been given special temperature treatment to ready them for early forcing are sold as prepared hyacinths. Others, as a result of special treatment by Dutch bulb growers, produce from each bulb several smaller and more graceful spikes than is normal. These are sold as multiflora hyacinths. The Roman hyacinth (*H. o. albulus*) is a native of southern France. Its stems are frailer than those of the common hyacinth and its bells fewer and more widely set. Usually they are white, but

vary toward pale blue. This sort blooms much earlier than common hyacinths, but is less hardy to cold.

Garden and Landscape Uses. For those who enjoy mechanical precision Dutch hyacinths are most satisfactory plants to fill spring flower beds. They delighted generations of European gardeners who worked out "color schemes" based on geometrical patterns with bed areas planted solidly to different hues, a central patch of pink perhaps, margined with blue, or vice versa. The more daring mixed two or more colors to achieve often more pleasing pepper-and-salt effects. In attempts to be different, British gardeners developed the practice of intermingling with hyacinths other plants such as pansies, English daisies, and polyanthus primroses. They usually produced less pleasing results. To achieve the greatest uniformity newly pur-

Bed of hyacinths

Border of hyacinths

Second-year bulbs flower less rigidly than first-year ones

chased bulbs must be planted each autumn, a costly procedure, and expense has proven a powerful factor in the decline in popularity of this kind of formal bedding. In any case it never appealed to Americans to the same extent as to Europeans.

Fortunately there are more imaginative and less expensive ways of using Dutch hyacinths to achieve good effects in gardens. They can be planted in somewhat irregular groups, with the bulbs not spaced precisely the same distance apart, in openings along the fronts of shrub borders. Nearby shrubs must be kinds that do not fill the surface soil with greedy roots. Another possibility is to use them in similar groups in mixed flower borders and, after their foliage has died, to overplant them with annuals. For both purposes second-year bulbs, those that have spent their first blooming season in a formal flower bed, may be used. Once planted, they may remain undisturbed. In most gardens Dutch hyacinths gradually deteriorate and finally fail to bloom altogether. In the few years that follow the first, the blooms gradually lose their massiveness and assume some of the characteristics of their wild ancestors. They become slenderer and smaller, with flowers more unevenly placed. They acquire grace, but lose the grandeur that makes them so impressive for use in formal flower beds. Fortunately they do not part with their fragrance and their colors are undiminished in loveliness.

Cultivation. Growing hyacinths is not difficult. They are responsive to well-drained, moderately fertile soils and full sun. They are planted as early in fall as the bulbs can be obtained, with their tops cov-

ered to a depth of 2 to 3 inches. Under favorable circumstances they increase in number and after the passage of several years it may be necessary to lift them, immediately their foliage has died, sort them to size and replant them. In intervening years they benefit from an annual top dressing with a complete fertilizer in spring.

Dutch hyacinths planted in formal beds are usually spaced 5 to 6 inches apart and set with their bases 5 inches beneath the surface. Plant them in early fall after spading the soil to a depth of 8 to 10 inches and making it agreeable to the roots by mixing in compost or other organic matter, except manure, and a dressing of bonemeal or other slow-acting fertilizer. Where winters are severe a protective cover of salt hay, branches of evergreens, or other suitable material may be placed over the beds after the soil is frozen an inch or so deep. This is removed in spring.

After the floral display is finished it is usual to lift hyacinths from formal beds to make way for plants that will provide the summer display. They should be dug carefully with as many roots and as much soil adhering to them as possible and be planted temporarily in a shaded location where they can be kept moist until the foliage dies naturally. At this time they need not be set deeply. It is enough if the bulbs are just covered. They are set closely together, but not crowded to the extent that the foliage is deprived of light and air. When the leaves have completely died the bulbs are taken up, cleaned of the remains of dead leaves, and stored in trays or flats in a cool, dry, shaded place until the fall planting season. Such bulbs never pro-

duce as large and uniform flower spikes as newly purchased ones, but, if they have been carefully handled, they will make a creditable display in their second year. The annual taking up of hyacinth bulbs from formal beds is necessitated by the need to plant other flowers in their place for summer show and also because after the first year the bulbs throw smaller and less uniform flower spikes. Hyacinths that are not in formal beds may remain undisturbed after blooming, but care must be taken not to remove their foliage until it has died naturally.

For forcing into early bloom Dutch hyacinths are available as normally harvested bulbs, the same as are used for outdoor plantings, and as "prepared" bulbs. The latter are grown and treated in such a way by the Dutch bulb growers that they can be brought into bloom at least a month earlier than unprepared bulbs. Except for very early forcing ordinary bulbs are used. Hyacinths for forcing are planted in fall in pots or pans (shallow pots) in any ordinary well-drained soil.

To obtain the largest spikes of bloom, the biggest bulbs sold, those sometimes called exhibition size, should be used, but

Forcing hyacinths: (a) Potting the bulbs in fall

(b) Covering the potted bulbs with sandy soil

(c) After several weeks, removed from the soil

(d) Covering to provide complete darkness to cause leaves and flower stalks to elongate

(e) After sufficient height is attained, cover is removed; plants are pale yellow

(f) Exposed to light they soon become green

(g) In full bloom

very attractive results can also be had from smaller, bedding size bulbs. In any case, they should be plump and heavy and planted with their tips just showing above the soil surface. Single bulbs may be accommodated in 4-inch pots or, the largest ones in 5-inch pots, or three may be set in a 6-inch pan. The next step is important. They must spend several weeks in a place conducive to strong root growth. One method to assure this is to bury them outdoors or in a cold frame under 8 inches of sand or sandy soil and, after its surface is frozen to a depth of an inch or two, to cover it with salt hay, straw, leaves, or other suitable insulation. Alternatively, they may be put in a cool, moist cellar or similar place where the temperature can be held as close to 40°F as possible. During this rooting period they must never become dry. The objective is to encourage root, but not top growth. This requires a continuously moist, but not waterlogged soil and coolness without actual freezing; in frozen soil root growth does not take place. Forcing, which must not begin until

the containers are well filled with roots, may be done in a greenhouse, home, or other warm place.

The earliest blooms may be had in December. To secure these, the largest-sized prepared bulbs are planted in October. By late November or early December they should be rooted sufficiently to begin forcing. Then they are placed in a temperature of 60°F. They are kept without light for a week and then are gradually accustomed to full sunlight and the temperature is raised five to ten degrees. When the flower buds show color the temperature is lowered to 50°F. This hardens the plants and stiffens the foliage. Blooms will be had in three or four weeks from the time forcing begins. The best varieties for very early forcing are 'Bismark' (blue-flowered), 'Pink Pearl' (pink), and 'L'Innocence' (white).

Forcing unprepared bulbs may be begun about Christmas, and successional batches may be brought indoors until spring approaches. When first brought in, they are kept in the dark until the shoots are a few inches tall and leaves and flower spikes are fairly well developed; then they are gradually exposed to full sunlight. For the earliest ones brought in, a temperature of 55 to 60°F is sufficient, but if fast results

are desired this may be raised to 65 to 70°F after a week. When the flowers show color the temperature should be lowered to 50 to 55°F to harden the plants. Under this treatment flowers from bulbs brought indoors early are had in three to four weeks from the time forcing begins; from bulbs brought indoors later in the season, in about two weeks. For the earliest forcing of unprepared bulbs satisfactory varieties are 'Bismark', 'Dr. Lieber', and 'Ostara', with blue flowers; 'Lady Derby', 'Nimrod', and 'Pink Pearl', with pink blooms; 'Jan Bos', with red blooms; and the white-flowered 'L'Innocence' and 'Edelweiss'. For the latest forcing 'King of the Blues', 'Queen of the Blues', 'Queen of the Pinks', and 'Queen of the Whites' are preferred. Other kinds, in addition to those recommended for earliest forcing, may be used for mid-season blooming. Here belong such varieties as 'Grand Maitre' and 'Myosotis', with blue flowers; the pink-flowered 'General DeWitt' and 'Gertrude'; red-flowered 'La Victoire', and 'Prince Henry'; and 'Yellow Hammer', with pale yellow blooms.

Roman hyacinths are naturally earlier bloomers than Dutch hyacinths and force even more readily than prepared bulbs of the latter. For forcing they are handled in exactly the same way except that they are planted as early as the bulbs can be obtained in the fall. Because they come to flower so quickly it is not the practice to bury them outdoors or in a cold frame after planting, but to put them in a cool, dark place to make sufficient root growth before they are subjected to forcing temperatures. With little trouble Roman hyacinths can be had in bloom well before Christmas.

Growing hyacinths without soil in special glasses and bowls is more commonly done in Europe than America. Yet, provided a place where the temperature can be held between 40 and 50°F during the rooting period is available, they are equally as successful west as east of the Atlantic. They will not prosper if started in the high temperature of the ordinary

Bulb starting into growth in hyacinth glass

American home. The bulbs may be set individually in hyacinth glasses constructed with a cupped top to contain the bulb and a base that holds water into which the roots grow, or they may be planted in pebbles or other non-nutrient medium in decorative bowls that are without drainage holes. In Europe "bulb fiber," consisting of turfy peat with some crushed oyster shells and small pieces of charcoal mixed in, is commonly used. Both Roman and Dutch hyacinths are successful when grown in this way; the cynthellas are especially charming. The purpose of the pebbles or fiber is to hold the bulbs in place and give anchorage to their roots. The nourishment needed to develop fine flower spikes is contained in the bulbs. All that is needed is water, enough roots to absorb sufficient water, warmth (not too much until a good mass of roots has developed), and, after the shoots are 3 or 4 inches high, light. Planting presents no problems. Hyacinth glasses are filled with water (to which a few pieces of charcoal are added) so that it just touches the bases of the bulbs. For preference rainwater is used, but tap water will do. In bowls the bulbs are set closely together with the pebbles or fiber packed about their bases just high enough to hold them in position and water is filled in to just reach the bulbs. During the rooting period and later water must be added from time to time to maintain the desired level. At least eight weeks in cool conditions are needed before forcing is begun by bringing the bulbs into warmth. Then a sunny window in a cool room or at least well away from radiators or other sources of intense heat affords a suitable location. For the first few days to a week, until the leaves green, they must be shaded from strong sun.

Hyacinth bulbs that have been forced in pebbles, bulb fiber, or water are of no further use and should be discarded after blooming. Those forced in soil have limited use for planting in the outdoor garden if they receive good care during and after their season of bloom. This involves keeping them growing as long as possible under favorable conditions in a greenhouse or similar place. They need regular watering and occasional applications of dilute fertilizer until the foliage begins to die naturally, when fertilizing should be stopped and watering is gradually reduced and finally completely withheld. When planted in the garden such bulbs produce only second-rate flowers. The effort is scarcely worthwhile.

HYBANTHUS (Hyb-ánthus). Herbaceous perennials, subshrubby, or rarely shrubby, constitute *Hybanthus*, of the violet family VIOLACEAE. Formerly named *Ionidium*, they are inhabitants of warm and warm-temperate parts of the Americas, including the West Indies. There are 150 species. The name, from the Greek *hybos*, a hump or bump, and *anthos*, a flower, is of unexplained application.

Hybanthuses have alternate or more rarely opposite, undivided leaves. Their blooms, solitary from the leaf axils or in terminal racemes, have five small sepals and five petals, the bottom one larger, sometimes very much so than the others, long-clawed, and distinctly pouched or concave. There are five separate stamens and one style. The fruits are capsules. Some kinds, especially *H. ipecacuanha*, have been used medicinally as substitutes for ipecac.

Native of the West Indies, **H. linearifolium** (syns. *Ionidium linearifolium, Viola linearifolia*) is a herbaceous perennial up to about 1½ feet tall. It has linear to obovate leaves up to 2 inches long and about ⅓ inch wide. The little flowers are bluish or bluish-white.

Garden Uses and Cultivation. Little known in cultivation, the kind described is sometimes planted in warm countries. It is propagated by seed.

HYBOPHRYNIUM (Hybo-phrynium). The only species of *Hybophrynium*, of the maranta family MARANTACEAE, is native to tropical West Africa. Its name comes from the Greek *hybos*, a hump, and *Phrynium*, the name of a related genus.

A graceful, evergreen herbaceous perennial of bamboo-like aspect, **H. braunianum** (syns. *Trachyphrynium braunianum, Bamburanta arnoldiana*) has arching, reedlike stems with along their lengths two rows of very short-stalked, pointed, oblong-elliptic, *Maranta*-like, hairless leaves with blades up to 6 inches long by approximately one-half as wide, the lateral veins diverging from the midrib at an angle of forty-five degrees. The little-branched or branchless flower spikes, shorter than the leaves, are terminal. The asymmetrical flowers have three sepals, three petals united at their bases, one three stamen, and petal-like staminodes (sterile stamens). The style is stout. The fruits are deeply three-lobed capsules.

Garden and Landscape Uses and Cultivation. An elegant foliage plant for lightly shaded places outdoors in the tropics and frost-free or practically frost-free subtropics and for pots and tubs indoors and beds in conservatories, this species thrives in fertile, porous, well-drained soils that do not lack for moisture. Its needs and care are those of *Calathea* and *Maranta*. Propagation is by division.

HYBRID. In common usage the term hybrid has generally been applied only to the offspring of cross-breeding between two or more species of the same or different genera. If the parents are of different genera the offspring are identified appropriately as bigeneric or trigeneric hybrids. Offspring of cross-breeding between variants of the same species have been known as crosses or cross-breds. But geneticists now accept as hybrids the results of any breeding between individuals that differ genetically in one or more genes and so what formerly were crosses or cross-breds can now properly be called hybrids.

HYDNOPHYTUM (Hydno-phytum). The curious plants contained in this genus of the madder family RUBIACEAE attract attention because in their homelands the large, swollen, deformed, tuberous bases of their stems are tunneled into and inhabited by ants, often of a fierce, biting nature. This does not occur in regions where the native ants are not adapted to this way of life. There are about eighty species of *Hydnophytum*, a genus native to Malaysia, Indochina, Indonesia, and islands of the Pacific, and very like *Myrmecodia*. The name comes from the Greek *hydnon*, a truffle, and was applied because of something of a resemblance between the tuberous swellings of hydnophytums and truffles.

Hydnophytums are epiphytes, they perch on trees, but abstract no nourishment from them. They have opposite, fleshy leaves and small, white flowers solitary or in clusters from the leaf axils. The blooms are funnel- or salver-shaped. The fruits are small drupes containing two seedlike stones.

Occasionally grown **H. formicarum,** of Malaya, develops a tuberous base 4 to 5 inches in diameter to its branched, leafy stem. Unlike those of some species the tubers and branches are spineless. The short-stalked, elliptic evergreen leaves are up to 5 inches long by one-half as wide.

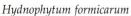

Hydnophytum formicarum

Hydnophytum formicarum (flowers)

The small flowers are succeeded by two-seeded, reddish-yellow, berry-like fruits.

Garden Uses and Cultivation. Hydnophytums appeal to lovers of the curious and unusual. They are easily grown in the humid tropics and in tropical greenhouses. Osmunda fiber, tree fern fiber, and other rooting mediums kept moist, but not constantly saturated, and suitable for epiphytic orchids, suit hydnophytums. Shade from strong sun is needed. Propagation is easy by fresh seed.

HYDRANGEA (Hydrán-gea). Consisting chiefly of shrubs, but including some clinging vines and small trees, the genus *Hydrangea* inhabits North and South America and Asia. It belongs in the saxifrage family SAXIFRAGACEAE or, if one accepts the segregation favored by some botanists, to the hydrangea family HYDRANGEACEAE. There are 115 species. The name, from the Greek *hydor*, water, and *aggeion,* a vessel, alludes to the shape of the fruits.

Hydrangeas have deciduous or evergreen, opposite, stalked, usually toothed and sometimes lobed leaves. Their flowers are in flat-topped, globular, or pyramidal, often large clusters. The individual blooms are prevailingly small, except that often the outer ones of each cluster (and in some horticultural varieties the inner ones) are much enlarged. Such flowers are without stamens or pistils and so are sterile. The flowers have usually five, rarely four or six each sepals and petals, eight to twenty, but most commonly ten stamens, and two to five styles. The sepals are the showy elements of the sterile flowers. The fruits are dry capsules containing many small seeds and opening from the top.

Best known are the hills-of-snow, hortensia, lacecap, and peegee hydrangeas. These splendid kinds have been planted so abundantly in parts of North America that they tend to become tiresome, but overplanting does not distract from their very real merits as garden ornamentals. In addition to their employment as outdoor

shrubs, hortensias are popular for growing in pots and tubs.

Hills-of-snow hydrangea (**H. arborescens grandiflora**), which has large globular clusters of nearly all sterile white flowers in June or July, is a variety of a species native from New York to Iowa, Florida, and Louisiana. The species **H. arborescens**

Hydrangea arborescens grandiflora

Hydrangea arborescens grandiflora (flowers)

Hydrangea arborescens

is a loose, straggling shrub, 3 to 6 feet in height, with ovate leaves without hairs or sometimes slightly pubescent on their undersides, and somewhat rounded flower clusters 3 to 6 inches across of mostly small fertile flowers and a few outer large, showy, sterile ones. The flowers are white. Other varieties of *H. arborescens* are *H. a. discolor* (syn. *H. cinerea*), native in the mountains from North Carolina to Georgia and Alabama, with leaves with densely-gray-hairy undersides and flower clusters with few or no sterile blooms. The leaves of *H. a. radiata* (syn. *H. radiata*), a native of mountainous parts of North Carolina and South Carolina, have white-hairy undersides. The heads of white flowers have few sterile ones.

Hortensia and lacecap hydrangeas are chiefly horticultural varieties derived from *H. macrophylla*, *H. m. normalis*, and *H. m. serrata*. Typical **H. macrophylla** (syn. *H. 'Otaksa'*) is actually a garden variety that originated in Japan from a species native to limited coastal regions of that country. Because the variety was described and named as a species before the true species was recognized as such, a technicality of botanical nomenclature necessitates the retention of the binomial *H. macrophylla* for the garden variety and the trinomial *H. m. normalis* for the natural species. From 5 to 8 feet tall, *H. macrophylla* is a wide, rounded shrub, deciduous in cold climates and more or less evergreen in milder ones. It has thickish, hairless, coarsely-toothed, rather lustrous, ovate leaves 5 to 9 inches long. Its white, blue, or pink flowers, all or nearly all sterile, are in large spherical heads. As it grows in the wild **H. m. normalis** is 3 to 10 feet tall and almost hairless. It has somewhat fleshy, broad-ovate

to broad-obovate, coarsely-toothed leaves, abruptly-pointed at their apexes and 4 to 8 inches long. The flowers, in wide, freely-branched, flattish-topped clusters or heads, are blue or pink. Tiny and mostly fertile, each has ten stamens and usually three styles, but a few of the outer ones of each cluster are sterile and up to 2 inches or more across. This species seems to be less cold-resistant than *H. macrophylla* and its other varieties. The tea-of-heaven hydrangea (*H. m. serrata* syns. *H. acuminata*, *H. serrata*, *H. thunbergii*), native of Japan and Quelpart Island off the coast of Korea, is up to about 5 feet high and has thin, dull, coarsely-toothed, hairless or hairy leaves up to 6 inches long that when young have a decidedly "sugary" taste. An inhabitant

Hydrangea macrophylla variety

Hydrangea macrophylla serrata

A hortensia hydrangea as a pot plant

A well-flowered hortensia hydrangea

tain a trading station on an artificial island called Deshima in Nagasaki Bay, Japan was closed to Westerners. The great Swedish botanist and physician Carl Thunberg became a member of this Dutch group and to the best of his very limited opportunities studied the flowers of the strange land to which he had come. Under heavy guard he was permitted to make one trip to Yedo (Tokyo), but most of his botanizing was confined to studying the hay brought from the mainland to feed livestock on Deshima and inspecting plants brought to him from time to time by interested Japanese. Among the latter was a plant then completely new to science and to which Thunberg applied the name *Viburnum macrophyllum*. Later it was named *H. macrophylla*. Shortly afterward another specimen was brought to Thunberg, this of a plant now named *H. m. serrata* and to which Thunberg applied the name *Viburnum serratum*. Later, living plants of hortensia hydrangeas were introduced from Japan to Europe, the first to come to France.

Hortensia hydrangeas range in height from 2 to 8 feet. Most modern varieties have resulted from the efforts of Dutch, French, German, and Swiss plant breeders, and most have been developed and selected with special reference to their suitability for cultivation as pot plants. The individual flowers of their huge heads vary from ¾ inch to 1¼ inches or more in diameter and in color from pure white to rich blue and deep red. The margins of the petal-like sepals may be irregularly-toothed and ragged or quite smooth. Several hundred varieties have been raised and named. Those available are described in catalogs of specialists.

Another group of hortensia varieties appears to have been derived from *H. m. ser-*

of mountain woodlands, this is less robust than *H. macrophylla normalis* and has more slender stems, proportionately narrower leaves, and smaller flowers. From the dried leaves of *H. m. serrata* a tea is made.

It is not difficult for Americans to recall the year in which *H. macrophylla* was first seen by a Western botanist. It was 1776. At that time, except for a small group of Dutch representatives permitted to main-

A lacecap hydrangea

Hydrangea macrophylla variegata

rata hybridized with *H. macrophylla* or *H. m. normalis.* These typically have elliptic to lanceolate, dull leaves 3 to 7 inches long, and more or less hairy and flat flower clusters about 3 inches across with a few small sterile blooms and more numerous fertile ones. Varieties of this complex well worth growing include especially fine *H. m.* 'Grayswood', a bushy, 6-foot-tall shrub with dome-shaped flower heads with about nine large sterile flowers surrounding the small blue or pink fertile ones. The sterile blooms, which are at first white or bluish-pink, change to vivid crimson, a color which they hold for a long period. Another variety worth cultivating is *H. m.* 'Rosalba', which has a flat-topped head of flowers, the central fertile ones blue or pink and the six or seven sterile ones at first white, but becoming blotched with crimson and producing the two-toned effect that inspired the designation 'Rosalba'. In addition to the marginal sterile blooms there is often a single one at the center of the cluster of fertile flowers. The variety *H. m. prolifera* is distinguished by its dense head of double flowers.

Lacecap hydrangeas are similar to hortensias except that their heads of bloom are flatter and consist of large numbers of tiny fertile flowers surrounded by a ring of large sterile ones. Like hortensias, they are horticultural varieties of *H. macrophylla* or are hybrids between it and *H. m. serrata.* Among the comparatively few outstanding sorts are *H. m.* 'Blue Wave', a strong grower with flowers from pink to pale blue according to the availability of aluminum in the soil; *H. m.* 'Lanarth White', a compact, slender-branched kind, with pink or blue fertile flowers and pure white

Hydrangea paniculata grandiflora

sterile ones; *H. m. mariesii,* with blooms usually pink, but occasionally blue and with small sterile flowers intermixed with as well as a row of large sterile flowers encircling the fertile ones; and *H. m.* 'White Wave', which has flattish flower heads with blue or pink fertile flowers sur-

rounded by about eight large, white or faintly blush-colored sterile blooms. This is vigorous and very free blooming. There are two lacecaps with attractively variegated foliage. Of these, *H. m. quadricolor* is the better. Its beautiful leaves are bright green and grayish-green or sea-green, and

Hydrangea paniculata grandiflora (flowers)

Hydrangea paniculata

yellow, and cream. Its flowers are pale blue or pale pink. The other variegated kind is *H. m. maculata* with milky-white flowers and leaves margined and spotted with yellowish-white. It is decidedly less attractive than *H. m. quadricolor.*

The peegee hydrangea (*H. paniculata grandiflora*) has a colloquial name reflecting the nurserymen's abbreviation "p. g." for *paniculata grandiflora*. It has in late summer and fall huge pyramidal clusters of mostly sterile, showy white flowers. These slowly fade to greenish, purplish, and finally sear brown. The peegee is the commonest variety of *H. paniculata*, but there are other good ones and the species itself is handsome. Its blooms are less massive than those of the peegee. Native of eastern Asia, *H. paniculata* is a tall shrub or small tree up to 25 feet in height. It has ovate to elliptic leaves 3 to 6 inches long, somewhat hairy above and on the veins of their undersides. The flower clusters may be 1 foot in length and consist of numerous small, fuzzy-looking, fertile flowers and fewer large, long-stalked, persistent, white, sterile blooms that become purplish as they age. Variety *H. p. praecox* blooms a month to six weeks earlier and *H. p. tardiva* later than typical *H. paniculata*.

The oak-leaved hydrangea (*H. quercifolia*), a very beautiful species restricted as a native from Georgia to Florida and Mississippi, is hardy in southern New England. This and *H. paniculata* and its varieties are the only cultivated hydrangeas with flowers in pyramidal panicles. Up to 6 feet tall, *H. quercifolia* has deeply-three-to five-lobed leaves whitish-pubescent on their undersides that in fall assume rich tones of bronzy-purple. Its 1-foot-long

Hydrangea quercifolia

Hydrangea quercifolia (flowers)

flower clusters contain many long-stalked, showy, sterile blooms as well as smaller, fertile ones. The flowers are white, but become purple as they age.

Eastern Asian *H. aspera* (syn. *H. villosa*), neither it nor its varieties hardy in the north, is up to 12 feet tall and has the branchlets and branches of the flower clusters furnished with stiff hairs. It succeeds better in alkaline soils than most hydrangeas. Its lanceolate, toothed leaves with rough-hairy undersides are up to 1 foot long and 4 inches wide. The flat-topped, much-branched clusters of flowers are of small, purplish-pink fertile blooms with blue stamens and styles, and white to pink or purplish sterile ones. Ovate to broadly-ovate leaves with rough-hairy under surfaces are a distinguished feature of *H. a. robusta*. From 6 to 12 feet tall, *H. a. strigosa* (syn. *H. strigosa*) has elliptic to oblong-ovate leaves clothed especially on their undersides with a velvet of more or less bristly hairs that stand outward from the under surface or are curled. The flowers are creamy-white. Variety *H. a. sargentiana* (syn. *H. sargentiana*) is an attractive sort with young shoots clothed with a moss of stiff, nearly transparent, bristly hairs. Its leaves, broadly-ovate and 6 inches to 1 foot long on the main stems, smaller on the flowering shoots, are dull dark green. Their upper sides are minutely-hairy, below they are paler and bristly-hairy. The flowers are attractive. The fertile ones are deep rosy-lavender, the sterile, mostly outer, ones are pinkish-white.

The climbing hydrangea (*H. anomala*) is a handsome, self-clinging, deciduous vine hardy about as far north as New York City. Native of the Himalayas, this must not be confused with related *Schizophragma*, which is often called climbing-hydrangea. They are easy to tell apart be-

Hydrangea aspera

Hydrangea aspera sargentiana

Hydrangea anomala petiolaris

Hydrangea anomala petiolaris (flowers)

cause the sterile blooms of the hydrangea have all four of the petal-like sepals large and of equal size, whereas in *Schizophragma* there is only one enlarged sepal. The climbing hydrangea may attain a height of 75 feet or more. It attaches itself firmly to its support by aerial rootlets in the manner of English ivy (*Hedera*). Its pointed, broad-ovate leaves are sharply-toothed and up to 4 inches across. They are lustrous dark green and nearly hairless. The flower clusters, borne in early summer, are 7 to 10 inches across and consist of numerous small white flowers with nine to fifteen stamens, surrounded by a dozen or so much larger, long-stalked, white sterile blooms. Hardier and satisfactory through much of New England, *H. a.* *petiolaris* (syns. *H. petiolaris, H. scandens*), of Japan, Sakhalin Island, Quelpart Island (Korea), and Taiwan, differs from the typical species in having more coarsely-toothed leaves and flatter clusters of flowers with fifteen to twenty-two stamens.

Other kinds worth planting for ornament include these: **H. heteromalla** (syns. *H. bretschneideri, H. xanthoneura*) is a hardy

Hydrangea heteromala

species of the Himalayan region. Up to 8 feet tall, it has hairy branchlets and branches of the flower clusters and ovate to elliptic leaves 4 to 8 inches long, with hairless to white-hairy undersides. The white fertile and sterile flowers are in flat-topped clusters 6 inches to 1 foot across, the sterile ones become purplish as they age. *H. integerrima,* the only truly evergreen hydrangea considered here and the only one dealt with that has toothless leaves, a native of Chile, is not hardy in the north. Up to 50 feet tall, it clings to its supports by aerial rootlets. Its leathery, smooth, green leaves are 2 to 6 inches long and ovate or slightly obovate. The deep clusters, up to 6 inches long and chiefly of small greenish fertile flowers, occasionally develop a few large, white sterile blooms. *H. involucrata,* an attractive Japanese species that blooms in late summer, is 3 to 6 feet tall and has ellipticoblong to oblong, bristle-toothed leaves,

pubescent on both surfaces, and up to 10 inches long, and pinkish or bluish flowers, or the long-stalked sterile ones nearly white, in heads 4 to 5 inches across. A distinguishing feature is that before the blooms expand the flower heads are enclosed by about six oval to nearly round, white-downy bracts about 1 inch long.

Garden and Landscape Uses. As outdoor ornamentals the best hydrangeas must be ranked among our finest hardy, deciduous, flowering shrubs. They are useful in masses for large-scale effects and as single specimens and may also be planted as informal hedges. For seaside planting no shrubs surpass in beauty and magnificence of floral display adaptable varieties of the hortensias, and these, too, are most excellent shrubs for cultivating in tubs for the summer embellishment of terraces, patios, steps, and suchlike places. Their bold foliage and massive heads of bloom associate well with buildings and other masonry features. The lacecap kinds are elegant for open woodlands and other places in light shade. Of comparable quality and uses are the sun-loving hills-of-snow hydrangea and *H. paniculata* and its ubiquitous variety the peegee hydrangea. The peegee and its parent type can be trained to tree form or as large bushes as fancy dictates. Serving a quite different purpose is the climbing hydrangea. Its functional use is to clothe masonry, tree trunks, and other supports to which it can attach itself by stem rootlets without this being objectionable. It is not appropriate for planting against wooden houses or surfaces that must be painted from time to time. For growing in shade the bold-foliaged oak-leaved hydrangea has much to

recommend it. Even in climates too cold for it to bloom reliably, it is worth cultivating for its handsome leaves. Cut blooms of hydrangeas last well as fresh flowers and those of *H. paniculata* and *H. macrophylla* and their varieties, as well as some other kinds, if allowed to dry slowly while standing with their stems in water, can be used as longtime everlastings.

Hydrangeas vary in hardiness. The most cold-resistant of the hortensias and other varieties of *H. macrophylla* and the oak-leaved hydrangea are satisfactory at New York City and in sheltered places in southern New England, but in colder regions are likely to have their flower buds killed even though the plants live and send up strong shoots each year. The hills-of-snow hydrangea and other variants of *H. arborescens* as well as the species itself succeed throughout most of New England as does *H. paniculata* and its variety the peegee hydrangea. The last two are the hardiest of all hydrangeas. Much more tender *H. aspera* and its varieties cannot be relied upon in climates harsher than that of the coastal plain of Virginia.

Cultivation. Hydrangeas appreciate fertile, porous soils that are never exceptionally dry, but are not waterlogged and have a slightly acid reaction. A reasonable admixture of organic matter is favorable to their best growth and is especially desirable for such woodland kinds as the lacecap varieties of *H. macrophylla* and the oak-leaved hydrangea. However, a soil excessively rich with organic matter can result in over-vigorous, soft shoot growth that may not winter or flower well. The woodlanders need light shade, and all kinds tolerate such conditions even though they

Hydrangea heteromala (flowers)

Hydrangea integerrima

In a tub, this hortensia hydrangea decorates a terrace

bloom more freely in full sun. Adequate supplies of moisture during droughty summer weather are essential for the best results. Hydrangeas allowed to wilt repeatedly for lack of ground moisture are bound to suffer and bloom indifferently. An organic mulch, such as compost, wood chips, peat moss, or other suitable material, is helpful in retaining moisture and promoting vigorous growth. An annual spring application of a complete fertilizer is also stimulating. Hydrangeas are easy to transplant. The best season to do this is early spring. Except with very small plants a ball of earth should be kept intact about the roots when transplanting.

Flower color of pink- and blue-flowered sorts is determined by the availability of aluminum in the soil. In alkaline soils this element is held in such a way that it is unavailable to the plants, in acid soils the roots can absorb it. The exact color of the blooms is closely tied to the pH of the soil, but is influenced also by the variety. Some "blue" more readily than others. With pH 4.5 to 5 or 5.5 blue flowers can be expected, although they may be mauvish as pH 5.5 is approached; from 5.5 to 6.5 the flowers are likely to be mauve verging to blue at the lower pH level, to pink at the higher one; with a pH of 7 to 7.5 the flowers will be pink. Alkalinity above pH 7.5 is likely to result in poor growth and chlorotic (yellowed) foliage. Chlorosis can be corrected by watering the plants with chelated iron at the rate of ¼ ounce to each gallon of water or by spraying the foliage with a solution of chelated iron. To acidify the soil to encourage "bluing" of the flowers, watering with aluminum sulfate at the rate ¼ ounce to a gallon of water, is done. It is good practice

to add to the solution iron sulfate at the same rate and to soak the soil several times at weekly intervals in spring and again in fall. To encourage pink blooms on plants in soil that normally gives blue flowers apply lime to the soil at the rate of a pound to

A twin-trunked tree-form *Hydrangea paniculata*

every ten feet of surface once or twice a year until the desired result is attained. It takes some weeks or months to effect marked "bluing" or "pinking."

Pruning is an important operation in the successful cultivation of hydrangeas and must be accommodated to the growth habits of particular kinds. Broadly, these plants fall into two groups, those represented by *H. paniculata* and its varieties including the peegee, which bear their blooms in late summer or fall at the ends of shoots developed during the current flowering season, and others that develop their flower clusters from short extensions of shoots produced during the previous year. Hydrangeas belonging to the first group are pruned in late winter or spring. The operation consists of cutting out all weak, crowded, and unwanted shoots and shortening those that remain to within 1 inch to 3 inches of their bases unless it is desired that the specimen grow taller, in which case a few selected shoots intended to be developed as permanent branches are shortened to one-third to two-thirds of their lengths. It should be emphasized that annual pruning to control the size of the plant and to secure larger flower heads, while practicable, is not essential. Specimens may be left to develop naturally.

Standard or tree-form specimens with single, branchless trunks and rounded heads of branches, foliage, and flowers can be had with *H. paniculata* and its varieties by suitable pruning and training. To do this, begin with a young plant. Select a stout shoot from the base. Tie it to a stake and pinch out or cut off all side shoots. When the retained shoot reaches a height of 4 to 6 feet pinch out its top and allow branches to develop from its upper part. Cut these back each late winter or spring to a length of 6 or 8 inches until a head of appropriate size is developed. From then on prune annually by thinning out weak shoots and cutting all others back to a length of 2 to 3 inches.

Typical of the second group, the kinds that flower from previous year's shoots, are the hortensia and lacecap varieties of *H. macrophylla*. Pruning of these should be done in summer as soon as the flowers have faded and strong new shoots are developing from the lower parts of the stems. The objective is to retain a framework of old wood and an adequate number of the stoutest new shoots to bear blooms the following year and to cut out the old flowering shoots as low as practicable without losing desirable strong new shoots arising from them. At the same time all weak and spindly shoots, old or new, are cut out. No further pruning in fall, winter, or spring must be done unless occasioned by winter-killing. Many hortensias produce flowers only from the terminal buds of shoots produced during the late summer and fall of the previous season and if these are destroyed by winter cold or are pruned away the result is no bloom. Some varieties have the ability to develop flower buds from lateral shoots that grow from the previous year's canes. With these the destruction of the terminal buds is not fatal to flowering, but the quality of the blooms is lower than those from terminal buds, which emphasizes the need to do everything possible to preserve the buds at the ends of the shoots of hydrangeas that bloom from the previous year's wood, which means all kinds except *H. paniculata* and *H. arborescens* and their varieties.

Following a severe winter the more tender hydrangeas, such as varieties of *H. macrophylla* and *H. quercifolia*, may suffer some killing back of the shoots and it is then necessary to cut these back to below the point of injury in spring. In cold localities protection can be given by tying the shoots together after leaf drop in fall, constructing a wooden framework around the plant and filling it to above the top of the plant with sifted sandy soil. Framework and soil are removed before new growth begins in spring.

Tub plants of hortensia hydrangeas grown for summer decoration of terraces, patios, steps, and other locations in association with architectural features or formal gardens are taken from their winter quarters and placed outdoors as soon in the spring as all danger of frost has passed. At that same time some of the surface soil is removed and replaced with a rich, fertile mixture and regular watering is begun. From spring until fall the soil must never be allowed to dry and weekly or semiweekly applications of dilute liquid fertilizer should be given. Specimens cultivated in this manner are pruned in late summer as advised for outdoor plants. In fall they remain outside until lightly touched by frost, then they are removed to a fairly light, cool, frost-free cellar or other place where the temperature can be kept between 35 and 45°F and where good air circulation is assured. During the winter the soil is kept almost dry.

For growing in pots as decorative flowering plants varieties of *H. macrophylla* are used extensively. They are forced into early bloom in greenhouses, are sold by millions, and are especially popular for Easter, Mother's Day, and Memorial Day holidays. For spring blooming, plants are propagated from stem or leaf bud cuttings made from February to April or, for plants to be finished in 4-inch pots, until as late as June. In a month or less they are rooted and ready for potting. In commercial practice they are often placed individually directly in 4-, 5-, or 6-inch pots, but where labor costs are of less significance it is better to pot them first in 2½- or 3-inch pots and transfer them later to containers 5 or 6 inches in diameter. Under favorable conditions young hydrangeas grow rapidly and the transfer to larger pots must be made promptly as soon as the roots have permeated the soil in the smaller containers and before they are at all crowded, which means in three weeks or less after the first potting. The soil should be coarse, porous, and fertile. If colored-flower varieties are being grown and blue flowers are desired it should have a pH of about 5, for pink blooms 6.5 to 7. Fertilizers added to soils for blue-flowered plants should contain little phosphorus, but those for pink-bloomed specimens should have a high phosphorus content. The shoots of the young plants are pinched once, or with early propagations twice, to develop branches, but pinching must not be done after June. During the summer the plants are set outdoors in a sunny location, either plunged to the rims of their receptacles in sand, ashes, soil, or other such material or stood directly on the ground. They should be spaced so they are not crowded and, if plunged, must be located where subsurface drainage is adequate to carry moisture away rapidly. Hydrangeas are "thirsty" subjects and need to be watered copiously and frequently, but not to the extent that the soil remains like mud for long periods. It is decidedly harmful to allow them to become so dry that the foliage wilts. During summer, fertilizing is done to maintain vigor and promote growth. With colored-flower varieties choice of fertilizers should depend to some extent on whether the plants are to have blue or pink blooms. If the former, the fertilizer must be low in phosphorus, if the latter a comparatively high phosphorus level is desirable.

Before the arrival of fall frosts the plants are placed in deep cold frames or are otherwise protected from freezing temperatures and watering is gradually reduced. From early November on they must be in a cool, frost-free place where the temperature never exceeds 50°F and is kept as close as possible to 40°F. Well-protected cold frames and storage sheds are employed to provide the needed protection. During the dormant period the soil is maintained in a nearly dry condition, which, together with low temperature, causes the leaves to drop, a desirable happening. Fallen leaves are collected promptly and removed to circumvent the spread of botrytis disease which causes the buds to rot. Good air circulation is also important in minimizing danger of this disease doing damage.

Forcing may begin any time from the end of December to late March. The later forcing begins the less chance there is of shoots being blind (not producing flowers). This condition is especially likely when the low temperature resting period has been too short as it may be if the fall has been exceptionally warm and forcing is begun early. Forcing begins by removing the plants to a greenhouse and watering them regularly. If they are to be repotted into larger pots this is done after the buds swell and the young leaves begin to expand. In the beginning a night temperature of 45 to 50°F is adequate, but as growth develops this may be increased to 55 or even 60°F. Always an increase during the day of five or ten degrees above the night temperature is allowable. During the forcing period hydrangeas need full sun and plenty of water, but not so much that the soil is constantly saturated. Spraying the foliage with water on sunny days promotes growth, but must not be done so late in the day that the leaves remain wet after nightfall.

An alternative method of producing pot plants for late spring and summer blooming is available. The young plants from spring propagations are planted in sunny outdoor nursery beds as soon as the weather is warm and settled and are carefully dug just before the first frosts and potted into containers just large enough to accommodate their root balls comfortably. The newly potted plants are thoroughly watered and stood in a cold frame, and kept lightly shaded, sprinkled with water, and covered with the frame sash for about two weeks to encourage new root growth. Then shade is removed, ventilation given freely, watering gradually reduced and the plants treated thereafter as advised above for those grown throughout in pots.

The propagation of hydrangeas is simple. Natural species can be raised from seeds. New varieties are produced in the same way, but horticultural varieties cannot be multiplied in that manner. Many do not produce seeds, and seedlings of those that do vary considerably, and do not duplicate the parent. Seeds are sown in a greenhouse or cold frame in late winter or spring in pots or flats of sifted sandy, peaty soil. The seeds are scattered thinly and covered very shallowly and the receptacle is covered with a sheet of glass and shaded. The soil must never become dry. As soon as the seedlings are big enough to handle they are transplanted to individual small pots, flats, or to a bed in a cold frame and are kept lightly shaded and evenly moist.

Cuttings is a more common means of propagation. One method is to use hardwood cuttings, pieces of current year's shoots consisting of three or four joints or nodes and cut cleanly across at bottom and top just beneath and above a node. Hardwood cuttings are made in fall, and in mild localities the cuttings are planted directly in the open garden with their tips just showing above the soil surface. In harsher climates they are tied in bundles and buried in sand until spring and then planted in the garden. Leafy cuttings consisting of terminal pieces of stem made in summer and planted under mist or in a humid, shaded cold frame or greenhouse, afford a popular means of securing increase for garden use. For greenhouse cultivation stem cuttings, terminal or consisting of a section of a stem containing one or more nodes, are used. If stock is scarce leaf-bud cuttings are satisfactory. These are made by cutting through the stem 1 inch below and ¼ inch above the same node and then splitting the piece lengthwise to form two leaf-bud cuttings each with a single bud. The cuttings, stem or leaf-bud, are planted in sand or a mixture of sand and peat moss in a propagating bench where bottom heat of 65°F and an atmospheric temperature of 55 to 60°F are maintained. If not under mist the cuttings should be lightly sprayed at frequent intervals with water and be shaded from sun.

Diseases and Pests. Hydrangeas are subject to bud blight or botrytis, leaf spots, powdery mildew, rust, and virus ring-spot diseases. Temperatures above 100°F can result in sun scald of the foliage, and chlorosis (yellowing) of the leaves may occur if the soil is too alkaline. The chief insect pests are aphids, leaf tier, rose chafer, red spider mite, oyster shell scale, and nematodes.

HYDRASTIS (Hydrás-tis)—Goldenseal. This is another of that notable number of genera in the wild represented only by species native to eastern North America and eastern Asia. They supply silent evidence to the one-time existence of a land bridge across the Bering Strait by which plants, animals, and man made their way from one continental land mass to the other. Again like a fair number of the genera to which reference is made above, *Hydrastis* consists of only two species, one in the United States and, in this case, one in China (it is not, as sometimes stated, native to Japan). It belongs in the buttercup family RANUNCULACEAE. The name may refer to the similarity of the leaves of these plants to those of *Hydrophyllum* of the water leaf family HYDROPHYLLACEAE.

These are deciduous, herbaceous, perennials with rhizomes from which spring stems bearing alternate leaves and solitary terminal flowers. The latter are without petals, but have three sepals that look like petals and fall when the blooms open. There are numerous stamens and many short pistils. The fruits are red berries in heads. Only the American species seems to be grown. In addition to its ornamental value it is cultivated as a commercial drug plant. It was employed by the Indians medicinally and as a dye.

The goldenseal (*H. canadensis*) inhabits rich woodlands from Vermont to Michigan, Minnesota, Virginia, Tennessee, and Arkansas. From 8 inches to 2 feet tall, each pubescent stem has a solitary basal leaf and two leaves near its top. They have blades rounded to heart-shaped in outline, deeply-five-lobed, and double-toothed. When full grown they are up to 1 foot across, smaller at flowering time. The greenish-white flowers, on short pubescent stalks, are ½ inch or slightly more in diameter. They appear in spring and are followed by dense clusters of berries that in late summer ripen to orange-red. Because of the medicinal value of its knotted yellow rhizomes goldenseal has been collected to such an extent that it is close to extinction in accessible places in the wild. It should never be wantonly taken.

Garden Uses and Cultivation. Goldenseal is an interesting plant for woodlands and for inclusion in gardens of native and medicinal plants. It needs soil containing an abundance of organic matter, fairly moist, but not wet, and slightly acid to neutral. Planting may be done in early spring or early fall. Increase by division is practicable at those same seasons. Seeds, sown in sandy peaty soil in a cold frame in spring or fall and kept evenly moist and shaded afford another satisfactory way of securing new plants.

HYDRIASTELE (Hydriastè-le). About nine species of Australia and New Guinea constitute *Hydriastele*, of the palm family PALMAE. They are rare in cultivation and plants grown as *H. wendlandiana* are usually species of *Ptychosperma*, generally *P. elegans*. The name, from the Greek *hydor*, water, and *stele*, a column or stem, refers to these palms usually growing near springs, and to their trunks.

Hydriasteles are tall trees with pinnately-divided leaves with the leaflets unequally spaced, and the upper ones much wider than those below. The ends of the leaflets are broad, blunt, and raggedly-toothed, with the front margin prolonged and tail-like. The fruits are egg-shaped to ellipsoid and up to ⅓ inch long.

New Guinean *H. rostrata*, introduced to Florida late in the 1950s, twelve years later had formed clusters of stems 2 to 3 inches in diameter and 15 to 20 feet in height. A

Hydrastis canadensis

native of northeastern Australia, *H. wend-landiana* has leaves of many leaflets up to 1½ feet long.

Garden and Landscape Uses and Cultivation. Of interest to collectors of palms, the sorts of this genus require a humid tropical environment. For more information see Palms.

HYDRILLA (Hyd-rílla). The name of this genus of the frog's bit family HYDROCHAR-ITACEAE is derived from the Greek *hydor*, water, in allusion to the plant's habitat. The only species, *Hydrilla verticillata*, is an underwater native aquatic of central Europe, Asia, and Australia.

Very similar to *Elodea densa*, it can most conveniently be distinguished from it by examining the margins of the leaves which are rough in *Hydrilla*, smooth in the *Elodea*. Additionally, the midrib of the leaf is sometimes reddish in *Hydrilla*, but not in the other. The leaves of *Hydrilla* are linear or oblong and are in whorls (circles) of four to eight on slender, freely-branching stems. They are ¼ to ⅓ inch long. The flowers are minute, the males solitary in the leaf axils and with three sepals, petals, and stamens, the females solitary or in pairs and with three each of sepals, petals, and stigmas. A variable plant, *H. verticillata* occurs in more than one variety; *H. v. crispa* much resembles and is sometimes confused with *Lagarosiphon muscoides major*, but the leaves of the latter are not in whorls.

Garden Uses and Cultivation. These are the same as for *Elodea*.

HYDROCHARIS (Hydró-charis)—Frog's Bit. The genus *Hydrocharis*, of the frog's bit family HYDROCHARITACEAE, occurs natively in Europe, Asia, Africa, and Australia and is represented in cultivation by one of its six species. The name, from the Greek *hydor*, water, and *charis*, grace, refers to the appearance and habitats of these plants. Another plant called frog's bit is the American *Limnobium spongia*.

Hydrocharises are aquatics with runner-like stems and floating or somewhat aerial leaves. Their usually unisexual flowers have three each sepals and petals, three or a multiple of three stamens, and six two-parted styles. The fruits are berry-like.

The European frog's bit (*H. morsus-ranae*) has stems ending in floating rosettes of glossy, long-stalked, heart- to kidney-shaped leaves. Its attractive flowers, the sexes on different plants, have three white-bordered, green sepals and the same number of white, yellow-spotted petals. The flowers arise from between a pair of bracts, the males stalked, about 1 inch in diameter and two to four together, the females stalkless and smaller.

Garden Uses and Cultivation. Although not suitable for small aquariums, European frog's bit does well in large tanks and

Hydrocharis morsus-ranae

is also suitable for sunny pools and ponds. It thrives in alkaline water with a positive calcium content, that is underlaid with a fairly deep layer of nutritious mud into which it can root. It forms attractive patches of floating foliage and blooms throughout the summer. This plant increases freely by offsets and by resting buds that form in fall, sink to the bottom, and in spring grow into new plants. It is hardy where there is a sufficient depth of water to keep the roots from freezing.

HYDROCHARITACEAE—Frog's Bit Family. Consisting of eighty species of fresh water and marine aquatic monocotyledons accommodated in sixteen genera, the frog's bit family has a wide natural distribution especially in the tropics and subtropics. It is represented in cultivation by a few fresh water kinds grown in pools and aquariums. A few of its sorts are free-floating,

but the majority are submersed and root into soil bottoms.

The leaves of plants of the frog's bit family may be all basal and often crowded, or alternate, opposite, or whorled (in circles of three or more) along stems. They vary greatly in size, in outline range from ribbon- to heart-shaped. The flowers, solitary or in umbels, are generally unisexual with the sexes on different plants; more rarely they are bisexual. They are symmetrical and arise from bractlike spathes. They have usually three sepals and three petals. Male blooms have three to many separate or united stamens, females three to six branched or branchless styles. The fruits are berry-like. Cultivated genera are *Elodea, Hydrilla, Hydrocharis, Lagarosiphon, Limnobium, Stratiotes,* and *Vallisneria.*

HYDROCLEYS (Hydrò-cleys) — Water-Poppy. Although botanically unrelated, *Hydrocleys*, of the butomus family BUTO-MACEAE, in its vegetative stage has much the aspect of a waterlily, but its blooms are quite different. They more nearly resemble those of *Limnocharis*, with which *Hydro-cleys* was once united, but differ in having six or fewer rather than numerous pistils, and in the stigma being at the end of a long style instead of stalkless. The three or four species are natives of warm parts of South America. The name comes from the Greek *hydor*, water, and *kleis*, a key. It has also been spelled *Hydrocleis*.

Members of this genus are herbaceous perennial aquatics with mostly floating, broad, ovate to rounded leaves. Their short-lived flowers have three persistent sepals, three petals, and many stamens. The fruits are clusters of follicles.

The water-poppy (*H. nymphoides* syn. *Limnocharis humboldtii*) has prostrate, root-

Hydrocleys nymphoides

Hydrocotyle sibthorpioides

Hydrocotyle moschata

ing stems, thick leaves with long stalks and broad-ovate nearly round blades 2 to 3 inches across, with heart-shaped bases. The leaves usually float, but sometimes rise above the water. They have glossy upper surfaces and are lightly hairy beneath. The solitary, light yellow, broad-petaled blooms, 2 to 2½ inches wide, are lifted well out of the water. They have usually six pistils. Each flower lasts only a day, but they are produced in succession over a long period. The fertile stamens are purple or violet.

Garden and Landscape Uses and Cultivation. Not hardy to frost, the water-poppy is an admirable permanent decoration for pools in the tropics and warm subtropics and for summer use outdoors elsewhere and in greenhouses. Its care is very simple. It thrives in moderately fertile, wet soil and may be planted at the margins of pools where its stems can trail into the water or in containers or in soil bottoms 6 or 9 inches beneath the surface. Propagation is very easy by division at any time, preferably in spring. Plants can be raised from seeds sown in pans, the soil surface covered with ¼ inch of sand, submerged an inch or two below the surface of water held at about 70°F.

HYDROCOTYLE (Hydrocót-yle) — Pennywort. Of the 100 tropical and temperate region, low herbaceous plants included in *Hydrocotyle*, a few find favor with gardeners. The genus belongs in the carrot family UMBELLIFERAE. Its name, from the Greek *hydor*, water, and *kotyle*, a hollow, alludes to the cuplike hollow in the center of each leaf.

Hydrocotyles are creepers with rounded, peltate (with the stalk attached to the center of the leaf), sometimes lobed, rarely compound (consisting of more than one leaflet) leaves, usually round-toothed at their margins and palmately (in hand-fashion) veined. The tiny white or greenish flowers, in small umbels, are of minor ornamental significance. Their parts are too small for easy observation. The fruits are tiny and seedlike. The chief attraction is the neat foliage.

Native to tropical Asia and Africa, *H. sibthorpioides* (syn. *H. rotundifolia*) has established itself in lawns in parts of the United States including Pennsylvania, Virginia, Indiana, and Kentucky. Its nearly round leaves, ⅓ inch or a little more or less in diameter, are shallowly five- to seven-lobed. Native North American species that are natives also of South America include *H. americana*, with orbicular to broadly-ovate leaves, shallowly six- to ten-lobed and from ⅓ inch to 2 inches across; *H. umbellata*, with peltate, orbicular leaves up to 3 inches broad and shallowly-lobed or round-toothed; *H. verticillata*, with peltate leaves up to 2½ inches in diameter, usually with eight to fourteen lobes; and *H. ranunculoides*, with rounded kidney-shaped, deeply-five-lobed or six-lobed leaves.

A charming little New Zealander, *H. moschata* is about 1 inch high. It has tiny, rounded leaves notched about one-third from margin to stalk. Another New Zealander, *H. dissecta* forms dense patches an inch or two high of beautiful foliage. Its more or less hairy leaves ½ to 1 inch across are deeply cleft into three to seven

Hydrocotyle dissecta

Hydrocotyle vulgaris

deeply-toothed lobes. From Tasmania comes *H. peduncularis,* a kind by some authorities considered to be the same as *H. sibthorpioides.* This has very small, five-lobed, orbicular heart-shaped leaves that form a dense, matted groundcover. The marsh pennywort of Europe (*H. vulgaris*) has round, peltate leaves up to 1 inch across and round-toothed or slightly-lobed at the margins.

Garden Uses. Hydrocotyles are of use in rock gardens, bog gardens, and as low groundcovers in damp soil both outdoors and in greenhouses. Occasionally they are employed for carpet bedding. The smaller-leaved sorts are attractive for growing in shallow pans in greenhouses.

Cultivation. So long as the soil is damp or wet the cultivation of pennyworts is simple. They flourish in sun or light shade and are easily increased by division. Some are quite rampant and must be restrained from overrunning more delicate neighbors, by pulling out invasive running stems. Propagation is by division and by seed.

HYDROLEA (Hydrò-lea). This American, African, and Asian genus of the tropics and subtropics belongs in the water leaf family HYDROPHYLLACEAE. It comprises twenty species of annuals, herbaceous perennials, and subshrubs. The name, from the Greek *hydor,* water, alludes to the preference of *Hydrolea* for moist or wet soils.

Hydroleas have often spiny stems and alternate, ovate to lanceolate, toothless leaves. The wheel- to shallowly-bell-shaped flowers, usually clustered but sometimes solitary, have five-lobed calyxes and corollas and five stamens with stalks dilated at their bases. The fruits are spherical capsules.

South American *H. spinosa* is sometimes cultivated. From 2 to 4 feet tall, it branches freely, and has stems with long, sharp spines. Its lanceolate, elliptic, or oblong, hairy leaves are 1 inch to 3 inches long. The ½-inch-wide, bright blue, fragrant blooms are in terminal clusters. Variety *H. s. inermis* is without spines.

Garden Uses and Cultivation. In warm countries this perennial is sometimes planted in informal landscapes where the soil is moist. It is propagated by seed.

HYDROPHYLLACEAE—Water Leaf Family. Of nearly cosmopolitan natural distribution, but absent from Australia, the water leaf family is especially abundant in western North America. It is composed of 250 species of dicotyledons classified in eighteen genera. Its sorts are annuals, herbaceous perennials, or less often subshrubs. Those cultivated are esteemed for their attractive blooms, and wigandias as well for their impressively large leaves.

Plants of this family commonly have more or less bristly hairs or are glandular. Their alternate or opposite leaves, often in basal rosettes, are undivided or are pinnate or less often palmate. The symmetrical flowers are in branched inflorescences, the arms of which frequently are coiled outward in fiddle-head fashion. They have a calyx of five lobes or five nearly separate sepals, a usually five-lobed, bell-, funnel-, or wheel-shaped corolla, generally five stamens of the same or different lengths, and one or two styles. The fruits are capsules. Cultivated genera include *Emmenanthe, Eriodictyon, Hesperochiron, Hydrolea, Hydrophyllum, Nemophila, Phacelia, Pholistoma, Romanzoffia, Turricula,* and *Wigandia.*

HYDROPHYLLUM (Hydro-phýllum)—Water Leaf. Neither the botanical name *Hydrophyllum,* derived from the Greek *hydor,* water, and *phyllon,* a leaf, nor its literal translation water leaf, which is the common name of this genus, has any obvious application. The group belongs in the water leaf family HYDROPHYLLACEAE and consists of eight chiefly woodland species of biennials and deciduous herbaceous perennials, all natives of North America. More familiar cultivated genera belonging in the same family are *Nemophila* and *Phacelia.* Why hydrophyllums are not more popular is difficult to understand; they are elegant, decorative, and of easy cultivation.

Hydrophyllums have thin, pinnately- or palmately- (maple-like) lobed leaves and clusters of bell-shaped white, purple, or blue flowers with long-projecting stamens. The flowers are in repeatedly-branched clusters. They have somewhat the aspect of polemoniums, which belong in the phlox family POLEMONIACEAE, a group closely related to the *Hydrophyllaceae.* The perennial kinds of water leaf have thick horizontal rhizomes.

The commonest eastern American species is *H. virginianum,* which grows in wet and moist places in woodlands and in the open from Quebec to North Dakota, South Carolina, Kentucky, Arkansas, and Kansas. From 1 foot to 2½ feet in height this has main stem leaves 4 to 8 inches long and deeply-pinnately-divided into usually five, more rarely seven or nine, toothed lobes, the basal pair of which are often again lobed. Its dense clusters of white to light pinkish-purple flowers are bristly-hairy. The stamens are long-protruding. From the above *H. macrophyllum* differs chiefly in the hairs of its flower clusters being longer and not bristly. It inhabits fertile woodlands from Ohio to Illinois, West Virginia, North Carolina, and Alabama.

Toothed stem leaves, five- to nine-lobed in palmate-fashion like maple leaves, are characteristic of *H. appendiculatum* and *H. canadense.* Both occur in rich moist woods, the former from Ohio to Minnesota, Pennsylvania, Tennessee, and Missouri, the lat-

Hydrophyllum virginianum

Hydrophyllum canadense

Hydrophyllum canadense (flowers)

ter from Vermont to Michigan, Illinois, Missouri, Georgia, and Alabama. From 1 foot to 2 feet tall, **H. appendiculatum** has densely-hairy branches and stalks to its flower clusters. Its white to pinkish-purple blooms rise mostly above the foliage. The stamens barely protrude. The similarly colored flowers of **H. canadense** are usually partly hidden by the upper leaves, and the branches and stalks of its flower clusters are almost or quite hairless. Its stamens scarcely protrude from the corollas.

The western American **H. capitatum** ranges in the wild from Montana to British Columbia, Colorado, and California. Attaining a height of 8 inches or more, it has leaves 2 to 3 inches long, with blades roughly ovate in outline, grayish-pubescent, and pinnately-cleft into five to seven divisions, which are again lobed. The flowers are on stalks shorter than the leaves.

Garden and Landscape Uses and Cultivation. These plants are useful for massing in open woodlands and other partly shaded places where the soil is dampish, but not waterlogged. They need very little care and are attractive for colonizing in naturalistic surroundings. They are easily increased by division and by seed.

HYDROPONICS or NUTRICULTURE. The science and art of cultivating plants that normally grow in soil without using soil or such organic soil substitutes as peat moss is called hydroponics or nutriculture. Widely promoted in the 1930s and 1940s as a highly efficient and practical method for amateur and commercial growers to adopt, it has failed to live up to early expectations. It is, however, employed to a considerable extent as a technique of scientific investigation and, to a much lesser

degree, and mostly in regions where there is little or no soil or where the soil available is unsuitable for growth, in raising plants for home or commercial use. Plants that have been successfully grown by this method include carnations, gardenias, roses, many annuals, cucumbers, endive, lettuce, radishes, and tomatoes. One of the most successful, but under less compelling circumstances surely not economically sound examples of the employment of hydroponics was the production on barren Ascension Island during World War II of large quantities of cucumbers, lettuce, radishes, and tomatoes to supply military forces stationed there. So far as is known the nutritional quality of crops grown hydroponically differs in no way from those raised in soil.

The word hydroponics in the early 1930s was a new one invented by Dr. W. F. Gericke, who in California, carried out extensive experiments with cultivating plants without soil. But the idea was not new. Scientists have grown plants in soilless solutions since at least the beginning of the eighteenth century. Dr. Gericke, however, developed refined techniques that under ideal conditions produced good results and published the results of his research. Soon, what proved to be overoptimistic, even extravagant claims were being made by others for the virtues of the hydroponic method and a great deal of amateur interest was stirred up, largely as a result of the persuasions of irresponsible contributors to the gardening press and promotional advertising by dealers in supplies needed by hydroponic gardeners.

The advantages claimed for hydroponics, none substantiated by later experience, were greater uniformity of growth

and higher yields, freedom from or greater resistance to pests and diseases, and practicability of closer spacing of plants than in rich soil, and the need for less water and less labor. It must be clearly understood that to grow plants hydroponically requires at least as much skill and generally a greater knowledge of plant physiology than does soil cultivation. The plants' environmental needs other than the character of the rooting medium remain the same. To achieve comparable results light, temperature, and other requirements are not altered, nor is the need to combat pests and diseases. All in all, except on a strictly experimental basis, it is better that amateur gardeners forego hydroponics.

There are two chief systems of hydroponics. In one the plants are grown with their roots in nothing but water containing minute and very accurately measured amounts of nutrients, in the other they root into gravel, aggregate, sand, or such similar inert inorganic material as vermiculite, bathed at intervals with nutrient solution. The last technique has the advantages of offering better support so that the plants grow erectly and of assuring the roots adequate supplies of air. With many plants it is necessary, if their roots are constantly surrounded with liquid, to provide supports for their upper parts and to bubble air through the solution to provide the roots with needed oxygen.

Water-cultured plants may be accommodated individually in crockery jars, bottles blackened on the outside to exclude light, or more together in wood, metal, or concrete tanks 6 inches to 1½ feet deep, of any convenient length and width, coated on the inside with asphaltum paint or fitted with polyethylene plastic liners to prevent contamination of the nutrient solution by contact with the material of which the tanks are made. A tray with a wire mesh bottom containing excelsior, straw, or other litter in which seeds are sown or seedlings raised in sand or vermiculite are set, is positioned a few inches above the tank. The roots grow down into the nutrient solution. This method is less used that the next.

Sand, gravel, finely crushed stone, cinders, vermiculite, and similar sterile aggregates afford better root holds than water. They can be used in crocks or other drained containers or in tanks, benches, or beds painted on their insides as recommended for water culture and constructed so that they drain readily. This last can be done by sloping their bottoms slightly to a low end fitted with a drainage hole. With long installations it is more practicable to have the bottoms of the benches or beds arched slightly along their centers so that the water solution exits through holes spaced every 1¼ feet or so along the bottoms of the sides into conduits that carry it to a storage receptacle for recirculation.

Flooding the aggregates with nutrient solution two, three, or more times a day as may be needed can be done in various ways. For small operations a watering can fitted with a spray nozzle is satisfactory. For larger ones overhead spraying of the rooting medium with nutrient solution is sometimes adopted, but a more usual method is to subirrigate. This is done by flooding the medium from below at intervals, a procedure usually automated by use of a time switch and pump, then draining it into a reservoir in readiness for recirculating at the next flooding. Whatever method is employed, the nutrient solution should be discarded and renewed every two weeks. At that time, to guard against nutrient build-up in the rooting medium flush it thoroughly with plain water.

Nutrient solutions must be very finely adjusted to the needs of the plants. Many have been devised, mostly based on the use of pure chemicals, but it is not impossible to achieve acceptable results at least over the period of the few weeks or months needed to mature some crops, by the use of less expensive soluble chemical fertilizers as basic materials. Here are two sample formulas for nutrient solutions and one concentrate of minor elements, which are part of them.

NUTRIENT SOLUTIONS
8.1 oz. nitrate of soda (15.5 percent N)
1.3 oz. monammonium phosphate (12 percent N, 56 percent P_2O_5)
5.9 oz. potassium sulfate (48 percent K_2O)
1.0 oz. nitrate of lime (13 percent N)
3.9 oz. magnesium sulfate (Epsom salts)
⅚ pt. minor elements concentrate
   All dissolved in 100 gallons of water
10.5 oz. nitrate of soda (15.5 percent N)

5.6 oz. superphosphate (14 percent P_2O_5)
4.9 oz. potassium sulfate (48 percent K_2O)
3.8 oz. magnesium sulfate (Epsom salts)
⅚ pt. minor elements concentrate
   All dissolved in 100 gallons of water

MINOR ELEMENTS CONCENTRATE
2 oz. boric acid
3 oz. manganese sulfate
20 oz. ferric citrate
   All dissolved in 20 gallons of water

The acidity of the nutrient solution is important. For most plants pH 6 is satisfactory but for azaleas and other acid-soil sorts pH 4.5 to 5.5 is recommended; for roses and some others pH 6 to 7. Adjustments are made to increase acidity by adding dilute sulfuric acid (three parts in seven of water), to increase alkalinity by adding small amounts of sodium hydroxide. When making such adjustments add extremely small amounts between repeated tests for pH until the desired level is reached.

HYDROSME. See Amorphophallus.

HYGROPHILA (Hygró-phila). This is a tropical genus of some eighty species of bog and marsh plants. Belonging in the acanthus family ACANTHACEAE, it has a name betraying its love of wet habitats derived from the Greek *hygros*, wet, and *phileo*, love.

Hygrophilas are erect or diffuse annuals or herbaceous perennials. They have opposite, undivided leaves, and flowers, sometimes associated with strong spines, in dense clusters in the leaf axils or more rarely solitary. The blooms have a deeply-five- or sometimes four-lobed calyx and a two-lipped, tubular corolla with the upper lip erect, concave, and with two teeth or lobes and the lower three-lobed. There are

Hygrophila stricta

four fertile stamens and one style. The fruits are capsules.

About 2 feet tall, *H. stricta* has numerous erect, reddish-brown stems, like the foliage softly-hairy. The leaves have long stalks. Their broad-ovate to elliptic blades have wedge-shaped bases and are up to about 3½ inches long by 2½ inches wide. The flowers are violet-blue, about ⅝ inch in length. African *H. gigas* is about 2 feet tall, with narrow-elliptic to lanceolate leaves some 4 inches long by ½ to ¾ inch wide. Its pale violet flowers are 1 inch to 1¼ inches long.

Hygrophila gigas

Other sorts sometimes cultivated include these: *H. difformis,* of tropical Asia, has sprawling, rooting stems up to 2 feet long. Its leaves are variously shaped, those submerged, up to 4½ inches long, pinnately-cleft or pinnately-divided, and flimsy. The thicker and smaller aerial leaves are lanceolate to ovate. Pale violet streaked with red-violet on their insides, the flowers, one to three from the leaf axils, are ½ inch long. *H. lacustris,* of the American tropics, has hairy aerial stems and lanceolate leaves up to 3 inches long. The ¼-inch-long flowers are white. *H. salicifolia,* of southeastern Asia and Indonesia, usually branches freely and has nearly stalkless, linear-lanceolate to lanceolate leaves up to 5 inches long, and from the leaf axils violet flowers about ¾ inch long.

Garden and Landscape Uses and Cultivation. Although not especially showy, these are attractive and interesting plants for growing in warm climates in mud at watersides or even where the soil in which they are rooted is covered with about 1 inch of water. They succeed in full sun or where there is shade for part of each day. Increase is easy by seeds, division, and cuttings.

HYLINE (Hy-lì-ne). Two species of Brazilian bulb plants are the only ones of *Hyline,* of the amaryllis family AMARYLLIDACEAE.

They differ from their near relative *Hymen-ocallis* in having perianth segments separate instead of joined partway and in their ovaries containing numerous ovules. The name, from the Greek *hyle*, a woodland, refers to the natural habitats in which these plants are commonly found.

Rare in cultivation, **H. worsleyi** has up to fourteen pointed leaves 10 to 20 inches in length and about 2½ inches wide. Its blooms, usually two on a stalk 1 foot tall or a little taller, open at night and fade the next morning. Up to 6 inches in diameter, they are white with greenish bases. Each has six long, slender perianth segments (petals) that become twisted and recurved. The six stamens sit upon the lowest petal. There is one style. The fruits are unknown, but are presumably capsules.

Garden and Landscape Uses and Cultivation. A choice and rare plant for fanciers and collectors, *H. worsleyi* responds to locations and treatment that suit *Eucharis* and tropical species of *Hymenocallis*. It is increased by offsets.

HYLOCEREUS (Hylo-cèreus) — Night-Blooming-Cereus. The species of *Hylocereus*, of the cactus family CACTACEAE, are generally similar, differing chiefly in minor details. They are high-climbing forest plants, often epiphytic, which means that they grow on trees without rooting into the ground, but take no nourishment from their hosts. There are twenty-one species, indigenous from Mexico to northern South America, and in the West Indies. The name is derived from the Greek *hyle*, wood, and the name of the genus *Cereus*. Here belong some of the plants called night-blooming-cereuses. That name is also used for some other kinds of cactuses including *Selenicereus*.

Hylocereuses have long-jointed, branching, typically triangular, more or less winged stems with aerial roots and areoles (specialized parts of cactus stems from which spines, bristles, and hairs may arise) with a tuft of felt and, in nearly all kinds, a cluster of short spines. The blooms are huge and nocturnal. They are funnel-shaped with the outside of the perianth tube and the ovary covered with large, leafy scales, but without wool, hairs, or spines in their axils. This last characteristic differentiates them from *Wilmattea*. The scales merge into the outer perianth segments and these gradually into the petal-like inner ones. The blooms are rarely red, usually white. They have numerous stamens in two rings and a thick, many-lobed style as long or longer. The fruits of most species are edible. They are large, have persistent leafy bracts, and contain black seeds. Few kinds are cultivated.

The common night-blooming-cereus (*H. undatus*) is often misnamed *H. triangularis*. True *H. triangularis* is very much rarer in cultivation. Plentiful throughout the tropics

Hylocereus undatus, its flower closing the day after the night it opened

Hylocereus, undetermined species

and subtropics of both the New World and the Old World, to the latter of which it was introduced from the Americas by man, **H. undatus** has very extensive, mostly three-winged, clambering stems 2 to 4 inches in diameter and with thin, markedly scalloped edges, which are hard and horny when old. From the areoles, spaced 1¼ to 1½ inches apart, arise one to three small spines. About 1 foot in length, the blooms have reflexed, yellowish-green outer perianth segments (petals) and pure white, erect inner ones. The stalks of the stamens and the styles are creamy-white. The latter have up to twenty-four slender branches. Red, often with large leafy scales, the oblongish, edible fruits are 4 to 4½ inches long. True **H. triangularis**, native of Jamaica and common there in

coastal areas, has sharply-three-angled stems 1¼ to 1½ inches in width, with many aerial roots and, from each areole, six to eight spines. Its flowers, about 8 inches long, have white inner petals. Its blooms, similar to those of *H. undatus*, West Indian **H. trigonus** differs from that species in its stems being only about 1 inch in diameter. They are three-angled and have very wavy, but not horny, margins. The spines are mostly in clusters of eight.

Other species are sometimes cultivated. From Costa Rica comes **H. costaricensis**, with bluish or grayish, usually three-angled stems up to 4 inches in width. Its spine clusters are at first usually accompanied by a pair of white bristles. The strongly fragrant blooms, 1 foot long or longer, are white with reddish outer petals. Large and red, its pear-shaped fruits are edible. Native of Trinidad and Tobago, **H. lemairei** has three-angled stems that root along one side and are about 1 inch wide. Usually there is a pair of short spines from each areole. The rather unpleasantly scented blooms, approximately 10 inches long, have white inner petals and outer ones that are reddish. The lobes of the stigma are divided to their middles with the divisions often notched at their tips. The fruits are purple and up to 3 inches long. With reddish-purple, short-tubed flowers 4 to 4½ inches long that close very early in the day, **H. stenopterus**, of Costa Rica, is a weak vine with stems about 1¼ inches in diameter that have three slender ribs. The yellow spines are solitary or in twos or threes. The perianth segments are all similar. The stamens and the white style, which is longer, protrude.

Garden and Landscape Uses and Cultivation. The popular night-blooming *H. undatus* is frequently cultivated in the tropics as a hedge and for clambering over walls, tree trunks, and other supports. Other kinds with stout stems can be used similarly and those of weaker growth as vines. They are amenable to greenhouse cultivation, doing best where the minimum winter temperature is about 55°F. The stout-stemmed kinds are good understocks upon which other cactuses are grafted. All species like a little shade from very strong sun. For their general cultural needs see Cactuses.

HYLOMECON (Hylomè-con). The only species of this poppy relative is native to temperate Asia. A hardy herbaceous perennial, *Hylomecon japonicum* is similar in appearance to *Chelidonium* and by some botanists is included there. It belongs in the poppy family PAPAVERACEAE, and has a name derived from the Greek *hyle*, wood, and *mecon*, a poppy.

Up to 1 foot tall, *H. japonicum* has leaves up to 1 foot long, with two or three pairs of lanceolate-oblong, irregularly-toothed leaflets. The upfacing, golden-yellow blooms, 1½ to 2 inches across, on stalks up to 2 inches long, are displayed in early summer. They are solitary or paired in the leaf axils, have two early deciduous sepals, four petals, many stamens, and a short style tipped with a two-lobed stigma. The fruits are slender capsules.

This is attractive for rock gardens and semiformal areas. It succeeds best in deep soil that contains an abundance of leaf mold, peat moss, or other decayed organic matter. Propagation is easy by seed and by division in early spring.

HYMENAEA (Hymen-aèa)—West-Indian-Locust or Algarrobo. The twenty to thirty species of *Hymenaea*, of the pea family LEGUMINOSAE, are widely distributed from Mexico to South America and the West Indies, with the greatest concentration of species in Brazilian Amazonia. One species inhabits East Africa and Malagasy (Madagascar). The name, derived from that of Hymen, the Greek god of marriage, alludes to the paired leaflets of the leaves. Some species are commercially important as sources of hard resins called copal.

Hymenaeas are trees with alternate leaves, technically pinnate, each of a pair of thick lustrous leaflets. The white or purplish, quite large flowers are in panicles. Not pea-like, they have five sepals, five petals, ten stamens, and a single style. The large, woody, dark brown, rough seed pods contain several large seeds surrounded by sweet, edible, but ill-scented pulp.

The West-Indian-locust or algarrobo (*H. courbaril*), sometimes 180 feet tall but usually less than one-half that height, has a large, spreading crown. Handsome, usually evergreen, and indigenous from Mexico to South America and the West Indies, this has short-stalked leaves, paler beneath than on their upper surfaces, and without teeth or hairs. The broad, thick-stalked flower clusters are about 4 inches long. The whitish blooms, about 1½ inches in diameter, have hairy sepals, elliptic petals, and ten white stamens with red anthers. The thick-walled seed pods, roughly oblong and 2 to 4 inches in length by up to 2 inches wide, do not open. They contain pockets of gum and several red seeds.

Where the West-Indian-locust is native its resin is used as incense and as cement for repairing crockery. The resin is exploited commercially for the manufacture of varnishes, and to some extent for medical uses. It is collected from living trees, but chiefly as accumulations that have trickled into the soil, have formed sizable lumps, and have been buried for some time. From sites where old trees have died large quantities of what is misleadingly called fossil copal are obtained. The lumber is of good quality.

Garden and Landscape Uses and Cultivation. The West-Indian-locust is an impressive species of considerable ornamental merit, useful as a roadside and shade tree in the tropics. Because its fruits have an unpleasant odor it should not be planted where this is likely to be objectionable as, for instance, near dwellings. West-Indian-locust prospers in a variety of soils, including those of limestone origin. It may be propagated by seeds, by cuttings set in a greenhouse propagating bed with some bottom heat, and by air layering. Small specimens are sometimes included in greenhouse collections of useful plants. They grow readily in a humid atmosphere in a minimum temperature of 60°F. They are pruned to size and shape and repotted in late winter. Fertile, coarse, porous soil suits them. When well rooted they benefit from applications of dilute liquid fertilizer. Watering is done to keep the soil fairly moist from spring to fall, somewhat drier in winter.

HYMENANDRA (Hymen-ándra). One species constitutes *Hymenandra* of the myrsine family MYRSINACEAE. Its name, from the Greek *hymen*, a membrane, and *andros*, man, alludes to a membrane that joins the anthers.

A native of Assam, *H. wallichii* (syn. *Ardisia hymenandra*) is a handsome, stout evergreen shrub 2 to 4 feet tall. It has glossy, leathery, practically stalkless, oblanceolate to obovate, toothed leaves up to 1 foot long with a very conspicuous midrib and finer veins angling at nearly right angles from it. In umbels from the leaf axils the whitish to pink flowers have five each sepals, petals, and stamens, and one style. The stalks of the umbels are raspberry-

Hymenandra wallichii, in bud

pink. The fruits are subspherical and berry-like.

Garden and Landscape Uses and Cultivation. These are as for *Ardisia*.

HYMENANTHERA (Hymen-ánthera). The unusual botanical placement of this genus of ten species of shrubs and small trees intrigues all interested in such matters. Native to New Zealand, Australia, Tasmania, and Norfolk Island, *Hymenanthera* is cousin to pansies and violets, although its members look very unlike those familiar flowers. It belongs in the violet family VIOLACEAE and has a name that calls attention to its anthers having terminal membranes. The name derives from the Greek *hymen*, a membrane, and the Latin *anthera*, an anther.

Hymenantheras are rigidly branched, and evergreen or partially so. The distinction between them and nearly related *Melicytus* is not very clear. Usually in *Hymenanthera* the flowers have styles with only two branches and, except in one species, anthers that are separate. The small leaves, alternate or grouped, toothed or toothless, have thickened margins. Of little or no decorative appeal, the unisexual or bisexual blooms are solitary or clustered. Unlike pansies and violets they are symmetrical. They develop from the leaf axils or from the naked parts of the branches below the leaves. Each has a calyx of five deep lobes or nearly separate sepals. There are five each petals and almost stalkless anthers, the latter are united by a five-toothed membrane that extends above them. The fruits are spherical, one- to few-seeded berries. As is true of many New Zealand genera, the species are variable and sometimes difficult to identify with precision. It seems certain that natural hybridization plays a part in this confusion. In practice, hymenantheras behave as though each were individually male or female. Only the latter bear fruits.

One of the hardiest sorts, **H. crassifolia,** of New Zealand, is a rounded shrub, low and spreading, or erect, and up to 6 feet tall. Its flat, rigid branches have spinelike ends. The leathery, very short-stalked, toothless or obscurely-toothed leaves are linear-obovate to spatula-shaped, and have blades ½ to ¾ inch long. Solitary or in twos or threes, the lemon-yellow flowers are about ⅛ inch across. The oblongish berries, white or purplish and ¼ inch long, make a good lasting display in fall. Sometimes 10 feet tall, but usually lower, **H. obovata,** of New Zealand, differs from *H. crassifolia* in being probably less hardy and having pale yellow flowers. Also, it is commonly erect in habit and has leaves 1 inch long or longer.

About as hardy as *H. crassifolia,* is **H. angustifolia** (syn. *H. dentata angustifolia*), a native of New Zealand and perhaps Tasmania. A usually erect but sometimes spreading shrub up to 9 feet tall, it has slender, interlacing branches, and few-toothed or toothless, narrow-oblong to linear leaves ½ inch to 1¼ inches long and up to ⅙ inch wide. Its brownish-yellow flowers, about ⅛ inch wide, are usually solitary. Stained with purple, the white berries, about ⅙ inch in diameter, contain one or two seeds.

Other New Zealand natives, less hardy than *H. crassifolia,* are **H. chathamica** and **H. novae-zelandiae.** These are up to 10 feet in height and have larger and proportionately broader leaves than those discussed above. The leathery, prominently veined leaves of **H. chathamica** have stalks over ⅓ inch long, and narrowly- to broadly-lanceolate, blunt-toothed blades 2 to 4½ inches long by up to 2 inches wide. The flowers, clustered along the branches, are white and purple. The berries, about ¼ inch in diameter, are white, sometimes flecked with purple. The leaves of **H. novae-zelandiae** are leathery, broad-ovate to broad-elliptic, and have round-toothed or shallowly-wavy margins. They have stalks under ¼ inch long, and blades from 1¼ to 2¼ inches long by ¾ inch to 2½ inches wide. The flowers are in clusters, often along the stems beneath the leaves. They are ⅙ inch in diameter. The berries, up to ⅙ inch across, are purplish.

Garden and Landscape Uses. These rarely cultivated shrubs are chiefly for lovers of the unusual and for inclusion in botanical collections. None is reliably hardy in the north, although in very sheltered places *H. crassifolia* lived outdoors at New York City for several years, only to succumb to an unusually severe winter. Shrub borders and rock gardens in California and other mild-climate areas suggest themselves as suitable sites for hymenantheras. To assure maximum displays of berries, a preponderance, in a proportion of up to six or seven to one, of female over male plants should be planted fairly close to each other. Hy-menantheras are not demanding as to soil, succeeding in any well-drained one of moderate fertility, not excessively dry. They appreciate full sun.

Cultivation. Hymenantheras need little care. The only pruning needed is any to thin out the branches or to shape the plants. It is done in spring. Propagation is by seeds sown in spring in a cold frame or cool greenhouse and by summer cuttings under mist or in a greenhouse propagating bench. Because seeds produce approximately equal numbers of male and female plants and only the latter fruit, propagation by cuttings of plants of known sex is usually preferable.

HYMENOCALLIS (Hymen-ocállis) — Spider-Lily, Basket Flower or Ismene or Peruvian-Daffodil. About thirty species of tender bulb plants of the amaryllis family AMARYLLIDACEAE constitute *Hymenocallis.* The name comes from the Greek *hymen,* a membrane, and *kallos,* beauty, and alludes to the connecting tissue that joins the stamens together and forms a cup in the center of the flower. In the wild, the genus is confined to the New World and is native from the southern United States to South America. It includes the plants previously separated as *Ismene,* now regarded as a subgenus of *Hymenocallis.* Gardeners sometimes confuse *Hymenocallis* with the closely related Old World genus *Pancratium* and occasionally wrongly apply that name to its species. True pancratiums are little known in America. They differ from *Hymenocallis* in having in each of the three compartments of the ovary numerous ovules one above the other. In *Hymenocallis* the ovules in each compartment are usually two, occasionally as many as eight, and are side by side.

There are evergreen and deciduous hymenocallises. Their leaves, stalked or not, are strap-shaped to broadly-ovate. Their leafless flower stalks arise directly from the bulbs. They carry one to many blooms at their tops, if two or more in umbels. Except in one species, *H. amancaes,* and hybrids of it, the blooms are white. The perianth is tubular and has six wide-spreading segments (petals, or more correctly, tepals). There are six stamens with their lower parts connected by a membrane that forms a staminal cup or saucer in the center of the flower. A rounded stigma terminates the long, slender style. The ovary is behind (below) the petals. The fruits are capsules.

Hymenocallises may be conveniently separated into spider-lilies and basket flowers or ismenes. Basket flowers or ismenes have blooms with staminal cups 1½ to 3 inches long, remindful of the trumpets of daffodils. Their stamens are incurved and extend 1 inch or less beyond the rim of the cup. In spider-lilies the staminal cups are proportionately shorter, and the free parts of the stamens much longer and erect or spreading.

Spider-lilies that bloom in winter or early spring include the beautiful evergreen **H. speciosa,** of the West Indies. Its leaves have stalks up to 7 inches long, and oblong or elliptic-oblong blades 1 foot to 2½ feet in length and one-fifth to one-third as broad as they are long. The glaucous flower stalks are commonly shorter than the leaves. Each carries an umbel of up to twelve stalked blooms. Their perianth tubes are 2½ to 3½ inches long, their petals 3½ to 6 inches long, and their funnel-shaped staminal cups 1 inch to 2 inches long. The free parts of the stamens are from a little more than 1 inch to 2 inches in length. Similar to *H. speciosa,* and perhaps only a variety of it, is West Indian **H. fragrans,** also an evergreen. Its leaf blades slightly exceed 1 foot in length and have stalks up to 3 inches long. Another fine kind, probably West Indian, **H. ovata** has pointed, broad-elliptic leaves with blades 8 inches to 1 foot long by 3½ to 4½ inches wide. Five to ten blooms top each flower stalk. Their perianth tubes are up to 4 inches in length, the funnel-shaped staminal cups 1 inch high, and the free parts of the stamens and the petals, 1½ to 1¾ inches in length. This evergreen kind is sometimes misnamed *H. amoena.*

Hymenocallis caribaea at the Royal Botanic Garden, Edinburgh, Scotland

The evergreen leaves of **H. caribaea** of the West Indies, are stalkless and taper to their bases. They are strap-shaped to oblanceolate, 1 foot to 3 feet long, and 2 to 3 inches or rather more wide. The sharp-angled flower stems, about as long as the foliage, carry eight to twelve individually stalkless blooms with perianth tubes 1½ to 3 inches long. The funnel-shaped staminal cup is ¾ to 1 inch long or slightly longer and has upturned edges. The free portions of the stamens are 1¼ to 2 inches in length. Strap-shaped to oblanceolate leaves that taper gradually to their bases

Hymenocallis expansa at the Royal Botanic Gardens, Kew, England

Hymenocallis littoralis at The New York Botanical Garden

are also characteristic of **H. expansa**, but the much longer perianth tubes of its flowers at once sets this apart from *H. caribaea*. The perianth tube is from slightly over 3 to a little over 4 inches long. Also, the petals, usually considerably larger than those of *H. caribaea*, are 3½ to 5½ inches long. The staminal cup, with erect edges, is narrowly-funnel-shaped and 1 inch to 1⅖ inches long. This species is evergreen.

Spider-lilies that bloom in late spring or summer include **H. littoralis,** a tropical American, evergreen species with stalkless, pointed, strap-shaped, bright green

leaves 1½ to 3 feet long or longer by 1 inch to 1½ inches wide. There are four to twelve individually stalkless flowers atop each 1½- to 2½-foot common stalk. Their green-tinged perianth tubes are 6 to 7 inches long. The lower parts of the narrow, 3- to 5-inch-long recurved petals are erect and hug the funnel-shaped, toothed staminal cup. The free parts of the stamens are 2 to 3 inches long.

An attractive hybrid, **H. macrostephana** has as parents *H. speciosa* and *H. narcissiflora*. Evergreen, its oblong-oblanceolate leaves taper sharply toward their bases

and are about 2 feet long by 3 to 3½ inches broad. The flower stalks are 1 foot to 1½ feet long and are topped by six to ten short-stalked blooms with perianth tubes 2½ to 3½ inches long. The petals are 3½ to 4½ inches in length and the margins of the staminal cups are nearly erect. The cups are 2 to 2½ inches long and up to 3 inches in diameter. The 1-inch-long free parts of the stamens tend to be incurved. Two fine varieties of this hybrid are cultivated, 'Advance' and 'Daphne'.

Evergreen **H. tubiflora,** of northeastern South America, has flowers, produced in spring or summer, without individual stalks. In clusters of five to twenty, they have perianth tubes 6 to 9 inches long. The funnel-shaped staminal cups spread but slightly at their edges and are about ¾ inch, the petals 3½ to 5 inches long. The free parts of the stamens are 1¾ to 2½ inches in length. This native of northeastern South America has longish-stalked, lanceolate-elliptic, broad-elliptic, or ovate leaves with blades up to 1 foot long by 3 to 6 inches wide. Native of Guatemala and Ecuador, spring- or summer-blooming **H. tenuiflora** has about six stalkless, arching, linear leaves 1½ to 2½ feet long by about 2 inches wide. Its slightly fragrant flowers have slender perianth tubes up to 6 inches in length and very narrow petals about two-thirds as long. It has white blooms with greenish perianth tubes. The funnel-shaped staminal cup is about ¾ inch long.

Naturalized in Africa and once thought to be native there, **H. pedalis** (syn. *H. senegambica*) is actually endemic to eastern South America. Its leaves, tapering from their middles to both ends, are up to 4 feet long by 3 inches broad. In umbels of few

Hymenocallis 'Advance'

to twelve or more, the flowers are borne in summer. Their perianths, without individual stalks, have tubes 5 to 9 inches long and slender lobes (petals) up to 5½ inches in length. The staminal cup is 1 inch to nearly 1½ inches long. This species is evergreen.

Mexican *H. harrisiana* has lustrous, stalkless, strap-shaped, evergreen leaves from 8 inches to 1 foot long and up to 2 inches wide. The blooms, individually stalkless and usually three or fewer together, are displayed in summer. They have slender perianth tubes 3½ to 5 inches long. The petals are up to 3 inches in length. The staminal cup is ½ to ¾ inch long and about as broad. It has spreading margins. The free parts of the stamens are 1 inch to 1½ inches long. A deciduous Mexican species, summer-flowering *H. horsmannii* has oblanceolate leaves tapered to their bases and 6 inches to 1 foot long by up to 1¾ inches wide. The flowering stalk carries one to four blooms without individual stalks and 4 to 5½ inches long. The staminal cup, about 1 inch long, is greatly exceeded by the narrow, recurved petals.

Deciduous *H. longipetala* (syn. *Elisena longipetala*), of Peru, has linear leaves about 2 feet long and two-edged flower stalks up to 3 feet long, carrying umbels of five to ten very short-stalked white blooms with narrow, wavy petals, slender and somewhat recurved at their ends and 3 to 4 inches long. The staminal cup, its margin reflexed, is 1¼ inches long. This blooms in summer. At The New York Botanical Garden it lived permanently outdoors at the base of a south-facing wall of a greenhouse for two decades, but did not survive away from this protection and source of mild warmth.

Kinds native to the southern United States, all spring- or early summer-bloomers, include several of interest. Here belongs *H. rotata* (syn. *H. lacera*). A variable, deciduous kind indigenous from North Carolina to Florida, its stalkless, linear to sword-shaped leaves up to 2 feet long and up to 2 inches broad, are glaucous and slightly channeled toward their bases. The two-edged flower stalks have up to six very fragrant, individually stalkless blooms with green perianth tubes 3 to 4 inches long and slender, recurved, longer petals. The staminal cup is saucer-shaped and up to 1½ inches long. The free parts of the stamens are as long. Native of southern Florida, including the Keys, and the West Indies, and tolerant of saline soils, *H. latifolia* (syn. *H. keyensis*) is much like *H. caribaea* and in gardens frequently passes under that name. From *H. caribaea* it differs in the flowers having a corolla with a tube longer than the lobes (petals) and in the leaves being markedly arching. This species forms large clumps of evergreen foliage up to 2 feet high above which are displayed white, fragrant flowers. It has a spherical-ovoid bulb and shallowly-channeled leaves up to 2½ feet long, much narrowed toward their bases. The flattened, sharp-edged flowering stalks, scarcely as long as the longest leaves, have umbels of ten to sixteen slender-tubed blooms with narrow petals. Endemic to Florida, *H. palmeri*, sometimes called alligator-lily, has 1-foot-long linear leaves under ½ inch wide and, on stalks up to 1½ feet long, solitary, fragrant, white flowers. The blooms are up to 3 inches long and have slender petals of about the same length and yellowish-green corolla tubes. The staminal cup, about 2 inches wide, has two long and one short tooth alternate with the stamens. Inhabiting swampy woodlands from Georgia to Indiana and Louisiana, *H. caroliniana* (syn. *H. occidentalis*) has up to twelve glaucous, linear-oblanceolate leaves up to 2 feet long by 2 inches wide. Its 1- to 2½-foot-tall flower stalks bear two to seven very slender-tubed 2- to 5-inch-long blooms with petals up to 4 inches long and a staminal cup approximately 1½ inches long.

Other spider-lilies from the southern United States and Mexico are likely to be brought into gardens. Mostly deciduous spring- or summer-bloomers, they are often difficult to identify as to species. One such is *H. liriosome*, a fragrant-flowered native of Louisiana and Texas. This has leaves up to 1½ inches wide and two-edged flowering stalks in spring topped with a cluster of short-tubed flowers with the stamens arising from indentations in the staminal cup. This spider-lily inhabits wet soils and shallow water.

Basket flowers or ismenes are summer-bloomers. They include two deciduous species that are cultivated and hybrids between them. Best known is the common basket flower, ismene, or Peruvian-daffodil (*H. narcissiflora* syns. *H. calathina*, *Ismene calathina*). The lower parts of the leaves of this sheathe each other closely to give the impression of a thick stem with the free, strap-shaped portions of the leaves sprouting from its top. The free parts are up to 2 feet long and are 1 inch to 2 inches wide. From among them come the 1- to 1½-foot-long flowering stalks each with normally two to five stalked

Hymenocallis horsmannii

Hymenocallis caroliniana

blooms with green perianth tubes 2½ to 4 inches in length and spreading, lanceolate petals about as long. The funnel-shaped staminal cup is 2 inches long and a little wider. It is striped with green and fringed at its edges. The inturned, free parts of the stamens are approximately ½ inch long. This is endemic to the Peruvian and Bolivian Andes.

The only yellow-flowered *Hymenocallis* is *H. amancaes.* This native of Peru also belongs to the ismene group. The lower parts of its leaves sheathe each other to form a thick false stem about 9 inches long. The free parts of the leaves, 1½ feet long and 1 inch to 2 inches wide, spread from the top of the apparent stems. The stalks that carry the flower clusters are 6 inches to 1 foot long. Each bears two to five golden-yellow blooms with perianth tubes 2 to 3 inches long and petals about as long. The funnel- to bell-shaped staminal cup is 2 to 2½ inches long and 2½ to 3½ inches wide. The inturned free parts of the stamens are up to ¾ inch long.

A hybrid between the last species and *H. narcissiflora,* the very lovely *H. spofforthiae,* is most commonly known by its variety *H. s.* 'Sulphur Queen', a charming kind with a false stem formed of the bases of the leaves up to 1 foot long. The free portions of the leaves are up to 2 feet in length. This hybrid is intermediate between its parents and has soft sulfur-yellow flowers. Another deciduous hybrid, between *H. narcissiflora* and *H. longipetala,* has white flowers and is intermediate between its parents. It is known as *H. festalis* (syn. *Ismene festalis).*

Garden and Landscape Uses. Spiderlilies are admirable for informal beds and borders, in sun or part-shade, and for growing in containers. In the lower south indigenous species are excellent for native plant gardens. Most evergreen kinds succeed only in high temperatures and humid atmospheres. Except in the tropics they are plants for warm conservatories and greenhouses, where they flourish in ground beds or containers without great trouble. Deciduous species are more temperate in their requirements and will live permanently outdoors in subtropical or warm-temperate climates, such as those of the southern United States. None is hardy in the north.

Basket flowers or ismenes may be left in the ground over winter in climates where little frost is experienced. In the north they are useful for grouping in beds and borders outdoors, and may be kept from year to year by storing them over winter indoors. They are excellent for warm, sheltered locations.

Cultivation. Hymenocallises grow best in fertile, loamy, well-drained soil that never lacks for moisture during their season of growth. They are propagated by offsets, bulb cuttings, and seeds, the latter sown shallowly in sandy peaty soil in a temperature of 65 to 75°F. From a spring sowing seedlings ready for 3-inch pots are had in about a year. At their first transplanting they are spaced 2 to 2½ inches apart in flats. In succession, as root growth makes necessary, they are transferred to larger pots and when two years old should be ready for containers 6 or 7 inches in diameter. The following spring they may be put into 9- or 10-inch pots or tubs. When three years old they will probably begin blooming. The removal of offsets for propagation is done in spring. If the offsets are small they are treated like year-old seedlings.

Routine greenhouse care of evergreen kinds consists of providing a humid atmosphere, light shade from strong sun, and a minimum winter temperature of 60°F. During the day this may rise five or ten degrees. Summer temperatures will naturally be higher. Minimum winter temperatures for deciduous kinds may be about 55°F. All kinds need abundant water when in active growth. Deciduous kinds are kept dry during their dormant season, watering being resumed when new growth begins in spring. Evergreen kinds have no period of dormancy, but they do go through a season of partial rest when growth is at a standstill and only sufficient water to keep the foliage from wilting is needed. With winter-blooming kinds the season of semirest is in high summer, with summer-blooming kinds, in winter.

Repotting large specimens of spiderlilies is done at intervals of several years only. Root disturbance is resented. In intervening years they are generously supplied with dilute liquid fertilizer when in active growth.

Outdoor cultivation of ismenes or basket flowers in climates too cold for the bulbs to live permanently outside involves digging them in fall just before the first frost with as many roots attached as possible, drying them off for a short time in an upside-down position (so that any moisture runs away from the bulbs) and then storing them over winter with their roots packed in nearly dry earth in a temperature of 55 to 60°F. Not until the ground is warm and the weather is really settled in spring are they planted outdoors. After they are, growth is remarkably rapid and flowers soon appear. These plants need deep, fertile, well-drained soil, and a sunny location. The bulbs are set with their tips at a depth of 3 or 4 inches, and 8 inches to 1 foot apart. Ismenes respond to deep watering during long spells of dry weather. They increase plentifully by natural division of the bulbs.

HYMENOCYCLUS. See Malephora.

HYMENOPAPPUS (Hymeno-páppus). This North American genus belongs to the daisy family COMPOSITAE and comprises about fifteen species. Its members are annuals, biennials, and herbaceous perennials. The name is from the Greek *hymen,* a membrane, and *pappos,* a pappus or tuft of hairs.

The leaves of *Hymenopappus* are alternate, and pinnately-lobed. Except in one species the yellow or whitish flower heads are without ray florets (those that in daisies and similar flowers are petal-like). They are composed of all disk florets (of the type that in daisies form the eye of the flower head). The bracts of the involucres (collars at the backs of the flower heads) are in two or three rows. The innermost at least have somewhat petal-like white or yellowish tips.

A tap-rooted biennial that inhabits prairies and dry woodlands from South Carolina to Illinois, Kansas, Florida, and Texas, *H. scabiosaeus* (syn. *H. carolinensis)* is 1½ to 3 feet tall. It has hairy, branching stems, and once- or twice-pinnately-lobed, or occasionally lobeless leaves, white-hairy on their undersides. The largest, 3½ to 9 inches long, are the basal ones, above they are gradually reduced in size. Several to many in loose clusters, the ¾-inch-wide flower heads have the bracts of the involucres white or yellowish at their apexes.

Garden and Landscape Uses and Cultivation. The species discussed above is suitable for use in informal areas, flower borders, and native plant gardens. It is easily raised from seed and flourishes in sunny places in well-drained fertile soil.

HYMENOSPORUM (Hymenós-porum) — Sweetshade. Only in Australia and New Guinea does the one species of this genus occur natively. It belongs in the pittosporum family PITTOSPORACEAE and differs from *Pittosporum* in having winged seeds without sticky coatings. Its name comes from the Greek *hymen,* a membrane, and *sporos,* a seed, and alludes to the wings of the seeds.

A handsome, evergreen, flowering tree, *Hymenosporum flavum* in America is sometimes called sweetshade. In cultivation in the United States it is usually not more than about 20 feet tall, but in its homelands it sometimes attains a height of 60 or 70 feet. Its alternate leaves, in rather rosette-like clusters near the branch ends, are elliptic to obovate; ordinarily 3 to 6 inches long, they are rarely bigger. They are neither lobed nor toothed and are hairless. The highly fragrant flowers, clear yellow with a touch of red in their throats, are in loose, umbel-like panicles at the branch ends. They come in spring and are about 1½ inches long. They have five each sepals, petals, and stamens, and a short style. The petals narrow toward their bases to form what botanists call claws. They are joined into a 1-inch-long, hairy corolla tube. The stalked seed capsules, about 1 inch long, contain many seeds.

Garden and Landscape Uses and Cultivation. In climates where not more than a

Hydrophyllum capitatum

Hydrocleys nymphoides

Idesia polycarpa in fruit

Hypericum cerastoides

Iboza riparia

Iberis sempervirens

Iberis umbellata

few degrees of frost are experienced, *Hymenosporum* is easy to satisfy and attractive. It is appropriate as lawn specimens and for displaying in other ways. It succeeds in most parts of Florida and should be tried more freely elsewhere where conditions are likely to be right for it. It thrives in any reasonably good soil. Propagation is by seeds and by cuttings.

HYMENOXYS (Hymenóx-ys). Lovers of uncommonly cultivated plants will find *Hymenoxys*, of the daisy family COMPOSITAE, of some interest. Although less showy perhaps than their cousins the blanket flowers (*Gaillardia*) and sneeze weeds (*Helenium*), hymenoxyses are certainly sufficiently attractive to warrant places in rock gardens and other informal plantings. Cultivated kinds are scarcely robust enough to maintain themselves successfully in competition with vigorous flower border perennials. This genus consists of twenty-six species of annuals, herbaceous perennials, and subshrubs, all natives of North and South America. Its name, derived from the Greek *hymen*, a membrane, and *oxys*, sharp, alludes to the pointed pappus scales of the fruits. Plants now included in *Hymenoxys* have often been grown in the past under the synonyms *Actinea, Actinella, Rydbergia,* and *Tetraneuris*.

Hymenoxys

The lobed or lobeless leaves of *Hymenoxys* are mostly basal or are distributed along the stems as well as clustered at the base of the plant. Usually they are impressed with tiny, yellowish, translucent glands and the foliage when brushed or bruised is more or less aromatic. The yellow, daisy-type flower heads are solitary or in clusters. The petal-like ray florets commonly become papery and reflexed and with age assume a whitish color. The fruits are seedlike achenes. From *Helenium* these plants differ in having the bracts of the involucre (collar of leafy organs behind the flower head) erect rather than reflexed, and from *Gaillardia* in being without narrow or bristle-like scales among the disk florets. The three genera are closely allied.

One cultivated species, **H. linearifolia** (syns. *Actinea linearifolia, Tetraneuris lineari-*folia), is an annual. A hairy, slender, branching plant, erect and up to 1¼ feet tall, its lower leaves are spatula-shaped and often have a few short lobes. Its stem leaves are linear, without lobes, and about 1½ inches long. The flower heads are solitary and ¾ to 1 inch in diameter. This species is a native of the plains from Louisiana and Kansas to New Mexico. Of the cultivated herbaceous perennial kinds, two have lobeless or only slightly-lobed leaves, all basal, and two have leafy stems and leaves, markedly pinnately-lobed. Ranging as a native from Texas to southcentral Canada, *H. acaulis* (syns. *Actinea simplex, Actinella acaulis*) is a tufted, cushion-like perennial with linear to narrowly-oblanceolate leaves from ½ inch to 2½ inches long and solitary flower heads ¾ inch to 1½ inches across on stems 2 inches to over 1 foot long. This species is quite variable. A form with woolly-hairy leaves is distinguished as *H. a. caespitosa*, and *H. a. glabra* has leaves that become almost hairless with age. The other cultivated kind with leafless stems, **H. scaposa**, ranges as a wildling from Mexico, New Mexico, and Texas to Kansas and Colorado. It is a plant of dry soils, occasionally 1 foot in height, but more commonly not over one-half as tall. Its leaves are narrowly-linear, lobeless, and up to 4 inches in length. They are conspicuously hairy at first, but may become nearly hairless with age. The flower heads are solitary and up to 1½ inches in diameter. This species is quite similar to *H. acaulis*, the differences being mainly technical. The variety *H. s. linearis*, forms a low, woody, moundlike subshrub with leaves narrower than those of the typical species.

Previously called *Rydbergia grandiflora* and *Actinella grandiflora*, the handsome species now named **H. grandiflora** is an alpine endemic of the Rocky Mountains. It has a thick taproot and one to few stout stems 6 inches to somewhat over 1 foot in height that bear a few, mostly deeply-lobed leaves, which like the stems are furnished with woolly hairs. The golden flower heads are light bright suns, up to 3 inches or slightly more in diameter. This is truly handsome. A short-lived perennial or perhaps only a biennial, **H. cooperi** is a leafy-stemmed kind that may reach a height of 2 feet. It has pinnately-divided, somewhat pubescent leaves and flower heads in clusters at the tops of the stems, each about 1½ inches in diameter. This is indigenous from Arizona and eastern California to Idaho. The plant sometimes called *H. californica* is *Lasthenia coronaria*.

Garden Uses and Cultivation. These plants are primarily rock garden subjects, but annual *H. linearifolia* may also be used to grace the fronts of flower beds and borders and its blooms have some merit as cut flowers. It is easily raised from seeds sown in well-drained soil in a sunny location in early spring or in regions of fairly mild winters in fall. The seeds are raked into the soil surface, and the young plants are thinned to 4 to 6 inches apart. No special care is needed. Ordinarily staking is not necessary. Perennial kinds are easily raised from seeds sown indoors in a temperature of about 60°F in late winter, or outdoors or in a cold frame in early spring in very well-drained, gritty soil. The seedlings are transplanted individually to small pots and when well established are transferred to dryish locations in deep, gritty soil in sunny parts of the rock garden. No special care is needed, but in cold climates a light winter covering of branches of evergreens is beneficial.

HYOPHORBE (Hyophór-be)—Pignut Palm, Bottle Palm, Spindle Palm. The name of this genus is contrived from the Greek *hys*, a pig, and *phorbe*, food for fodder. It alludes to the fruits providing food for hogs in Mauritius, one of the Mascarene Islands to which group of islands the genus is endemic. Belonging to the palm family PALMAE, as accepted here *Hyophorbe* includes plants some authorities segregate as *Mascarena*. It consists of five species.

Hyophorbes have single trunks of approximately uniform thickness or spindle-shaped, and with a swollen base. The trunk is crowned with a few stiffish, arching, pinnate leaves, and the bases of the leaf stalks form a columnar crownshaft that looks like an extension of the trunk. The flower clusters appearing from below the crownshaft spray outward in bushy masses and have several spathes that soon fall. The tiny, yellowish, unisexual flowers are in groups of four to seven each having one female at its base and the other flowers males. The olive-like, aromatic fruits, in large clusters, are green to purplish, up to 1 inch long, and contain a single seed.

The bottle palm (*H. lagenicaulis* syn. *Mascarena lagenicaulis*) acquired its vernacular name from the shape of its trunk, which is much swollen below and at the top narrows gradually to a long bottle

Hyophorbe lagenicaulis at Fairchild Tropical Garden, Miami, Florida

Hyophorbe verschaffeltii

Hyoscyamus niger

neck. Up to 30 feet tall, but often lower, its leaves have on each side of the midrib forty to seventy ascending leaflets up to 1½ feet long by 2 inches wide and with three or four strong veins. The spindle palm (*H. verschaffeltii* syn. *Mascarena verschaffeltii*) reaches a maximum height of 60 feet. Its stout, spindle-shaped trunk is less obese than that of the bottle palm, and without the bottle neck of that species, and its leaflets, thirty to forty on each side of the midrib and up to 2 feet long and about 1 inch wide, have only one prominent vein and tend to droop.

Slender-trunked *H. indica* attains a height of 40 to 50 feet. Its sparse crown is of leaves up to 6 feet long and with about fifty pairs of leaflets. The pear-shaped fruits, 1 inch to 1½ inches long, contain a seed one and one-half times as long as broad. Very similar to the last, *H. vaughanii* has leaves with relatively broader leaflets and oblong fruits 1½ to almost 2 inches in length, each containing a globose seed.

Garden and Landscape Uses and Cultivation. These handsome trees of rather formal appearance can be used effectively as single specimens and in groups, and to form avenues and line driveways. They grow well in sun or part-shade, but under the latter conditions are slimmer-trunked. Because they are frost-tender they are suitable for outdoor cultivation only in southern Florida, Hawaii, and areas with similar climates. They will grow in any ordinary garden soil. They are attractive in large pots and tubs. In greenhouses they need a humid atmosphere, shade from strong summer sun, and a minimum winter temperature of 60°F. Temperatures on winter days may be five or ten degrees higher; at

other seasons night and day temperatures may, with advantage, be considerably higher. Watering should be done often enough to keep the soil always evenly moist, but not waterlogged, and from spring through fall dilute liquid fertilizer may be applied biweekly to specimens that have filled their containers with roots. Container-grown specimens need fertile, porous soil and the containers must be well drained. For more information see Palms.

HYOSCYAMUS (Hyos-cyamus) — Henbane. This group of poisonous plants consists of fifteen species of the Mediterranean region. One, the henbane (*Hyoscyamus niger*), has been naturalized in North America since before 1672. The genus belongs in the nightshade family SOLANACEAE, an assemblage noted for its food crops, including tomatoes and potatoes, as well as for its more menacing members, such as deadly nightshade, jimson weed, and henbane. The generic name is a modification of the ancient Greek name for henbane, which came from the Greek words *hyos*, a hog, and *kyamos*, a bean, and alludes to the fruits being eaten by hogs.

Species of *Hyoscyamus* are coarse, erect, or prostrate annuals, biennials, or rarely herbaceous perennials, with largish, usually pinnately-lobed or coarsely-toothed leaves. The stalkless flowers, from the upper leaf axils, have five-toothed calyxes that enlarge as the seed capsules develop. They are in leafy, spikelike clusters. Their dingy yellow or purplish corollas are narrowly-bell- to funnel-shaped and five-lobed. Not infrequently they are split down one side. There are five stamens and one style. The fruits are capsules.

The henbane (*H. niger*) is a leafy biennial or annual up to 3 feet in height. Its leaves, 4 to 8 inches long and ovate or broad-elliptic in general outline, have few irregularly sized large teeth or shallow lobes. The upper leaves are without stalks, the lower have short ones. The flowers, about 1¼ inches long, are on their outsides a drab buff-yellow veined with purple, in their throats a dull purple. The fruits of henbane, like those of other species of the genus, open by a lid that forms the top of the capsule. It is said that the henbane capsule was the model for one of the ornaments of the headdress of Jewish high priests. A related species, *H. albus*, differs in having all its leaves stalked and yellowish corollas without purple veining. This is native to the Mediterranean region. Native to Crete, Rhodes, Turkey, and Egypt, *H. aureus* is a sprawling perennial with stems 1 foot to 2 feet long and ovate to nearly circular, woolly and sometimes sticky, sharply-toothed leaves. The stamens and style of the 1-inch-long, stalked, bright yellow flowers protrude.

As a medicinal plant henbane has been employed as a narcotic for a very long time. It was well known to the ancients, including Dioscorides. By some henbane is considered to be the source of the "juice of cursed hebenon," the "leprous distillment" that Shakespeare described Hamlet's uncle as pouring into the ear of the King. Others favor the yew (*Taxus*) as the source of Shakespeare's deadly hebenon.

Garden Uses. The horticultural importance of henbane is minor; it may be included in gardens of medicinal plants. Although not particularly likely to appeal to children or others given to eating strange vegetation on impulse, as are the berries of deadly nightshade, for example, it would be unwise to plant it or other sorts of this genus where even slight danger of such experiment exists.

Cultivation. Henbane grows in any ordinary, fertile, well-drained garden soil, being especially partial to those that contain lime. It thrives especially well near the sea. Seeds are sown from May to July and the seedlings transplanted to where they are to remain, or to nursery beds from which they are moved in fall or early the following spring to their blooming quarters. A distance of 1½ to 2 feet apart is satisfactory final spacing. Sometimes, probably when they are old, the seeds do not germinate promptly, but may take several months to sprout.

HYPERICACEAE—St.-John's-Wort Family. By some authorities included in the *Guttiferae*, the St.-John's-wort family maintained as a separate entity is composed of about eight genera involving approximately 350 species of dicotyledons, natives in many parts of the world. A few are cultivated as ornamentals, others are pestiferous weeds, some poisoning livestock that eat them.

The family includes trees, shrubs, a few woody vines, annuals, and herbaceous perennials. They have resinous sap and undivided, opposite or whorled (in circles of three or more) leaves generally with tiny translucent or black dots. The symmetrical flowers are in branched clusters. They have four or five sepals often unequal in size and united at their bases, as many petals as sepals, numerous stamens usually in several bundles or groups with the stalks of each joined at their bases, less often united in this fashion into one group. There are three to five separate or basally-united styles. The fruits are capsules or berries. Genera in cultivation are *Cratoxylum*, *Hypericum*, and *Triadenum*.

HYPERICUM (Hy-péricum)—St.-John's-Wort, Aaron's Beard, St. Andrew's Cross, St.-Peter's-Wort, Tutsan. Although more correctly *Hy-perìcum*, the pronunciation *Hy-péricum* is almost always adopted by English-speaking peoples for the name of this genus of the St.-John's-wort family HYPERICACEAE. The group it identifies consists of some 300 species of shrubs, subshrubs, herbaceous perennials, and annuals chiefly of temperate and subtropical regions of the northern hemisphere. Its name, from the Greek *hyper*, above, and *eikon*, a picture, alludes to branches being placed, in a pagan festival (celebrated on what now is St. John's Day), above images to ward off evil spirits. Sorts with flowers with four instead of five petals, sometimes segregated as *Ascyrum*, are here accepted in *Hypericum*.

Hypericums have opposite, undivided leaves dotted with tiny glands clearly visible when the leaf is held to the light. Their prevailingly yellow, rarely pink or purplish, small to large flowers have four or five often unequal-sized sepals, four or five petals, numerous stamens commonly joined at their bases into three to five bundles, and two to five styles that in young flowers are often tightly pressed together so they appear to be one. The fruits are usually capsules, those of a few kinds berries.

The most handsome shrubby St.-John's-wort is the hybrid *H.* 'Rowallane'. Its parents *H. hookeranum rogersii* and *H. leschenaultii*, this sometimes misidentified as *H. rogersii*, originated in the famous Irish garden Rowallane. Reliably hardy and semievergreen in fairly mild climates only, in southern New England the above-ground parts of this sort are usually killed back severely in winter. Nevertheless, new shoots that bloom the first year arise from the base. Up to 6 feet tall, *H.* 'Rowallane' has leaves up to 2½ inches long and clusters of three or more buttercup-yellow, saucer-shaped blooms each 2 to 3½ inches in diameter.

Another magnificent shrub, *H.* 'Hidcote', is of somewhat obscure ancestry. It may be a Chinese species brought to England in the 1920s or possibly a hybrid between *H. forrestii* and *H. calycinum*. First observed in the famous Hidcote Manor gardens in England in the 1940s, in favorable climates it is an evergreen or nearly evergreen shrub up to 4 or 5 feet high, broader than tall. It has lanceolate leaves with dark green upper surfaces and paler under ones with a network of clearly visible veins. The rich golden-yellow flowers 2 to 3 inches in diameter and shallowly-saucer-shaped are borne in clusters of few over a long late summer and fall season. Hardy in southern New England, it there is often killed to the ground in winter, but recovers and blooms the same year on shoots that grow from the base. A hypericum named 'Sungold' is essentially similar to 'Hidcote'.

Closely allied to 'Hidcote' and possibly a parent of it, **H. forrestii** (syn. *H. patulum forrestii*) has in gardens frequently been misnamed *H. patulum henryi*. Native to China and the Himalayas, this is a 5- to 6-foot-tall, deciduous or nearly deciduous, upright shrub with pendulous branches and short-stalked, ovate to lanceolate leaves up to 1¾ inches long and ¾ inch wide, their rounded ends with a little sharp point. Borne singly or in branched clusters of three or five, the golden-yellow, slightly cupped flowers are 1½ to 2 inches wide. Their stamens, about one-half as long as the petals, are in five bundles. The styles are separate. Another Chinese of this relationship, **H. beanii** (syn. *H. patulum henryi*) differs from *H. forrestii* chiefly in its flowers having much narrower and pointed sepals than the

Hypericum forrestii

broad-elliptic to ovate ones of that species, stamens one-half to almost three-quarters as long as the petals, and styles two-thirds as long as the ovary. Also, the leaves are without any tiny point at their blunt tips. The horticultural variety 'Gold Cup' differs from *H. beanii* in its leaves being lanceolate, its flower buds nearly twice instead of scarcely more as long as wide, and in its blooms, which are golden-yellow with paler edges to the petals, having shorter stamens. The small loosely-spreading, evergreen shrub 'Eastleigh Gold', which originated in Hillier's Nurseries in England in 1964, may be a variety of *H. beanii* or a hybrid between it and *H. stellatum*. It has lustrous, elliptic leaves up to 2 inches long and saucer-shaped flowers 2 inches wide or slightly wider, golden-yellow and with comparatively long stamens. Yet another Chinese species once named *H. patulum henryi* is related *H. pseudohenryi*, which has these identifying floral characteristics. The sepals are ovate to oblong. The stamens are three-quarters as long or longer than the petals. The styles only slightly exceed the ovary in length.

The tutsan (**H. androsaemum**) is distinct from all other kinds discussed here in hav-

Hypericum androsaemum (flowers)

Hypericum androsaemum (fruits)

Hypericum inodorum 'Elstead' (in fruit)

ing berries instead of capsules as fruits. Furthermore, they are the chief ornamental feature of this European and north African subshrub. They outdo the light yellow blooms in attractiveness. The name tutsan, a corruption of the French *toute-saine* (heal-all), alludes to the many virtues this plant was once supposed to possess. Bushy and 2 to 3 feet tall, it has stalkless, blunt-ovate leaves up to 4 inches long by somewhat more than one-half as wide, and heart-shaped at their bases. In branched clusters of three to nine at the stem and branch ends, the pale yellow, ¾-inch-wide blooms, have petals very slightly longer than the sepals, stamens in five bundles, and three styles. The large-pea-sized, spherical, berrylike, juicy fruits change as they ripen to purple and finally almost black. Hybridized with *H. hircinum* this species produces rather variable **H. inodorum** (syns. *H. elatum, H. multiflorum*) a semievergreen shrub up to 5 feet in height the leaves of which when crushed are strongly aromatic. They are stalkless, ovate, and 1½ to 3 inches long. Produced at and near the shoot ends, the 1-inch-wide flowers are in branched clusters. They differ from those of the tutsan in having petals conspicuously longer than the sepals and styles at least twice as long as the ovary. Their sepals, unlike those of *H. hircinum,* are persistent into the fruiting stage. The fruits, slightly less fleshy than those of the tutsan and less globular, are reddish-brown. Low *H. inodorum* 'Elstead' has light orange-scarlet fruits. Unfortunately this last is subject to a debilitating rust disease that mars its foliage.

Native North American shrub hypericums, less spectacular than the finest

Asians, include a few of decided ornamental merit. All treated here are hardy in southern New England, some as their native ranges suggest, in more severe climates. Unless otherwise indicated all have flowers with five petals. Rarely attaining 1 foot in height, **H. buckleyi,** a rare native of the southern Appalachians, has prostrate, rooting, four-angled stems and may attain a width of a few feet. Its leaves, obovate to elliptic, are up to ¾ inch long. Solitary or in twos or threes, the ½- to 1-inch-wide flowers, borne at the apexes of the stems, are bright yellow. Becoming 6 feet tall, **H. densiflorum** occurs in damp and dry places from New Jersey to Missouri, Oklahoma, Alabama, and Louisiana. Much-branched in its upper parts, usually less well furnished below, this has linear to narrowly-elliptic or oblanceolate leaves rarely over ¾ inch long. It bears branched clusters of many yellow flowers from under to slightly over ½ inch in diameter. An inhabitant of moist soils along the southern shores of the Great Lakes, **H. frondosum** (syn. *H. aureum*), up to about 3 feet tall and bushy, has usually stalkless, linear to narrowly-oblong leaves ¾ inch to 1½ inches long. Its golden-yellow flowers ¾ inch to 1½ inches wide are in groups of seven or fewer at the branch ends. They have five styles. **H. hypericoides** (syn. *Ascyrum hypericoides*), the St. Andrew's cross, has four-petaled flowers and inhabits dry and moist, sandy and rocky soils from Massachusetts to Ohio, Missouri, Kansas, Florida, Texas, and the West Indies. It is a variable, often straggling shrub with stems 1½ to 2½ feet long, much-branched, and often more or less prostrate. In the warmer parts of its range it is evergreen. Linear to oblanceolate, its leaves are ¾ inch to 1½ inches long. The flowers, about ½ inch across, have narrowly-oblong-elliptic, bright yellow petals and two styles. Native from South Carolina to Indiana, Georgia, Alabama, and Mississippi, **H. kalmianum,** up to 3 feet tall, has narrowly-oblong to elliptic or ovate-lanceolate leaves 1½ to 2¼ inches in length. Its almost stalkless blooms 1¼ to nearly 2 inches wide are solitary or in twos or threes near the ends of the branches. The seed capsules are never fully divided into more than one compartment. Native of dry sandy soils from New Jersey to Pennsylvania, Florida, and Texas, and in Kentucky and Missouri, **H. stans** (syn. *Ascyrum stans*), the St.-Peter's-wort differs from similar *H. hy-*

Hypericum densiflorum

Hypericum calycinum as a groundcover

Hypericum calycinum (flowers)

pericoides in its flowers having three or four styles, their four petals being broader and obovate, and in its leaves being elliptic-oblong.

Excellent groundcovers are *H. calycinum*, in Great Britain, but not in America, called rose-of-Sharon and also known as Aaron's beard, and *H. moseranum,* the latter a hybrid between *H. calycinum* and *H. patulum* that is also appropriate for rock gardens. Popular on the West Coast, **H. calycinum** is a native of southeast Europe and Asia Minor. It survives outdoors in sheltered places in southern New England, but does not grow there with the abandon it displays in milder climes. One of the finest of the genus and evergreen or nearly so, this spreads by underground stolons to form mats of leafy growths about 1 foot high. It has upturned, solitary or occasionally paired, golden-yellow blooms 3 to 4 inches in diameter. These it produces over a long summer season. Its leaves are ovate-oblong to oblong, 2 to 4 inches long, on their undersides glaucous. The stamens are in five clusters. There are five spreading styles. Raised in France in 1887, **H. moseranum** has characteristics midway between those of its parents. A subshrub 1 foot to 2 feet tall not spreading by stolons, it has spreading or arching reddish branches up to 1½ feet long. Its ovate leaves, up to 2¼ inches in length and about one-half as wide, have glaucous undersides and a tiny projecting point at their otherwise blunt apexes. In clusters of five or fewer or occasionally solitary, the yellow flowers are 2 to 2½ inches in diameter. This hybrid survives in southern New England. Although its branches are killed back most winters it renews itself from the base and the new shoots bloom the first summer. A weaker grower with smaller blooms, *H. m. tricolor* has leaves variegated with white and margined with pink or red.

Suitable for rock gardens, in addition to *H. moseranum* and its variety just described, are a few more low, shrubby, subshrubby, and herbaceous perennial St.-John's-worts. These belong here: **H. ae-**

Hypericum moseranum

gypticum, not as its name suggests native of Egypt, but an inhabitant of the Mediterranean region, is hardy in mild climates only. An evergreen, much-branched shrublet up to about 1 foot tall, it has crowded, gray-green, ovate or obovate leaves up to ¼ inch long and solitary light golden-yellow blooms ¼ to ½ inch in diameter, their petals more or less erect. **H. cerastoides** (syn. *H. rhodopeum*) is a pros-

Hypericum aegypticum

Hypericum cerastoides

trate or tufted subshrub from southeast Europe and Asia Minor. Not reliably hardy in the vicinity of New York City, it has crowded, branched stems up to about 6 inches long. The stalkless, glaucous-gray-green leaves, elliptic to broad-elliptic or ovate, are up to nearly 1 inch long. In many few-flowered clusters from the leaf axils, the lustrous yellow flowers 1¼ to 1¾ inches wide have three styles. **H. coris** is native from Spain to Italy. This is a subshrub 6 inches to 1 foot tall. It has semierect stems and blunt, recurved, linear, green leaves in whorls (circles) of three to six. They are about 1 inch long and have strongly evident midribs on their undersides. Marked with fine red lines, the ¾-inch-wide, golden-yellow flowers are in loose panicles. This is not hardy in the north. **H. empetrifolium,** hardy only where winters are not severe, is a charming evergreen shrub 1 foot or a little more in height. It has slender, strongly-angled, prostrate to erect stems and gray-green leaves in circles of three, linear, not over ½ inch in length, and with rolled-under edges. The golden-yellow flowers, ½ to ¾ inch wide, are in loose panicles. This is a native of southern Europe and Asia Minor. **H. olympicum** is a very attractive, variable subshrub, native of southeast Europe, Syria, and Asia Minor, and fairly hardy in sheltered places at New York City. From 9 inches to 1½ feet tall, it has spreading to ascending stems. Its entirely glaucous-gray-green leaves, conspicuously translucent-dotted and ½ to 1 inch long or longer, are oblong-lanceolate. The golden-yellow blooms, in clusters of up to five or sometimes single, are 1½ to 2½ inches wide or somewhat wider. Lovely *H. o. cit-*

Hypericum olympicum

rinum has blooms of pale yellow. **H. polyphyllum** is another variable species with glaucous foliage. From *H. olympicum* it differs in its flowers having pointed sepals edged with black dots. Its stems, prostrate or ascending, are up to 1 foot long and furnished with more or less pointed, broadly-ovate to elliptic or lanceolate leaves from tiny to up to more than 1 inch

long. The flowers, 1½ to 2 inches wide, are yellow sometimes marked with red and in crowded clusters at the stem ends. This very lovely sort, endemic in Turkey, is not reliably hardy in New York City. **H. reptans,** of the Himalayas, is perhaps hardy about as far north as Philadelphia. It spreads to form low mats of wiry stems and thin, light green, broad-elliptic leaves that turn brown or reddish in fall. The golden-yellow flowers, tinged on their outsides with red, and about 1¾ inches in diameter, are in terminal clusters.

Garden and Landscape Uses. The taller shrub St.-John's-worts are excellent for supplying bright flowers during a long summer period after most shrubs have passed out of bloom. The North Americans are appropriate for informal landscapes and native plant gardens. All prefer full sun, but stand part-day shade. Well-drained, fertile earth is best to their liking. Most of the European and Asian kinds prosper in limestone soils.

An outstanding groundcover that does well under trees and in other shaded locations and in sun where the soil does not lack moisture, H. calycinum, unfortunately, is not hardy enough to be relied upon for such usage north of about Washington, D.C. The other recommended groundcover, H. buckleyi, is hardier. Although in its wild state it usually inhabits shady, dampish places, in cultivation it blooms more freely in full sun.

Cultivation. No particular care is needed by the majority of St.-John's-worts. A few not likely to be attempted except by the most ardent rock garden fans are challenging and even some of the low kinds described here sometimes die rather inexplicably. Possibly they are rather short-lived by nature, but more likely, when grown near the limits of their climatic tolerance unusual weather or some other trying circumstance is responsible for this. The low rock garden St.-John's-worts are for the most part more or less tender in the north, and certainly in the vicinity of New York City, are more likely to survive if well-drained, sheltered locations are chosen for them, and if they are given the protection in winter of a covering of branches of evergreens or salt hay. In the north it is a good plan to keep young stock coming along in small pots in a cold frame as replacement for possible losses. These hypericums transplant better from pots than from open ground beds. Propagation of H. calycinum, H. buckleyi, and others that have creeping rhizomes or rooting stems is easy by division in spring or early fall. Where available seeds of these and other sorts afford ready means of increase and cuttings made in summer of firm shoots may be rooted in a cold frame or greenhouse propagating bench or under mist.

HYPHAENE (Hyphaè-ne)—Doum Palm, Gingerbread Palm. Most palms never branch, but many species of this Old World genus normally have trunks with widely-spreading limbs that divide and redivide in very characteristic fashion so that older specimens have more the aspect of Yucca, Pandanus, or Dracaena than of a conventional palm. The genus Hyphaene belongs in the palm family PALMAE. Its name

is derived from the Greek hyphaino, to entwine, and refers to the fibers of the fruits. There are fewer than thirty species.

Doum palms have fan-shaped leaves and male and female flowers on separate trees. The blooms are in thick-branched clusters that originate among the leaves. There are about thirty species in Africa, Arabia, and Malagasy (Madagascar) and one in India that are difficult to distinguish from each other especially when juvenile. The hard, horny, dry kernals of mature fruits are used as vegetable ivory for making buttons, beads, and trinkets. The unripe kernals of young fruits and the outer parts of mature ones are edible. The leaves are used for thatching and for making baskets and other domestic articles and when young are browsed by camels. Doum palms are trees of deserts and other dry open areas, never of forests, although they sometimes form considerable colonies.

Best known is the Egyptian doum or gingerbread palm (**H. thebaica**), which is common along the valley of the Nile and in other parts of Egypt and in the Sudan and in Israel. It is called gingerbread palm because the edible parts of its fruits have much the appearance and consistency, but not the flavor, of gingerbread. This attains a height of 20 to 30 feet and may have a spread of one-half to two-thirds its height. Rarely it is branchless. Its nearly round, rigid leaves have blades 2 to 2½ feet across divided to their middles or beyond into many narrow segments each with a strong mid-vein. The leafstalk is very spiny. The orange-yellow fruits about 3 inches long are ovoid or oblong.

Garden and Landscape Uses and Cultivation. Doum palms are little known in the United States, but it seems likely that they would succeed in the warmer parts and especially in desert areas. Like other arid-region palms they need well-drained soil, full sun, and access for their roots to moisture. They are considered difficult to cultivate in greenhouses perhaps because the germinating seedlings develop a very long root structure called a hypocotyl before any leaves or secondary roots appear, and if this is seriously damaged, as is likely at the first transplanting, or if it is crowded or twisted in a shallow pot, the young plants die or are severely stunted. For the best chance of success seeds should be sown as recommended for Jubaeopsis. For further information see Palms.

HYPOCALYMMA (Hypo-calýmma)—Swan-River-Myrtle. Belonging in the myrtle family MYRTACEAE, the eighteen species of this genus are endemic to Australia. They are opposite-leaved shrubs with small, axillary clusters of white, pink, or yellow flowers resembling those of Leptospermum, but having many spreading stamens. The flowers have five sepals and five spreading petals. The name comes from the

Greek hypo, under, and kalymma, a veil, and alludes to the manner in which the calyx falls. The fruits are capsules.

The Swan-river-myrtle (**Hypocalymma robustum**) is erect, about 3 feet tall, hairless, and has rigid, spreading, narrowly-linear-lanceolate, thick leaves about 1 inch in length. They are in four ranks. The purplish-pink flowers, ⅜ inch across, have rounded petals and slightly longer, yellow-tipped stamens. The flowers are stalkless and in pairs.

Hypocalymma robustum

Garden and Landscape Uses and Cultivation. In California and places with similar, practically frost-free, climates the Swan-river-myrtle prospers and is effective in beds, borders, foundation plantings and other locations where a fine-textured, low, evergreen, flowering shrub can be displayed advantageously. It is pleasing for cool greenhouses where it may be had in bloom early in the year. It grows without difficulty in well-drained pots in porous, fertile, peaty soil watered to keep it always evenly moist, but not constantly saturated. Full sun and an airy, well-ventilated, sunny greenhouse with a minimum winter night temperature of 40 to 50°F provides satisfactory environmental conditions. In summer the plants may be buried to the rims of their pots outdoors. Pruning back and repotting is done in spring after flowering is through. To assure compactness and shapeliness, it is desirable to pinch out the tips of the shoots of pot-grown specimens once or twice during the summer. Propagation is easy by seeds and by cuttings.

HYPOCHOERIS (Hypo-chòeris)—Cat's Ear. Of minor horticultural interest, this genus of the daisy family COMPOSITAE, the name of which is sometimes spelled Hypochaeris, includes possibly 100 species of annuals and herbaceous perennials. The greatest concentration of kinds in the wild is in South America, but the group is indigenous also in Europe and the Mediterranean region, and is naturalized in North America. The name is a modification of one applied by Theophrastus to these or related plants.

These plants have mostly basal, lobed or toothed leaves, and yellow flower heads, composed like those of dandelions of all strap-shaped florets, and solitary or clustered. The seedlike fruits or achenes are furnished with tufts of fine feathery hairs that enable them to be blown for long distances by a slight breeze.

Native of the European Alps, *Hypochoeris uniflora* is a hardy perennial with basal rosettes of spreading, oblong-lanceolate, usually toothed, hairy leaves and one to three smaller leaves near the bases of the stems. The stems, 8 inches to 1¼ feet tall, are swollen and hollow below the solitary golden-yellow flower heads. The heads are 1½ to 3 inches in diameter, and have collars (involucres) at their backs of shaggy-haired, blackish bracts that have comblike edges. An attractive alpine from high altitudes in the Andes, *H. meyeniana* is a perennial with a deep, woody taproot and a basal rosette of 2- to 4-inch-long, spreading, elliptic, coarsely-toothed leaves. The stalkless or almost stalkless, yellow dandelion-type flower head, 1 inch to 1½ inches wide, nestles at the center of the rosette.

Hypochoeris meyeniana

Garden Uses and Cultivation. These plants are appropriate for rock gardens, and *H. uniflora* for the fronts of flower beds. In sunny locations, where the ground is not so fertile that it induces gross growth, they are decidedly attractive. Propagation is most surely achieved by seed.

HYPOCYRTA. See Nematanthus and Alloplectus.

HYPOESTES (Hypo-éstes)—Freckleface. The name *Hypoestes* is that of a genus of possible 150 species of the acanthus family ACANTHACEAE. Derived from the Greek *hypo*, under, and *estia*, a house, it alludes to the calyxes of the flowers being covered by the bracts.

Indigenous to the Old World tropics and subtropics and especially abundant in Madagascar, *Hypoestes* includes shrubs, subshrubs, and herbaceous perennials. Its members have undivided, toothed or toothless leaves, and spikelets of flowers in heads or loose spikes. Each spikelet contains one bloom and the rudiment of another. The blooms have five sepals and a slender, tubular corolla, expanded toward its top and two-lipped. There are two stamens and a short style with a pair of unequal lobes. The fruits are small capsules containing two or four seeds.

Hypoestes phyllostachya

The pretty little plant called freckleface (**H. phyllostachya**) is sometimes misidentified as *H. sanguinolenta*, a name that properly belongs to another species, one with green leaves veined with fiery red. Freckleface is a charming and fairly recent addition to the tropical plants available to American gardeners. A herbaceous perennial or low subshrub, it has long-stalked, pointed-ovate, downy, opposite leaves along slender, ribbed, purplish-green stems. They are freely besprinkled with bright pink spots of various sizes and shapes. The lilac flowers are without much decorative merit. Variety *H. p.* 'Splash' has leaves more lavishly mottled with spots of deeper pink.

Entirely different from freckleface, **H. aristata,** of South Africa, is an evergreen subshrub 2 to 5 feet tall, grown for its attractive blooms. It has stalked, toothless, softly downy, ovate leaves 2 to 3 inches in length. Its 1-inch-long, rosy-purple flowers, somewhat bell-shaped at their throats, have short petals marked with darker purple and white. They are in long spikes, much resembling those of certain salvias, of fairly widely-spaced tiers, each tier with a pair of sizable, stalkless, leaflike bracts. Most widely distributed of African species in the wild **H. verticillaris** occurs as a native from

Hypoestes aristata

Hypoestes verticillaris

South Africa to tropical Africa. A hairy herbaceous plant up to about 1½ feet tall, it has pointed, elliptic-lanceolate leaves 2 to 3½ inches long and lavender-rose flowers spotted with magenta. Both the upper and lower lip are strongly reflexed.

Garden and Landscape Uses and Cultivation. Freckleface is chiefly grown in greenhouses and windows for its interesting foliage. In the tropics and warm subtropics it can be grown outdoors. It thrives in any good soil, indoors in temperatures of 55 to 70°F where the atmosphere is reasonably humid. Light shade from strong sun is beneficial. The soil must be moderately moist. Occasional pinching out of the tips of the shoots or shearing is required to encourage branching. Propagation is very easy by cuttings.

The other species discussed above can be grown outdoors in mild, practically frostless, California-type climates, and in greenhouses. Outdoors, *H. aristata* is excellent for grouping in flower beds. Its blooms are fine for cutting. It prospers in ordinary fertile soil, indoors under conditions that suit such plants as tender buddleias, and *Leonotis*. Plants that will bloom the first year are easily had from seeds and cuttings. During their early stages the tips of their shoots should be pinched out once or twice to encourage branching. The only other attentions needed are watering to keep the soil moderately moist, staking to keep the plants neat, and for specimens that have filled their containers with roots, weekly applications of some dilute liquid fertilizer.

HYPOLEPIS (Hypó-lepis). About forty-five species of chiefly tropical evergreen ferns, but some of New Zealand, Japan, and South Africa, constitute *Hypolepis*, of the pteris family PTERIDACEAE. They are not common in cultivation. The name is derived from the Greek *hypo*, under, and *lepis*, a scale, and alludes to the location of the clusters of spore capsules.

Hypolepises have creeping, usually red-hairy rhizomes and hairy or hairless, papery leaves two or more times-pinnately-divided. The small, round assemblages of spore cases are located at bases of indentations in the leaf margins and are covered with a reflexed portion of the margin or are further away from the margins and not covered.

An endemic of lowland forests in New Zealand, *H. tenuifolia* creeps widely. Its three-times-pinnate, broadly-triangular fronds have blades 10 inches to 2½ feet long by two-thirds as broad. Their primary divisions, spreading and often arched, are ovate-oblong to ovate-lanceolate and up to

Hypolepis punctata

1½ feet long by 9 inches broad. The final divisions are toothed. Widely dispersed in the tropics, *H. punctata* has slender to stout, hairy rhizomes and very hairy, twice-pinnate, triangular fronds with blades up to 1½ feet long by about 1 foot wide. They have stalked leaflets, those above alternate, the lower ones opposite. The ultimate segments are wavy and sometimes obscurely toothed. Tropical America is the native home of *H. repens*, which has somewhat prickly, erect fronds 4 to 6 feet tall, four-times-pinnately-divided.

Garden and Landscape Uses and Cultivation. These ferns are chiefly of interest to collectors. Not hardy in the north, they may be grown outdoors in ferneries, rock gardens, and other places in climates approximately as mild as those of their homeland, and in cool greenhouses. They are of easy culture, thriving in coarse, loose, well-drained peaty soil that never dries, but is not constantly wet. A humid atmosphere and shade from strong sun

are essential. A greenhouse winter night temperature of 50 to 55°F is satisfactory, by day it should be a few degrees higher. Multiplication is by division and spores. For further information see Ferns.

HYPOPITYS. See Monotropa.

HYPOXIS (Hy-póxis)—Star-Grass. Herbaceous perennials of the amaryllis family AMARYLLIDACEAE compose this genus, which is widely dispersed in temperate, subtropical, and tropical parts of the Old World and the New World. The majority of its approximately 100 species are natives of the southern hemisphere. Some are from regions north of the equator, including the United States. Most are without garden merit. The name comes from the Greek *hypoxys*, subacid, and was used by Dioscorides for another plant.

Star-grasses have corms (solid bulblike organs), tubers, or short rhizomes, and tufts of basal, linear, usually hairy leaves. Their starry blooms are generally in irregular, few-flowered racemes or slender-stalked umbels, or more rarely are solitary. They have short perianth tubes, six nearly equal petals (more correctly, tepals), six stamens, a short style, and three erect stigmas. The fruits are capsules.

Native to sparse, dry woodlands and thickets from Maine to Manitoba, Georgia, Mississippi, and Texas, *Hypoxis hirsuta* has flower stalks shorter than the foliage, and from 4 inches to over 1 foot tall. The linear, hairy leaves, 6 inches to 2 feet long, are from very slender to nearly ½ inch wide. Star-shaped, and ½ to 1 inch in diameter, the bright yellow blooms, two to six at the end of the common stalk, have fairly long individual stalks.

Hypoxis hygrometrica

Hypoxis stellata

Hypoxis, undetermined species

Hypoxis multiceps

Golden star or golden weather glass (*H. hygrometrica*) is an Australian, in its homeland a common inhabitant of wet grasslands and forest clearings. It has a fleshy, cylindrical tuber, and sparsely-hairy, grasslike leaves up to 10 inches long. The flower stalks, shorter than the foliage, often bear only one, sometimes two or three, golden-yellow blooms, ¾ to 1 inch wide, and with petals greenish or paler on their backs than on their faces. This is not hardy in the north.

South African *H. stellata* (syn. *Spiloxene capensis*) is a charming nonhardy sort that attains a height of 6 to 9 inches. It has several hairless, smooth-edged or finely-toothed leaves up to 1 foot long. Its hollow flower stalks terminate in solitary, starry blooms ¾ inch to 4 inches in diameter, with widely-spreading petals. The flowers are yellow, pink, or white, with all six, three, or none of the petals having dark purple, sometimes bluish-green or yellow, often iridescent blotches at their bases, and with a dark center line up their backs. A form with white petals blotched at their bases with purple, and with purple stamens has been called *H. s. elegans*. Another South African, nonhardy *H. rooperi* has strap-shaped, curving leaves up to 1 foot long by 1½ inches wide, nearly hairless above and softly-hairy on their undersides and margins. The racemes, sprouting from the leaf axils and terminating in stalks decidedly shorter than the leaves, are of several blooms with spreading, nearly 1-inch-long, yellow corolla segments (petals). The three inner segments are much broader than the three outer ones. Also native to South Africa, *H. multiceps* has a stout rootstock clothed with the fibrous bases of old leaves and slender, linear, recurved leaves up to 1 foot long. In clusters of usually about five, the bright yellow flowers have petals with greenish and hairy undersides.

Garden and Landscape Uses and Cultivation. For naturalizing mostly in partially shaded places and accommodating in wild gardens native American star-grasses are of some little interest, and in climates where they are hardy those native in the southern hemisphere may be used similarly. Especially lovely *H. stellata* is excellent for outdoor cultivation in California and other regions with Mediterranean-type climates. It is also delightful for growing in pots or pans (shallow pots) in a cool, sunny greenhouse under conditions that suit freesias, babianas, and ixias.

HYPSELA (Hyp-sèla). The distribution in the wild of this genus of the bellflower family CAMPANULACEAE is of interest to students of plant geography. It is one of a small group represented only in the native floras of South America, New Zealand, and Australia. Of *Hypsela*, one species occurs from Ecuador to Tierra del Fuego, one is endemic to New Zealand, and two are from Australia. Only the first appears to be cultivated. The name, from the Greek *hypselos*, high, was probably applied in recognition that the kind first described came from high altitudes in the Andes.

Hypselas are creeping, evergreen herbaceous perennials with rooting stems and alternate, sometimes clustered, toothed or

Hypsela reniformis

toothless leaves. Their small, solitary, stalked flowers, from the leaf axils, have five-lobed calyxes, and tubular corollas not slit longitudinally as are those of related *Pratia* and *Lobelia*. There are five pointed corolla lobes, asymmetrically arranged, and five stamens that closely surround the style, which ends in a two-lobed stigma. The berry-like fruits contain many small seeds.

South American *H. reniformis,* which includes the population previously segregated as *H. longiflora* (syn. *Pratia longiflora*), is rarely over 1 inch in height, and forms carpets of bright green foliage against which are displayed the yellow-eyed, slightly pink-tinged, white blooms, ⅓ inch long or a little longer, with dark violet anthers. The elliptic-ovate to nearly round or kidney-shaped leaves are up to about ¾ inch long. The flowers, on stalks about ½ inch long, have corolla tubes about ¼ inch long.

Garden Uses and Cultivation. The species described is a choice plant for the collector of rare alpines. It is suitable for growing in pans (shallow pots) in alpine greenhouses and in favored regions, such as parts of the Pacific Northwest, for rock gardens. It is not hardy in the north. It prefers a peaty, reasonably moist soil, and part shade. Increase is by division and by seed.

HYSSOP is *Hyssopus officinalis.* Giant-hyssop is *Agastache,* hedge-hyssop *Gratiola officinalis,* water-hyssop *Bacopa.*

HYSSOPUS (Hyssòp-us)—Hyssop. Generally considered to consist of one species but by some botanists as many as fifteen, the genus *Hyssopus* contains the plant that is called hyssop, although it certainly is not the hyssop of the Bible, that "groweth out of the wall" because it neither conforms to biblical descriptions nor was it native to Palestine. The Bible references are thought to be to a species of caper (*Capparis*) or any of several other plants. Our plant belongs in the mint family LABIATAE and is native of rocky places, screes, and dry banks from southern Europe to central Asia. It is naturalized in parts of North America. Hyssop is more or less evergreen and blooms in summer. Its name comes from *hyssopos,* an old Greek one used for the plant by Dioscorides.

Hyssop is a good bee plant and its virtues are employed to give flavor to liqueurs including chartreuse and absinthe. In folk medicine tea made from the fresh green tops was used in treating arthritis and other ills. The old herbalists favored it for coughs, asthma, and other pulmonary troubles. As a potherb it is put into soups, and sometimes it is added as a flavoring to salads. It must be used sparingly, however, as its flavor is too strong for most modern tastes.

Hyssopus officinalis

From nearly related *Satureja,* hyssop (*H. officinalis*) differs in its blooms having protruding stamens. The five nearly equal teeth of their fifteen-ribbed tubular calyxes distinguish it from thyme (*Thymus*). Hyssop has square stems, is much branched, woody in its lower parts, herbaceous above, and aromatic with a mintlike odor when crushed. It is 1 foot to 2 feet tall and has opposite, narrow-elliptic or linear, hairless leaves ¾ inch to 1½ inches long, with sunken glands. Its asymmetrical flowers in whorls (circles of several) form fairly dense, long, narrow, one-sided spikes with the lower whorls of flowers often interrupted, that is, separated by short sections of naked stem. They have tubular-bell-shaped calyxes and straight-tubed, two-lipped corollas, under ½ inch long, and the upper lip notched and the lower three-lobed, with the middle lobe larger than the others. There are four projecting, spreading stamens of two lengths. Typically the blooms are blue or violet, but in *H. o. albus* they are white, and in *H. o. rubra,* red. Hyssop is a hardy perennial subshrub.

Garden Uses. In herb gardens and collections of plants that have been used medicinally hyssop is rightfully included, and it is not without merit as an occasional specimen in perennial borders and informal landscapes. It loves warmth and sun and does well in thoroughly drained, light soils including limestone ones. In olden days hyssop was prominent among "strewing herbs," kinds scattered on floors to scent the air and mask noisome odors.

Cultivation. Hyssop is easily raised from seeds sown in early spring where the plants are to remain, or the seedlings can be transplanted. If they are to be undisturbed they may be in rows 1 foot to 1½ feet apart; if they are transplanted a spacing of 1 foot between plants is about right.

Increase may also be had by division, best done in early spring, and by cuttings, in summer, in a cold frame, greenhouse, or shaded place outdoors. For drying as a culinary herb hyssop is cut just as the flower ends open, tied in bundles, and hung upside down in a dry, airy, shaded place. Hyssop is a hardy perennial.

HYSTERIONICA (Hysteri-ónica). Herbaceous perennials of the daisy family COMPOSITAE compose this South American genus of a dozen species. They are usually hairy and have undivided, toothless, linear to lanceolate leaves. The flower heads, consisting of a central eye of bisexual disk florets surrounded by petal-like ray florets that are mostly female, are solitary, and yellow, orange, or red. The seedlike fruits are achenes. The meaning of the name *Hysterionica* is obscure.

Occasionally cultivated, *H. montevidensis* (syn. *Erigeron dubius*) is a hairy, abundantly foliaged species about 1 foot tall. Its leaves are linear, sometimes sparsely toothed, ½ to 1 inch long, and often glandular. The flower heads are about ½ inch in diameter.

Garden Uses and Cultivation. Hysterionicas are hardy only in regions of mild winters. They do not stand hard freezing. They grow satisfactorily in ordinary well-drained soil in sunny locations and are propagated by seed. Sometimes they are treated as annuals.

HYSTRIX (Hýs-trix)—Bottle Brush Grass. Half a dozen species of perennial grasses of the grass family GRAMINEAE, compose this genus represented in the native floras of North America, China, India and New Zealand. Referring to the shaggy, bristly flower spikes, its name comes from the Greek *hystrix,* a porcupine. These plants have upright stems and flat leaves. Their loose flower spikes, erect or nodding, are composed of usually two- to four-, rarely one-flowered, stalkless spikelets.

The bottle brush grass (*Hystrix patula*) is endemic to North America. It inhabits woods from Nova Scotia to Quebec, North Dakota, Georgia, and Oklahoma. Its stems, from creeping bases, are 2 to 4 feet tall, its leaves ⅓ to ½ inch wide. Its nodding flower spikes are furnished with loosely-spreading bristles ½ inch to 1½ inches in length. Their spikelets, mostly commonly in pairs, spread horizontally as they mature and soon drop.

Garden and Landscape Uses and Cultivation. The bottle brush grass is sometimes grown in flower borders and is well suited for naturalizing in informal places. Its plumes are useful for cutting for fresh or dried flower arrangements. The plant is easily grown in any ordinary garden soil, not excessively dry, in sun or part-shade. It is usually propagated by seed and by division.

I

IBERIS (I-bèris)—Candytuft. Confined in the wild to Europe, North Africa, and western Asia, *Iberis*, of the mustard family CRUCIFERAE, contains several well-known, and some lesser known, worthwhile kinds. Its species number thirty, and include annuals, herbaceous perennials, and small subshrubs. The name is derived from Iberia, the ancient name for Spain; many species are natives there.

Candytufts may be hairless or hairy. Their round stems bear alternate, linear to obovate leaves that may be pinnately-cleft or not. The flowers, white, lilac, pink, or purple, are in umbel-like clusters or in racemes that often elongate as the fruits develop. As with most other members of the mustard family, they have four sepals, four spreading petals, and six stamens four of which exceed the others in length. In *Iberis* the two outer petals are very much larger than the two inner ones, which gives the blooms an irregular appearance. The fruits, seed pods of the type called siliques, are flat, rounded at their bases, and often notched at their apexes. The seeds, one in each of the two compartments of the pods, are often winged.

The most popular perennial kind, sometimes called edging candytuft, and often just evergreen candytuft, is *I. sempervirens*

Iberis sempervirens

Iberis sempervirens (flowers)

(syn. *I. garrexiana*), a native of high mountains in the Mediterranean region. Cultivated in several horticultural varieties, it is hardy. Edging candytuft is a procumbent, somewhat diffuse to compact, hairless subshrub, up to 1 foot in height, with flexible younger branches, and linear to oblanceolate or spatula-shaped, blunt, thickish, flat, lobeless, toothless leaves up to 1½ inches long and ¹⁄₁₀ inch wide or somewhat wider. The flowers, in lateral racemes that lengthen as they pass into fruit, are white. The broadly-winged, ovate seed pods about ¼ inch across are sharply notched at their apexes. Variety *I. s. correifolia* is compact, with flowers in racemes that at first are very flat-topped. Horticultural varieties generally more compact than the typical species include derivatives of both it and *I. s. correifolia*. They are listed in dealers' catalogs under names such as 'Snowflake', 'Little Gem', and 'Purity'. A rather unattractive double-flowered variety exists, and some varieties have variegated foliage.

Equally excellent and as hardy as *I. sempervirens*, smaller *I. saxatilis* differs from

that in its racemes of flowers being terminal on the stems instead of lateral. An evergreen subshrub 3 to 6 inches tall, it has prostrate branches and numerous erect flowering shoots. Its leaves, up to ¾ inch long, are pointed-linear, lobeless, and under ¹⁄₁₀ inch broad. Those of the flowering shoots are flat, but the leaves of non-flowering shoots are semicylindrical. When very young their margins are fringed with hairs, but these soon fall. The white flowers are in squat clusters that elongate as the broadly-winged, shallowly-notched seed pods, ¼ inch or so across, form. Variety *I. s. cinerea* has grayish-hairy foliage and seed pods sharply notched.

Iberis saxatilis

Less hardy perennial, evergreen candytufts are *I. semperflorens*, *I. gibraltarica*, and *I. pruitii*. None has proved reliably hardy at The New York Botanical Garden, although the two last survived in sheltered places for several relatively mild winters. The only truly winter-flowering species is *I. semperflorens*, a kind in the wild confined to western Italy and Sicily, where it inhabits sea cliffs. It is distinguished from the other sorts here described by its scarcely-notched seed pods being much broader than long as well as by its time of bloom. A hairless, procumbent shrub up to 2½ feet in height, it has flat, broadly-spatula-shaped, lobeless, fleshy leaves, the lower ones up to 3 inches long or slightly longer and ½ inch broad, the upper ones considerably smaller. The white flowers are in dense clusters that elongate as the fruits form. This is not hardy in the north.

The Gibraltar candytuft (*I. gibraltarica*) inhabits cool, shady places on the famous rock after which it is named and occurs also in Morocco. Handsome, with sometimes white, but usually pale lilac to reddish-lilac flowers in clusters that do not lengthen markedly as seed pods mature, it is a dense evergreen subshrub up to 1 foot tall. Its fleshy leaves, sometimes toothed near their apexes, are broadly-spatula-shaped and up to 1 inch long by one-half as broad. The flat flower clusters are almost or quite 2 inches across. The seed pods are deeply notched and broadly winged.

Variable *I. pruitii* embraces kinds previously distinguished as *I. tenoreana, I. lagascana,* and *I. jordanii,* as well as other components, both perennials and annuals, sometimes treated as distinct species. From 2 to 6 inches in height, or sometimes perhaps slightly taller, this species characteristically forms low clumps and has rather fleshy, blunt leaves, often with a few teeth near their tips. Those on the lower parts of the plants are obovate-spatula-shaped, those above, narrower. The flowers are in compact, flattish clusters that do not elongate as fruits develop. The fruits, up to 1/3 inch across, are angled-elliptic, broadly winged, and deeply notched. This species occurs at high elevations in the Mediterranean region.

Annual candytuft

Annual candytutfs, horticultural developments of *I. amara* and *I. umbellata* and hybrids between them, are popular. Horticultural varieties have flowers in white and many shades of lilac, pink, red, and purple. Those derived from the first species are called rocket candytufts, those from the latter globe candytufts. The names allude to the forms of the flower clusters. Commonly not over 1 foot tall, but sometimes a little taller, *I. amara* is

erect, branched above, leafy, and sparingly-hairy on its lower parts. Its leaves, nearly always with a few irregular lobes or large teeth, are spatula-shaped to oblanceolate, and 1 inch to 4 inches long. As a wild plant the blooms are white or purplish. The seed pods are up to 1/5 inch across and shallowly or deeply notched. The flower clusters elongate markedly as seed pods develop. This fragrant-flowered species is native chiefly of western Europe. From it *I. umbellata,* mostly a taller plant, differs in having pale pink to purplish or purple-red, nonfragrant flowers in clusters that do not lengthen appreciably as they pass into fruit. Its pointed, linear-lanceolate leaves are scarcely or not toothed. The broadly-winged, deeply-notched seed pods are about 1/3 inch wide.

Another candytuft sometimes cultivated, *I. taurica* (syn. *I. simplex*), is an annual, a biennial, or a short-lived perennial 2 to 9 inches in height. It has linear-spatula-shaped leaves usually without teeth or at most with minute ones. The purplish-pink to white flowers are in dense clusters that do not lengthen. The broadly-winged, deeply-notched seed pods are about 1/4 inch in diameter. This is a native of Asia Minor. Native of the Pyrenees, annual *I. bernardiana* is attractive and up to 6 inches tall. It has compact rosettes of deep green, lobed, spatula-shaped leaves and crowded heads of light pink flowers.

Iberis bernardiana

Garden and Landscape Uses. Cultivated candytufts are all attractive and easy to grow. The perennials serve well in rock gardens, dry walls, at the fronts of flower borders and shrub plantings, and as edgings, the annuals are effective in flower beds and as pot plants, and are grown for cut flowers. For pot plants as well as to supply flowers for cutting, they may be bloomed in winter in cool greenhouses. They are grateful plants that respond to minimum care. Their only demands are good soil drainage and full sun. Ground that lies wet, especially in winter, is not tolerated. All kinds thrive in limestone soils and the addition of lime or crushed limestone to earths that are pronouncedly

acid is beneficial; these plants, however, tolerate slight to moderate acidity without apparent harm.

Cultivation. Perennial kinds are best planted in early spring or early fall. The only care needed by established specimens is a light shearing as soon as blooming is over to remove the old flower heads and encourage compact growth. Cuttings root with great facility and quickly in propagating benches in cool greenhouses, in cold frames, under Mason jars, or elsewhere where a humid atmosphere and shade from strong sun can be provided. If taken in late spring or early summer they become sturdy, small plants by fall, but it is not until their second spring that they are big enough to make any considerable show of bloom.

Annual candytufts for summer display may be raised from seeds sown where the plants are to bloom. This is usually done in early spring, but in regions of fairly mild winters fall sowing is practicable and earlier flowers are had in that way. The seedlings are thinned to 6 inches apart or, if grown in rows spaced 1 foot or more apart for cutting, to 4 inches apart. It is also possible to secure earlier bloom by sowing indoors in a temperature of about 60°F some six weeks before it is deemed safe to transplant the young plants to the garden and to grow the seedlings, transplanted 2 inches apart in flats, in a sunny, airy greenhouse with a night temperature of 50°F until planting out time. So handled, the young plants may be set out about 6 inches apart as soon as danger from frost is over.

For late winter and spring blooming in greenhouses annual candytufts are excellent as pot plants and to supply cut flowers, and the perennials also make effective pot plants when forced in a greenhouse to bloom at that season. The seeds of the annual kinds are sown in September, and for succession again in January. The seedlings are transferred individually to 2½-inch pots and from those to benches, or better still ground beds (because they like best a cool root run) of fertile, porous soil. They are set in rows 1 foot apart with 4 inches between plants in the rows. An alternative method is to sow thinly directly in the beds or benches in rows spaced 1 foot apart, and to thin the seedlings to about 4 inches apart. This is likely to give more flower spikes, but of less high quality than from transplanted plants. High temperatures must be avoided. At night the thermometer should never register more than 50°F and two or three degrees lower is better. A rise of five to ten degrees, depending upon the brightness of the weather, is allowed during the day. On all favorable occasions the greenhouse must be ventilated as freely as possible. If plants are to be flowered in pots rather than in beds or benches essentially the same treatment is given, the only difference being that instead of transplanting from 2½-inch pots to beds or benches the young plants are potted into containers 5 inches in diameter. When they have filled these pots with roots weekly applications of dilute liquid fertilizer are supplied.

To have plants of *I. sempervirens* or other perennial kinds in bloom indoors in late winter and spring sturdy two-year-old specimens are dug from nursery beds in early fall and potted individually in pots or pans (shallow pots) sufficiently large to accommodate the root balls without crowding. After potting, the containers are buried to their rims in a bed of sand, peat moss, or other loose material in a cold frame where they remain until early the following year. Then they are brought into a sunny greenhouse where the night temperature is 45 to 50°F, and the day temperature only five to ten degrees higher, and are kept watered and supplied with an occasional application of dilute liquid fertilizer. After they are through blooming if they are planted outdoors they will flower there the following spring.

IBERVILLEA (Iber-víllea)—Globe Berry. The botanically perplexing genus *Ibervillea*, of the gourd family CUCURBITACEAE, is endemic to the southwestern United States and northern Mexico. By different authorities it is regarded as consisting of one variable or of a few closely related species. The derivation of its name is unknown.

Ibervilleas are tuberous-rooted, branching, tendril-climbing, perennial vines very like *Melothria*, but differing in the female flowers not having a disk at the bottom of the style. They have alternate, stalked, palmately- (in hand-fashion) lobed leaves, with the lobes usually again lobed or toothed, and male and female flowers on separate plants. The greenish-yellow blooms have tubular, five-lobed calyxes, and corollas of five petals. The male flowers, usually clustered or in racemes, or rarely solitary, have three stalkless stamens, the females, always solitary, a style ending in a three-lobed stigma. The fruits are spherical and when ripe bright red or orange.

Native from Texas to Oklahoma and Mexico, *I. lindheimeri* has slender stems and mostly three- or sometimes five-lobed, toothed leaves up to 4½ inches across. Its flowers are up to ⅓ inch long, the fruits ¾ inch to 1½ inches in diameter. Variants with more finely dissected foliage and smallish fruits are sometimes distinguished as *I. tripartita*, and *I. tenuisecta*. An inhabitant of deserts on both sides of the Gulf of California, **I. sonorae** has a root usually projecting above the ground, but sometimes subterranean, usually from 3 to 6 inches in diameter, but sometimes very much bigger. Its leaves, mostly up to 4 inches in diameter, are more dissected than those of typical *I. lindheimeri*.

Ibervillea lindheimeri

Ibervillea sonorae

Garden and Landscape Uses and Cultivation. An attractive vine for covering fences, trellis, and similar supports, *I. lindheimeri* displays its colorful fruits in late summer and fall. Branches bearing these may be cut and used effectively in fall arrangements with gourds and other decorative fruits. This vine is not winter hardy in the north, but may be grown as an annual. It succeeds with little care in fairly good soil in sunny locations. In the south seeds may be sown outdoors in spring where the plants are to remain. In the north it is better to start plants indoors early and set them in the garden after there is no longer danger of frost. In warm, dry regions *I. sonorae* may be planted permanently outdoors. It is also sometimes grown in pots in greenhouse collections of succulents and in window gardens. This needs very well-drained soil and exposure to full sun, with indoor, winter temperatures of 50°F at night, five to fifteen degrees higher by day. Water moderately when in growth, not at all when the plant is dormant.

IBICELLA (Ibicél-la). This group of three species of South American herbaceous plants includes one ornamental, rather unusual flower garden plant. The genus is a member of the martynia family MARTYNI-

ACEAE. Its name, one previously applied to a section of the related genus *Proboscidea*, is a diminutive of the name of the animal ibex. It alludes to the horns on the fruits.

Ibicellas are softly-hairy and clammy or sticky. They have broad-ovate to nearly round, lobeless leaves and attractive flowers in compact, terminal clusters. The blooms have five sepals, the two lower much broader than the upper, a five-lobed, obliquely-bell-shaped corolla, four fertile stamens, and usually one staminode (abortive stamen). The fruits are large, woody, ovoid-cylindrical capsules with a pair of long, slender upcurved horns.

Ibicella lutea

Native from Brazil to Argentina, **Ibicella lutea** (syns. *Proboscidea lutea, Martynia lutea*) is a vigorous, spreading, slightly ill-scented annual about 1½ feet tall, with thick, succulent stems and nearly round, toothless leaves up to 1 foot across. Its 1-inch-long flowers are golden-yellow, spotted in their throats with crimson or deep orange. The fruits are 6 to 8 inches long. In its native land the young ones are pickled and eaten.

Garden Uses and Cultivation. For creating bold, unusual effects in flower gardens, the large, undivided leaves and showy blooms of *I. lutea* are effective. They suggest the lushness of the humid tropics. The plant needs full sun and fertile soil. Its seeds germinate erratically. To promote even sprouting, soak them in tepid water for twenty-four hours and remove their outer husks. In the far south sow them outdoors in early spring, but elsewhere it is desirable to start them indoors and set the young plants in the garden after the weather is settled and warm about the time it is safe to plant out peppers and eggplants. It takes twenty weeks or more from seed sowing to first blooming. Cover the seeds with soil to a depth of about ½ inch. Indoors put them to germinate in a temperature of about 75°F. Pot the young plants individually in 3-inch pots and if growth demands repot them later into pots 4 or 5 inches in diameter. Except for a final short period of hardening off in a cold frame or sheltered place outdoors before planting out time, grow them in a temperature of 60°F at night, five to fifteen degrees higher by day. In the garden plant them 2 to 3 feet apart.

IBIDIUM. See Spiranthes.

IBOZA (I-bòza). This genus of about a dozen African species is distinct from others of the mint family LABIATAE in having terminal panicles of tiny unisexual flowers. Its name is a Zulu one. The Zulus used *Iboza riparia* medicinally.

Ibozas are subshrubs or herbaceous perennials with undivided, usually toothed, opposite leaves. Their tubular flowers have minute, three-lobed calyxes and four- or five-lobed, slender-tubed corollas. The corolla lobes (petals) are of unequal size. Male flowers, slightly larger than females, have four stamens and a nonfunctional ovary and style. Female flowers have one style and often nonfunctual stamens (staminodes). The fruits consist of four erect, one-seeded nutlets, often referred to as seeds.

Iboza riparia

The only species cultivated is *I. riparia* (syn. *Moschosma riparium*), a winter-blooming subshrub up to 5 or 6 feet tall. Erect, and branching freely, it has squarish branches and thickish, broadly-ovate, coarsely-toothed leaves 1 inch to 2 inches long. As known in gardens the flowers are creamy-white with prominent dark anthers, but in the wild they vary from whitish to pale lilac. The very numerous blooms have corolla tubes ⅛ inch long or slightly longer and are in large, loose, showy panicles. The entire plant is glandular, slightly clammy, and has a strong musklike odor. A similar kind with smaller, thicker, more deeply-toothed and more strongly glandular-pubescent stems and foliage has been described as *I. galpinii,* but as intermediates between it and typical *I. riparia* are common it would seem at most to be a variety of the latter.

Garden and Landscape Uses. Only in regions not subject to frost and not excessively humid is *I. riparia* adapted for outdoor cultivation. It is admirable for flower beds and borders and for the fronts of shrubberies, but is without value as a cut flower. It is excellent as a pot plant for the winter adornment of greenhouses and conservatories, but under room conditions the flowers soon shatter, and for this reason and because the plants do not pack or travel well they are of no interest to commercial florists.

Cultivation. A vigorous grower, *I. riparia* responds to fertile, well-drained soil kept moderately moist, but not excessively wet. It grows well fully exposed or with a little shade to temper the intensity of the strongest summer sun. The plants are

Iboza riparia (flowers)

pruned back quite severely after they are through blooming. Propagation is usually by cuttings, more rarely by seeds.

In greenhouses the common practice is to raise new plants each year from cuttings taken from March to July, the earlier ones producing specimens that bloom in 8- or 9-inch pots, the later ones smaller plants. During their early stages the tips of their shoots are pinched out occasionally to induce branching, the last pinch being given in early August. Ibozas prosper under conditions that suit chrysanthemums. They must not be permitted to suffer from dryness, and whenever conditions permit the greenhouse must be ventilated freely. When the containers in which they are to bloom are filled with roots the plants benefit greatly from regular applications of dilute liquid fertilizer. From fall until spring a winter night temperature of 50°F with a daytime rise of five or ten degrees is satisfactory, but somewhat earlier bloom is had and the foliage may hold better if it is held at 55°F until after flowering is through. In late winter the plants are cut back, fertilized, and placed in a slightly warmer greenhouse to induce the production of new shoots suitable as cuttings. Occasionally it may be necessary to remove yellowed or dead leaves from ibozas. This should always be done with an upward tug. If the pull is downward a long strip of bark is removed from the stem along with the leaf.

ICACINACEAE—Icacina Family. Trees, shrubs, woody vines, and a few herbaceous plants totaling 400 species of dicotyledons distributed among fifty-eight genera constitute this family. Nearly all have alternate, a few opposite leaves, which are usually leathery and without lobes or teeth. Generally in panicle-like clusters, less commonly in panicles, racemes, or spikes, the usually bisexual flowers have five- or four-lobed calyxes or none, five or four petals, rarely united, five or four stamens, one style, and three, or less often two or five stigmas. The fruits are usually one-seeded drupes, sometimes samaras. Genera cultivated are *Pennantia* and *Villaresia*.

ICACOREA. See Ardisia.

ICE PLANT is *Mesembryanthemum crystallinum.*

ICELAND POPPY is *Papaver nudicaule.*

IDAHO PLUME is *Holodiscus discolor.*

IDESIA (Idès-ia). Named in honor of Eberhard Ysbrant Ides, a seventeenth-century Dutch traveler in China, *Idesia,* of the flacourtia family FLACOURTIACEAE, consists of one hardy, deciduous tree with horizontally-spreading branches in distinct tiers and shoots with thick pith.

Idesia polycarpa

Idesia polycarpa (fruits)

Native to Japan, Taiwan, and China, *I. polycarpa* is up to 50 feet tall. It has alternate, long-stalked, pointed-ovate leaves with widely-spaced teeth and heart-shaped bases. Somewhat resembling those of *Catalpa*, but smaller and thicker, the leaves are mostly about 6 inches long by almost as broad. Occasionally they are one-half as big again. The mostly unisexual, fragrant, yellowish-green flowers are without petals and have three to six, but usually five sepals. The females are about ⅓ inch, the males about ½ inch, in diameter. Charac-

teristically male and female blooms are on separate trees. Following pollination, the females develop fleshy, many-seeded berries about the size of peas that hang from the ends of the branches in grapelike clusters 6 to 10 inches long and remain for many months. When they first ripen, they are bright orange-red to deep red and highly ornamental, but after several weeks they become blackish. Varieties are *I. p.*

vestita, with densely-pubescent under surfaces to its leaves, and *I. p. microcarpa*, which has fruits about one-half as big as those of the typical species.

Garden and Landscape Uses. The prime value of this tree as an ornamental is the beauty of the great show of berries that female specimens are capable of making in fall. This they do only if a male is near, and, as one male produces pollen enough to impregnate several females, the ideal arrangement is to plant the trees in the proportion of anything up to eight or ten females to one male. Unfortunately the sexes of specimens raised from seeds cannot be determined until they bloom. The sex of vegetatively propagated specimens is, of course, the same as that of the parent plant. Cut branches with berries can be used effectively for indoor decorations and are likely to cause much favorable comment when exhibited at fall flower shows. The hardiness of *I. polycarpa* is related to the source of the original stock. Specimens raised from Japanese parent stock are not hardy north of Philadelphia, but stock of Chinese origin succeeds at New York City and in sheltered places as far north as Boston. This tree thrives in any reasonably fertile garden soil in full sun.

Cultivation. Idesias are easily raised from seeds and may be increased by cuttings of young leafy shoots in summer and by root cuttings. They require no special care.